Collins
TURKISH
DICTIONARY
ESSENTIAL EDITION

Published by Collins
An imprint of HarperCollins Publishers
Westerhill Road
Bishopbriggs
Glasgow G64 2QT

HarperCollins Publishers
Macken House
39/40 Mayor Street Upper
Dublin 1, D01 C9W8, Ireland
First Edition 2019

6

© HarperCollins Publishers 2019

ISBN 978-0-00-827065-0

Collins® is a registered trademark of
HarperCollins Publishers Limited

www.collinsdictionary.com

Typeset by Davidson Publishing
Solutions, Glasgow

Printed and bound by CPI Group (UK)
Ltd, Croydon, CR0 4YY

Entered words that we have reason to
believe constitute trademarks have
been designated as such. However,
neither the presence nor absence of
such designation should be regarded
as affecting the legal status of any
trademark.

The contents of this publication are
believed correct at the time of printing.
Nevertheless the Publisher can accept
no responsibility for errors or omissions,
changes in the detail given or for any
expense or loss thereby caused.

HarperCollins does not warrant that
any website mentioned in this title will
be provided uninterrupted, that any
website will be error free, that defects
will be corrected, or that the website
or the server that makes it available are
free of viruses or bugs. For full terms
and conditions please refer to the site
terms provided on the website.

A catalogue record for this book is
available from the British Library.

If you would like to comment on any
aspect of this book, please contact us
at the given address or online.
E-mail: dictionaries@harpercollins.co.uk

Acknowledgements
We would like to thank those authors
and publishers who kindly gave
permission for copyright material to be
used in the Collins Corpus. We would
also like to thank Times Newspapers Ltd
for providing valuable data.

İÇİNDEKİLER

CONTENTS

GİRİŞ

Bu Türkçe sözlüğü almaya karar verdiğiniz için teşekkür ederiz, umarız bu sözlüğü evde, tatilde ya da iş yerinizde kullanmaktan keyif alır ve faydalanırsınız.

INTRODUCTION

We are delighted that you have decided to buy this Turkish dictionary and hope you will enjoy and benefit from using it at home, on holiday, or at work.

KISALTMALAR		ABBREVIATIONS
sıfat	*adj*	adjective
zarf	*adv*	adverb
ünlem	*excl*	exclamation
konuşma dili (!argo)	*inf (!)*	colloquial (! offensive)
edat	*prep*	preposition
zarf	*pron*	pronoun
isim	*n*	noun
dişil	*f*	feminine
eril	*m*	masculine
cinssiz	*nt*	neuter
çoğul	*pl*	plural
fiil	*v*	verb

TURKISH PRONUNCIATION

VOWELS

a	[a]	kapı	like *a* in c*a*r
e	[e]	gelir	like *e* in p*e*t
ı	[ə]	kapı	like *e* in op*e*n
i	[i]	iki	like *i* in mach*i*ne
o	[o]	mor	like *o* in m*o*re
ö	[ø]	öğrenci	like *u* in b*u*rn
u	[u]	uyku	like *u* in r*u*de
ü	[y]	üzgün	like *u* in c*u*be

CONSONANTS

c	[j]	cam	like *j* in *j*ohn
ç	[tʃ]	çağdaş	like *ch* in *ch*ain or *c* in *c*ello
ğ	[:]	ağaç	silent letter, which doubles the length of the previous vowel
j	[ʒ]	ajans	like *s* in mea*s*ure
ş	[ʃ]	şeftali	like *sh* in *sh*are or *s* in *s*ugar

b, d, g, h, k, l, m, n, p, r, s, t, v, y, and z are pronounced as in English.

STRESS
The rules of stress in Turkish are as follows:

(a)   The main stress usually occurs on the last syllable of a word:
        ara'ba (car), ka'dın (woman), or'tak (partner)

(b)   For proper names, the stress occurs on the penultimate syllable,
        unless the penultimate syllable is light and the antepenultimate
        syllable is heavy:
            Penultimate:
            An'talya, O'regon, İs'tanbul
            Antepenultimate:
            'Ankara

(c)   The regular stress pattern occurs on words where suffixes are added
        to stems. The stress shifts away from the stem as suffixes are
        concatenated:
            el'ma (apple)
            elma'lar (apples)
            elmalar'ım (my apples)

In the phonetic transcription, the symbol ['] precedes the syllable on which the
stress falls.

İNGİLİZCE TELAFFUZ

İngilizce Örnek	Açıklamalar
[ɑː] father	Türkçede karşılığı tam olarak bulunmaz. Uzatılmış *a* sesinin sonuna *ğ* eklenmiş hâlidir.
[ʌ] b**u**t, c**o**me	Türkçedeki *a* sesidir. Örnek olarak *kapı* verilebilir
[æ] m**a**n, c**a**t	Türkçede tam olarak karşılığı bulunmaz. *a* ile *e* sesleri arasındaki bir sese benzer.
[ə] fath**e**r, **a**go	Türkçede tam olarak karşılığı bulunmaz. *a* ile *ı* sesleri arasındaki bir sese benzer.
[ə] b**i**rd, h**ea**rd	*Köprü*, *Göz* gibi sözcüklerdeki *ö* sesinin biraz daha uzatılmış hâlidir.
[ɛ] g**e**t, b**e**d	Türkçedeki *e* sesinin tam karşılığıdır. Örnek olarak *Eylül* verilebilir.
[i] **i**t, b**i**g	Türkçedeki *i* sesinin tam karşılığıdır. Örnek olarak *Simit* verilebilir.
[i] t**ea**, s**ee**	Türkçedeki *i* sesinin uzatılmış hâlidir.
[ɔ] h**o**t, w**a**sh	Türkçede tam olarak karşılığı bulunmaz. Yine de *o* sesine çok benzer. Tam olarak *o* sesinin sonuna hafif bir *a* eklenmiş hâli denilebilir.
[ɔ] s**a**w, **a**ll	Türkçede tam olarak karşılığı bulunmaz. Uzunca söylenen *oğ* sesine benzer.
[u] p**u**t, b**oo**k	Türkçedeki *u* sesinin karşılığıdır. Örnek olarak *dokuz* verilebilir.
[u] t**oo**, y**ou**	Türkçede tam olarak karşılığı bulunmaz. Uzunca söylenen *ıu* sesine benzer.

[ai]	fly, high	Hızlıca *ai* sesinin çıkarılmasına benzer.
[au]	how, house	Hızlıca *au* sesinin çıkarılmasına benzer.
[εə]	there, bear	Hızlıca *eı* sesinin çıkarılmasına benzer.
[ei]	day, obey	Hızlıca *ei* sesinin çıkarılmasına benzer.
[iə]	here, hear	Hızlıca *iı* sesinin çıkarılmasına benzer.
[əu]	go, note	Hızlıca *ıu* sesinin çıkarılmasına benzer. Fakat buradaki *ı* sesi, *ı* ile *a* arası bir sestir.
[əi]	boy, oil	Hızlıca *oi* sesinin çıkarılmasına benzer.
[uə]	poor, sure	Hızlıca *ıuı* sesinin çıkarılmasına benzer. Buradaki ikinci *ı* sesi yine *ı* ile *a* arası bir sestir.

[ʤ]	gin, judge	Türkçedeki *c* sesinin tam karşılığıdır. Örnek olarak Cuma verilebilir.
[ŋ]	sing	Türkçede tam olarak karşılığı bulunmaz. *ng* sesinin çıkartılmasına benzer fakat sondaki *g* sesi tam olarak söylenmez, böylelikle uzatılmış bir *n* sesine benzer bir ses elde edilir.
[k]	come, mock	Türkçedeki *k* sesinin tam karşılığıdır. Örnek olarak kapı verilebilir.
[z]	rose, zebra	Türkçedeki *z* sesinin tam karşılığıdır. Örnek olarak zor verilebilir.

[ʃ]	**sh**e, ma**ch**ine	Türkçedeki ş sesinin tam karşılığıdır. Örnek olarak şeref verilebilir.
[tʃ]	**ch**in, ri**ch**	Türkçedeki ç sesinin tam karşılığıdır. Örnek olarak çocuk verilebilir.
[w]	**w**ater, **wh**ich	Türkçede tam olarak karşılığı bulunmaz. v sesinden önce u sesi varmış gibi okunur fakat u sesinin yalnızca son kısmı söylenir.
[ʒ]	vi**s**ion	Türkçedeki j sesinin tam karşılığıdır. Örnek olarak ajanda verilebilir.
[θ]	**th**ink, my**th**	Türkçede tam olarak karşılığı bulunmaz. t ile s sesleri arasındaki bir sese benzer. Bu sesi çıkartmak için dil dişler arasında sıkıştırılarak sert bir şekilde t sesi çıkartılmaya çalışılır.
[ð]	**th**is, **th**e	Türkçede tam olarak karşılığı bulunmaz. d ile s sesleri arasındaki bir sese benzer. Bu sesi çıkartmak için dil dişler arasında sıkıştırılarak sert bir şekilde d sesi çıkartılmaya çalışılır.

Fonetik çevriyazıda, [*] simgesi, İngiliz İngilizcesinde ardından gelen sözcük sesli harf ile başlıyorsa çok hafif şekilde telaffuz edilen sözcük sonundaki "r" harfini temsil eder. Fonetik çevriyazıda, ['] simgesi vurgunun olduğu heceden önce kullanılır.

SAYILAR		NUMBERS
sıfır	0	zero
bir	1	one
iki	2	two
üç	3	three
dört	4	four
beş	5	five
altı	6	six
yedi	7	seven
sekiz	8	eight
dokuz	9	nine
on	10	ten
on bir	11	eleven
on iki	12	twelve
on üç	13	thirteen
on dört	14	fourteen
on beş	15	fifteen
on altı	16	sixteen
on yedi	17	seventeen
on sekiz	18	eighteen
on dokuz	19	nineteen
yirmi	20	twenty

yirmi bir	21	twenty-one
yirmi iki	22	twenty-two
yirmi üç	23	twenty-three
otuz	30	thirty
otuz bir	31	thirty-one
kırk	40	forty
elli	50	fifty
altmış	60	sixty
yetmiş	70	seventy
seksen	80	eighty
doksan	90	ninety
yüz	100	one hundred
yüz on	110	one hundred and ten
iki yüz	200	two hundred
iki yüz elli	250	two hundred and fifty
bin	1 000	one thousand
bir milyon	1 000 000	one million

HAFTANIN GÜNLERİ

Pazartesi	Monday
Salı	Tuesday
Çarşamba	Wednesday
Perşembe	Thursday
Cuma	Friday
Cumartesi	Saturday
Pazar	Sunday

DAYS OF THE WEEK

AYLAR

Ocak	January
Şubat	February
Mart	March
Nisan	April
Mayıs	May
Haziran	June
Temmuz	July
Ağustos	August
Eylül	September
Ekim	October
Kasım	November
Aralık	December

MONTHS

Turkish–English

Türkçe–İngilizce

a

AB [ap] *abbr* EU
abajur [abaʒur] *n* lampshade
abartı [abartə] *n* exaggeration
abartmak [abartmak] *v*
exaggerate
ABD [abd] *n* USA
abonelik [abonelik] *n* s
ubscription
abonman [abonman] *n* **abonman**
kartı *n* season ticket; **tren**
abonmanı *n* railcard
Abu Dabi [abudabi] *n* Abu Dhabi
acaip [adʒaip] *adj* odd, weird
acele [adʒele] *n* hurry ▷ *v* **acele**
etmek *v* hurry, hurry up; **Acelem**
var I'm in a hurry
acemi [adʒemi] *adj* green
(inexperienced)
acemice [adʒemidʒe] *adj* poorly
acenta [adʒenta] *n* **seyahat**
acentası *n* travel agency, travel
agent's, *(kişi)* travel agent

acı [adʒə] *adj (tat)* bitter ▷ *n* pain,
(biber) chilli; **acı çekmek** *v*
suffer; **sıla acısı çeken** *adj*
homesick; **Burası acıyor** I have
a pain here
acık [adʒək] *n* **acıklı bir şekilde**
adv sadly
acılı [adʒələ] *adj* painful, spicy
acıma [adʒəma] *n (duygu)* pity
acımak [adʒəmak] *v* pity
acımasız [adʒəmasəz] *adj*
ruthless
acınası [adʒənasə] *adj* pathetic
acil [adʒil] *adj* immediate; **acil**
çıkış kapısı *n* emergency exit;
acil durum *n* emergency; **acil iniş**
n emergency landing; **kaza & acil**
servis *n* accident & emergency
department
aç [atʃ] *adj (karın)* hungry; **kurt**
gibi aç *adj* ravenous; **Aç değilim**
I'm not hungry
açacak [atʃadʒak] *n* **kalem**
açacağı *n* pencil sharpener;
kutu açacağı *n* can-opener,
tin-opener; **şişe açacağı** *n*
bottle-opener
açgözlü [atʃgøzly] *adj* greedy
açı [atʃə] *n* angle; **bakış açısı** *n*
aspect; **dik açı** *n* right angle
açığa çıkarmak *v* bare
açık [atʃək] *adj (hava vb)* clear,
(kapı, pencere vb) open, *(kavram)*
obvious, *(renk)* light *(not dark)*
▷ *adv* on ▷ *n (finans)* deficit; **açık**
arttırma *n* auction; **açık çek** *n*
blank cheque; **açık büfe** *n* buffet;
açık fikirli *adj* broad-minded; **açık**
görüşlü *adj* liberal; **açık hava** *adj*
outdoor; **açık havada** *adv*

out-of-doors, outdoors; **açık iş** n vacancy; **açık renk** (ten/saç) adj fair (light colour); **açık saçık** adj obscene; **açık sözlü** adj outspoken, straightforward; **açıkça fikrini söylemek** v speak up; **açıklık kazandırmak** v clarify; **mali açıklık** n shortfall; **rüzgara açık** adj bleak; **rekabete açık** adj competitive; **Açık mısınız?** Are you open?; **Banka bugün açık mı?** Is the bank open today?; **Bugün açık mı?** Is it open today?; **Müze ne zaman açık?** When is the museum open?; **Saray ne zaman açık?** When is the palace open?; **Tapınak ne zaman açık?** When is the temple open?; **Yarın açık mı?** Is it open tomorrow?

açıkça [atʃəktʃa] adv apparently, clearly

açıkçası [atʃəktʃasə] adv obviously

açıklama [atʃəklama] n (beyan) statement, (izah) explanation

açıklamak [atʃəklamak] vi explain; **kamuoyuna açıklamak** v issue

açıklık [atʃəklək] n (aralık) aperture

açılır [atʃələr] adj **üstü açılır araba** n convertible

açılış [atʃələʃ] n **açılış saatleri** npl opening hours; **açılış sayfası** n home page

açlık [atʃlək] n hunger; **açlık çekmek** v starve; **Açım** I'm hungry

açmak [atʃmak] v turn on, (paket) unwrap, (paket, fermuar vb) undo, (rulo/sargı) unroll ▷ vt (kapı vb) open, (sargı) unwind; **çiçek**

açmak v blossom, flower; **fermuarı açmak** v unzip; **şalter açmak** v switch on; **oturum açmak** v log in, log on; **yol açmak** v cause

ad [ad] n (gramer) noun, (kişi) name; **adın baş harfleri** n initials; **adının ön harflerini yazmak** v initial; **ön ad** n first name; **ön adı** n Christian name; **diğer adıyla** prep alias; **takma ad** n alias, nickname, pseudonym; **... adına yer ayırtmıştım** I booked a room in the name of...; **Adınız ne?** What's your name?; **Benim adım...** My name is...

ada [ada] n island; **ıssız ada** n desert island; **Mauritius Adası** n Mauritius

Ada [ada] n **Bahama Adaları** n Bahamas; **Batı Hint Adaları** npl West Indian, West Indies; **Faroe Adaları** npl Faroe Islands; **Kanarya Adaları** n Canaries; **Polonezya Adaları** n Polynesia

adalet [adalet] n justice

adaletsizlik [adaletsizlik] n injustice

adam [adam] n guy; **bilim adamı** n scientist; **iş adamı** n businessman; **kardan adam** n snowman

adanmış [adanməʃ] adj dedicated

adaptör [adaptør] n adaptor

aday [adaj] n candidate; **aday göstermek** v nominate

adaylık [adajlək] n nomination

adet [adet] n (gelenek) custom

adım [adəm] n footstep, pace, step; **adım adım** adv gradually;

uygun adım yürümek *v* march;
uygun adım yürümek *v* keep up
with
adımlamak [adəmlamak] *v* tread
adil [adil] *adj* fair *(reasonable)*
adres [adres] *n* address *(location)*;
adres defteri *n* address book;
adres listesi *n* mailing list;
e-posta adresi *n* email address;
ev adresi *n* home address;
internet adresi *n* web address;
Adresi yazar mısınız lütfen? Will
you write down the address,
please?; **İnternet adresi…** The
website address is…;
**Mektuplarımı şu adrese
gönderin lütfen** Please send my
mail on to this address
Adriyatik [adrijatik] *adj* Adriatic
Adriyatik Denizi
[adrijatikdenizi] *n* Adriatic Sea
adsız [adsəz] *adj* anonymous
aerobik [aerobik] *npl* aerobics
aerosol [aerosol] *n* aerosol
aferin [aferin] *excl* well done!
affedersiniz [affedersiniz]
excuse me, sorry
Afgan [afgan] *adj* Afghan ▷ *n*
Afghan
Afganistan [afganistan] *n*
Afghanistan
afiyet [afijet] *n* appetite;
Afiyet olsun! Enjoy your meal!
afiyette [afijette] *adj* well
Afrika [afrika] *n* Africa;
Güney Afrika *adj* South Africa,
South African; **Kuzey Afrika** *adj*
North Africa, North African;
Orta Afrika Cumhuriyeti *n*
Central African Republic

Afrikaanca [afrikaandʒa] *n*
Afrikaans
Afrikalı [afrikalə] *adj* African ▷ *n*
African; **Güney Afrikalı** *n* South
African; **Kuzey Afrikalı** *n* North
African
Afrikaner [afrikaner] *n* Afrikaner
ağ [a:] *n* web, *(bilişim)* network;
örümcek ağı *n* cobweb
ağaç [a:adʒ] *n* **köknar ağacı** *n* fir
(tree)
ağaç [a:atʃ] *n* tree ▷ *adj* wooden;
ağaç üflemeli *(çalgı)* *n*
woodwind; **ağaç gövdesi** *n* trunk;
ağaç işleri *n* woodwork; **huş
ağacı** *n* birch; **kayın ağacı** *n* beech
(tree); **Noel ağacı** *n* Christmas
tree; **porsuk ağacı** *n* yew; **zeytin
ağacı** *n* olive tree
ağartıcı [a:artədʒə] *n* bleach
ağartılmış [a:artəlməʃ] *adj*
bleached
ağır [a:ər] *adj* heavy; **ağır bir
şekilde** *adv* heavily; **ağır yük
taşıma aracı** *n* HGV; **Bu çok ağır**
This is too heavy
ağırlık [a:ərlək] *n* weight; **ağırlık
kaldırma** *n* weightlifting; **kağıt
ağırlığı** *n* paperweight
ağız [a:əz] *n* mouth, *(çaydanlık vb)*
rim; **ağız dalaşı** *v* squabble; **dört
yol ağzı** *n* crossroads; **kol ağzı** *n*
sleeve
ağlamak [a:lamak] *n* cry ▷ *v* cry,
weep; **hıçkırarak ağlamak** *v* sob
ağrı [a:rə] *n* ache; **ağrı kesici** *n*
painkiller; **baş ağrısı** *n* headache;
diş ağrısı *n* toothache; **kulak
ağrısı** *n* earache; **mide ağrısı** *n*
stomachache; **sırt ağrısı** *n*

back pain, backache; **Ağrıyor**
It's sore

ağrılı [a:rələ] *adj* sore

ağrımak [a:rəmak] *v* ache

Ağustos [a:ustos] *n* August

ahbap [ahbap] *n* mate

ahçı [ahtʃə] *n* cook

ahır [ahər] *n* stable

ahlak [ahlak] *n* **ahlak dışı** *adj*
immoral; **ahlak kuralları** *npl*
morals

ahlaki [ahlaki] *adj* ethical, moral

ahmak [ahmak] *n* fool

ahpap [ahpap] *n* chap

ahtapot [ahtapot] *n* octopus

ahududu [ahududu] *n* raspberry

AIDS [aids] *n* AIDS

aile [aile] *n* family; **aile oyunları** *n*
board game; **eşinin ailesi** *npl*
in-laws; **koruyucu aile**
bakımındaki çocuk *n* foster child;
koruyucu aile olmak *v* foster;
Aile odası ayırtmak istiyorum
I want to reserve a family room;
Aile odası istiyorum I'd like to
book a family room; **Ailemle**
geldim I'm here with my family

ait [ait] *n* **ait olmak** *v* belong,
belong to; **Georgia'ya ait** *adj*
Georgian; **Hollanda'ya ait** *n*
Dutch; **Lübnan'a ait** *n* Lebanese;
Meksika'ya ait *n* Mexican

ajans [aʒans] *n* agency

ak [ak] *n* **yumurta akı** *n* egg white

akademi [akademi] *n* academy;
akademik yıl *n* academic year

akademik [akademik] *adj*
academic

akbaba [akbaba] *n* vulture

akciğer [akdʒiier] *n* lung

akçaağaç [aktʃaa:atʃ] *n* maple

Akdeniz [akdeniz] *adj*
Mediterranean ▷ *n* Mediterranean

akdiken [akdiken] *n* hawthorn

akıcı [akədʒə] *adj* fluent

akıl [akəl] *adj* mental; **akıl**
hastanesi *n* psychiatric ward;
akıllı dokunuş *n* touchpad; **akıllı**
telefon *n* smart phone; **akıllıca**
olmayan *adj* unwise

akıllı [akəllə] *adj* brainy, wise

akıllıca [akəllədʒa] *adj* advisable,
rational

akım [akəm] *n* current *(electricity)*;
moda akımı *n* trend

akın [akən] *n* **akın etmek** *v* invade

akıntı [akəntə] *n* *(nezle)* catarrh

akış [akəʃ] *n* current *(flow)*

akmak [akmak] *v* flow ▷ *vt* pour

akne [akne] *n* spot *(blemish)*

akordiyon [akordijon] *n*
accordion

akraba [akraba] *adj* related;
en yakın akraba *n* next-of-kin

akrep [akrep] *n* scorpion

Akrep [akrep] *n* **Akrep burcu** *n*
Scorpio

akrobat [akrobat] *n* acrobat

aksesuar [aksesuar] *n* accessory

aksi [aksi] *prep* **saatin aksi**
yönünde *adv* anticlockwise;
ya da aksine *adv* vice versa

akşam [akʃam] *n* evening, in the
evening; **akşam okulu** *n* evening
class; **akşam yemeği** *n* dinner;
akşamdan kalma *n* hangover;
hafif akşam yemeği *n* supper;
kahvaltı ve akşam yemeği dahil
n half board; **İyi akşamlar** Good
evening; **Bu akşam ne**

yapıyorsunuz? What are you doing this evening?; **Burada akşamları yapılabilecek ne var?** What is there to do in the evenings?; **Masa bu akşam saat dokuz için rezerve edildi** The table is booked for nine o'clock this evening

aktarım [aktarəm] *n (doku/organ)* transplant; **kan aktarımı** *n* transfusion

aktif [aktif] *adj* active

aktivite [aktivite] *n* **aktivite tatili** *n* activity holiday

aktör [aktør] *n* actor

akupunktur [akupuŋtur] *n* acupuncture

akustik [akustik] *adj* acoustic

akü [aky] *n* **Akü çalışmıyor** The battery is flat; **Yeni bir akü gerekiyor** I need a new battery

akvaryum [akvarjum] *n* aquarium

alabalık [alabalək] *n* trout

alabora [alabora] *v* **alabora olmak** *v* capsize

alacakaranlık [aladʒakaranlək] *n* dusk

alakasız [alakasəz] *adj* irrelevant

alan [alan] *n (ölçü birimi)* area, *(yer)* site; **alan kodu** *n* postcode; **çalışma alanı** *n* workspace; **çöp döküm alanı** *n* rubbish dump; **çim alan** *n* lawn; **fuar alanı** *n* fairground; **inşaat alanı** *n* building site; **kapalı alan** *adj* indoor; **konaklama alanı** *n* service area; **koruma alanı** *n* reserve *(land)*; **oyun alanı** *n* playground, playing field;

paten alanı *n* rink, skating rink

alarm [alarm] *n* alarm; **duman alarmı** *n* smoke alarm; **hırsız alarmı** *n* burglar alarm; **yangın alarmı** *n* fire alarm; **yanlış alarm** *n* false alarm

alay [alaj] *n (askeri)* regiment, *(tören/gelin)* procession; **alay etmek** *v* mock; **alay etmek** *v* scoff; **ince alay** *n* irony; **tören alayı** *n* parade

alaycı [alajdʒə] *adj* ironic, sarcastic

albay [albaj] *n* colonel

albüm [albym] *n (müzik, fotoğraf)* album; **fotoğraf albümü** *n* photo album

alçak [altʃak] *adj* lousy; **alçak gönüllü** *adj* humble, modest

aldırmak [aldərmak] *vi* mind

alerji [alerʒi] *n* allergy; **buğday alerjisi** *n* wheat intolerance; **fıstık alerjisi** *n* nut allergy, peanut allergy

alerjik [alerʒik] *adj* allergic

alet [alet] *n* instrument; **kayıt aleti** *n* recorder *(scribe)*; **şarj aleti** *n* charger; **müzik aleti** *n* musical instrument

alev [alev] *n* flame; **parlak alev** *n* blaze

alfabe [alfabe] *n* alphabet

alıcı [alədʒə] *n* buyer, receiver *(electronic)*, *(kişi)* recipient

alım [aləm] *n* **bagaj alım** *n* baggage reclaim

alın [alən] *n* forehead

alınmış [alənməʃ] *adj* **satın alınmış** *adj* bought

alıntı [aləntə] *n* quotation, quote ▷ *v* **alıntı yapmak** *v* quote

alışılagelmiş [aləʃəlagelmiʃ] *adj*
usual

alışılmadık [aləʃəlmadək] *adj*
unusual

alışkanlık [aləʃkanlək] *n* habit

alışveriş [aləʃveriʃ] *n* shopping;
alışveriş çantası *n* shopping bag;
alışveriş merkezi *n* shopping
centre; **alışveriş torbası** *n* carrier
bag

alkış [alkəʃ] *n* applause

alkışlamak [alkəʃlamak] *v*
applaud

alkışlanmak [alkəʃlanmak] *vi*
clap

alkol [alkol] *n* alcohol; **alkollü içki**
npl spirits; **düşük alkollü** *adj*
low-alcohol; **Bunda alkol var mı?**
Does that contain alcohol?

alkolik [alkolik] *n* alcoholic

alkollü [alkolly] *adj* alcoholic

alkolsüz [alkolsyz] *adj*
alcohol-free

Allah [allah] *n* Allah

allık [allək] *n* blusher

alma [alma] *n* **eleman alma** *n*
recruitment

almak [almak] *v* get, get *(to a
place)*, receive ▷ *vt* take, take
(time); **askıya alma** *n* suspension;
askıya almak *v* suspend; **ödünç
almak** *v* borrow; **garantiye
almak** *v* ensure; **gözaltına alma** *n*
detention; **geri almak** *v* take
back; **hafife almak** *v*
underestimate; **içeri almak** *v*
admit *(allow in)*; **içeriye almak** *v*
let in; **ileriye almak** *v* put forward;
işe alma *n* employment; **işe
almak** *v* employ; **miras almak** *v*

inherit; **nefes alma** *n* breathing;
nefes almak *v* breathe, breathe
in; **not almak** *v* jot down, note
down; **risk almak** *v* risk; **satın
alma** *(şirket)* *n* buyout; **satın
almak** *v* buy, purchase; **sıkı
tedbirler almak** *v* crack down on;
toz almak *vt* dust; **yönetimi ele
almak** *v* take over; **yeniden ele
almak** *vt* reconsider; **yerden
almak** *v* pick up; **yerini alma** *n*
replacement; **yerini almak** *v*
replace

Alman [alman] *adj* German ▷ *n*
German *(person)*

Almanca [almandʒa] *n (dil)*
German *(language)*

Almanya [almanja] *n* Germany

Alpler [alpler] *npl* Alps

alt [alt] *n* **alt geçit** *n* underpass; **alt
kat** *adj* downstairs; **alt katta** *adv*
downstairs; **altını çizmek** *v*
underline; **el altında** *adj* handy;
en alt *adj* bottom; **yerin altında**
adv underground

alternatif [alternatif] *adj*
alternative

altgeçit [altgetʃit] *n* subway

altı [altə] *number* six

altın [altən] *adj (metal)* golden ▷ *n
(metal)* gold; **altın kaplama** *n*
gold-plated

altıncı [altəndʒə] *adj* sixth

altında [altənda] *adv* below,
underneath ▷ *prep* below, beneath,
under, underneath

altmış [altməʃ] *number* sixty

altyapı [altjapə] *n* infrastructure

altyazı [altjazə] *npl* subtitles

altyazılı [altjazələ] *adj* subtitled

alüminyum [alyminjum] *n*
aluminium

Alzheimer [alsheimer] *n*
Alzheimer hastalığı *n*
Alzheimer's disease

amaç [amatʃ] *n* cause *(ideals)*,
objective

amaçsız [amatʃsəz] *adj* senseless

amatör [amatør] *n* amateur

ambulans [ambulans] *n*
Ambulans çağırın Call an
ambulance

amca [amdʒa] *n* uncle

ameliyat [amelijat] *n* surgery
(operation), *(tıp)* operation
(surgery); **ameliyat etmek** *v*
operate *(to perform surgery)*;
ameliyat odası *n* operating
theatre

Amerika [amerika] *n* America;
Güney Amerika *adj* South
America, South American; **Kuzey
Amerika** *adj* North America,
North American; **Latin Amerika**
adj Latin America, Latin American;
Orta Amerika *n* Central America

Amerikalı [amerikalə] *n*
American; **Güney Amerikalı** *n*
South American; **Kuzey
Amerikalı** *n* North American

Amerikan [amerikan] *adj*
American; **Amerikan futbolu** *n*
American football

amir [amir] *n (iş)* supervisor

amper [amper] *n* amp

ampul [ampul] *n* light bulb,
(elektrik) bulb *(electricity)*

an [an] *n* moment; **aynı anda** *adv*
simultaneously; **aynı anda olan**
adj simultaneous; **bir anlık** *adj*

momentary; **şu an** *n* present *(time
being)*; **şu anda** *adv* currently,
presently

ana [ana] *n* base, lead *(position)*;
ana okulu *n* infant school; **ana
yemek** *n* main course; **deniz
anası** *n* jellyfish

anadil [anadil] *n* mother tongue;
anadilini konuşan *n* native
speaker

anafikir [anafikir] *n* basis

anahtar [anahtar] *n (kilit)* key *(for
lock)*; **araba anahtarları** *npl* car
keys; **İngiliz anahtarı** *n* spanner;
Anahtar alabilir miyim? Can I
have a key?; **Anahtar lütfen** The
key, please; **Anahtar uymuyor**
The key doesn't work; **Anahtarı
nereden alacağız?** Where do we
get the key...?; **Anahtarım
çalışmıyor** My key doesn't work;
Anahtarımı unuttum I've
forgotten the key; **Anahtarla
sorunum var** I'm having trouble
with the key; **Anahtarları
arabada bıraktım** I left the keys in
the car; **Ayrılırken anahtarı
nereye bırakacağız?** Where do
we hand in the key when we're
leaving?; **Bu anahtar nerenin?**
What's this key for?; **Bu kapının
anahtarı hangisi?** Which is the
key for this door?; **Hangisi ön
kapının anahtarı?** Which is the
key for the front door?; **Hangisi
garaj anahtarı?** Which is the key
for the garage?; **Yedek bir
anahtar istiyoruz** We need a
second key

anahtarlık [anahtarlək] *n* keyring

anakara [anakara] *n* mainland

analiz [analiz] *n* **sistem analizcisi** *n* systems analyst

ananas [ananas] *n* pineapple

anason [anason] *n* aniseed

anavatan [anavatan] *n* homeland

anayol [anajol] *n* main road

ancak [a:ndʒak] *adv* however

ançuez [antʃuez] *n* anchovy

And Dağları [andda:larə] *npl* Andes

Andora [andora] *n* Andorra

anestetik [anestetik] *n* anaesthetic

anestezi [anestezi] *n* **genel anestezi** *n* general anaesthetic; **lokal anestezi** *n* local anaesthetic

Angola [angola] *adj* Angolan ▷ *n* Angola

Angolalı [angolalə] *n* Angolan

anında [anənda] *adv* immediately

anıt [anət] *n* memorial, monument

ani [ani] *adj* abrupt, sudden; **ani rüzgar** *n* gust; **ani yükselme** *n* surge

aniden [aniden] *adv* abruptly, suddenly

anjin [anʒin] *n* angina

ankesör [aŋesør] *n* **ankesörlü telefon** *n* payphone

anket [aŋet] *n* questionnaire

anlam [anlam] *n* meaning; **anlamına gelmek** *v* stand for

anlama [anlama] *n* comprehension

anlamak [anlamak] *v* understand; **halden anlama** *n* sympathy; **halden anlamak** *v* sympathize; **yanlış anlama** *n* misunderstanding; **yanlış anlamak** *v* misunderstand; **Anladım** I understand

anlamsız [anlamsəz] *adj* pointless

anlaşılır [anlaʃələr] *adj* understandable

anlaşma [anlaʃma] *n* agreement, deal, *(tarih)* treaty

anlaşmazlık [anlaʃmazlək] *n* disagreement

anlatıcı [anlatədʒə] *n* teller

anlatım [anlatəm] *n* expression

anlatmak [anlatmak] *vt* tell

anlayış [anlajəʃ] *adj* understanding

anlayışlı [anlajəʃlə] *adj* sympathetic

anlık [anlək] *adj* **bir anlığına** *adv* momentarily

anma [anma] *n* **anma yazısı** *(ölünün ardından)* *n* obituary

anmalık [anmalək] *n* souvenir

anne [anne] *n* mother, mum; **üvey anne** *n* stepmother; **isim annesi** *n* godmother; **ninenin annesi** *n* great-grandmother; **taşıyıcı anne** *n* surrogate mother

annecim [annedʒim] *n* mummy *(mother)*

annelik [annelik] *n* maternal

anons [anons] *n* **anons etmek** *v* page

anorak [anorak] *n* anorak

anoreksi [anoreksi] *n* anorexia

anoreksik [anoreksik] *adj* anorexic

anormal [anormal] *adj* abnormal

ansiklopedi [ansiklopedi] *n* encyclopaedia

Antarktik [antarktik] *n* Antarctic

anten [anten] *n* aerial

antibiyotik [antibijotik] *n*
antibiotic

antidepresan [antidepresan] *n*
antidepressant

antifriz [antifriz] *n* antifreeze

antihistamin [antihistamin] *n*
antihistamine

antika [antika] *n* antique;
antikacı dükkanı *n* antique shop

antikor [antikor] *n* antibody

antilop [antilop] *n* antelope

antiseptik [antiseptik] *n*
antiseptic

antivirüs [antivirys] *n* antivirus

antre [antre] *n* hallway

antreman [antreman] *n*
antreman giysisi *n* tracksuit

apaçık [apatʃək] *adj* blatant

apandisit [apandisit] *n*
appendicitis

apartman [apartman] *n*
apartman dairesi *n* apartment,
flat; **... adına bir apartman
dairesi ayırtmıştık** We've booked
an apartment in the name of...;
**Bir apartman dairesi
bakıyorduk** We're looking for an
apartment

aperatif [aperatif] *n* **Aperatif
almak istiyoruz** We'd like an aperitif

apse [apse] *n* abscess; **Burası apse
yaptı** I have an abscess

aptal [aptal] *adj* stupid

aptalca [aptaldʒa] *adj* silly

ara [ara] *n (konser, tiyatro)*
interval; **bir ara** *adv* sometime;
bu arada *adv* meantime;
devre arası *n* half-time;
reklam arası *n* commercial break;
tavan arası *n* loft

araba [araba] *n* car; **araba
anahtarları** *npl* car keys; **araba
kazası** *n* crash; **araba kiralama** *n*
car hire; **araba sigortası** *n* car
insurance; **araba tutması** *n* travel
sickness; **arabalı feribot** *n*
car-ferry; **arabayı çekmek** *v* tow
away; **at arabası** *n* buggy, cart;
üstü açılır araba *n* convertible;
bebek arabası *n* pram; **birini
arabayla evine bırakma** *n* lift
(free ride); **devriye arabası** *n*
patrol car; **el arabası** *n*
wheelbarrow; **içkili araba
kullanma** *n* drink-driving; **kiralık
araba** *n* hire car, hired car, rental
car; **şirket arabası** *n* company
car; **market arabası** *n* shopping
trolley; **sedan araba** *n* saloon car;
yarış arabası *n* racing car; **yük
arabası** *n* lorry; **Araba çalışmıyor**
The car won't start; **Araba
güvertesine nasıl gidebilirim?**
How do I get to the car deck?;
Araba kaydı The car skidded;
Araba kiralamak istiyorum I
want to hire a car; **Araba ne
zaman hazır olur?** When will the
car be ready?; **Arabada stereo
var mı?** Is there a stereo in the
car?; **Arabam bozuldu** My car has
broken down; **Arabamı çarptım**
I've crashed my car; **Arabamı
nereye park edebilirim?** Where
can I park the car?; **Arabamı
soydular** My car has been broken
into; **Arabanın garantisi var** The
car is still under warranty;
Arabanızı çeker misiniz lütfen?
Could you move your car, please?;

Arabayı buraya mı geri getirmem gerekiyor Do I have to return the car here?; **Arabayı yıkamak istiyorum** I would like to wash the car; **Beş günlüğüne bir araba kiralamak istiyorum** I want to hire a car for five days; **Beni arabayla alabilir misiniz?** Can you take me by car?; **Birisine araba çarptı** Someone has been knocked down by a car; **Hafta sonu için bir araba kiralamak istiyorum** I want to hire a car for the weekend

aracılık [aradʒələk] n **hakem aracılığıyla çözümleme** n arbitration

araç [aratʃ] n device, (mekanik) tool, (otomobil) vehicle; **ağır yük taşıma aracı** n HGV; **üstü kapalı yük aracı** n van; **kar temizleme aracı** n snowplough; **karşılıklı sefer yapan araç** n shuttle; **kurtarma aracı** n breakdown van; **uzay aracı** n spacecraft

Aralık [aralək] n (ay) December; **Otuz bir Aralık Cuma günü** on Friday the thirty first of December

arama [arama] n search; **arama ekibi** n search party; **arama motoru** n search engine

aramak [aramak] v ask for, look for, look up, search, seek ▷ vt call; **geri aramak** v call back, phone back, ring back; **telefonla aramak** v ring up; **... ı arıyoruz** We're looking for...; **Dışarıyı aramak istiyorum, hat bağlar mısınız?** I want to make an outside call, can I have a line?

Arap [arap] adj Arab, Arabic ▷ n Arab; **Birleşik Arap Emirlikleri** npl United Arab Emirates

Arapça [araptʃa] n Arabic (language)

arasında [arasənda] prep among, between

arasıra [arasəra] adj occasional

araştırma [araʃtərma] n enquiry, research; **pazar araştırması** n market research

araştırmak [araʃtərmak] v enquire, explore

arazi [arazi] n **bina ve etrafındaki arazi** npl premises

arazide [arazide] n cross-country

ardıç [ardətʃ] n **ardıç kuşu** n thrush

ardıl [ardəl] adj successive

arduvaz [arduvaz] n slate

argo [argo] n slang

arı [arə] n bee; **hezen arısı** n bumblebee

arındırmak [arəndərmak] v **önyargılardan arındırma** n liberation

arıza [arəza] n breakdown; **Arızalı** It's faulty

arife [arife] n eve; **büyük perhizin arife günü** n Shrove Tuesday; **Noel arifesi** n Christmas Eve

Arjantin [arʒantin] adj Argentinian ▷ n Argentina

Arjantinli [arʒantinli] n (kişi) Argentinian (person)

arka [arka] adj back, rear ▷ n behind, rear; **arka ayna** n rear-view mirror; **arka plan** n background; **arkaya dönmek** v turn round, turn around; **Hangisi**

arka kapının anahtarı? Which is the key for the back door?

Arka [arka] *abr* **Lütfen Arka Sayfaya Bakınız** *abbr* PTO

arkada [arkada] *adv* back ▷ *prep* behind

arkadaş [arkadaʃ] *n* friend; *v* friend *(social media)* **arkadaşlıktan çıkarmak** unfriend; **erkek arkadaş** *n* boyfriend; **iş arkadaşı** *n* associate; **kalem arkadaşı** *n* penfriend; **kız arkadaş** *n* girlfriend; **oda arkadaşı** *n* roommate; **sınıf arkadaşı** *n* classmate; **Arkadaşlarımla geldim** I'm here with my friends; **Buraya arkadaşlarımı görmeye geldim** I'm here visiting friends

arkasında [arkasənda] *adv* behind

arkeolog [arkeolog] *n* archaeologist

arkeoloji [arkeoloʒi] *n* archaeology

armağan [arma:an] *n* gift, present *(gift)*; **birine ufak bir armağan alma** *n* treat; **Bir çocuk için armağan almak istiyordum** I'm looking for a present for a child; **Bu armağan sizin için** This is a gift for you; **Eşime bir armağan almak istiyordum** I'm looking for a present for my husband, I'm looking for a present for my wife

armonika [armonika] *n* mouth organ

armut [armut] *n* pear

Arnavut [arnavut] *adj* Albanian ▷ *n (kişi)* Albanian *(person)*

Arnavutça [arnavuttʃa] *n (dil)* Albanian *(language)*

Arnavutluk [arnavutluk] *n* Albania

aromaterapi [aromaterapi] *n* aromatherapy

arpa [arpa] *n* barley

arsa [arsa] *n* plot *(piece of land)*

arsız [arsəz] *adj* cheeky

arşiv [arʃiv] *n* archive

art arda [artarda] *adj* **ardı ardına** *adj* consecutive

artık [artək] *adv* yet *(interrogative)*; **artık yıl** *n* leap year; **artık yemek** *npl* leftovers

artış [artəʃ] *n* increase

artmak [artmak] *v* increase; **gitgide artarak** *adv* increasingly

artrit [artrit] *n* **Artrit hastasıyım** I suffer from arthritis

arttırmak [arttərmak] *v* **açık arttırma** *n* auction

arzu [arzu] *n* desire ▷ *v* **arzu etmek** *v* desire

as [as] *n* ace; **as solist** *n* lead singer

asansör [asansør] *n* **Asansör nerede?** Where is the lift?; **Asansör var mı?** Is there a lift?; **Tekerlekli sandalyeler için asansör var mı?** Do you have a lift for wheelchairs?

asfalt [asfalt] *n* tarmac

asık [asək] *adj* **suratı asık** *adj* sulky

asılmak [asəlmak] *vi* hang

asi [asi] *adj* disobedient

asistan [asistan] *n* assistant; **kişisel asistan** *n* personal assistant, PA

asit [asit] *n* acid; **asit yağmuru** *n* acid rain

asker [asker] *n* soldier; **asker traşı** *n* crew cut; **askeri öğrenci** *n* cadet

askeri [askeri] *adj* military

askı [askə] *n* hanger; **askıya alma** *n* suspension; **askıya almak** *v* suspend; **elbise askısı** *n* coathanger; **kol askısı** *(sağlık) n* sling; **pantolon askıları** *npl* braces

askılık [askələk] *n* rack

asla [asla] *adv* never

aslan [aslan] *n* lion, *(dişi)* lioness

Aslan [aslan] *n* **Aslan burcu** *n* Leo

aslında [aslənda] *adv* actually, basically

asma [asma] *n (bitki)* vine; **asma köprü** *n* suspension bridge; **asma kilit** *n* padlock

asmak [asmak] *vt* hang; **suratını asmak** *v* sulk

aspirin [aspirin] *n* aspirin; **Aspirin alamıyorum** I can't take aspirin; **Aspirin rica ediyorum** I'd like some aspirin

ast [ast] *n* inferior

astar [astar] *n (kumaş)* lining

astım [astəm] *n* asthma; **Astımım var** I suffer from asthma

astroloji [astroloʒi] *n* astrology

astronomi [astronomi] *n* astronomy

astronot [astronot] *n* astronaut

Asya [asja] *adj* Asian ▷ *n* Asia

Asyalı [asjalə] *adj* Asiatic ▷ *n* Asian

aşağı [aʃa:ə] *adj (durum)* inferior, *(konum)* low ▷ *adv (konum)* low; **aşağıya inmek** *v* come down; **baş aşağı** *adv* upside down; **daha aşağı** *adj* lower

aşağıda [aʃa:əda] *adv* down

aşçı [aʃtʃə] *n* **Aşçının özel tercihi nedir?** What is the chef's speciality?

aşçıbaşı [aʃtʃəbaʃə] *n* chef

aşçılık [aʃtʃələk] *n* cookery

aşı [aʃə] *n (tıp)* jab, *(tıp)* vaccination; **Aşı yaptırmam gerek** I need a vaccination

aşık [aʃək] *n* lover

aşılamak [aʃəlamak] *v* vaccinate

aşırı [aʃərə] *adj* excessive, extreme; **aşırı derecede** *adv* extremely, terribly; **aşırı derecede korkmuş** *adj* terrified; **aşırı duygusal** *adj* soppy; **aşırı kilolu** *adj* overweight; **aşırı uçta** *n* extremist

aşırıcılık [aʃərədʒələk] *n* extremism

aşırma [aʃərma] *n (dükkanda)* shoplifting

aşina [aʃina] *adj* **aşina olmayan** *adj* unfamiliar

at [at] *n (hayvan)* horse; **at arabası** *n* buggy, cart; **at nalı** *n* horseshoe; **at yarışı** *n* horse racing; **ata binme** *n* riding; **sallanan at** *n* rocking horse; **yarış atı** *n* racehorse; **At yarışı görmek isterdim** I'd like to see a horse race; **Ata binebilir miyiz?** Can we go horse riding?; **Ata binmeye gidelim** Let's go horse riding

ata [ata] *n* ancestor

atamak [atamak] *v* appoint

atardamar [atardamar] *n* artery

atasözü [atasözy] *n* proverb

ataş [ataʃ] *n* paperclip

ateş [ateʃ] *n* shot, *(sağlık)* fever; **ateş etme** *n* shooting; **ateş etmek** *vt* shoot; **ateşe dayanıklı** *adj* ovenproof; **şenlik ateşi** *n* bonfire; **Ateşi çok yüksek** He has a fever

ateşkes [ateʃkes] n ceasefire, truce

ateşleme [ateʃleme] n ignition

atık [atək] v **atık boşaltmak** vt drain ▷ n **atık borusu** n drain, drainpipe

atıştırma [atəʃtərma] n snack

atkı [atkə] n *(giysi)* muffler

atkuyruğu [atkujru:u] n ponytail

atlama [atlama] n **sırıkla atlama** n pole vault; **uzun atlama** n long jump; **yüksek atlama** n high jump

atlamak [atlamak] vi jump ▷ vt skip; **engel atlama** n show-jumping; **hızla atlamak** v plunge ▷ n **uzun atlama** n jump

Atlantik [atlantik] n Atlantic

atlas [atlas] n atlas

atlet [atlet] n athlete, vest

atletik [atletik] adj athletic

atletizm [atletizm] npl athletics

atlıkarınca [atləkarəndʒa] n merry-go-round

ATM [atm] abr **Buralarda ATM var mı?** Is there a cash machine here?; **En yakın ATM nerede?** Where is the nearest cash machine?

atma [atma] n **işten atma** n sack *(dismissal)*

atmak [atmak] v dump, scrap, throw away, throw out, toss ▷ vt throw; **çığlık atmak** v scream; **e-posta atmak** v email *(a person)*; **göz atmak** vi browse; **hapse atmak** v jail; **işten atmak** v sack; **şaplak atmak** v spank; **mesaj atmak** v text; **tehlikeye atmak** v endanger; **tokat atmak** v smack

atmosfer [atmosfer] n atmosphere

atom [atom] n atom; **atom bombası** n atom bomb

atölye [atølje] n workshop

au-pair [aupair] n au pair

av [av] n hunting; **balık avlamak** n fishing; **kaçak avlanmış** adj poached *(caught illegally)*

avanak [avanak] n twit

avara [avara] v **avara etmek** v bounce

avare [avare] n rambler

avcı [avdʒə] n hunter

avlamak [avlamak] v hunt; **balık avlamak** n fish

avlu [avlu] n courtyard, yard *(enclosure)*

avokado [avokado] **(avokadolar)** n avocado

avro [avro] n euro

Avrupa [avrupa] adj European ▷ n Europe; **Avrupa Birliği** n European Union

Avrupalı [avrupalə] n European

avuçiçi [avutʃitʃi] n palm *(part of hand)*

avukat [avukat] n attorney, lawyer

Avustralasya [avustralasja] n Australasia

Avustralya [avustralja] n Australia

Avustralyalı [avustraljalə] adj Australian ▷ n Australian

Avusturya [avusturja] adj Austrian ▷ n Austria

Avusturyalı [avusturjalə] n Austrian

ay [aj] n *(uydu)* moon, *(zaman)* month; **bir ay önce** a month ago; **bir ay sonra** in a month's time;

Beş ay sonra doğuracağım I'm due in five months

ayak, ayaklar [ajak, ajaklar] *n* foot; **ayağını yere vurmak** *v* stamp; **ayak parmağı** *n* toe; **ayak uzmanı** *n* chiropodist; **ayaklarını sürüyerek yürümek** *v* shuffle; **ayaklı merdiven** *n* stepladder; **çıplak ayak** *adj* barefoot; **çıplak ayakla** *adv* barefoot; **karbon ayak izi** *n* carbon footprint; **yangılı ayak şişi** *n* bunion; **Ayaklarım ağrıyor** My feet are sore

ayak bileği [ajakbileji:] *n* ankle

ayakizi [ajakizi] *n* footprint

ayakkabı [ajakkabə] *n* shoe; **ayakkabı bağı** *n* shoelace; **ayakkabı cilası** *n* shoe polish; **lastik spor ayakkabısı** *npl* trainers; **spor ayakkabısı** *npl* sneakers; **Ayakkabılar hangi katta?** Which floor are shoes on?; **Ayakkabılarımın topuklarını değiştirebilir misiniz?** Can you re-heel these shoes?; **Ayakkabımda delik var** I have a hole in my shoe; **Bu ayakkabıları tamir edebilir misiniz?** Can you repair these shoes?

ayakkabıcı [ajakkabədʒə] *n* shoe shop

ayaklanma [ajaklanma] *n* outbreak, riot

ayaklar [ajaklar] *npl* feet

ayarlama [ajarlama] *n* adjustment, set

ayarlamak [ajarlamak] *v* adjust ▷ *vt* set

ayarlanabilir [ajarlanabilir] *adj* adjustable

ayartma [ajartma] *n* temptation

ayçiçeği [ajtʃitʃeji:] *n* sunflower

aygır [ajgər] *n* **deniz aygırı** *n* walrus

aygıt [ajgət] *n* apparatus

ayı [ajə] *n* bear; **kutup ayısı** *n* polar bear; **oyuncak ayı** *n* teddy bear

ayık [ajək] *adj* sober

ayırılmak [ajərəlmak] *v* part with

ayırım [ajərəm] *n* **cinsiyet ayrımcılığı yapan** *adj* sexist

ayırmak [ajərmak] *vt* separate, split

ayırt [ajərt] *n* **ayırt etmek** *v* distinguish

ayin [ajin] *n* (kilise) mass (church), (tören) ritual; **Ayin ne zaman?** When is mass?

ayinsel [ajinsel] *adj* ritual

aylık [ajlək] *adj* (zaman) monthly

ayna [ajna] *n* mirror; **arka ayna** *n* rear-view mirror; **yan ayna** *n* wing mirror

aynasız [ajnasəz] *n* cop

aynı [ajnə] *adj* same; **aynı anda** *adv* simultaneously; **aynı anda olan** *adj* simultaneous; **aynı fikirde olmak** *v* agree; **Bana da aynısından** I'll have the same

ayraç [ajratʃ] *n* **kitap ayracı** *n* bookmark

ayrı [ajrə] *adj* separate ▷ *adv* apart; **ayrı olarak** *adv* separately ▷ *n* **sürüden ayrılmış** *n* stray; **Hesabı ayrı alalım** Separate bills, please; **sütü ayrı getirin** with the milk separate

ayrıca [ajrədʒa] *prep* plus

ayrıcalık [ajrədʒalək] *n* concession, privilege

ayrılış [ajrələʃ] n parting
ayrılma [ajrəlma] n separation
ayrılmak [ajrəlmak] v leave, split up; **biryerden ayrılmak** v leave; **Yarın sabah onda ayrılıyorum** I will be leaving tomorrow morning at ten a.m.
ayrılmış [ajrəlməʃ] adj reserved
ayrımcılık [ajrəmdʒələk] n discrimination
ayrıntı [ajrəntə] n detail
ayrıntılı [ajrəntələ] adj detailed
az [az] adj slight; **az görülür** adj rare (uncommon); **az pişmiş** adj rare (undercooked); **daha az** pron (miktar olarak) less, (sayıca) fewer; **en az** adj least, minimum; **en aza indirgemek** v minimize; **en azından** adv at least
az-yağlı [azja:lə] adj low-fat
azalma [azalma] n decrease
azalmak [azalmak] v decrease, go down
azaltma [azaltma] n cutback
azaltmak [azaltmak] v diminish, reduce
azap [azap] n vicdan azabı n remorse
azarlamak [azarlamak] v scold, tell off
Azerbaycan [azerbajdʒan] adj Azerbaijani ▷ n Azerbaijan
Azerbaycanlı [azerbajdʒanlə] n Azerbaijani
azgın [azgən] adj fierce
azıcık [azədʒək] adv slightly
azınlık [azənlək] n minority
aziz [aziz] n saint
azmetmek [azmetmek] v persevere

b

baba [baba] n dad, father, (mafya) godfather (criminal leader); **üvey baba** n stepfather; **dedenin babası** n great-grandfather; **isim babası** (vaftiz) n godfather (baptism)
babacığım [babadʒʒəm] n daddy
babalık [babalək] n babalık izni n paternity leave
baca [badʒa] n chimney
bacak [badʒak] n leg; **Bacağım kaşınıyor** My leg itches; **Bacağıma kramp girdi** I've got cramp in my leg; **Bacağımı oynatamıyorum** I can't move my leg; **Bacağını incitti** She has hurt her leg; **Bacağını oynatamıyor** He can't move his leg
badana [badana] n plaster (for wall); **yeniden badana yapmak** v redecorate
badanalamak [badanalamak] v whitewash

badem [badem] *n* almond; **badem ezmesi** *n* marzipan

bademcik [bademdʒik] *n* **bademcik iltihabı** *n* tonsillitis

bademcikler [bademdʒikler] *npl* tonsils

badminton [badminton] *n* badminton; **badminton topu** *n* shuttlecock

bagaj [bagaʒ] *n* baggage, luggage; **bagaj alım** *n* baggage reclaim; **bagaj emanet dolabı** *n* left-luggage locker; **bagaj limiti** *n* baggage allowance; **bagaj trolleyi** *n* luggage trolley; **el bagajı** *n* hand luggage; **emanet bagaj** *n* left-luggage; **emanet bagaj bürosu** *n* left-luggage office; **fazla bagaj** *n* excess baggage; **port bagaj** *n* luggage rack, roof rack; **... uçağının bagajları nerede?** Where is the luggage for the flight from...?; **Bagaj limiti ne kadar?** What is the baggage allowance?; **Bagajım çıkmadı** My luggage hasn't arrived; **Bagajım hasar görmüş** My luggage has been damaged; **Bagajım kaybolmuş** My luggage has been lost; **Bagajımı sigorta ettirebilir miyim?** Can I insure my luggage?; **Bagajımız çıkmadı** Our luggage has not arrived; **Bagajlarımı nerede check-in yaptırabilirim** Where do I check in my luggage?

bağ [ba:] *n* bond, *(üzüm)* vineyard; **ayakkabı bağı** *n* shoelace; **göz bağı** *n* blindfold; **isteğe bağlı** *adj* optional

bağdaşım [ba:daʃəm] *n* **gerçeklerle bağdaşmayan** *adj* unrealistic

bağımlı [ba:əmlə] *adj* addicted ▷ *n* addict

bağımlılık [ba:əmlələk] *n* **uyuşturucu bağımlısı** *n* drug addict

bağımsız [ba:əmsəz] *adj* independent; **bağımsız olarak** *adv* freelance

bağımsızlık [ba:əmsəzlək] *n* independence

bağırmak [ba:ərmak] *v* shout, yell

bağırsak [ba:ərsak] *n* gut

bağırsaklar [ba:ərsaklar] *npl* bowels

bağırtı [ba:ərtə] *n* shout

bağışıklık [ba:əʃəklək] *n* **bağışıklık sistemi** *n* immune system

bağışlama [ba:əʃlama] *n* pardon

bağışlamak [ba:əʃlamak] *v* donate, forgive; **hayatını bağışlamak** *v* spare

bağlamak [ba:lamak] *v* attach, tie, *(kablo)* connect, *(tekne)* moor; **birini bağlamak** *v* tie up; **gözlerini bağlamak** *v* blindfold

bağlanmak [ba:lanmak] *v* **Minimum bağlanma süresi ne kadar?** What's the minimum amount of time?

bağlantı [ba:lantə] *n* conjunction, connection, joint *(junction)*; **bağlantı yolu** *n* slip road; **Bağlantı çok yavaş** The connection seems very slow; **Bağlantı uçağımı kaçırdım** I've missed my connection

Bahama [bahama] n **Bahama Adaları** n Bahamas
bahane [bahane] n pretext
bahar [bahar] n springtime; **bahar temizliği** n spring-cleaning
baharat [baharat] n spice; **köri baharatı** n curry powder; **tuzlu ve baharatlı** adj savoury
bahçe [bahtʃe] n garden; **bahçe kulübesi** n shed; **bahçe merkezi** n garden centre; **bahçe sulama bidonu** n watering can; **hayvanat bahçesi** n zoo; **meyve bahçesi** n orchard; **Bahçeleri gezebilir miyiz?** Can we visit the gardens?
bahçecilik [bahtʃedʒilik] n gardening
bahçıvan [bahtʃəvan] n gardener
bahis [bahis] n bet; **bahis bayii** n betting shop ▷ v **bahse girmek** vi bet
Bahreyn [bahrejn] n Bahrain
bahriyeli [bahrijeli] n sailor
bahsetmek [bahsetmek] v mention
bahşiş [bahʃiʃ] n tip (reward) ▷ v **bahşiş vermek** vt tip (reward); **Bahşiş vermek adet midir?** Is it usual to give a tip?; **Ne kadar bahşiş vermem gerek?** How much should I give as a tip?
bakan [bakan] n (hükümet) minister (government)
bakanlık [bakanlək] n ministry (government)
bakıcı [bakədʒə] n (apartman, ev) caretaker; **çocuk bakıcısı** n childminder, nanny; **bebek bakıcısı** n babysitter
bakım [bakəm] n (araba vb)

maintenance, (hasta vb) care; **çocuk bakımı** n childcare; **yüz bakımı** n facial; **yoğun bakım ünitesi** n intensive care unit
bakınmak [bakənmak] v look round
bakır [bakər] n copper
bakış [bakəʃ] n glance, look; **bakış açısı** n aspect; **bakış noktası** n standpoint, viewpoint; **yaşama bakış** n outlook
bakire [bakire] n virgin
bakiye [bakije] n bank balance
bakkal [bakkal] n grocer, shopkeeper, (dükkan) grocer's
bakla [bakla] n (sebze) broad bean
bakliyat [baklijat] npl pulses
bakmak [bakmak] v look after, (hasta vb) care, (karşılıklı) face; **öfkeyle bakmak** v glare; **bebek bakma** n babysitting; **bebek bakmak** v babysit; **boşluğa bakmak** v stare; **şaşı bakmak** v squint
bakteri [bakteri] npl bacteria
bal [bal] n honey
balayı [balajə] n honeymoon
bale [bale] n ballet; **bale patiği** npl ballet shoes; **Baleye nereden bilet alabilirim?** Where can I buy tickets for the ballet?
balerin [balerin] n ballerina
balet [balet] n ballet dancer
balığı [balʒə] n **yılan balığı** n eel
balık [balək] n fish; **balık avlamak** n fish, fishing; **Japon balığı** n goldfish; **kılıç balığı** n swordfish; **köpek balığı** n shark; **mezgit balığı** n haddock; **morina balığı** n cod; **ringa balığı** n herring; **som**

balığı n salmon; **tatlısu balığı** n freshwater fish; **ton balığı** n tuna; **tuzlanıp tütsülenmiş ringa balığı** n kipper; **İçinde balık olmayan bir yemek yapabilir misiniz?** Could you prepare a meal without fish?; **İçinde et / balık olmayan ne yemekleriniz var mı?** Which dishes have no meat / fish?; **Balık alayım** I'll have the fish; **Balık yemiyorum** I don't eat fish; **Balıklarınız taze mi, dondurulmuş mu?** Is the fish fresh or frozen?; **Balıklardan ne var?** What fish dishes do you have?; **Bu yemekte balık suyu var mı?** Is this cooked in fish stock?; **Burada balık avlanabilir mi?** Can we fish here?; **Burada balık avlayabilir miyim?** Am I allowed to fish here?; **Nerede balık tutabilirim?** Where can I go fishing?

Balık [balək] n **Balık burcu** n Pisces

balıkadam [baləkadam] n **balıkadam kıyafeti** n wetsuit

balıkçı [baləktʃə] **(balıkçılar)** n fisherman, (dükkan) fishmonger; **balıkçı teknesi** n fishing boat; **olta balıkçısı** n angler

balıkçıl [baləktʃəl] n **balıkçıl kuşu** n heron

balıkçılık [baləktʃələk] n **olta balıkçılığı** n angling

balina [balina] n whale

balkabağı [balkaba:ə] n pumpkin

Balkan [balkan] adj Balkan

balkon [balkon] n balcony; **Balkonlu odanız var mı?** Do you have a room with a balcony?

balmumu [balmumu] n wax

balo [balo] n ball (dance); **balo kostümü** n fancy dress

balon [balon] n balloon; **balonlu çiklet** n bubble gum

balta [balta] n axe

bambu [bambu] n bamboo

banço [bantʃo] **(bançolar)** n banjo

band [band] n **elastik band** n rubber band

bandaj [bandaʒ] n bandage

bando [bando] n **bando takımı** n brass band

bank [baŋ] n bench

banka [baŋa] n bank (finance); **banka ödeme emri** n standing order; **banka ücretleri** npl bank charges; **banka hesabı** n bank account; **banka kartı** n debit card; **ticaret bankası** n merchant bank; **Banka bugün açık mı?** Is the bank open today?; **Banka buraya ne kadar uzakta?** How far is the bank?; **Banka ne zaman açılıyor?** When does the bank open?; **Banka ne zaman kapanıyor?** When does the bank close?; **Bankamdan para transferi yapmak istiyorum** I would like to transfer some money from my bank in...; **Burada banka var mı?** Is there a bank here?; **Yakınlarda bir banka var mı?** Is there a bank nearby?

bankacı [baŋadʒə] n banker

bankamatik [baŋamatik] n cash dispenser

banknot [baŋnot] n banknote

banliyö [banlijø] *adj* suburban ▷ *n* suburb

bant [bant] *n* band *(strip)*; **cırt bant** *n* Velcro®; **geniş bant** *n* broadband; **lastik bant** *n* elastic band; **saç bandı** *n* hairband; **taşıyıcı bant** *n* conveyor belt; **yara bandı** *n* Elastoplast®, plaster *(for wound)*

banyo [banjo] *n* bath, bathroom; **banyo havlusu** *n* bath towel; **köpüklü banyo** *n* bubble bath; **Banyo taşıyor** The bathroom is flooded; **Banyoda tutunma rayı var mı?** Are there support railings in the bathroom?; **Odada banyo var mı?** Does the room have a private bathroom?

Baptist [baptist] *n* Baptist

bar [bar] *n* bar *(alcohol)*; **bar işletmecisi** *n* publican; **snack bar** *n* snack bar; **İyi bir bar biliyor musunuz?** Where is there a nice bar?; **Bar ne tarafta?** Where is the bar?

baraj [baraʒ] *n* dam

baraka [baraka] *n* hut

Barbados [barbados] *n* Barbados

barbar [barbar] *adj* barbaric

barbekü [barbeky] *n* barbecue; **Barbekü kısmı nerede?** Where is the barbecue area?

bardak [bardak] *n* **cam bardak** *n* glass *(vessel)*; **Bir bardak limonata lütfen** A glass of lemonade, please; **Bir bardak su** a glass of water; **Temiz bir bardak alabilir miyim lütfen?** Can I have a clean glass, please?

barınak [barənak] *n* shelter

barındırmak [barəndərmak] *v* accommodate

barış [barəʃ] *n* peace

barışçıl [barəʃtʃəl] *adj* peaceful

bariyer [barijer] *n* barrier

bariz [bariz] *adj* glaring

barmen [barmen] **(barmenler)** *n* barman, bartender; **kadın barmen** *n* barmaid

bas [bas] *n* bass; **bas davul** *n* bass drum

basın [basən] *n* **basın toplantısı** *n* press conference; **Basın büronuz var mı?** Do you have a press office?

basınç [basəntʃ] *n* pressure

basit [basit] *adj* simple

basitçe [basittʃe] *adv* simply

basitleştirmek [basitleʃtirmek] *v* simplify

Bask [bask] *adj* Basque ▷ *n* **Bask dili** *n* Basque *(language)*

basketbol [basketbol] *n* basketball

baskı [baskə] *n (gazete, dergi)* edition, *(matbaa)* print; **baskı hatası** *n* misprint; **baskı yapmak** *v* lean on, pressure; **ikinci baskı kitap** *n* paperback

baskın [baskən] *n* raid; **baskın yapmak** *v* raid

baskısı [baskəsə] *n* **deneme baskısı** *n* proof *(for checking)*

Basklı [basklə] *n (kişi)* Basque *(person)*

basmak [basmak] *v (matbaa)* print; **su basmak** *(vt)* *vi* flood

basmakalıp [basmakaləp] *n* stereotype

bastırmak [bastərmak] *v* press; **bastırarak söndürmek** *v* stub out

baston [baston] *n* walking stick

basur [basur] *npl* piles

baş [baʃ] *adj* chief, *(tepede)* principal ▷ *n (vücut)* head *(body part)*, *(yönetim)* head *(principal)*; **adın baş harfleri** *n* initials; **baş ağrısı** *n* headache; **baş aşağı** *adv* upside down; **baş belası** *n* pest; **baş eğmek** *v* bow; **baş parmak** *n* thumb ▷ *v* **başı çekmek** *v* head; **başı dönmüş** *adj* dizzy; **başıyla onaylamak** *v* nod; **baştan başa** *prep* throughout; **merdiven başı** *n* landing; **saat başı** *adv* hourly

Başak [baʃak] *n* **Başak burcu** *n* Virgo

başarı [baʃarə] *n* achievement, success ▷ *v* **başarısız olmak** *vi* fail

başarılı [baʃarələ] *adj* successful

başarısız [baʃarəsəz] *adj* unsuccessful

başarısızlık [baʃarəsəzlək] *n* failure

başarıyla [baʃarəjla] *adv* successfully

başarmak [baʃarmak] *v* achieve, succeed

başbakan [baʃbakan] *n* prime minister

başına [baʃəna] *prep* per

başka [baʃka] *adj*, *adv* **başka bir yerde** *adv* elsewhere; **başka türlü** *adv* otherwise; **ilgisini başka yöne çekmek** *v* distract; **Başka bir oda istiyorum** I'd like another room; **Başka bir yol var mı?** Is there a diversion?; **Başka neyiniz var?** Have you anything else?; **Başka odanız var mı?** Do you have any others?; **Bunun başka**

rengi var mı? Do you have this in another colour?

başkaldırmak [baʃkaldərmak] *v* riot

başkan [baʃkan] **(başkanlar)** *n* chairman, *(şirket)* president, *(okul)* prefect; **belediye başkanı** *n* mayor

başkent [baʃkent] *n* capital

başlama [baʃlama] *n* **başlama vuruşu** *n* kick-off; **başlama vuruşu yapmak** *v* kick off

başlamak [baʃlamak] *v* begin ▷ *vt* start

başlangıç [baʃlangətʃ] *adj (ilk)* initial ▷ *n* beginning, *(çıkış)* outset, *(iş, yarış vb)* start; **başlangıç olarak** *adv* originally

başlangıçta [baʃlangətʃta] *adv* initially

başlatmak [baʃlatmak] *vi* start ▷ *vt* launch

başlayan [baʃlajan] *adj* **yeni başlayan** *n* beginner

başlıca [baʃlədʒa] *adv* mainly, primarily

başlık [baʃlək] *n* caption, *(haber)* headline, *(kitap, albüm vb)* title; **duş başlığı** *n* shower cap

başpiskopos [baʃpiskopos] *n* archbishop

başrol [baʃrol] *n (oyun/film)* lead *(in play/film)*

baştanbaşa [baʃtanbaʃa] *adj* thorough

başucu [baʃudʒu] *n* **başucu lambası** *n* bedside lamp

başvurmak [baʃvurmak] *v* resort to

başvuru [baʃvuru] *n* application; **başvuru formu** *n* application form

başvurucu [baʃvurudʒu] *n* applicant

bataklık [bataklək] *n* bog, marsh, swamp

batı [batə] *adj* west, western ▷ *n* west; **batıya doğru** *adj* westbound

Batı [batə] *n* **Batı Hint Adaları** *npl* West Indian, West Indies

batıl [batəl] *adj* **batıl inançları olan** *adj* superstitious

batmak [batmak] *vi* sink

battal [battal] *adj* **battal boy yatak** *n* king-size bed

battaniye [battanije] *n* blanket; **elektrikli battaniye** *n* electric blanket; **Bana bir battaniye daha getirir misiniz lütfen?** Please bring me an extra blanket

Bay [baj] *n* Mr

bayağı [baja:ə] *adv (oldukça)* pretty

bayan [bajan] *n (evlenmemiş kadınlara hitap şekli)* Miss, *(evli olup olmadığını belirtmeyenler için)* Ms, *(hanım)* Mrs; **Bayanlar tuvaleti nerede?** Where is the ladies?; **Bir bayan doktorla konuşmak istiyorum** I'd like to speak to a female doctor; **Bir bayan polisle konuşmak istiyorum** I want to speak to a policewoman

bayat [bajat] *adj* stale

bayılmak [bajəlmak] *v* faint, pass out; **Bayıldı** She has fainted

bayii [bajii] *n* **bahis bayii** *n* betting shop; **gazete bayii** *n* newsagent

baykuş [bajkuʃ] *n* owl

bayrak [bajrak] *n* flag

Bayram [bajram] *n* **Musevilerin Fısıh Bayramı** *n* Passover

bazen [bazen] *adv* sometimes

bazı [bazə] *pron* some

bebe [bebe] *n* **bebe sandalyesi** *n* highchair

bebek [bebek] *n* baby; **ıslak bebek mendili** *n* baby wipe; **bebe bisküvisi** *n* rusk; **bebek arabası** *n* pram; **bebek bakıcısı** *n* babysitter; **bebek bakma** *n* babysitting; **bebek bakmak** *v* babysit; **bebek bezi** *n* nappy; **bebek karyolası** *n* cot; **bebek sütü** *n* baby milk; **oyuncak bebek** *n* doll; **Bebeği nerede emzirebilirim?** Where can I breast-feed the baby?; **Bebeğin altını nerede değiştirebilirim?** Where can I change the baby?; **Bebek sandalyeniz var mı?** Do you have a baby seat?; **Bebekli aileler için kolaylıklarınız var mı?** Are there facilities for parents with babies?

beceri [bedʒeri] *n* skill

becerikli [bedʒerikli] *adj* skilful, skilled

beceriksiz [bedʒeriksiz] *adj* awkward

becermek [bedʒermek] *v* manage

bedava [bedava] *adj* free *(no cost)*

bedbin [bedbin] *adj* moody

beden [beden] *n* body; **bedenine göre büyük** *adj* outsize

beğenmek [bejenmek] *n* **kendini beğenmiş** *adj* arrogant, bigheaded

bej [beʒ] *adj* beige

bekar [bekar] *n* bachelor; **bekarlığa veda partisi** *(erkek) n* stag night; **Bekarım** I'm single

bekçi [bektʃi] *n* warden

bekle [bekle] *n* **Lütfen beni bekleyin** Please wait for me

bekleme [bekleme] *adj* **beklemede bilet** *n* stand-by ticket

beklemek [beklemek] *v* wait for ▷ *vt* wait; **bekleme listesi** *n* waiting list; **bekleme odası** *n* waiting room; **olması beklenen** *adj* due; **uçuş bekleme salonu** *n* departure lounge; **yatmayıp beklemek** *v* wait up

beklenti [beklenti] *n* **gelecek beklentisi** *n* prospect

bekleyiş [beklejiʃ] *n* **kuşku ve gerilimli bekleyiş** *n* suspense

bektaşi [bektaʃi] *n* **bektaşi üzümü** *n* gooseberry

bel [bel] *n* waist; **bel çantası** *n* bum bag, money belt

bela [bela] *n* **baş belası** *n* pest

Belarus [belarus] *adj* Belarussian

Belarusca [belarusdʒa] *n* Belarussian *(language)*

Belaruslu [belaruslu] *n* Belarussian *(person)*

Belçika [beltʃika] *adj* Belgian ▷ *n* Belgium

Belçikalı [beltʃikalə] *n* Belgian

belediye [beledije] *n* **belediye başkanı** *n* mayor; **belediye binası** *n* town hall; **belediye meclis üyesi** *n* councillor

belge [belge] *n* document, *(döküm)* transcript; **hasta belgesi** *n* sick note; **sağlık belges** *n* medical certificate; **sigorta belgesi** *n* insurance certificate; **Bu belgenin fotokopisini çektirmek istiyorum** I want to copy this document

belgeleme [belgeleme] *n* documentation

belgeler [belgeler] *npl* documents

belgesel [belgesel] *n* documentary

belirgin [belirgin] *adj* distinctive

belirlemek [belirlemek] *v* **kimlik belirlemek** *v* identify

belirleyici [belirlejidʒi] *adj* decisive

belirsiz [belirsiz] *adj* uncertain, vague; **belli belirsiz** *adj* subtle

belirsizlik [belirsizlik] *n* uncertainty

belirteç [belirtetʃ] *n* adverb

belirti [belirti] *n* trace, *(hastalık)* symptom

belirtmek [belirtmek] *v* specify; **miktar belirtmek** *v* quantify

belkemiği [belkeməə] *n* spine

belki [beːlki] *adv* maybe, perhaps

bellek [bellek] *n* memory

belli [belli] *adj* **belli belirsiz** *adj* subtle; **ne yapacağı belli olmayan** *adj* unpredictable

ben [ben] *pron (kişi)* I, me; **... a geldiğimizde beni uyarır mısınız?** Please let me know wher we get to...; **Ben dondurma alayım** I'd like an ice cream; **Ben gelmiyorum** I'm not coming

bencil [bendʒil] *adj* self-centred, selfish

bengaldeş [bengaldeʃ] *n*
  Bengaldeş ile ilgili *n* Bangladeshi
Bengaldeş [bengaldeʃ] *n*
  Bangladesh
Bengaldeşli [bengaldeʃli] *n*
  Bangladeshi
benim [benim] *adj* my ▷ *pron* mine;
  Benim adım... My name is...;
  Pardon, orası benim yerim
  Excuse me, that's my seat
bent [bent] *n* embankment
benzemek [benzemek] *v* take
  after
benzer [benzer] *adj* similar
benzerlik [benzerlik] *n*
  resemblance, similarity
benzetmek [benzetmek] *v*
  resemble
benzin [benzin] *n* petrol; **benzin**
  deposu *n* petrol tank; **benzin**
  istasyonu *n* petrol station, service
  station; **kurşunsuz benzin** *n*
  unleaded petrol; **Benzin bitti** The
  petrol has run out; **Benzinim bitti**
  I've run out of petrol; **Buraya en**
  yakın benzin istasyonu nerede?
  Is there a petrol station near here?;
  Depo benzin sızdırıyor The
  petrol tank is leaking
beraber [beraber] *adv* **beraber**
  yaşamak *v* live together
berabere [berabere] *n* **berabere**
  kalmak *vt* draw (*equal with*)
berbat [berbat] *adj* awful, nasty;
  berbat etmek *v* spoil, wreck;
  berbat etmek *v* mess up; **Hava**
  çok berbat! What awful weather!
berber [berber] *n* barber
bere [bere] *n* (*giyim*) beret,
  (*tıp*) bruise

beri [beri] *prep* **den beri** *prep* since;
  o zamandan beri *adv* since;
  Dünden beri kusuyorum I've
  been sick since yesterday
beslemek [beslemek] *vt* feed
beslenme [beslenme] *n* nutrition;
  yetersiz beslenme *n*
  malnutrition
besleyici [beslejidʒi] *adj* nutritious
  ▷ *n* (*gıda*) nutrient
beste [beste] *n* composition
besteci [bestedʒi] *n* composer
beş [beʃ] *number* five; **Beş ay sonra**
  doğuracağım I'm due in five
  months; **Beş günlüğüne bir**
  araba kiralamak istiyorum I
  want to hire a car for five days; **Beş**
  numaralı kabin nerede? Where is
  cabin number five?; **Beş yüz...**
  rica ediyorum I'd like five
  hundred...
beşik [beʃik] *n* cradle
beşinci [beʃindʒi] *adj* fifth
betimleme [betimleme] *n*
  description
betimlemek [betimlemek] *v*
  describe
beton [beton] *n* concrete
bey [bej] *n* master
beyan [bejan] *n* **özür beyan**
  etmek *v* excuse
beyaz [bejaz] *adj* white; **beyaz**
  güvercin *n* dove; **beyaz saçlı** *adj*
  grey-haired; **beyaz yazı tahtası** *n*
  whiteboard; **İyi bir beyaz şarap**
  tavsiye edebilir misiniz? Can you
  recommend a good white wine?;
  Bir şişe beyaz şarap a bottle of
  white wine; **Bir sürahi beyaz**
  şarap a carafe of white wine;

Siyah beyaz in black and white

beyin [bejin] n brain

beyzbol [bejzbol] n baseball; **beyzbol kepi** n baseball cap

bez [bez] n **bebek bezi** n nappy; **kurulama bezi** n dishcloth

beze [beze] n gland, *(tatlı)* meringue

bezelye [bezelje] npl peas

bıçak [bətʃak] n blade, knife; **çatal, bıçak, kaşık** n cutlery; **traş bıçağı** n razor, razor blade

bıçaklamak [bətʃaklamak] v stab

bıkmış [bəkməʃ] adj fed up

bıldırcın [bəldərdʒən] n quail

bırakmak [bərakmak] vt keep, quit, stop; **birini arabayla evine bırakma** n lift *(free ride)*; **serbest bırakma** n release ▷ v **serbest bırakmak** v release

bıyık [bəjək] n moustache, whiskers

biber [biber] n pepper; **kırmızı toz biber** n paprika

biberiye [biberije] n rosemary

biberlik [biberlik] n peppermill

biberon [biberon] n baby's bottle

biçim [bitʃim] n **dikdörtgen biçiminde** adj rectangular; **etkili bir biçimde** adv efficiently; **şalvar biçimi** adj baggy; **yaşam biçimi** n lifestyle

biçmek [bitʃmek] v mow; **çim biçme makinesi** n lawnmower, mower ▷ v **fiyat biçmek** vt charge *(price)*

bidon [bidon] n **bahçe sulama bidonu** n watering can

biftek [biftek] n rump steak, steak

bigudi [bigudi] n curler

bikini [bikini] n bikini

bilanço [bilantʃo] n balance sheet

bilardo [bilardo] n billiards

bildik [bildik] adj familiar

bildirim [bildirim] n notification; **bildirimde bulunmak** v notify

bile [bile] adv even

bilek [bilek] n wrist

bileşen [bileʃen] adj component ▷ n component, element

bilet [bilet] n ticket; **beklemede bilet** n stand-by ticket; **bilet gişesi** n booking office, box office, ticket office; **bilet kontrolörü** n ticket inspector; **bilet otomatı** n ticket machine; **bilet turnikesi** n ticket barrier; **günlük bilet** n day return; **gidiş-dönüş bilet** n return ticket; **otobüs bileti** n bus ticket; **otopark bileti** n parking ticket; **tek gidiş bileti** n one-way ticket; **tek yön bilet** n single ticket; **... a gidiş dönüş iki bilet** two return tickets to...; **iki bilet, lütfen** I'd like two tickets, please; **Baleye nereden bilet alabilirim?** Where can I buy tickets for the ballet?; **Bilet almam gerekiyor mu?** Do I need to buy a car-parking ticket?; **Bilet makinası çalışmıyor** The ticket machine isn't working; **Bilet makinası nasıl çalışıyor?** How does the ticket machine work?; **Bilet makinası nerede?** Where is the ticket machine?; **Biletimi değiştirmek istiyorum** I want to change my ticket; **Biletimi kaybettim** I've lost my ticket; **Biletler ne kadar?** How much are the tickets?; **Biletleri**

buradan alabilir miyim? Can I buy the tickets here?; **Biletleri siz ayırtır mısınız lütfen?** Can you book the tickets for us?; **Bir çocuk bileti** a child's ticket; **Bir bilet, lütfen** A ticket, please; **Birkaç seyahati içeren bilet satıyor musunuz?** Do you have multi-journey tickets?; **Bu akşam için iki bilet almak istiyorum** I'd like two tickets for tonight; **Bu akşam için iki bilet lütfen** Two tickets for tonight, please; **Gidiş dönüş bilet ne kadar?** How much is a return ticket?; **Haftalık bir bilet lütfen** A book of tickets, please; **Konser biletlerini nereden alabilirim?** Where can I buy tickets for the concert?; **Nereden bilet alabilirim?** Where can I get tickets?, Where do I buy a ticket?; **Nereden bilet alabiliriz?** Where can we get tickets?; **Tek gidiş bilet ne kadar?** How much is a single ticket?

biletçi [bilettʃi] n bus conductor, ticket collector

bilgi [bilgi] n information, knowledge; **bilgi tazeleme eğitimi** n refresher course; **bilgi vermek** v inform; **bilgi yarışması** n quiz; **teknik bilgi** n know-how; **temel bilgiler** npl basics; **... hakkında bilgi istiyordum** I'd like some information about...

bilgiç [bilgitʃ] n know-all

bilgilendirici [bilgilendiridʒi] adj informative

bilgili [bilgili] adj knowledgeable

bilgisayar [bilgisajar] n computer; **bilgisayar çalışması** n computing; **bilgisayar bilimi** n computer science; **bilgisayar hafızası** hard disk; **bilgisayar oyunu** n computer game; **dizüstü bilgisayarı** n laptop; **Bilgisayar odası nerede?** Where is the computer room?; **Bilgisayarınızı kullanabilir miyim?** May I use your computer?; **Bu bilgisayarda CD yapabilir miyim?** Can I make CDs at this computer?

bilim [bilim] n science; **bilgisayar bilimi** n computer science; **bilim adamı** n scientist; **bilim kurgu** n science fiction; **din bilimi** n theology; **doğa bilimleri uzmanı** n naturalist; **elektronik bilimi** npl electronics; **genetik bilimi** n genetics; **insan bilimi** n anthropology

bilimsel [bilimsel] adj scientific

bilinçli [bilintʃli] adj conscious

bilinçlilik [bilintʃlilik] n consciousness

bilinçsiz [bilintʃsiz] adj unconscious

bilinen [bilinen] adj known

bilinmeyen [bilinmejen] adj bilinmeyen numaralar npl directory enquiries

bilinmez [bilinmez] adj unknown

bilmece [bilmedʒe] n puzzle

bilmek [bilmek] v know; **Bilmiyorum** I don't know

bin [bin] number (sayı) thousand

bina [bina] n **belediye binası** n town hall; **bina sorumlusu** n janitor; **bina ve etrafındaki arazi** npl premises; **Binada asansör var**

mı? Is there a lift in the building?
binici [binidʒi] n rider
binicilik [binidʒilik] n horse riding
bininci [binindʒi] adj thousandth
▷ n thousandth
biniş [biniʃ] n **biniş kartı** n
boarding card, boarding pass;
Biniş kartım burada Here is my
boarding card
binmek [binmek] v get on ▷ vt
(hayvana) ride; **ata binme** n
riding; **bisiklete binme** n cycle
(bike), cycling; **Ata binebilir
miyiz?** Can we go horse riding?;
Ata binmeye gidelim Let's go
horse riding
bir [bɪrr] art a, an ▷ pron one; **... a
bir bilet** a single to... ▷ number
one; **ağır bir şekilde** adv heavily;
başka bir yerde adv elsewhere;
bir anlığına adv momentarily; **bir
anlık** adj momentary; **bir ara** adv
sometime; **bir araya gelmek** v
get together; **bir kaşık dolusu** n
spoonful; **bir şey** pron something;
bir seferinde adv once; **bir
seferlik** n one-off; **bir sonraki** adv
next; **bir yerde** adv someplace,
somewhere; **dokuzda bir** n ninth;
her bir pron each; **herhangi bir
şey** pron anything; **herhangi bir
yer** adv anywhere; **kötü bir
şekilde** adv badly; **Ayrıca bir
ücret ödenmesi gerekiyor mu?**
Is there a supplement to pay?; **bir
ay önce** a month ago; **bir ay
sonra** in a month's time; **bir hafta
önce** a week ago; **bir hafta sonra**
in a week's time; **Bana bir otelde
yer ayırtabilir misiniz?** Can you

book me into a hotel?; **Bir
apartman dairesi bakıyorduk**
We're looking for an apartment;
Bir araç ve dört kişi ne kadar?
How much is the crossing for a car
and four people?; **Bir araç ve iki
kişi ne kadar?** How much is it for a
car with two people?; **Bir çay
lütfen** A tea, please; **Bir çekme
bira lütfen** A draught beer,
please; **Bir çocuğum var** I have a
child; **Bir büroda çalışıyorum** I
work in an office; **Bir bilet, lütfen**
A ticket, please; **Bir dakika lütfen**
Just a moment, please; **Bir
fabrikada çalışıyorum** I work in a
factory; **Bir günlük kayak kartı
almak istiyorum** I'd like a ski pass
for a day; **Bir gece daha kalmak
istiyorum** I want to stay an extra
night; **Bir haftalığı ne kadar?**
How much is it for a week?; **Bir
kahve lütfen** A coffee, please; **Bir
şey içmek ister misiniz?** Would
you like a drink?; **Bir metro
haritası lütfen** Could I have a
map of the tube, please?; **Bir oda
kiralamak istiyorum** I'd like to
rent a room; **Bir otel arıyoruz**
We're looking for a hotel; **Bir otel
tavsiye edebilir misiniz?** Can you
recommend a hotel?; **Bir saatlik
internet bağlantısı kaça?** How
much is it to log on for an hour?;
Bir tarife alabilir miyim, lütfen?
Can I have a timetable, please?;
**Bir torba daha alabilir miyim
lütfen?** Can I have an extra bag,
please?; **Bir villa kiralamak
istiyorum** I'd like to rent a villa;

Hafta sonu için bir araba kiralamak istiyorum I want to hire a car for the weekend; **Haftalık bir bilet lütfen** A book of tickets, please; **Size bir içki ısmarlayabilir miyim?** Can I get you a drink?; **Standart bir kabin bileti** a standard class cabin

bira [bira] n beer; **bira fabrikası** n brewery; **hafif bira** n lager; **Bir çekme bira lütfen** A draught beer, please; **Bir bira daha lütfen** Another beer, please

birader [birader] n **kayın birader** n brother-in-law

birahane [birahane] n pub

biraz [biraz] pron some; **Bana biraz borç verebilir misiniz?** Could you lend me some money?

birey [birej] adj individual

bireysel [birejsel] adj **Bireysel kaza sigortası yaptırmak istiyorum** I'd like to arrange personal accident insurance

biri [biri] pron either; **biri bizi gözetliyor** n reality TV; **birinin hesabına borç kaydetmek** v debit; **herhangi biri** pron anybody, anyone

birikim [birikim] npl savings

birikinti [birikinti] n drift; **su birikintisi** n puddle

birikmek [birikmek] v mount up

biriktirmek [biriktirmek] v put aside, save up

birinci [birindʒi] num **birinci sınıf** adj first-class; **... a birinci sınıf bir gidiş dönüş bilet** a first-class return to...; **Biletimi birinci sınıfa çevirmek istiyorum** I want to

upgrade my ticket; **Birinci sınıf bir kabin** a first-class cabin; **Birinci sınıf seyahat etmek istiyorum** I would like to travel first-class

birisi [birisi] pron somebody, someone

birkaç [birkatʃ] adj few, several ▷ pron few, several

birleşik [birleʃik] adj united; **Birleşik Arap Emirlikleri** npl United Arab Emirates; **Birleşik Devletler** n US, (Amerika) United States; **Birleşik Krallık** (İngiltere) n UK, United Kingdom

birleşim [birleʃim] n **cinsel birleşim** n sexual intercourse

birleşme [birleʃme] n conjugation

birleştirme [birleʃtirme] n combination

birleştirmek [birleʃtirmek] v combine, (kişileri) unite, (parçaları) link (up) ▷ vi join

birlik [birlik] n union, (dernek) association; **Avrupa Birliği** n European Union; **oy birliği** n consensus

birlikler [birlikler] npl (askeri) troops

birlikte [birlikte] adv together; **birlikte yatmak** v sleep together; **bununla birlikte** adv nevertheless; **hep birlikte** adv altogether; **Hepsini birlikte yazın lütfen** All together, please

bisiklet [bisiklet] n bicycle, bike; **üç tekerlekli bisiklet** n tricycle; **bisiklet pompası** n bicycle pump ▷ v **bisiklet sürmek** v cycle; **bisiklet yolu** n cycle path;

bisiklet yolu n cycle lane;
bisiklete binme n cycle (bike),
cycling; **dağ bisikleti** n mountain
bike; **tandem bisiklet** n tandem;
Bisiklet kiralamak istiyorum
I want to hire a bike; **Bisiklet
vitesli mi?** Does the bike have
gears?; **Bisikleti ne zaman geri
getirmem gerekiyor?** When is
the bike due back?; **Bisikletimi
buraya bırakabilir miyim?** Can
I keep my bike here?; **Bisikletin
frenleri var mı?** Does the bike
have brakes?; **Bisikletin geri
frenleri var mı?** Does the bike
have back-pedal brakes?;
Bisikletin lambaları var mı?
Does the bike have lights?; **En
yakın bisiklet tamircisi nerede?**
Where is the nearest bike repair
shop?; **Nereden bisiklet
kiralayabilirim?** Where can I hire
a bike?
bisikletçi [bisiklettʃi] n cyclist
bisküvi [biskyvi] n biscuit; **bebe
bisküvisi** n rusk
bit [bit] npl (saç) lice
bitişiğinde [bitiʃəənde] prep near
bitişik [bitiʃik] adj adjacent;
bitişik nizam ev n semi,
semi-detached house
bitki [bitki] n plant; **bitki örtüsü** n
vegetation; **bitki çayı** n herbal
tea; **bitki yetiştirmek** vi grow;
**Yerel bitkileri ve ağaçları
görmek isterdik** We'd like to see
local plants and trees
bitkin [bitkin] adj shaky
bitmek [bitmek] v (tükenmek) run
out of ▷ vt (son bulmak) finish

bitmiş [bitmiʃ] adj over
bit pazarı [bitpazarə] n flea
market
biyo-çözünür [bijotʃøzynyr] adj
biodegradable
biyokimya [bijokimja] n
biochemistry
biyoloji [bijoloʒi] n biology
biyolojik [bijoloʒik] adj biological
biyometrik [bijometrik] adj
biometric
biz [biz] pron us, we, (kendimiz)
ourselves; **Bizi davet ettiğiniz
için çok teşekkürler** It's very kind
of you to invite us
bizim [bizim] adj our
bizimki [bizimki] pron ours
BlackBerry [pladʒkberrj] n
BlackBerry®
blazer [plazer] n blazer
blog [plog] n blog; **blog yazarı** n
blogger; **blog yazısı** n blogpost
▷ v **blog yazmak** v blog
blok [plok] n block (solid piece),
(bina) block (buildings)
bloke [ploke] v **bloke etmek** v block
blöf [pløf] n bluff ▷ v **blöf yapmak**
v bluff
blucin [pludʒin] npl denims, jeans;
blucin kumaşı n denim
bluz [pluz] n blouse
bodrum [bodrum] n basement
boğa [boa:] n bull
Boğa [boa:] n **Boğa burcu** n Taurus
boğaz [boa:z] n throat
boğazlamak [boa:zlamak] v
strangle
boğmak [boymak] v suffocate
boğucu [bou:dʒu] adj stifling
boğulmak [bou:lmak] v **boğucu**

sıcak *adj* sweltering; **suda boğulmak** *v* drown

boks [boks] *n* box, boxing

bokser [bokser] *n* **bokser şort** *npl* boxer shorts

boksör [boksør] *n* boxer

Bolivya [bolivja] *adj* Bolivian ▷ *n* Bolivia

Bolivyalı [bolivjalə] *n* Bolivian

bomba [bomba] *n* bomb; **atom bombası** *n* atom bomb; **gözyaşı bombası** *n* teargas; **saatli bomba** *n* time bomb

bombacı [bombadʒə] *n* **intihar bombacısı** *n* suicide bomber

bombalama [bombalama] *n* bombing

bombalamak [bombalamak] *vt* bomb

boncuk [bondʒuk] *n* bead

borazan [borazan] *n* trumpet

borç [bortʃ] *n* debt; **birinin hesabına borç kaydetmek** *v* debit; **borçlu olmak** *v* owe; **vadesi geçmiş borç** *npl* arrears

bornoz [bornoz] *n* bathrobe

borsa [borsa] *n* stock exchange, stock market

borsacı [borsadʒə] *n* stockbroker

boru [boru] *n* pipe; **atık borusu** *n* drain, drainpipe; **boru hattı** *n* pipeline; **egzos borusu** *n* exhaust pipe; **lağım borusu** *n* sewer

Bosna [bosna] *adj* Bosnian ▷ *n* Bosnia

Bosna-Hersek [bosnahersek] *n* Bosnia and Herzegovina

Bosnalı [bosnalə] *n (kişi)* Bosnian *(person)*

boş [boʃ] *adj (daire, ev, sandalye)* vacant, *(insan)* idle, *(kağıt, zihin)* blank, *(mekan)* empty; **boş durmak** *v* mess about; **boş vakit** *n* leisure; **boş zaman** *n* spare time

boşaltmak [boʃaltmak] *v* unpack, *(bina)* evacuate, *(yük)* unload ▷ *vt* empty; **atık boşaltmak** *vt* drain

boşanma [boʃanma] *n* divorce

boşanmış [boʃanməʃ] *adj* divorced; **Boşandım** I'm divorced

boşluk [boʃluk] *n (konum)* slot, *(mekan)* space, *(uzay, geometri)* void, *(yazı, zihin)* blank; **boşluğa bakmak** *v* stare; **boşluk payı** *(tavanda)* n headroom; **karın boşluğu ile ilgili** *adj* coeliac

bot [bot] *n* **Fiyata botlar da dahil mi?** Does the price include boots?; **Kayak botu kiralamak istiyorum** I want to hire boots

Botsvana [botsvana] *n* Botswana

bovling [bovling] *n* tenpin bowling

bowling [bovling] *n* bowling; **bowling salonu** *n* bowling alley

boy [boj] *n* **battal boy yatak** *n* king-size bed; **boy göstermek** *v* turn up; **orta boy** *adj* medium-sized; **uzun boylu** *adj* tall; **Boyunuz kaç?** How tall are you?

boya [boja] *n (giysi)* dye, *(yapı)* paint; **boya fırçası** *n* paintbrush; **mum boya** *n* crayon; **Dip boya yapar mısınız lütfen?** Can you dye my roots, please?; **Saçımı boyar mısınız lütfen?** Can you dye my hair, please?

boyalı [bojalə] *adj* tinted

boyama [bojama] *n* colouring

boyamak [bojamak] v dye ▷ vt
paint

boylam [bojlam] n longitude

boynuz [bojnuz] n horn

boyun [bojun] n neck; **boyun
eğmek** v obey

boyunca [bojundʒa] prep along

boyut [bojut] n extent, size; **üç
boyutlu** adj three-dimensional

bozkır [bozkər] n moor

bozmak [bozmak] v break down;
kararı bozmak v overrule; **sinir
bozucu** adj annoying; **sinirini
bozmak** v annoy

bozuk [bozuk] adj **Arabam
bozuldu** My car has broken down;
**Bana... lık bozuk para verebilir
misiniz?** Could you give me
change of...?; **Biraz bozuk para
verebilir misiniz?** Can you give
me some change, please?; **Bozuk
param yok** I don't have anything
smaller; **Bozuk paranız var mı?**
Do you have any small change?; **Et
bozulmuş** This meat is off;
**Kusura bakmayın, hiç bozuk
param yok** Sorry, I don't have any
change; **Taksimetre bozuk** The
meter is broken; **Telefon için
bozuk para rica ediyorum** I'd like
some coins for the phone, please

böbrek [bøbrek] n kidney

böbürlenmek [bøbyrlenmek] v
boast

böcek [bødʒek] n beetle, bug,
insect; **böcek ilacı** n insect
repellent; **böcek zehiri** n
pesticide; **cırcır böceği** n cricket
(insect); **hamam böceği** n
cockroach; **uç uç böceği** n

ladybird; **Böcek ilacınız var mı?**
Do you have insect repellent?;
Odamda böcek var There are
bugs in my room

böğürtlen [bø:yrtlen] n
blackberry

bölge [bølge] n district, region,
(arazi) territory, (kent) precinct,
(savaş, kuraklık) zone, (seçim)
ward (area); **kırsal bölge** n
countryside; **kilisenin dini
bölgesi** n parish; **seçmen
bölgesi** n constituency,
electorate; **yayalara özel bölge** n
pedestrian precinct; **Bu bölgenin
haritasını nereden alabilirim**
Where can I buy a map of the
region?

bölgesel [bølgesel] adj regional

bölme [bølme] n division

bölmek [bølmek] vt divide

bölüm [bølym] n (bina, konum)
section, (dizi) episode, (idari)
department, (kitap) chapter

börek [børek] n pie

böyle [bøjle] adj such

böylesine [bøjlesine] adv such

brendi [brendi] n brandy; **Ben
brendi alayım** I'll have a brandy

Brezilya [brezilja] adj Brazilian
▷ n Brazil

Brezilyalı [breziljalə] n Brazilian

brifing [brifing] n briefing

brokoli [brokoli] n broccoli

bronşit [bronʃit] n bronchitis

bronz [bronz] n bronze;
bronzlaşmış ten n tan

bronzlaşma [bronzlaʃma] n
suntan

bronzlaşmak [bronzlaʃmak] n

bronzlaşma losyonu n suntan lotion

broş [broʃ] n brooch

broşür [broʃyr] n brochure, leaflet, pamphlet; **tanıtma broşürü** n prospectus; **... hakkında broşürünüz var mı?** Do you have any leaflets about...?; **Broşürünüz var mı?** Do you have any leaflets?

Brüksel lahanası [bryksellahanasə] n Brussels sprouts

bu [bu] adj that, this ▷ pron this; **bu arada** adv meantime; **bu gece** adv tonight; **bununla birlikte** adv nevertheless; **ya o, ya bu** conj either (... or); **Bu akşam ne yapıyorsunuz?** What are you doing this evening?; **Bu anahtar nerenin?** What's this key for?; **Bu armağan sizin için** This is a gift for you; **Bu elbiseyi deneyebilir miyim?** Can I try on this dress?; **Bu eşim** This is my husband, This is my wife; **Bu ilacı kullanıyorum** I'm on this medication; **Bu kadar yeter, sağolun** That's enough, thank you; **Bu koltuk boş mu?** Is this seat free?; **Bu mektubu postalamak istiyorum** I'd like to send this letter; **Bu ne demek?** What does this mean?; **Bu otobüs... a gider mi?** Does this bus go to...?; **Bu pantalonu deneyebilir miyim?** Can I try on these trousers?; **Bu partnerim** This is my partner; **Bu sabahtan beri kusuyorum** I've been sick since this morning; **Bunu**

değiştirmek istiyorum I'd like to exchange this; **Bunu kasaya koyun lütfen** Put that in the safe, please; **Bunun içinde ne var?** What is in this?

buçuk [butʃuk] n **Saat iki buçuk** It's half past two; **Saat neredeyse iki buçuk** It's almost half past two

Buda [buda] n Buddha

Budist [budist] adj Buddhist ▷ n Buddhist

Budizm [budizm] n Buddhism

bugün [bugyn] adv today; **Banka bugün açık mı?** Is the bank open today?; **Bugün açık mı?** Is it open today?; **Bugün deniz dalgalı mı?** Is the sea rough today?; **Bugün günlerden ne?** What day is it today?; **Bugün ne yapmak istersiniz?** What would you like to do today?; **Bugünün tarihi nedir?** What is today's date?

bugünlerde [bugynlerde] adv nowadays

buğday [bu:daj] n wheat; **buğday alerjisi** n wheat intolerance

buğu [bu:u] n condensation

buhar [buhar] n steam

buji [buʒi] n spark plug

buket [buket] n bouquet

bukle [bukle] n (saç) curl, (saç) lock (hair)

bulantı [bulantə] n nausea; **hamilelik bulantısı** n morning sickness

bulaşıcı [bulaʃədʒə] adj catching, contagious, infectious; **Bulaşıcı mı?** Is it infectious?

bulaşık [bulaʃək] n **bulaşık deterjanı** n washing-up liquid;

between (*arasında*)
> **between** you and me
> *senin ve benim aramda*

from (*-den/dan*)
> **from Izmir**
> *İzmir'den*

in (*-de/da, -in içinde*)
> **in** Ankara   **in** the room
> *Ankara'da*   *odada*

into (*-in içine doğru, -e doğru*)
> Get **into** the car.
> *Arabaya gir.*

of (*-ın/in*)
> at the front **of** the house
> *evin önünde*

on (*-in üzerinde*)
> The cat is **on** the sofa.
> *Kedi koltuğun üzerindedir.*

over (*üzerinde- arada boşluk olacak şekilde*)
> The plane is flying **over** the city.
> *Uçak şehrin üzerinde uçuyor.*

to (*-e/a, -e doğru*)
> **to** London   I am going **to** London.
> *Londra'ya*   *Ben Londra'ya gidiyorum.*

under (*-in altında*)
> The dog is **under** the table.
> *Köpek masanın altında.*

with (*ile*)
> Come **with** me.   Water **with** ice.
> *Benimle gel.*   *Buzlu su.*

without (*-siz, -sız*)
> **without** him   **without** milk
> *Onsuz*   *sütsüz*

ice, please; **Buz pateni yapmak için nereye gidebiliriz?** Where can we go ice-skating?

buzdağı [buzda:ə] n iceberg

buzdolabı [buzdolabə] n fridge, refrigerator

buzlu [buzlu] adj frosty, icy

buzul [buzul] n glacier

Buzul [buzul] n **Kuzey Buzul Kuşağı** n Arctic Circle

büfe [byfe] n (dükkan) kiosk, (mobilya) sideboard; **açık büfe** n buffet

bükmek [bykmek] vt twist

bükülmüş [bykylmyʃ] adj bent (not straight)

büro [byro] n office; **danışma bürosu** n inquiries office; **döviz bürosu** n bureau de change; **emanet bagaj bürosu** n left-luggage office; **enformasyon bürosu** n information office; **turizm bürosu** n tourist office; **Basın büronuz var mı?** Do you have a press office?; **Büronuza nasıl gelebilirim?** How do I get to your office?; **Bir büroda çalışıyorum** I work in an office; **Turizm bürosu nerede?** Where is the tourist office?

bürokrasi [byrokrasi] n bureaucracy

büsbütün [bysbytyn] adv quite

bütçe [byttʃe] n budget

bütün [bytyn] adj complete, (bölünmemiş) intact, (hepsi) all, (tamamı) entire, (tüm) whole ▷ n (tamamı) whole; **Bütün gün hiç kimseyi değil, sadece kendimizi görmek isterdik!** We'd like to see

nobody but us all day!

bütünleyici [bytynlejidʒi] adj complementary

bütünüyle [bytynyjle] adv entirely, quite

büyü [byjy] n magic, spell (magic)

büyücü [byjydʒy] n sorcerer

büyük [byjyk] adj big, (iri) large, (müthiş) great ▷ n major; **çok büyük** adj tremendous; **büyük çoğunluk** n majority; **büyük karides** npl scampi; **büyük mağaza** n department store; **büyük perhizin arife günü** n Shrove Tuesday; **büyük yolcu gemisi** n liner; **bedenine göre büyük** adj outsize; **daha büyük** adj bigger; **yaşça en büyük** adj eldest; **Çok büyük** It's too big; **Büyük beden var mı?** Do you have a large?; **Bunun bir büyük bedeni var mı?** Do you have this in a bigger size?; **Daha büyük bir odanız var mı?** Do you have a bigger one?; **Ekstra büyük beden var mı?** Do you have an extra large?; **Ev oldukça büyük** The house is quite big

Büyük [byjyk] adj **Büyük perhizin ilk Çarşambası** n Ash Wednesday

büyükanne [byjykanne] n grandmother; **büyükanne ve büyükbaba** npl grandparents

büyükbaba [byjykbaba] n grandfather; **büyükanne ve büyükbaba** npl grandparents

büyükelçi [byjykeltʃi] n ambassador

büyüleyici [byjylejidʒi] adj fascinating

büyülü [byjyly] *adj* magic
büyüme [byjyme] *n* growth
büyümek [byjymek] *v* grow up
  ▷ *vi* grow
büyüteç [byjytetʃ] *n* magnifying
  glass
büyütme [byjytme] *n*
  enlargement
büyütmek [byjytmek] *v* **gözünde**
  büyütmek *v* overestimate

cadde [dʒadde] *n* street
cadı [dʒadə] *n* witch
cahil [dʒahil] *adj* ignorant
cam [dʒam] *n* glass; **ön cam** *n*
  windscreen; **çift cam** *n* double
  glazing; **cam bardak** *n* glass
  (vessel); **cam kenarı koltuğu** *n*
  window seat; **cam sileceği** *n*
  windscreen wiper; **pencere camı**
  n window pane
cami [dʒami] *n* mosque; **Cami**
  nerede var? Where is there a
  mosque?
cam yünü [dʒamjyny] *n*
  fibreglass
can [dʒan] *v* **can kurtaran** *adj*
  life-saving; **can sıkıntısı** *n*
  boredom; **can sıkmak** *v* bore
  (be dull); **canı sıkılmış** *adj*
  bored; **canı sıkkın** *adj*
  depressed
canavar [dʒanavar] *n* monster

cankurtaran [dʒaŋurtaran] *n*
(sahil) lifeguard, *(tıp)* ambulance;
cankurtaran sandalı *n* lifeboat;
cankurtaran simidi *n* lifebelt;
cankurtaran yeleği *n* life jacket;
Cankurtaran çağırın! Get the
lifeguard!; **Cankurtaran var mı?**
Is there a lifeguard?

canlandırmak [dʒanlandərmak]
v revive; **gözünde canlandırmak**
v visualize

canlı [dʒanlə] *adj (hayatta)* alive,
(parlak) vivid, *(yaşayan)* live ▷ *n*
(yaşayan) living; **Canlı müzik
dinleyebileceğimiz bir yer var
mı?** Where can we hear live
music?

cari [dʒari] *adj* **cari hesap** *n*
current account

casus [dʒasus] *n* spy ▷ *v* **casusluk
etmek** *v* spy

casusluk [dʒasusluk] *n* espionage,
spying

catering [dʒatering] *n* catering

caz [dʒaz] *n* jazz

cazibe [dʒazibe] *n* **cazibesine
kapılmak** *v* fall for

CD [si:di:] *n* CD; **CD ne zaman
hazır olur?** When will the CD be
ready?

CD-ROM [si:di:rom] *n*
CD-ROM

cehalet [dʒehalet] *n* ignorance

cehennem [dʒehennem] *n* hell

ceket [dʒeket] *n* jacket

cenaze [dʒenaze] *n* funeral;
cenaze kaldırıcısı *n* undertaker;
**cenazenin gömülmeye ya da
yakılmaya hazırlandığı oda** *n*
funeral parlour

cenin [dʒenin] *n* foetus

cennet [dʒennet] *n* heaven,
paradise

centilmen [dʒentilmen]
(centilmenler) *n* gentleman

CEO [dʒeo] *abbr* CEO

cep [dʒep] *n* pocket; **cep harçlığı** *n*
pocket money; **cep hesap
makinesi** *n* pocket calculator; **cep
matarası** *n* flask; **cep numarası** *n*
mobile number; **cep telefonu** *n*
mobile phone

cephane [dʒephane] *n*
ammunition

cephe [dʒephe] *n* frontier

cereyan [dʒerejan] *n* draught

cerrah [dʒerrah] *n* surgeon

cerrahi [dʒerrahi] *n* **kozmetik
cerrahi** *n* cosmetic surgery;
plastik cerrahi *n* plastic surgery

cesaret [dʒesaret] *n* bravery,
courage; **cesaret verici** *adj*
encouraging; **cesaretini kırmak** *v*
discourage

ceset [dʒeset] *n* corpse

cesur [dʒesur] *adj* brave, daring

cetvel [dʒetvel] *n* ruler *(measure)*

ceviz [dʒeviz] *n* walnut; **Hindistan
cevizi** *n* coconut; **küçük
Hindistan cevizi** *n* nutmeg

ceza [dʒeza] *n* fine, punishment,
sentence *(punishment)*; **dayak
cezası** *n* corporal punishment;
idam cezası *n* capital
punishment; **Ceza ne kadar?**
How much is the fine?; **Cezayı
nereye yatıracağım?** Where do I
pay the fine?

cezalandırmak [dʒezalandərmak]
v penalize, punish

Cezayir [dʒezajir] *adj* Algerian ▷ *n* Algeria

Cezayirli [dʒezajirli] *n* Algerian

cezve [dʒezve] *n* coffeepot

check-in [dʒhedʒkin] *v* **... uçağı için nerede check-in yaptırabilirim?** Where do I check in for the flight to...?; **Check-in yaptırmak istiyorum lütfen** I'd like to check in, please; **En son kaçta check-in yaptırmam gerekiyor?** When is the latest I can check in?; **Kaçta check-in yaptırmam gerekiyor?** When do I have to check in?

cımbız [dʒəmbəz] *npl* tweezers

cırcır [dʒərdʒər] *n* **cırcır böceği** *n* cricket *(insect)*

cırt [dʒərt] *n* **cırt bant** *n* Velcro®

cıva [dʒəva] *n* mercury

cıyaklamak [dʒəjaklamak] *v* squeak

ciddi [dʒiddi] *adj* serious; **Ciddi bir şey mi?** Is it serious?

ciddiyetle [dʒiddijetle] *adv* seriously

ciğer [dʒijer] *n* **Ciğer yiyemem** I can't eat liver

cihaz [dʒihaz] *n* appliance; **üfleme cihazı** *n* Breathalyser®; **çağrı cihazı** *n* bleeper, pager; **gizli dinleme cihazı yerleştirilmiş** *adj* bugged; **işitme cihazı** *n* hearing aid; **inhalasyon cihazı** *n* inhaler; **otopark ödeme cihazı** *n* parking meter; **ses kayıt cihazı** *n* recorder *(music)*, tape recorder; **yağmurlama cihazı** *n* sprinkler

cila [dʒila] *n* polish, *(vernik)* varnish; **ayakkabı cilası** *n* shoe polish; **tırnak cilası** *n* nail varnish

cilalamak [dʒilalamak] *v* polish, varnish

cilt [dʒilt] *n* skin

cimnastik [dʒimnastik] *n* **Cimnastik salonu nerede?** Where is the gym?

cin [dʒin] *n (alkol)* gin; **Ben bir cin tonik alayım lütfen** I'll have a gin and tonic, please

cinayet [dʒinajet] *n* murder

cins [dʒins] *adj* pedigree ▷ *n (hayvan)* breed

cinsel [dʒinsel] *adj* sexual; **cinsel birleşim** *n* sexual intercourse

cinsiyet [dʒinsijet] *n* gender, *(seks)* sex; **cinsiyet ayrımcılığı** *n* sexism; **cinsiyet ayrımcılığı yapan** *adj* sexist

cips [dʒips] *n* crisps

civar [dʒivar] *adv* **Civarda ilginç yürüyüş yerleri var mı?** Are there any interesting walks nearby?

civciv [dʒivdʒiv] *n* chick

coğrafya [dʒoɣrafja] *n* geography

conta [dʒonta] *n* gasket

coşku [dʒoʃku] *n* ecstasy

cömert [dʒømert] *adj* generous

cömertlik [dʒømertlik] *n* generosity

cross-country [dʒrossdʒountrj] *n* **Cross-country kayağı kiralamak istiyorum** I want to hire cross-country skis; **Cross-country kayağı yapmak mümkün mü?** Is it possible to go cross-country skiing?

Cuma [dʒuma] *n* Friday; **Kutsal Cuma** *n* Good Friday; **Cuma günü** on Friday; **Cuma günü için iki**

bilet almak istiyorum I'd like two tickets for next Friday

Cumartesi [dʒumartesi] n Saturday; **önümüzdeki Cumartesi** next Saturday; **bu Cumartesi** this Saturday; **Cumartesi günü** on Saturday; **Cumartesileri** on Saturdays; **geçen Cumartesi** last Saturday; **her Cumartesi** every Saturday; **Cumartesileri** on Saturdays

cumhuriyet [dʒumhurijet] n republic

Cumhuriyet [dʒumhurijet] n **Çek Cumhuriyeti** n Czech Republic; **Dominik Cumhuriyeti** n Dominican Republic; **Orta Afrika Cumhuriyeti** n Central African Republic

cüce [dʒydʒe] **(cüceler)** n dwarf (inf!)

cümle [dʒymle] n sentence (words)

cüret [dʒyret] n nerve (boldness) ▷v **cüret etmek** v dare

cüzdan [dʒyzdan] n (erkek) wallet, (kadın) purse; **evlilik cüzdanı** n marriage certificate; **nüfus cüzdanı** n birth certificate; **Cüzdanım çalındı** My wallet has been stolen; **Cüzdanımı kaybettim** I've lost my wallet

CV [siːviː] n CV

Ç

çaba [tʃaba] n effort, try

çabalamak [tʃabalamak] v go after, try

çabucak [tʃabudʒak] adv promptly

çabuk [tʃabuk] adj prompt, quick; **çabuk kızan** adj irritable

çabukça [tʃabuktʃa] adv quickly

Çad [tʃad] n Chad

çadır [tʃadər] n tent; **çadır direği** n tent pole; **çadır kazığı** n tent peg; **Çadırımızı buraya kurabilir miyiz?** Can we pitch our tent here?; **Çadırın bir geceliği ne kadar?** How much is it per night for a tent?; **Çadırın bir haftalığı ne kadar?** How much is it per week for a tent?; **Bir çadır yeri istiyoruz** We'd like a site for a tent

Çağ [tʃaː] n **Orta Çağ** n Middle Ages

çağdaş [tʃaːdaʃ] adj contemporary

çağlayan [tʃaːlajan] n cataract (waterfall)

çağlayanlar [tʃaːlajanlar] *npl* rapids

çağrı [tʃaːrə] *n* call; **çağrı cihazı** *n* bleeper, pager; **çağrı merkezi** *n* call centre; **uyarı çağrısı** *n* alarm call

çakı [tʃakə] *n* penknife

çakıl [tʃakəl] *n* gravel; **çakıl taşı** *n* pebble

çakırkeyif [tʃakərkejif] *adj* tipsy

çakışmak [tʃakəʃmak] *v* coincide

çakmak [tʃakmak] *n* cigarette lighter, lighter

çalgıcı [tʃalgədʒe] *n* **sokak çalgıcısı** *n* busker

çalı [tʃalə] *n* bush, shrub; **çalı fasulyesi** *n* French beans, runner bean; **çalı meyvesi** *n* berry

çalıkuşu [tʃaləkuʃu] *n* wren

çalılık [tʃaləlak] *n* bush *(thicket)*

çalışan [tʃaləʃan] *n* **serbest çalışan** *adj* self-employed

çalışma [tʃaləʃma] *n* **çalışma alanı** *n* workspace; **çalışma köşesi** *n* workstation; **yol yapım çalışması** *npl* roadworks

çalışmak [tʃaləʃmak] *v* study ▷ *vt* work; **çalışma izni** *n* work permit; **çalışma köşesi** *n* work station; **çalışma saatleri** *npl* office hours; **bilgisayar çalışması** *n* computing; **esnek çalışma saati** *n* flexitime; **köle gibi çalışmak** *v* slave; **... a çalışıyorum** I work for...; **Çalışıyorum** I work; **Nerede çalışıyorsunuz?** Where do you work?; **Sizinle çalışmak bir zevkti** It's been a pleasure working with you

çalkalamak [tʃalkalamak] *vt* shake

çalkalanmak [tʃalkalanmak] *vi* shake

çalkantı [tʃalkantə] *n* turbulence

çalma [tʃalma] *v* **çalma tonu** *n* ringtone

çalmak [tʃalmak] *v* steal, *(zil/çan)* ring ▷ *vt* play *(music)*; **ıslık çalmak** *v* whistle; **çalar saat** *n* alarm clock; **CD çalar** *n* CD player; **kapıyı çalmak** *v* knock *(on the door etc.)*

çam [tʃam] *n* pine

çamaşır [tʃamaʃər] *n* laundry, washing; **çamaşır ipi** *n* clothes line, washing line; **çamaşır kurutma makinesi** *n* spin dryer, tumble dryer; **çamaşır makinesi** *n* washing machine; **çamaşır mandalı** *n* clothes peg; **çamaşır odası** *n* utility room; **çamaşır tozu** *n* washing powder; **iç çamaşırı** *n* lingerie, underwear; **Çamaşır makineleri nerede?** Where are the washing machines?; **Çamaşır makinesi nasıl çalışıyor?** How does the washing machine work?; **Çamaşır servisi var mı?** Is there a laundry service?; **Çamaşır tozunuz var mı?** Do you have washing powder?; **Çamaşırlarımı nerede yıkayabilirim?** Where can I do some washing?

çamaşırhane [tʃamaʃərhane] *n* Launderette®

çamur [tʃamur] *n* mud; **sulu çamur** *n* slush

çamurlu [tʃamurlu] *adj* muddy

çamurluk [tʃamurluk] n
mudguard

çan [tʃan] n **çan sesi** n toll

çanak [tʃanak] n **çanak çömlek** n
pottery; **uydu çanak** n satellite
dish

çanta [tʃanta] n handbag;
alışveriş çantası n shopping bag;
bel çantası n bum bag, money
belt; **evrak çantası** n briefcase;
gecelik seyahat çantası n
overnight bag; **ilk yardım çantası**
n first-aid kit; **okul çantası** n
schoolbag; **omuz çantası** n
satchel; **sırt çantası** n backpack,
holdall, rucksack; **sırt çantasıyla
dolaşan gezgin** backpacker; **sırt
çantasıyla gezme** n backpacking;
tuvalet çantası n sponge bag,
toilet bag

çap [tʃap] n diameter

çapa [tʃapa] n anchor

çapkın [tʃapkən] adj **yalı çapkını** n
kingfisher

çapraz [tʃapraz] n cross

çaput [tʃaput] n rag

çarkıfelek [tʃarkəfelek] n
çarkıfelek meyvası n passion
fruit

çarpıcı [tʃarpədʒə] adj striking

çarpışma [tʃarpəʃma] n collision

çarpışmak [tʃarpəʃmak] v collide
▷ vi (araçla) crash

çarpma [tʃarpma] n bump, hit;
elektrik çarpması n electric
shock; **güneş çarpması** n
sunstroke

çarpmak [tʃarpmak] v
(matematik) multiply; **çarparak
kapatmak** v slam; **çarpma işlemi**

n multiplication; **kazara çarpmak**
v bump into; **vasıta ile çarpmak**
vi crash

çarşaf [tʃarʃaf] n sheet; **yatak
çarşafı** n bed linen; **Çarşaflar kirli**
The sheets are dirty; **Çarşaflarım
kirli** My sheets are dirty

Çarşamba [tʃarʃamba] n
Wednesday; **Büyük perhizin ilk
Çarşambası** n Ash Wednesday;
Çarşamba günü on Wednesday

çatal [tʃatal] n fork; **çatal, bıçak,
kaşık** n cutlery; **Temiz bir çatal
alabilir miyim lütfen?** Could I
have a clean fork please?

çatı [tʃatə] n roof; **Çatı akıyor** The
roof leaks

çatışma [tʃatəʃma] n conflict

çatışmak [tʃatəʃmak] vi clash

çatlak [tʃatlak] adj cracked ▷ n
crack (fracture)

çatlatmak [tʃatlatmak] vi crack

çatmak [tʃatmak] n **kaşlarını
çatmak** v frown

çavdar [tʃavdar] n rye

çavuş [tʃavuʃ] n sergeant

çay [tʃaj] n tea; **çay fincanı** n
teacup; **çay kaşığı** n teaspoon;
çay saati n teatime; **bitki çayı** n
herbal tea; **torba çay** n tea bag;
Bir çay daha alabilir miyiz?
Could we have another cup of tea,
please?; **Bir çay lütfen** A tea,
please

çaydanlık [tʃajdanlək] n kettle,
teapot

çayır [tʃajər] n meadow

Çeçenistan [tʃetʃenistan] n
Chechnya

çek [tʃek] n cheque; **açık çek** n

blank cheque; **çek defteri** n chequebook; **hediye çeki** n gift voucher; **seyahat çeki** n traveller's cheque; **Çek bozdurabilir miyim?** Can I cash a cheque?; **Çek bozdurmak istiyorum lütfen** I want to cash a cheque, please; **Çekle ödeme yapabilir miyim?** Can I pay by cheque?; **Bu seyahat çeklerini bozdurmak istiyorum** I want to change these traveller's cheques; **Seyahat çeki kabul ediyor musunuz?** Do you accept traveller's cheques?; **Seyahat çeklerimi burada bozdurabilir miyim?** Can I change my traveller's cheques here?

çek-yat [tʃekjat] n sofa bed

Çek [tʃek] adj Czech ▷ n (kişi) Czech (person); **Çek Cumhuriyeti** n Czech Republic; **Çek dili** (dil) n Czech (language)

çekici [tʃekidʒi] adj attractive; **ilgi çekici** adj interesting; **Çok çekicisiniz** You are very attractive

çekiç [tʃekitʃ] n hammer

çekiliş [tʃekiliʃ] n draw (tie), raffle

çekilmek [tʃekilmek] v opt out

çekim [tʃekim] n attraction, charm; **yeniden çekim** n remake

çekirdek [tʃekirdek] n pip; **çekirdekli kısım** (meyve) n core; **kahve çekirdeği** n coffee bean; **metal çekirdek** n pellet

çekirge [tʃekirge] n grasshopper; **sopa çekirgesi** n stick insect

çekme [tʃekme] n withdrawal

çekmece [tʃekmedʒe] n drawer;

Çekmece takılmış The drawer is jammed

çekmek [tʃekmek] v attract, withdraw, (ağırlık) weigh ▷ vt pull; **açlık çekmek** v starve; **acı çekmek** v suffer; **arabayı çekmek** v tow away; **başı çekmek** v head; **burnunu çekmek** v sniff; **dikkatini çekmek** v point out; **fişten çekmek** v unplug; **fotoğrafını çekmek** v photograph; **fotokopisini çekmek** v photocopy; **halat çekme oyunu** n tug-of-war; **hesabından çekilen para** n debit; **iç çekme** n sigh; **ilgisini başka yöne çekmek** v distract; **kürek çekmek** v row (in boat); **kenara çekmek** v (araç) pull out, (araç) pull up; **sınav çekmek** n press-up; **röntgenini çekmek** v X-ray

çelik [tʃelik] n steel; **paslanmaz çelik** n stainless steel

çelişki [tʃeliʃki] n contradiction

çelişmek [tʃeliʃmek] v contradict

çene [tʃene] n chin, jaw

çerçeve [tʃertʃeve] n frame; **resim çerçevesi** n picture frame

çeşit [tʃeʃit] n assortment, sort, variety; **çeşitlilik göstermek** v vary

çeşitli [tʃeʃitli] adj miscellaneous, varied, various

çeşitlilik [tʃeʃitlilik] n **çeşitlilik göstermek** v range

çeşme [tʃeʃme] n fountain

çeşni [tʃeʃni] n seasoning

çete [tʃete] n gang

çetin [tʃetin] adj **çetin sınav** n ordeal

çevirimiçi [tʃevirimitʃi] *adj* online

çevirme [tʃevirme] *n (trafik)* roadblock

çevirmek [tʃevirmek] *v* **elektrik düğmesini çevirmek** *v* switch; **geri çevirmek** *v* turn down

çevre [tʃevre] *n* environment, vicinity ▷ *npl* surroundings; **çevre dostu** *adj* ecofriendly, environmentally friendly; **çevre yolu** *n* bypass, ring road

çevrebilim [tʃevrebilim] *n* ecology

çevrelemek [tʃevrelemek] *v* surround

çevresel [tʃevresel] *adj* environmental

çeyrek [tʃejrek] *n* quarter; **çeyrek final** *n* quarter final; **Saat ikiyi çeyrek geçiyor** It's quarter past two

çığ [tʃɣ] *n* avalanche; **Çığ tehlikesi var mı?** Is there a danger of avalanches?

çığlık [tʃɣlək] *n* scream ▷ *v* **çığlık atmak** *v* scream

çıkarıcı [tʃəkarədʒə] *n* **oje çıkarıcı** *n* nail-polish remover

çıkarma [tʃəkarma] *n* **çıkarma işlemi** *v* subtract

çıkarmak [tʃəkarmak] *v* leave out, stick out, take away, *(matematik)* deduct; **üstünü çıkarmak** *v* take off; **diş çıkarmak** *v* teethe; **elden çıkarmak** *v* sell off; **işten çıkarma *(ihtiyaç fazlası olarak)*** *n* redundancy; **işten çıkarmak** *v* lay off

çıkartmak [tʃəkartmak] *v* **işten çıkarmak** *v* dismiss;

ortaya çıkarmak *v* disclose

çıkış [tʃəkəʃ] *n* checkout, exit, way out ▷ *v* **çıkış yapmak** *v* check out; **yangın çıkışı** *n* fire escape; **... çıkışı nerede?** Which exit for...?; **Çıkış nerede?** Where is the exit?

çıkış, kapı [tʃəkəʃkapə] *n* **acil çıkış kapısı** *n* emergency exit

çıkmak [tʃəkmak] *v* come out, get out; **dışarı çıkmak** *n* go out, outing; **iki katına çıkmak** *vt* double; **karşı çıkmak** *v* oppose; **ortaya çıkmak** *v* show up; **sahip çıkmak** *v* own up; **sıradan çıkmak** *v* fall out; **tura çıkmak** *v* tour; **yürüyüşe çıkma** *n* hike; **yola çıkmak** *v* go away, start off; **zahmetli bir yürüyüşe çıkmak** *v* trek

çıkmaz [tʃəkmaz] *n* **çıkmaz sokak** *n* dead end

çıktı [tʃəktə] *n (bilgisayar)* printout

çıldırmak [tʃəldərmak] *n* **öfkeden çıldırmış** *adj* furious

çılgın [tʃəlgən] *adj* crazy, frantic, mad *(angry)*

çılgınca [tʃəlgəndʒa] *adv* madly

çılgınlık [tʃəlgənlək] *n* madness, mania

çıngırak [tʃəngərak] *n* rattle; **çıngıraklı yılan** *n* rattlesnake

çıplak [tʃəplak] *adj* bare, naked, nude ▷ *n* nude; **çıplak ayak** *adj* barefoot; **çıplak ayakla** *adv* barefoot ▷ *v* **sığ suda çıplak ayak yürümek** *v* paddle

çırak [tʃərak] *n* apprentice

çırpıcı [tʃərpədʒə] *n* whisk

çırpmak [tʃərpmak] *n* **kanat çırpmak** *v* flap

çiçek [tʃitʃek] n flower ▷ v **çiçek açmak** v blossom, flower; **çiçek saksısı** n plant pot; **çiçek tozu** n pollen; **çuha çiçeği** n primrose; **düğün çiçeği** n buttercup; **inci çiçeği** n lily of the valley; **kadife çiçeği** n marigold; **saksı çiçeği** n pot plant

çiçekçi [tʃitʃektʃi] n florist

çift [tʃift] adj double ▷ n couple, pair; **çift cam** n double glazing; **çift kişilik yatak** n double bed; **çift odaklı gözlük** npl bifocals; **çift tırnak** npl quotation marks; **çift yatak** npl twin beds; **çift yataklı oda** n twin room, twin-bedded room; **çift-şeritli yol** n dual carriageway; **Çift yataklı bir oda rica ediyorum** I'd like a room with a double bed

çiftçi [tʃifttʃi] n farmer

çiftçilik [tʃifttʃilik] n farming

çiftlik [tʃiftlik] n farm; **çiftlik evi** n farmhouse

çiğ [tʃiji] adj (pişmemiş) raw; **Çiğ yumurta yiyemiyorum** I can't eat raw eggs

çiğdem [tʃijidem] n (çiçek) crocus

çiğnemek [tʃijinemek] v chew

çiklet [tʃiklet] n chewing gum; **balonlu çiklet** n bubble gum

çikolata [tʃikolata] n chocolate; **sade çikolata** n plain chocolate; **sütlü çikolata** n milk chocolate

çile [tʃile] n **çileden çıkaran** adj infuriating

çilek [tʃilek] n strawberry

çilingir [tʃilingir] n locksmith

çiller [tʃiller] npl freckles

çim [tʃim] n **çim alan** n lawn;

çim biçme makinesi n lawnmower, mower

çimdiklemek [tʃimdiklemek] vt pinch

çimento [tʃimento] n cement

Çin [tʃin] adj Chinese ▷ n China; **Çin çubuğu** npl chopsticks

Çince [tʃindʒe] n (dil) Chinese (language)

çingene [tʃingene] n gypsy

çinko [tʃinjo] n zinc

Çinli [tʃinli] n (kişi) Chinese (person)

çip [tʃip] n (elektronik) chip (electronic); **silikon çip** n silicon chip

çirkin [tʃirkin] adj ugly

çisenti [tʃisenti] n drizzle

çit [tʃit] n (çalılık) hedge, (tahta, tel örgü) fence

çivi [tʃivi] n nail

çizelge [tʃizelge] n **hesap çizelgesi** n spreadsheet

çizgi [tʃizgi] n line; **çizgi öykü** n comic strip; **eğik çizgi** n forward slash; **geriye yatık çizgi** n backslash; **taç çizgisi** n touchline

çizgili [tʃizgili] adj striped, stripy

çizim [tʃizim] n drawing

çizme [tʃizme] n (ayakkabı) boot, (boyasını vb) scratch; **lastik çizme** npl wellies; **lastik çizmeler** npl wellingtons

çizmek [tʃizmek] v (arabanın boyasını vb) scratch ▷ vt (resim) draw (sketch); **altını çizmek** v underline

çoban [tʃoban] n shepherd; **İskoç çoban köpeği** n collie; **çoban köğeği** n sheepdog; **çoban püskülü** n holly

çocuk [tʃodʒuk] **(çocuklar)** n
child, kid; **çocuk bakıcısı** n
childminder, nanny; **çocuk**
bakımı n childcare; **çocuk felci** n
polio; **çocuk şarkıları** n nursery
rhyme; **çocuk odası** n nursery;
çocuk oyun grubu n playgroup;
çocuk tacizi n child abuse;
koruyucu aile bakımındaki
çocuk n foster child; **oğlan**
çocuğu n boy; **okul çocukları** n
schoolchildren; **vaftiz çocuğu** n
godchild; **yeni yürümeye**
başlayan çocuk n toddler; **İki**
yaşında bir çocuk için çocuk
koltuğu istiyorum I'd like a child
seat for a two-year-old child;
Çocuğum hasta My child is ill;
Çocuğum kayıp My child is
missing; **Çocuğum yok** I don't
have any children; **Çocuk bu**
pasaportta The child is on this
passport; **Çocuk havuzu var mı?**
Is there a children's pool?; **Çocuk**
koltuğu var mı? Do you have a
child's seat?; **Çocuk menüsü var**
mı? Do you have a children's
menu?; **Çocuk porsiyonu**
yapıyor musunuz? Do you have
children's portions?; **Çocuklar bu**
pasaportta The children are on
this passport; **Çocuklar için**
etkinlikleriniz var mı? Do you
have activities for children?;
Çocuklar için güvenli mi?,
Çocuklara verilebilir mi? Is it safe
for children?; **Çocuklar için**
kolaylıklarınız neler? Do you
have facilities for children?;
Çocuklar için neler var? What is

there for children to do?; **Çocuklar**
için yüzme havuzu var mı? Is
there a paddling pool for the
children?; **Çocuklara indirim var**
mı? Are there any reductions for
children?; **Çocukları alıyor**
musunuz? Is it okay to take
children?; **Çocuklarım arabada**
My children are in the car; **Üç**
çocuğum var I have three
children; **Bir çocuğum var** I have
a child; **Bir çocuk bileti** a child's
ticket; **Bir çocuk için armağan**
almak istiyordum I'm looking for
a present for a child; **Bu akşam**
çocuklara bakacak birine
ihtiyacım var I need someone to
look after the children tonight
çocukça [tʃodʒuktʃa] adj childish
çocukluk [tʃodʒukluk] n
childhood
çoğul [tʃou:l] n plural
çoğunluk [tʃou:nluk] n büyük
çoğunluk n majority
çoğunlukla [tʃou:nlukla] adv
mostly
çok [tʃok] adj many ▷ adv very ▷ n
plenty ▷ pron many, most
(majority); **çok önemli** adj
momentous; **çok büyük** adj
tremendous; **çok güzel** adj
gorgeous; **çok gizli** adj top-secret;
çok iyi n fine; **çok komik** adj
hilarious; **çok pişmiş** adj
overdone; **çok sevinmiş** adj
thrilled; **çok uluslu** n
multinational; **çok yönlü** n
versatile; **en çok** adv most, most
(superlative); **Çok az İngilizce**
konuşabiliyorum I speak very

little English; **Çok üzgünüm** I'm very sorry; **Çok çekicisiniz** You are very attractive; **Çok naziksiniz** That's very kind of you; **Çok sıcak** It's very hot; **Çok teşekkürler** Thank you very much; **Çok yakın** It's very near; **Beni davet ettiğiniz için çok teşekkürler** It's very kind of you to invite me; **Bu yemek çok yağlı** The food is very greasy; **Kar çok şiddetli** The snow is very heavy

çokça [tʃoktʃa] *adv* much

çoksatar [tʃoksatar] *n* bestseller

çorap [tʃorap] *n* sock; **külotlu çorap** *npl* tights; **naylon çorap** *n* stocking

çorba [tʃorba] *n* soup; **çorba kaşığı** *n* tablespoon; **et ya da sebze suyuna çorba** *n* broth; **Günün çorbası ne?** What is the soup of the day?

çökmek [tʃøkmek] *v* collapse; **diz çökmek** *v* kneel, kneel down

çöl [tʃøl] *n* desert; **çöl faresi** *n* gerbil

çömelmek [tʃømelmek] *v* crouch down

çömlek [tʃømlek] *n* **çanak çömlek** *n* pottery

çöp [tʃøp] *n* garbage, litter, rubbish, trash; **çöp döküm alanı** *n* rubbish dump; **çöp kutusu** *n* litter bin; **çöp sepeti** *n* dustbin, wastepaper basket; **çöp tenekesi** *n* bin; **Çöpü nereye bırakacağız?** Where do we leave the rubbish?

çöpçü [tʃøptʃy] **(çöpçüler)** *n* dustman

çöplük [tʃøplyk] *n* dump

çörek [tʃørek] *n* bun; **çörek ve kahve ya da çaydan oluşan kahvaltı** *n* continental breakfast

çözmek [tʃøzmek] *v* figure out, solve, work out, *(bağcık)* untie

çözücü [tʃøzydʒy] *n* solvent; **buz çözücü** *n* de-icer

çözüm [tʃøzym] *n* solution

çözümleme [tʃøzymleme] *n* analysis

çözümlemek [tʃøzymlemek] *v* analyse; **hakem aracılığıyla çözümleme** *n* arbitration

çözünür [tʃøzynyr] *adj* soluble

çubuk [tʃubuk] *n* bar *(strip)*, *(demir)* rod; **Çin çubuğu** *npl* chopsticks; **çubuk buz** *n* ice lolly; **kulak çubuğu** *n* cotton bud; **yağ çubuğu** *n* dipstick

çuha [tʃuha] *n* **çuha çiçeği** *n* primrose

çukur [tʃukur] *n* **foseptik çukuru** *n* septic tank; **yol çukuru** *n* pothole

çuval [tʃuval] *n* sack *(container)*

çünkü [tʃynky] *conj* because

çürük [tʃyryk] *n* **vişne çürüğü renginde** *adj* maroon

çürümek [tʃyrymek] *v* decay, rot

çürümüş [tʃyrymyʃ] *adj* rotten

d

da [da] *prep* on

dağ [da:] *n* mountain; **dağ bisikleti** *n* mountain bike; **Dağ manzaralı bir oda rica ediyorum** I'd like a room with a view of the mountains; **En yakın dağ kulübesi nerede?** Where is the nearest mountain hut?; **En yakın dağ kurtarma ekibi nerede?** Where is the nearest mountain rescue service post?

dağarcık [da:ardʒək] *n* **sözcük dağarcığı** *n* vocabulary

dağcı [da:dʒə] *n* mountaineer, *(tırmanıcı)* climber

dağcılık [da:dʒələk] *n* mountaineering, *(tırmanıcılık)* climbing

dağınık [da:ənək] *adj* untidy

dağınıklık [da:ənəklək] *n* mess

dağıtıcı [da:ətədʒə] *n* dispenser

dağıtım [da:ətəm] *n* **gazete**

dağıtım *n* paper round

dağıtmak [da:ətmak] *v* distribute, *(vermek)* give out

dağlık [da:lək] *adj* mountainous

daha [daha] *adv* more; **daha aşağı** *adj* lower; **daha az** *pron* less, *(miktar olarak)* less, *(sayıca)* fewer; **daha önce** *adv* earlier; **daha önceden** *adv* beforehand, previously; **daha önceden olmamış** *adj* unprecedented; **daha önemsiz bir göreve kaydırmak** *v* relegate; **daha büyük** *adj* bigger; **daha erken** *adv* sooner; **daha fazla** *pron* more; **daha genç** *adj* younger; **daha ileri, daha ileriye** *adv* further; **daha iyi, daha iyisi** *adv* better; **daha kötü, daha kötüsü** *adv* worse; **daha sonra** *adv* later; **daha uzun** *adv* longer; **daha yaşlı** *adj* elder; **Biraz daha yavaş konuşabilir misiniz lütfen?** Could you speak more slowly, please?; **Daha fazla çarşafa ihtiyacımız var** We need more sheets; **Daha fazla battaniyeye ihtiyacımız var** We need more blankets; **Daha fazla tabak çanağa ihtiyacımız var** We need more crockery

dahi [dahi] *adv (o da)* also ▷ *n (zeki)* genius

dahil [dahil] *adj* included ▷ *prep* including; **dahil etmek** *v* include, involve; **Fiyata neler dahil?** What is included in the price?; **KDV dahil mi?** Is VAT included?; **Sebze de dahil mi?** Are the vegetables included?; **Servis dahil mi?**

Is service included?

dahili [dahili] *adj* **Dahili ht numara** extension

daimi [daimi] *adj* continual ▷ *adv* continually

daire [daire] *n* circle; **apartman dairesi** *n* flat; **evlendirme dairesi** *n* registry office; **stüdyo daire** *n* studio flat; **yarım daire** *n* semicircle

dairesel [dairesel] *adj* circular

dairesi [dairesi] *n* **apartman dairesi** *n* apartment

dakika [dakika] *n* minute; **Her yirmi dakikada bir otobüs var** The bus runs every twenty minutes; **On dakika geciktik** We are ten minutes late; **Tren on dakika rötarlı** The train is running ten minutes late

daktilo [daktilo] *n* typewriter

daktilograf [daktilograf] *n* typist

dal [dal] *n (ağaç vb)* branch

dalaş [dalaʃ] *n* **ağız dalaşı** *v* squabble

daldırmak [daldərmak] *vt* dip

dalga [dalga] *n* wave *v* **dalga geçmek** *v* kid

dalgaboyu [dalgaboju] *n* wavelength

dalgalı [dalgalə] *adj* wavy

dalgıç [dalgətʃ] *n* diver

dalgın [dalgən] *adj* absent-minded

dalış [daləʃ] *n* dive; **tüplü dalış** *n* scuba diving

dalma [dalma] *n (denize)* diving

dalmak [dalmak] *v (deniz vb)* dive; **Burada dalınacak en iyi yer neresi?** Where is the best place to dive?; **Dalmak istiyorum**

I'd like to go diving

dama [dama] *n* **dama oyunu** *npl* draughts

damar [damar] *n* vein

damat [damat] **(damatlar)** *n (kızının kocası)* son-in-law, *(gelinin kocası)* bridegroom, groom

damga [damga] *n* stamp; **posta damgası** *n* postmark

damıtımevi [damətəmevi] *n* distillery

damla [damla] *n* drip, drop; **göz damlası** *npl* eye drops

damlalık [damlalək] *n* **damlalıklı eviye** *n* draining board

damlamak [damlamak] *v* drip

dan [dan] *conj* than ▷ *prep* from, off

dana [dana] **(danalar)** *n* calf; **dana eti** *n* veal

danışma [danəʃma] *n* inquiry desk; **danışma bürosu** *n* inquiries office

danışmak [danəʃmak] *v* consult

danışman [danəʃman] *n* consultant *(adviser)*; **hukuk danışmanı** *n* solicitor

Danimarka [danimarka] *adj* Danish ▷ *n* Denmark; **Danimarka dili** *(dil)* *n* Danish *(language)*

Danimarkalı [danimarkalə] *n* Dane

dans [dans] *n* dance *v* **dans etmek** *v* dance; **danslı toplantı** *n* dancing; **salon dansı** *n* ballroom dancing; **step dansı** *n* tap-dancing; **Dans etmek için nereye gidebiliriz?** Where can we go dancing?; **Dans etmek ister misiniz?** Would you like to dance?;

Dans etmek istiyorum I feel like dancing; **Dans etmem pek** I don't really dance

dansçı [danstʃə] n dancer

dantel [dantel] n lace

dar [dar] adj narrow; **dar görüşlü** adj narrow-minded; **dar sokak** n alley; **dar yol** n lane

daracık [daradʒək] adj skin-tight

darbe [darbe] n bash v **darbe yemek** vi strike

darlık [darlək] n austerity

darphane [darphane] n mint (coins)

dart [dart] n **dart oku** n dart; **dart oyunu** npl darts

dava [dava] npl proceedings v **dava etmek** v sue

davalı [davalə] n defendant

davar [davar] npl cattle

davet [davet] n invitation; **davet etmek** v invite; **davetsiz misafir** n intruder

davranış [davranəʃ] n behaviour

davranmak [davranmak] v (hareket) act, (muamele) treat, (tavır) behave

davul [davul] n drum; **bas davul** n bass drum

davulcu [davuldʒu] n drummer

dayak [dajak] v **dayak cezası** n corporal punishment

dayanan [dajanan] adj based

dayanıklılık [dajanəklələk] n stamina

dayanılmaz [dajanəlmaz] adj unbearable

dayanmak [dajanmak] v bear up

dazlak [dazlak] adj bald; **dazlak kafa** n skinhead

de [de] prep on

de, da [deda] prep at

debriyaj [debrijaʒ] n clutch

dede [dede] n granddad, grandfather, grandpa; **dedenin babası** n great-grandfather

dedektif [dedektif] n detective

dedikodu [dedikodu] n gossip; **dedikodu yapmak** v gossip

defalarca [defalardʒa] adv repeatedly

define [define] n treasure

defne [defne] n **defne yaprağı** n bay leaf

defter [defter] n **adres defteri** n address book; **çek defteri** n chequebook; **digital not defteri** n e-book; **karalama defteri** n scrapbook; **not defteri** n jotter, notebook, notepad

değer [de:er] n value, worth; **dikkate değer** adj remarkable; **görülmeye değer** adj spectacular; **resmedilmeye değer** adj picturesque; **Tamir ettirmeye değer mi?** Is it worth repairing?

değerlendirmek [de:erlendirmek] v regard

değerli [de:erli] adj precious, valuable; **değerli eşyalar** npl valuables; **Değerli eşyalarımı kasaya koymak istiyorum** I'd like to put my valuables in the safe; **Değerli eşyalarımı nereye bırakabilirim?** Where can I leave my valuables?

değersiz [de:ersiz] adj worthless

değil [deji:l] adv not, no; **iyi değil** adj unwell; **net değil** adj unclear;

Aç değilim I'm not hungry;
Bir şey değil You're welcome;
Bundan memnun değilim I'm
not satisfied with this; **Bunun
tadı pek iyi değil** It doesn't taste
very nice; **Sorun değil** No
problem; **Uzak değil** It's not far
değirmen [deji:rmen] *n* mill,
windmill
değişik [deji:ʃik] *adj* different;
değişiklik yapmak *v* modify
değişiklik [deji:ʃiklik] *n*
modification; **iklim değişikliği** *n*
climate change
değişim [deji:ʃim] *n* change
değişken [deji:ʃken] *adj* variable
değişmemiş [deji:ʃmemiʃ] *adj*
unchanged
değiştirilebilir [deji:ʃtirilebilir]
adj changeable
değiştirmek [deji:ʃtirmek] *v*
alter, swap ▷ *vi* change ▷ *vt*
change, *(dönüştürmek)* convert;
güzergah değiştirme *n* detour;
kılık değiştirmek *v* disguise;
yer değiştirme *n* shift *v* **yer
değiştirmek** *v* shift
değnek [de:inek] *n* **koltuk
değneği** *n* crutch
dehşet [dehʃet] *n* horror;
dehşet verici *adj* horrifying,
outrageous *v* **dehşete
düşürmek** *v* terrify
deklare [deklare] *adj* **deklare
etmek** *v* declare; **İzin verilen
miktarda içki deklare etmek
istiyorum** I have the allowed
amount of alcohol to declare;
**İzin verilen miktarda sigara
deklare etmek istiyorum**

I have the allowed amount of
tobacco to declare
dekoratör [dekoratør] *n*
decorator
dekore etmek *v* decorate
delege [delege] *n* delegate
deli [deli] *adj* insane
delici [delidʒi] *n* piercing
delik [delik] *adj (kulak vb)* pierced
▷ *n (çorap, duvar vb)* hole; **burun
deliği** *n* nostril; **musluk deliği** *n*
plughole
delikanlı [delikanlə] *n* lad
delil [delil] *n* clue
delmek [delmek] *v* bore *(drill)*,
pierce, *(iğneyle)* prick ▷ *vt*
(matkapla) drill
demet [demet] *n* bunch
demir [demir] *n* iron; **demir
dövmek** *v* forge
demirci [demirdʒi] *n* **demirci
dükkanı** *n* ironmonger's
demiryolu [demirjolu] *n* railway
demo [demo] *n* demo
demokrasi [demokrasi] *n*
democracy
demokratik [demokratik] *adj*
democratic
den [den] *conj* than ▷ *prep* from, off
deneme [deneme] *n* essay;
deneme baskısı *n* proof *(for
checking)*; **deneme sınavı** *adj*
mock; **deneme süresi** *n* trial
period
denemek [denemek] *v* rehearse,
test, try out, *(giysi)* try on;
Deneyebilir miyim? Can I try it on?
denetçi [denettʃi] *n* surveyor,
(maliye) auditor, *(müfettiş)*
inspector

denetim [denetim] *n* check;
hesap denetimi *n* audit; **yazım**
denetimi *n* spellchecker

denetlemek [denetlemek] *v*
supervise, *(teftiş)* inspect ▷ *vt*
(kontrol) check; **hesapları**
denetlemek *v* audit

deney [denej] *n* experiment;
deney tüpü *n* test tube

deneyim [denejim] *n* experience;
iş deneyimi *n* work experience

deneyimli [denejimli] *adj*
experienced

deneyimsiz [denejimsiz] *adj*
inexperienced

denge [denge] *n (durum)* stability,
(fizik) balance

dengede [dengede] *adj* stable

dengeli [dengeli] *adj* balanced

dengesiz [dengesiz] *adj* unstable

dengesizlik [dengesizlik] *n*
instability

deniz [deniz] *adj (askeri)* naval ▷ *n*
(coğrafya) sea; **deniz anası** *n*
jellyfish; **deniz aygırı** *n* walrus;
deniz ürünü *n* seafood; **deniz**
feneri *n* lighthouse; **deniz kazası**
n shipwreck; **deniz kazası**
geçirmiş *adj* shipwrecked; **deniz**
kıyısı *n* seaside, *(sahil)* seashore;
deniz kızı *n* mermaid; **deniz**
motoru *n* motorboat; **deniz**
seviyesi *n* sea level; **deniz suyu** *n*
sea water; **deniz tarağı** *n* scallop;
deniz tutmuş *adj* seasick; **deniz**
yatağı *n* Lilo®; **kabuklu deniz**
ürünü *n* shellfish; **Karayip denizi**
n Caribbean; **Bugün deniz dalgalı**
mı? Is the sea rough today?; **Deniz**
manzaralı bir oda rica ediyorum
I'd like a room with a view of the
sea

Deniz [deniz] *n* **Kızıl Deniz** *n* Red
Sea; **Kuzey Denizi** *n* North Sea

denizaltı [denizaltə] *n* submarine

deniz anası [denizanasə] *n*
Burada deniz anası var mı? Are
there jellyfish here?

denizaşırı [denizaʃərə] *adv*
overseas

denizci [denizdʒi] **(denizciler)** *n*
seaman

denizcilik [denizdʒilik] *adj*
denizcilikle ilgili *adj* maritime

denk [deŋ] *n (eşit)* equivalent,
(uygun) match *(partnership)*

deodoran [deodoran] *n*
deodorant

deodorant [deodorant] *n* **ter**
önleyici deodorant *n*
antiperspirant

depo [depo] *n* storage, store,
warehouse; **benzin deposu** *n*
petrol tank; **depoyu doldurmak** *v*
stock up on; **su deposu** *n* reservoir

depolamak [depolamak] *v* store

depozito [depozito] *n* deposit

deprem [deprem] *n* earthquake

depresyon [depresjon] *n*
depression

dere [dere] *n* stream

derece [deredʒe] *n (düzey)* grade,
(sıcaklık) degree; **aşırı derecede**
adv extremely, terribly; **aşırı**
derecede korkmuş *adj* terrified;
derece derece *adj* gradual;
Fahrenheit derece *n* degree
Fahrenheit; **lisans derecesi**
(edebiyat) *abbr* BA; **son derece**
adv awfully; **Santigrat derece** *n*

degree centigrade, degree Celsius
derecede [deredʒede] *adv* **dikkat**
çekecek derecede *adv*
remarkably
dergi [dergi] *n* magazine
(periodical); **mizah dergisi** *n*
comic book; **Dergi nereden**
alabilirim? Where can I buy a
magazine?
derhal [derhal] *adj* instant ▷ *adv*
instantly
deri [deri] *n (hayvan, giysi vb)*
leather
derin [derin] *adj* deep
derinden [derinden] *adv* deeply
derinlemesine [derinlemesine]
adv thoroughly
derinlik [derinlik] *n* depth
derlemek [derlemek] *v* **derleyip**
toplamak *v* tidy up
derli toplu *adj* tidy ▷ *adv* neatly
dernek [dernek] *n* **yardım**
derneği *n* charity; **yardım**
derneği dükkanı *n* charity shop
ders [ders] *n* lecture, *(ahlaki)*
moral, *(özel)* tutorial, *(sınıf)*
lesson; **ders kitabı** *n* schoolbook,
textbook ▷ *v* **ders vermek** *v*
lecture; **direksiyon dersi** *n*
driving lesson; **Ders alabilir**
miyiz? Can we take lessons?; **Ders**
veriyor musunuz? Do you give
lessons?; **Kayak dersleri veriyor**
musunuz? Do you organise skiing
lessons?
destek [destek] *n (bağ, kuşak vb)*
brace *(fastening)*, *(manevi)*
support; **destek olmak** *v* back up;
mali destek *n* sponsorship; **mali**
destek sağlamak *v* subsidize

destekleme [destekleme] *n*
backing
desteklemek [desteklemek] *v*
support
deterjan [deterʒan] *n* detergent;
bulaşık deterjanı *n* washing-up
liquid
dev [dev] *n* giant ▷ *adj* **dev gibi** *adj*
giant
devalüasyon [devalyasjon] *n*
devaluation
devam [devam] **devam etmek** *v*
carry on, continue, go on;
doldurmaya devam etmek *v*
refill
devamı [devamə] *n* sequel
devasa [devasa] *adj* gigantic,
mammoth
deve [deve] *n* camel; **deve dikeni** *n*
thistle
devekuşu [devekuʃu] *n* ostrich
devir [devir] *n* **sermaye devri** *n*
turnover
devirmek [devirmek] *v*
(düşürmek) knock down ▷ *vt*
(dökmek) tip *(incline)*
devlet [devlet] *v* **devlet koleji** *n*
public school
Devlet [devlet] *n* **Birleşik**
Devletler *n* US, *(Amerika)* United
States
devralma [devralma] *n* takeover
devre [devre] *n* circuit; **devre**
arası *n* half-time; **devre mülk** *n*
timeshare
Devre [devre] *n* **Kapalı Devre**
Televizyon Sistemi *n* CCTV
devrim [devrim] *n* revolution
devrimci [devrimdʒi] *adj*
revolutionary

devriye [devrije] n patrol; **devriye arabası** n patrol car

deyim [dejim] n saying

dezavantaj [dezavantaʒ] n disadvantage

dezenfektan [dezenfektan] n disinfectant

dırdır [dərdər] n **dırdır etmek** v nag

dış [dəʃ] adj (harici) external, (iç karşıtı) out, (yapı vb) exterior; **ahlak dışı** adj immoral; **dışa dönük** adj outgoing; **dışarı çıkmak** n outing; **gerçek dışı** adj unreal; **olasılık dışı** adj unlikely; **sezon dışı, on dışında** adv off-season

dışarı [dəʃarə] adj outside v **dışarda tutmak** v keep out; **Dışarıyı aramak istiyorum, hat bağlar mısınız?** I want to make an outside call, can I have a line?

dışarıda [dəʃarəda] adv out, outside; **Dışarıda** He's out

dışarısı [dəʃarəsə] n outside

dışında [dəʃənda] n (haricinde) exception ▷ prep outside, (ondan ayrı olarak) apart from, (onu hariç tutarak) excluding; **dışında tutmak** v exclude

digital [digital] adj digital **not defteri** n e-book

diğer [djier] adj another, other ▷ adv else; **diğer adıyla** prep alias

dijital [diʒital] adj digital; **dijital fotoğraf makinesi** n digital camera; **dijital radyo** n digital radio; **dijital saat** n digital watch; **dijital televizyon** n digital television; **Bu dijital kameraya hafıza kartı almak istiyorum**

lütfen A memory card for this digital camera, please

dik [dik] adj (yokuş vb) steep ▷ adv upright; **dik açı** n right angle

dikdörtgen [dikdørtgen] n rectangle; **dikdörtgen biçiminde** adj rectangular; **dikdörtgen şeklinde** adj oblong

diken [diken] n thorn; **deve dikeni** n thistle; **diken diken olmuş tüyler** mpl goose pimples; **dikenli tel** n barbed wire

dikey [dikej] adj vertical

dikiş [dikiʃ] n (eylem) sewing, (giysinin) seam, (tıp, nakış vb) stitch; **dikiş makinesi** n sewing machine

dikkat [dikkat] n attention; **dikkat çekecek derecede** adv remarkably; **dikkat çeken** adj noticeable v **dikkat etmek** v watch out; **dikkat etmek** v spot; **dikkate değer** adj remarkable; **dikkatini çekmek** v point out

dikkatinize [dikkatinize] abbr NB (notabene)

dikkatli [dikkatli] adj careful ▷ adv carefully

dikkatsiz [dikkatsiz] adj careless

dikmek [dikmek] v put up, sew, (bitki) plant, (onarmak) sew up, (tıp, nakış vb) stitch; **gözünü dikmek** v gaze

diktatör [diktatør] n dictator

dikte [dikte] n dictation

dil [dil] n (anatomi) tongue, (lisan) language; **Çek dili** (dil) n Czech (language); **Bask dili** n Basque (language); **Burma dili** (dil) n Burmese (language);

dil laboratuvarı n language laboratory; **dil okulu** n language school; **Danimarka dili** (dil) n Danish (language); **Estonya dili** (dil) n Estonian (language); **iki dilli** adj bilingual; **işaret dili** n sign language; **modern diller** npl modern languages; **Malta dili** (dil) n Maltese (language); **Maori dili** (dil) n Maori (language); **Hangi dilleri konuşabiliyorsunuz?** What languages do you speak?

dilbilim [dilbilim] adj linguistic

dilbilimci [dilbilimdʒi] n linguist

dilek [dilek] n wish

dilekçe [dilektʃe] n petition

dilemek [dilemek] v wish

dilenci [dilendʒi] n beggar

dilenmek [dilenmek] v beg

dilim [dilim] n slice; **dilimli grafik** n pie chart; **zaman dilimi** n time zone

dilimlemek [dilimlemek] v slice

dilsiz [dilsiz] adj dumb

din [din] n religion; **din bilimi** n theology; **kilisenin dini bölgesi** n parish

dinamik [dinamik] adj dynamic

dindirmek [dindirmek] v (acı) relieve

dingil [dingil] n axle

dini [dini] adj religious

dinlemek [dinlemek] v listen; **gizli dinleme cihazı yerleştirilmiş** adj bugged; **söz dinlemek** v listen to

dinlememek [dinlememek] v **söz dinlememek** v disobey

dinlendirici [dinlendiridʒi] adj restful

dinlenme [dinlenme] n rest, the rest; **dinlenme günü** (Yahudiler için Cumartesi, Hristiyanlar için Pazar) n Sabbath

dinlenmek [dinlenmek] vi rest

dinleyici [dinlejidʒi] n listener

dinleyiciler [dinlejidʒiler] n audience

dinozor [dinozor] n dinosaur

dip [dip] n bottom

diploma [diploma] n diploma

diplomat [diplomat] n diplomat

diplomatik [diplomatik] adj diplomatic

direk [direk] n pole, (çit) post (stake), (elektrik, telgraf) pole, (kale, gemi) mast; **çadır direği** n tent pole; **elektrik direği** n pylon; **lamba direği** n lamppost

direksiyon [direksijon] n steering wheel; **direksiyon öğretmeni** n driving instructor; **direksiyon dersi** n driving lesson; **direksiyon sınavı** n driving test; **direksiyonu kırmak** v swerve

direktör [direktør] n director

direnme [direnme] n resistance

direnmek [direnmek] v resist

dirsek [dirsek] n elbow

disiplin [disiplin] n discipline

disk [disk] n disc, disk; **disk kayması** n slipped disc; **disk sürücü** n disk drive; **kompakt disk** n compact disc

disket [disket] n diskette, floppy disk

disk jokey [diskʒokej] n disc jockey

disko [disko] n disco

disleksi [disleksi] n dyslexia

disleksik [disleksik] *adj* dyslexic
distribütör [distribytør] *n* distributor
diş [diʃ] *adj* dental ▷ *n* tooth; **diş ağrısı** *n* toothache; **diş çıkarmak** *v* teethe; **diş fırçası** *n* toothbrush; **diş ipi** *n* dental floss; **diş macunu** *n* toothpaste; **takma dişler** *npl* dentures; **yirmi yaş dişi** *n* wisdom tooth; **Bu dişim ağrıyor** This tooth hurts; **Diş sigortam var mı bilmiyorum?** I don't know if I have dental insurance; **Diş sigortam yok** I don't have dental insurance; **Dişim kırıldı** I've broken a tooth
dişçi [diʃtʃi] *n* dentist; **Dişçiye ihtiyacım var** I need a dentist
dişli [diʃli] *n* gear *(mechanism)*
divan [divan] *n* settee
diyabetik [dijabetik] *adj* diabetic
diyagonal [dijagonal] *adj* diagonal
diyagram [dijagram] *n* diagram
diyalekt [dijalekt] *n* dialect
diyalog [dijalog] *n* dialogue
diyet [dijet] *n* diet *v* **diyet yapmak** *v* diet
diz [diz] *n* knee; **diz çökmek** *v* kneel, kneel down
dizayn [dizajn] *n* design
dizel [dizel] *n* diesel; **...lık dizel lütfen** ... worth of diesel, please
dizgin [dizgin] *npl (at)* reins
dizi [dizi] *n* sequence, series; **televizyon dizisi** *n* soap opera
dizin [dizin] *n (sayısal)* index *(numerical scale)*
dizkapağı [dizkapa:ə] *n* kneecap

dizüstü [dizysty] *n* **dizüstü bilgisayarı** *n* laptop; **Burada dizüstü bilgisayarımı kullanabilir miyim?** Can I use my own laptop here?
DJ [di:dʒej] *n* DJ
DNA [de:ena:] *n* DNA
doğa [doa:] *n* nature; **doğa bilimleri uzmanı** *n* naturalist; **vahşi doğa** *n* wildlife
doğal [doa:l] *adj* natural; **doğal gaz** *n* natural gas; **doğal kaynaklar** *npl* natural resources; **doğal olarak** *adv* naturally; **doğal yiyecek** *npl* wholefoods
doğan [doa:n] *adj* **yeni doğan** *adj* newborn
doğaüstü [doa:ysty] *adj* supernatural
doğmuş [doymuʃ] *adj* born
doğrama [doyrama] *n* chop
doğramacı [doyramadʒə] *n* joiner
doğramak [doyramak] *v* hack, *(et, sebze)* chop
doğru [doyru] *adj (çizgi)* straight, *(işlem, hareket)* correct, *(işlem, hareket)* right *(correct)*, *(söz, eylem, sonuç)* accurate; **batıya doğru** *adj* westbound; **doğru dürüst** *adv* proper, properly; **doğru olarak** *adv* accurately, correctly, right; **doğru olmayan** *adj* inaccurate; **...e doğru** *(yön)* *prep* towards; **geriye doğru** *adv* backwards; **kuzeye doğru** *adj* northbound; **yana doğru** *adv* sideways; **yukarıya doğru** *adv* upwards
doğrudan doğruya [doyrudandoyruja] *adv* directly

doğrulamak [doɣrulamak] v
confirm
doğrulma [doɣrulma] n rise
doğrulmak [doɣrulmak] v rise
doğruluk [doɣruluk] n accuracy
doğu [dou:] adj east, eastern ▷ n
east; **doğu yönünde** adj
eastbound
Doğu [dou:] n Orient; **Orta Doğu**
n Middle East; **Uzak Doğu** n Far
East
doğum [dou:m] n birth; **doğum
öncesi** adj antenatal; **doğum
günü** n birthday; **doğum
hastanesi** n maternity hospital;
doğum izni n maternity leave;
doğum kontrol hapı n
contraceptive; **doğum kontrolü**
n birth control, contraception;
doğum yeri n birthplace, place of
birth
doğurgan [dou:rgan] adj fertile
doğusunda [dou:sunda] adv east
doğuş [dou:ʃ] n birth; **gün doğuşu**
n sunrise
dok [dok] n dock
doksan [doksan] number ninety
doktor [doktor] n doctor; **Bana bir
doktor gerek** I need a doctor; **Bir
bayan doktorla konuşmak
istiyorum** I'd like to speak to a
female doctor; **Bir doktor çağırın**
Call a doctor!; **Doktordan
randevu alabilir miyim?** Can I
have an appointment with the
doctor?; **Doktorla konuşmak
istiyorum lütfen** I'd like to speak
to a doctor; **Nöbetçi doktoru
çağırın lütfen** Please call the
emergency doctor

doktora [doktora] n PhD
dokunaklı [dokunaklə] adj
(konuşma) touching, (sahne, film)
moving
dokunmak [dokunmak] v touch;
akıllı dokunuş n touchpad
dokuz [dokuz] number nine;
dokuzda bir n ninth; **Masa bu
akşam saat dokuz için rezerve
edildi** The table is booked for nine
o'clock this evening
dokuzuncu [dokuzundʒu] adj
ninth
dolambaçlı [dolambatʃlə] adj
tricky
dolandırıcı [dolandərədʒə] n
cheat
dolandırıcılık [dolandərədʒələk]
n (hileli iş) scam, (sahte para vb)
fraud
dolandırmak [dolandərmak] v
cheat
dolap [dolap] n (hile) trick,
(mobilya) cupboard; **bagaj
emanet dolabı** n left-luggage
locker; **kilitli dolap** n locker;
mutfak dolabı n dresser
dolar [dolar] n dollar; **Dolar kabul
ediyor musunuz?** Do you take
dollars?
dolaşım [dolaʃəm] n **kan dolaşımı**
n circulation
dolaşmak [dolaʃmak] v wander;
sırt çantasıyla dolaşan gezgin
backpacker
dolayı [dolajə] prep due to
dolaylı [dolajlə] adj indirect
doldurmak [doldurmak] v fill in,
(benzin deposu) fill up ▷ vt (içini)
fill; **depoyu doldurmak** v stock

up on; **doldurmaya devam
etmek** v refill; **tıkabasa
doldurmak** vi cram
dolgu [dolgu] n **Dolgum düştü** A
filling has fallen out; **Geçici dolgu
yapabilir misiniz?** Can you do a
temporary filling?
dolmakalem [dolmakalem] n
fountain pen
dolu [dolu] adj full ▷ n (hava) hail;
bir kaşık dolusu n spoonful ▷ v
dolu yağmak v hail; **enerji dolu**
adj energetic; **tıkabasa dolu** adj
crammed
dolunay [dolunaj] n full moon
domates [domates]
(domatesler) n tomato;
domates sosu n tomato sauce
Dominik [dominik] n **Dominik
Cumhuriyeti** n Dominican
Republic
domino [domino] n domino;
domino oyunu npl dominoes
domuz [domuz] n pig; **domuz eti**
n pork; **domuz pastırması** n
bacon; **domuz pirzolası** n pork
chop
don [don] n (hava) frost
donanım [donanəm] n equipment
donanımlı [donanəmlə] adj
equipped
donanma [donanma] n (deniz)
navy
dondurma [dondurma] n ice
cream; **Ben dondurma alayım** I'd
like an ice cream
dondurmak [dondurmak] vi freeze
dondurucu [dondurudʒu] adj
(çok soğuk) freezing ▷ n
(derin) freezer

donmuş [donmuʃ] adj frozen
donut® [donut] n doughnut
dosdoğru [dosdoɣru] adv straight
on
dost [dost] n friend; **çevre dostu**
adj ecofriendly, environmentally
friendly; **kullanıcı dostu** adj
user-friendly; **yakın dost** n pal
dostça [dosttʃa] adj friendly
dostluk [dostluk] n friendship
dosya [dosja] n file (folder), folder
dosyalamak [dosjalamak] v file
(folder)
doz [doz] n dose
dozda [dozda] n **yüksek dozda** n
overdose
dökmek [døkmek] vt spill
döküm [døkym] n **çöp döküm
alanı** n rubbish dump
dönem [dønem] n period,
(akademik dönem) term (division
of year), (belirli bir süre) spell
(time); **40 günlük Paskalya
dönemi** n Lent
dönemeç [dønemetʃ] n hard
shoulder
döner [døner] adj turning; **döner
kavşak** n roundabout
döngü [døngy] n cycle (recurring
period)
dönme [dønme] n turn
dönmek [dønmek] v go back ▷ vi
turn; **arkaya dönmek** v turn
round, turn around; **başı dönmüş**
adj dizzy; **eski haline dönmek** n
relapse; **geri dönmek** v return,
reverse, turn back
dönük [dønyk] n **dışa dönük** adj
outgoing
dönüş [dønyʃ] n turning; **gidiş**

dönüş yolculuk *n* round trip; **gidiş-dönüş bilet** *n* return ticket; **... a gidiş dönüş iki bilet** two return tickets to...; **Gidiş dönüş bilet ne kadar?** How much is a return ticket?

dönüştürmek [dønyʃtyrmek] *v* transform; **geri dönüştürmek** *n* recycle, recycling

dönüşüm [dønyʃym] *n* transformation; **şişe geri dönüşüm kutusu** *n* bottle bank

dördüncü [dørdyndʒy] *adj* fourth

dört [dørt] *number* four; **dört çekerli** *n* four-wheel drive; **Bu akşam saat sekiz için dört kişilik bir masa ayırtmak istiyordum** I'd like to book a table for four people for tonight at eight o'clock; **Bu dört kartpostal için pul alacaktım... a gidecek** Can I have stamps for four postcards to...; **Dört kişilik bir kamper ne kadar?** How much is it for a camper with four people?; **Dört kişilik bir masa lütfen** A table for four people, please

dört yol [dørtjol] *n* **dört yol ağzı** *n* crossroads

döviz [døviz] *n* **döviz bürosu** *n* bureau de change; **döviz kuru** *n* exchange rate, rate of exchange; **Burada döviz bürosu var mı?** Is there a bureau de change here?; **Döviz bürosu arıyorum** I need to find a bureau de change; **Döviz bürosu ne zaman açılıyor?** When is the bureau de change open?; **Döviz kuru ne kadar?** What's the exchange rate?; **Nereden döviz**

alabilirim? Where can I change some money?

dövme [døvme] *n* tattoo

dövmek [døvmek] *v* beat *(strike)*

dövüş [døvyʃ] *n* fight; **hayvan dövüşleri** *n* blood sports

dövüşme [døvyʃme] *n* fighting

dram [dram] *n* drama

dramatik [dramatik] *adj* dramatic

dua [dua] *n* prayer; **dua etmek** *v* pray

dublör [duplør] **(dublörler)** *n* stuntman, stunt

dudak [dudak] *n* lip; **dudak kremi** *n* lip salve; **dudak okuma** *v* lip-read

dul [dul] *n (kocası/karısı ölmüş)* widow, widower

duman [duman] *mpl (pis kokulu)* fumes ▷ *n* smoke; **duman alarmı** *n* smoke alarm; **Odada duman kokusu var** My room smells of smoke

dur [dur] *interj* **Burada durun lütfen** Stop here, please; **Lütfen durun** Please stop the bus

durak [durak] *n* stop; **otobüs durağı** *n* bus stop; **... için hangi durakta inmem gerek?** Which stop is it for...?; **... a kaç durak var?** How many stops is it to...?; **Bir sonraki durak neresi?** What is the next stop?; **Otobüs durağı buraya ne kadar uzakta?** How far is the bus stop?; **Sonraki durak... mı?** Is the next stop...?; **Taksi durağı nerede?** Where is the taxi stand?

duraklama [duraklama] *n* pause

duraksama [duraksama] *n* halt

duraksamak [duraksamak] v
hesitate

durdurma [durdurma] n stop

durdurmak [durdurmak] vi stop

durgun [durgun] adj still

durgunluk [durgunluk] n (piyasa)
recession

durmak [durmak] v stop; **ayakta
durmak** v stand

durulama [durulama] n rinse

durulamak [durulamak] v rinse

durum [durum] n situation,
(ruhsal) state; **acil durum** n
emergency; **ruh durumu** n mood

duruşma [duruʃma] n trial

duş [duʃ] n shower; **duş başlığı** n
shower cap; **duş jeli** n shower gel;
Burada duş var mı? Are there
showers?; **Duş çalışmıyor** The
shower doesn't work; **Duş kirli**
The shower is dirty; **Duş soğuk
akıyor** The showers are cold;
Duşlar nerede? Where are the
showers?

duty-free [dutʃfree] adj duty-free
▷ n duty-free; **Duty-free nerede?**
Where is the duty-free shopping?

duvar [duvar] n wall; **duvar kağıdı**
n wallpaper; **güvenlik duvarı** n
firewall

duvarcı [duvardʒə] n bricklayer

duvardan duvara halı
[duvardanduvarahalə] n fitted
carpet

duyarlı [dujarlə] adj sensitive,
(tensel) sensuous

duyarsız [dujarsəz] adj
insensitive

duygu [dujgu] n emotion; **mizah
duygusu** n sense of humour

duygulanmış [dujgulanməʃ] adj
touched

duygusal [dujgusal] adj
emotional, sentimental; **aşırı
duygusal** adj soppy

duymak [dujmak] v hear, feel;
gerek duymak v need; **kuşku
duymak** v doubt; **saygı duymak**
v respect

duyu [duju] n sense

duyurmak [dujurmak] v
announce

duyuru [dujuru] n announcement

düğme [dy:me] n (giysi, elektrik)
button; **elektrik düğmesi** n
switch v **elektrik düğmesini
çevirmek** v switch; **kol
düğmeleri** npl cufflinks; **Hangi
düğmeye basacağım?** Which
button do I press?

düğüm [dy:ym] n knot

düğün [dy:yn] n wedding; **düğün
çiçeği** n buttercup; **Buraya bir
düğüne geldik** We are here for a
wedding

dükkan [dykkan] n shop; **antikacı
dükkanı** n antique shop; **demirci
dükkanı** n ironmonger's; **hediye
dükkanı** n gift shop; **içki satan
dükkan** n off-licence; **kuyumcu
dükkanı** n jeweller's; **yardım
derneği dükkanı** n charity shop;
Dükkanlar kaçta kapanıyor?
What time do the shops close?

dün [dyn] adv yesterday

dünya [dynja] n world; **Üçüncü
Dünya** n Third World; **Dünya
Kupası** n World Cup

dürbün [dyrbyn] n binoculars

dürtmek [dyrtmek] v poke

dürüst [dyryst] *adj* honest,
truthful; **dürüst olmayan** *adj*
dishonest; **doğru dürüst** *adv*
proper, properly
dürüstçe [dyrysttʃe] *adv* honestly
dürüstlük [dyrystlyk] *n* fairness,
honesty
düş [dyʃ] *n (rüya)* dream; **düş
görmek** *v* dream; **düş kırıklığı** *n*
disappointment
düşman [dyʃman] *n* enemy
düşmanca [dyʃmandʒa] *adj*
hostile, unfriendly
düşmanlık [dyʃmanlək] *n*
hostility; **düşmanlığını
kazanmak** *v* antagonize
düşmek [dyʃmek] *v* fall down ▷ *vi*
fall
düşük [dyʃyk] *adj* low; **düşük
alkollü** *adj* low-alcohol; **düşük
ücretli** *adj* underpaid; **düşük
yapmak** *n* miscarriage; **en düşük**
adj minimal
düşünce [dyʃyndʒe] *n* thought
düşünceli [dyʃyndʒeli] *adj*
thoughtful, *(özenli)* considerate
düşüncesiz [dyʃyndʒesiz] *adj*
thoughtless
düşünmek [dyʃynmek] *v* think
düşürmek [dyʃyrmek] *v* lower ▷ *vt*
drop
düşüş [dyʃyʃ] *n* fall
düz [dyz] *adj (düzgün)* even,
(desensiz, süssüz) plain, *(yassı)*
flat; **düz ekran** *adj* flat-screen
düzelti [dyzelti] *n* correction
düzeltme [dyzeltme] *n*
regulation
düzeltmek [dyzeltmek] *v*
(hata, yanlış) correct, *(hatalı bir*

davranış) rectify; **kesip
düzeltmek** *v* trim
düzen [dyzen] *n* order; **düzenli
olarak** *adv* regularly
düzenbaz [dyzenbaz] *n* crook,
crook *(swindler)*
düzenleme [dyzenleme] *n*
(aranjman) arrangement, *(masa
vb)* layout
düzenlemek [dyzenlemek] *v*
(masa, eşya vb) set out, *(toplantı)*
arrange; **yeniden düzenlemek** *v*
reorganize
düzenleyen [dyzenlejen] *v*
eğlence düzenleyen *n*
entertainer
düzenli [dyzenli] *adj* regular
düzensiz [dyzensiz] *adj* irregular
düzey [dyzej] *n* level
düzine [dyzine] *n* dozen
düzlem [dyzlem] *n* plane *(surface)*
düzmece [dyzmedʒe] *adj* false
DVD [dvd] *n* DVD; **DVD oynatıcı** *n*
DVD player; **DVD yazıcı** *n* DVD
burner

e

ebat [ebat] *n* dimension
ebe [ebe] **(ebeler)** *n* midwife
ebediyen [ebedijen] *adv* forever
ebeveyn [ebevejn] *n* parent;
yalnız ebeveyn *n* single parent
ebeveynler [ebevejnler] *npl*
parents
e-bilet [ebilet] *n* e-ticket
eczacı [edʒzadʒə] *n* chemist,
pharmacist
eczane [edʒzane] *n* chemist('s),
pharmacy; **En yakın eczane
nerede?** Where is the nearest
chemist?; **Hangi eczane nöbetçi?**
Which pharmacy provides
emergency service?
edebiyat [edebijat] *n* literature
eder [eder] *n* cost
editör [editør] *n* editor
efsane [efsane] *n* legend, myth
egzema [egzema] *n* eczema
egzersiz [egzersiz] *n* exercise

egzos [egzos] *adj* **egzos borusu** *n*
exhaust pipe; **egzos gazı** *npl*
exhaust fumes; **Egzos patladı**
The exhaust is broken
egzotik [egzotik] *adj* exotic
eğe [e:e] *n* file *(tool)*
eğer [e:er] *conj* if
eğik [eji:k] *adj* **eğik çizgi** *n* forward
slash
eğilim [eji:lim] *n* tendency;
eğilim göstermek *v* tend
eğilmek [eji:lmek] *v (ayak
uçlarına doğru)* bend over,
(kıvrılarak) bend down
eğitilmiş [eji:tilmiʃ] *adj* trained
eğitim [eji:tim] *n (kurs)* training,
(okul) education; **üniversite
sonrası eğitim yapan öğrenci** *n*
postgraduate; **bilgi tazeleme
eğitimi** *n* refresher course;
eğitim kursu *n* training course;
ileri eğitim *n* further education;
yüksek eğitim *n* higher
education; **yetişkin eğitimi** *n*
adult education
eğitimli [eji:timli] *adj*
educated
eğitimsel [eji:timsel] *adj*
educational
eğitmek [eji:tmek] *vt* train
eğitmen [eji:tmen] *n (spor vb)*
trainer
eğlence [e:lendʒe] *n* fun;
eğlence düzenleyen *n*
entertainer; **eğlence merkezi** *n*
leisure centre; **eğlence sanayii** *n*
show business; **konulu eğlence
parkı** *n* theme park
eğlendirici [e:lendiridʒi] *adj*
entertaining, fun

eğlendirmek [e:lendirmek] v
entertain, *(şakayla)* amuse
eğmek [e:mek] n **baş eğmek** v
bow; **boyun eğmek** v obey
eğrelti otu [e:reltiotu] n fern
ehliyet [ehlijet] n licence; **sürücü
ehliyeti** n driving licence; **İşte
ehliyetim** Here is my driving
licence; **Ehliyet numaram...** My
driving licence number is...;
Ehliyetim üzerimde değil I don't
have my driving licence on me
ejderha [eʒderha] n dragon
ek [ek] adj additional ▷ n
attachment
Ekim [ekim] n *(ay)* October; **Üç
Ekim Pazar** It's Sunday the third
of October
ekip [ekip] n team; **arama ekibi** n
search party
eklemek [eklemek] v add
ekli [ekli] adj attached
ekmek [ekmek] n bread; **ekmek
kırıntısı** n breadcrumbs, crumb;
ekmek kızartma makinesi n
toaster; **ekmek kutusu** n bread
bin; **esmer ekmek** n brown bread;
yuvarlak ekmek n bread roll;
**Biraz daha ekmek getirir
misiniz?** Please bring more bread;
Biraz daha ekmek ister misiniz?
Would you like some bread?
ekmekçi [ekmektʃi] n *(fırın)*
bakery
ekolojik [ekoloʒik] adj ecological
ekonomi [ekonomi] adj economic
▷ n economy ▷ npl economics;
ekonomi yapmak v economize
ekonomik [ekonomik] adj
economical

ekonomist [ekonomist] n
economist
ekose [ekose] adj tartan
ekran [ekran] n screen; **düz ekran**
adj flat-screen; **ekranı yukarı
kaydırmak** v scroll up; **ekranı
aşağı kaydırmak** v scroll down;
ekran koruyucusu n screen-saver;
plazma ekran n plasma screen
eksantrik [eksantrik] adj
eccentric
eksi [eksi] prep minus
eksik [eksik] adj incomplete
eksiklik [eksiklik] n lack,
shortcoming
ekskavatör [ekskavatør] n digger
ekstra [ekstra] adj **Ekstra büyük
beden var mı?** Do you have an
extra large?; **Yanında ekstra...
istiyorum lütfen** I'd like it with
extra..., please
ekşi [ekʃi] adj sour
ekşime [ekʃime] n **mide ekşimesi**
n heartburn
Ekvador [ekvador] n Ecuador
ekvator [ekvator] n equator
Ekvator [ekvator] n **Ekvator
Ginesi** n Equatorial Guinea
el [el] n hand; **el altında** adj handy;
el arabası n wheelbarrow; **el
bagajı** n hand luggage; **el feneri** n
torch; **el freni** n handbrake; **el
sallamak** v wave; **el yapımı** adj
handmade; **el yazısı** n handwriting;
elden çıkarmak v sell off; **eli sıkı**
adj mean; **elle yapmak** v handle;
elle yoklamak v grope; **ikinci el**
adj secondhand; **sağ elini
kullanan** adj right-handed;
yeniden ele almak vt reconsider;

Ellerimi nerede yıkayabilirim?
Where can I wash my hands?
elastik [elastik] *adj* **elastik band** *n*
rubber band
elbise [elbise] *n* clothes; **elbise
askısı** *n* coathanger; **gece
elbisesi** *n* evening dress; **takım
elbise** *n* suit; **Bu elbiseyi
deneyebilir miyim?** Can I try on
this dress?
elçilik [eltʃilik] *n* embassy; **Elçiliğe
telefon etmem gerek** I need to
call the embassy
eldiven [eldiven] *n* glove; **fırın
eldiveni** *n* oven glove; **lastik
eldiven** *npl* rubber gloves;
parmaksız eldiven *n* mitten
elek [elek] *n* sieve
elektrik [elektrik] *n* electricity;
elektriği kapamak *v* switch off;
elektrik çarpması *n* electric
shock *v* **elektrik düğmesi** *n*
switch; **elektrik düğmesini
çevirmek** *v* switch; **elektrik
direği** *n* pylon; **elektrik kesintisi**
n power cut; **elektrik süpürgesi** *n*
Hoover®, vacuum cleaner;
elektrikli battaniye *n* electric
blanket; **Elektrik ücrete dahil
mi?** Is the cost of electricity
included?; **Elektrik için ayrıca
para ödememiz gerekiyor mu?**
Do we have to pay extra for
electricity?; **Elektrik sayacı
nerede?** Where is the electricity
meter?; **Elektrik yok** There is no
electricity
elektrikçi [elektriktʃi] *n* electrician
elektrikli [elektrikli] *adj* electric,
electrical

elektronik [elektronik] *adj*
electronic; **elektronik bilimi** *npl*
electronics *n* **elektronik kitap
okuyucu** *n* e-reader; **elektronik
sigara** *n* e-cigarette; *v* **elektronik
sigara içmek** *v* vape
eleman [eleman] *n* staff
(workers); **eleman alma** *n*
recruitment; **satış elemanı** *n*
sales rep, shop assistant
eleme [eleme] *v* **ön eleme listesi**
n shortlist
eleştiri [eleʃtiri] *n (kitap, film vb)*
review
eleştirmek [eleʃtirmek] *v* criticize
eleştirmen [eleʃtirmen] *n* critic
elişi [eliʃi] *n* **elişiyle süslemek** *v*
embroider
elkoymak [elkojmak] *v* confiscate
elli [elli] *number* fifty; **Elli
yaşındayım** I'm fifty years old
elma [elma] *n* apple; **elma şarabı**
n cider; **elmalı turta** *n* apple pie
elmacık [elmadʒək] *n* **elmacık
kemiği** *n* cheekbone
elmas [elmas] *n* diamond
elti [elti] *n* sister-in-law
elveda [elveda] *excl* farewell!
elverişsiz [elveriʃsiz] *adj*
unfavourable
elyazması [eljazmasə] *n*
manuscript
e-mail [i:meil] *n* **istenmeyen
e-mail** *n* spam
emanet [emanet] *v* **bagaj
emanet dolabı** *n* left-luggage
locker; **emanet bagaj** *n*
left-luggage; **emanet bagaj
bürosu** *n* left-luggage office
emaye [emaje] *n* enamel

emek [emek] n labour
emeklemek [emeklemek] v crawl
emekli [emekli] adj retired ▷ n
old-age pensioner, pensioner;
emekli maaşı n pension; **emekli
olmak** v retire; **Emekliyim** I'm
retired
emeklilik [emeklilik] n retirement
emektar [emektar] adj veteran ▷ n
veteran
emin [emin] adj sure; **emin
olmayan** adj unsure
emir [emir] n command, order;
banka ödeme emri n standing
order
emlakçı [emlaktʃə] n estate agent
emmek [emmek] v suck
emniyet [emnijet] n safety;
emniyet kemeri n safety belt,
seatbelt
emoji [eməʊdʒɪ] n emoji
emzirmek [emzirmek] v
breast-feed
en [en] n **en alt** adj bottom; **en az**
adj least, minimum; **en aza
indirgemek** v minimize; **en
azından** adv at least; **en çok** adv
most, most (superlative); **en
düşük** adj minimal; **en fazla** adj
maximum; **en genç** adj youngest;
en iyi adj best; **en iyi şekilde** adv
ideally; **en iyisi** adv best; **en kısa
zamanda** adv asap (as soon as
possible); **en kötü** adj worst; **en
yakın akraba** n next-of-kin;
eninde sonunda adv ultimately;
yaşça en büyük adj eldest;
**Buraya en yakın metro
istasyonu nerede?** Where is the
nearest tube station?; **Buraya en**

yakın otobüs durağı nerede?
Where is the nearest bus stop?;
En geç ne zaman? By what time?;
En sevdiğiniz içki hangisi? What
is your favourite drink?; **En ucuz
bilet olsun lütfen** I'd like the
cheapest ticket, please; **En yakın
bisiklet tamircisi nerede?** Where
is the nearest bike repair shop?;
**En yakın gazete satan dükkan
nerede?** Where is the nearest shop
which sells newspapers?; **Umarım
en kısa zamanda tekrar birlikte
çalışabiliriz** I hope we can work
together again soon
endişe [endiʃe] n anxiety; **endişe
etmek** vt fret; **endişe verici** adj
worrying
endişeli [endiʃeli] adj
apprehensive, worried
Endonezya [endonezja] adj
Indonesian ▷ n Indonesia
Endonezyalı [endonezjalə] n
Indonesian (person)
endüstri [endystri] n industry
endüstriyel [endystrijel] adj
industrial
enerji [enerʒi] n energy; **enerji
dolu** adj energetic; **güneş enerjisi**
n solar power
enerjik [enerʒik] adj lively
enfeksiyon [enfeksijon] n
infection
enfes [enfes] adj delicious; **Enfesti**
That was delicious; **Yemek
enfesti** The dinner was delicious
enflasyon [enflasjon] n inflation
enformasyon [enformasjon] n
enformasyon bürosu n
information office

Enformasyon [enformasjon] *n*
Enformasyon Teknolojisi *n* IT
engebe [engebe] *n* **engebeli yol** *n*
track
engel [engel] *n* block *(obstruction)*,
drawback, hurdle, obstacle,
setback; **engel atlama** *n* show
jumping
engellenmiş [engellenmiʃ] *adj*
frustrated
engelli [engelli] *adj* disabled
enginar [enginar] *n* artichoke
enjeksiyon [enʒeksijon] *n*
injection
enjekte [enʒekte] *n* **enjekte**
etmek *v* inject
enkaz [eŋaz] *n* wreck, wreckage
enlem [enlem] *n* latitude
enstantane [enstantane] *n*
snapshot
enstitü [enstity] *n* institute
ensülin [ensylin] *n* insulin
entellektüel [entellektyel] *adj*
intellectual ▷ *n* intellectual
envanter [envanter] *n* inventory
E-posta [eposta] *n* **E-posta**
adresim... My email address is...;
E-posta adresiniz nedir? What is
your email address?; **E-posta**
gönderebilir miyim? Can I send
an email?; **E-postamı aldınız mı?**
Did you get my email?; **E-postanız**
var mı? Do you have an email?
e-posta [eposta] *n* email; **e-posta**
adresi *n* email address; **e-posta**
atmak *v* email *(a person)*;
E-postanızı alabilir miyim? Can I
have your email?
ergen [ergen] *n* adolescent, teenager
ergenler [ergenler] *npl* teens

ergenlik [ergenlik] *n* adolescence
erik [erik] *n* plum; **kuru erik** *n* prune
erimek [erimek] *vt* dissolve
erişilebilir [eriʃilebilir] *adj*
accessible
erişkin [eriʃkin] *n* grown-up
erişmek [eriʃmek] *v* access
eritmek [eritmek] *vi* melt
Eritre [eritre] *n* Eritrea
erkek [erkek] *adj* male ▷ *n* man,
male; **erkek arkadaş** *n* boyfriend;
erkek öğrenci *n* schoolboy;
erkek Fatma *n* tomboy; **erkek**
kardeş *n* brother; **erkek polis** *n*
police officer, policeman; **erkek**
torun *n* grandson; **erkekler**
tuvaleti *n* gents'; **Fransız erkek** *n*
Frenchman; **üvey erkek kardeş**
n stepbrother
erkeksi [erkeksi] *adj* masculine
erken [erken] *adj* early, premature
▷ *adv* early; **daha erken** *adv*
sooner; **Daha erken bir uçak**
tercih ederim I would prefer an
earlier flight; **Erken/ geç geldik**
We arrived early/late
Ermeni [ermeni] *adj* Armenian ▷ *n*
(kişi) Armenian *(person)*
Ermenice [ermenidʒe] *n (dil)*
Armenian *(language)*
Ermenistan [ermenistan] *n*
Armenia
eroin [eroin] *n* heroin
erotik [erotik] *adj* erotic
ertelemek [ertelemek] *v*
postpone, put off
erzak [erzak] *npl* supplies
eser [eser] *n* **sanat eseri** *n* work
of art
esinti [esinti] *n* blow

eski [eski] *adj* ancient, *(ölmüş)* late *(dead)*, *(önceki)* former; **eski grubun yerini alan yeni grup** *n* relay; **eski haline dönmek** *n* relapse; **eski karı** *n* ex-wife; **eski koca** *n* ex-husband; **eski moda** *adj* old-fashioned; **eski püskü** *adj* shabby; **eski ve hoş** *adj* quaint

eskimiş [eskimiʃ] *adj* worn

esmek [esmek] *v (rüzgar)* wind *(coil around)*, *(rüzgar)* wind *(with a blow etc.)*

esmer [esmer] *adj* brown; **esmer ekmek** *n* brown bread; **esmer pirinç** *n* brown rice

esnek [esnek] *adj* flexible, *(materyal)* stretchy; **esnek çalışma saati** *n* flexitime; **esnek olmayan** *adj* inflexible

esnemek [esnemek] *v* yawn

esnetmek [esnetmek] *vi* stretch

esprili [esprili] *adj* witty

esrar [esrar] *n (bitki)* cannabis

Estonya [estonja] *adj* Estonian ▷ *n* Estonia; **Estonya dili** *(dil)* *n* Estonian *(language)*

Estonyalı [estonjalə] *n (kişi)* Estonian *(person)*

eş [eʃ] *n (karıkoca)* spouse; **eşinin ailesi** *npl* in-laws

eşarp [eʃarp] **(eşarplar)** *n* headscarf, scarf

eşek [eʃek] *n* donkey

eşekarısı [eʃekarəsə] *n* wasp

eşik [eʃik] *n* **kapı eşiği** *n* doorstep

eşit [eʃit] *adj* equal

eşitlemek [eʃitlemek] *v* equal, equalize

eşitlik [eʃitlik] *n (matematik)* equation, *(siyasi)* equality

eşkin [eʃkin] *n* **eşkin gitmek** *v* canter

eşkiya [eʃkija] *n* thug

eşlik [eʃlik] *n* **eşlik etmek** *v (refakat)* escort, *(yanında gitmek)* accompany

eşofman [eʃofman] *n* shell suit

eşsiz [eʃsiz] *adj* unique

eşya [eʃja] *npl* belongings; **değerli eşyalar** *npl* valuables; **indirimli fiyatla sunulan eşya** *n* special offer; **kayıp eşya bürosu** *n* lost-property office

et [et] *n (yiyecek)* meat; **dana eti** *n* veal; **domuz eti** *n* pork; **et sosu** *n* gravy; **et ya da sebze suyuna çorba** *n* broth; **geyik eti** *n* venison; **kırmızı et** *n* red meat; **kemikli et** *n* joint *(meat)*; **koyun eti** *n* mutton; **sığır eti** *n* beef; **Bu yemeğin içinde et suyu var mı?** Is this cooked in meat stock?; **Et bozulmuş** This meat is off; **Et sevmem** I don't like meat; **Et soğuk** The meat is cold; **Et yemiyorum** I don't eat meat; **Et yiyor musunuz?** Do you eat meat?; **Kırmızı et yemiyorum** I don't eat red meat

etek [etek] *n (giysi)* skirt; **mini etek** *n* miniskirt

eteklerinde [eteklerinde] *npl* outskirts

e-ticaret [etidʒaret] *n* e-commerce

etiket [etiket] *n (bilişim)* tag, *(defter vb)* sticker, *(fiyat vb)* label

etki [etki] *n* effect, *(nüfuz)* influence, *(sonuç)* impact; **etkili bir biçimde** *adv* efficiently; **etkili**

bir şekilde *adv* effectively; **yan etki** *n* side effect
etkilemek [etkilemek] *v* influence, *(bir sonuç yaratarak)* affect, *(iz bırakmak)* impress
etkilenmiş [etkilenmiʃ] *adj* impressed
etkileyici [etkilejidʒi] *adj* impressive
etkili [etkili] *adj* effective
etkin [etkin] *adj (nüfuzlu)* efficient
etkinlik [etkinlik] *n* activity
etmek [etmek] *prep* **acele etmek** *v* hurry, hurry up; **akın etmek** *v* invade; **alay etmek** *v* mock; **ameliyat etmek** *v* operate *(to perform surgery)*; **anons etmek** *v* page; **arzu etmek** *v* desire; **ateş etmek** *vt* shoot; **ayırt etmek** *v* distinguish; **ısrar etmek** *v* insist; **özür beyan etmek** *v* excuse; **berbat etmek** *v* spoil, wreck; **casusluk etmek** *v* spy; **cüret etmek** *v* dare; **dahil etmek** *v* include, involve; **dans etmek** *v* dance; **dava etmek** *v* sue; **davet etmek** *v* invite; **dırdır etmek** *v* nag; **devam etmek** *v* carry on, continue, go on; **dikkat etmek** *v* watch out; **dua etmek** *v* pray; **eşlik etmek** *v (refakat)* escort, *(yanında gitmek)* accompany; **endişe etmek** *vt* fret; **enjekte etmek** *v* inject; **feda etmek** *n* sacrifice; **feryat etmek** *v* shriek; **finanse etmek** *v* finance, sponsor; **flört etmek** *v* flirt; **garanti etmek** *v* guarantee; **göç etmek** *v* emigrate; **gemiyle yolculuk etmek** *n* sail; **hak**

etmek *v* deserve; **hizmet etmek** *v* serve, service; **ibadet etmek** *v* worship; **icat etmek** *v* invent; **idam etmek** *v* execute; **idare etmek** *v* go round, manipulate; **ifade etmek** *v* express, state; **ihanet etmek** *v* betray; **ihmal etmek** *v* neglect; **ihraç etmek** *v* export; **ikna etme** *v* persuade; **iltifat etmek** *v* compliment; **işaret etmek** *v* sign; **işkence etmek** *v* torture; **inkar etmek** *v* deny; **inşa etmek** *vt* build; **iptal etmek** *vt* call off, cancel; **israf etmek** *v* waste; **istifa etmek** *v* resign; **ithal etmek** *v* import; **itiraf etmek** *v* confess; **kabul etmek** *v* accept, *(itiraf)* admit *(confess)*; **kötü muamele etmek** *v* ill-treat; **şarj etmek** *(elektrik)* *v* charge *(electricity)*; **mahkum etmek** *v* sentence; **merak etmek** *v* wonder; **modernize etmek** *v* modernize; **nefret etmek** *v* hate; **organize etmek** *v* organize; **park etmek** *v* park; **pazarlık etmek** *v* haggle; **protesto etmek** *v* protest; **rahatsız etmek** *v* disturb; **restore etmek** *v* restore; **rezerve etmek** *v* book; **rica etmek** *v* appeal, request; **sırılsıklam etmek** *v* drench; **söz etmek** *v* refer; **seyahat etmek** *vi* travel; **sohbet etmek** *v* chat; **sterilize etmek** *v* sterilize; **tahrip etmek** *n* vandalize; **taklit etmek** *v* imitate; **talep etmek** *v* claim, demand; **tecavüz etmek** *v* rape; **tedavi etmek** *vt* cure; **tehdit etmek** *v* threaten; **teklif etmek** *v* offer; **telaffuz etmek** v pronounce, spell; **telafi etmek** v compensate; **telaş etmek** vi rush; **telefon etmek** v phone; **teşekkür etmek** v thank; **temin etmek** v supply; **temsil etmek** v represent; **tercüme etmek** v translate; **teslim etmek** vt deliver; **umut etmek** v hope; **vekalet etmek** v substitute; **yardım etmek** vt help; **yok etmek** v destroy; **zahmet etmek** v bother; **ziyaret etmek** v visit; **zorbalık etmek** v bully; **Bunu iade etmek istiyorum** I'd like to return this; **Dans etmek ister misiniz?** Would you like to dance?

etnik [etnik] adj ethnic

etraf [etraf] adv **bina ve etrafındaki arazi** npl premises; **Bize etrafı gösterebilir misiniz?** Could you show us around?

etrafında [etrafǝnda] prep around

etrafını [etrafǝnǝ] prep round

Etyopya [etjopja] adj Ethiopian ▷ n Ethiopia

Etyopyalı [etjopjalǝ] n Ethiopian

ev [ev] n home, house; **çiftlik evi** n farmhouse; **birini arabayla evine bırakma** n lift (free ride); **ev adresi** n home address; **ev ödevi** n homework; **ev hayvanı** n pet; **ev işi** n housework; **ev şarabı** n house wine; **ev sahibesi** n landlady; **ev sahibi** n host (entertains), landlord; **ev yapımı** adj home-made; **evde kalmak** v stay in; **kişinin evinin önündeki özel yol** n driveway; **müstakil ev** n detached house; **sıra evler** adj

terraced; **taşınabilir ev** n mobile home; **tatil evi** n holiday home; **Ayrılmadan önce evi temizlememiz gerekiyor mu?** Do we have to clean the house before we leave?; **Ev oldukça büyük** The house is quite big; **Eve gitmek istiyorum** I'd like to go home; **Eve ne zaman gideceksiniz?** When do you go home?; **Eve ne zaman isterseniz o zaman dönebilirsiniz** Come home whenever you like; **Evi aramak ister misiniz?** Would you like to phone home?; **Evi arayabilir miyim?** May I phone home?

evcil [evdʒil] adj tame

evde [evde] adv home; **Akşam saat on bire kadar evde olun lütfen** Please come home by 11p.m.

evet [evet] excl yes; **Evet, çok isterdim** Yes, I'd love to; **Evet, bekarım** Yes, I'm single

eviye [evije] n **damlalıklı eviye** n draining board

evkadını [evkadǝnǝ] n housewife

evlat [evlat] n **üvey kız evlat** n stepdaughter; **evlat edinilmiş** adj adopted; **kız evlat** n daughter

evlendirme [evlendirme] n **evlendirme dairesi** n registry office

evlenmek [evlenmek] v marry; **yeniden evlenmek** v remarry

evlenmemiş [evlenmemiʃ] adj unmarried

evli [evli] adj married

evlilik [evlilik] n marriage; **evlilik**

cüzdanı n marriage certificate;
evlilik yıldönümü n wedding
anniversary; **şirket evliliği** n
merger; **Evliyim** I'm married
evrak [evrak] n documents,
papers; **evrak çantası** n briefcase;
evrak işi n paperwork;
Evraklarım burada Here are my
vehicle documents
evren [evren] n universe
evrim [evrim] n evolution
evsiz [evsiz] adj homeless
eylem [ejlem] n action
Eylül [ejlyl] n September
ezberlemek [ezberlemek] v
memorize
ezme [ezme] n squash, (yiyecek)
dip (food, sauce); **badem ezmesi**
n marzipan; **fıstık ezmesi** n
peanut butter; **yulaf ezmesi** n
oatmeal, porridge
ezmek [ezmek] v squash,
(arabayla) run over, (sıkıştırarak)
crush

f

fabrika [fabrika] n factory;
bira fabrikası n brewery; **Bir
fabrikada çalışıyorum** I work
in a factory
fagot [fagot] n bassoon
fahişe [fahiʃe] n prostitute
Fahrenheit [fahrenheit] n
Fahrenheit derece n degree
Fahrenheit
faiz [faiz] n interest (income);
faiz oranı n interest rate
fakat [fakat] conj but
faks [faks] n fax; **Buradan faks
çekebilir miyim?** Can I send a fax
from here?; **Faks çekmek
istiyorum** I want to send a fax;
Faks göndermek ne kadar? How
much is it to send a fax?; **Faks
numarası nedir?** What is the fax
number?; **Faksınız var mı?** Do
you have a fax?; **Faksınızı bir
daha gönderin** Please resend

your fax; **Faksınızda bir sorun var** There is a problem with your fax; **Kullanabileceğim bir faks makinesi var mı?** Is there a fax machine I can use?

fakslamak [fakslamak] *v* fax

fakülte [fakylte] *n* faculty; **hukuk fakültesi** *n* law school

fal [fal] *n* fortune; **yıldız falı** *n* horoscope

fanatik [fanatik] *n* fanatic

fanila [fanila] *n* flannel

far [far] *n* headlight; **göz farı** *n* eye shadow; **Farlar çalışmıyor** The headlights are not working

faraş [faraʃ] *n* dustpan

fare [fare] **(fareler)** *n* mouse; **çöl faresi** *n* gerbil; **fare pedi** *n* mouse mat; **kobay faresi** *n* guinea pig (rodent)

fark [fark] *n* difference; **fark gözetme** *n* distinction; **farkına varma** *n* notice (note); **farkına varmak** *v* notice, realize; **Farketmez** It doesn't matter

farkında [farkənda] *adj* aware

farklı [farklə] *adj* different; **farklı olarak** *prep* unlike; **Farklı bir şey istiyordum** I would like something different

Faroe [faroe] *adj* **Faroe Adaları** *npl* Faroe Islands

farzetmek [farzetmek] *v* presume

Fas [fas] *adj* Moroccan ▷ *n* Morocco

Faslı [faslə] *n* Moroccan

fasulye [fasulje] *n* bean; **çalı fasulyesi** *n* French beans, runner bean; **fasulye filizi** *npl* beansprouts

fatura [fatura] *n* invoice; **telefon faturası** *n* phone bill

faturalamak [faturalamak] *v* invoice

faul [faul] *n* foul

fayans [fajans] *n* tile; **fayans döşeli** *adj* tiled

fazla [fazla] *adj* much, surplus ▷ *pron* more, much; **daha fazla** *pron* more; **en fazla** *adj* maximum; **fazla bagaj** *n* excess baggage; **fazla fiyat isteme** *n* surcharge; **fazla fiyat istemek** *v* overcharge; **fazla mesai** *n* overtime; **fazla para çekme** *n* overdraft; **hesabından fazla para çekmiş** *adj* overdrawn; **Çok fazla... koymuşsunuz** There's too much... in it; **Daha fazla çarşafa ihtiyacımız var** We need more sheets; **Daha fazla battaniyeye ihtiyacımız var** We need more blankets; **Daha fazla tabak çanağa ihtiyacımız var** We need more crockery; **Taksimetrenin gösterdiğinden daha fazla** It's more than on the meter

fazlalık [fazlalək] *n* surplus

feda [feda] *n* sacrifice ▷ *v* **feda etmek** *n* sacrifice

fedai [fedai] *n* bouncer

felaket [felaket] *n* disaster, (doğal afet) catastrophe

felç [feltʃ] *n* paralysis; **çocuk felci** *n* polio

felçli [feltʃli] *adj* paralysed

felsefe [felsefe] *n* philosophy

feminist [feminist] *n* feminist

fener [fener] *n* flashlight; **deniz feneri** *n* lighthouse; **el feneri** *n* torch

ferah [ferah] *adv (geniş)* wide;
iç ferahlatıcı *adj* refreshing
ferahlamak [ferahlamak] *v*
freshen up
feribot [feribot] *n* ferry; **arabalı**
feribot *n* car ferry; **... feribotuna**
nereden binebiliriz? Where do
we catch the ferry to...?; **... a**
feribot var mı? Is there a car ferry
to...?
fermuar [fermuar] *n* zip;
fermuarı açmak *v* unzip
fersiz [fersiz] *adj* dull
feryat [ferjat] *n* scream, cry ▷ *v*
feryat etmek *v* shriek
feshetmek [feshetmek] *v* abolish
fesleğen [fesle:en] *n* basil
festival [festival] *n* festival
fıçı [fətʃə] *n* barrel
fındık [fəndək] *n* hazelnut; **fındık**
fıstık *n* nut *(food)*
fırça [fərtʃa] *n* brush; **boya fırçası**
n paintbrush; **diş fırçası** *n*
toothbrush; **saç fırçası** *n*
hairbrush; **tırnak fırçası** *n*
nailbrush
fırçalamak [fərtʃalamak] *v* brush
fırın [fərən] *n* oven; **fırın eldiveni**
n oven glove; **fırında pişirilmiş**
adj baked; **fırında pişirme** *n*
baking; **fırında pişirmek** *v* bake;
mikrodalga fırın *n* microwave
oven
fırıncı [fərəndʒə] *n* baker
fırlatmak [fərlatmak] *v* pitch
fırsat [fərsat] *n (durum)* occasion,
(olanak) opportunity
fırtına [fərtəna] *n* storm; **gök**
gürültülü fırtına *n*
thunderstorm; **kar fırtınası** *n*

blizzard, snowstorm; **Fırtına**
çıkabilir mi? Do you think there
will be a storm?
fırtınalı [fərtənalə] *adj* stormy
Fısıh [fəsəh] *n* **Musevilerin Fısıh**
Bayramı *n* Passover
fısıldamak [fəsəldamak] *v*
whisper
fıstık [fəstək] *n* **fındık fıstık** *n* nut
(food); **fıstık alerjisi** *n* nut allergy,
peanut allergy; **fıstık ezmesi** *n*
peanut butter; **Hint fıstığı** *n*
cashew; **İçinde fındık fıstık**
olmayan bir yemek yapabilir
misiniz? Could you prepare a meal
without nuts?; **Bunda fıstık var**
mı? Does that contain peanuts?;
Fıstığa alerjim var I'm allergic to
peanuts
fıtık [fətək] *n* hernia
fibre [fibre] *n* fibre
fidye [fidje] *n* ransom
fiil [fiil] *n* verb
Fiji [fiʒi] *n* Fiji
fikir [fikir] *n (bir konuda)* opinion,
(düşünce) idea; **açık fikirli** *adj*
broad-minded; **açıkça fikrini**
söylemek *v* speak up; **aynı**
fikirde olmak *v* agree
fiks [fiks] *adj* **fiks mönü** *n* set
menu; **Fiks menü alalım** We'll
take the set menu; **Fiks menü ne**
kadar? How much is the set
menu?; **Fiks menünüz var mı?**
Do you have a set-price menu?
fil [fil] *n* elephant
fildişi [fildiʃi] *n* ivory
fileto [fileto] *n* fillet ▷ *v* **fileto**
kesmek *v* fillet
Filipinli [filipinli] **(Filipinler)** *adj*

Filipino ▷ n Filipino
Filistin [filistin] adj Palestinian ▷ n
Palestine
Filistinli [filistinli] n Palestinian
filiz [filiz] n **fasulye filizi** npl
beansprouts
film [film] n (fotoğraf vb) film,
(sinema) movie; **film müziği** n
soundtrack; **film yıldızı** n film
star; **korku filmi** n horror film;
kovboy filmi n western; **Bu filmi
banyo edebilir misiniz lütfen?**
Can you develop this film, please?;
**Bu makine için renkli film
istiyorum** I need a colour film for
this camera; **Burada film
çekebilir miyim?** Can I film here?;
**Film görmek için nereye
gidebiliriz?** Where can we go to
see a film?; **Film kaçta başlıyor?**
When does the film start?; **Film
takıldı** The film has jammed;
Renkli film istiyorum lütfen A
colour film, please; **Sinemada
hangi film oynuyor?** Which film
is on at the cinema?
filo [filo] n fleet
filtre [filtre] n filter
Fin [fin] adj Finnish ▷ n Finn
final [final] n final; **çeyrek final** n
quarter final; **yarı final** n
semifinal
finans [finans] n finance ▷ v
finanse etmek v finance, sponsor
finansör [finansør] n sponsor
fincan [findʒan] n **çay fincanı** n
teacup; **fincan tabağı** n saucer;
**Bir fincan kahve daha alabilir
miyiz?** Could we have another cup
of coffee, please?

Finlandiya [finlandija] n Finland
Finli [finli] n Finnish
firma [firma] m firm
fiş [fiʃ] n receipt; **fişten çekmek** v
unplug; **Fiş istiyorum lütfen** I
need a receipt, please
fişek [fiʃek] n (silah) cartridge
fitil [fitil] n **fitilli kadife** n corduroy
fitted çarşaf [fittedtʃarʃaf] n
fitted sheet
fiyasko [fijasko] n flop
fiyat [fijat] n price; **fazla fiyat
isteme** n surcharge ▷ v **fazla fiyat
istemek** v overcharge; **fiyat
biçmek** vt charge (price); **fiyat
listesi** n price list; **fiyat vermek**
(açık arttırmada) vi bid (at auction);
indirimli fiyatla sunulan eşya n
special offer; **perakende fiyatı** n
retail price; **satış fiyatı** n selling
price; **yarı fiyatı** adj half-price;
yarı fiyatına adv half-price;
Fiyata botlar da dahil mi? Does
the price include boots?; **Fiyata
neler dahil?** What is included in
the price?; **Fiyata sıcak su dahil
mi?** Is hot water included in the
price?; **Fiyata sopalar da dahil
mi?** Does the price include poles?;
**Fiyata tam kapsamlı sigorta
dahil mi?** Is fully comprehensive
insurance included in the price?;
Fiyatı yazar mısınız? Please write
down the price
fizik [fizik] n (görünüş) physical ▷
npl physics
fizikçi [fiziktʃi] n physicist
fiziksel [fiziksel] adj physical
fizyoterapi [fizjoterapi] n
physiotherapy

fizyoterapist [fizjoterapist] *n*
physiotherapist

flamingo [flamingo] *n* flamingo

flaş [flaʃ] *n* flash; **Flaş çalışmıyor**
The flash is not working

flora [flora] *n* flora

floresan [floresan] *adj* fluorescent

flört [fløɾt] *n* flirt ▷ *v* **flört etmek** *v*
flirt

flüt [flyt] *n* flute

fobi [fobi] *n* phobia

fok [fok] *n* seal *(animal)*

folklor [folklor] *n* folklore

folyo [foljo] *n* foil

fon [fon] *n (destek)* grant, *(mali
birikim)* pool *(resources)*

form [form] *n* form; **başvuru
formu** *n* application form; **istek
formu** *n* claim form; **sipariş
formu** *n* order form

formalite [formalite] *n* formality

format [format] *n* format

formatlamak [formatlamak] *v*
format

formül [formyl] *n* formula

forum [foɾəm] *n* forum

foseptik [foseptik] *adj* **foseptik
çukuru** *n* septic tank

fotoğraf [fotoɣɾaf] *n* photo,
photograph; **dijital fotoğraf
makinesi** *n* digital camera;
fotoğraf albümü *n* photo album;
fotoğraf makinesi *n* camera ▷ *v*
başkasının fotoğrafına girmek *v*
photobomb; **fotoğrafını çekmek**
v photograph; **fotoğraflı telefon**
n camera phone; **Bu fotoğrafları
CD'ye yükleybilir misiniz lütfen?**
Can you put these photos on CD,
please?; **Fotoğraf inidirebilir**

miyim? Can I download photos to
here?; **Fotoğraflar kaça malolur?**
How much do the photos cost?;
**Fotoğraflar ne zaman hazır
olur?** When will the photos be
ready?; **Fotoğrafları mat kağıda
basın lütfen** I'd like the photos
matt; **Fotoğrafları parlak
kağıda basın lütfen** I'd like the
photos glossy

fotoğrafçı [fotoɣɾaftʃə] *n*
photographer

fotoğrafçılık [fotoɣɾaftʃələk] *n*
photography

fotokopi [fotokopi] *n* photocopy;
fotokopi makinesi *n* photocopier
▷ *v* **fotokopisini çekmek** *v*
photocopy; **Bunun fotokopisini
istiyorum lütfen** I'd like a
photocopy of this, please; **Bunun
renkli fotokopisini istiyorum
lütfen** I'd like a colour photocopy
of this, please; **Nerede fotokopi
çektirebilirim?** Where can I get
some photocopying done?

fön [føn] *n* blow-dry; **Kesip fön
çekin lütfen** A cut and blow-dry,
please

Fransa [fransa] *n* France

Fransız [fransəz] *adj* French ▷ *n*
French; **Fransız erkek** *n*
Frenchman; **Fransız kadın** *n*
Frenchwoman

fren [fren] *n* brake; **el freni** *n*
handbrake; **fren lambası** *n* brake
light; **Bisikletin frenleri var mı?**
Does the bike have brakes?;
Bisikletin geri frenleri var mı?
Does the bike have back-pedal
brakes?; **Frenler çalışmıyor** The

brakes are not working, The
brakes don't work

Frenk [freŋ] **Frenk soğanı** *mpl*
chives; **kırmızı Frenk üzümü** *n*
redcurrant

frenlemek [frenlemek] *v* brake

frikik [frikik] *n* free kick

fuar [fuar] *n* fair; **fuar alanı** *n*
fairground

full-board [fullboard] *n*
Full-board ne kadar? How much
is full board?

futbol [futbol] *n* football;
Amerikan futbolu *n* American
football; **futbol maçı** *n* football
match; **Futbol maçı görmek
isterdim** I'd like to see a football
match; **Futbol oynayalım** Let's
play football

futbolcu [futboldʒu] *n* football
player, footballer

füze [fyze] *n* missile

g

Gabon [gabon] *n* Gabon

gaddar [gaddar] *adj* cruel

gaf [gaf] *n* blunder

gaga [gaga] *n* beak

Gal [gal] *adj* Welsh

gala [gala] *n* premiere

galeri [galeri] *n* gallery; **sanat
galerisi** *n* art gallery

Galler [galler] *n* Wales

Galli [galli] *n* Welsh

Gambiya [gambija] *n* Gambia

Gana [gana] *adj* Ghanaian ▷ *n*
Ghana

Ganalı [ganalə] *n* Ghanaian

gangster [gangster] *n* gangster

garaj [garaʒ] *n* garage; **Hangisi
garaj anahtarı?** Which is the key
for the garage?

garanti [garanti] *n* guarantee,
warranty ▷ *v* **garanti etmek** *v*
guarantee; **garantiye almak** *v*
ensure; **Arabanın garantisi var**

The car is still under warranty; **Hala garantisi var** It's still under guarantee

gardrop [gardrop] n wardrobe

gargara [gargara] n mouthwash

garip [garip] adj strange

garson [garson] n waiter; **kadın garson** n waitress

gaspetmek [gaspetmek] v hijack

gayda [gajda] npl bagpipes

gaz [gaz] n gas; **doğal gaz** n natural gas; **egzos gazı** npl exhaust fumes; **gaz pedalı** n accelerator; **gazlı ocak** n gas cooker; **tüp gaz** n camping gas; **Gaz kokusu alıyorum** I can smell gas; **Gaz sayacı nerede?** Where is the gas meter?; **Gaz tüpümü doldurabilir misiniz?** Do you have a refill for my gas lighter?

gazete [gazete] n newspaper; **gazete bayii** n newsagent; **gazete dağıtım** n paper round; **gazete kesiği** n cutting; **En yakın gazete satan dükkan nerede?** Where is the nearest shop which sells newspapers?; **Gazete almak istiyorum** I would like a newspaper; **Gazete nereden alabilirim?** Where can I buy a newspaper?; **Gazete satıyor musunuz?** Do you have newspapers?

gazeteci [gazetedʒi] n journalist

gazetecilik [gazetedʒilik] n journalism

gazyağı [gazjaːə] n kerosene

gebe [gebe] adj pregnant

gebelik [gebelik] n pregnancy

gece [gedʒe] n at night, night; **bu gece** adv tonight; **dün gece** n last night; **gece elbisesi** n evening dress; **gece hayatı** n nightlife; **gece kulübü** n nightclub; **gece nöbeti** n nightshift; **gece okulu** n night school; **kına gecesi** n hen night; **İki gece kalmak istiyorum** I'd like to stay for two nights; **İyi geceler** Good night; **Çadırın bir geceliği ne kadar?** How much is it per night for a tent?; **Bir gece daha kalmak istiyorum** I want to stay an extra night; **Geceliği ne kadar?** How much is it per night?

gecekondu [gedʒekondu] n slum

gecelik [gedʒelik] n nightdress, nightie, (hafif) negligee; **gecelik seyahat çantası** n overnight bag

geceyarısı [gedʒejarəsə] n midnight, at midnight

gecikme [gedʒikme] n delay

gecikmek [gedʒikmek] v delay

gecikmeli [gedʒikmeli] adj delayed, late (delayed)

geç [getʃ] adv late; **geç saatlere kadar oturmak** v stay up; **Çok geç** It's too late

geçen [getʃen] adj past, last; **geçen hafta** last week

geçer [getʃer] n (standartlara uygun) pass (meets standard)

geçerli [getʃerli] adj valid

geçersiz [getʃersiz] adj void

geçici [getʃidʒi] adj temporary, (bir süreliğine) provisional; **geçici görevli** n temp; **yol kenarında geçici park yeri** n layby

geçilmek [getʃilmek] vi pass

geçim [getʃim] n geçimini sağlamak v provide for

geçinmek [getʃinmek] v live on
geçirmek [getʃirmek] v go
through; **gözden geçirmek**
(yeniden) v revise; **iç geçirmek** n
sigh; **şok geçirmek** v shock
geçiş [getʃiʃ] n transition; **geçiş
hakkı** n right of way
geçit [getʃit] n crossing, passage
(route), *(dağ)* pass *(in mountains)*;
alt geçit n underpass; **ışıklı yaya
geçidi** n pelican crossing;
hemzemin geçit n level crossing;
şeritli yaya geçidi n zebra
crossing; **yaya geçidi** n
pedestrian crossing
geçmek [getʃmek] v go by,
(deneyim/ameliyat) undergo ▷ vt
pass; **dalga geçmek** v kid;
karşıdan karşıya geçmek vt
cross; **yanından geçmek** v go
past
geçmiş [getʃmiʃ] adj gone, past ▷ n
past; **ödeme günü geçmiş** adj
overdue; **günü geçmiş** adj
out-of-date; **modası geçmiş** adj
obsolete; **vadesi geçmiş borç** npl
arrears
gedik [gedik] n *(yer)* gap
geğirme [geʒi:rme] n burp
geğirmek [geʒi:rmek] vi burp
gelebilirsiniz v **Gelebilirsiniz!**
Come in!
gelecek [geledʒek] adj coming,
future, next ▷ n future; **gelecek
beklentisi** n prospect
gelen [gelen] **gelen kutusu** n
inbox; **yeni gelen** n newcomer
gelenek [gelenek] n tradition
geleneksel [geleneksel] adj *(töre)*
traditional

gelgit [gelgit] n tide
gelin [gelin] n daughter-in-law,
(damadın eşi) bride; **gelin teli** n
tinsel
gelincik [gelindʒik] n *(çiçek)*
poppy, *(hayvan)* weasel
gelinlik [gelinlik] n wedding dress
gelir [gelir] n *(maaş)* income ▷ npl
(aylık kazanç) earnings, *(toplanan
para)* proceeds; **gelir vergisi** n
income tax; **vergi geliri** n revenue
gelişigüzel [geliʃigyzel] adv
casually ▷ n chance
gelişme [geliʃme] n *(büyüme)*
development, *(iyileşme)*
improvement
gelişmek [geliʃmek] vt develop;
gelişmekte olan ülke n
developing country
gelişmemiş [geliʃmemiʃ] adj
immature
geliştirmek [geliʃtirmek] v
improve ▷ vi *(büyüme)* develop;
vücut geliştirme n bodybuilding
gelmek [gelmek] v come, come
from; **anlamına gelmek** v stand
for; **üstesinden gelmek** v master,
overcome, tackle; **bir araya
gelmek** v get together; **gündeme
gelmek** v come up; **geri gelmek** v
come back; **kendine gelmek** v
come round, regain; **yeniden bir
araya gelme** n reunion
gemi [gemi] n ship; **büyük yolcu
gemisi** n liner; **gemi gezisi** n
cruise; **gemi teknesi** n hull; **gemi
yapımı** n shipbuilding ▷ v **gemiyle
yolculuk etmek** n sail
gen [gen] n gene
genç [gentʃ] adj young; **daha genç**

adj younger; **en genç** *adj*
youngest; **genç kız** *n* lass;
gençlerin kaldığı otel *n* youth
hostel

gençlik [gentʃlik] *n* youth; **gençlik
klubü** *n* youth club

genel [genel] *adj* general ▷ *n*
general; **genel anestezi** *n* general
anaesthetic; **genel kültür** *n*
general knowledge; **genel müdür**
n managing director; **genel
merkez** *n* HQ; **genel seçim** *n*
general election

genellemek [genellemek] *v*
generalize

genellikle [genellikle] *adv*
generally, usually

genetik [genetik] *adj* genetic;
genetik bilimi *n* genetics;
genetik olarak değiştirilmiş *adj*
genetically-modified

geniş [geniʃ] *adj (ferah, yaygın)*
extensive, *(yayvan)* broad,
(yayvan) wide; **geniş bant** *n*
broadband

genişlik [geniʃlik] *n* width

Georgia [georgia] *n (Amerikan
eyaleti)* Georgia *(US state)*;
Georgia'ya ait *adj* Georgian

gerçek [gertʃek] *adj (durum)* real,
(mücevher) genuine, *(söz)* true ▷ *n*
actual, *(bilgi)* fact, *(doğruluk)*
truth; **gerçek dışı** *adj* unreal;
gerçeklerle bağdaşmayan *adj*
unrealistic; **gerçek kahveniz var
mı?** Have you got real coffee?

gerçekçi [gertʃektʃi] *adj* realistic

gerçekleştirmek
[gertʃekleʃtirmek] *v* fulfil

gerçeklik [gertʃeklik] *n* reality;

sanal gerçeklik *n* virtual reality

gerçekten [gertʃekten] *adv*
indeed, really, truly

gerçi [gertʃi] *adv* though

gerek [gerek] *adj* necessary; **gerek
duymak** *v* need; **Bana bir doktor
gerek** I need a doctor; **Geri
dönmeniz gerekiyor** You have to
turn round; **Ne giymem
gerekiyor?** What should I wear?;
Ne kadar almam gerekiyor?
How much should I take?

gerekli [gerekli] *adj* necessary

gereklilik [gereklilik] *n* necessity

gereksinim [gereksinim] *n*
requirement

gereksiz [gereksiz] *adj*
unnecessary

gerektirmek [gerektirmek] *v*
require

gergin [gergin] *adj (huzursuz)*
tense, *(sinirleri yay gibi)* uptight,
(sinirli) edgy

gerginlik [gerginlik] *n* tension;
gerginlik yaratıcı *adj* stressful

geri [geri] *adv* back; **geri almak** *v*
take back; **geri aramak** *v* call back,
phone back, ring back; **geri ödeme**
n repayment; **geri ödemek** *v* pay
back, repay; **geri çevirmek** *v* turn
down; **geri dönüş** *n* return
(coming back); **geri dönüştürmek**
n recycle, recycling; **geri
döndürmek** *vi* return; **geri
dönmek** *v* return, reverse, turn
back; **geri göndermek** *v* send
back; **geri gelmek** *v* come back;
geri getirmek *v* bring back, get
back; **geri gitmek** *v* move back;
geri kalmak *v* back out; **geri**

koymak v put back; **geri sarmak** v rewind; **geri tepmek** v backfire; **geri vermek** v give back; **geride kalmak** v lag behind; **geriye yatık çizgi** n backslash; **Arabayı buraya mı geri getirmem gerekiyor** Do I have to return the car here?; **Bisikleti ne zaman geri getirmem gerekiyor?** When is the bike due back?; **Geri dönmeniz gerekiyor** You have to turn round; **Kaçta geri döneriz?** When do we get back?; **Lütfen beni geri arayın** Please call me back; **Paramı geri alabilir miyim?** Can I have a refund?, Can I have my money back?; **Paramı geri istiyorum** I want my money back

geribildirim [geribildirim] n feedback

gerilim [gerilim] n tension; **kuşku ve gerilimli bekleyiş** n suspense

gerilmiş [gerilmiʃ] adj stressed

geriye [gerije] adv **geriye doğru** adv backwards

germek [germek] v tighten, stretch; **psikolojik anlamda germek** v strain

getiri [getiri] n return (yield)

getirmek [getirmek] v bring ▷ vt fetch; **geri getirmek** v bring back, get back

gevelemek [gevelemek] v waffle

gevrek [gevrek] adj crispy, (çıtır çıtır) crisp; **mısır gevreği** n cornflakes; **tahıl gevreği** n cereal

gevşek [gevʃek] adj (düğüm vb) loose, (sarkmış karın vb) flabby, (tavır) slack

gevşeme [gevʃeme] n relaxation

gevşemek [gevʃemek] vi relax

gevşetici [gevʃetidʒi] adj relaxing

geyik [gejik] **(geyikler)** n deer; **geyik eti** n venison; **ren geyiği** n reindeer

gezegen [gezegen] n planet

gezgin [gezgin] n tourist, traveller **sırt çantasıyla dolaşan gezgin** backpacker

gezi [gezi] n excursion, tour; **gemi gezisi** n cruise; **keşif gezisi** n expedition

gezinti [gezinti] n (at/araba/bisiklet) ride; **gezinti yeri** n promenade

gezmek [gezmek] v walk, go out, tour; **gezip görme** n sightseeing; **sırt çantasıyla gezme** n backpacking

gıda [gəda] n food; **gıda zehirlenmesi** n food poisoning

gıdıklamak [gədəklamak] v tickle

gibi [gibi] adv as ▷ prep like; **dev gibi** adj giant; **sırık gibi** n lanky

giden [giden] adj **güneye giden** adj southbound

gidermek [gidermek] v eliminate

gidiş [gidiʃ] n departure; **dörtnala gidiş** n gallop; **gidiş dönüş yolculuk** n round trip; **gidiş-dönüş bilet** n return ticket; **tek gidiş bileti** n one-way ticket; **... a gidiş dönüş iki bilet** two return tickets to...; **Gidiş dönüş bilet ne kadar?** How much is a return ticket?; **Tek gidiş bilet ne kadar?** How much is a single ticket?

gidon [gidon] npl handlebars

Gine [gine] n Guinea; **Ekvator Ginesi** n Equatorial Guinea

giriş [giriʃ] *n* entry, *(geçiş)* access, *(havaalanı)* check-in, *(kapı)* entrance, *(yer, nokta)* way in; **giriş ücreti** *n* admission charge, entrance fee; **giriş hakkı** *n* admittance ▷ *v* **giriş yapmak** *v* check in; **Engelli kişiler için girişiniz var mı?** Do you provide access for people with disabilities?; **Giriş vizem var** I have an entry visa; **Tekerlekli sandalye girişi olan bir oda istiyorum** I need a room with wheelchair access

girişim [giriʃim] *n* attempt, *(inisiyatif)* initiative

girmek [girmek] *v* get into, *(içeriye)* come in, *(içeriye)* go in ▷ *vt (bir yere)* enter; **bahse girme** *n* betting; **bahse girmek** *vi* bet; **kuyruğa girmek** *v* queue; **mekana girmek** *v* get in; **yeniden sınava girmek** *v* resit

gişe [giʃe] *n* **bilet gişesi** *n* booking office, box office, ticket office

git [git] *v* **Gidin buradan!** Go away!

gitar [gitar] *n* guitar

gitmek [gitmek] *v* go; **önden gitmek** *v* go ahead; **geri gitmek** *v* move back; **ileri gitmek** *v* move forward; **tırıs gitmek** *v* trot; **uçup gitmek** *v* fly away; **... a gitmek istiyorduk** We'd like to go to...; **... a gitmek istiyorum** I'm going to...; **Eve gitmek istiyorum** I'd like to go home; **Gitme zamanı geldi mi?** Is it time to go?; **Sörf için nereye gitmek gerek?** Where can you go surfing?; **Tırmanmaya gitmek isterdim** I'd like to go climbing

giyim [gijim] *n* clothing

giyinik [gijinik] *adj* dressed

giyinmek [gijinmek] *vi* dress

giymek [gijmek] *vt* wear

giysi [gijsi] *n (elbise)* dress, *(kıyafet)* garment; **antreman giysisi** *n* tracksuit; **spor giysisi** *n* sportswear; **Giysi kuralı var mı?** Is there a dress-code?

giysiler [gijsiler] *n* clothes

giz [giz] *n* mystery; **çok gizli** *adj* top-secret

gizem [gizem] *n* mystery

gizemli [gizemli] *adj* mysterious

gizli [gizli] *adj* confidential, secret; **gizli buz** *n* black ice; **gizli dinleme cihazı yerleştirilmiş** *adj* bugged; **gizli plan** *v* plot *(conspire)*; **gizli servis** *n* secret service

gizlice [gizlidʒe] *adv* secretly

glükoz [glykoz] *n* glucose

glüten [glyten] *n* gluten

GM [gm] *abbr* GM

gofret [gofret] *n* wafer

gol [gol] *n* goal, *(Amerikan futbolunda)* touchdown

golf [golf] *n* golf; **golf klübü** *n* golf club *(society)*; **golf sahası** *n* golf course; **golf sopası** *n* golf club *(stick)*, tee; **Buraya yakın bir golf sahası var mı?** Is there a public golf course near here?; **Golf sopaları kiralıyorlar mı?** Do they hire out golf clubs?; **Nerede golf oynayabilirim?** Where can I play golf?

Google® [google] *v* Google®

goril [goril] *n* gorilla

göbek [gøbek] *n* belly, navel; **göbek deliği** *n* belly button

göç [gøtʃ] *n* migration; **göç etmek** *v* emigrate

göçme [gøtʃme] *n* immigration

göçmen [gøtʃmen] *adj* migrant ▷ *n* immigrant, migrant

göçük [gøtʃyk] *n* dent

göçürmek [gøtʃyrmek] *v* dent

göğüs [gø:ys] *n* breast, bust, chest; **Göğsümde bir ağrı var** I have a pain in my chest

gök [gøk] *n* sky; **gök gürültülü** *adj* thundery; **gök gürültülü fırtına** *n* thunderstorm; **gök gürültüsü** *n* thunder

gökdelen [gøkdelen] *n* high-rise, skyscraper

gökkuşağı [gøkkuʃa:ə] *n* rainbow

göktaşı [gøktaʃə] *n* meteorite

göl [gøl] *n* lake

gölcük [gøldʒyk] *n* pond

gölge [gølge] *n* (*birinin ya da bir şeyin*) shadow, (*tente, ağaç altı*) shade

gömlek [gømlek] *n* shirt; **iç gömleği** *n* slip (*underwear*); **polo gömlek** *n* polo shirt

gömmek [gømmek] *v* bury

gönderen [gønderen] *n* sender

gönderme [gønderme] *n* (*kaynak*) reference

göndermek [gøndermek] *v* send, send out; **geri göndermek** *v* send back

gönenç [gønentʃ] *n* prosperity

gönül [gjønylj] *n* heart, mind, affection; **alçak gönüllü** *adj* humble, modest; **gönüllü olarak** *adv* voluntarily; **gönüllü olmak** *n* volunteer

gönüllü [gønylly] *adj* voluntary;

gönüllü olmak *n* volunteer

gönülsüz [gønylsyz] *adj* reluctant

gönülsüzce [gønylsyzdʒe] *adv* reluctantly

göre [gøre] *prep* according to; **bedenine göre büyük** *adj* outsize; **göreceli olarak** *adv* comparatively, relatively

göreceli [gøredʒeli] *n* relative

görenek [gørenek] *n* custom; **göreneklere uymayan** *adj* unconventional

görev [gørev] *n* duty, task, (*ödev vb*) assignment, (*pozisyon*) post (*position*); **daha önemsiz bir göreve kaydırmak** *v* relegate

görevli [gørevli] *adj* assigned ▷ *n* official, employee; **görevli memur** (*polis/asker*) *n* officer; **güvenlik görevlisi** *n* security guard; **geçici görevli** *n* temp; **hapishane görevlisi** *n* prison officer; **hükümet görevlisi** *n* civil servant; **oda görevlisi** *n* chambermaid; **polis görevlisi** *n* police officer; **sahil koruma görevlisi** *n* coastguard; **sınav görevlisi** *n* examiner; **sosyal hizmetler görevlisi** *n* social worker; **Görevliyi gördünüz mü?** Have you seen the guard?

görgü [gørgy] *npl* manners

görkem [gørkem] *n* majesty

görkemli [gørkemli] *adj* glorious, splendid

görmek [gørmek] *vt* see; **düş görmek** *v* dream; **görme yetisi** *n* eyesight; **gezip görme** *n* sightseeing; **hor görme** *n* contempt

görsel [gørsel] *adj* visual
görünmek [gørynmek] *v* appear, seem; **yapar gibi görünmek** *v* pretend
görünmez [gørynmez] *adj* invisible
görünür [gørynyr] *adj* apparent, visible
görünüş [gørynyʃ] *n* appearance
görüş [gøryʃ] *n* view, *(fikir)* remark, *(göz)* sight, *(göz)* visibility; **açık görüşlü** *adj* liberal; **dar görüşlü** *adj* narrow-minded; **görüşe katılmamak** *v* disagree; **ortak görüş** *n* communion; **Görüşürüz** See you later
görüşme [gøryʃme] *n* interview ▷ **görüşme yapmak** *v* interview; **telefon görüşmesi** *n* phonecall
görüşmeci [gøryʃmedʒi] *n* interviewer, negotiator
görüşmek [gøryʃmek] *v* discuss, negotiate
görüşmeler [gøryʃmeler] *npl* negotiations
gösterge [gøsterge] *n* indicator; **gösterge tablosu** *n* dashboard
gösteri [gøsteri] *n (eğlence)* show, *(politik)* demonstration; **havai fişek gosterlleri** *npl* fireworks; **Gösteri için nereye gidebiliriz?** Where can we go to see a show?
gösterici [gøsteridʒi] *n* demonstrator
gösterim [gøsterim] *n (film vb)* showing; **yeniden gösterim** *n* replay
gösteriş [gøsteriʃ] *n* show-off; **gösteriş yapmak** *v* show off
gösterişli [gøsteriʃli] *adj* grand

göstermek [gøstermek] *v* show ▷ *vi* point; **aday göstermek** *v* nominate; **çeşitlilik göstermek** *v* range, vary; **boy göstermek** *v* turn up; **eğilim göstermek** *v* tend; **haklılığını göstermek** *v* justify; **kendini göstermek** *v* stand out; **tepki göstermek** *v* react; **yeniden göstermek** *v* replay; **yol göstermek** *vt* lead
gövde [gøvde] *n* **ağaç gövdesi** *n* trunk
göz [gøz] *n* eye; **göz atmak** *vi* browse; **göz önünde tutarak** *prep* considering; **göz bağı** *n* blindfold; **göz damlası** *npl* eye drops; **göz farı** *n* eye shadow; **göz kamaştırıcı** *adj* glamorous, stunning; **göz kapağı** *n* eyelid; **göz kırpmak** *v* wink; **göz kırpmak** *v* blink; **gözünü dikmek** *v* gaze; **gözünü dikmek** *v* look, look at; **gözünü korkutmak** *v* intimidate; **gözünde büyütmek** *v* overestimate; **gözünde canlandırmak** *v* visualize; **gözden geçirmek** *(yeniden) v* revise; **gözden kaybolma** *n* disappearance; **gözden kaybolmak** *v* disappear; **gözlerini bağlamak** *v* blindfold; **torpido gözü** *n* glove compartment; **Gözüme bir şey kaçtı** I have something in my eye; **Gözlerim yanıyor** My eyes are sore
gözaltı [gøzaltə] *n* **gözaltına alma** *n* detention
gözatmak [gøzatmak] *v* glance
gözbebeği [gøzbebeji:] *n* pupil *(eye)*

gözcü [gøzdʒy] n monitor; **sınav gözcüsü** n invigilator

gözde [gøzde] adj favourite ▷ n favourite

gözden [gøzden] n **gözden kaçırmak** v overlook

gözetim [gøzetim] n oversight *(supervision)*

gözetlemek [gøzetlemek] v pry ▷ vt watch

gözetmek [gøzetmek] v protect, look after, consider, respect; **fark gözetme** n distinction

gözlemci [gøzlemdʒi] adj observant ▷ n observer

gözlemek [gøzlemek] v watch, observe; **kuş gözleme** n birdwatching

gözlemevi [gøzlemevi] n observatory

gözlemlemek [gøzlemlemek] v observe

gözlük [gøzlyk] npl glasses, spectacles; **çift odaklı gözlük** npl bifocals; **güneş gözlüğü** npl sunglasses; **koruma gözlüğü** npl goggles; **Gözlüklerimi tamir edebilir misiniz?** Can you repair my glasses?

gözlükçü [gøzlyktʃy] n optician

gözyaşı [gøzjaʃə] n tear *(from eye)*; **gözyaşı bombası** n teargas

GPS [dʒiːpiːes] n **GPS sistemi** n GPS; **GPS var mı?** Does it have GPS?

grafik [grafik] n graph ▷ npl graphics; **dilimli grafik** n pie chart

grafiti [grafiti] n graffiti

gram [gram] n gramme

gramatik [gramatik] adj grammatical

gramer [gramer] n grammar

granit [granit] n granite

grev [grev] n strike; **grev yapmak** vi strike *(suspend work)*; **grev vardı, o yüzden** because of a strike

grevci [grevdʒi] n striker

greyfurt [grejfurt] n grapefruit

gri [gri] adj grey

grip [grip] n flu, influenza; **kuş gribi** n bird flu; **Grip geçiriyorum** I've got flu; **Yakınlarda grip atlattım** I had flu recently

Grönland [grønland] n Greenland

grup [grup] n group; **çocuk oyun grubu** n playgroup; **eski grubun yerini alan yeni grup** n relay; **kan grubu** n blood group; **sözcük grubu** n phrase; **Grup indirimi var mı?** Are there any reductions for groups?; **Kan grubum O pozitif** My blood group is O positive

Guatemala [guatemala] n Guatemala

guguk [guguk] n **guguk kuşu** n cuckoo

gurur [gurur] n pride

gururlu [gururlu] adj proud

gübre [gybre] n fertilizer, manure

gücendirmek [gydʒendirmek] v offend

güç [gytʃ] adj *(zor)* difficult ▷ n *(erk)* power, *(kuvvet)* force, *(kuvvet)* strength; **gücü yetmek** v afford; **insan gücü** n manpower

güçlendirmek [gytʃlendirmek] v strengthen

güçlü [gytʃly] *adj* powerful, strong
güçlük [gytʃlyk] *n* difficulty, trouble; **güçlük çıkaran** *n* troublemaker
güçlükle [gytʃlykle] *adv* hardly
güfte [gyfte] *npl* lyrics
gül [gyl] *n* rose
gülmek [gylmek] *v* laugh; **kahkahayla gülmek** *v* laugh; **kıs kıs gülmek** *v* snigger
gülümseme [gylymseme] *n* smile
gülümsemek [gylymsemek] *v* smile
gülünç [gylyntʃ] *adj* ridiculous
gülüş [gylyʃ] *n* laugh
gümrük [gymryk] *n* customs, (customs) duty; **gümrük memuru** *n* customs officer; **gümrük tarifesi** *n* tariff; **Bunun için gümrük ödemem gerekiyor mu?** Do I have to pay duty on this?
gümüş [gymyʃ] *n* silver
gün [gyn] *n* day; **dinlenme günü** (*Yahudiler için Cumartesi, Hristiyanlar için Pazar*) *n* Sabbath; **doğum günü** *n* birthday; **gün ışığı** *n* sunlight, sunshine; **gün batımı** *n* sunset; **gün doğuşu** *n* sunrise; **günü geçmiş** *adj* out-of-date; **her gün** *adv* daily; **resmi tatil günü** *n* public holiday; **Sevgililer Günü** *n* Valentine's Day; **tam gün** *adv* full-time; **yarım gün** *adv* part-time; **ödeme günü geçmiş** *adj* overdue; **Beş günlüğüne bir araba kiralamak istiyorum** I want to hire a car for five days; **Bugün günlerden ne?** What day is it today?; **Günün çorbası ne?** What is the soup of

the day?; **Günün yemeği ne?** What is the dish of the day?; **Harika bir gün!** What a lovely day!; **Müze her gün açık mı?** Is the museum open every day?; **öbür gün** the day after tomorrow
günah [gynah] *n* sin
güncel [gyndʒel] *adj* current, (*haber vb*) topical, (*yenilenmiş*) up-to-date; **güncel haberler** *npl* current affairs
güncellemek [gyndʒellemek] *v* update
gündem [gyndem] *n* agenda; **gündeme gelmek** *v* come up
gündüz [gyndyz] *n* daytime
güneş [gyneʃ] *adj* solar ▷ *n* sun; **güneş çarpması** *n* sunstroke; **güneş enerjisi** *n* solar power; **güneş gözlüğü** *npl* sunglasses; **güneş kremi** *n* suncream; **güneş sistemi** *n* solar system; **güneş sonrası krem** *n* after sun lotion; **güneş yağı** *n* suntan oil; **güneş yanığı** *adj* sunburn, sunburnt; **güneşte yanmak** *v* sunbathe; **güneşte yanmış** *adj* tanned; **güneşlenme yatağı** *n* sunbed; **koruyucu güneş kremi** *n* sunblock
güneşli [gyneʃli] *adj* sunny
güneşlik [gyneʃlik] *n* sunscreen
güney [gynej] *adj* south, southern ▷ *n* south; **güneye giden** *adj* southbound; **Güney Afrika** *adj* South Africa, South African; **Güney Afrikalı** *n* South African; **Güney Amerika** *adj* South America, South American; **Güney Amerikalı** *n* South American;

Güney Kore n South Korea;
Güney Kutbu n South Pole, the
Antarctic, Antarctica
güneybatı [gynejbatə] n
southwest
güneyde [gynejde] adv south
güneydoğu [gynejdou:] n
southeast
günlük [gynlyk] adj daily ▷ n diary;
günlük bilet n day return; **günlük
ifadeler sözlüğü** n phrasebook
Gürcistan [gyrdʒistan] n Georgia
(country)
Gürcü [gyrdʒy] n Georgian
(inhabitant of Georgia)
güreş [gyreʃ] n wrestling
güreşçi [gyreʃdʒi] n wrestler
gürültü [gyrylty] n noise; **gök
gürültülü** adj thundery; **gök
gürültülü fırtına** n
thunderstorm; **gök gürültüsü** n
thunder; **Gürültüden
uyuyamıyorum** I can't sleep for
the noise
gürültülü [gyryltyly] adj loud,
noisy
gütmek [gytmek] n **kin gütmek** v
spite
güve [gyve] n moth
güveç [gyvetʃ] n casserole, stew
güven [gyven] n confidence
(trust), trust; **güven verici** adj
reassuring; **güven vermek** v
reassure; **güvenine bağlı olmak** v
depend; **kendine güvenen** adj
confident, self-assured
güvence [gyvendʒe] n **güvence
vermek** v assure
güvenen [gyvenen] adj trusting
güvenilir [gyvenilir] adj reliable

güvenilmez [gyvenilmez] adj
unreliable
güvenli [gyvenli] adj safe, secure
güvenlik [gyvenlik] n safety,
security; **güvenlik duvarı** n
firewall; **güvenlik görevlisi** n
security guard; **sosyal güvenlik** n
social security
güvenmek [gyvenmek] v count
on, rely on, trust
güvensiz [gyvensiz] adj insecure
güvercin [gyverdʒin] n pigeon;
beyaz güvercin n dove
güverte [gyverte] n deck; **Araba
güvertesine nasıl gidebilirim?**
How do I get to the car deck?;
Güverteye çıkabilir miyiz? Can
we go out on deck?
Güyan [gyjan] n Guyana
güzel [gyzel] adj beautiful; **çok
güzel** adj gorgeous; **güzel
manzaralı yer** n beauty spot
güzellik [gyzellik] n beauty;
güzellik salonu n beauty salon
güzergah [gyzergah] n itinerary,
route; **güzergah değiştirme** n
detour

h

hafife almak v underestimate
hafta [hafta] n week; **hafta içi** n
weekday; **hafta sonu** n weekend;
iki hafta n fortnight; **bir hafta**
önce a week ago; **bir hafta sonra**
in a week's time; **bundan bir**
hafta önce the week before last;
Bir haftalığı ne kadar? How
much is it for a week?; **geçen**
hafta last week; **gelecek hafta**
next week; **Odanın haftalığı ne**
kadar? How much is it per week?
haftalık [haftalək] adj weekly;
Haftalık bir bilet lütfen A book
of tickets, please; **Haftalık kart**
kaça? How much is a pass per
week?; **Haftalık kayak kartı rica**
ediyorum? I'd like a ski pass for a
week; **Haftalık tarifeniz nedir?**
What are your rates per week?
haham [haham] n rabbi
hain [hain] adj (cadı vb) wicked ▷ n
(kötü) villain
Haiti [haiti] n Haiti
hak [hak] n right; **özlük hakları** n
civil rights; **geçiş hakkı** n right of
way; **giriş hakkı** n admittance;
hak etmek v deserve; **haklı**
olarak adv rightly; **haklılığını**
göstermek v justify; **insan**
hakları npl human rights; **telif**
hakkı n copyright; **Yol hakkı**
sizin değildi It wasn't your right
of way
hakaret [hakaret] n insult
hakaretamiz [hakaretamiz] adj
abusive
hakem [hakem] n referee, umpire;
hakem aracılığıyla çözümleme
n arbitration

haber [haber] n news,
information, knowledge; **güncel**
haberler npl current affairs;
haber sunucusu n newsreader;
Gecikeceğiniz zaman lütfen
bize haber verin Please call us if
you'll be late; **Haberler kaçta?**
When is the news?; **Polise haber**
vermemiz gerekiyor We will
have to report it to the police
haberler [haberler] npl news
hac [hadʒ] n pilgrimage
hacı [hadʒə] n pilgrim
hacim [hadʒim] n volume
hacker [hadʒker] n hacker
hafıza [hafəza] n memory;
bilgisayar hafızası hard disk;
hafıza kartı n memory card
hafif [hafif] adj light (not heavy);
hafif akşam yemeği n supper;
hafif bira n lager; **hafif rüzgar** n
breeze; **hafif vuruş** n tap;

hakim [hakim] **sulh hakimi** *n* magistrate

hakimiyet [hakimijet] *n* curb

hakkında [hakkənda] *prep* about

haksız [haksəz] *adj* unfair

hal [hal] *n* condition, state; **eski haline dönmek** *n* relapse; **halden anlama** *n* sympathy; **halden anlamak** *v* sympathize; **hali vakti yerinde** *adj* well-off; **medeni hal** *n* marital status; **ruh hali** *n* temper

hala [hala] *adv* still

halat [halat] *n* rope; **halat çekme oyunu** *n* tug-of-war

halef [halef] *n* successor

half-board [halfboard] *n* **Half-board ne kadar?** How much is half board?

halı [halə] *n* carpet; **küçük halı** *n* rug

halk [halk] *adj* public ▷ *n* public; **halk müziği** *n* folk music; **halkla ilişkiler** *npl* public relations; **hane halkı** *n* household; **Kale halka açık mı?** Is the castle open to the public?; **Manastır halka açık mı?** Is the monastery open to the public?; **Saray halka açık mı?** Is the palace open to the public?; **Tapınak halka açık mı?** Is the temple open to the public?

halka [halka] *n (çember)* round *(circle)*, *(zincir)* link

halletmek [halletmek] *v* deal with, sort out

halterci [halterdʒi] *n* weightlifter

halükar [halykar] *adv* **her halükarda** *adv* anyhow

hamak [hamak] *n* hammock

hamal [hamal] *n* porter

hamam [hamam] *n* baths; **hamam böceği** *n* cockroach

hamburger [hamburger] *n* beefburger, hamburger

hamile [hamile] *adj* pregnant; **Hamileyim** I'm pregnant; **Hamile kalmamak için bir şey istiyorum** I need contraception

hamilelik [hamilelik] *n* pregnancy; **hamilelik bulantısı** *n* morning sickness

hamster [hamster] *n* hamster

hamur [hamur] *n* dough, pastry; **hamur yuvarı** *n* dumpling; **milföy hamuru** *n* puff pastry; **sulu hamur** *n* batter; **un kurabiyesi hamuru** *n* shortcrust pastry

han [han] *n* inn

handikap [handikap] *n* handicap; **Handikapım...** My handicap is...; **Handikapınız kaç?** What's your handicap?

handsfree [handsfree] *adj* hands-free; **handsfree set** *n* hands-free kit

hane [hane] *n* house; **hane halkı** *n* household

hang-gliding [hanggliding] *n* hang-gliding; **Hang-gliding yapmak isterdim** I'd like to go hang-gliding

hangi [hangi] *adj* which ▷ *pron* which; **Ayakkabılar hangi katta?** Which floor are shoes on?; **Hangi düğmeye basacağım?** Which button do I press?; **Hangi eczane nöbetçi?** Which pharmacy provides emergency service?

hanım [hanəm] *n* Mrs, Miss;
**... hanımla konuşabilir miyim
lütfen?** Can I speak to Ms...,
please?

hanımeli [hanəmeli] *n* honeysuckle

hantal [hantal] *adj* gross *(income
etc.)*

hap [hap] *n* pill, tablet; **doğum
kontrol hapı** *n* contraceptive;
uyku hapı *n* sleeping pill

hapis [hapis] *n* **hapse atmak** *v* jail

hapishane [hapishane] *n* jail,
prison; **hapishane görevlisi** *n*
prison officer

hapşırmak [hapʃərmak] *v* sneeze

hararet [hararet] *n* heat; **Motor
hararet yapıyor** The engine is
overheating

harcamak [hardʒamak] *v* spend,
use up

harcamalar [hardʒamalar] *npl*
expenditure

harç [hartʃ] *n* mortar *(plaster)*

harçlık [hartʃlək] *n* **cep harçlığı** *n*
pocket money

hardal [hardal] *n* mustard; **hardal
otu** *n* rape *(plant)*

harekat [harekat] *n* **yeraltı
harekatı** *n* underground

hareket [hareket] *n* act, move,
movement; **bir yerden hareket
etmek** *v* depart

hareketsiz [hareketsiz] *adj*
motionless

harf [harf] *n* letter *(a, b, c)*; **adın
baş harfleri** *n* initials; **adının ön
harflerini yazmak** *v* initial; **harfi
harfine** *adv* literally

hariç [haritʃ] *prep* except; **liste
harici** *adj* unlisted

harika [harika] *adj* fantastic,
magnificent, marvellous,
smashing, wonderful

harita [harita] *n* chart, map;
sokak haritası *n* street map; **yol
haritası** *n* road map; **... haritası
var mı?** Have you got a map of...?;
... yol haritası istiyorum
I need a road map of...; **Ülkenin
haritasını nereden alabilirim?**
Where can I buy a map of the
country?; **Bölgenin haritasını
nereden alabilirim?** Where can I
buy a map of the area?; **Bir metro
haritası lütfen** Could I have a
map of the tube, please?; **Bu
bölgenin haritasını nereden
alabilirim?** Where can I buy a map
of the region?; **Harita alabilir
miyim?** Can I have a map?;
**Haritada yerini gösterebilir
misiniz?** Can you show me where
it is on the map?; **Kentin
haritasını nereden alabilirim?**
Where can I buy a map of the city?;
Kentin yol haritasını istiyorum
I want a street map of the city;
Metro haritası var mı? Do you
have a map of the tube?; **Nerede
olduğumuzu haritada
gösterebilir misiniz?** Can you
show me where we are on the map?

harp [harp] *n (müzik)* harp

hasar [hasar] *n* damage; **Bagajım
hasar görmüş** My luggage has
been damaged; **Valizim hasar
görmüş** My suitcase has arrived
damaged

hasat [hasat] *n* harvest; **hasat
kaldırmak** *v* harvest

haset [haset] n envy
hasetlenmek [hasetlenmek] v
envy
hasılat [hasəlat] npl takings
hassas [hassas] adj delicate,
touchy
hasta [hasta] adj ill, sick ▷ n
patient; **hasta belgesi** n sick
note; **şeker hastası** n diabetic
hastalık [hastalək] n illness,
sickness; **Alzheimer hastalığı** n
Alzheimer's disease; **hastalık
ödentisi** n sick pay; **hastalık izni**
n sick leave; **şeker hastalığı** n
diabetes
hastalıklı [hastaləklə] adj frail
hastane [hastane] n hospital; **akıl
hastanesi** n psychiatric hospital;
doğum hastanesi n maternity
hospital; **Hastane nerede?**
Where is the hospital?;
Hastanede çalışıyorum I work in
a hospital; **Hastaneye
götürmemiz gerek** We must get
him to hospital; **Hastaneye
gitmesi gerekiyor mu?** Will he
have to go to hospital?, Will she
have to go to hospital?;
Hastaneye nasıl gidebilirim?
How do I get to the hospital?
haşlama [haʃlama] adj boiled;
haşlanmış yumurta n boiled
egg
hat [hat] n line; **boru hattı** n
pipeline; **yardım hattı** n helpline;
**... için nerede hat değiştirmem
gerek?** Where do I change for...?;
... a hangi hat gider? Which line
should I take for...?; **Hat kesildi**
I've been cut off; **Hat meşgul** It's

engaged; **Hattı düşüremiyorum**
I can't get through
hata [hata] n fault (defect), fault
(mistake), mistake, oversight, slip
slip-up; **baskı hatası** n misprint
▷ v **hata yapmak** v mistake, slip
up; **Hata bende değildi** It wasn't
my fault
hatalı [hatalə] adj faulty, mistaken
hatchback [hatdʒhbadʒk] n
hatchback
hatıra [hatəra] n memento
hatırlamak [hatərlamak] v
remember
hatırlatıcı [hatərlatədʒə] n
reminder
hatırlatmak [hatərlatmak] v
remind
hatta [hatta] adv even, (bilgisayar)
online
hava [hava] n air, (meteoroloji)
weather; **açık hava** adj outdoor;
açık havada adv out-of-doors,
outdoors; **hava sahası** n airspace;
hava tahmini n weather forecast;
hava trafik kontrolörü n
air-traffic controller; **hava yastığı**
n airbag; **havaya uçmak** vi blow;
Hava çok berbat! What awful
weather!; **Hava değişecek mi?** Is
the weather going to change?;
**Hava postası ile ne kadar
zamanda gider?** How long will it
take by air?; **Hava tahmini nasıl?**
What's the weather forecast?;
Hava yarın nasıl olacak? What
will the weather be like
tomorrow?; **Tekerleklerin
havasını kontrol eder misiniz
lütfen?** Can you check the air,

please?; **Umarım hava böyle kalır** I hope the weather stays like this; **Umarım hava düzelir** I hope the weather improves

Hava [hava] *n* **Hava Kuvvetleri** *n* Air Force

hava alanı [havaalanə] *n* airport; **hava alanı otobüsü** *n* airport bus

havaalanı [havaalanə] *n* airport; **Havaalanına nasıl gidebilirim?** How do I get to the airport?; **Havaalanına otobüs var mı?** Is there a bus to the airport?; **Havaalanına taksi ne kadar?** How much is the taxi to the airport?

havai fişek [havaifiʃek] *n* **havai fişek gösterileri** *npl* fireworks

havalandırma [havalandərma] *n* air conditioning, ventilation

havalandırmalı [havalandərmalə] *adj* air-conditioned

havale [havale] *n* **posta havalesi** *n* postal order

havalı [havalə] *adj* cool (*stylish*)

havan [havan] *n* **havan topu** *n* mortar (*military*)

havasız [havasəz] *adj* stuffy

havaya [havaja] *n* **havaya uçurmak** *v* blow up

havayolu [havajolu] *n* airline

havlamak [havlamak] *v* bark

havlu [havlu] *n* towel; **banyo havlusu** *n* bath towel; **kurulama havlusu** *n* dish towel; **mutfak havlusu** *n* tea towel; **yüz havlusu** *n* face cloth; **Bana bir havlu verebilir misiniz?** Could you lend me a towel?; **Birkaç tane daha**

havlu getirir misiniz lütfen? Please bring me more towels; **Havlu kalmamış** The towels have run out

havuç [havutʃ] *n* carrot; **yabani havuç** *n* parsnip

havuz [havuz] *n* pool (*water*); **kum havuzu** *n* sandpit; **sığ havuz** *n* paddling pool; **yüzme havuzu** *n* swimming pool; **Açık yüzme havuzu mu?** Is it an outdoor pool?; **Çocuk havuzu var mı?** Is there a children's pool?; **Havuz ısıtılmış mı?** Is the pool heated?; **Yüzme havuzu nerede?** Where is the public swimming pool?; **Yüzme havuzu var mı/Yüzme havuzunuz var mı?** Is there a swimming pool?

haya [haja] *n* (anatomi) testicle

hayal [hajal] *n* imagination; **hayal kırıklığına uğramış** *adj* disappointed; **hayal kırıklığına uğratmak** *v* disappoint, let down

hayalet [hajalet] *n* ghost

hayali [hajali] *adj* imaginary

hayat [hajat] *n* life; **gece hayatı** *n* nightlife; **hayat pahalılığı** *n* cost of living; **hayatını bağışlamak** *v* spare; **hayatta kalan** *n* survivor; **hayatta kalmak** *v* survive

hayıflanmak [hajəflanmak] *v* regret

hayır [hajər] no

hayranlık [hajranlək] *n* admiration; **hayranlık duymak** *v* admire

hayret [hajret] *n* amazement, surprise; **hayret verici** *adj* amazing

haysiyet [hajsijet] *n* dignity
hayvan [hajvan] *n* animal; **ev
hayvanı** *n* pet; **hayvan dövüşleri**
n blood sports
hayvanat [hajvanat] *npl* fauna;
hayvanat bahçesi *n* zoo
hayvanbilim [hajvanbilim] *n*
zoology
haz [haz] *n* delight, zest
(*excitement*)
hazımsızlık [hazəmsəzlək] *n*
indigestion
hazır [hazər] *adj* finished, ready;
hazır bir şekilde *adv* readily;
hazır mutfak *n* fitted kitchen;
hazır yemek *n* ready-cooked,
takeaway; **Araba ne zaman
hazır olur?** When will the car be
ready?; **CD ne zaman hazır olur?**
When will the CD be ready?; **Hazır
değilim** I'm not ready; **Hazır
mısınız?** Are you ready?; **Ne
zaman hazır olur?** When will it be
ready?
hazırlama [hazərlama] *v* prepare
hazırlanmış [hazərlanməʃ] *adj*
prepared
hazırlık [hazərlək] *n* preparation
Haziran [haziran] *n* June; **bütün
Haziran boyunca** for the whole of
June; **Haziran başında** at the
beginning of June; **Haziran
sonunda** at the end of June; **On
beş Haziran Pazartesi** It's
Monday the fifteenth of June
hece [hedʒe] *n* syllable
heceleme [hedʒeleme] *n* spelling
hedef [hedef] *n* aim, target
hedeflemek [hedeflemek] *v* aim
hediye [hedije] *n* gift; **hediye çeki**
n gift voucher; **hediye dükkanı** *n*
gift shop; **Hediye paketi yapar
mısınız?** Please can you gift-wrap
it?; **Hediyelik eşya nereden
alabilirim?** Where can I buy gifts?;
Hediyelik eşyanız var mı? Do
you have souvenirs?
hekim [hekim] *n* doctor;
pratisyen hekim *n* GP
helal [helal] *adj* permissible; **Helal
yemeğiniz var mı?** Do you have
halal dishes?
helikopter [helikopter] *n*
helicopter
helva [helva] *n* **pamuk helva** *n*
candyfloss
hemen [hemen] *adv* nearly,
immediately; **hemen hemen** *adv*
nearly; **Hemen mi ödemem
gerekiyor?** Do I have to pay it
straightaway?; **Hemen yapabilir
misiniz?** Can you do it
straightaway?
hemoroid [hemoroid] *npl*
haemorrhoids
hemşire [hemʃire] *n* nurse;
**Hemşireyle konuşmak
istiyorum** I'd like to speak to a
nurse
hemzemin [hemzemin] *n*
hemzemin geçit *n* level crossing
hendek [hendek] *n* ditch, moat
hentbol [hentbol] *n* handball
henüz [henyz] *adv* just, yet (*with
negative*)
hep [hep] *adj* **hep birlikte** *adv*
altogether
hepsi [hepsi] *pron* all; **hepsini
satmak** *v* sell out; **Hepsi küçük
harf** all lower case; **Hepsini**

birlikte yazın lütfen All together, please

her [her] *adj* any, every; **her bir** *pron* each; **her gün** *adv* daily; **her halükarda** *adv* anyhow; **her iki** *adj* both; **her ikisi de** *pron* both; **her ne kadar** *conj* though; **her yıl** *adv* annually, yearly; **her yerde** *adv* everywhere; **her zaman** *adv* always; **Müze her gün açık mı?** Is the museum open every day?

herhangi [herhangi] *adj* some ▷ *pron* any; **herhangi bir şey** *pron* anything; **herhangi bir yer** *adv* anywhere; **herhangi biri** *pron* anybody, anyone

herif [herif] *n* bloke

herkes [herkes] *pron* everybody, everyone

herşey [herʃej] *pron* everything

hesap [hesap] *n* bill (account), (banka) account (in bank); **banka hesabı** *n* bank account ▷ *v* **birinin hesabına borç kaydetmek** *v* debit; **cari hesap** *n* current account; **cep hesap makinesi** *n* pocket calculator; **hesaba katmak** *v* consider, reckon; **hesaba katmamak** *v* rule out ▷ *n* **hesabından çekilen para** *n* debit; **hesabından fazla para çekmiş** *adj* overdrawn; **hesap özeti** *n* bank statement; **hesap çizelgesi** *n* spreadsheet; **hesap denetimi** *n* audit; **hesap makinesi** *n* calculator; **hesap numarası** *n* account number; **hesap vermek** *v* account for ▷ *v* **hesapları denetlemek** *v* audit; **ortak hesap** *n* joint account; **Ayrıntılı hesap**

alabilir miyim? Can I have an itemized bill?; **Hesabı alalım lütfen** Please bring the bill; **Hesabı ayrı alalım** Separate bills, please; **Hesabıma yazın** Put it on my bill; **Hesabımdan para transferi yapmak istiyorum** I would like to transfer some money from my account; **Hesapta bir yanlışlık var** The bill is wrong

hesaplama [hesaplama] *n* calculation

hesaplamak [hesaplamak] *v* calculate

heteroseksüel [heteroseksyel] *adj* heterosexual

heves [heves] *n* enthusiasm

hevesli [hevesli] *adj* enthusiastic

heybe [hejbe] *n* saddlebag

heyecan [hejedʒan] *n* thrill; **heyecan verici** *adj* exciting, thrilling

heyecanlı [hejedʒanlə] *adj* excited

heykel [hejkel] *n* sculpture, statue

heykeltraş [hejkeltraʃ] *n* sculptor

hıçkırık [hətʃkərək] *npl* hiccups

hıçkırmak [hətʃkərmak] *v* **hıçkırarak ağlamak** *v* sob

hırdavat [hərdavat] *n* hardware

hırka [hərka] *n* cardigan

hırlamak [hərlamak] *v* growl, snarl

hırs [hərs] *n* ambition

hırsız [hərsəz] *n* burglar, thief; **hırsız alarmı** *n* burglar alarm

hırsızlık [hərsəzlək] *n* break-in, burglary, theft; **kimlik hırsızlığı** *n* identity theft; **Bir hırsızlığı bildirmek istiyorum** I want to report a theft

hırslı [hərslə] *adj* ambitious
Hırvat [hərvat] *adj* Croatian ▷ *n* (kişi) Croatian *(person)*
Hırvatça [hərvattʃa] *n* (dil) Croatian *(language)*
Hırvatistan [hərvatistan] *n* Croatia
hız [həz] *n* speed; **hız sınırı** *n* speed limit; **hız yapmak** *v* speeding ▷ *v* **hızla atlamak** *v* plunge; **hızla koşmak** *v* dash, sprint; **Bu yolda hız limiti nedir?** What is the speed limit on this road?
hızlanma [həzlanma] *n* acceleration
hızlanmak [həzlanmak] *v* accelerate, speed up
hızlı [həzlə] *adj* fast ▷ *adv* fast; **Çok hızlı gidiyordu** He was driving too fast; **Çok hızlı gidiyordunuz** You were driving too fast
hızölçer [həzøltʃer] *n* speedometer
hi-fi [hifi] *n* hifi
hiç [hitʃ] *adj* no ▷ *adv* ever; **hiç durmadan** *adv* non-stop; **hiç kimse** *pron* no one, nobody; **... a hiç gittiniz mi?** Have you ever been to...?; **Hiç param yok** I have no money
hiçbir [hitʃbir] *pron* neither; **hiçbir şey** *n* nothing; **hiçbir yerde** *adv* nowhere
hiçbiri [hitʃbiri] *pron* none ▷ *sfb* neither
hiddet [hiddet] *n* rage
hidrojen [hidroʒen] *n* hydrogen
hijyen [hiʒen] *n* hygiene
hikaye [hikaje] *n* tale
hindi [hindi] *n* turkey

Hindistan [hindistan] *n* India; **Hindistan cevizi** *n* coconut; **küçük Hindistan cevizi** *n* nutmeg
Hindu [hindu] *adj* Hindu ▷ *n* Hindu
Hinduizm [hinduizm] *n* Hinduism
Hint [hint] *adj* Indian; **Batı Hint Adaları** *npl* West Indian, West Indies; **Hint fıstığı** *n* cashew; **Hint keneviri** *(yaprakları esrar olarak kullanılır)* *n* marijuana; **Hint Okyanusu** *n* Indian Ocean
Hintli [hintli] *n* Indian
hipermarket [hipermarket] *n* hypermarket
hipopotam [hipopotam] **(hipopotamlar)** *n* hippopotamus, hippo
hippi [hippi] *n* hippie
his [his] *n* feeling
hisar [hisar] *n* fort
hisse [hisse] *n* share; **hisse sahibi** *n* shareholder
hissedar [hissedar] *n* stockholder
hissetmek [hissetmek] *v* feel
hitap [hitap] *n* address *(speech)*
HIV [hiv] *n* **HIV'li olmayan** *adj* HIV-negative; **HIV'li** *adj* HIV-positive; **HIV'liyim** I am HIV positive
hizmet [hizmet] *n* service; **hizmet eden** *n* server *(person)*; **hizmet etmek** *v* serve, service; **hizmet sınıfı** *n* business class; **sosyal hizmetler** *npl* social services; **sosyal hizmetler görevlisi** *n* social worker
hizmetçi [hizmettʃi] *n* servant; **hizmetçi kadın** *n* maid

hobi [hobi] n hobby

hokey [hokej] n hockey; **buz hokeyi** n ice hockey

hokkabaz [hokkabaz] n juggler

Hollanda [hollanda] n Holland ▷ npl Netherlands

Hollandalı [hollandalə] **(Hollandalı erkekler)** n Dutchman, Dutchwoman, Dutch

homeopati [homeopati] n homeopathy

homeopatik [homeopatik] adj homeopathic

Honduras [honduras] n Honduras

hoparlör [hoparlør] n loudspeaker

hor [hor] adj **hor görme** n contempt

hor görmek [horgørmek] v despise

horlamak [horlamak] v snore

hormon [hormon] n hormone

horoz [horoz] n cock, cockerel

hortum [hortum] n hose, hosepipe

hostes [hostes] n air hostess, steward; **uçuş hostesi** n flight attendant

hoş [hoʃ] adj lovely, nice, pleasant, pretty; **eski ve hoş** adj quaint; **hoş bir şekilde** adv prettily; **hoş olmayan** adj unpleasant

hoşça [hoʃtʃa] adv beautifully

hoşçakal [hoʃtʃakal] excl bye!, bye-bye!, goodbye!

hoşgeldiniz [hoʃgeldiniz] excl welcome!

hoşgörülü [hoʃgøryly] adj tolerant

hoşgörüsüz [hoʃgørysyz] adj intolerant

hoşlanmak [hoʃlanmak] v enjoy

hoşlanmamak [hoʃlanmamak] v dislike

hoşnut [hoʃnut] adj delighted

hoşnutsuz [hoʃnutsuz] adj dissatisfied

hoverkraft [hoverkraft] n hovercraft

Hristiyan [hristijan] adj Christian ▷ n Christian

Hristiyanlık [hristijanlək] n Christianity

hukuk [hukuk] n law; **hukuk danışmanı** n solicitor; **hukuk fakültesi** n law school

huni [huni] n funnel

hurra [hurra] excl hooray!

huş [huʃ] n **huş ağacı** n birch

huy [huj] n nature, temper; **iyi huylu** adj good-natured

huysuz [hujsuz] adj bad-tempered, grumpy

huzurevi [huzurevi] n (yaşlılar için) nursing home

huzursuz [huzursuz] adj restless

hücre [hydʒre] n cell

hüküm [hykym] n judgement; **yanlış hüküm vermek** v misjudge

hükümdar [hykymdar] n ruler (commander)

hükümet [hykymet] n government; **hükümet görevlisi** n civil servant

hükümlü [hykymly] n inmate ▷ v convict

hümanist [hymanist] adj humanitarian

I

ığğ [ələdʒa] *excl* ugh
ılıca [ələdʒa] *n* spa
ılık [ələk] *adj* lukewarm, warm
ılımlı [ələmlə] *adj* medium (between extremes), mild, moderate
ılımlılık [ələmləl</_>ək] *n* moderation
IQ [ajkju:] *abbr* IQ
Irak [ərak] *adj* Iraqi ▷ *n* Iraq
Iraklı [əraklə] *n* Iraqi
ırk [ərk] *n* race (origin); **ırkla ilgili** *adj* racial
ırkçı [ərktʃə] *adj* racist ▷ *n* racist
ırkçılık [ərktʃələk] *n* racism
ırmak [ərmak] *n* river; **ırmak kıyısı** *n* bank (ridge)
ısı [əsə] *n* heat
ısınma [əsənma] *n* küresel **ısınma** *n* global warming
ısırgan [əsərgan] *n* nettle
ısırıcı [əsərədʒə] *adj* stingy
ısırma [əsərma] *n* bite

ısırmak [əsərmak] *n* bite
ısıtıcı [əsətədʒə] *n* heater
ısıtma [əsətma] *n* heating; **Isıtma çalışmıyor** The heating doesn't work
ısıtmak [əsətmak] *v* heat, warm up; **merkezi ısıtma** *n* central heating
ıslak [əslak] *adj* moist, soaked, soggy, wet; **ıslak bebek mendili** *n* baby wipe
ıslatmak [əslatmak] *v* soak
ıslık [əslək] *n* whistle; **ıslık çalmak** *v* whistle
ısmarlamak [əsmarlamak] *v* order (request)
ıspanak [əspanak] *n* spinach
ısrar [əsrar] *n* insistence; **ısrar etmek** *v* insist
ısrarlı [əsrarlə] *adj* persistent
ıssız [əssəz] *n* **ıssız ada** *n* desert island
ıstaka [əstaka] *n* cue (billiards)
ıstakoz [əstakoz] *n* lobster
ıstırap [əstərap] *n* agony
ışık [əʃək] *n* light; **ışığı söndürmek** *v* turn out; **ışıklı yaya geçidi** *n* pelican crossing; **gün ışığı** *n* sunlight, sunshine; **projektör ışığı** *n* floodlight; **tehlike uyarı ışığı** *npl* hazard warning lights; **trafik ışıkları** *npl* traffic lights; **Işığı söndürebilir miyim?** Can I switch the light off?; **Işığı yakabilir miyim?** Can I switch the light on?; **Işık yanmıyor** The light doesn't work; **Işıkta bakabilir miyim?** May I take it over to the light?; **Yağ ikaz ışığı yanıyor** The oil warning light won't go off

ışıklandırma [əʃəklandərma] *n*
lighting

ışın [əʃən] *n* beam

ızgara [əzgara] *n* grid, grill ▷ *v*
ızgara yapmak *v* grill

ızgarada [əzgarada] *adj* grilled

iade [iade] *n* returning, giving
back; **iadeli taahhütlü** *n* recorded
delivery; **para iadesi** *n* rebate,
refund; **para iadesi yapmak** *v*
refund; **vergi iadesi** *n* tax return;
**İadeli taahhütlü ne kadar
sürer?** How long will it take by
registered post?; **Bunu iade
etmek istiyorum** I'd like to return
this

ibadet [ibadet] *v* **ibadet etmek** *v*
worship

icap ettirmek [idʒapettirmek] *v*
call for

icat [idʒat] *n* invention; **icat
etmek** *v* invent

iç [itʃ] *adj* inner, *(organ vb)* internal
▷ *n* interior; **ülke içi** *adj* domestic;
hafta içi *n* weekday; **iç çamaşırı** *n*
lingerie, underwear; **iç çekme,iç
geçirmek** *n* sigh; **iç ferahlatıcı** *adj*
refreshing; **iç gömleği** *n* slip

(underwear); **iç lastik** n inner tube; **iç mimar** n interior designer; **iç rahatlığı** n relief; **iç savaş** n civil war; **içine kapanık** adj self-conscious

içecek [itʃedʒek] n drink, soft drink; **serinletici içecek** npl refreshments

içeri [itʃeri] prep into; **içeri almak** v admit (allow in)

içeride [itʃeride] adv indoors, inside ▷ prep inside; **İçeride** It's inside

içerik [itʃerik] n context

içerisi [itʃerisi] n inside

içerlemiş [itʃerlemiʃ] adj resentful

içermek [itʃermek] v contain

içgüdü [itʃgydy] n instinct

için [itʃin] prep for, owing to; **Engelli kişiler için kolaylıklarınız nelerdir?** What facilities do you have for people with disabilities?; **Engelli için tuvaletiniz var mı?** Are there any accessible toilets?

içinde [itʃinde] prep in, within (space)

içinden [itʃinden] prep through

içine [itʃine] prep within (term)

iç karartıcı adj depressing, dismal

içki [itʃki] n booze; **alkollü içki** npl spirits; **içki satan dükkan** n off-licence; **içkili araba kullanma** n drink-driving; **yemek öncesi içki** n aperitif

içmek [itʃmek] vt drink; **ölçüsüz içme** n binge drinking; **içme suyu** n drinking water ▷ v **sigara içmek** v smoke; **Bir şey içmek ister misiniz?** Would you like a drink?; **Ne içmek istersiniz?** What would

you like to drink?; **içmiyorum** I'm not drinking

içten [itʃten] adj sincere

içtenlikle [itʃtenlikle] adv frankly, sincerely

idam [idam] n execution; **idam cezası** n capital punishment; **idam etmek** v execute

idare [idare] n management, direction; **idare etmek** v go round, manipulate; **idare etmek** v control

idari [idari] adj administrative

iddia [iddia] n allegation; **iddia edilen** adj alleged

ideal [ideal] adj ideal

ideoloji [ideoloʒi] n ideology

idrar [idrar] n urine

ifade [ifade] n expression; **günlük ifadeler sözlüğü** n phrasebook; **ifade etmek** v express, state

ifşa [ifʃa] n **ifşa etmek** v reveal

iğne [jine] n needle; **kilitli iğne** n safety pin; **toplu iğne** n pin; **iğne ipliğiniz var mı?** Do you have a needle and thread?

iğrenç [jirentʃ] adj disgusting, filthy, obnoxious, repulsive, revolting

ihanet [ihanet] n **ihanet etmek** v betray

ihmal [ihmal] n neglect; **ihmal edilmiş** adj neglected ▷ v **ihmal etmek** v neglect

ihracat [ihradʒat] n export

ihraç [ihratʃ] v **ihraç etmek** v export

ihtiyaç [ihtijatʃ] n need; **ihtiyaca uyarlanmış** adj customized; **Ütüye ihtiyacım var** I need an

iron; **Bir ihtiyacınız var mı?** Do you need anything?; **Yardıma ihtiyacım var** I need assistance
ikaz [ikaz] n warning; **Yağ ikaz ışığı yanıyor** The oil warning light won't go off
iken [iken] conj as, while
iki [iki] num two; **her iki/her ikisi de** pron both; **iki dilli** adj bilingual; **iki hafta** n fortnight; **iki katına çıkmak** vt double; **iki kere** adv twice; **iki kişilik oda** n double room; **iki nokta üst üste** n colon; **İki bilet, lütfen** I'd like two tickets, please; **İki gece kalmak istiyorum** I'd like to stay for two nights; **İki yaşında bir çocuk için çocuk koltuğu istiyorum** I'd like a child seat for a two-year-old child; **İki yüz... rica ediyorum** I'd like two hundred...; **İki yüz iki numaralı odanın anahtarı lütfen** the key for room number two hundred and two; **Saat ikiye çeyrek var** It's quarter to two; **Saat yedi buçuğa iki kişilik bir rezervasyon yaptırmak istiyorum** I'd like to make a reservation for half past seven for two people; **Yarın akşam için iki kişilik bir masa ayırtmak istiyordum** I'd like to book a table for two people for tomorrow night; **Yolculuk iki saat sürüyor** The journey takes two hours
ikilem [ikilem] n dilemma
ikinci [ikindʒi] n second, (yarışma) runner-up; **ikinci baskı kitap** n paperback; **ikinci el** adj secondhand; **ikinci kalite** adj

second-rate; **ikinci olarak** adv secondly; **ikinci sınıf** adj economy class, second class, second-class; **Soldan ikinci sokağa dönün** Take the second turning on your left
ikiz [ikiz] n twin
İkizler [ikizler] n **İkizler burcu** n Gemini
iklim [iklim] n climate; **iklim değişikliği** n climate change
ikmal [ikmal] n **yakıt ikmali yapmak** v refuel
ikna [ikna] n persuasion; **ikna edici** adj persuasive; **ikna etme** v persuade
ikon [ikon] n icon
ikrar [ikrar] n acknowledgement
ilaç [ilatʃ] n drug, medicine, remedy; **böcek ilacı** n insect repellent; **ilaç yazmak** v prescribe; **Bu ilacı alıyorum zaten** I'm already taking this medicine
ilahi [ilahi] n hymn
ilan [ilan] n notice; **ilan tahtası** n bulletin board, notice board; **küçük ilanlar** npl small ads
ilave [ilave] adj (fazladan) extra ▷ n (ek) supplement
ilaveten [ilaveten] adv extra
ile [ile] prep with
ileri [ileri] adj advanced; **daha ileri/daha ileriye** adv further; **ileri dönüştürmek** v upcycle; **ileri eğitim** n further education; **ileri gitmek** v move forward; **ileriye almak** v put forward
ileriye [ilerije] adv forward
ilerleme [ilerleme] n advance, progress

ilerlemek [ilerlemek] v advance
iletişim [iletiʃim] n communication;
  iletişim kurmak v communicate
iletlemek [iletlemek] v forward
ilgi [ilgi] n (merak) interest
  (curiosity); **ilgi çekici** adj
  interesting; **ilgisini başka yöne
  çekmek** v distract
ilgilenmek [ilgilenmek] v interest
ilgili [ilgili] adj concerned,
  interested ▷ prep concerning; **ırkla
  ilgili** adj racial; **Bengaldeş ile ilgili**
  n Bangladeshi; **denizcilikle ilgili**
  adj maritime; **ilgili olarak** prep
  regarding
ilginç [ilgintʃ] adj interesting;
  **Gidilecek ilginç yerler önerebilir
  misiniz?** Can you suggest
  somewhere interesting to go?
ilik [ilik] n (anatomi) marrow
ilişki [iliʃki] n relation, relationship;
  halkla ilişkiler npl public relations
ilişkin [iliʃkin] adj relevant
ilk [ilk] adj first, primary ▷ n first;
  Büyük perhizin ilk Çarşambası n
  Ash Wednesday; **ilk yardım** n first
  aid; **ilk yardım çantası** n first-aid
  kit; **... a ilk otobüs kaçta?** When
  is the first bus to...?; **... a ilk tren
  kaçta?** When is the first train
  to...?; **İlk teleferik kaçta?** When
  does the first chair-lift go?; **İlk
  vapur kaçta?** When is the first
  boat?; **Bu benim... a ilk gelişim**
  This is my first trip to...; **Sağdan
  ilk sokağa dönün** Take the first
  turning on your right
ilkbahar [ilkbahar] n spring
  (season)
ilke [ilke] n principle

ilkel [ilkel] adj primitive, uncivilized
ilkin [ilkin] adv first
ilkokul [ilkokul] n elementary
  school, primary school
illet [illet] n disease
illüzyonist [illyzjonist] n conjurer
iltifat [iltifat] n compliment;
  iltifat etmek v compliment
iltihap [iltihap] n inflammation;
  bademcik iltihabı n tonsillitis;
  karaciğer iltihabı n hepatitis;
  mafsal iltihabı n arthritis
im [im] n tick
ima [ima] n hint ▷ v **imada
  bulunmak** v hint
imdat [imdat] excl help!
imge [imge] n image
imha [imha] n destruction
imkansız [imkansəz] adj
  impossible
imleç [imletʃ] n cursor
imparator [imparator]
  (imparatoriçe) n emperor
imparatorluk [imparatorluk] n
  empire
imza [imza] n autograph,
  signature
inanç [inantʃ] n belief, faith; **batıl
  inançları olan** adj superstitious
inandırıcı [inandərədʒə] adj
  convincing, credible
inandırmak [inandərmak] v
  convince, rope in ▷ vi believe
inanılmaz [inanəlmaz] adj
  incredible, unbelievable ▷ afj
  fabulous
inanmak [inanmak] vt believe
inatçı [inattʃə] adj stubborn
ince [indʒe] adj thin, (vücut vb)
  slim; **ince alay** n irony

inceleme [indʒeleme] *n* survey
incelemek [indʒelemek] *v*
examine
incelik [indʒelik] *n* tact
incelikli [indʒelikli] *adj* tactful
inci [indʒi] *n* pearl; **inci çiçeği** *n*
lily of the valley
incil [indʒil] *n* gospel
İncil [indʒil] *n* Bible
incinmiş [indʒinmiʃ] *adj* hurt
incir [indʒir] *n* fig
incitmek [indʒitmek] *vt* hurt;
Acıyor It hurts
inç [intʃ] *n* inch
indeks [indeks] *n* index *(list)*
indirgemek [indirgemek] *v* **en
aza indirgemek** *v* minimize
indirim [indirim] *n* discount,
reduction; **öğrenci indirimi** *n*
student discount; **indirimli
fiyatla sunulan eşya** *n* special
offer; **Çocuklara indirim var mı?**
Are there any reductions for
children?; **Öğrenci indirimi var
mı?** Are there any reductions for
students?; **Engelli için
indiriminiz var mı?** Is there a
reduction for people with
disabilities?; **Bu kartla indirim
alabilir miyim?** Is there a
reduction with this pass?; **Grup
indirimi var mı?** Are there any
reductions for groups?; **Yaşlılara
indirim var mı?** Are there any
reductions for senior citizens?
indirme [indirme] *n (bilgisayar)*
download
indirmek [indirmek] *v (bilgisayar)*
download; **denize indirmek** *v*
launch; **yere indirmek** *v* ground

inek [inek] *n* cow
ineklemek [ineklemek] *v* swot
İngiliz [ingiliz] *adj* British, English
▷ *n* Englishman, British; **İngiliz
anahtarı** *n* spanner; **İngiliz kadın**
n Englishwoman
İngilizce [ingilizdʒe] *n* English
(language); **İngilizce bilen bir
doktor var mı?** Is there a doctor
who speaks English?; **İngilizce
bilen biri var mı?** Does anyone
speak English?; **İngilizce biliyor
musunuz?** Do you speak English?;
İngilizce bilmiyorum I don't
speak English; **İngilizce
broşürünüz var mı?** Do you have
a leaflet in English?; **İngilizce film
var mı?** Are there any films in
English?; **İngilizce kılavuzunuz
var mı?** Do you have a guide book
in English?; **İngilizce konuşan bir
rehber var mı?** Is there a guide
who speaks English?; **İngilizce
rehberli turunuz var mı?** Is there
a guided tour in English?; **Çok az
İngilizce konuşabiliyorum** I
speak very little English
İngiltere [ingiltere] *n* England
inhalasyon [inhalasjon] *n*
inhalasyon cihazı *n* inhaler
iniş [iniʃ] *n* **acil iniş** *n* emergency
landing; **iniş yapmak** *vi* land;
Bu iniş zor mu? How difficult is
this slope?; **Yokuş iniş kayağı
kiralamak istiyorum** I want to
hire downhill skis
inkar [iŋar] *n* denial; **inkar
edilemez** *adj* undeniable; **inkar
etmek** *v* deny
inlemek [inlemek] *v* groan, moan

inmek [inmek] v get off,
(alçalmak) descend; **aşağıya
inmek** v come down

insan [insan] *adj* human; **insan
bilimi** n anthropology; **insan
gücü** n manpower; **insan hakları**
npl human rights

insanlar, kişi [insanlar, kişi] *npl*
people

insanlık [insanlək] n mankind

insanoğlu [insanoɣlu] n human
being

inşa [inʃa] n construction; **inşa
etmek** vt build

inşaat [inʃaat] n **inşaat alanı** n
building site

inşaatçı [inʃaattʃə] n builder

interkom [interkom] n intercom

internet [internet] n internet;
internet adresi n web address;
internet kafe n internet café;
internet kamerası n webcam;
internet kullanıcısı n internet
user; **internet meme** n meme;
internet sitesi n website;
internet suçu n cybercrime;
internet tarayıcı n web browser;
Buralarda internet kafe var mı?
Are there any internet cafés here?;
**Odada internet bağlantısı var
mı?** Is there an internet
connection in the room?

intihar [intihar] n suicide; **intihar
bombacısı** n suicide bomber

intikam [intikam] n revenge

İÖ [iə] *abbr* BC

ip [ip] n rope, string; **çamaşır ipi** n
clothes line, washing line; **diş ipi** n
dental floss

ipek [ipek] n silk

iplik [iplik] n thread; **iğne ipliğiniz
var mı?** Do you have a needle and
thread?

iPod® [ipod] n iPod®

iptal [iptal] n cancellation; **iptal
etmek** vt call off, cancel; **iptal
olan uçuş var mı?** Are there any
cancellations?

irade [irade] n will *(motivation)*,
willpower

İran [iran] *adj* Iranian ▷ n Iran

İranlı [iranlə] *adj* Persian ▷ n *(kişi)*
Iranian *(person)*

iri [iri] *adj* large, big; **iri parça** n
lump

iribaş [iribaʃ] n tadpole

irin [irin] n pus

iris [iris] n iris

irkilmek [irkilmek] v startle

İrlanda [irlanda] *adj* Irish ▷ n Eire,
Ireland; **Kuzey İrlanda** n
Northern Ireland, Ulster

İrlandalı [irlandalə] **(İrlandalı
adamlar)** n *(erkek)* Irishman,
(kadın) Irishwoman, Irish

İsa [isa] n Christ, Jesus

ishal [ishal] n diarrhoea; **ishal
oldum** I have diarrhoea

isim [isim] n name; **isim annesi** n
godmother; **isim babası** *(vaftiz)* n
godfather *(baptism)*

İskandinav [iskandinav] *adj*
Scandinavian

İskandinavya [iskandinavja] n
Scandinavia

iskele [iskele] n *(deniz)* quay,
(inşaat) scaffolding

iskelet [iskelet] n skeleton

İskoç [iskotʃ] *adj* Scots, Scottish
▷ n Scotswoman, *(erkek)*

Scotsman, Scot; **İskoç çoban köpeği** n collie
İskoçya [iskotʃja] n Scotland
İslami [islami] adj Islamic
İspanya [ispanja] n Spain
İspanyol [ispanjol] adj Spanish ⊳ n Spaniard, Spanish
israf [israf] n waste; **israf etmek** v waste
İsrail [israil] adj Israeli ⊳ n Israel
İsrailli [israilli] n Israeli
İSS [ieses] abbr ISP
istasyon [istasjon] n station; **benzin istasyonu** n petrol station, service station; **metro istasyonu** n metro station; **polis istasyonu** n police station; **radyo istasyonu** n radio station; **tren istasyonu** n railway station; **Buraya en yakın benzin istasyonu nerede?** Is there a petrol station near here?; **Tren istasyonuna en kolay nasıl gidebilirim?** What's the best way to get to the railway station?
istek [istek] n wish, request; **isteğe bağlı** adj optional; **istek formu** n claim form
istekli [istekli] adj keen, willing
istemek [istemek] v want; **fazla fiyat isteme** n surcharge
istenmeyen [istenmejen] adj **istenmeyen e-mail** n spam
istifa [istifa] n resignation; **istifa etmek** v resign
istridye [istridje] n oyster
İsveç [isvetʃ] adj Swedish ⊳ n Sweden
İsveçli [isvetʃli] n Swede, Swedish
İsviçre [isvitʃre] adj Swiss ⊳ n Switzerland

İsviçreli [isvitʃreli] n Swiss
isyankar [isjaŋar] adj rebellious
iş [iʃ] n job, work; **ağaç işleri** n woodwork; **açık iş** n vacancy; **ev işi** n housework; **evrak işi** n paperwork; **her gün işe trenle giden kimse** n commuter; **her gün işi ile evi arasında gidip gelmek** v commute; **iş adamı** n businessman; **iş arkadaşı** n associate; **iş bulma kurumu** n job centre; **iş kadını** n businesswoman; **iş saatleri dışında** adv off-peak; **iş seyahati** n business trip; **işe alma** n employment; **işe almak** v employ; **işten atma** n sack (dismissal); **işten çıkarılmış** (ihtiyaç fazlası olarak) adj redundant; **işten çıkarma** (ihtiyaç fazlası olarak) n redundancy; **işten çıkarmak** v dismiss, lay off; **musluk işleri** n plumbing; **usta işi** adj ingenious; **yazlık iş** n holiday job; **Buraya iş için geldim** I'm here for work
işaret [iʃaret] n mark, sign, signal; **ünlem işareti** n exclamation mark; **işaret dili** n sign language; **işaret etmek** v sign; **işaret parmağı** n index finger; **sınır işareti** n landmark; **soru işareti** n question mark; **ters tırnak işareti** npl inverted commas; **trafik işareti** n road sign; **at işaretini bulamıyorum** I can't find the 'at' sign
işaretlemek [iʃaretlemek] v indicate, mark (make sign)
işbirliği [iʃbirləə] n cooperation; **işbirliği yapmak** v collaborate

işçi [iʃtʃi] **(işçiler)** n workman, employee, labourer, worker; **işçi sınıfı** adj working-class

işgal [iʃgal] n occupation (invasion)

işgücü [iʃgydʒy] n workforce

işitme [iʃitme] n hearing; **işitme cihazı** n hearing aid; **İşitme aracı kullanıyorum** I have a hearing aid; **İşitme özürlüler için cihaz var mı?** Is there an induction loop?

işitmek [iʃitmek] v hear

işkence [iʃkendʒe] n torture ▷ v **işkence etmek** v torture

işlem [iʃlem] n process, transaction; **çarpma işlemi** n multiplication; **çıkarma işlemi** v subtract

işlemek [iʃlemek] v commit, operate (to function)

işletme [iʃletme] n **bar işletmecisi** n publican; **işletme masrafları** npl overheads

işsiz [issiz] adj unemployed

işsizlik [iʃsizlik] n unemployment

işsiz [iʃʃiz] adj jobless

iştah [iʃtah] n appetite

işveren [iʃveren] n employer

işyeri [iʃjeri] n workplace

itaatkar [itaatkar] adj obedient

İtalya [italja] n Italy

İtalyan [italjan] adj Italian ▷ n (kişi) Italian (person)

İtalyanca [italjandʒa] n (dil) Italian (language)

itfaiye [itfaije] n fire brigade; **itfaiyeyi çağırın** Please call the fire brigade

itfaiyeci [itfaijedʒi] **(itfaiyeciler)** n firefighter

ithaf [ithaf] n dedication

ithal [ithal] n import ▷ v **ithal etmek** v import

itici [itidʒi] adj hideous, repellent

itimatname [itimatname] n credentials

itiraf [itiraf] n confession; **itiraf etmek** v confess

itiraz [itiraz] n objection, reservation

ittifak [ittifak] n alliance

ittirmek [ittirmek] vt push

ivedi [ivedi] adj urgent

ivedilik [ivedilik] n urgency

iyi [iji] adj good ▷ adv all right, well; **çok iyi** n fine; **daha iyi/daha iyisi** adv better; **en iyi/en iyisi** adv best; **en iyi şekilde** adv ideally; **iyi değil** adj unwell; **iyi huylu** adj good-natured; **iyi kalpli** adj kind; **iyi yüreklilik** n kindness; **iyi yetiştirilmiş** adj well-behaved; **İyi akşamlar** Good evening; **İyi bir beyaz şarap tavsiye edebilir misiniz?** Can you recommend a good white wine?; **İyi bir kırmızı şarap tavsiye edebilir misiniz?** Can you recommend a good red wine?; **İyi bir kulüp biliyor musunuz?** Where is there a good club?; **İyi bir şarap tavsiye edebilir misiniz?** Can you recommend a good wine?; **İyi bir restoran tavsiye edebilir misiniz?** Can you recommend a good restaurant?; **İyi günler** Good afternoon; **İyi geceler** Good night; **İyi konserler var mı?** Are there any good concerts on?; **İyi uyudunuz mu?** Did you sleep well?; **İyi yolculuklar!** Have a good trip!;

Buralarda iyi bir plaj var mı?
Are there any good beaches near
here?; **Gidilecek iyi bir yer biliyor
musunuz?** Do you know a good
place to go?; **Hiç iyi değil** He's not
well

iyileşme [ijileʃme] *n* recovery
iyileşmek [ijileʃmek] *v* heal ▷ *vi*
recover
iyilikle [ijilikle] *adv* kindly
iyimser [ijimser] *adj* optimistic
▷ *n* optimist
iyimserlik [ijimserlik] *n* optimism
iz [iz] *n* footprint, mark, trace; **iz
sürmek** *v* retrace; **izini sürmek** *v*
track down; **karbon ayak izi** *n*
carbon footprint; **parmak izi** *n*
fingerprint
izci [izdʒi] *n* scout
izin [izin] *n* permit, *(birine bir şey
yapmak için verilen)* permission,
(işten alınan) time off, *(işten izne
ayrılmak)* leave; **çalışma izni** *n*
work permit; **babalık izni** *n*
paternity leave; **doğum izni** *n*
maternity leave; **hastalık izni** *n*
sick leave; **izin vermek** *n* allow,
let, permit; **kayak izni** *n* ski pass;
**Avlanma izin belgesi gerekiyor
mu?** Do you need a fishing permit?
İzlanda [izlanda] *adj* Icelandic
▷ *n* Iceland
İzlandalı [izlandalə] *n* Icelandic
izlemek [izlemek] *vt* follow
izlenim [izlenim] *n* impression
izleyen [izlejen] *adj* following
izleyici [izlejidʒi] *n* onlooker,
spectator, viewer
izmarit [izmarit] *n (sigara)* stub

j

jackpot [ʒdekpot] *n* jackpot
jaluzi [ʒaluzi] *n* blind, Venetian
blind
Jamaika [ʒamaika] *adj* Jamaican
Jamaikalı [ʒamaikalə] *n* Jamaican
jambon [ʒambon] *n* ham
jant [ʒant] *n* **jant kapağı** *n*
hubcap; **jant teli** *n* spoke
Japon [ʒapon] *adj* Japanese ▷ *n
(kişi)* Japanese *(person)*; **Japon
balığı** *n* goldfish
Japonca [ʒapondʒa] *n (dil)*
Japanese *(language)*
Japonya [ʒaponja] *n* Japan
jartiyer [ʒartijer] *npl* suspenders
jel [ʒel] *n* **duş jeli** *n* shower gel
jeneratör [ʒeneratør] *n* generator
jeoloji [ʒeoloʒi] *n* geology
jest [ʒest] *n* gesture
jet [ʒet] *n* jet; **jumbo jet** *n* jumbo
jet
jet-ski [ʒetski] *n* **Jet-ski nereden**

kiralayabilirim? Where can I hire a jet-ski?

jeton [ʒeton] n **jetonlu makine** n slot machine

jimnastik [ʒimnastik] npl gymnastics; **jimnastik salonu** n gym

jimnastikçi [ʒimnastiktʃi] n gymnast

jinekolog [ʒinekolog] n gynaecologist

jogging [ʒogging] n jogging ▷ v **jogging yapmak** v jog; **Nerede jogging yapabilirim?** Where can I go jogging?

jokey [ʒokej] n jockey

joystick [ʒojstik] n joystick

jöle [ʒøle] n (saç) gel, (tatlı) jelly; **saç jölesi** n hair gel

judo [ʒudo] n judo

jumbo [ʒumbo] adj **jumbo jet** n jumbo jet

jüpon [ʒypon] n underskirt

jüri [ʒyri] n jury; **jüri kararı** n verdict

k

kaba [kaba] adj (aceleyle yapılmış) rough, (davranış) rude, (iş vb) crude, (insan) vulgar, (kumaş, sakal vb) coarse; **kaba şaka** n prank

kabaca [kabadʒa] adv grossly, roughly

kabak [kabak] n courgette, zucchini

kabakulak [kabakulak] n mumps

kaban [kaban] n coat

kabara [kabara] n stud

kabarcık [kabardʒək] n bubble; **sulu kabarcık** n blister

kabartmak [kabartmak] v raise; **kabartma tozu** n baking powder

kabız [kabəz] adj constipated; **Kabızlık çekiyorum** I'm constipated

kabile [kabile] n tribe

kabin [kabin] n cabin; **kabin mürettebatı** n cabin crew; **Beş**

numaralı kabin nerede? Where is cabin number five?; **Standart bir kabin bileti** a standard class cabin
kabine [kabine] n cabinet
kablo [kaplo] n cable, flex; **kablolu yayın** n cable television; **takviye kablosu** npl jump leads; **uzatma kablosu** n extension cable
kablosuz [kaplosuz] adj **Odada kablosuz internet bağlantısı var mı?** Does the room have wireless internet access?
kabuk [kabuk] n shell; **kabuklu deniz ürünü** n shellfish; **kabuksuz sümüklüböcek** n slug; **limon kabuğu** n zest (lemon-peel); **meyva kabuğu** n peel
kabul [kabul] n admission; **kabul edilebilir** adj acceptable; **kabul edilemez** adj unacceptable; **kabul etmek** v accept, (itiraf) admit (confess)
kabullenmek [kabullenmek] n **yenilgiyi kabullenmek** v give in
kaburga [kaburga] n rib
kabza [kabza] n hold, handle; **kısa kabzalı tabanca** n pistol
kaç [katʃ] num how many?, how much?; **... a kaç durak var?** How many stops is it to...?; **Boyunuz kaç?** How tall are you?; **Kaç yaşındasınız?** How old are you?; **Kaça olur?** How much will it be?; **Kaçıncı katta?** What floor is it on?; **Kaçta kapatıyorsunuz?** What time do you close?; **Sabah kaçta kalkıyorsunuz?** What time do you get up?; **Tren... a kaçta varıyor?** What time does the train arrive

in...?; **Tren kaçta kalkacak?** What time does the train leave?
kaçak [katʃak] n **kaçak avlanmış** adj poached (caught illegally)
kaçakçı [katʃaktʃə] n smuggler; **kaçakçılık yapmak** v smuggle
kaçakçılık [katʃaktʃələk] n smuggling
kaçık [katʃək] adj mad (insane) ▷ n lunatic, nutter (inf, pej); **keyfi kaçık** adj upset
kaçınılmaz [katʃənəlmaz] adj inevitable, unavoidable; **kaçınılmaz bir şekilde** adv necessarily
kaçırmak [katʃərmak] v (adam) kidnap, (birini) abduct ▷ vt (treni, otobüsü) miss; **gözden kaçırmak** v overlook; **keyfini kaçırmak** v upset
kaçış [katʃəʃ] n escape
kaçmak [katʃmak] v avoid, flee, (uzaklara) run away ▷ vi escape; **kenara kaçmak** v dodge; **okuldan kaçmak** v play truant
kadar [kadar] conj (zaman, olay vb) until ▷ prep as, (yer) until; **...'e kadar** (zaman) prep till; **...e kadar** (yer) prep till; **her ne kadar** conj though
kadeh [kadeh] n glass, cup; **kadeh kaldırmak** n toast (tribute); **şarap kadehi** n wineglass
kader [kader] n destiny, fate
kadın [kadən] adj female ▷ n woman, female; **İngiliz kadın** n Englishwoman; **Fransız kadın** n Frenchwoman; **hizmetçi kadın** n maid; **iş kadını** n businesswoman; **kadın barmen** n barmaid; **kadın**

garson n waitress; **kadın kahraman** n heroine; **kadın oyuncu** n actress; **kadın polis** n police officer, policewoman; **kadın postacı** n postwoman; **kadın sporcu** n sportswoman; **kadınlar tuvaleti** n ladies'
kadınsı [kadənsə] adj feminine
kadife [kadife] n velvet; **fitilli kadife** n corduroy; **kadife çiçeği** n marigold
kadro [kadro] n **oyuncu kadrosu** n cast
kafa [kafa] n head; **dazlak kafa** n skinhead; **kafası karışık** adj confused; **kafası karışmış** adj puzzled; **kafasını takmış** adj preoccupied
kafatası [kafatasə] n skull
kafe [kafe] n café
kafein [kafein] n caffeine
kafeinsiz [kafeinsiz] adj decaffeinated; **kafeinsiz kahve** n decaffeinated coffee
kafes [kafes] n cage
kafeterya [kafeterja] n cafeteria
Kafkas [kafkas] n Caucasus
kağıt [ka:ət] n paper; **aydınger kağıdı** n tracing paper; **duvar kağıdı** n wallpaper; **kağıt ağırlığı** n paperweight; **kağıt mendil** n tissue (anatomy), tissue (paper); **kağıt parçası** n slip (paper); **kağıt peçete** n serviette; **karalama kağıdı** n scrap paper; **not kağıdı** n notepaper; **paket kağıdı** n wrapping paper; **tuvalet kağıdı** n toilet paper, toilet roll; **yazı kağıdı** n writing paper; **Tuvalet kağıdı yok** There is no toilet paper

kahkaha [kahkaha] n laughter ▷ v **kahkahayla gülmek** v laugh
kahkül [kahkyl] n fringe
kahraman [kahraman] n hero; **kadın kahraman** n heroine
kahvaltı [kahvaltə] n breakfast; **kahvaltı ve akşam yemeği dahil** n half board; **yatak ve kahvaltı** n bed and breakfast, B&B; **kahvaltı dahil** with breakfast; **kahvaltı hariç** without breakfast; **Kahvaltı dahil mi?** Is breakfast included?; **Kahvaltı kaçta?** What time is breakfast?; **Kahvaltı nerede veriliyor?** Where is breakfast served?; **Kahvaltıda ne yemek istersiniz?** What would you like for breakfast?; **Odamda kahvaltı edebilir miyim?** Can I have breakfast in my room?
kahve [kahve] n coffee; **kafeinsiz kahve** n decaffeinated coffee; **kahve çekirdeği** n coffee bean; **sütsüz kahve** n black coffee; **Bir fincan kahve daha alabilir miyiz?** Could we have another cup of coffee, please?; **Bir kahve lütfen** A coffee, please; **gerçek kahveniz var mı?** Have you got real coffee?; **Kahve lekesi** This stain is coffee; **Salonda kahve içebilir miyiz?** Could we have coffee in the lounge?; **Sütlü kahve lütfen** A white coffee, please; **Taze kahveniz var mı?** Have you got fresh coffee?
kahverengi [kahverengi] adj brown
kakao [kakao] n cocoa
kaktüs [kaktys] n cactus

kalabalık [kalabalək] *adj* crowded
▷ *n* crowd, host *(multitude)*

kalamar [kalamar] *n* squid

kalan [kalan] *adj* remaining;
hayatta kalan *n* survivor

kalay [kalaj] *n* tin; **kalay yaldızı** *n*
tinfoil

kalça [kaltʃa] *n* hip ▷ *npl* buttocks

kaldırım [kaldərəm] *n* pavement;
kaldırım taşı *n* kerb

kaldırmak [kaldərmak] *v* hold up,
remove, *(yukarıya)* lift; **ağırlık**
kaldırma *n* weightlifting; **hasat**
kaldırmak *v* harvest; **kadeh**
kaldırmak *n* toast *(tribute)*;
yürürlükten kaldırma *n* abolition

kale [kale] *n* *(şato vb)* castle;
kumdan kale *n* sandcastle; **Kale**
halka açık mı? Is the castle open
to the public?; **Kaleyi görebilir**
miyiz? Can we visit the castle?

kaleci [kaledʒi] *n* goalkeeper

kalem [kalem] *n* pen; **kalem**
açacağı *n* pencil sharpener;
kalem arkadaşı *n* penfriend; **keçe**
kalem *n* felt-tip pen; **kurşun**
kalem *n* pencil; **tükenmez kalem**
n Biro®; **Tükenmez kalem** *n*
ballpoint pen; **Kaleminiz var mı?**
Do you have a pen I could borrow?

kalemlik [kalemlik] *n* pencil case

kalıcı [kalədʒə] *adj* permanent;
kalıcı bir şekilde *adv* permanently

kalın [kalən] *adj* thick; **pamuklu**
kalın tişört *n* sweatshirt

kalınlık [kalənlək] *n* thickness

kalıntı [kaləntə] *npl* remains

kalıp [kaləp] *n* *(dikiş)* pattern, *(pasta,
jöle, briket vb)* mould *(shape)*

kalış [kaləʃ] *n* stay

kalıtsal [kalətsal] *adj* hereditary

kalite [kalite] *n* quality; **ikinci**
kalite *adj* second-rate

kalkan [kalkan] *n* shield

kalkış [kalkəʃ] *n* departure, *(uçak)*
takeoff

kalkışmak [kalkəʃmak] *v* attempt

kalkmak [kalkmak] *v* get up;
ayağa kalkmak *v* stand up

kalma [kalma] *adj* remaining;
akşamdan kalma *n* hangover

kalmak [kalmak] *v* remain, stay;
berabere kalmak *vt* draw *(equal
with)*; **geri kalmak** *v* back out;
geride kalmak *v* lag behind;
hayatta kalmak *v* survive;
kalacak yer *n* accommodation;
kısılıp kalmak *adj* stranded;
Otelde kalıyorum I'm staying at a
hotel

kalori [kalori] *n* calorie

kalorifer [kalorifer] *n* heating;
Kalorifer nasıl çalışıyor? How
does the heating work?; **Odada**
kalorifer var mı? Does the room
have heating?

kalp [kalp] *n* heart; **iyi kalpli** *adj*
kind; **kalbi kırık** *adj* heartbroken;
kalp krizi *n* heart attack; **kalp pili**
n pacemaker; **Kalp hastasıyım** I
have a heart condition

kalsiyum [kalsijum] *n* calcium

Kamboçya [kambotʃja] *adj*
Cambodian ▷ *n* Cambodia

Kamboçyalı [kambotʃjalə] *n* *(kişi)*
Cambodian *(person)*

kamera [kamera] *n* camera; **araç**
içi kamera *n* dashcam; **internet**
kamerası *n* webcam; **video**
kamera *n* camcorder; **video**

kamerası n video camera; **Bu dijital kameraya hafıza kartı almak istiyorum lütfen** A memory card for this digital camera, please; **Bu video kamera için teyp alabilir miyim?** Can I have a tape for this video camera, please?; **Kameram tutukluk yapıyor** My camera is sticking

kameraman [kameraman] **(kameramanlar)** n cameraman

Kamerun [kamerun] n Cameroon

kamış [kaməʃ] n reed

kamp [kamp] n camp ▷ v **kamp yapmak** v camp; **kamp yeri** n campsite; **karavan kampı** n caravan site

kampanya [kampanja] n campaign

kampçı [kamptʃə] n camper

kamping [kamping] n camping

kampüs [kampys] n campus

kamulaştırmak [kamulaʃtərmak] v nationalize

kamuoyu [kamuoju] n public opinion; **kamuoyu yoklaması** n opinion poll, poll; **kamuoyuna açıklamak** v issue

kamyon [kamjon] n truck; **kamyon şoförü** n lorry driver, truck driver; **taşınma kamyonu** n removal van

kan [kan] n blood; **kan aktarımı** n transfusion; **kan dolaşımı** n circulation; **kan grubu** n blood group; **kan kırmızısı** adj scarlet; **kan nakli** n blood transfusion; **kan testi** n blood test; **kan zehirlenmesi** n blood poisoning; **Kan grubum O pozitif** My blood

group is O positive; **Kan lekesi** This stain is blood

Kanada [kanada] adj Canadian ▷ n Canada

Kanadalı [kanadalə] n Canadian

kanal [kanal] n canal, channel

kanama [kanama] n bleeding; **burun kanaması** n nosebleed

kanamak [kanamak] vi bleed

kanarya [kanarja] n canary

Kanarya [kanarja] n **Kanarya Adaları** n Canaries

kanat [kanat] n wing; **kanat çırpmak** v flap; **sağ kanat** adj right-wing

kanca [kandʒa] n hook, peg

kancık [kandʒək] n bitch

kandırmak [kandərmak] v fool, trick

kanepe [kanepe] n couch, (koltuk) sofa

kanguru [kanguru] n kangaroo

kanıt [kanət] n evidence, proof (evidence)

kanıtlamak [kanətlamak] v prove; **bulgularla kanıtlamak** v demonstrate

kaniş [kaniʃ] n poodle

kanlı [kanlə] adj bloody

kano [kano] n canoe; **kano sporu** n canoeing; **Kano sporu nerede yapabiliriz?** Where can we go canoeing?

kanser [kanser] n (hastalık) cancer (illness)

kansız [kansəz] adj anaemic

kantin [kantin] n canteen

kap [kap] n container; **yumurta kabı** n eggcup

kapa [kapa] v **Pencereyi**

kapatabilir miyim? May I close the window?

kapak [kapak] n lid; **göz kapağı** n eyelid; **jant kapağı** n hubcap; **motor kapağı** n bonnet (car)

kapalı [kapalə] adj closed ▷ adv off; **üstü kapalı yük aracı** n van; **kapalı alan** adj indoor; **kapalı yer korkusu olan** adj claustrophobic; **Kapalı Devre Televizyon Sistemi** n CCTV

kapamak [kapamak] v go off; **elektriği kapamak** v switch off

kapanık [kapanək] adj **içine kapanık** adj self-conscious

kapanış [kapanəʃ] n closure; **kapanış saati** n closing time

kaparo [kaparo] n deposit; **Kaparo ne kadar?** How much is the deposit?; **Kaparomı geri alabilir miyim?** Can I have my deposit back, please?

kapasite [kapasite] n capacity

kapatmak [kapatmak] v close, shut down, turn off ▷ vt shut, (fermuar) zip (up); **çarparak kapatmak** v slam; **oturum kapatmak** v log off, log out; **telefonu kapatmak** v hang up

kapı [kapə] n door, gate; **kapı eşiği** n doorstep; **kapı kolu** n door handle; **kapı telefonu** n entry phone; **kapı zili** n doorbell ▷ v **kapıyı çalmak** v knock (on the door etc.); **... numaralı kapıya gidiniz** Please go to gate...; **Bu kapının anahtarı hangisi?** Which is the key for this door?; **Hangisi arka kapının anahtarı?** Which is the key for the back door?;

Hangisi ön kapının anahtarı? Which is the key for the front door?; **Kapı açılmıyor** The door won't open; **Kapı kapanmıyor** The door won't close; **Kapı kilitlenmiyor** The door won't lock; **Kapının kolu çıktı** The door handle has come off; **Kapınızı kilitleyin** Keep the door locked

kapıcı [kapədʒə] **(kapıcılar)** n doorman

kapılmak [kapəlmak] v **cazibesine kapılmak** v fall for; **paniğe kapılmak** v panic

kapitalizm [kapitalizm] n capitalism

kapkaççı [kapkatʃtʃə] n mugger

kapkaççılık [kapkatʃtʃələk] n mugging

kaplama [kaplama] n coating; **altın kaplama** n gold-plated

kaplan [kaplan] n tiger

kaplumbağa [kaplumba:a] n tortoise; **su kaplumbağası** n turtle

kapmak [kapmak] v snatch

kapsamlı [kapsamlə] adj comprehensive, inclusive ▷ adv overall

kapsül [kapsyl] n capsule

kaptan [kaptan] n captain

kapüşon [kapyʃon] n hood

kar [kar] n snow; **kar fırtınası** n blizzard, snowstorm; **kar tanesi** n snowflake; **kar temizleme aracı** n snowplough; **kar topu** n snowball ▷ v **kar yağmak** v snow; **kardan adam** n snowman; **sulu kar** n sleet; **... yolunda kar var mı?** Is the road to... snowed up?;

Kar çok şiddetli The snow is very heavy; **Kar durumu nasıl?** What are the snow conditions?; **Kar nasıl?** What is the snow like?; **Kar yağacak mı dersiniz?** Do you think it will snow?; **Kar yağıyor** It's snowing; **Kar zinciri almam gerekiyor mu?** Do I need snow chains?

kara [kara] n (coğrafya) land; **kara kurbağa** n toad

karaağaç [karaa:atʃ] n elm

karabasan [karabasan] n nightmare

karaciğer [karadʒjier] n liver; **karaciğer iltihabı** n hepatitis

kara hindiba [karahindiba] n dandelion

karakol [karakol] n police station; **Polis karakolu nerede?** Where is the police station?; **Polis karakolunu arıyorum** I need to find a police station

karakter [karakter] n character

karakteristik [karakteristik] n characteristic

karalama [karalama] n sketch; **karalama defteri** n scrapbook; **karalama kağıdı** n scrap paper

karalamak [karalamak] v scribble; **karalama yapmak** v sketch

karamela [karamela] n toffee

karamelâ [karamela:] n caramel

karanfil [karanfil] n (çiçek) carnation, (baharat) clove

karanlık [karanlək] adj dark ▷ n dark, darkness; **Karanlık** It's dark

karantina [karantina] n quarantine

karaoke [karaoke] n karaoke

karar [karar] n decision; **jüri kararı** n verdict; **karar vermek** v decide; **kararı bozmak** v overrule

kararlı [kararlə] adj determined

kararlılık [kararlələk] n resolution

kararsız [kararsəz] adj indecisive, undecided

karartma [karartma] n blackout, curfew

karatahta [karatahta] n blackboard

karatavuk [karatavuk] n blackbird

karate [karate] n karate

karavan [karavan] n camper, caravan; **karavan kampı** n caravan site; **Karavanımızı buraya park edebilir miyiz?** Can we park our caravan here?; **Karavanımızla kamp edebileceğimiz bir yer arıyoruz** We'd like a site for a caravan

Karayip [karajip] adj Caribbean

karayolu [karajolu] n road; **Bu bölgenin karayolları haritası var mı?** Do you have a road map of this area?

karbon [karbon] n carbon; **karbon ayak izi** n carbon footprint

karbonat [karbonat] n bicarbonate of soda

karbonhidrat [karbonhidrat] n carbohydrate

karbüratör [karbyratør] n carburettor

kardeş [kardeʃ] n sibling; **erkek kardeş** n brother; **üvey erkek kardeş** n stepbrother

kardeşler [kardeʃler] npl siblings

kare [kare] *adj* square ▷ *n* square
kareli [kareli] *adj* checked
karga [karga] *n* crow
kargaşa [kargaʃa] *n* chaos, muddle
kargo [kargo] *n* cargo
karı [karə] **(karılar)** *n (eş)* wife;
　eski karı *n* ex-wife
karın [karən] *n* abdomen, tummy;
　karın boşluğu ile ilgili *adj* coeliac
karınca [karəndʒa] *n* ant
karışık [karəʃək] *adj* mixed ▷ *n*
　(şeker/çiçek) mix; **kafası karışık**
　adj confused; **karışık salata** *n*
　mixed salad
karışıklık [karəʃəklək] *m*
　confusion ▷ *n* mix-up
karışım [karəʃəm] *n* mixture
karıştırmak [karəʃtərmak] *v*
　(fikir) confuse, *(salata, baharat vb)*
　mix up ▷ *vt (çorba vb)* stir, *(nesne)*
　mix
karides [karides] *n* prawn; **büyük**
　karides *npl* scampi; **ufak karides**
　n shrimp
karikatür [karikatyr] *n* cartoon
kariyer [karijer] *n* career
karmakarışık [karmakarəʃək] *adj*
　chaotic
karnabahar [karnabahar] *n*
　cauliflower
karnaval [karnaval] *n* carnival
karne [karne] *n* report card
karpuz [karpuz] *n* watermelon
karşı [karʃə] *adj* opposed ▷ *prep*
　against, versus; **karşı çıkan** *adj*
　opposing; **karşı çıkmak** *v* oppose;
　karşıdan karşıya geçmek *vt*
　cross
karşılama [karʃəlama] *n* welcome
karşılamak [karʃəlamak] *v*

welcome; **zararını karşılamak** *v*
reimburse
karşılık [karʃələk] *n* **karşılıklı**
sefer yapan araç *n* shuttle ▷ *v*
karşılıklı yapmak *v* exchange
karşılıklı [karʃələklə] *adj*
　alternate, mutual ▷ *adv* opposite
karşın [karʃən] *prep* despite
karşısında [karʃəsənda] *prep*
　opposite
karşıt [karʃət] *adj* opposite ▷ *n*
　opponent
karşıtlık [karʃətlək] *n* contrast
karşıya [karʃəja] *prep* across
kart [kart] *n* card; **abonman kartı**
　n season ticket; **üyelik kartı** *n*
　membership card; **banka kartı** *n*
　debit card; **biniş kartı** *n* boarding
　card, boarding pass; **hafıza kartı**
　n memory card; **kartlı telefon** *n*
　cardphone; **kimlik kartı** *n* badge,
　identity card, ID card; **kredi kartı**
　n credit card; **kredi kartı şifresi**
　npl PIN; **Noel kartı** *n* Christmas
　card; **oyun kartı** *n* playing card;
　tebrik kartı *n* greetings card;
　telefon kartı *n* phonecard,
　top-up card; **Banka kartı alıyor**
　musunuz?/Banka kartı kabul
　ediyor musunuz? Do you take
　debit cards?; **Biniş kartım burada**
　Here is my boarding card; **Bu kartı**
　bu makinede kullanabilir miyim?
　Can I use my card with this cash
　machine?; **Bu kartları nereden**
　postalayabilirim? Where can I
　post these cards?; **Buyurun**
　kartım Here is my card; **Kartım**
　çalındı My card has been stolen;
　Kartımı iptal ettirmek istiyorum

I need to cancel my card; **Kartınız var mı?** Do you have a business card?; **Kartınızı alabilir miyim?** Can I have your card?; **Kredi kartı kabul ediyor musunuz?** Do you take credit cards?; **Kredi kartıma nakit ödeme alabilir miyim?** Can I get a cash advance with my credit card?; **Kredi kartıyla ödeme yapabilir miyim?** Can I pay by credit card?; **Makine kartımı yuttu** The cash machine swallowed my card; **Nakit almak için kartımı kullanabilir miyim?** Can I use my card to get cash?; **Nereden otobüs kartı alabilirim?** Where can I buy a bus card?; **Telefon kartı nereden alabilirim** Where can I buy a top-up card?; **Telefon kartı satıyor musunuz?** Do you sell phone cards?; **Uluslararası telefon kartı satıyor musunuz?** Do you sell international phone cards?; **Yirmibeş euroluk telefon kartı rica ediyorum** I'd like a twenty-five euro phone card

kartal [kartal] n eagle
karton [karton] n carbboard; **karton kutu** n carton
kartpostal [kartpostal] n postcard; **Bu dört kartpostal için pul alacaktım... a gidecek** Can I have stamps for four postcards to...; **Kartpostal bakıyordum** I'm looking for postcards; **Kartpostal satıyor musunuz?** Do you have any postcards?; **Nereden kartpostal alabilirim?** Where can I buy some postcards?

karyola [karjola] n bed; **bebek karyolası** n cot; **portatif karyola** n camp bed
kas [kas] adj muscular ▷ n muscle
kasa [kasa] n safe; **yazar kasa** n till; **Bunu kasaya koyun lütfen** Put that in the safe, please; **Kasada eşyalarım vardı** I have some things in the safe
kasap [kasap] n butcher, butcher's
kase [kase] n bowl
kaset [kaset] n cassette
Kasım [kasəm] n (ay) November
kasımpatı [kasəmpatə] n chrysanthemum
kasırga [kasərga] n hurricane, tornado
kasıt [kasət] n purpose, intention; **kasıtlı olarak** adv deliberately; **kasıtsız olarak** adv inadvertently
kasıtlı [kasətlə] adj deliberate, intentional
kasıtsız [kasətsəz] adj unintentional
kasiyer [kasijer] n cashier
kask [kask] n (motosiklet) helmet; **Kask alabilir miyim?** Can I have a helmet?
kastetmek [kastetmek] v mean
kasvetli [kasvetli] adj gloomy
kaş [kaʃ] n eyebrow; **kaşlarını çatmak** v frown
kaşer [kaʃer] adj kosher
kaşık [kaʃək] n spoon; **çay kaşığı** n teaspoon; **çorba kaşığı** n tablespoon; **bir kaşık dolusu** n spoonful; **tatlı kaşığı** n dessert spoon; **Temiz bir kaşık alabilir miyim lütfen** Could I have a clean spoon, please?

kaşınmak [kaʃənmak] v itch
kaşıntılı [kaʃəntələ] adj itchy
kaşif [kaʃif] n explorer
kaşmir [kaʃmir] n cashmere
kat [kat] n (giysi, kağıt vb) fold ▷ adj
  alt kat adj downstairs ▷ adv **alt
  katta** adv downstairs; **üç katı** adj
  treble, triple; **üst katta** adv
  upstairs; **iki katına çıkmak** vt
  double; **zemin kat** n ground floor
katalitik [katalitik] adj **katalitik
  konvertör** n catalytic converter
katalog [katalog] n catalogue;
  Katalog istiyorum I'd like a
  catalogue
Katar [katar] n Qatar
katarakt [katarakt] n cataract
  (eye)
katedral [katedral] n cathedral;
  Katedral ne zaman açık? When
  is the cathedral open?
kategori [kategori] n category
katı [katə] adj (durum) stark,
  (kumaş vb) stiff, (kural vb) strict,
  (maddenin hali) solid; **katı bir
  şekilde** adv strictly
katılım [katələm] n attendance
katılmak [katəlmak] v attend,
  participate ▷ vi join; **partiye
  katılmak** v party; **Size katılabilir
  miyim?** Can I join you?
katır [katər] n mule
katil [katil] n killer, murderer
katkı [katkə] n contribution; **katkı
  maddesi** n additive, preservative;
  katkıda bulunmak v contribute
katlamak [katlamak] vt fold
katlanır [katlanər] adj folding
katletmek [katletmek] v murder
katliam [katliam] n massacre

katman [katman] n layer
Katolik [katolik] adj Catholic ▷ n
  Catholic; **Roma Katoliği/Roma
  Katolik** n Roman Catholic
kavak [kavak] n poplar
kaval [kaval] n **kaval kemiği** n
  shin
kavanoz [kavanoz] n jar; **reçel
  kavanozu** n jam jar
kavga [kavga] n quarrel, scrap
  (dispute); **yaşam kavgası** n
  survival
kavramak [kavramak] v grab,
  grasp; **sımsıkı kavramak** v grip
kavrulmuş [kavrulmuʃ] adj roast
kavşak [kavʃak] n junction; **döner
  kavşak** n roundabout; **... kavşağı
  nerede?** Which junction is it for...?;
  **Araba... numaralı kavşağa
  yakın** The car is near junction
  number...; **Bir sonraki
  kavşaktan sağa dönün** Go right
  at the next junction; **Bir sonraki
  kavşaktan sola dönün** Go left at
  the next junction
kavun [kavun] n melon
kaya [kaja] n rock
kayak [kajak] n ski; **kayak
  alıştırma pisti** n nursery slope;
  kayak izni n ski pass ▷ v **kayak
  yapmak** v ski; **su kayağı** n
  water-skiing; **Burada kayak
  kiralayabilir miyiz?** Can we hire
  skis here?; **Burada kayak okulu
  var mı?** Is there a ski school?;
  **Cross-country kayağı yapmak
  mümkün mü?** Is it possible to go
  cross-country skiing?; **Haftalık
  kayak kartı rica ediyorum?** I'd
  like a ski pass for a week; **Kayak**

dersleri veriyor musunuz? Do you organise skiing lessons?; **Kayak güzergahlarının haritası var mı?** Do you have a map of the ski runs?; **Kayak gereçlerini nereden kiralayabilirim?** Where can I hire skiing equipment?; **Kayak kartı ne kadar?** How much is a ski pass?; **Kayak kartı nereden alabilirim?** Where can I buy a ski pass?; **Kayak kiralamak istiyorum** I want to hire skis; **Kayak sopası kiralamak istiyorum** I want to hire ski poles; **Kayak yapmak istiyorum** I'd like to go skiing; **Yokuş iniş kayağı kiralamak istiyorum** I want to hire downhill skis

kayakçı [kajaktʃə] n skier

kayalık [kajalək] n cliff

kaybetmek [kajbetmek] vt lose

kaybolmak [kajbolmak] vi lose; **gözden kaybolma** n disappearance; **gözden kaybolmak** v disappear

kaydetmek [kajdetmek] v record, tape; **birinin hesabına borç kaydetmek** v debit

kaydolmak [kajdolmak] v sign on

kaygan [kajgan] adj slippery

kayın [kajən] n **kayın ağacı** n beech (tree); **kayın birader** n brother-in-law

kayınpeder [kajənpeder] **(kayınpederler)** n father-in-law

kayınvalide [kajənvalide] **(kayınvalideler)** n mother-in-law

kayıp [kajəp] adj lost, missing ▷ n loss; **kayıp eşya bürosu** n lost-property office; **kaybolup bulunmuş** n lost-and-found; **Çocuğum kayıp** My child is missing; **Bagajım kaybolmuş** My luggage has been lost; **Kızım kayıp** My daughter is missing; **Kızım kayboldu** My daughter is lost; **Oğlum kayıp** My son is missing; **Oğlum kayboldu** My son is lost

kayısı [kajəsə] n apricot

kayış [kajəʃ] n strap; **saat kayışı** n watch strap; **soğutucu kayışı** n fan belt

kayıt [kajət] n record, recording, register, registration; **kayıt aleti** n recorder (scribe) ▷ v **kayıt yaptırmak** v register; **ses kayıt cihazı** n recorder (music), tape recorder

kayıtlı [kajətlə] adj registered

kayma [kajma] n slide; **toprak kayması** n landslide

kaymak [kajmak] v skid, slide ▷ vi slip; **disk kayması** n slipped disc; **kayma sporu** n skiing; **kızak kayma** n tobogganing; **kızak kaymak** n sledging; **patenle kaymak** n rollerskating

kaynak [kajnak] adj (çıkış noktası) origin ▷ n (destek) resource; **doğal kaynaklar** npl natural resources; **parasal kaynak** npl funds

kaynamış [kajnaməʃ] adj boiled

kaynar [kajnar] adj boiling

kaynaştırmak [kajnaʃtərmak] v merge

kaynatmak [kajnatmak] vt boil; **yavaş yavaş kaynatmak** v simmer

kaypak [kajpak] *adj* shifty
kaytarmak [kajtarmak] *v* skive
kaz [kaz] **(kazlar)** *n* goose
kaza [kaza] *n* accident; **araba
kazası** *n* crash; **deniz kazası** *n*
shipwreck; **deniz kazası geçirmiş**
adj shipwrecked; **kaza & acil
servis** *n* accident & emergency
department; **kaza sigortası** *n*
accident insurance; **kaza sonucu**
adj accidental; **Bir kaza oldu!**
There's been an accident!;
**Bireysel kaza sigortası
yaptırmak istiyorum** I'd like to
arrange personal accident
insurance; **Kaza geçirdim** I've
been in an accident, I've had an
accident; **Kaza geçirirsem ne
yapmam gerekiyor?** What do I do
if I have an accident?
kazak [kazak] *n* jersey, jumper,
pullover, sweater; **polo yakalı
kazak** *n* polo-necked sweater
Kazakistan [kazakistan] *n*
Kazakhstan
kazan [kazan] *n* boiler
kazanan [kazanan] *adj* winning
kazanç [kazantʃ] *n* gain, profit
kazançlı [kazantʃlə] *adj* lucrative,
profitable
kazandırmak [kazandərmak] *v*
açıklık kazandırmak *v* clarify
kazanma [kazanma] *n* winner
kazanmak [kazanmak] *v* earn,
win ▷ *vt* gain; **düşmanlığını
kazanmak** *v* antagonize
kazara [kazara] *adv* accidentally,
by chance, by accident
kazık [kazək] *n (pahalı)* rip-off;
çadır kazığı *n* tent peg

kazıklamak [kazəklamak] *v* rip
off
kazımak [kazəmak] *v* engrave
kazma [kazma] *n* pick
kazmak [kazmak] *vt* dig
kâfi [ka:fi] *adj* enough ▷ *pron*
enough
KDV [kdv] *abbr* VAT; **KDV dahil mi?**
Is VAT included?
kebap [kebap] *n* kebab; **kebap şişi**
n skewer
keçe [ketʃe] *n* felt; **keçe kalem** *n*
felt-tip pen
keçi [ketʃi] *n* goat
keder [keder] *n* grief
kedi [kedi] *n* cat; **kedi yavrusu** *n*
kitten
kefalet [kefalet] *n* bail
kehanet [kehanet] *n* premonition
kehribar [kehribar] *n* amber
kek [kek] *n* cake; **şekerli kek süsü**
n frosting
kekelemek [kekelemek] *v*
stammer, stutter
kekik [kekik] *n* thyme
keklik [keklik] *n* partridge
kel [kel] *adj* bald
kelebek [kelebek] *n (hayvan)*
butterfly
kelepçe [keleptʃe] *npl* handcuffs
keler [keler] *n* **su keleri** *m* newt
keman [keman] *n* violin
kemancı [kemandʒə] *n* violinist
kemer [kemer] *n* arch, belt;
emniyet kemeri *n* safety belt,
seatbelt; **kemer tokası** *n* buckle
kemik [kemik] *n* bone; **elmacık
kemiği** *n* cheekbone; **kaval
kemiği** *n* shin; **köprücük kemiği**
n collarbone; **kürek kemiği** *n*

shoulder blade; **kemikli et** *n* joint *(meat)*; **leğen kemiği** *n* pelvis
kemirgen [kemirgen] *n* rodent
kenar [kenar] *n* **cam kenarı koltuğu** *n* window seat; **kenara çekmek** *v (araç)* pull out, *(araç)* pull up; **kenara kaçmak** *v* dodge; **yol kenarında geçici park yeri** *n* layby
kendi [kendi] *adj* own; **kendinden memnun** *adj* smug; **kendine güvenen** *adj* self-assured; **kendine gelmek** *v* regain; **kendini beğenmiş** *adj* arrogant, bigheaded
kendileri [kendileri] *pron* themselves
kendiliğinden [kendiləənden] *adj* spontaneous
kendim [kendim] *pron* myself
kendin [kendin] *pron* yourself, yourself *(intensifier)*, yourself *(polite)*
kendine [kendine] *adv* **kendine gelmek** *v* come round
kendiniz [kendiniz] *pron* yourselves *(intensifier)*, yourselves *(polite)*, yourselves *(reflexive)*
kendin-yap [kendinjap] *n* DIY
kendisi [kendisi] *pron* itself, *(erkek)* himself, *(kadın)* herself
kenevir [kenevir] *n* **Hint keneviri** *(yaprakları esrar olarak kullanılır)* *n* marijuana
kent [kent] *n* city, town; **kent merkezi** *adv* city centre; **kent merkezinde** *adv* downtown; **Kent merkezine lütfen** Please take me to the city centre; **Kent turunuz var mı?** Are there any

sightseeing tours of the town?; **Kente otobüs var mı?** Is there a bus to the city?; **Kente taksi ne kadar?** How much is the taxi fare into town?; **Kenti gezecek kadar zamanımız var mı?** Do we have time to visit the town?; **Kentin haritasını nereden alabilirim?** Where can I buy a map of the city?; **Kentin yol haritasını istiyorum** I want a street map of the city
Kenya [kenja] *adj* Kenyan ▷ *n* Kenya
Kenyalı [kenjalə] *n* Kenyan
kep [kep] *n* cap; **beyzbol kepi** *n* baseball cap
kepaze [kepaze] *adj* miserable
kepçe [keptʃe] *n (mutfak)* ladle
kepek [kepek] *n* bran, *(saç)* dandruff; **kepekli undan yapılmış** *adj* wholemeal
kepenk [kepeŋ] *n* shutters
kereste [kereste] *n* timber
kerevit [kerevit] *n* crayfish
kereviz [kereviz] *n* **kereviz sapı** *n* celery
kertenkele [kerteŋele] *n* lizard
keseye uygun [kesejeujgun] *adj* affordable
kesici [kesidʒi] *n* **ağrı kesici** *n* painkiller
kesilmek [kesilmek] *v (bağlantı)* disconnect
kesin [kesin] *adj* certain, definite
kesinlik [kesinlik] *n* certainty
kesinlikle [kesinlikle] *adv* absolutely, certainly, definitely
kesinti [kesinti] *n* deduction, interruption; **elektrik kesintisi** *n* power cut

kesintisiz [kesintisiz] *adj* continuous

keski [keski] *n* chisel

keskin [keskin] *adj* sharp

kesme [kesme] *n* cut

kesme imi [kesmeimi] *n* apostrophe

kesmek [kesmek] *v* cut, cut down, cut off; **fileto kesmek** *v* fillet; **kesip düzeltmek** *v* trim; **sözünü kesmek** *v* interrupt

kestane [kestane] *n* chestnut

kestirme [kestirme] *adj* direct ▷ *n (uyku)* nap; **kestirme yol** *n* shortcut; **saç kestirme** *n* haircut

kestirmek [kestirmek] *v* doze

keşfetmek [keʃfetmek] *v* discover

keşif [keʃif] *n* **keşif gezisi** *n* expedition

keşiş [keʃiʃ] *n* monk

ketçap [kettʃap] *n* ketchup

keten [keten] *n (kumaş)* linen

ketlenme [ketlenme] *n* inhibition

keyif [kejif] *n* pleasure, joy; **keyfi kaçık** *adj* upset; **keyfini kaçırmak** *v* upset; **keyif verici** *adj* delightful

kıbrıs [kəbrəs] *n* Cyprus

Kıbrıs [kəbrəs] *adj* Cypriot

Kıbrıslı [kəbrəslə] *n (kişi)* Cypriot *(person)*

kıç [kətʃ] *n* backside, bum

kıkırdamak [kəkərdamak] *v* giggle

kılavuz [kəlavuz] *n* guide; **kullanım kılavuzu** *n* manual; **... kılavuzunuz var mı?** Do you have a guide book in...?; **İngilizce kılavuzunuz var mı?** Do you have a guide book in English?

kılıç [kələtʃ] *n* sword; **kılıç balığı** *n* swordfish

kılıf [kələf] *n* cover, case; **yastık kılıfı** *n* pillowcase

kılık [kələk] *n* outfit; **kılık değiştirmek** *v* disguise

kıllı [kəllə] *adj* hairy

kımıldamak [kəməldamak] *vi* move; **Kımıldayamıyor** She can't move

kımıldatmak [kəməldatmak] *vt* move

kına [kəna] *n* **kına gecesi** *n* hen night

kınamak [kənamak] *v* condemn

kırat [kərat] *n* carat

kırbaç [kərbatʃ] *n* whip

Kırgızistan [kərgəzistan] *n* Kyrgyzstan

kırık [kərək] *adj* broken, broken down ▷ *n* break, fracture; **düş kırıklığı** *n* disappointment; **hayal kırıklığına uğramış** *adj* disappointed; **hayal kırıklığına uğratmak** *v* disappoint, let down; **kalbi kırık** *adj* heartbroken

kırılgan [kərəlgan] *adj* fragile

kırılmaz [kərəlmaz] *adj* unbreakable

kırıntı [kərəntə] *n* fragment, piece; **ekmek kırıntısı** *n* breadcrumbs, crumb

kırışık [kərəʃək] *adj* creased ▷ *n* wrinkle

kırışıklık [kərəʃəklək] *n* crease

kırışmış [kərəʃməʃ] *adj* wrinkled

kırk [kərk] *number* forty

kırmak [kərmak] *v* break up ▷ *vt* break; **cesaretini kırmak** *v* discourage; **direksiyonu kırmak** *v*

swerve; **onur kırmak** v insult
kırmızı [kərməzə] adj red; **kan
kırmızısı** adj scarlet; **kırmızı et** n
red meat; **kırmızı Frenk üzümü** n
redcurrant; **kırmızı şarap** n red
wine; **kırmızı toz biber** n paprika;
kırmızı turp n radish; **kırmızı
yaban mersini** n cranberry; **İyi
bir kırmızı şarap tavsiye
edebilir misiniz?** Can you
recommend a good red wine?; **Bir
şişe kırmızı şarap** a bottle of red
wine; **Bir sürahi kırmızı şarap** a
carafe of red wine; **Kırmızı et
yemiyorum** I don't eat red meat
kırpmak [kərpmak] v **göz
kırpmak** v wink; **göz kırpmak** v
blink
kırsal [kərsal] adj rural; **kırsal
bölge** n countryside
kırtasiye [kərtasije] n stationery
kırtasiyeci [kərtasijedʒi] n
stationer's
kısa [kəsa] adj brief, short; **en kısa
zamanda** adv asap (as soon as
possible); **kısa öykü** n short story;
kısa kabzalı tabanca n pistol;
kısa kürek n paddle; **kısa kollu**
adj short-sleeved; **kısa menzilli
silah** n shotgun; **kısa mesafe hız
koşusu** n sprint; **kısa mesafe
koşucusu** n sprinter; **kısa not** n
memo; **kısa ve öz** adj concise;
kısa zamanda adv shortly, soon
kısaca [kəsadʒa] adv briefly
kısalmak [kəsalmak] v shrink
kısalmış [kəsalməʃ] adj shrunk
kısaltma [kəsaltma] n
abbreviation, acronym
kısım [kəsəm] n part, section;

çekirdekli kısım (meyve) n core;
**Bu kısım doğru dürüst
çalışmıyor** This part doesn't work
properly
kıskanç [kəskantʃ] adj envious,
jealous
kısmen [kəsmen] adv partly
kısmi [kəsmi] adj partial
kısrak [kəsrak] n mare
kış [kəʃ] n winter; **kış sporları** npl
winter sports
kışkırtmak [kəʃkərtmak] v tempt
kıt [kət] adj scarce
kıta [kəta] n continent
kıtlık [kətlək] n famine
kıvılcım [kəvəldʒəm] n spark
kıvırcık [kəvərdʒək] adj curly;
Saçım doğuştan kıvırcık My hair
is naturally curly
kıvrılmak [kəvrəlmak] v bend
kıvrım [kəvrəm] n turning
kıyafet [kəjafet] n dress, clothes;
balıkadam kıyafeti n wetsuit
kıyaslama [kəjaslama] n
comparison
kıyaslamak [kəjaslamak] v
compare
kıyaslanabilir [kəjaslanabilir]
adj comparable
kıyı [kəjə] n coast, shore; **ırmak
kıyısı** n bank (ridge); **deniz kıyısı**
n seaside, (sahil) seashore
kıyma [kəjma] n mince
kıymık [kəjmək] n splinter
kız [kəz] n girl; **deniz kızı** n
mermaid; **kız arkadaş** n
girlfriend; **kız öğrenci** n
schoolgirl; **kız evlat** n daughter;
kız kurusu n spinster; **kız torun** n
granddaughter; **vaftiz kızı** n

goddaughter; **üvey kız evlat** n
stepdaughter

kızak [kəzak] n sledge, toboggan;
kızak kayma n tobogganing;
kızak kaymak n sledging; **Kızak
kaymak için nereye gitmemiz
gerek?** Where can we go sledging?

kızamık [kəzamək] npl measles;
Yakınlarda kızamık geçirdim
I had measles recently

kızamıkçık [kəzaməktʃək] n
German measles

kızarıklık [kəzarəklək] n rash

kızarmak [kəzarmak] v blush;
yüz kızarması n flush; **yüzü
kızarmak** v flush

kızarmış [kəzarməʃ] adj fried

kızartma [kəzartma] v deep-fry;
ekmek kızartma makinesi n
toaster; **kızartma tavası** n frying
pan; **patates kızartması** npl chips

kızartmak [kəzartmak] v fry

kızdırmak [kəzdərmak] vt tease

kızgın [kəzgən] adj angry, inflamed

kızıl [kəzəl] adj red; **Kızıl Deniz** n
Red Sea; **kızıl saçlı** n red-haired,
redhead

kızılgerdan [kəzəlgerdan] n robin

Kızılhaç [kəzəlhatʃ] n Red Cross

kızılımsı [kəzələmsə] adj **kızılımsı
sarı saçlı** adj ginger

kızışmak [kəzəʃmak] v heat up

kızkardeş [kəzkardeʃ] n sister;
üvey kızkardeş n stepsister

kızlık [kəzlək] n **kızlık soyadı** n
maiden name

ki [ki] conj that

kibar [kibar] adj gentle, polite

kibarca [kibardʒa] adv
gently, politely

kibarlık [kibarlək] n politeness

kibirli [kibirli] adj stuck-up

kil [kil] n clay

kiler [kiler] n larder

kilise [kilise] n church; **kilise
kulesi** n steeple; **kilise kulesinin
sivri tepesi** n spire; **kilisenin dini
bölgesi** n parish; **Kiliseyi
gezebilir miyiz?** Can we visit the
church?

kilit [kilit] n lock (door); **asma kilit**
n padlock; **kilidi açmak** v unlock;
kilitli dolap n locker; **kilitli iğne** n
safety pin; **Kilit alabilir miyim?**
Can I have a lock?; **Kilit kırılmış**
The lock is broken

kilitlemek [kilitlemek] vt lock

kilitlmek [kilitlmek] v lock out

kilo [kilo] n kilo; **aşırı kilolu** adj
overweight

kilometre [kilometre] n kilometre

kilt [kilt] n kilt

kim [kim] pron who; **Kim arıyor?**
Who's calling?; **Kim o?** Who is it?;
Kime şikayet edebilirim? Who
can I complain to?; **Kiminle
görüşüyorum?** Who am I talking to?

kime [kime] adj whose ▷ pron
whom

kimi [kimi] pron whom

kimin [kimin] pron whose

kimlik [kimlik] n identification,
identity; **kimliği belirsiz** adj
unidentified; **kimlik belirlemek** v
identify; **kimlik hırsızlığı** n
identity theft; **kimlik kartı** n
badge, identity card, ID card

kimse [kimse] pron somebody,
someone; **hiç kimse** pron
no one, nobody

kimsesiz [kimsesiz] *n* orphan
kimya [kimja] *n* chemistry
kimyasal [kimjasal] *n* chemical
kimyon [kimjon] *n* cumin
kin [kin] *n* grudge; **kin gütmek** *v* spite
kinci [kindʒi] *adj* spiteful
kincilik [kindʒilik] *n* spite
kir [kir] *n* dirt
kira [kira] *n* rent, rental; **kira sözleşmesi** *n* lease; **kiralık araba** *n* rental car; **DVD kiralayabilir miyim?** Do you rent DVDs?
kiracı [kiradʒə] *n* tenant
kiralama [kiralama] *n* hire
kiralamak [kiralamak] *v* hire, lease, rent; **araba kiralama** *n* car hire; **oto kiralama** *n* car rental; **Paten nereden kiralayabiliriz?** Where can we hire skates?
kiralık [kiralək] *n* **kiralık araba** *n* hire car, hired car; **kiralık oda** *n* bedsit
kiraz [kiraz] *n* cherry
kireç [kiretʃ] *n* lime *(compound)*; **kireç taşı** *n* limestone
kiriş [kiriʃ] *n (anatomi)* tendon
kirlenmiş [kirlenmiʃ] *adj* polluted
kirletmek [kirletmek] *v* pollute
kirli [kirli] *adj* dirty, foul, messy; **Çatal bıçak kirli** My cutlery is dirty; **Çarşaflarım kirli** My sheets are dirty
kirlilik [kirlilik] *n* pollution
kirpi [kirpi] *n* hedgehog
kirpik [kirpik] *n* eyelash
kist [kist] *n* cyst
kişi [kiʃi] *n* person; **çift kişilik yatak** *n* double bed; **iki kişilik oda** *n* double room; **kişinin evinin**

önündeki özel yol *n* driveway; **tek kişilik oda** *n* single room; **Bir araç ve iki kişi ne kadar?** How much is it for a car with two people?; **Bu akşam için üç kişilik bir masa ayırtmak istiyordum** I'd like to book a table for three people for tonight; **Bu akşam saat sekiz için dört kişilik bir masa ayırtmak istiyordum** I'd like to book a table for four people for tonight at eight o'clock; **Dört kişilik bir kamper ne kadar?** How much is it for a camper with four people?; **Dört kişilik bir masa lütfen** A table for four people, please; **Kişi başına ne kadar?** How much is it per person?; **Saat yedi buçuğa iki kişilik bir rezervasyon yaptırmak istiyorum** I'd like to make a reservation for half past seven for two people; **Yarın akşam için iki kişilik bir masa ayırtmak istiyorum** I'd like to book a table for two people for tomorrow night
kişilik [kiʃilik] *n* personality
kişisel [kiʃisel] *adj* personal; **kişisel asistan** *n* personal assistant, PA; **kişisel müzik çalar** *n* personal stereo; **kişisel olarak** *adv* personally; **kişisel organizatör** *n* personal organizer; **Bu benim kişisel kullanımım için** It is for my own personal use
kişniş [kiʃniʃ] *n* coriander
kitap [kitap] *n* book; **ders kitabı** *n* schoolbook, textbook; **ikinci baskı kitap** *n* paperback; **kitap**

ayracı n bookmark; **kitap rafı** n bookshelf; **referans kitabı** n handbook; **yemek kitabı** n cookbook, cookery book

kitapçı [kitaptʃə] n bookshop

kitapçık [kitaptʃək] n booklet

kitaplık [kitaplək] n bookcase

kitle [kitlə] n mass; **kitle fonlaması** n crowdfunding

kivi [kivi] n (kuş) kiwi

klarnet [klarnet] n clarinet

klasik [klasik] adj classic, classical ▷ n classic

klasör [klasør] n ring binder

klavye [klavje] n keyboard

klima [klima] n air conditioner; **Klima çalışmıyor** The air conditioning doesn't work; **Klima var mı?** Does it have air conditioning?; **Odada klima var mı?** Does the room have air conditioning?

klinik [klinik] n surgery (doctor's)

klips [klips] n clip

klon [klon] n clone

klonlamak [klonlamak] v clone

klor [klor] n chlorine

klüp [klyp] n club (group)

km/s [kilometrefanje] abbr km/h

kobay [kobaj] n guinea pig (for experiment); **kobay faresi** n guinea pig (rodent)

koca [kodʒa] n (eş) husband; **eski koca** n ex-husband

kocaman [kodʒaman] adj huge

koç [kotʃ] n ram, (spor) coach (trainer)

Koç [kotʃ] n **Koç burcu** n Aries

kod [kod] n code; **alan kodu** n postcode; **telefon kodu** n dialling code; **İngiltere'nin kodu kaç?** What is the dialling code for the UK?

koğuş [kou:ʃ] n ward (hospital room); **... hangi koğuşta?** Which ward is... in?

kokain [kokain] n cocaine

koklamak [koklamak] vt smell

kokmak [kokmak] vi smell; **kötü kokmak** v stink

kokpit [kokpit] n cockpit

kokteyl [koktejl] n cocktail; **Kokteyl yapıyor musunuz?** Do you sell cocktails?

koku [koku] n aroma, odour, scent, smell; **kokulu otlar** n herbs; **pis kokulu** adj smelly; **Garip bir koku var** There's a funny smell; **Gaz kokusu alıyorum** I can smell gas

kokuşmuş [kokuʃmuʃ] adj vile

kol [kol] n arm, handle, lever; **kapı kolu** n door handle; **kısa kollu** adj short-sleeved; **kol ağzı** n sleeve; **kol askısı** (sağlık) n sling; **kol düğmeleri** npl cufflinks; **kol saati** n watch; **vites kolu** n gear lever, gear stick, gearshift; **Kapının kolu çıktı** The door handle has come off; **Kolu çıktı** The handle has come off; **Kolumu oynatamıyorum** I can't move my arm; **Kolunu incitti** He has hurt his arm

Kola [kola] n Coke®

kolay [kolaj] adj easy; **kolay gıdıklanan** adj ticklish; **En kolay alanlar nereleri?** Which are the easiest runs?

kolaylıkla [kolajləkla] adv easily

kolaylıklar [kolajləklar] npl facilities

kolçak [koltʃak] n bracelet

kolej [koleʒ] n **devlet koleji** n public school

koleksiyon [koleksijon] n collection

kolektif [kolektif] adj collective ▷ n collective

kolesterol [kolesterol] n cholesterol

kolleksiyoncu [kolleksijondʒu] n collector

Kolombiya [kolombija] adj Colombian ▷ n Colombia

Kolombiyalı [kolombijalə] n Colombian

kolsuz [kolsuz] adj (giysi) sleeveless

koltuk [koltuk] n armchair, easy chair, (politika) seat (constituency); **cam kenarı koltuğu** n window seat; **koltuk değneği** n crutch; **koridor koltuğu** n aisle seat; **Çocuk koltuğu var mı?** Do you have a child's seat?; **Bu koltuk boş mu?** Is this seat free?; **Koltuğum koridor tarafında olsun** I'd like an aisle seat; **Koltuğum pencere kenarında olsun** I'd like a window seat; **Sigara içilen bölümde bir koltuk lütfen** I'd like a seat in the smoking area; **Sigara içilmeyen bölümde bir koltuk lütfen** I'd like a non-smoking seat

koltukaltı [koltukaltə] n armpit

kolye [kolje] n necklace

koma [koma] n coma

komedi [komedi] n comedy

komedyen [komedjen] n comedian

komik [komik] adj funny ▷ n comic; **çok komik** adj hilarious

komisyon [komisjon] n commission; **Komisyon alıyor musunuz?** Do you charge commission?; **Komisyon ne kadar?** What's the commission?

komisyoncu [komisjondʒu] n broker

komite [komite] n committee

komodin [komodin] n bedside table, chest of drawers

kompakt [kompakt] adj **kompakt disk** n compact disc

kompartıman [kompartəman] n compartment; **Sigara içilmeyen kompartmanda yer ayırtmak istiyorum** I want to book a seat in a non-smoking compartment

kompleks [kompleks] n complex

komplike [komplike] adj complex, complicated

kompliman [kompliman] n compliment

komplo [komplo] n conspiracy ▷ v plot (secret plan)

komşu [komʃu] n neighbour

komut [komut] n order, command ▷ v **komut vermek** v order (command)

komünizm [komynizm] n communism

konak [konak] n mansion

konaklama [konaklama] n stopover

konaklamak [konaklamak] v **konaklama alanı** n service area

konçerto [kontʃerto] **(konçertolar)** n concerto

konferans [konferans] n conference; **Konferans**

merkezine lütfen Please take me
to the conference centre
konfeti [konfeti] *npl* confetti
konfor [konfor] *npl* comforts,
conveniences; **konfor ve rahatlık**
npl mod cons
Kongo [kongo] *n* Congo
koni [koni] *n* cone
konser [konser] *n* concert; **İyi**
konserler var mı? Are there any
good concerts on?; **Konser**
biletlerini nereden alabilirim?
Where can I buy tickets for the
concert?; **Konser salonunda bu**
gece ne var? What's on tonight at
the concert hall?
konserve [konserve] *n*
kutulanmış konserve *adj* tinned
konsol [konsol] *n* **oyun konsolu** *n*
games console
konsolos [konsolos] *n* consul
konsolosluk [konsolosluk] *n*
consulate
kontakt [kontakt] *n* **kontakt lens**
npl contact lenses
kontrabas [kontrabas] *n* double
bass
kontrat [kontrat] *n* contract
kontrol [kontrol] *n* control;
doğum kontrol hapı *n*
contraceptive; **doğum kontrolü**
n birth control, contraception;
kontrol edilemez *adj*
uncontrollable; **kontrol lambası**
n pilot light; **pasaport kontrol** *n*
passport control; **bilet**
kontrolörü *n* ticket inspector;
hava trafik kontrolörü *n*
air-traffic controller
kontrplak [kontrplak] *n* plywood

kontuar [kontuar] *n* counter
konu [konu] *n* subject, theme;
(bilgisayar) thread, **konulu**
eğlence parkı *n* theme park
konuk [konuk] *n* guest
konukevi [konukevi] *n*
guesthouse
konukseverlik [konukseverlik] *n*
hospitality
konuşan [konuʃan] *n* **anadilini**
konuşan *n* native speaker
konuşkan [konuʃkan] *adj*
talkative
konuşlanmış [konuʃlanməʃ] *adj*
situated
konuşma [konuʃma] *n*
conversation, speech, talk; **abuk**
sabuk konuşma *n* rave
konuşmacı [konuʃmadʒə] *n*
speaker
konuşmak [konuʃmak] *v* speak
▷ *vi* talk; **biriyle konuşmak** *v* talk
to; **... ile konuşmak istiyorum**
lütfen I'd like to speak to...,
please; **... konuşabiliyorum** I
speak...; **Müdürle konuşmak**
istiyorum lütfen I'd like to speak
to the manager, please
konut [konut] *n* house; **konut**
kredisi *n* mortgage; **sosyal**
konut *n* council house
konvensiyonel [konvensijonel]
adj (alışılmış) conventional
konvertibl [konvertipl] *adj*
convertible
konvertör [konvertør] *n* **katalitik**
konvertör *n* catalytic converter
konvoy [konvoj] *n* convoy
kopmak [kopmak] *vt* snap; **ödü**
kopmak *adj* petrified

kopya [kopja] n (nüsha) copy (written text), (taklit) replica

kopyalamak [kopjalamak] v copy

Kore [kore] adj Korean ▷ n Korea; **Güney Kore** n South Korea; **Kuzey Kore** n North Korea

Korece [koredʒe] n (dil) Korean (language)

Koreli [koreli] n (kişi) Korean (person)

koridor [koridor] n aisle, corridor; **koridor koltuğu** n aisle seat; **Koltuğum koridor tarafında olsun** I'd like an aisle seat

korkak [korkak] n coward

korkakça [korkaktʃa] adj cowardly

korkmak [korkmak] v fear

korkmuş [korkmuʃ] adj afraid, frightened, scared

korku [korku] n fear, fright; **kapalı yer korkusu olan** adj claustrophobic ▷ v **korkarak titremek** v shudder; **korku filmi** n horror film; **yükseklik korkusu** n vertigo

korkuluk [korkuluk] n scarecrow

korkunç [korkuntʃ] adj appalling, disastrous, dreadful, horrendous, horrible, terrible

korkutmak [korkutmak] v frighten, scare; **gözünü korkutmak** v intimidate

korkutucu [korkutudʒu] adj scary

kornet [kornet] n cornet

korno [korno] n French horn

koro [koro] n choir

korsan [korsan] n (deniz) pirate, (uçak/hava) hijacker

kort [kort] n tenis kortu n tennis court; **Kort rezervasyonunu**

nerede yapabilirim? Where can I book a court?; **Tenis kortu kiralamak kaça?** How much is it to hire a tennis court?

koruluk [koruluk] n wood (forest)

koruma [koruma] n conservation, protection; **özel koruma** n bodyguard; **koruma gözlüğü** npl goggles

korumak [korumak] v defend, guard, protect; **koruma alanı** n reserve (land); **koruma altına alma** n custody; **sahil koruma görevlisi** n coastguard

koruyucu [korujudʒu] adj **ekran koruyucusu** n screen-saver; **koruyucu güneş kremi** n sunblock

Kosova [kosova] n Kosovo

Kosta Rika [kostarika] n Costa Rica

kostüm [kostym] n costume; **balo kostümü** n fancy dress

koşer [koʃer] adj, adv **Koşer yemeğiniz var mı?** Do you have kosher dishes?

koşma [koʃma] n running

koşmak [koʃmak] vt run; **dörtnala koşmak** n gallop; **hızla koşmak** v dash, sprint

koşturmak [koʃturmak] vi run

koşu [koʃu] n run, running; **kısa mesafe hız koşusu** n sprint

koşucu [koʃudʒu] n runner; **kısa mesafe koşucusu** n sprinter

koşul [koʃul] n condition

koşullar [koʃullar] npl circumstances

koşullu [koʃullu] adj conditional

koşulsuz [koʃulsuz] adj unconditional

kota [kota] n quota

kova [kova] n bucket, pail

Kova [kova] n **Kova burcu** n Aquarius

kovalamaca [kovalamadʒa] n pursuit

kovboy [kovboj] n cowboy; **kovboy filmi** n western

kovmak [kovmak] v expel

kovuşturma [kovuʃturma] n prosecution

koyak [kojak] n ravine

koymak [kojmak] v lay, put; **geri koymak** v put back; **yıldız koymak** v star; **yoluna koymak** v settle

koyulmak [kojulmak] v **yola koyulmak** v set off

koyun [kojun] n sheep, (dişi) ewe; **koyun eti** n mutton; **koyun postu** n sheepskin

kozalak [kozalak] n conifer

kozmetik [kozmetik] n **kozmetik cerrahi** n cosmetic surgery

köfte [køfte] n meatball

kök [køk] n root

köknar [køknar] n **köknar ağacı** n fir (tree)

köle [køle] n slave

kömür [kømyr] n coal; **kömür ocağı** n colliery; **odun kömürü** n charcoal

köpek [kjøpek] n dog; **İskoç çoban köpeği** n collie; **köpek balığı** n shark; **köpek kulübesi** n kennel; **rehber köpek** n guide dog; **yavru köpek** n puppy; **Rehber köpeğim var** I have a guide dog

köprü [køpry] n bridge; **asma köprü** n suspension bridge

köprücük [køprydʒyk] n **köprücük kemiği** n collarbone

köpük [køpyk] n foam; **köpük krema** n mousse, whipped cream; **köpüklü banyo** n bubble bath; **traş köpüğü** n shaving foam

köpüklü [køpykly] adj fizzy

kör [kør] adj blind, (bıçak/makas) blunt; **renk körü** adj colour-blind; **Körüm** I'm blind

körfez [kørfez] n bay

Körfez [kørfez] n **Körfez Ülkeleri** npl Gulf States

köri [køri] n curry; **köri baharatı** n curry powder

köstebek [køstebek] n (casus) mole (infiltrator), (hayvan) mole (mammal)

köşe [køʃe] n corner; **çalışma köşesi** n work station, workstation; **köşeli parantezler** npl brackets; **Köşede** It's on the corner; **Köşeyi dönünce** It's round the corner

kötü [køty] adj bad, vicious; **daha kötü/daha kötüsü** adv worse; **en kötü** adj worst; **kötü bir şekilde** adv badly; **kötü kokmak** v stink; **kötü muamele etmek** v ill-treat; **kötü niyetli** adj malicious; **kötüye kullanmak** v abuse

kötücül [køtydʒyl] adj evil, malignant

kötülemek [køtylemek] v deteriorate

kötüleşmek [køtyleʃmek] v worsen

kötülük [køtylyk] n vice

kötümser [køtymser] adj pessimistic ▷ n pessimist

köy [køj] n village

kraker [kraker] n cracker

kral [kral] n king, monarch

kraliçe [kralitʃe] n queen

kraliyet [kralijet] adj royal ▷ n monarchy

krallık [krallək] n kingdom; **Birleşik Krallık** (İngiltere) n United Kingdom

kramp [kramp] n spasm

kravat [kravat] n tie; **papyon kravat** n bow tie

kredi [kredi] n credit, loan; **konut kredisi** n mortgage; **kredi kartı** n credit card; **kredi kartı şifresi** npl PIN; **Kredi kartı kabul ediyor musunuz?** Do you take credit cards?; **Kredi kartıma nakit ödeme alabilir miyim?** Can I get a cash advance with my credit card?; **Kredi kartıyla ödeme yapabilir miyim?** Can I pay by credit card?

krek [krek] n (kokain) crack (cocaine)

krem [krem] n cream; **dudak kremi** n lip salve; **güneş kremi** n suncream; **güneş sonrası krem** n after sun lotion; **koruyucu güneş kremi** n sunblock; **saç kremi** n conditioner; **traş kremi** n shaving cream

krema [krema] n cream, custard; **köpük krema** n mousse, whipped cream; **kremalı pasta** n gateau

krematoryum [krematorjum] **(krematoryumlar)** n crematorium

krep [krep] n (yiyecek) pancake

kreş [kreʃ] n crêche, nursery school

kriket [kriket] n cricket (game)

kriko [kriko] n jack

kristal [kristal] n crystal

kriter [kriter] n criterion

kritik [kritik] adj critical

kriz [kriz] n crisis; **kalp krizi** n heart attack; **sinir krizi** n nervous breakdown

krom [krom] n **krom kaplı** n chrome

kronik [kronik] adj chronic

kronometre [kronometre] n stopwatch

krüsifi [krysifi] n crucifix

ksilofon [ksilofon] n xylophone

kuaför [kuafør] n hairdresser, hairdresser's

kuartet [kuartet] n quartet

kucak [kudʒak] n lap

kucaklama [kudʒaklama] n cuddle, hug

kucaklamak [kudʒaklamak] v cuddle ▷ vt hug

kuduz [kuduz] n rabies

kuğu [kuːu] n swan

kukla [kukla] n puppet

kulak [kulak] n ear; **kulak ağrısı** n earache; **kulak çubuğu** n cotton bud; **kulak tıkacı** npl earplugs; **kulak zarı** n eardrum

kulaklık [kulaklək] npl earphones, headphones; **Kulaklık var mı?** Does it have headphones?

kule [kule] n tower; **kilise kulesi** n steeple; **kilise kulesinin sivri tepesi** n spire

kullanıcı [kullanədʒə] n user; **internet kullanıcısı** n internet user; **kullanıcı dostu** adj user-friendly

kullanılmış [kullanəlməʃ] adj used

kullanım [kullanəm] *n* use; **son kullanım tarihi** *n* best-before date, expiry date; **tek kullanımlık** *adj* disposable

kullanmak [kullanmak] *v* apply, use; **içkili araba kullanma** *n* drink-driving; **kötüye kullanmak** *v* abuse; **yeniden kullanmak** *v* reuse

kulübe [kulybe] *n* cabin, cottage; **bahçe kulübesi** *n* shed; **köpek kulübesi** *n* kennel; **telefon kulübesi** *n* call box, phonebox

kulüp [kulyp] *n* club; **gece kulübü** *n* nightclub; **İyi bir kulüp biliyor musunuz?** Where is there a good club?

kum [kum] *n* grit, sand; **kum havuzu** *n* sandpit; **kum tepesi** *n* sand dune; **kumdan kale** *n* sandcastle

kumanda [kumanda] *n, v* **uazaktan kumanda** *n* remote control; **uzaktan kumandalı** *adj* radio-controlled; **Kumanda kilitlendi** The controls have jammed; **Kumandaların nasıl çalıştığını gösterir misiniz?** Can you show me how the controls work?

kumar [kumar] *n* gambling ▷ *v* **kumar oynamak** *v* gamble

kumarcı [kumardʒə] *n* gambler

kumarhane [kumarhane] *n* casino

kumaş [kumaʃ] *n* cloth, fabric

kumaşı [kumaʃə] *n* **blucin kumaşı** *n* denim

kumbara [kumbara] *n* piggybank

kumpir [kumpir] **(kumpirler)** *n* baked potato, jacket potato

kumral [kumral] *adj* auburn

kumsal [kumsal] *n* beach; **Buraya yakın sakin bir kumsal var mı?** Is there a quiet beach near here?

kumtaşı [kumtaʃə] *n* sandstone

kundaklama [kundaklama] *n* arson

kunduz [kunduz] *n* beaver

kupa [kupa] *n (kahve)* mug, *(spor)* trophy; **Dünya Kupası** *n* World Cup

kupkuru [kupkuru] *adj* bone dry

kupon [kupon] *n* voucher

kur [kur] *n (para)* currency; **döviz kuru** *n* exchange rate, rate of exchange

kura [kura] *n* draw *(lottery)*

kuraklık [kuraklək] *n* drought

kural [kural] *n* rule; **ahlak kuralları** *npl* morals; **trafik kuralları** *n* Highway Code

kuram [kuram] *n* theory

Kuran [kuran] *n* Koran

kurbağa [kurba:a] *n* frog; **kara kurbağa** *n* toad

kurbağalama [kurba:alama] *n (yüzme)* breaststroke

kurban [kurban] *n (kişi)* victim

kurdele [kurdele] *n* ribbon

kurgu [kurgu] *n* fiction; **bilim kurgu** *n* science fiction

kurmak [kurmak] *v* **iletişim kurmak** *v* communicate; **temas kurmak** *v* contact

kurnaz [kurnaz] *adj* cunning, sly

kurs [kurs] *n* course; **eğitim kursu** *n* training course

kursiyer [kursijer] *n* trainee

kurşun [kurʃun] *n (metal)* lead *(metal)*, *(silah)* bullet; **kurşun**

kalem n pencil; **kurşunsuz benzin** n unleaded petrol

kurşunsuz [kurʃunsuz] adj lead-free ⊳ n unleaded; **...lık kurşunsuz benzin lütfen** ... worth of premium unleaded, please

kurt [kurt] **(kurtlar)** n wolf; **kurt gibi aç** adj ravenous

kurtarma [kurtarma] n rescue

kurtarmak [kurtarmak] v rescue, save; **kurtarma aracı** n breakdown van

kurtçuk [kurtʧuk] n grub

kuru [kuru] adj dried, dry; **kız kurusu** n spinster; **kuru üzüm** n raisin, sultana; **kuru erik** n prune; **kuru temizleme** n dry-cleaning; **Bunu kuru temizleyiciye vermek istiyorum** I need this dry-cleaned

kurul [kurul] n board (meeting)

kurulamak [kurulamak] v dry; **kurulama bezi** n dishcloth; **kurulama havlusu** n dish towel

kurum [kurum] n (enstitü) institution; **iş bulma kurumu** n job centre

kuru temizleyici [kurutemizlejidʒi] n dry-cleaner's

kurutmak [kurutmak] v dry; **çamaşır kurutma makinesi** n spin dryer; **Çamaşırlarımı kurutabileceğim bir yer var mı?** Is there somewhere to dry clothes?

kurutucu [kurutudʒu] n dryer

kurye [kurje] n courier; **Kuryeyle göndermek istiyorum** I want to send this by courier

kusmak [kusmak] v throw up, vomit; **Kusuyor** She has been sick

kusur [kusur] n defect, flaw

kuş [kuʃ] n bird; **ardıç kuşu** n thrush; **balıkçıl kuşu** n heron; **guguk kuşu** n cuckoo; **kuş gözleme** n birdwatching; **kuş gribi** n bird flu; **muhabbet kuşu** n budgerigar; **tavus kuşu** n peacock; **yırtıcı kuş** n bird of prey

kuşak [kuʃak] n (jenerasyon) generation; **burçlar kuşağı** n zodiac

kuşet [kuʃet] n couchette; **kuşetli vagon** n sleeping car; **a bir kuşetli bilet ayırtmak istiyorum** I want to book a sleeper to...; **Kuşetlide yer ayırtabilir miyim?** Can I reserve a sleeper?

kuşkonmaz [kuʃkonmaz] n asparagus

kuşku [kuʃku] n doubt ⊳ v **kuşku duymak** v doubt; **kuşku götürmez bir şekilde** adv undoubtedly; **kuşku ve gerilimli bekleyiş** n suspense

kuşkulanmak [kuʃkulanmak] v suspect

kuşkulu [kuʃkulu] adj doubtful, dubious, sceptical, suspicious

kuşüzümü [kuʃyzymy] n blackcurrant, currant

kutlama [kutlama] n celebration

kutlamak [kutlamak] v celebrate, congratulate

kutsal [kutsal] adj holy, sacred; **Kutsal Cuma** n Good Friday

kutsamak [kutsamak] v bless

kutu [kutu] n box; **çöp kutusu** n litter bin; **buz kutusu** n icebox; **ekmek kutusu** n bread bin; **gelen**

kutusu n inbox; **karton kutu** n carton; **kutu açacağı** n can-opener, tin-opener; **kutulanmış konserve** adj tinned; **şişe geri dönüşüm kutusu** n bottle bank; **posta kutusu** n letterbox, mailbox, postbox; **sigorta kutusu** n fuse box; **teneke kutu** n canister; **vites kutusu** n gear box

kutulanmış [kutulanməʃ] adj canned

kutup [kutup] adj polar; **kutup ayısı** n polar bear

Kutup [kutup] n Pole; **Güney Kutbu** n South Pole, the Antarctic, Antarctica; **Kuzey Kutbu** n North Pole, the Arctic

Kuveyt [kuvejt] adj Kuwaiti ▷ n Kuwait

Kuveytli [kuvejtli] n Kuwaiti

Kuvvet [kuvvet] n strength, power, force; **Hava Kuvvetleri** n Air Force

kuvvetli [kuvvetli] adv strongly

kuyruk [kujruk] n (hayvan vb) tail, (insan sırası) queue ▷ v **kuyruğa girmek** v queue; **kuyruklu yıldız** n comet; **Kuyruğun sonu burası mı?** Is this the end of the queue?

kuyu [kuju] n well; **petrol kuyusu** n oil well

kuyumcu [kujumdʒu] n jeweller; **kuyumcu dükkanı** n jeweller's

kuzen [kuzen] n cousin

kuzey [kuzej] adj north, northern ▷ n north; **kuzeye doğru** adj northbound; **Kuzey Afrika** adj North Africa, North African; **Kuzey Afrikalı** n North African;

Kuzey Amerika adj North America, North American; **Kuzey Amerikalı** n North American; **Kuzey İrlanda** n Northern Ireland; **Kuzey Buzul Kuşağı** n Arctic Circle; **Kuzey Denizi** n North Sea; **Kuzey Kore** n North Korea; **Kuzey Kutbu** n North Pole, the Arctic; **Kuzey Okyanusu** n Arctic Ocean

kuzeybatı [kuzejbatə] n northwest

kuzeyde [kuzejde] adv north

kuzeydoğu [kuzejdou:] n northeast

kuzgunî [kuzguni:] n raven

kuzu [kuzu] n lamb

Küba [kyba] adj Cuban ▷ n Cuba

Kübalı [kybalə] n Cuban

kübik [kybik] adj cubic

küçük [kytʃyk] adj minute, small ▷ n little, minor; **küçük halı** n rug; **küçük Hindistan cevizi** n nutmeg; **küçük ilanlar** npl small ads; **küçük sandal** n dinghy; **yaşça küçük** adj junior; **Çok küçük** It's too small; **Bunun bir küçük bedeni var mı?** Do you have this in a smaller size?; **Küçük beden var mı?** Do you have a small?

küf [kyf] n mould (fungus)

küflü [kyfly] adj mouldy

küfretmek [kyfretmek] v swear

küfür [kyfyr] n curse, swearword

kül [kyl] n **yanıp kül olmak** v burn down; **Kül tablası alabilir miyim?** May I have an ashtray?

küllük [kyllyk] n ashtray

külot [kylot] npl briefs, panties,

pants, *(kadın)* knickers; **külotlu çorap** *npl* tights

kültür [kyltyr] *n* culture; **genel kültür** *n* general knowledge

kültürel [kyltyrel] *adj* cultural

küp [kyp] *n* cube; **küp buz** *n* ice cube

küpe [kype] *n* earring

kürdan [kyrdan] *n* toothpick; **kürdan gibi** *adj* skinny

kürek [kyrek] *n* oar, shovel, spade; **kısa kürek** *n* paddle; **kürek çekmek** *v* row *(in boat)*; **kürek kemiği** *n* shoulder blade; **kürek sporu** *n* rowing; **kürek teknesi** *n* rowing boat

küresel [kyresel] *adj* global; **küresel ısınma** *n* global warming

küreselleşme [kyreselleʃme] *n* globalization

kürk [kyrk] *n* fur, *(giysi)* fur coat

kürtaj [kyrtaʒ] *n* abortion

kütle [kytle] *n* mass *(amount)*

kütüphane [kytyphane] *n* library

kütüphaneci [kytyphanedʒi] *n* librarian

küvet [kyvet] *n* bathtub

labirent [labirent] *n* maze

laboratuvar [laboratuvar] *n* lab, laboratory; **dil laboratuvarı** *n* language laboratory

lacivert [ladʒivert] *adj* navy-blue

lagün [lagyn] *n* lagoon

lağım [laːəm] *adj* **lağım borusu** *n* sewer

lahana [lahana] *n* cabbage; **Brüksel lahanası** *npl* sprouts; **lahana salatası** *n* coleslaw

lake [lake] *n* lacquer

lale [lalje] *n* tulip

lamba [ljamba] *n* lamp; **ön lamba** *n* headlamp, headlight; **başucu lambası** *n* bedside lamp; **fren lambası** *n* brake light; **kontrol lambası** *n* pilot light; **lamba direği** *n* lamppost; **sis lambası** *n* fog light; **sokak lambası** *n* streetlamp; **spot lambası** *n* spotlight; **yan lambalar** *n*

sidelight; **Lamba çalışmıyor**
The lamp is not working
lanet [lanet] *adj* damn
Laos [laos] *n* Laos
larenjit [larenʒit] *n* laryngitis
larva [larva] *n* maggot
lastik [lastik] *n* elastic, rubber,
tyre; **iç lastik** *n* inner tube; **lastik
çizme** *npl* wellies; **lastik çizmeler**
npl wellingtons; **lastik bant** *n*
elastic band; **lastik eldiven** *npl*
rubber gloves; **lastik spor
ayakkabısı** *npl* trainers; **Lastiğim
indi/Lastiğim patladı** I have a flat
tyre; **Lastik patladı** The tyre has
burst; **Lastikleri kontrol eder
misiniz lütfen?** Can you check
the tyres, please?
Latin [ljatin] *n* Latin; **Latin
Amerika** Latin America, Latin
American
Latviya [ljatvija] *adj* Latvian ▷ *n*
Latvia
lav [lav] *n* lava
lavabo [lavabo] *n* sink, washbasin;
Lavabo kirli The washbasin is
dirty
lavanta [lavanta] *n* lavender
lazer [lazer] *n* laser
lazımlık [lazəmlək] *n* potty
leğen [le:en] *n* basin; **leğen
kemiği** *n* pelvis
leke [leke] *n* smudge, stain;
leke çıkarıcı *n* stain remover;
Bu lekeyi çıkarabilir misiniz?
Can you remove this stain?;
Kahve lekesi This stain is coffee;
Kan lekesi This stain is blood;
Şarap lekesi This stain is wine;
Yağ lekesi This stain is oil

lekelemek [lekelemek] *v* stain
lens [lens] *n* lens; **kontakt lens** *npl*
contact lenses; **Lens solüsyonu**
cleansing solution for contact
lenses; **Lens takıyorum** I wear
contact lenses
leopar [leopar] *n* leopard
leotard [leotard] *n* leotard
Letonca [letondʒa] *n (dil)* Latvian
(language)
Letonyalı [letonjalə] *n (kişi)*
Latvian *(person)*
leydi [lejdi] *n* lady
leylak [lejlak] *n* lilac; **leylak renkli**
adj lilac; **pembemsi leylak rengi**
adj mauve
lezzet [lezzet] *n* flavour; **lezzet
katıcı** *n* flavouring
lezzetli [lezzetli] *adj* delicious,
tasteful, tasty
Liberya [liberja] *adj* Liberian ▷ *n*
Liberia
Liberyalı [liberjalə] *n* Liberian
Libya [libja] *adj* Libyan ▷ *n* Libya
Libyalı [libjalə] *n* Libyan
lider [lider] *n* leader
lig [lig] *n* league
Lihtenştayn [lihtenʃtajn] *n*
Liechtenstein
likör [likør] *n* liqueur; **Likör olarak
neleriniz var?** What liqueurs do
you have?
liman [liman] *n* harbour, port
(ships); **yat limanı** *n* marina
limit [limit] *n* limit; **bagaj limiti** *n*
baggage allowance; **Bagaj limiti
ne kadar?** What is the baggage
allowance?; **Bu yolda hız limiti
nedir?** What is the speed limit on
this road?

limon [limon] *n* lemon; **limon kabuğu** *n* zest *(lemon-peel)*; **yeşil limon** *n* lime *(fruit)*; **limonlu** with lemon

limonata [limonata] *n* lemonade; **Bir bardak limonata lütfen** A glass of lemonade, please

limonluk [limonluk] *n* conservatory

limuzin [limuzin] *n* limousine

lisans [lisans] *n* licence, certificate; **lisans derecesi** *(edebiyat) abbr* BA

liste [liste] *n* list; **adres listesi** *n* mailing list; **ön eleme listesi** *n* shortlist; **bekleme listesi** *n* waiting list; **fiyat listesi** *n* price list; **liste harici** *adj* unlisted; **şarap listesi** *n* wine list; **Şarap listesi lütfen** The wine list, please

listelemek [listelemek] *n* list

litre [litre] *n* litre

Litvanca [litvandʒa] *n (dil)* Lithuanian *(language)*

Litvanya [litvanja] *adj* Lithuanian ▷ *n* Lithuania

Litvanyalı [litvanjalə] *n (kişi)* Lithuanian *(person)*

lobi [lobi] *n* lobby; **Lobide buluşuruz** I'll meet you in the lobby

logo [logo] *n* logo

lokal [lokal] *n* **lokal anestezi** *n* local anaesthetic

lokanta [lokanta] *n* restaurant; **lokanta müşterisi** *n* diner

lolipop [lolipop] *n* lollipop, lolly

Londra [londra] *n* London

losyon [losjon] *n* lotion; **bronzlaşma losyonu** *n* suntan lotion; **traş losyonu** *n* aftershave; **yüz temizleme losyonu** *n* cleansing lotion

loş [loʃ] *adj* dim

lösemi [løsemi] *n* leukaemia

lunapark [lunapark] *n* funfair

Lübnan [lybnan] *n* Lebanon

Lübnanlı [lybnanlə] *n* Lebanese

lüks [lyks] *adj* luxurious ▷ *n* luxury

Lüksemburg [lyksemburg] *n* Luxembourg

lütfen [lytfen] *excl* please; **Lütfen Arka Sayfaya Bakınız** *abbr* PTO *(please turn over)*; **... koymayın lütfen** I'd like it without..., please; **Adresi yazar mısınız lütfen?** Will you write down the address, please?; **buzlu lütfen** With ice, please; **Binmeme yardım eder misiniz lütfen?** Can you help me get on, please?; **Biraz daha yavaş konuşabilir misiniz lütfen?** Could you speak more slowly, please?; **Burada durun lütfen** Stop here, please; **Burada ineyim lütfen** Please let me off; **Buranın sahibiyle konuşabilir miyim lütfen** Could I speak to the owner, please?; **Daha yüksek sesle konuşabilir misiniz lütfen?** Could you speak louder, please?; **Deneyebilir miyim lütfen?** Can I test it, please?; **Gecikeceğiniz zaman lütfen bize haber verin** Please call us if you'll be late; **Hesabı alalım lütfen** Please bring the bill; **Lütfen bana bir iğne yapın** Please give me an injection; **Lütfen beni bekleyin** Please wait for me; **Lütfen durun** Please stop the bus; **Menü lütfen** The menu, please; **Sarar mısınız lütfen?** Could you wrap it up for me, please?; **Tekrar eder misiniz lütfen?** Could you repeat that, please?; **Temiz bir kaşık alabilir miyim lütfen?** Could I have a clean spoon, please?; **Tuzu uzatır mısınız lütfen?** Pass the salt, please; **Yanında ekstra... istiyorum lütfen** I'd like it with extra..., please; **Yazabilir misiniz lütfen** Could you write that down, please?

maaş [maaʃ] *n* pay, salary; **emekli maaşı** *n* pension; **yüksek maaşlı** *adj* well-paid
mabed [mabed] *n* shrine
Macar [madʒar] *adj* Hungarian ▷ *n* Hungarian
Macaristan [madʒaristan] *n* Hungary
macera [madʒera] *n* adventure
maceraperest [madʒeraperest] *adj* adventurous
macun [madʒun] *n* paste; **diş macunu** *n* toothpaste
maç [matʃ] *n* match *(sport)*; **futbol maçı** *n* football match; **kendi sahasında maç** *n* home match; **rakip sahada maç** *n* away match; **Futbol maçı görmek isterdim** I'd like to see a football match
Madagaskar [madagaskar] *n* Madagascar
madalya [madalja] *n* medal

madalyon [madaljon] *n* locket, medallion

madam [madam] *n* madam

madde [madde] *n* stuff, substance, *(dizi)* item, *(fizik)* matter, *(yasa vb)* clause; **katkı maddesi** *n* additive, preservative; **patlayıcı madde** *n* explosive; **yiyecek maddeleri** *npl* groceries

maden [maden] *n* mineral; **maden ocağı** *n* mine; **maden suyu** *n* mineral water, sparkling water; **Bir şişe maden suyu** a bottle of mineral water

madenci [madendʒi] *n* miner

madencilik [madendʒilik] *n* mining

madensel [madensel] *adj* mineral

mafsal [mafsal] *n* joint; **mafsal iltihabı** *n* arthritis

magazin [magazin] *n* **online magazin** *n* webzine

mağara [ma:ara] *n* cave

mağaza [ma:aza] *v* large shop; **büyük mağaza** *n* department store

mahalle [mahalle] *n* neighbourhood

mahcup [mahdʒup] *adj* ashamed

mahkeme [mahkeme] *n* court, tribunal

mahkum [mahkum] *n* prisoner ▷ *v* **mahkum etmek** *v* sentence

mahvetmek [mahvetmek] *v* ruin

mahvolmuş [mahvolmuʃ] *adj* devastated

mahzen [mahzen] *n* cellar

makale [makale] *n* article

makara [makara] *n* reel

makarna [makarna] *n* pasta ▷ *npl* macaroni

makas [makas] *npl* scissors, *(tırnak/saç/tel/çalı)* clippers; **tırnak makası** *n* nail scissors

makaslamak [makaslamak] *v* cut up

makine [makine] *n* engine, machine; **çamaşır kurutma makinesi** *n* spin dryer, tumble dryer; **çamaşır makinesi** *n* washing machine; **çim biçme makinesi** *n* lawnmower, mower; **bulaşık makinesi** *n* dishwasher; **cep hesap makinesi** *n* pocket calculator; **dijital fotoğraf makinesi** *n* digital camera; **dikiş makinesi** *n* sewing machine; **ekmek kızartma makinesi** *n* toaster; **fotoğraf makinesi** *n* camera; **fotokopi makinesi** *n* photocopier; **hesap makinesi** *n* calculator; **jetonlu makine** *n* slot machine; **makinede yıkanabilir** *n* machine washable; **makineli tüfek** *n* machine gun; **otomatik satış makinesi** *n* vending machine; **saç kurutma makinesi** *n* hairdryer; **slot makinesi** *n* fruit machine; **traş makinesi** *n* shaver; **Çamaşır makinesi nasıl çalışıyor?** How does the washing machine work?; **Bilet makinası çalışmıyor** The ticket machine isn't working; **Bilet makinası nasıl çalışıyor?** How does the ticket machine work?; **Bilet makinası nerede?** Where is the ticket machine?; **Bu kartı bu makinede kullanabilir miyim?**

Can I use my card with this cash machine?; **Kullanabileceğim bir faks makinesi var mı?** Is there a fax machine I can use?; **Makine kartımı yuttu** The cash machine swallowed my card

maksat [maksat] n purpose

maksimum [maksimum] n maximum

makul [makul] adv reasonably

makyaj [makjaʒ] n make-up; **makyaj malzemeleri** npl toiletries; **makyaj malzemesi** npl cosmetics

mala [mala] n trowel

Malawi [malavi] n Malawi

Malezya [malezja] adj Malaysian ▷ n Malaysia

Malezyalı [malezjalə] n Malaysian

mali [mali] adj financial, fiscal; **mali açıklık** n shortfall; **mali destek** n sponsorship; **mali destek sağlamak** v subsidize; **mali yıl** n financial year, fiscal year

malikane [malikane] n estate, stately home

mallar [mallar] npl goods

malt [malt] n **malt viskisi** n malt whisky

Malta [malta] adj Maltese ▷ n Malta; **Malta dili** (dil) n Maltese (language)

Maltalı [maltalə] n (kişi) Maltese (person)

malzeme [malzeme] n ingredient, material; **makyaj malzemeleri** npl toiletries; **makyaj malzemesi** npl cosmetics; **malzeme temin etme** n supply

mama [mama] n **mama önlüğü** n

bib; **Mama sandalyeniz var mı?** Do you have a high chair?

mamut [mamut] n mammoth

manastır [manastər] n abbey, convent, monastery; **Manastır halka açık mı?** Is the monastery open to the public?

manav [manav] n greengrocer's

manda [manda] n buffalo

mandal [mandal] n **çamaşır mandalı** n clothes peg

mandalina [mandalina] n clementine, mandarin (fruit), tangerine

mandıra [mandəra] n dairy

manevi [manevi] adj spiritual

mangetout [mangetout] n mangetout

mango [mango] n mango

manikür [manikyr] n manicure ▷ v **manikür yapmak** n manicure

manken [maɲen] n **vitrin mankeni** n dummy

mantar [mantar] n (botanik) mushroom, (botanik) toadstool, (eşya) cork

mantık [mantək] n reason

mantıklı [mantəklə] adj logical, reasonable

mantıksız [mantəksəz] adj unreasonable

manyak [manjak] n madman, maniac

manzara [manzara] n landscape, scenery; **güzel manzaralı yer** n beauty spot

Maori [maori] adj Maori ▷ n (kişi) Maori (person); **Maori dili** (dil) n Maori (language)

marangoz [marangoz] n carpenter

marangozluk [marangozluk] *n* carpentry

maraton [maraton] *n* marathon

margarin [margarin] *n* margarine

marka [marka] *n* brand, brand name, *(ticaret)* trademark

marker [marker] *n* highlighter

market [market] *n* **market arabası** *n* shopping trolley

Marksizm [marksizm] *n* Marxism

marmelat [marmelat] *n* marmalade

marş [marʃ] *n* anthem; **milli marş** *n* national anthem

Mart [mart] *n* March

martı [martə] *n* seagull

marul [marul] *n* lettuce

masa [masa] *n* table *(furniture)*; **masa örtüsü** *n* tablecloth; **masa tenisi** *n* table tennis; **servis masası** *n* trolley; **tuvalet masası** *n* dressing table; **Dört kişilik bir masa lütfen** A table for four people, please

masaj [masaʒ] *n* massage

masal [masal] *n* story, tale; **peri masalı** *n* fairytale

masif [masif] *adj* massive

maske [maske] *n* mask

maskeli [maskeli] *adj* masked

masraf [masraf] *n* expense; **işletme masrafları** *npl* overheads

masraflar [masraflar] *npl* expenses

masum [masum] *adj* innocent

maşa [maʃa] *n* **saç maşası** *npl* straighteners

matara [matara] *n* **cep matarası** *n* flask

matbaacı [matbaadʒə] *n* printer *(person)*

matem [matem] *n* mourning

matematik [matematik] *npl* mathematics, maths

matematiksel [matematiksel] *adj* mathematical

matine [matine] *n* matinée; **Sekiz matinesine iki bilet lütfen** two for the eight o'clock showing

matkap [matkap] *n* drill; **pnömatik matkap** *n* pneumatic drill

maun [maun] *n* mahogany

mavi [mavi] *adj* blue

mavna [mavna] *n* barge

maya [maja] *n* yeast

maydanoz [majdanoz] *n* parsley

Mayıs [majəs] *n* May

maymun [majmun] *n* monkey

mayo [majo] *n* bathing suit, swimming costume, swimsuit

mayonez [majonez] *n* mayonnaise

mecburi [medʒburi] *adj* **mecburi yön** *(trafik)* *n* diversion

meclis [medʒlis] *n* *(belediye vb)* council; **belediye meclis üyesi** *n* councillor

medeni [medeni] *adj* **medeni hal** *n* marital status

meditasyon [meditasjon] *n* meditation

medya [medja] *npl* media

mega [mega] *adj* mega

mekanik [mekanik] *adj* mechanical

mekanizma [mekanizma] *n* machinery, mechanism

Mekke [mekke] *n* Mecca

Meksika [meksika] *n* Mexico

Meksikalı [meksikalə] *n* Mexican

mektup [mektup] *n* letter
(*message*); **Bu mektubu
postalamak istiyorum** I'd like to
send this letter
melankoli [melaŋoli] *npl* blues
melas [melas] *n* treacle
melek [melek] *n* angel
melez [melez] *n* mongrel
melodi [melodi] *n* melody, tune
memeli [memeli] *n* mammal
memnun [memnun] *adj* glad,
pleased; **kendinden memnun** *adj*
smug
memur [memur] *n* official,
employee; **Çin'de yüksek memur**
n mandarin (*official*); **görevli
memur** (*polis/asker*) *n* officer;
gümrük memuru *n* customs
officer; **tasfiye memuru** *n*
receiver (*person*); **trafik memuru**
n traffic warden
mendil [mendil] *n* handkerchief,
hankie; **ıslak bebek mendili** *n*
baby wipe; **kağıt mendil** *n* tissue
(*anatomy*), tissue (*paper*)
menenjit [menenʒit] *n* meningitis
menopoz [menopoz] *n*
menopause
mensup [mensup] *n* **ordu
mensubu** *n* (*erkek*) serviceman,
(*kadın*) servicewoman
menteşe [menteʃe] *n* hinge
menü [meny] *n* menu; **Çocuk
menüsü var mı?** Do you have a
children's menu?; **Fiks menü
alalım** We'll take the set menu;
Fiks menü ne kadar? How much
is the set menu?; **Fiks menünüz
var mı?** Do you have a set-price
menu?; **Menü lütfen** The menu,

please; **Tatlı menüsü lütfen**
The dessert menu, please
menzil [menzil] *n* **kısa menzilli
silah** *n* shotgun
merak [merak] *n* curiosity ▷ *v*
merak etmek *v* wonder
meraklı [meraklə] *adj* curious,
inquisitive, nosy
mercan [merdʒan] *n* coral
mercanköşk [merdʒaŋøʃk] *n*
marjoram, (*yabani*) oregano
mercimek [merdʒimek] *npl* lentils
merdiven [merdiven] *n* staircase;
ayaklı merdiven *n* stepladder;
merdiven başı *n* landing; **taşınır
merdiven** *n* ladder; **yürüyen
merdiven** *n* escalator
merdivenler [merdivenler] *npl*
stairs
merhaba [merhaba] *excl* hello!
merhamet [merhamet] *n* mercy
merhem [merhem] *n* ointment
merkez [merkez] *n* centre ▷ *npl*
headquarters; **alışveriş merkezi**
n shopping centre; **çağrı merkezi**
n call centre; **bahçe merkezi** *n*
garden centre; **eğlence merkezi**
n leisure centre; **genel merkez** *n*
HQ; **kent merkezi** *adv* city centre;
kent merkezinde *adv* downtown;
şehir merkezi *n* town centre;
merkezi ısıtma *n* central heating;
yönetim merkezi *n* head office;
ziyaretçi merkezi *n* visitor
centre; **Kent merkezine lütfen**
Please take me to the city centre;
**Şehir merkezinden ne kadar
uzaktayız?** How far are we from
the town centre?; **Şehir
merkezine en kolay nasıl**

gidebilirim? What's the best way to get to the city centre?

merkezi [merkezi] *adj* central

mermer [mermer] *n* marble

mesafe [mesafe] *n* distance, space; **kısa mesafe hız koşusu** *n* sprint; **kısa mesafe koşucusu** *n* sprinter

mesai [mesai] *n* work; **fazla mesai** *n* overtime

mesaj [mesaʒ] *n* message, text message; **mesaj atmak** *v* text; **Bana mesaj var mı?** Are there any messages for me?; **Mesaj bırakabilir miyim?** Can I leave a message?; **Sekreterine mesaj bırakabilir miyim?** Can I leave a message with his secretary?

mesele [mesele] *n* issue

meskun [meskun] *adj* residential; **meskun olmayan** *adj* uninhabited

meslek [meslek] *n* occupation *(work)*, profession

meslekdaş [meslekdaʃ] *n* colleague

mesleki [mesleki] *n* vocational

meşe [meʃe] *n* oak; **meşe palamudu** *n* acorn

meşgul [meʃgul] *adj* busy; **meşgul sinyali** *n* busy signal, engaged tone; **Kusura bakmayın, meşgulüm** Sorry, I'm busy

metabolizma [metabolizma] *n* metabolism

metal [metal] *n* metal; **metal çekirdek** *n* pellet

metazori [metazori] *adj* compulsory

Methodist [methodist] *adj*

Methodist mezhebine ait *n* Methodist

metin [metin] *n* text

metre [metre] *n* metre; **şerit metre** *n* tape measure

metres [metres] *n* mistress

metrik [metrik] *adj* metric

metro [metro] *n* underground, tube; **metro istasyonu** *n* metro station, tube station; **Bir metro haritası lütfen** Could I have a map of the tube, please?; **Buraya en yakın metro istasyonu nerede?/En yakın metro istasyonu nerede?** Where is the nearest tube station?; **En yakın metro istasyonuna nasıl gidebilirim?** How do I get to the nearest tube station?; **Metro haritası var mı?** Do you have a map of the tube?

mevsim [mevsim] *n* season

mevsimlik [mevsimlik] *n* seasonal

mevzuat [mevzuat] *n* legislation

meydan [mejdan] *n* **meydan okuma** *v* challenge

meyve [mejve] *n* fruit *(botany)*, fruit *(collectively)*; **çalı meyvesi** *n* berry; **meyve bahçesi** *n* orchard; **meyve salatası** *n* fruit salad; **meyve suyu** *n* fruit juice, juice; **çarkıfelek meyvası** *n* passion fruit; **meyva kabuğu** *n* peel

mezar [mezar] *n* grave; **mezar taşı** *n* gravestone

mezarlık [mezarlək] *n* cemetery, graveyard

mezgit [mezgit] *n* whiting; **mezgit balığı** *n* haddock

mezhep [meshep] n sect;
Methodist mezhebine ait n
Methodist; **Quaker**
mezhebinden n Quaker
mezun [mezun] n **üniversite**
mezunu n graduate,
undergraduate
mezuniyet [mezunijet] n
graduation
mıknatıs [məknatəs] n magnet
mıknatıslı [məknatəslə] adj
magnetic
mırıldanmak [mərəldanmak] v
mutter, (kedi gibi) purr
mısır [məsər] b maize ▷ n (sebze)
corn; **bebe mısır** n sweetcorn;
mısır gevreği n cornflakes; **mısır**
nişastası n cornflour; **patlamış**
mısır n popcorn
Mısır [məsər] adj Egyptian ▷ n
(ülke) Egypt
Mısırlı [məsərlə] n Egyptian
mızrak [məzrak] n javelin
mide [mide] n stomach; **mide**
ağrısı n stomachache; **mide**
bulandırıcı adj sickening; **mide**
ekşimesi n heartburn
midilli [midilli] n pony
midye [midje] n mussel
migren [migren] n migraine
mikroçip [mikrotʃip] n microchip
mikrodalga [mikrodalga] n
mikrodalga fırın n microwave
oven
mikrofon [mikrofon] n
microphone, mike; **Mikrofon var**
mı? Does it have a microphone?
mikrop [mikrop] n germ
mikroskop [mikroskop] n
microscope

mikser [mikser] n blender,
liquidizer, mixer
miktar [miktar] n amount,
quantity; **miktar belirtmek** v
quantify
mil [mil] n mile; **mil ölçer** n
mileometer; **mil hesabıyla**
uzaklık n mileage
milenyum [milenjum] n
millennium
milföy [milføj] n **milföy hamuru**
n puff pastry
milimetre [milimetre] n
millimetre
milkshake [milkshake] n
milkshake
millet [millet] n nation; **Birleşmiş**
Milletler n UN, United Nations
milli [milli] adj **milli marş** n
national anthem; **milli park** n
national park
mil/saat [milsaat] abbr mph
milyar [miljar] n billion
milyon [miljon] n million
milyoner [miljoner] n millionaire
mimar [mimar] n architect; **iç**
mimar n interior designer
mimarlık [mimarlək] n
architecture
mini [mini] adj mini; **mini etek** n
miniskirt
minibar [minibar] n minibar
minibüs [minibys] n minibus
minimum [minimum] adj
minimum; **Minimum bağlanma**
süresi ne kadar? What's the
minimum amount of time?
minyatür [minjatyr] adj
miniature ▷ n miniature
miras [miras] n heritage,

inheritance; **miras almak** v
inherit

misafir [misafir] n guest, visitor;
davetsiz misafir n intruder

misyoner [misjoner] n missionary

miting [miting] n rally

mitoloji [mitoloʒi] n mythology

miyop [mijop] adj near-sighted,
short-sighted

mizah [mizah] n humour; **mizah
dergisi** n comic book; **mizah
duygusu** n sense of humour

MMS [ememes] n MMS

mobil [mobil] n mobile

mobilya [mobilja] n furniture

mobilyalı [mobiljalə] adj
furnished

moda [moda] n fashion; **eski
moda** adj old-fashioned; **moda
akımı** n trend; **modası geçmiş** adj
obsolete; **modaya uygun** adj
fashionable, trendy; **modaya
uymayan** adj unfashionable

model [model] n model ▷ v
modelini yapmak v model; **saç
modeli** n hairdo, hairstyle

modem [modem] n modem

modern [modern] adj modern;
modern diller npl modern
languages

modernize [modernize] v
modernize etmek v modernize

modül [modyl] n module

Moğol [moɣol] adj Mongolian

Moğolca [moɣoldʒa] n (dil)
Mongolian (language)

Moğolistan [moɣolistan] n
Mongolia

mola [mola] n break; **yemek
molası** n lunch break; **Ne zaman**

mola veriyoruz? When do we
stop next?; **Yemek molası ne
zaman?** Where do we stop for
lunch?

Moldova [moldova] adj Moldovan
▷ n Moldova

Moldovalı [moldovalə] n
Moldovan

molekül [molekyl] n molecule

Monako [monako] n Monaco

Mongolistanlı [mongolistanlə] n
(kişi) Mongolian (person)

moped [moped] n moped; **Moped
kiralamak istiyorum** I want to
hire a moped

mor [mor] adj purple

moral [moral] n morale

morfin [morfin] n morphine

morg [morg] n morgue

morina [morina] n **morina balığı**
n cod

Moritanya [moritanja] n
Mauritania

Morse [morse] n (alfabe) Morse

motel [motel] n motel

motivasyon [motivasjon] n
motivation

motor [motor] n motor; **arama
motoru** n search engine; **deniz
motoru** n motorboat; **motor
kapağı** n bonnet (car); **motor
teknisyeni** n motor mechanic;
sürat motoru n speedboat

motorsiklet [motorsiklet] n
Motosiklet kiralamak istiyorum
I want to hire a motorbike

motosiklet [motosiklet] n
motorbike, motorcycle

motosikletçi [motosiklettʃi] n
motorcyclist

mozaik [mozaik] n mosaic

Mozambik [mozambik] n Mozambique

mönü [møny] n menu; **fiks mönü** n set menu

MP3 [empi:ytʃ] n **MP3 çalar** n MP3 player

MP4 [empi:dørt] n **MP4 çalar** n MP4 player

MS [ms] abbr AD ▷ n (hastalık) MS

muamele [muamele] n treatment; **kötü muamele etmek** v ill-treat

muazzam [muazzam] adj enormous

mucit [mudʒit] n inventor

mucize [mudʒize] n miracle

muhabbet [muhabbet] n **muhabbet kuşu** n budgerigar; **muhabbet kuşu** n budgie

muhabir [muhabir] n correspondent, reporter

muhafazakâr [muhafazaka:r] adj conservative

muhakkak [muhakkak] adv surely

muhalefet [muhalefet] n opposition

muharebe [muharebe] n battle; **muharebe zırhlısı** n battleship

muhasebeci [muhasebedʒi] n accountant

muhasebecilik [muhasebedʒilik] n accountancy

muhbir [muhbir] n grass (informer)

muhteşem [muhteʃem] adj superb

muhteviyat [muhtevijat] n content ▷ npl contents (list)

mukavva [mukavva] n cardboard, hardboard

muktedir [muktedir] adj able, capable

multipl skleroz n multiple sclerosis

mum [mum] n candle; **mum boya** n crayon

mumya [mumja] n mummy (body)

Musevi [musevi] n Jew ▷ adj Jewish; **Musevilerin Fısıh Bayramı** n Passover

musluk [musluk] n tap; **musluk deliği** n plughole; **musluk işleri** n plumbing

muslukçu [muslukʧu] n plumber

muson [muson] n monsoon

muşamba [muʃamba] n **yer muşambası** n lino

mutabık [mutabək] adj agreed

mutfak [mutfak] n kitchen; **hazır mutfak** n fitted kitchen; **mutfak dolabı** n dresser; **mutfak havlusu** n tea towel; **mutfak robotu** n food processor

mutlu [mutlu] adj happy; **Mutlu Yıllar!** Happy New Year!

mutluluk [mutluluk] n bliss, happiness

mutsuz [mutsuz] adj unhappy

muz [muz] n banana

mücadele [mydʒadele] n struggle

mücevher [mydʒevher] n gem, jewel

mücevherat [mydʒevherat] n jewellery

müdahale [mydahale] n interruption

müdür [mydyr] n headteacher,

manager, principal, *(kadın)*
manageress; **genel müdür** *n*
managing director; **müdür**
yardımcısı *n* deputy head;
Müdürle konuşmak istiyorum
lütfen I'd like to speak to the
manager, please
müflis [myflis] *adj* bankrupt
müfredat [myfredat] *n*
curriculum, syllabus
mühendis [myhendis] *n* engineer
mühendislik [myhendislik] *n*
engineering
mühlet [myhlet] *n* notice
(termination)
mühür [myhyr] *n* seal *(mark)*
mühürlemek [myhyrlemek] *v*
seal
mükemmel [mykemmel] *adj*
excellent, outstanding, perfect;
mükemmel bir şekilde *adv*
perfectly; **Yemek mükemmeldi**
The lunch was excellent
mükemmellik [mykemmellik] *n*
perfection
mülk [mylk] *n* property; **özel mülk**
n private property; **devre mülk** *n*
timeshare
mülkiyet [mylkijet] *n* possession
münazara [mynazara] *n*
discussion
mürekkep [myrekkep] *n* ink
mürettebat [myrettebat] *n*
crew; **kabin mürettebatı** *n*
cabin crew
müshil [myshil] *n* laxative
müsli [mysli] *n* muesli
Müslüman [myslyman] *adj*
Moslem, Muslim
▷ *n* Moslem, Muslim

Müslümanlık [myslymanlək] *n*
Islam
müsrüf [mysryf] *v* **müsrüflük**
etmek *v* squander
müstakil [mystakil] *adj*
self-contained; **müstakil ev** *n*
detached house
müstesna [mystesna] *adj*
exceptional
müşterek [myfterek] *adj* common
müşteri [myfteri] *n* client,
customer; **lokanta müşterisi** *n*
diner
mütercim [myterdʒim] *n*
interpreter
müteşekkir [myteʃekkir] *adj*
grateful
müthiş [mythiʃ] *adj* terrific
müttefik [myttefik] *n* ally
müze [myze] *n* museum; **Müze**
öğleden sonra açık mı? Is the
museum open in the afternoon?;
Müze her gün açık mı? Is the
museum open every day?; **Müze**
ne zaman açık? When is the
museum open?; **Müze Pazar**
günleri açık mı? Is the museum
open on Sundays?; **Müze**
sabahları açık mı? Is the museum
open in the morning?
müzik [myzik] *adj* musical ▷ *n*
music; **film müziği** *n* soundtrack;
halk müziği *n* folk music; **kişisel**
müzik çalar *n* personal stereo;
müzik aleti *n* musical instrument;
müzik seti *n* music centre; **Canlı**
müzik dinleyebileceğimiz bir
yer var mı? Where can we hear
live music?
müzikal [myzikal] *n* musical

müzisyen [myzisjen] *n* musician, player *(instrumentalist)*; **Yerel müzisyenleri dinleyebileceğimiz bir yer var mı?** Where can we hear local musicians play?

müzmin [myzmin] *adj* obstinate

Myanmar [mjanmar] *n* Myanmar

nabız [nabəz] *n* pulse

nadiren [nadiren] *adv* rarely, scarcely, seldom

nahoş [nahoʃ] *adj* embarrassing

nakış [nakəʃ] *n* embroidery

nakil [nakil] *n* transfer; **kan nakli** *n* blood transfusion

nakit [nakit] *n* cash; **Üzerimde nakit yok** I don't have any cash; **Nakit almak için kartımı kullanabilir miyim?** Can I use my card to get cash?; **Nakit ödemelere indirim yapıyor musunuz?** Do you offer a discount for cash?

nakliye [naklije] *n* freight

nal [nal] *n* **at nalı** *n* horseshoe

namına [naməna] *n* on behalf of

namussuz [namussuz] *adj* bent *(inf: dishonest)*

nane [nane] *n (bitki/şeker)* mint *(herb/sweet)*; **nane şekeri** *n* peppermint

nankör [naŋør] *adj* ungrateful

nar [nar] *n* pomegranate

nasıl [nasəl] *adj* what ▷ *adv* how;
... merkezine nasıl gidebilirim?
How do I get to the centre of...?;
... na nasıl gidebilirim? How do
I get to...?; **... na nasıl gidebiliriz?**
How do we get to...?; **Bilet
makinası nasıl çalışıyor?** How
does the ticket machine work?;
Bu nasıl çalışıyor? How does
this work?; **Bu yemeği nasıl
pişiriyorsunuz?** How do you
cook this dish?; **Bunun nasıl
yapıldığını biliyor musunuz?** Do
you know how to do this?; **Hava
yarın nasıl olacak?** What will the
weather be like tomorrow?; **Kar
nasıl?** What is the snow like?;
**Kumandaların nasıl çalıştığını
gösterir misiniz?** Can you show
me how the controls work?; **Nasıl
alacağım?** How should I take it?;
Nasıl okunuyor? How do you
pronounce it?; **Nasıl yazılıyor?**
How do you spell it?; **Nasılsınız?**
How are you?; **Oraya nasıl
gidebilirim?** How do I get there?

nasılsa [nasəlsa] *adv* somehow

NATO [nato] *abbr* NATO

naylon [najlon] *n* nylon; **naylon
çorap** *n* stocking; **naylon torba** *n*
plastic bag, polythene bag

nazik [nazik] *adj* polite; **Çok
naziksiniz** That's very kind of you

ne [ne] *adj* what ▷ *conj* neither
▷ *pron* what; **ne yapacağı belli
olmayan** *adj* unpredictable; **... a
ne zaman varırız?** What time do
we get to...?; **Adınız ne?** What's

your name?; **Bu ne demek?** What
does this mean?; **Bu nedir?** What
is it?; **Bu yemeğin içinde ne var?**
What is in this dish?; **Bunun
içinde ne var?** What is in this?;
Burada neler yapabiliriz? What
is there to do here?; **Buraya özel
ne var?** What is the house
speciality?; **Ne giymem
gerekiyor?** What should I wear?;
Ne içmek istersiniz? What would
you like to drink?; **Ne işle
meşgulsünüz?** What do you do?;
Ne oldu? What happened?; **Ne
zaman kalkıyor?** What time does
it leave?; **Otobüs ne zaman
geliyor?** What time does the bus
arrive?; **Otobüs ne zaman
kalkacak?** What time does the bus
leave?; **Sandviç olarak ne var?**
What kind of sandwiches do you
have?

neden [neden] *n* cause *(reason)*

nedime [nedime] *n* bridesmaid

nefes [nefes] *n* breath; **nefes alma**
n breathing; **nefes almak** *v*
breathe, breathe in; **nefes
vermek** *v* breathe out

nefis [nefis] *adj* excellent; **Nefisti**
That was delicious; **Yemek nefisti**
The meal was delicious

nefret [nefret] *n* hatred ▷ *v* **nefret
etmek** *v* hate; **nefret etmek** *v*
resent

nehir [nehir] *n* river; **Nehirde
tekne turu var mı?** Are there any
boat trips on the river?; **Nehirde
yüzülebilir mi?** Can one swim in
the river?

nektarin [nektarin] *n* nectarine

nem [nem] n humidity, moisture
nemlendirici [nemlendiridʒi] n
moisturizer
nemli [nemli] adj damp, humid
neon [neon] n neon
Nepal [nepal] n Nepal
nerede [nerede] adv where ▷ conj
where; **Bunu nerede tamir
ettirebilirim?** Where can I get this
repaired?; **Duşlar nerede?** Where
are the showers?; **Nerede
buluşabiliriz?** Where can we
meet?; **Nerede buluşalım?** Where
shall we meet?; **Nerede
kalıyorsunuz?** Where are you
staying?; **Nerede
oturuyorsunuz?** Where do you
live?
nereden [nereden] pron, conj
... ın neresindensiniz? What part
of... are you from?
neredeyse [neredejse] adv almost
nergiz [nergiz] n daffodil
nesne [nesne] n object
neşe [neʃe] n joy
neşeli [neʃeli] adj cheerful, jolly ▷ n
smiley
net [net] adj, adv **net değil** adj
unclear
netbol [netbol] n netball
network [netvork] n **şirketiçi
network** n intranet
neyse [nejse] adv anyway
nice [nidʒe] adj **Nice Yıllara!**
Happy birthday!
niçin [nitʃin] adv why
Nijer [niʒer] n Niger
Nijerya [niʒerja] adj Nigerian ▷ n
Nigeria
Nijeryalı [niʒerjalə] n Nigerian

Nikaragua [nikaragua] adj
Nicaraguan ▷ n Nicaragua
Nikaragualı [nikaragualə] n
Nicaraguan
nikotin [nikotin] n nicotine
nine [nine] n grandma, granny;
ninenin annesi n great-
grandmother
ninni [ninni] n lullaby
Nisan [nisan] n April; **1 Nisan
Şakası** n April Fools' Day
nişan [niʃan] n (belirti) token;
nişan yüzüğü n engagement ring
nişanlı [niʃanlə] adj engaged ▷ n
(erkek) fiancé, (kadın) fiancée;
Nişanlıyım I'm engaged
nişasta [niʃasta] n starch; **mısır
nişastası** n cornflour
nitekim [nitekim] adv
consequently
nitelemek [nitelemek] v qualify
nitelik [nitelik] n qualification
nitelikli [nitelikli] adj qualified
niteliksiz [niteliksiz] adj unskilled
nitrojen [nitroʒen] n nitrogen
niyet [nijet] n intention; **kötü
niyetli** adj malicious
niyetlenmek [nijetlenmek] v
intend to
nizam [nizam] n **bitişik nizam ev**
n semi, semi-detached house
Noel [noel] n Christmas, Xmas;
Noel ağacı n Christmas tree; **Noel
arifesi** n Christmas Eve; **Noel
öncesi** n advent; **Noel kartı** n
Christmas card; **Noel şarkısı** n
carol; **Mutlu Noeller!** Merry
Christmas!
nohut [nohut] n chickpea
nokta [nokta] n (gramer) full stop,

(şekil) dot, *(yer)* point; **bakış noktası** *n* standpoint, viewpoint; **iki nokta üst üste** *n* colon; **noktalı virgül** *n* semicolon

noktalama [noktalama] *n* punctuation

noodle [noodle] *npl* noodles

normal [normal] *adj* normal; **Normal postayla ne kadar sürer?** How long will it take by normal post?

normalde [normalde] *adv* normally

Norveç [norvetʃ] *adj* Norwegian ▷ *n* Norway

Norveççe [norvetʃtʃe] *adj* Norwegian ▷ *n (dil)* Norwegian *(language)*

Norveçli [norvetʃli] *n (kişi)* Norwegian *(person)*

not [not] *n (mesaj)* note *(message)*; **digital not defteri** *n* e-book; **kısa not** *n* memo; **not almak** *v* jot down, note down; **not defteri** *n* jotter, notebook, notepad; **not kağıdı** *n* notepaper ▷ *v* **not vermek** *v* mark *(grade)*

nota [nota] *n* score *(of music)*, *(müzik)* note *(music)*

nöbet [nøbet] *n* seizure; **öfke nöbeti** *n* tantrum; **gece nöbeti** *n* nightshift; **sara nöbeti** *n* epileptic seizure

nöbetçi [nøbettʃi] *n* guard

nörotik [nørotik] *adj* neurotic

numara [numara] *n* number; **bilinmeyen numaralar** *npl* directory enquiries; **cep numarası** *n* mobile number; **hesap numarası** *n* account number; **oda numarası** *n* room number; **referans numarası** *n* reference number; **telefon numarası** *n* phone number; **yanlış numara** *n* wrong number; **... numaralı kapıya gidiniz** Please go to gate...; **Ayakkabı numaram altı** My feet are a size six; **İki yüz iki numaralı odanın anahtarı lütfen** the key for room number two hundred and two; **Üç numaralı pompa lütfen** Pump number three, please; **Beş numaralı kabin nerede?** Where is cabin number five?; **Benim cep numaram...** My mobile number is...; **Bilinmeyen numaralar için hangi numarayı çevireceğim?** What is the number for directory enquiries?; **Ehliyet numaram...** My driving licence number is...; **Faks numarası nedir?** What is the fax number?; **Otuz numaralı vagon nerede?** Where is carriage number thirty?; **Telefon numaranızı alabilir miyim?** Can I have your phone number?; **Telefon numarası nedir?** What's the telephone number?

nüdist [nydist] *n* nudist

nüfus [nyfus] *n* population; **nüfus cüzdanı** *n* birth certificate; **nüfus sayımı** *n* census

nükleer [nykleer] *adj* atomic, nuclear

nükte [nykte] *n* wit

nükteli [nykteli] *adj* humorous

O

o [o] *pron (eşya/hayvan)* it, *(erkek)* he, *(kadın)* she; **o sırada** *adv* meanwhile; **ya o, ya bu** *conj* either *(.. or)*; **Onu tanıyor musunuz?** Do you know him?
obez [obez] *adj* obese
obua [obua] *n* oboe
ocak [odʒak] *n (fırın vb)* cooker; **gazlı ocak** *n* gas cooker; **kömür ocağı** *n* colliery; **maden ocağı** *n* mine; **taş ocağı** *n* quarry
Ocak [odʒak] *n (ay)* January
oda [oda] *n* room; **ameliyat odası** *n* operating theatre; **öğretmen odası** *n* staffroom; **çamaşır odası** *n* utility room; **çift yataklı oda** *n* twin room, twin-bedded room; **çocuk odası** *n* nursery; **bekleme odası** *n* waiting room; **cenazenin gömülmeye ya da yakılmaya hazırlandığı oda** *n* funeral parlour; **iki kişilik oda** *n* double

room; **kiralık oda** *n* bedsit; **oda arkadaşı** *n* roommate; **oda görevlisi** *n* chambermaid; **oda numarası** *n* room number; **oda servisi** *n* room service; **oturma odası** *n* living room, sitting room; **sohbet odası** *n* chatroom; **soyunma odası** *n (mağaza)* fitting room, *(spor)* changing room; **tek kişilik oda** *n* single room; **yatak odası** *n* bedroom; **yedek oda** *n* spare room; **Aile odası istiyorum** I'd like to book a family room; **İki kişilik bir oda ayırtmak istiyorum** I want to reserve a double room; **İki kişilik bir oda istiyorum** I'd like to book a double room; **Balkonlu odanız var mı?** Do you have a room with a balcony?; **Başka bir oda istiyorum** I'd like another room; **Bilgisayar odası nerede?** Where is the computer room?; **Bir oda kiralamak istiyorum** I'd like to rent a room; **Bu oda çok küçük** The room is too small; **Oda çok sıcak** The room is too hot; **Oda çok soğuk** The room is too cold; **Oda hesabıma yazın lütfen** Please charge it to my room; **Oda ne kadar?** How much is the room?; **Oda pis** The room is dirty; **Oda servisi var mı?** Is there room service?; **Oda temizlenmemiş** The room isn't clean; **Odada banyo var mı?** Does the room have a private bathroom?; **Odada bir sorun var** There's a problem with the room; **Odada duman kokusu var** My room smells of smoke; **Odada internet bağlantısı var mı?** Is there an internet connection in the room?; **Odada kablosuz internet bağlantısı var mı?** Does the room have wireless internet access?; **Odada kalorifer var mı?** Does the room have heating?; **Odada klima var mı?** Does the room have air conditioning?; **Odada televizyon var mı?** Does the room have a TV?; **Odada vantilatör var mı?** Does the room have a fan?; **Odamı değiştirebilir miyim?** Can I switch rooms?; **Odamı temizler misiniz lütfen** Can you clean the room, please?; **Odamda böcek var** There are bugs in my room; **Odamda kahvaltı edebilir miyim?** Can I have breakfast in my room?; **Odanız burası** This is your room; **Odanız var mı?** Do you have a room?; **Odayı görebilir miyim?** Can I see the room?; **Odayı kaçta boşaltmam gerek?** When do I have to vacate the room?; **Sessiz bir oda rica ediyorum** I'd like a quiet room; **Sigara içilebilen bir oda rica ediyorum** I'd like a smoking room; **Sigara içilemeyen bir oda rica ediyorum** I'd like a no smoking room; **Soyunma odaları ne tarafta?** Where are the changing rooms?; **Tek kişilik bir oda ayırtmak istiyorum** I want to reserve a single room

odak [odak] n focus; **çift odaklı gözlük** npl bifocals

odaklanmak [odaklanmak] v focus

odun [odun] n firewood, log; **odun kömürü** n charcoal

ofsayt [ofsajt] adj offside

Oğlak [oɣlak] n **Oğlak burcu** n Capricorn

oğlan [oɣlan] n **oğlan çocuğu** n boy

oğul [ou:l] n son; **üvey oğul** n stepson; **vaftiz oğlu** n godson; **Oğlum kayıp** My son is missing; **Oğlum kayboldu** My son is lost

oje [oʒe] n nail polish; **oje çıkarıcı** n nail-polish remover

ok [okej] n arrow; **dart oku** n dart

OK [okej] excl OK!

okey [okej] adj okay; **okey!** excl okay!

oklava [oklava] n rolling pin

oksijen [oksiʒen] n oxygen

okşama [okʃama] n stroke (apoplexy), stroke (hit)

okşamak [okʃamak] v stroke

okul [okul] n school; **akşam okulu** n evening class; **ana okulu** n infant school; **dil okulu** n language school; **gece okulu** n night school; **okul üniforması** n school uniform; **okul çantası** n schoolbag; **okul çocukları** n schoolchildren; **okuldan kaçmak** v play truant; **sanat okulu** n art school; **yatılı okul** n boarding school; **yüksek okul** n college; **Burada kayak okulu var mı?** Is there a ski school?; **Okuyorum** I'm still studying

okuma [okuma] n reading; **okuma yazması olmayan** adj illiterate

okumak [okumak] v read; **dudak okuma** v lip-read; **yüksek sesle okumak** v read out; **Okuyamıyorum** I can't read it

okunaklı [okunaklə] adj legible

okunaksız [okunaksəz] adj illegible

okutman [okutman] n lecturer

okuyucu [okujudʒu] n reader

okyanus [okjanus] n ocean; **Hint Okyanusu** n Indian Ocean; **Kuzey Okyanusu** n Arctic Ocean

Okyanusya [okjanusja] n Oceania

olağanüstü [ola:anysty] adj extraordinary

olan [olan] art **aynı anda olan** adj simultaneous

olanaklar [olanaklar] npl amenities

olarak [olarak] conj **düzenli olarak** adv regularly; **doğal olarak** adv naturally; **gönüllü olarak** adv voluntarily; **otomatik olarak** adv automatically; **tam olarak** adv exactly

olası [olasə] adj likely, possible, probable

olasılık [olasələk] n possibility, probability; **olasılık dışı** adj unlikely

olasılıkla [olasələkla] adv possibly, presumably, probably

olay [olaj] n affair, event, incident, occurrence; **önemli olay** n highlight

olaylı [olajlə] adj eventful

oldukça [olduktʃa] adv fairly, rather

olgun [olgun] adj (kişi) mature,

(mevye) ripe; **olgun öğrenci** n mature student

olmadıkça [olmadəktʃa] conj unless

olmak [olmak] v be, become, happen; **ait olmak** v belong, belong to; **alabora olmak** v capsize; **aynı fikirde olmak** v agree; **önemli olmak** v matter; **başarısız olmak** vi fail; **destek olmak** v back up; **doğru olarak** adv accurately; **emekli olmak** v retire; **gönüllü olmak** n volunteer; **sahip olmak** v have, own, possess; **sonucu olmak** v result in; **teslim olmak** v surrender; **var olmak** v exist; **yaklaşık olarak** adv approximately; **yanıp kül olmak** v burn down; **yapmak zorunda olmak** v have to; **yok olmak** v vanish; **Üye olmak gerekiyor mu?** Do you have to be a member?

olmayan [olmajan] prep **dürüst olmayan** adj dishonest; **doğru olmayan** adj inaccurate; **esnek olmayan** adj inflexible; **HIV'li olmayan** adj HIV-negative; **pahalı olmayan** adj inexpensive; **pratik olmayan** adj impractical; **tatmin edici olmayan** adj disappointing

olta [olta] n fishing rod, fishing tackle; **olta balıkçılığı** n angling; **olta balıkçısı** n angler

olumlu [olumlu] adj positive

olumsuz [olumsuz] adj negative ▷ n negative

oluşmak [oluʃmak] v consist of

oluşturmak [oluʃturmak] v make up

omlet [omlet] *n* omelette

omurga [omurga] *n* backbone

omurilik [omurilik] *n* spinal cord

omuz [omuz] *n* shoulder; **omuz çantası** *n* satchel; **omuz silkmek** *v* shrug; **Omuzumu incittim** I've hurt my shoulder

on [on] *number* ten; **on yıl** *n* decade; **On dakika geciktik** We are ten minutes late; **On yaşında** He is ten years old; **Saat ikiyi on geçiyor** It's ten past two; **Tren on dakika rötarlı** The train is running ten minutes late

ona [ona] *adj (kadın)* her ▷ *pron (erkek)* him, *(kadın)* her

onaltı [onaltə] *number* sixteen

onaltıncı [onaltəndʒə] *adj* sixteenth

onarmak [onarmak] *v* mend, repair

onay [onaj] *n* approval

onaylamak [onajlamak] *v* approve; **başıyla onaylamak** *v* nod

onbaşı [onbaʃə] *n* corporal

on beş [onbeʃ] *num* **On beş Haziran Pazartesi** It's Monday the fifteenth of June

onbeş [onbeʃ] *number* fifteen

onbeşinci [onbeʃindʒi] *adj* fifteenth

onbir [onbir] *number* eleven

onbirinci [onbirindʒi] *adj* eleventh

ondokuz [ondokuz] *number* nineteen

ondokuzuncu [ondokuzundʒu] *adj* nineteenth

ondördüncü [ondørdyndʒy] *adj* fourteenth

ondört [ondørt] *number* fourteen

oniki [oniki] *number* twelve

onikinci [onikindʒi] *adj* twelfth

onlar [onlar] *pron* they

onları [onlarə] *pron* them

onların [onlarən] *adj* their

onlarınki [onlarəɲi] *pron* theirs

onluk [onluk] *adj* decimal

ons [ons] *n* ounce

onsekiz [onsekiz] *number* eighteen

onsekizinci [onsekizindʒi] *adj* eighteenth

onsuz [onsuz] *prep* without

onsuz yapmak [onsuzjapmak] *v* do without

onu [onu] *adj* her ▷ *pron* her, him

onun [onun] *adj* its, *(erkek)* his ▷ *prep* of ▷ *pron (erkek)* his

onuncu [onundʒu] *adj* tenth ▷ *n* tenth

onunki [onuɲi] *pron (kadın)* hers

onur [onur] *n (şeref)* honour ▷ *v* **onur kırmak** *v* insult

onüç [onytʃ] *number* thirteen

onüçüncü [onytʃyndʒy] *adj* thirteenth

onyedi [onjedi] *number* seventeen

onyedinci [onjedindʒi] *adj* seventeenth

opera [opera] *n* opera

operasyon [operasjon] *n* operation *(undertaking)*

operatör [operatør] *n* operator; **tur operatörü** *n* tour operator

oran [oran] *n* proportion, rate, ratio; **faiz oranı** *n* interest rate

oranlamak [oranlamak] *v* rate

orantılı [orantələ] *adj* proportional

oraya [oraja] *prep* to

ordu [ordu] *n* army; **ordu mensubu** *n (erkek)* serviceman, *(kadın)* servicewoman

org [org] *n* organ *(music)*

organ [organ] *n* organ *(body part)*

organik [organik] *adj* organic

organizasyon [organisasjon] *n* organization

organizatör [organisatør] *n* **kişisel organizatör** *n* personal organizer

organize [organize] *adj* **organize etmek** *v* organize

organizma [organizma] *n* organism

orgazm [orgazm] *n* orgasm

orkestra [orkestra] *n* band *(musical group)*, orchestra; **orkestra şefi** *n* conductor

orkide [orkide] *n* orchid

orman [orman] *n* forest, jungle; **orman tavuğu** *n* grouse *(game bird)*; **yağmur ormanı** *n* rainforest

orta [orta] *adj* intermediate, mid ▷ *n* middle; **orta boy** *adj* medium-sized; **orta sınıf** *adj* middle-class; **orta yaşlı** *adj* middle-aged; **ortaya çıkarmak** *v* disclose; **ortaya çıkmak** *v* show up

Orta [orta] *n* middle; **Orta Afrika Cumhuriyeti** *n* Central African Republic; **Orta Amerika** *n* Central America; **Orta Çağ** *n* Middle Ages; **Orta Doğu** *n* Middle East

ortaçağ [ortatʃaː] *adj* mediaeval

ortak [ortak] *adj* joint; **ortak görüş** *n* communion; **ortak hesap** *n* joint account; **suç ortağı** *n* accomplice

ortalama [ortalama] *adj* average ▷ *n* average

ortaokul [ortaokul] *n* secondary school

oryantal [orjantal] *adj* oriental

ot [ot] *n* grass *(plant)*, *(esrar)* grass *(marijuana)*; **hardal otu** *n* rape *(plant)*; **kokulu otlar** *n* herbs; **süpürge otu** *n* heather; **yabani ot** *n* weed; **yabani ot öldürücü** *n* weedkiller

otel [otel] *n* hotel; **gençlerin kaldığı otel** *n* youth hostel; **Bana bir otelde yer ayırtabilir misiniz?** Can you book me into a hotel?; **Bir otel arıyoruz** We're looking for a hotel; **Bir otel tavsiye edebilir misiniz?** Can you recommend a hotel?; **Bu otele taksi ne kadar?** How much is the taxi fare to this hotel?; **Şu otele en kolay nasıl gidebilirim?** What's the best way to get to this hotel?; **Otelde kalıyorum** I'm staying at a hotel; **Oteli yönetiyor** He runs the hotel; **Otelinizde tekerlekli sandalye girişi var mı?** Is your hotel accessible to wheelchairs?

oto [oto] *n* car; **oto kiralama** *n* car rental; **oto yarışı** *n* motor racing; **oto yıkama** *n* car wash

otobüs [otobys] *n* bus; **hava alanı otobüsü** *n* airport bus; **otobüs bileti** *n* bus ticket; **otobüs durağı** *n* bus stop; **otobüs terminali** *n* bus station; **tur otobüsü** *n* coach *(vehicle)*; **... otobüsü ne kadarda bir geliyor?** How often are the buses to...?; **... otobüsü ne sıklıkta geliyor?** How frequent are the buses to...?; **... otobüsüne nereden binebilirim?** Where can I get a bus to...?, Where do I catch the bus to...?, Where do I get a bus for...?; **... a bir sonraki otobüs kaçta?** When is the next bus to...?; **... a ilk otobüs kaçta?** When is the first bus to...?; **... a otobüs var mı?** Is there a bus to...?; **... a son otobüs kaçta?** When is the last bus to...?; **Affedersiniz,... a hangi otobüs gidiyor?** Excuse me, which bus goes to...?; **Bu otobüs... a gider mi?** Does this bus go to...?; **Buraya en yakın otobüs durağı nerede?** Where is the nearest bus stop?; **Havaalanına otobüs var mı?** Is there a bus to the airport?; **Kente otobüs var mı?** Is there a bus to the city?; **Nereden otobüs kartı alabilirim?** Where can I buy a bus card?; **Otobüs durağı buraya ne kadar uzakta?** How far is the bus stop?; **Otobüs ne zaman geliyor?** What time does the bus arrive?; **Otobüs ne zaman kalkacak?** What time does the bus leave?; **Otobüs terminali nerede?** Where is the bus station?; **Otobüs terminaline ne kadar uzaktayız?** How far are we from the bus station?; **Plaja otobüs var mı?** Is there a bus to the beach?; **Son otobüs kaçta?** What time is the last bus?; **Tur otobüsü ne zaman kalkıyor?** When is the bus tour of the town?

otomat [otomat] *n* **bilet otomatı** *n* ticket machine

otomatik [otomatik] *adj* automatic; **otomatik ödeme** *n* direct debit; **otomatik olarak** *adv* automatically; **otomatik satış makinesi** *n* vending machine; **Bu araba otomatik mi?** Is it an automatic car?; **Otomatik olsun lütfen** An automatic, please

otopark [otopark] *n* car park; **otopark ödeme cihazı** *n* parking meter; **otopark bileti** *n* parking ticket; **Buralarda bir otopark var mı?** Is there a car park near here?

otostop [otostop] *n* hitchhike; **otostop yapma** *n* hitchhiking

otostopçu [otostoptʃu] *n* hitchhiker

otoyol [otojol] *n* motorway; **Bu otoyol ücretli mi?** Is there a toll on this motorway?; **Otoyola nereden gidebilirim?** How do I get to the motorway?; **Otoyolda trafik yoğun mu?** Is the traffic heavy on the motorway?

oturak [oturak] *n* **Oturağınız var mı?** Do you have a potty?

oturma [oturma] *n* **oturma odası** *n* living room

oturmak [oturmak] *v* occupy, sit down ▷ *vi* sit; **geç saatlere kadar oturmak** *v* stay up; **oturma odası** *n* sitting room; **Nereye oturabilirim** Where can I sit down?; **Oturabileceğim bir yer var mı?** Is there somewhere I can sit down?; **Oturabilir miyim?** Can I sit here?

oturum [oturum] *n* **oturum açmak** *v* log in, log on; **oturum kapatmak** *v* log off, log out

otuz [otuz] *number* thirty; **Otuz numaralı vagon nerede?** Where is carriage number thirty?

ova [ova] *n* plain

oval [oval] *adj* oval

ovalamak [ovalamak] *v* scrub

oy [oj] *n* vote; **oy birliği** *n* consensus; **oy propagandası yapmak** *v* canvass ▷ *v* **oy vermek** *v* vote

oybirliğiyle [ojbirləəjle] *adj* unanimous

oymak [ojmak] *vt (ağaç)* carve

oynamak [ojnamak] *vt* play *(in sport)*; **kumar oynamak** *v* gamble; **Tenis oynamak istiyoruz** We'd like to play tennis

oynatıcı [ojnatədʒə] *n* **DVD oynatıcı** *n* DVD player

oyuk [ojuk] *adj* hollow

oyun [ojun] *n* game, play; **aile oyunları** *n* board game; **çocuk oyun grubu** *n* playgroup; **bilgisayar oyunu** *n* computer game; **dama oyunu** *npl* draughts; **dart oyunu** *npl* darts; **domino oyunu** *npl* dominoes; **halat çekme oyunu** *n* tug-of-war; **oyun alanı** *n* playground, playing field; **oyun kartı** *n* playing card; **oyun konsolu** *n* games console; **oyun saati** *n* playtime; **oyun salonu** *n* amusement arcade; **oyun yazarı** *n* playwright; **Buralarda çocuk oyun alanı var mı?** Is there a play park near here?; **Oyun oynayabilir miyim?** Can I play video games?

oyunbozan [ojunbozan] *n* spoilsport

oyuncak [ojundʒak] *n* toy; **oyuncak ayı** *n* teddy bear; **oyuncak bebek** *n* doll

oyuncu [ojundʒu] *adj (oyunbaz)* playful ▷ *n (spor)* player *(of sport)*; **kadın oyuncu** *n* actress; **oyuncu kadrosu** *n* cast; **tenis oyuncusu** *n* tennis player

oyunculuk [ojundʒuluk] *n* acting

ozon [ozon] *n* ozone; **ozon tabakası** *n* ozone layer

Ö

öd [ød] n **ödü kopmak** adj petrified

ödeme [ødeme] n payment; **ödeme günü geçmiş** adj overdue; **banka ödeme emri** n standing order

ödemek [ødemek] vi pay; **geri ödeme** n repayment; **geri ödemek** v pay back, repay; **otomatik ödeme** n direct debit; **Ayrıca bir şey ödeyecek miyim?** Is there a supplement to pay?; **Şimdi mi ödemem gerekiyor?** Do I pay in advance?; **Şimdi mi ödeyeceğim, sonra mı?** Do I pay now or later?

ödenecek [ødenedʒek] adj payable

ödenti [ødenti] n income; **hastalık ödentisi** n sick pay

ödev [ødev] n role; **ev ödevi** n homework

ödül [ødyl] n award, prize, reward; **ödül töreni** n prize-giving

ödüllü [ødylly] n prizewinner

ödün [ødyn] n compromise; **ödün vermek** v compromise

ödünç [ødyntʃ] n **ödünç almak** v borrow; **ödünç vermek** v lend, loan

öfke [øfke] n anger; **öfke nöbeti** n tantrum; **öfkeden çıldırmış** adj furious; **öfkeyle bakmak** v glare

öfkeli [øfkeli] adj cross

öğle [ø:le] n midday, noon; **Öğlen** at midday

öğlen [ø:len] n midday, noon, at midday; **öğle yemeği** n lunch; **öğleden önce** abbr a.m.; **öğleden sonra** abbr afternoon, p.m.; **öğleden sonra** in the afternoon; **Öğle yemeğinde buluşabilir miyiz?** Can we meet for lunch?; **Öğlen boşum, yemek yiyebiliriz** I'm free for lunch; **Müze öğleden sonra açık mı?** Is the museum open in the afternoon?; **Saat öğlen on iki** It's twelve midday; **yarın öğleden sonra** tomorrow afternoon

öğrenci [ø:rendʒi] n learner, pupil (learner), student; **askeri öğrenci** n cadet; **öğrenci indirimi** n student discount; **öğrenci sürücü** n learner driver; **öğrenci yurdu** n hostel; **üniversite sonrası eğitim yapan öğrenci** n postgraduate; **erkek öğrenci** n schoolboy; **kız öğrenci** n schoolgirl; **olgun öğrenci** n mature student; **yatılı öğrenci** n boarder; **Öğrenci indirimi var mı?**

Are there any reductions for students?; **Öğrenciyim** I'm a student
öğrenmek [ø:renmek] v learn
öğretim [ø:retim] n tuition; **öğretim ücreti** npl tuition fees
öğretme [ø:retme] n teaching
öğretmek [ø:retmek] v teach
öğretmen [ø:retmen] n instructor, schoolteacher, teacher; **öğretmen odası** n staffroom; **özel öğretmen** n tutor; **direksiyon öğretmeni** n driving instructor; **yardımcı öğretmen** n classroom assistant; **yedek öğretmen** n supply teacher
öğün [ø:yn] n meal
öğüt [ø:yt] n advice, tip (suggestion)
öğütmek [ø:ytmek] vt grind
ökseotu [økseotu] n mistletoe
öksürmek [øksyrmek] vi cough; **Öksürüyorum** I have a cough
öksürük [øksyryk] n cough; **öksürük şurubu** n cough mixture; **Öksürüyorum** I have a cough
ölçek [ølt∫ek] n gauge
ölçmek [ølt∫mek] v gauge, measure
ölçü [ølt∫y] n scale (measure)
ölçüler [ølt∫yler] npl measurements
ölçüsüz [ølt∫ysyz] adj extortionate; **ölçüsüz içme** n binge drinking
öldürmek [øldyrmek] v kill
ölmek [ølmek] v die
ölü [øly] adj dead ▷ adv dead
ölüm [øljym] n death

ölümcül [ølymdʒyl] adj fatal, terminal ▷ adv terminally
ön [øn] adj front ▷ n front; **adının ön harflerini yazmak** v initial; **ön ad** n first name; **ön adı** n Christian name; **ön cam** n windscreen; **ön eleme listesi** n shortlist; **ön lamba** n headlamp, headlight; **ön plan** n foreground; **ön yemek** n starter; **önüne gelenle yatmak** v sleep around; **önden gitmek** v go ahead; **öne eğilmek** v lean forward; **göz önünde tutarak** prep considering; **Öne bakan koltuk olsun lütfen** Facing the front, please; **Hangisi ön kapının anahtarı?** Which is the key for the front door?
önce [øndʒe] conj before; **öğleden önce** abbr a.m.; **önceden ödenmiş** adj prepaid; **önceden rezervasyon** n advance booking; **daha önce** adv earlier; **daha önceden** adv beforehand, previously; **daha önceden olmamış** adj unprecedented; **doğum öncesi** adj antenatal; **Noel öncesi** n advent; **sondan bir önceki** adj penultimate; **tarih öncesi** adj prehistoric; **yemek öncesi içki** n aperitif; **önceki gün** the day before yesterday; **Ayrılmadan önce evi temizlememiz gerekiyor mu?** Do we have to clean the house before we leave?; **saat beşten önce** before five o'clock; **Daha önce bu modelde saç kesmiş miydiniz?** Have you cut my type of hair before?

önceden [øndʒeden] *adv* before
önceki [øndʒeki] *adj* preceding, previous ▷ *adv* formerly
öncelik [øndʒelik] *n* priority; **öncelik belirlemek** *v* put in; **öncelik getirmek** *v* bring forward
öncelikle [øndʒelikle] *adv* firstly
önde [ønde] *adv* ahead
önem [ønem] *n* importance, significance; **önemsiz şey** *n* trifle
önemli [ønemli] *adj* crucial, important, significant, vital; **önemli olay** *n* highlight; **önemli olmak** *v* matter; **çok önemli** *adj* momentous
önemsiz [ønemsiz] *adj* trivial, unimportant
öneri [øneri] *n* proposal, recommendation, suggestion
önermek [ønermek] *v* propose, suggest
öngörmek [øngørmek] *v* foresee, predict
önlem [ønlem] *n* caution, precaution
önleme [ønleme] *n* prevention
önlemek [ønlemek] *v* prevent; **ter önleyici deodorant** *n* antiperspirant
önlük [ønlyk] *n* apron, pinafore; **mama önlüğü** *n* bib
önsezi [ønsezi] *n* intuition
önünde [ønynde] *prep* before
önyargı [ønjargə] *n* prejudice; **önyargılardan arındırma** *n* liberation
önyargılı [ønjargələ] *adj* prejudiced
öpmek [øpmek] *v* kiss
öpücük [øpydʒyk] *n* kiss

ördek [ørdek] *n* duck
örgü [ørgy] *n* knitting; **örgü şişi** *n* knitting needle; **saç örgüsü** *n* pigtail, plait
örmek [ørmek] *vt* knit
örneğin [ørneji:n] *abbr* e.g., i.e.
örnek [ørnek] *adj* model ▷ *n* example, instance, sample
örtmek [ørtmek] *v* cover
örtü [ørty] *n* cover; **bitki örtüsü** *n* vegetation; **masa örtüsü** *n* tablecloth; **yatak örtüsü** *n* bedspread
örümcek [ørymdʒek] *n* spider; **örümcek ağı** *n* cobweb
ötesinde [øtesinde] *prep* beyond
övmek [øvmek] *v* praise
övücü [øvydʒy] *adj* complimentary
öykü [øjky] *n* story; **özyaşam öyküsü** *n* autobiography; **çizgi öykü** *n* comic strip; **kısa öykü** *n* short story; **yaşam öyküsü** *n* biography
öyle [øjle] *adv* so; **öyle ki** *conj* so (that)
öylesine [øjlesine] *adv* so
öyleyse [øjlejse] *adv* then
öz [øz] *adv* **kısa ve öz** *adj* concise
Özbekistan [øzbekistan] *n* Uzbekistan
özçekim [øztʃekim] *n* selfie
özdeş [øzdeʃ] *adj* identical
özdisiplin [øzdisiplin] *n* self-discipline
özel [øzel] *adj* private, special; **özel öğretmen** *n* tutor; **özel koruma** *n* bodyguard; **özel mülk** *n* private property; **özel yaşam** *n* privacy; **kişinin evinin önündeki özel yol** *n* driveway; **yayalara özel bölge** *n* pedestrian precinct; **Özel sağlık**

sigortam var I have private health insurance; **Sizinle özel olarak konuşabilir miyim?** Can I speak to you in private?

özelleştirmek [øzelleʃtirmek] v privatize

özellik [øzellik] adj particular ▷ n feature

özellikle [øzellikle] adv especially, particularly, specially, specifically

özellikler [øzellikler] npl specs

özen [øzen] n care, attention; **özenli bir şekilde** adv cautiously

özerk [øzerk] adj autonomous

özerklik [øzerklik] n autonomy

özet [øzet] n outline, summary; **hesap özeti** n bank statement

özetlemek [øzetlemek] v sum up, summarize

özgeçmiş [øzgetʃmiʃ] n curriculum vitae

özgü [øzgy] adj special, unique to; **Bu şehre özgü bir şey istiyorum** Have you anything typical of this town?; **Bu yöreye özgü bir şey denemek istiyorum lütfen** I'd like to try something local, please; **Bu yöreye özgü bir şey istiyorum** Do you have anything typical of this region?; **Yöreye özgü bir şey ısmarlamak istiyorum** I'd like to order something local

özgün [øzgyn] adj authentic, original

özgür [øzgyr] adj free (no restraint)

özgürlük [øzgyrlyk] n freedom

özgüven [øzgyven] n confidence (self-assurance)

özkontrol [øzkontrol] n self-control

özlemek [øzlemek] v long

özlü [øzly] adj lush

özlük [øzlyk] n person, individual; **özlük hakları** n civil rights

özsavunma [øssavunma] n self-defence

özür [øzyr] n alibi, apology, excuse ▷ v **özür beyan etmek** v excuse

özür dilemek [øzyrdilemek] v apologize

özürlü [øzyrly] adj disabled, with a disability; **Özürlüler için girişiniz var mı?** Do you provide access for people with disabilities?; **Özürlüler için indiriminiz var mı?** Is there a reduction for people with disabilities?; **Özürlüler için kolaylıklarınız nelerdir?** What facilities do you have for people with disabilities?; **Özürlüler için tuvaletiniz var mı?** Are there any accessible toilets?

özverili [øzverili] adj devoted

özyaşam [øzjaʃam] n **özyaşam öyküsü** n autobiography

p

paha [paha] n price, value; **paha biçmek** v appreciate

pahalı [pahalə] adj dear (expensive), expensive; **hayat pahalılığı** n cost of living; **pahalı olmayan** adj inexpensive; **pahalı sezon** n high season; **Çok pahalı** It's quite expensive; **Benim için çok pahalı** It's too expensive for me

paket [paket] n package, packet, parcel; **paket kağıdı** n wrapping paper; **paket tatil** n package holiday; **paket tur** n package tour; **paket yemek** n packed lunch; **sımsıkı paketlenmiş** adj compact; **Bu paket kaça gider?** How much is it to send this parcel?; **Bu paketi postalamak istiyorum** I'd like to send this parcel

paketleme [paketleme] n packaging

paketlemek [paketlemek] v wrap up ▷ vt pack

paketlenmiş [paketlenmiʃ] adj packed

Pakistan [pakistan] adj Pakistani ▷ n Pakistan

Pakistanlı [pakistanlə] n Pakistani

palamut [palamut] n **meşe palamudu** n acorn

palanga [palanga] n tackle

palmiye [palmije] n palm (tree)

palto [palto] n overcoat

palyaço [paljatʃo] n clown

pamuk [pamuk] n cotton wool, (bitki) cotton; **pamuk helva** n candyfloss; **pamuklu kalın tişört** n sweatshirt

Panama [panama] n Panama

pancar [pandʒar] n beetroot

panç [pantʃ] n punch (hot drink)

panda [panda] n panda

pandantif [pandantif] n pendant

pandispanya [pandispanja] n sponge (cake)

pandomim [pandomim] n pantomime

panik [panik] n panic, scare ▷ v **paniğe kapılmak** v panic

pansiyoner [pansijoner] n lodger

panter [panter] n panther

pantolon [pantolon] npl trousers; **pantolon askıları** npl braces

panzehir [panzehir] n antidote

papa [papa] n pope

papağan [papa:an] n parrot

papatya [papatja] n daisy

papaz [papaz] n **papaz yardımcısı** n vicar

papazlık [papazlək] n ministry (religion)

papyon [papjon] v **papyon kravat** n bow tie

para [para] n money; **fazla para çekme** n overdraft; **hesabından çekilen para** n debit; **hesabından fazla para çekmiş** adj overdrawn; **madeni para** n coin; **para iadesi** n rebate, refund ▷ v **para iadesi yapmak** v refund; **Bana acilen para gönderilmesini ayarlayabilir misiniz?** Can you arrange to have some money sent over urgently?; **Hesabımdan para transferi yapmak istiyorum** I would like to transfer some money from my account; **Hiç param yok** I have no money; **Param bitti** I have run out of money; **Paramı geri alabilir miyim?** Can I have my money back?; **Paramı geri istiyorum** I want my money back

para-sailing [parasailing] n **Para-sailing için nereye gitmek gerek?** Where can you go para-sailing?

parafin [parafin] n paraffin

paragliding [paragliding] n **Paragliding için nereye gidebiliriz?** Where can you go paragliding?

paragraf [paragraf] n paragraph

Paraguay [paraguaj] adj Paraguayan ▷ n Paraguay

Paraguaylı [paraguajlə] n Paraguayan

paralel [paralel] adj parallel

paramedik [paramedik] n paramedic

parantez [parantez] n **köşeli parantezler** npl brackets

parasal [parasal] adj monetary; **parasal kaynak** npl funds

parascending [parasdʒending] n **Parascending yapmak isterdim** I'd like to go parascending

parasetamol [parasetamol] n **Parasetamol rica ediyorum** I'd like some paracetamol

paraşüt [paraʃyt] n parachute

parça [partʃa] n bit, chip (small piece), chunk, part, piece, portion, scrap (small piece), (müzik) passage (musical); **iri parça** n lump; **kağıt parçası** n slip (paper); **yedek parça** n spare part

parçalamak [partʃalamak] vt smash

pardon [pardon] part **Pardon, anlayamadım** Sorry, I didn't catch that; **Pardon, orası benim yerim** Excuse me, that's my seat

parfüm [parfym] n perfume

park [park] n park; **konulu eğlence parkı** n theme park; **milli park** n national park; **park etme** n parking ▷ v **park etmek** v park; **yol kenarında geçici park yeri** n layby; **Arabamı buraya park edebilir miyim?** Can I park here?; **Arabamı nereye park edebilirim?** Where can I park the car?; **Karavanımızı buraya park edebilir miyiz?** Can we park our caravan here?; **Ne kadarlığına park edebilirim?** How long can I park here?; **Yanımıza park edebilir miyiz?** Can we park by our site?

parka [parka] n **su geçirmez parka** n cagoule

parkmetre [parkmetre] *n*
Parkmetre bozuk The parking
meter is broken; **Parkmetre için
bozuk paranız var mı?** Do you
have change for the parking
meter?

parkur [parkur] *n* **yarış parkuru** *n*
racecourse

parlak [parlak] *adj* bright, shiny;
parlak alev *n* blaze

parlamak [parlamak] *v* shine ▷ *vi*
flash

parlamento [parlamento] *n*
parliament

parmak [parmak] *n* finger; **ayak
parmağı** *n* toe; **baş parmak** *n*
thumb; **işaret parmağı** *n* index
finger; **parmak izi** *n* fingerprint;
parmaklarının ucunda yürüme
n tiptoe; **parmaksız eldiven** *n*
mitten

parmaklık [parmaklək] *n* rail ▷ *npl*
railings

parti [parti] *n (grup)* party *(group)*,
(sosyal etkinlik) party *(social
gathering)*; **bekarlığa veda
partisi** *(erkek) n* stag night;
yemekli parti *n* dinner party

partner [partner] *n* partner; **Bu
partnerim** This is my partner;
Partnerim var I have a partner

pas [pas] *n (metal)* rust;
paslanmaz çelik *n* stainless steel

pasaklı [pasaklə] *adj* sloppy

pasaport [pasaport] *n* passport;
pasaport kontrol *n* passport
control; **İşte pasaportum** Here is
my passport; **Çocuk bu
pasaportta** The child is on this
passport; **Çocuklar bu
pasaportta** The children are on
this passport; **Pasaportum
çalındı** My passport has been
stolen; **Pasaportumu kaybettim**
I've lost my passport;
Pasaportumu unutmuşum I've
forgotten my passport

pasif [pasif] *adj* passive

Pasifik [pasifik] *n* Pacific

Paskalya [paskalja] *n* Easter;
Paskalya yumurtası *n* Easter egg

paslı [paslə] *adj* rusty

paso [paso] *n* pass *(permit)*

paspas [paspas] *n (ayak silme)*
mat, *(yer silme)* mop

paspaslamak [paspaslamak] *v*
mop up

pasta [pasta] *n* cake; **kremalı
pasta** *n* gateau; **pastanın
üzerindeki şekerli süsleme** *n*
icing

pastırma [pastərma] *n* **domuz
pastırması** *n* bacon

pastörize [pastørize] *adj*
pasteurized

patates [patates] **(patatesler)** *n*
potato; **patates kızartması** *npl*
chips; **patates püresi** *n* mashed
potatoes; **patates soyucu** *n*
potato peeler

patavatsız [patavatsəz] *adj*
tactless

paten [paten] *npl* rollerskates; **buz
pateni** *n* ice-skating; **buz pateni
sahası** *n* ice rink; **paten alanı** *n*
rink, skating rink; **paten yapma** *n*
skating ▷ *v* **paten yapmak** *v*
skate; **patenle kaymak** *n*
rollerskating

patenler [patenler] *npl* skates

patik [patik] *n* **bale patiği** *npl*
ballet shoes

patika [patika] *n* footpath, lane
(driving), path; **Patikadan
ayrılmayın** Keep to the path

patlak [patlak] *n* puncture

patlama [patlama] *n* blast,
explosion; **patlama sesi** *n* bang

patlamak [patlamak] *v*
(delinerek) burst, *(havaya uçarak)*
explode, *(ses çıkararak)* bang

patlayıcı [patlajədʒə] *adj*
patlayıcı madde *n* explosive

patlıcan [patlədʒan] *n* aubergine

patron [patron] *n* boss; **patronluk
taslamak** *v* boss around

pay [paj] *n* share; **boşluk payı**
(tavanda) *n* headroom

payalamak [pajalamak] *v* tick off

paylaşmak [pajlaʃmak] *v* share,
(iş/masraf) club together;
(computer) post

paylaştırmak [pajlaʃtərmak] *v*
share out

pazar [pazar] *n* *(piyasa)* market;
pazar araştırması *n* market
research; **pazar yeri** *n* marketplace

Pazar [pazar] *n* Sunday; **Üç Ekim
Pazar** It's Sunday the third of
October; **Pazar günü** on Sunday

pazarlama [pazarlama] *n*
marketing

pazarlık [pazarlək] *n* bargain;
pazarlık etmek *v* haggle

Pazartesi [pazartesi] *n* Monday;
**Pazartesi'den Çarşamba'ya
kadar kalmak istiyorum** I want
to stay from Monday till
Wednesday; **Pazartesi'nden beri
kusuyorum** I've been sick since

Monday; **On beş Haziran
Pazartesi** It's Monday the
fifteenth of June; **Pazartesi günü**
on Monday

PC [pi.si:] *n* PC

PDF [pi:di:ef] *n* PDF

peçe [petʃe] *n* veil

peçete [petʃete] *n* napkin; **kağıt
peçete** *n* serviette

ped [ped] *n* pad, sanitary towel;
fare pedi *n* mouse mat

pedal [pedal] *n* pedal; **gaz pedalı** *n*
accelerator

pedofil [pedofil] *n* paedophile

pekala [pekala] *adv* fine

Pekin [pekin] *n* Beijing

Pekinez [pekinez] *n* Pekinese

pelikan [pelikan] *n* pelican

pembe [pembe] *adj* pink; **pembe
şarap** *n* rosé; **pembemsi leylak
rengi** *adj* mauve

penaltı [penaltə] *n* penalty

pencere [pendʒere] *n* window;
pencere camı *n* window pane;
pencere pervazı *n* windowsill;
**Koltuğum pencere kenarında
olsun** I'd like a window seat;
Pencere açılmıyor The window
won't open; **Pencereyi açabilir
miyim?** May I open the window?;
Pencereyi açamıyorum I can't
open the window; **Pencereyi
kapatabilir miyim?** May I close
the window?

pençe [pentʃe] *n* claw, paw

penguen [penguen] *n* penguin

peni [peni] *n* penny

penisilin [penisilin] *n* penicillin;
Penisiline alerjim var I'm allergic
to penicillin

pense [pense] *npl* pliers
pentatlon [pentatlon] *n*
pentathlon
perakende [perakende] *n* retail;
perakende fiyatı *n* retail price
perakendeci [perakendedʒi] *n*
retailer
perde [perde] *n* curtain, *(ses)* pitch
(sound)
performans [performans] *n*
performance *(functioning)*;
performans göstermek *v*
perform; **sahne performansı** *n*
performance *(artistic)*
perhiz [perhiz] *n* diet, fast; **büyük
perhizin arife günü** *n* Shrove
Tuesday; **Büyük perhizin ilk
Çarşambası** *n* Ash Wednesday
peri [peri] *n* fairy; **peri masalı** *n*
fairytale
perili [perili] *adj* haunted
perma [perma] *n* perm; **Saçım
permalı** My hair is permed
personel [personel] *n* personnel
perspektif [perspektif] *n*
perspective
Perşembe [perʃembe] *n* Thursday;
Perşembe günü on Thursday
Peru [peru] *adj* Peruvian ▷ *n* Peru
peruk [peruk] *n* wig; **yarım peruk**
n toupee
Perulu [perulu] *n* Peruvian
peş [peʃ] *n, v* **peşine takılmak** *v*
pursue
pet [pet] *nf* can
petrol [petrol] *n* **petrol kuyusu** *n*
oil well; **petrol platformu** *n* oil
rig, rig; **petrol rafinerisi** *n* oil
refinery; **petrol sızması** *n* oil slick
peynir [pejnir] *n* cheese; **süzme**

peynir *n* cottage cheese
pırasa [pərasa] *n* leek
pırıl pırıl [pərəlpərəl] *adj* brilliant
pijama [piʒama] *npl* pyjamas
piknik [piknik] *n* picnic
piksel [piksel] *n* pixel
pil [pil] *n* battery; **kalp pili** *n*
pacemaker; **Bu makineye uygun
pil var mı?** Do you have batteries
for this camera?; **Pil satıyor
musunuz?** Do you have any
batteries?
pilot [pilot] *n* pilot
pint [pint] *n (içki)* pint
piramit [piramit] *n* pyramid
pire [pire] *n* flea
pirinç [pirintʃ] *n (metal)* brass,
(yiyecek) rice; **esmer pirinç** *n*
brown rice
pirzola [pirzola] *n* cutlet; **domuz
pirzolası** *n* pork chop
pis [pis] *adj* dirty; **pis kokulu** *adj*
smelly; **Oda pis** The room is dirty;
Pis It's dirty
piskopos [piskopos] *n* bishop
pist [pist] *n* **kayak alıştırma pisti**
n nursery slope; **uçak pisti** *n*
runway; **yarış pisti** *n* racetrack
piston [piston] *n* piston
pişirme [piʃirme] *n* cooking
pişirmek [piʃirmek] *v* boil, cook;
fırında pişirme *n* baking; **fırında
pişirmek** *v* bake; **fırında
pişirilmiş** *adj* baked
pişmanlık [piʃmanlək] *n* regret
piyade [pijade] *n* infantry
piyango [pijango] *n* lottery
piyanist [pijanist] *n* pianist
piyano [pijano] *n* piano
pizza [pizza] *n* pizza

plaj [plaʒ] n beach; **Buralarda iyi bir plaj var mı?** Are there any good beaches near here?; **Plaj ne kadar uzakta?** How far is the beach?; **Plaja gidiyorum** I'm going to the beach; **Plaja otobüs var mı?** Is there a bus to the beach?; **Plajdan ne kadar uzaktayız?** How far are we from the beach?

plaka [plaka] n (otomobil) number plate

plaket [plaket] n plaque

plan [plan] n plan, scheme; **arka plan** n background; **ön plan** n foreground; **gizli plan** v plot (conspire); **şehir planlama** n town planning; **sokak planı** n street plan

planlama [planlama] n planning

planlamak [planlamak] v plan

planör [planør] n glider; **planörle uçma** n gliding

plastik [plastik] adj plastic ▷ n plastic; **plastik cerrahi** n plastic surgery

platform [platform] n platform; **petrol platformu** n oil rig, rig; **... treni hangi platformdan kalkıyor?** Which platform does the train for... leave from?; **... treninin kalkacağı platform burası mı?** Is this the right platform for the train to...?; **Tren hangi platformdan kalkıyor?** Which platform does the train leave from?

platin [platin] n platinum

PlayStation® [plajstation] n PlayStation®

plazma [plazma] n **plazma ekran** n plasma screen; **plazma TV** n plasma TV

pnömatik [pnømatik] adj **pnömatik matkap** n pneumatic drill

podcast [poddʒast] n podcast

pohpohlamak [pohpohlamak] v flatter

pohpohlanmış [pohpohlanməʃ] adj flattered

poker [poker] n poker

poliklinik [poliklinik] n clinic

polis [polis] n police; **erkek polis** n police officer, policeman; **kadın polis** n police officer, policewoman; **polis görevlisi** n police officer; **polis istasyonu** n police station; **Polis çağırın** Call the police; **Polis karakolu nerede?** Where is the police station?; **Polis karakolunu arıyorum** I need to find a police station; **Polise haber vermemiz gerekiyor** We will have to report it to the police; **Sigortam için polise bildirmemiz gerekiyor** I need a police report for my insurance

polisiye [polisije] n thriller

politik [politik] adj political

politika [politika] npl politics

politikacı [politikadʒə] n politician

polo [polo] n **polo gömlek** n polo shirt; **polo yakalı kazak** n polo-necked sweater

Polonezce [polonezdʒe] n (dil) Polynesian (language)

Polonezya [polonezja] adj Polynesian; **Polonezya Adaları** n Polynesia

Polonezyalı [polonezjalə] *n (kişi)* Polynesian *(person)*

Polonya [polonja] *adj* Polish ▷ *n* Poland

Polonyalı [polonjalə] *n* Polish

pompa [pompa] *n* pump; **bisiklet pompası** *n* bicycle pump; **Bisiklet pompanız var mı?** Do you have a bicycle pump?

pompalamak [pompalamak] *v* pump

popüler [popyler] *adj* popular; **popüler olmayan** *adj* unpopular

popülerlik [popylerlik] *n* popularity

porno [porno] *n* porn

pornografi [pornografi] *n* pornography

pornografik [pornografik] *adj* pornographic

porselen [porselen] *n* china

porsuk [porsuk] *n* badger; **porsuk ağacı** *n* yew

port [port] *n* **port bagaj** *n* luggage rack, roof rack

portakal [portakal] *n* orange; **portakal rengi** *adj* orange; **portakal suyu** *n* orange juice

portatif [portatif] *adj* portable; **portatif karyola** *n* camp bed

portbebe [portbebe] *n* carrycot

Portekiz [portekiz] *adj* Portuguese ▷ *n* Portugal

Portekizce [portekizdʒe] *n (dil)* Portuguese *(language)*

Portekizli [portekizli] *n (kişi)* Portuguese *(person)*

portföy [portføj] *n* portfolio

porto [porto] *n* **porto şarabı** *n* port *(wine)*

Portoriko [portoriko] *n* Puerto Rico

portre [portre] *n* portrait

post [post] *n* fleece; **koyun postu** *n* sheepskin

posta [posta] *n* mail, post *(mail)*; **istenmeyen posta** *n* junk mail; **posta ücreti** *n* postage; **posta damgası** *n* postmark; **posta havalesi** *n* postal order; **posta kutusu** *n* letterbox, mailbox, postbox; **sesli posta** *n* voicemail; **uçak postası** *n* airmail; **Acele posta ile ne kadar zamanda gider?** How long will it take by priority post?; **Normal postayla ne kadar sürer?** How long will it take by normal post?

postacı [postadʒə] **(postacılar)** *n* postman; **kadın postacı** *n* postwoman

postalamak [postalamak] *v* mail, post

postane [postane] *n* post office; **Postane ne zaman açılıyor?** When does the post office open?

poster [poster] *n* poster

potansiyel [potansijel] *adj* potential ▷ *n* potential

pound [pound] *n (İngiliz ağırlık birimi)* pound; **pound sterlin** *(İngiliz para birimi)* *n* pound sterling

pozisyon [pozisjon] *n* position

pratik [pratik] *adj* practical ▷ *n* practice; **pratik olarak** *adv* practically; **pratik olmayan** *adj* impractical; **pratik yapmak** *v* practise

pratisyen [pratisjen] *n* **pratisyen hekim** *n* GP

prens [prens] n prince
prenses [prenses] n princess
pres [pres] n press, *(spor)* push-up
Presbiteryan [presbiterjan] adj
Presbyterian ▷ n Presbyterian
prestij [prestiʒ] n prestige
prezervatif [prezervatif] n
condom
prim [prim] n bonus
priz [priz] n socket
profesör [profesør] n professor
profesyonel [profesjonel] adj
professional ▷ n professional
profesyonelce [profesjoneldʒe]
adv professionally
profil [profil] n profile; **profil
fotoğrafı** n profile picture
program [program] n program,
programme, schedule, timetable;
sohbet programı n chat show;
Programa uygun gidiyoruz We
are on schedule; **Programın
gerisindeyiz** We are slightly
behind schedule
programcı [programdʒə] n
programmer
programlama [programlama] n
programming
programlamak [programlamak]
v program
proje [proʒe] n project
projektör [proʒektør] n overhead
projector, projector; **projektör
ışığı** n floodlight
propaganda [propaganda] n
propaganda; **oy propagandası
yapmak** v canvass
protein [protein] n protein
Protestan [protestan] adj
Protestant ▷ n Protestant

protesto [protesto] n protest ▷ v
protesto etmek v protest
prova [prova] n rehearsal
psikiyatrik [psikijatrik] adj
psychiatric
psikiyatrist [psikijatrist] n
psychiatrist
psikolog [psikolog] n psychologist
psikoloji [psikoloʒi] n psychology
psikolojik [psikoloʒik] adj
psychological
psikoterapi [psikoterapi] n
psychotherapy
puding [puding] n pudding
pudra [pudra] n powder; **talk
pudrası** n talcum powder
pul [pul] n stamp, *(balık)* scale *(tiny
piece)*; **Pul nereden alabilirim?**
Where can I buy stamps?; **Pul
satan en yakın yer nerede?**
Where is the nearest shop which
sells stamps?; **Pul satıyor
musunuz?** Do you sell stamps?
pulluk [pulluk] n plough
punkçu [puɲtʃu] n punk
puro [puro] n cigar
puset [puset] n pushchair
pusula [pusula] n compass
pürüzsüz [pyryssyz] adj smooth
püskürtmek [pyskyrtmek] v
spray

q r

Quaker [kuaker] *n* **Quaker mezhebinden** *n* Quaker

radar [radar] *n* radar
radyasyon [radjasjon] *n* radiation
radyatör [radjatør] *n* radiator; **Radyatör sızıntı yapıyor** There is a leak in the radiator
radyo [radjo] *n* radio; **dijital radyo** *n* digital radio; **radyo istasyonu** *n* radio station; **Radyoyu açabilir miyim?** Can I switch the radio on?; **Radyoyu kapatabilir miyim?** Can I switch the radio off?
radyoaktif [radjoaktif] *adj* radioactive
raf [raf] **(raflar)** *n* shelf; **kitap rafı** *n* bookshelf; **şömine rafı** *n* mantelpiece
rafineri [rafineri] *n* refinery; **petrol rafinerisi** *n* oil refinery
rağmen [ra:men] *conj* although
rahat [rahat] *adj* comfortable, cosy, laid-back, relaxed

ʼahatlamış [rahatlaməʃ] *adj*
relieved

ʼahatlık [rahatlək] *n* peace,
comfort; **iç rahatlığı** *n* relief;
konfor ve rahatlık *npl* mod cons

ʼahatsız [rahatsəz] *adj*
inconvenient, uncomfortable;
rahatsız etmek *v* disturb

ʼahatsızlık [rahatsəzlək] *n*
inconvenience

ʼahibe [rahibe] *n* nun

ʼahip [rahip] *n* priest

ʼaket [raket] *n* racket *(racquet)*,
racquet; **tenis raketi** *n* tennis
racket; **Raket kiralıyorlar mı?**
Do they hire out rackets?; **Raket
nereden kiralayabilirim?** Where
can I hire a racket?

ʼakip [rakip] *adj* rival ▷ *n* adversary,
rival; **rakip sahada maç** *n* away
match

ʼakun [rakun] *n* racoon

Ramazan [ramazan] *n* Ramadan

ʼampa [rampa] *n* ramp

ʼandevu [randevu] *n* appointment,
engagement, rendezvous;
... ile randevum vardı I have an
appointment with...; **Doktordan
randevu alabilir miyim?** Can I have
an appointment with the doctor?;
Randevu almak istiyorum I'd like
to make an appointment;
Randevunuz var mıydı? Do you
have an appointment?

ʼanza [ranza] *n* berth, bunk, bunk
beds

ʼapor [rapor] *n* report ▷ *v* **rapor
vermek** *v* report

ʼaptiye [raptije] *n* drawing pin,
thumb tack

rastgele [rastgele] *adj* random

rastlantı [rastlantə] *n*
coincidence

ravent [ravent] *n* rhubarb

ray [raj] *n* rail

reaktör [reaktør] *n* reactor

reçel [retʃel] *n* jam; **reçel
kavanozu** *n* jam jar

reçete [retʃete] *n* prescription; **Bu
reçeteyi nerede yaptırabilirim**
Where can I get this prescription
made up?

reçine [retʃine] *n* resin

red [red] *n* refusal

reddetme [reddetme] *n* refuse

reddetmek [reddetmek] *v* refuse,
reject

reddeylemek [reddejlemek] *v*
ignore

referans [referans] *n* reference;
referans kitabı *n* handbook;
referans numarası *n* reference
number

refleks [refleks] *n* reflex

regl [regl] *n* menstruation

rehber [rehber] *n* **rehber köpek** *n*
guide dog; **rehberli tur** *n* guided
tour; **rehberlik etmek** *v* conduct;
telefon rehberi *n* telephone
directory; **telefon rehberi** *n*
directory; **tur rehberi** *n* tour
guide; **İngilizce rehberli turunuz
var mı?** Is there a guided tour in
English?; **Rehber köpeğim var**
I have a guide dog; **Rehberli tur
kaçta başlıyor?** What time does
the guided tour begin?; **Rehberli
yürüyüş var mı?** Are there any
guided walks?

rehberlik [rehberlik] *n* **Bana**

rehberlik eder misiniz lütfen
Can you guide me, please?
rehinci [rehindʒi] *n* pawnbroker
rehine [rehine] *n* hostage
rekabet [rekabet] *n* rivalry;
rekabete açık *adj* competitive
reklam [reklam] *n* ad, advert,
advertisement, commercial;
reklam arası *n* commercial break;
reklam yapmak *v* advertise
reklamcılık [reklamdʒələk] *n*
advertising
ren [ren] *v* **ren geyiği** *n* reindeer
rende [rende] *n* plane *(tool)*
rendelemek [rendelemek] *v*
grate
reng [reng] *n* **vişne çürüğü**
renginde *adj* maroon
renk [renk] *n* colour; **açık renk** *(ten/
saç)* *adj* fair *(light colour)*; **krem
renkli** *adj* cream; **leylak renkli** *adj*
lilac; **pembemsi leylak rengi** *adj*
mauve; **portakal rengi** *adj*
orange; **renk körü** *adj*
colour-blind; **renkli televizyon** *n*
colour television; **türkuvaz renkli**
adj turquoise; **Bu makine için
renkli film istiyorum** I need a
colour film for this camera; **Bu
rengi sevmedim** I don't like the
colour; **Bu renk olsun** This colour,
please; **Bunun başka rengi var
mı?** Do you have this in another
colour?; **Bunun renkli
fotokopisini istiyorum lütfen**
I'd like a colour photocopy of this,
please; **Renkli film istiyorum
lütfen** A colour film, please
renkli [renli] *adj* colourful,
in colour

resepsiyon [resepsijon] *n*
reception
resepsiyonist [resepsijonist] *n*
receptionist
resim [resim] *n* painting, picture;
resim çerçevesi *n* picture frame
resimleme [resimleme] *n (kitabı)*
illustration
resmi [resmi] *adj* formal; **resmi
olmayan** *adj* unofficial; **resmi
tatil günü** *n* public holiday
ressam [ressam] *n* painter
restoran [restoran] *n* restaurant;
**İyi bir restoran tavsiye edebilir
misiniz?** Can you recommend a
good restaurant?
restore [restore] *v* **restore etmek**
v restore
reşit [reʃit] *n, adj* adult; **reşit
olmayan** *adj* underage
revir [revir] *n* infirmary
revizyon [revizjon] *n* check-up,
revision
revolver [revolver] *n* revolver
rezene [rezene] *n* fennel
rezervasyon [rezervasjon] *n*
booking; **önceden rezervasyon**
advance booking; **rezerve etmek**
v book; **Masa bu akşam saat
dokuz için rezerve edildi** The
table is booked for nine o'clock thi
evening; **Rezervasyonumu
değiştirebilir miyim?** Can I
change my booking?;
**Rezervasyonumu iptal
ettirmek istiyorum** I want to
cancel my booking;
**Rezervasyonumu mektupla
teyid etmiştim** I confirmed my
booking by letter

rıhtım [rəhtəm] n jetty, pier

rica [ridʒa] n appeal, request ▷ v
  rica etmek v appeal, request

rimel [rimel] n eyeliner, mascara

ringa [ringa] n **ringa balığı** n
  herring

risk [risk] n risk ▷ v **risk almak** v
  risk

riskli [riskli] adj risky

ritim [ritim] n beat, rhythm

robot [robot] n robot; **mutfak
  robotu** n food processor

roket [roket] n rocket

rollercoaster [rollerdʒoaster] n
  rollercoaster

rom [rom] n rum

roman [roman] n novel

romancı [romandʒə] n novelist

Romanesk [romanesk] adj
  Romanesque

romantik [romantik] adj
  romantic

Romanya [romanja] n Romania

romatizma [romatizma] n
  rheumatism

Romen [romen] adj Roman,
  Romanian

römork [rømork] n trailer

röntgen [røntgen] n X-ray ▷ v
  röntgenini çekmek v X-ray

rugbi [rugbi] n rugby

ruh [ruh] n soul, spirit; **ruh
  durumu** n mood; **ruh hali** n
  temper

ruj [ruʒ] n lipstick

rulet [rulet] n roulette

Rumen [rumen] n (kişi) Romanian
  (person)

Rumence [rumendʒe] n (dil)
  Romanian (language)

Rus [rus] adj Russian ▷ n (kişi)
  Russian (person)

Rusça [rustʃa] n (dil) Russian
  (language)

Rusya [rusja] n Russia

rüşvet [ryʃvet] n bribery ▷ v **rüşvet
  vermek** v bribe

rütbe [rytbe] n rank (status)

rüzgar [ryzgar] n wind; **ani rüzgar**
  n gust; **hafif rüzgar** n breeze;
  şiddetli rüzgar n gale; **rüzgar
  sörfü** n windsurfing; **rüzgara
  açık** adj bleak; **Rüzgar sörfü
  yapmak istiyorum** I'd like to go
  windsurfing

rüzgarlı [ryzgarlə] adj windy

S

saat [saat] *n (fırın vb)* timer, *(genelde)* clock, *(zaman)* hour; **açılış saatleri** *npl* opening hours; **çalar saat** *n* alarm clock; **çalışma saatleri** *npl* office hours; **çay saati** *n* teatime; **dijital saat** *n* digital watch; **esnek çalışma saati** *n* flexitime; **geç saatlere kadar oturmak** *v* stay up; **iş saatleri dışında** *adv* off-peak; **kapanış saati** *n* closing time; **kol saati** *n* watch; **oyun saati** *n* playtime; **saat başı** *adv* hourly; **saat kayışı** *n* watch strap; **saat yönünde** *adv* clockwise; **saatin aksi yönünde** *adv* anticlockwise; **saatli bomba** *n* time bomb; **sıkışık saat** *npl* peak hours; **sıkışık saatler** *n* rush hour; **yarım saat** *n* half-hour; **ziyaret saatleri** *npl* visiting hours; **Bir saatlik internet bağlantısı kaça?** How much is it to log on for an hour?; **Saati ne kadar?** How much is it per hour?; **Yolculuk iki saat sürüyor** The journey takes two hours; **Ziyaret saatleri nedir?** When are visiting hours?

sabah [sabah] *n* in the morning, morning; **bu sabah** this morning; **Beni yarın sabah yedide uyandırır mısınız?** I'd like an alarm call for tomorrow morning at seven o'clock; **Bu sabahtan beri kusuyorum** I've been sick since this morning; **Müze sabahları açık mı?** Is the museum open in the morning?; **Otobüs sabah kaçta hareket ediyor?** When does the coach leave in the morning?; **yarın sabah** tomorrow morning; **Yarın sabah boşum** I'm free tomorrow morning; **Yarın sabah onda ayrılıyorum** I will be leaving tomorrow morning at ten a.m.

sabahlık [sabahlək] *n* dressing gown

sabır [sabər] *n* patience

sabırlı [sabərlə] *adj* patient

sabırsız [sabərsəz] *adj* impatient

sabırsızlık [sabərsəzlək] *n* impatience

sabırsızlıkla [sabərsəzləkla] *adv* impatiently

sabit [sabit] *adj (değişmez)* constant, *(dengeli)* steady

sabitlemek [sabitlemek] *vt* fix

sabitlenmiş [sabitlenmiʃ] *adj* fixed

sabotaj [sabotaʒ] *n* sabotage; **sabote etmek** *v* sabotage

sabretmek [sabretmek] v hang on
sabun [sabun] n soap; **sabun tozu**
n soap powder; **Sabun yok** There
is no soap
sabunluk [sabunluk] n soap dish
saç [satʃ] n hair; **beyaz saçlı** adj
grey-haired; **kızıl saçlı** n
red-haired, redhead; **kızılımsı sarı**
saçlı adj ginger; **saç örgüsü** n
pigtail, plait; **saç bandı** n
hairband; **saç fırçası** n hairbrush;
saç jölesi n hair gel; **saç kestirme**
n haircut; **saç kremi** n
conditioner; **saç kurutma**
makinesi n hairdryer; **saç maşası**
npl straighteners; **saç modeli** n
hairdo, hairstyle; **saç spreyi** n hair
spray; **saç tokası** n hairgrip; **Saç**
kurutma makinesine ihtiyacım
var I need a hair dryer; **Saçım**
doğuştan düz My hair is naturally
straight; **Saçım doğuştan**
kıvırcık My hair is naturally curly;
Saçım kuru I have dry hair; **Saçım**
permalı My hair is permed; **Saçım**
röfleli My hair is highlighted;
Saçım yağlı I have greasy hair;
Saçıma ne tavsiye edersiniz?
What do you recommend for my
hair?; **Saçımı boyar mısınız**
lütfen? Can you dye my hair,
please?; **Saçımı düzleştirebilir**
misiniz? Can you straighten my
hair?; **Saçımı yıkar mısınız**
lütfen? Can you wash my hair,
please?
saçma [satʃma] adj absurd ▷ n
nonsense
saçmalamak [satʃmalamak]
v rave

sadakat [sadakat] n loyalty
sadakatle [sadakatle] adv
faithfully
sadakatsiz [sadakatsiz] adj
unfaithful
sade [sade] adj plain; **sade**
çikolata n plain chocolate
sadece [sadedʒe] adj mere
sadık [sadək] adj faithful
saf [saf] adj daft, naive, pure
safari [safari] n safari
safir [safir] n sapphire
safra [safra] n **safra kesesi** n gall
bladder; **safra kesesi taşı** n
gallstone
safran [safran] n saffron
sağ [sa:] adj (yan, yön) right (not
left); **sağ elini kullanan** adj
right-handed; **sağ kanat** adj
right-wing; **sağdan trafik** n
right-hand drive; **Sağa dönün**
Turn right; **Sağdan ilk sokağa**
dönün Take the first turning on
your right
sağanak [sa:anak] n downpour
sağdıç [sa:dətʃ] n best man
sağduyu [sa:duju] n common
sense, discretion
sağduyulu [sa:dujulu] adj
sensible
sağır [sa:ər] adj deaf; **sağır edici**
adj deafening; **Sağırım** I'm deaf
sağlam [sa:lam] adj sound, tough
sağlamak [sa:lamak] v provide;
ürün sağlamak v yield; **geçimini**
sağlamak v provide for; **mali**
destek sağlamak v subsidize;
yarar sağlamak v benefit
sağlıcakla [sa:lədʒakla] excl
cheerio!

sağlık [sa:lək] *n* health; **sağlık belgesi** *n* medical certificate; **sağlıklı yaşam** *n* keep-fit; **Özel sağlık sigortam var** I have private health insurance; **Sağlık sigortam yok** I don't have health insurance

sağlıklı [sa:ləklə] *adj* healthy

sağlıksız [sa:ləksəz] *adj* unfit, unhealthy

sağmak [sa:mak] *v* milk

saha [saha] *n (spor)* pitch *(sport)*; **buz pateni sahası** *n* ice rink; **golf sahası** *n* golf course; **hava sahası** *n* airspace; **kendi sahasında maç** *n* home match; **rakip sahada maç** *n* away match

sahil [sahil] *n* **sahil koruma görevlisi** *n* coastguard

sahip [sahip] *n* owner; **ev sahibi** *n* host *(entertains)*, landlord; **ev sahibesi** *n* landlady; **hisse sahibi** *n* shareholder; **sahip çıkmak** *v* own up; **sahip olmak** *v* have, own, possess; **toprak sahibi** *n* landowner; **Buranın sahibiyle konuşabilir miyim lütfen** Could I speak to the owner, please?

sahipsiz [sahipsiz] *adj* unattended

sahne [sahne] *n (olay, bölüm)* scene, *(tiyatro mekan)* stage; **sahne performansı** *n* performance *(artistic)*

Sahra [sahra] *n* Sahara

sahte [sahte] *n* fake, forgery

sakal [sakal] *n* beard

sakallı [sakallə] *adj* bearded

sakar [sakar] *adj* clumsy

sakat [sakat] *n* invalid

sakatlık [sakatlək] *n* disability

sakınca [sakəndʒa] *n* **Sakıncası yok** I don't mind; **Sizce sakıncası var mı?** Do you mind?

sakız [sakəz] *n* gum

sakin [sakin] *adj* calm ▷ *n (konut)* inhabitant, *(konut)* resident

sakinleşmek [sakinleʃmek] *v* calm down

sakinleştirici [sakinleʃtiridʒi] *n* tranquillizer

saklamak [saklamak] *v (korumak)* reserve ▷ *vi* hide

saklambaç [saklambatʃ] *n* hide-and-seek

saklı [saklə] *adj* hidden

saksafon [saksafon] *n* saxophone

saksağan [saksa:an] *n* magpie

sal [sal] *n* float, raft

salak [salak] *n* idiot

salakça [salaktʃa] *adj* idiotic

salam [salam] *n* salami

salaş [salaʃ] *adj* naff

salata [salata] *n* salad; **karışık salata** *n* mixed salad; **lahana salatası** *n* coleslaw; **meyve salatası** *n* fruit salad; **salata sosu** *n* salad dressing; **sirkeli salata sosu** *n* vinaigrette; **yeşil salata** *n* green salad

salatalık [salatalək] *n* cucumber

saldırgan [saldərgan] *adj* aggressive, offensive

saldırı [saldərə] *n* attack, offence; **terörist saldırı** *n* terrorist attack; **Saldırıya uğradım** I've been attacked

saldırmak [saldərmak] *v* mug ▷ *vt* attack

salgın [salgən] *n* epidemic

Salı [salə] *n* Tuesday; **Salı günü** on Tuesday

salınmak [salənmak] *v* sway

sallamak [sallamak] *v* rock; **el sallamak** *v* wave

sallanan [sallanan] *adj* unsteady

sallanma [sallanma] *n* swing

sallanmak [sallanmak] *vi* swing; **sallanan at** *n* rocking horse; **sallanan sandalye** *n* rocking chair

salon [salon] *n* hall, lounge, saloon; **bowling salonu** *n* bowling alley; **güzellik salonu** *n* beauty salon; **jimnastik salonu** *n* gym; **oyun salonu** *n* amusement arcade; **salon dansı** *n* ballroom dancing; **transit yolcu salonu** *n* transit lounge; **uçuş bekleme salonu** *n* departure lounge; **yemek salonu** *n* dining room; **Konser salonunda bu gece ne var?** What's on tonight at the concert hall?; **Salonda kahve içebilir miyiz?** Could we have coffee in the lounge?

salyangoz [saljangoz] *n* snail

saman [saman] *n* hay, straw; **saman nezlesi** *n* hay fever; **saman yığını** *n* haystack; **saz ve saman çatılı** *adj* thatched

samanlık [samanlək] *n* barn

samimiyetsiz [samimijetsiz] *adj* insincere

sanal [sanal] *adj* virtual; **sanal gerçeklik** *n* virtual reality

sanat [sanat] *n* art; **sanat eseri** *n* work of art; **sanat galerisi** *n* art gallery; **sanat okulu** *n* art school

sanatçı [sanattʃə] *n* artist

sanatsal [sanatsal] *adj* artistic

sanayi [sanaji] *n* industry; **eğlence sanayii** *n* show business; **sanayi sitesi** *n* industrial estate

sandal [sandal] *n* **cankurtaran sandalı** *n* lifeboat

sandalet [sandalet] *n* sandal

sandalye [sandalje] *n* chair *(furniture)*, seat *(furniture)*; **bebe sandalyesi** *n* highchair; **sallanan sandalye** *n* rocking chair; **tekerlekli sandalye** *n* wheelchair; **Bebek sandalyeniz var mı?** Do you have a baby seat?; **Mama sandalyeniz var mı?** Do you have a high chair?

sandık [sandək] *n* chest *(storage)*

sandviç [sandvitʃ] *n* sandwich; **sosisli sandviç** *n* hot dog; **Sandviç olarak ne var?** What kind of sandwiches do you have?

sanık [sanək] *n* accused

San Marino [sanmarino] *n* San Marino

sansasyonel [sansasjonel] *adj* sensational

Santigrat [santigrat] *n* **Santigrat derece** *n* degree centigrade, degree Celsius

santimetre [santimetre] *n* centimetre

santral [santral] *n* switchboard

sap [sap] *n* **kereviz sapı** *n* celery; **saplı tencere** *n* saucepan

sara [sara] *n* epilepsy; **sara nöbeti** *n* epileptic seizure

saray [saraj] *n* palace; **Saray halka açık mı?** Is the palace open to the public?; **Saray ne zaman açık?** When is the palace open?

sardalya [sardalja] *n* sardine
sardunya [sardunja] *n* geranium
sargı [sargə] *n* bandage; **Sargı yapar mısınız?** I'd like a bandage; **Sargılarımı değiştirir misiniz?** I'd like a fresh bandage
sarhoş [sarhoʃ] *adj* drunk ▷ *n* drunk; **dut gibi sarhoş** *adj* pissed *(inf!)*
sarı [sarə] *adj* yellow; **kızılımsı sarı saçlı** *adj* ginger; **sarı şalgam** *n* swede; **yumurta sarısı** *n* egg yolk; **yumurtanın sarısı** *n* yolk
Sarı [sarə] *adj* **Sarı Sayfalar** *npl* Yellow Pages®
sarılık [sarələk] *n* jaundice
sarımsak [sarəmsak] *n* garlic; **Bunda sarımsak var mı?** Is there any garlic in it?
sarışın [sarəʃən] *adj* blonde; **Doğma büyüme sarışınım** My hair is naturally blonde
sarkmak [sarkmak] *v* to hang; **dışarıya sarkmak** *v* lean out
sarmak [sarmak] *v* bandage, do up, wrap; **geri sarmak** *v* rewind; **Sarar mısınız lütfen?** Could you wrap it up for me, please?
sarmaşık [sarmaʃək] *n* ivy
sarsılmış [sarsəlməʃ] *adj* shaken
sarsıntı [sarsəntə] *n* concussion
satıcı [satədʒə] **(satıcı kadınlar)** *n* saleswoman, *(erkek)* salesman, dealer, salesperson, supplier, vendor; **uyuşturucu satıcısı** *n* drug dealer
satın [satən] *v* **satın alınmış** *adj* bought; **satın alma** *(şirket)* *n* buyout; **satın almak** *v* buy
satış [satəʃ] *n* sale; **otomatik satış makinesi** *n* vending machine; **satış elemanı** *n* sales rep, shop assistant; **satış fiyatı** *n* selling price; **son satış tarihi** *n* sell-by date; **telefonla satış** *npl* telesales; **toptan satış** *adj* wholesale
satmak [satmak] *vt* sell; **hepsini satmak** *v* sell out; **perakende satmak** *v* retail
satnav [satnav] *n* sat nav
satranç [satrantʃ] *n* chess
sauna [sauna] *n* sauna
savaş [savaʃ] *n* war; **iç savaş** *n* civil war
savaşmak [savaʃmak] *v* fight
savruk [savruk] *adj* extravagant
savunma [savunma] *n* defence
savunmasız [savunmasəz] *adj* vulnerable
savunucu [savunudʒu] *n* defender
savurmak [savurmak] *v* fling
sayaç [sajatʃ] *n* meter; **Gaz sayacı nerede?** Where is the gas meter?
saydam [sajdam] *adj* transparent
sayfa [sajfa] *n* page; **açılış sayfası** *n* home page; **Lütfen Arka Sayfaya Bakınız** *abbr* PTO; **Sarı Sayfalar** *npl* Yellow Pages®
saygı [sajgə] *n* regard, respect ▷ *v* **saygı duymak** *v* respect
saygıdeğer [sajgəde:er] *adj* reputable, respectable
saygın [sajgən] *adj* prestigious
sayı [sajə] *n* number, *(maç/oyun)* score *(game/match)* ▷ *v* **sayı yapmak** *v* score
sayım [sajəm] *n* **nüfus sayımı** *n* census

sayımlama [sajǝmlama] *npl* statistics

sayısız [sajǝsǝz] *adj* numerous

saymak [sajmak] *v* count

sayvan [sajvan] *n* pavilion

saz [saz] *n* **saz ve saman çatılı** *adj* thatched

sci-fi [sdʒifi] *n* sci-fi

seans [seans] *n* session

sebep [sebep] *n* motive; **bu sebeple** *adv* therefore

sebze [sebze] *n* vegetable; **Sebze de dahil mi?** Are the vegetables included?; **Sebzeleriniz taze mi, dondurulmuş mu?** Are the vegetables fresh or frozen?

seçenek [setʃenek] *n* alternative, option

seçilmiş [setʃilmiʃ] *adj* chosen

seçim [setʃim] *n* choice, election; **genel seçim** *n* general election

seçme [setʃme] *n* selection

seçmek [setʃmek] *v* choose, elect, pick out, select

seçmen [setʃmen] *n* voter; **seçmen bölgesi** *n* constituency, electorate

sedan [sedan] *n* **sedan araba** *n* saloon car

sedye [sedje] *n* stretcher

sefalet [sefalet] *n* misery

sefer [sefer] *n* journey; **bir seferinde** *adv* once; **bir seferlik** *n* one-off; **karşılıklı sefer yapan araç** *n* shuttle

sehpa [sehpa] *n* coffee table

sekiz [sekiz] *number* eight; **Sekiz matinesine iki bilet lütfen** two for the eight o'clock showing

sekizinci [sekizindʒi] *adj* eighth ▷ *n* eighth

sekreter [sekreter] *n* secretary; **Sekreterine mesaj bırakabilir miyim?** Can I leave a message with his secretary?

seksen [seksen] *number* eighty

seksi [seksi] *adj* sexy

seksilik [seksilik] *n* sexuality

sektör [sektør] *n* sector

sel [sel] *n* flood

selam [selam] *excl* hi!

selamlamak [selamlamak] *v* greet, salute

selamlaşma [selamlaʃma] *n* greeting

sele [sele] *n* seat, saddle; **Bu sele rahat değil** The seat is uncomfy; **Sele çok alçak** The seat is too low; **Sele çok yüksek** The seat is too high

selef [selef] *n* predecessor

self-catering [selfdʒatering] *n* self-catering

selfservis [selfservis] *adj* self-service

seloteyp [selotejp] *n* Sellotape®

sembol [sembol] *n* symbol

semer [semer] *n* saddle

sen [sen] *pron* you (*singular*); **Seni seviyorum** I love you

sendelemek [sendelemek] *v* stagger

sendika [sendika] *n* trade union

sendikacı [sendikadʒǝ] *n* trade unionist

sendrom [sendrom] *n* **Down sendromu** *n* Down's syndrome

Senegal [senegal] *adj* Senegalese ▷ *n* Senegal

Senegalli [senegalli] n Senegalese
senfoni [senfoni] n symphony
senin [senin] adj your *(singular)*
sent [sent] n *(para birimi)* cent
sepet [sepet] n basket; **çöp sepeti**
n dustbin, wastepaper basket
sepetlemek [sepetlemek] v ditch
sera [sera] n greenhouse
seramik [seramik] adj ceramic
serbest [serbest] adj free,
independent; **serbest çalışan** adj
self-employed; **serbest bırakma**
n release; **serbest bırakmak** v
release; **Serbest çalışıyorum** I'm
self-employed
serçe [sertʃe] n sparrow
sergi [sergi] n exhibition
sergileme [sergileme] n display
sergilemek [sergilemek] v display
seri [seri] n serial
serin [serin] adj cool *(cold)*;
serinletici içecek npl
refreshments
sermaye [sermaje] n **sermaye**
devri n turnover
sermek [sermek] v **yere sermek** v
knock out
serpinti [serpinti] n spray
sersem [sersem] n **Uçak**
sersemiyim I'm suffering from jet
lag
serseri [serseri] n tramp *(beggar)*
sert [sert] adj hard *(firm, rigid)*
sertifika [sertifika] n certificate
servet [servet] n fortune
servis [servis] n service; **gizli**
servis n secret service; **kaza & acil**
servis n accident & emergency
department; **oda servisi** n room
service; **servis atmak** n serve;

servis ücreti n cover charge,
service charge; **servis masası** n
trolley; **servis tabağı** n dish
(plate); **Çamaşır servisi var mı?**
Is there a laundry service?; **Çocuk**
bakıcı servisiniz var mı? Is there
a child-minding service?; **Oda**
servisi var mı? Is there room
service?; **Servis berbattı** The
service was terrible; **Servis dahil**
mi? Is service included?; **Servisten**
şikayetçiyim I want to complain
about the service; **Tamir servisini**
çağırabilir misiniz lütfen? Call
the breakdown service, please
ses [ses] n sound, voice; **çan sesi** n
toll; **patlama sesi** n bang; **ses**
kayıt cihazı n recorder *(music)*,
tape recorder; **ses sınavı** n
audition; **sesli posta** n voicemail;
yüksek sesle adv aloud, loudly;
yüksek sesle okumak v read out
sessiz [sessiz] adj quiet, silent;
Sessiz bir oda rica ediyorum I'd
like a quiet room
sessizce [sessizdʒe] adv quietly
sessizlik [sessizlik] n silence
sevecen [sevedʒen] adj
affectionate
sevgi [sevgi] n love
sevgili [sevgili] adj dear *(loved)*
Sevgili [sevgili] n **Sevgililer Günü**
n Valentine's Day
sevgilim [sevgilim] n darling
sevimli [sevimli] adj charming,
cute
sevinmek [sevinmek] v to be
pleased; **çok sevinmiş** adj thrilled
seviye [sevije] n level; **deniz**
seviyesi n sea level

sevmek [sevmek] v like, love;
... severim I love ...; **Seni
seviyorum** I love you
seyahat [sejahat] n journey,
travel; **gecelik seyahat çantası** n
overnight bag; **iş seyahati** n
business trip; **seyahat acentası** n
travel agency, travel agent's, (kişi)
travel agent; **seyahat çeki** n
traveller's cheque; **seyahat etme**
n travelling ▷ v **seyahat etmek** vi
travel; **seyahat sigortası** n travel
insurance; **Seyahat bulantım
var** I get travel-sick; **Seyahat
sigortam yok** I don't have travel
insurance; **Tek başıma seyahat
ediyorum** I'm travelling alone
seyis [sejis] n groom
sezmek [sezmek] v guess
sezon [sezon] n season; **pahalı
sezon** n high season; **sezon dışı/
sezon dışında** adv off-season;
ucuz sezon n low season; **yaz
sezonu** n summertime
sıcak [sədʒak] adj hot; **boğucu
sıcak** adj sweltering; **sıcak su
torbası** n hot-water bottle;
Çok sıcak It's very hot; **Çok
sıcakladım** I'm too hot; **Biraz
fazla sıcak** It's a bit too hot;
Oda çok sıcak The room is
too hot; **Sıcak su yok** There
is no hot water
sıcaklık [sədʒaklək] n temperature
sıçan [sətʃan] n rat
sıçramak [sətʃramak] v leap
sıçratmak [sətʃratmak] v splash
sıfat [səfat] adj adjective
sıfır [səfər] **(sıfırlar)** n zero,
nil, nought

sığ [səɣ] adj shallow; **sığ havuz** n
paddling pool
sığınak [səɣnak] n refuge
sığınma [səɣnma] n asylum
sığınmacı [səɣnmadʒə] n asylum
seeker, refugee
sığır [səɣər] n cattle; **sığır eti** n beef
sık [sək] adj frequent, (orman)
dense; **sık sorulan sorular** n FAQ
(Frequently Asked Question)
sıkı [səkə] adj firm, tight; **eli sıkı** adj
mean; **sıkı tedbirler almak** v
crack down on; **sımsıkı
kavramak** v grip; **sımsıkı
paketlenmiş** adj compact
sıkıcı [səkədʒə] adj boring, drab
sıkılamak [səkəlamak] v tighten
sıkılmak [səkəlmak] v to get
bored; **canı sıkılmış** adj bored;
canı sıkkın adj depressed
sıkıntı [səkəntə] n nuisance;
can sıkıntısı n boredom
sıkışık [səkəʃək] adj **sıkışık saat**
npl peak hours; **sıkışık saatler** n
rush hour
sıkışmak [səkəʃmak] v squeeze in
sıkışmış [səkəʃməʃ] adj jammed
sıklık [səklək] n frequency
sıklıkla [səkləkla] adv often
sıkmak [səkmak] v squeeze;
can sıkmak v bore (be dull)
sıla [səla] n **sıla acısı çeken** adj
homesick
sınav [sənav] n exam, examination
(medical), examination (school);
çetin sınav n ordeal; **deneme
sınavı** adj mock; **direksiyon
sınavı** n driving test; **ses sınavı** n
audition; **sınav görevlisi** n
examiner; **sınav gözcüsü** n

invigilator ▷ v **sınavı kazanmak** v
pass *(an exam)*; **yeniden sınava
girmek** v resit

sınıf [sənəf] n class, classroom;
birinci sınıf adj first-class; **hizmet
sınıfı** n business class; **ikinci sınıf**
adj economy class, second class,
second-class; **işçi sınıfı** adj
working-class; **orta sınıf** adj
middle-class; **sınıf arkadaşı** n
classmate; **... a birinci sınıf bir
gidiş dönüş bilet** a first-class
return to...; **Birinci sınıf bir kabin**
a first-class cabin; **Birinci sınıf
seyahat etmek istiyorum** I
would like to travel first class

sınır [sənər] n border, boundary,
edge, limit, margin, range *(limits)*;
hız sınırı n speed limit; **sınır dışı
etmek** v deport; **sınır işareti** n
landmark; **yaş sınırı** n age limit

sınırlamak [sənərlamak] v restrict

sır [sər] n confidence *(secret)*, secret

sıra [səra] n order, *(dizi)* row *(line)*,
(okul) desk, *(oyun)* round *(series)*,
(taksi vb) rank *(line)*; **sıra evler** adj
terraced; **taksi sırası** n taxi rank

sırada [sərada] n while; **o sırada**
adv meanwhile

sıradağ [sərada:] n range
(mountains)

sıradan [səradan] adj ordinary ▷ n
routine; **sıradan çıkmak** v fall out

sıralamak [səralamak] v rank

sırasıyla [sərasəjla] adv
respectively

Sırbistan [sərbistan] n Serbia

sırık [sərək] n pole; **sırık gibi** n
lanky; **sırıkla atlama** n pole vault

sırılsıklam [sərəlsəklam] v

sırılsıklam etmek v drench

sırıtış [sərətəʃ] n grin

sırıtmak [sərətmak] v grin

Sırp [sərp] adj Serbian ▷ n *(kişi)*
Serbian *(person)*

Sırpça [sərptʃa] n *(dil)* Serbian
(language)

sırt [sərt] n back; **sırt ağrısı** n back
pain, backache; **sırt çantası** n
backpack, holdall, rucksack; **sırt
çantasıyla dolaşan gezgin**
backpacker; **sırt çantasıyla
gezme** n backpacking; **Sırtım
ağrıyor** My back is sore; **Sırtım
tutuldu** I've got a bad back;
sırtüstü yüzme n backstroke

sıtma [sətma] n malaria

sıvı [səvə] n liquid

sıvışmak [səvəʃmak] v get away

sızdırmak [səzdərmak] vi leak

sızıntı [səzəntə] n leak

sızma [səzma] n **petrol sızması** n
oil slick

siber [siber] adj **siber zorbalık** n
cyberbullying

Siberya [siberja] n Siberia

sidik [sidik] v urine; **sidik torbası**
n bladder

sifon [sifon] n **Tuvaletin sifonu
çalışmıyor** The toilet won't flush

sigara [sigara] n cigarette, *(argo)*
fag; **sigara içen** n smoker; **sigara
içilmeyen** adj non-smoking;
sigara içmek v smoke; **sigara
içmeyen** n non-smoker

sigorta [sigorta] n *(elektrik)* fuse,
(poliçe) insurance; **araba
sigortası** n car insurance; **kaza
sigortası** n accident insurance;
üçüncü kişi sorumluluk

sigortası *n* third-party insurance; **seyahat sigortası** *n* travel insurance; **sigorta belgesi** *n* insurance certificate; **sigorta kutusu** *n* fuse box; **sigorta poliçesi** *n* insurance policy; **yaşam sigortası** *n* life insurance; **İşte sigorta bilgilerim** Here are my insurance details; **Bireysel kaza sigortası yaptırmak istiyorum** I'd like to arrange personal accident insurance; **Diş sigortam var mı bilmiyorum?** I don't know if I have dental insurance; **Diş sigortam yok** I don't have dental insurance; **Fiyata tam kapsamlı sigorta dahil mi?** Is fully comprehensive insurance included in the price?; **Sağlık sigortam yok** I don't have health insurance; **Seyahat sigortam yok** I don't have travel insurance; **Sigorta attı** A fuse has blown; **Sigorta belgenizi görebilir miyim lütfen?** Can I see your insurance certificate please?; **Sigorta bilgilerim burada** Here are my insurance details; **Sigorta bilgilerinizi verin lütfen** Give me your insurance details, please; **Sigorta için fiş almam gerekiyor** I need a receipt for the insurance; **Sigortam için polise bildirmemiz gerekiyor** I need a police report for my insurance; **Sigortalıyım** I have insurance; **Sigortanız var mı?** Do you have insurance?; **Sigortayı tamir eder misiniz?** Can you mend a fuse?; **Sigota bunu öder mi?** Will the

insurance pay for it?; **Tam kapsamlı sigorta için ne kadar ekstra ödemem gerekiyor?** How much extra is comprehensive insurance cover?
sigortalamak [sigortalamak] *v* insure
sigortalı [sigortalə] *adj* insured
siğil [səəl] *n* wart
sihirbaz [sihirbaz] *n* magician
sihirli [sihirli] *adj* magical
Sikh [sikh] *adj* Sikh ▷ *n* Sikh
siklon [siklon] *n* cyclone
silah [silah] *n* gun, weapon; **kısa menzilli silah** *n* shotgun
silahlı [silahlə] *adj* armed
silecek [siledʒek] *n* **cam sileceği** *n* windscreen wiper; **Cam sileceklerinin deposunu doldurur musunuz lütfen?** Can you top up the windscreen washers?
silikon [silikon] *n* **silikon çip** *n* silicon chip
silindir [silindir] *n* cylinder, roller
silkmek [silkmek] *v* **omuz silkmek** *v* shrug
silmek [silmek] *v* delete, erase, *(silip çıkarmak)* cross out; **silerek temizlemek** *v* wipe; **silip temizlemek** *v* wipe up
simetrik [simetrik] *adj* symmetrical
simit [simit] *n* **cankurtaran simidi** *n* lifebelt
sinagog [sinagog] *n* synagogue; **Sinagog nerede var?** Where is there a synagogue?
sincap [sindʒap] *n* squirrel
sindirim [sindirim] *n* digestion

sindirmek [sindirmek] v digest

sinek [sinek] n fly

sinema [sinema] n cinema; **Bu gece sinemada ne var?** What's on tonight at the cinema?; **Sinemada hangi film oynuyor?** Which film is on at the cinema?; **Sinemada ne oynuyor?** What's on at the cinema?

sinir [sinir] n (anatomi) nerve (anat); **sinir bozucu** adj annoying, irritating, nerve-racking; **sinir krizi** n nervous breakdown; **sinirini bozmak** v annoy

sinirli [sinirli] adj nervous

sinüs [sinys] n sinus

sinyal [sinjal] n signal; **meşgul sinyali** n busy signal, engaged tone; **sinyal vermek** v signal; **telefon sinyali** n dialling tone

sipariş [sipariʃ] n order; **sipariş formu** n order form; **Sipariş verebilir miyim lütfen?** Can I order now, please?

siper [siper] n trench

siren [siren] n siren

sirk [sirk] n circus

sirke [sirke] n vinegar; **sirkeli salata sosu** n vinaigrette

sis [sis] n fog, mist; **sis lambası** n fog light

sisli [sisli] adj foggy, misty

sistem [sistem] n system; **bağışıklık sistemi** n immune system; **güneş sistemi** n solar system; **GPS sistemi** n GPS; **sistem analizcisi** n systems analyst; **Kapalı Devre Televizyon Sistemi** n CCTV

sistemli [sistemli] adj systematic

sistit [sistit] n cystitis

sitkom [sitkom] n sitcom

sivil [sivil] adj civilian ▷ n civilian

sivilce [sivildʒe] n acne, pimple, zit

sivilceli [sivildʒeli] adj spotty

sivrisinek [sivrisinek] n mosquito

siyah [sijah] adj black; **Siyah beyaz** in black and white

siz [siz] pron you (plural), you (singular polite); **Siz döndüğünüzde biz yatmış oluruz** We'll be in bed when you get back; **Siz nasılsınız?** And you?; **Sizden çok hoşlanıyorum** I like you very much; **Size katılabilir miyim?** Can I join you?; **Sizi yarın arayabilir miyim?** May I call you tomorrow?; **Sizinle özel olarak konuşabilir miyim?** Can I speak to you in private?; **Sizinle çalışmak bir zevkti** It's been a pleasure working with you; **Sizinle nasıl temas kurabilirim?** Where can I contact you?; **Sizinle tanışmak bir zevk** It was a pleasure to meet you

sizin [sizin] adj your (plural), your (singular polite)

sizinki [siziŋi] pron yours (plural), yours (singular), yours (singular polite)

skandal [skandal] n scandal

skateboard [skateboard] n skateboard; **skateboard yapma** n skateboarding; **Skateboarding yapmak isterdim** I'd like to go skateboarding

skleroz [skleroz] n **multipl skleroz** n multiple sclerosis

skuter [skuter] n scooter

Slovak [slovak] *adj* Slovak ▷ *n (kişi)* Slovak *(person)*

Slovakça [slovaktʃa] *n (dil)* Slovak *(language)*

Slovakya [slovakja] *n* Slovakia

Slovence [slovendʒe] *n (dil)* Slovenian *(language)*

Slovenya [slovenja] *adj* Slovenian ▷ *n* Slovenia

Slovenyalı [slovenjalə] *n (kişi)* Slovenian *(person)*

smokin [smokin] *n* dinner jacket, tuxedo

smoothie [smuəi] *n (sıvı meyve püresi)* smoothie

SMS [esemes] *n* SMS

snooker [snooker] *n* snooker

snowboard [snovboard] *n* **Snowboard kiralamak istiyorum** I want to hire a snowboard; **Snowboarding dersleri veriyor musunuz?** Do you organise snowboarding lessons?

soba [soba] *n* stove

sofistike [sofistike] *adj* sophisticated

soğan [soa:n] *n* onion, *(bitki)* bulb *(plant)*; **Frenk soğanı** *mpl* chives; **taze soğan** *n* spring onion

soğuk [sou:k] *adj* chilly, cold ▷ *n* cold; **Duş soğuk akıyor** The showers are cold; **Et soğuk** The meat is cold; **Oda çok soğuk** The room is too cold; **Soğuk algınlığı için bir şey rica ediyorum** I'd like something for a cold; **Soğuk algınlığım var** I have a cold

soğutmak [sou:tmak] *v* chill

soğutucu [sou:tudʒu] *n* fridge; **soğutucu kayışı** *n* fan belt

sohbet [sohbet] *n* chat ▷ *v* **sohbet etmek** *v* chat; **sohbet odası** *n* chatroom; **sohbet programı** *n* chat show

sokak [sokak] *n* street; **çıkmaz sokak** *n* dead end; **dar sokak** *n* alley; **sokak çalgıcısı** *n* busker; **sokak haritası** *n* street map; **sokak lambası** *n* streetlamp; **sokak planı** *n* street plan; **sokaklarda büyümüş** *adj* streetwise; **yan sokak** *n* side street; **Sağdan ilk sokağa dönün** Take the first turning on your right; **Soldan ikinci sokağa dönün** Take the second turning on your left

sokma [sokma] *n (arı, böcek)* sting

sokmak [sokmak] *v (arı, böcek vb)* sting

sol [sol] *adj* left, left-hand, *(politika)* left-wing ▷ *n* left; **soldan trafik** *n* left-hand drive; **Sola dönün** Turn left; **Soldan ikinci sokağa dönün** Take the second turning on your left

solak [solak] *adj* left-handed

soldaki [soldaki] *adv* left

solist [solist] *n* soloist; **as solist** *n* lead singer

sollamak [sollamak] *v* overtake

solmak [solmak] *v* fade, wilt

solucan [soludʒan] *n* worm

soluk [soluk] *adj* pale

solüsyon [solysjon] *n* **Lens solüsyonu** cleansing solution for contact lenses

som [som] *n* **som balığı** *n* salmon

Somali [somali] *adj* Somali ▷ *n* Somalia

Somalice [somalidʒe] n Somali (language)

Somalili [somalili] n (kişi) Somali (person)

somun [somun] **(somunlar)** n (ekmek) loaf; **vida somunu** n nut (device)

son [son] adj final, last, ultimate ▷ n end, ending, finish; **eninde sonunda** adv ultimately; **hafta sonu** n weekend; **son derece** adv awfully; **son kullanım tarihi** n best-before date, expiry date; **son olarak** adv lastly; **son satış tarihi** n sell-by date; **son teslim tarihi** n deadline; **son zamanlarda** adv lately, recently; **sondan bir önceki** adj penultimate; **... a son otobüs kaçta?** When is the last bus to...?; **... a son tren kaçta?** When is the last train to...?; **... a son vapur kaçta?** When is the last sailing to...?; **En son çıkış kaçta?** When is the last ascent?; **Haziran sonunda** at the end of June; **Kuyruğun sonu burası mı?** Is this the end of the queue?; **Son otobüs kaçta?** What time is the last bus?; **Son teleferik kaçta?** When does the last chair-lift go?; **Son vapur kaçta?** When is the last boat?

sonbahar [sonbahar] n autumn

sonda [sonda] adv last

sonlandırmak [sonlandərmak] v end, finalize

sonra [sonra] adv afterwards ▷ conj after; **öğleden sonra** abbr afternoon, p.m.; **bir sonraki** adv next; **daha sonra** adv later; **güneş**

sonrası krem n after sun lotion; **ondan sonra** conj then; **bir sonraki hafta** the week after next; **saat sekizden sonra** after eight o'clock

sonsuz [sonsuz] adj endless, eternal ▷ n eternity, infinitive

sonuç [sonutʃ] n conclusion, consequence, outcome, result; **kaza sonucu** adj accidental; **sonucu olmak** v result in

sonuçlar [sonutʃlar] npl repercussions

sonuçta [sonutʃta] adv eventually

sonunda [sonunda] adv finally

sopa [sopa] n (asa) staff (stick or rod), (çubuk) stick, (silah) club (weapon); **golf sopası** n golf club (game), tee; **sopa çekirgesi** n stick insect; **Golf sopaları kiralıyorlar mı?** Do they hire out golf clubs?

soprano [soprano] n soprano

sorbet [sorbet] n sorbet

sorgulamak [sorgulamak] v interrogate, query

sormak [sormak] v ask, question

soru [soru] n inquiry, query, question; **sık sorulan sorular** n FAQ (Frequently Asked Question); **soru işareti** n question mark

sorumlu [sorumlu] adj accountable, responsible; **bina sorumlusu** n janitor

sorumluluk [sorumluluk] n responsibility; **üçüncü kişi sorumluluk sigortası** n third-party insurance

sorumsuz [sorumsuz] adj irresponsible

sorun [sorun] n problem; **ufak sorun** n hitch; **Bir sorun çıkarsa kiminle temas kuracağız?** Who do we contact if there are problems?; **Odada bir sorun var** There's a problem with the room; **Sorun değil** No problem

soruşturma [soruʃturma] n inquest, investigation

soruşturmak [soruʃturmak] v inquire

sos [sos] n sauce; **domates sosu** n tomato sauce; **et sosu** n gravy; **salata sosu** n salad dressing; **sirkeli salata sosu** n vinaigrette; **soya sosu** n soy sauce; **terbiye sosu** n marinade; **terbiye sosuna yatırmak** v marinade

SOS [esoes] n SOS

sosis [sosis] n sausage; **sosisli sandviç** n hot dog

sosyal [sosjal] adj sociable, social; **sosyal güvenlik** n social security; **sosyal hizmetler** npl social services; **sosyal hizmetler görevlisi** n social worker; **sosyal medya** n social media

sosyalist [sosjalist] adj socialist ▷ n socialist

sosyalizm [sosjalizm] n socialism

soy [soj] n race; lineage; **soyu tükenmiş** adj extinct

soya [soja] n soya; **soya sosu** n soy sauce

soyadı [sojadə] n surname; **kızlık soyadı** n maiden name

soygun [sojgun] n hold-up, robbery

soyguncu [sojgundʒu] n robber

soymak [sojmak] v burgle, rob ▷ vt (meyva, deri vb) peel

soyunmak [sojunmak] v strip, undress; **soyunma odası** n (mağaza) fitting room, (spor) changing room

soyut [sojut] adj abstract

soyutlanmış [sojutlanməʃ] adj isolated

söğüt [sø:yt] n willow

sökmek [søkmek] v (parçalarına ayırmak) take apart, (vida) unscrew

sömestr [sømestr] n semester

sömürmek [sømyrmek] v exploit

sömürü [sømyry] n exploitation

söndürmek [søndyrmek] v put out, turn off; **bastırarak söndürmek** v stub out

söndürücü [søndyrydʒy] n (yangın) extinguisher; **yangın söndürücü** n fire extinguisher

sör [sør] n sir

sörf [sørf] n surf; **rüzgar sörfü** n windsurfing; **sörf tahtası** n surfboard; **sörf yapma** n surfing; **sörf yapmak** v surf; **Sörf için nereye gitmek gerek?** Where can you go surfing?

sörfçü [sørftʃy] n surfer

söylemek [søjlemek] v say; **açıkça fikrini söylemek** v speak up; **şarkı söyleme** n singing; **şarkı söylemek** v sing; **yalan söylemek** v lie

söylenti [søjlenti] n rumour

söz [søz] n promise; **açık sözlü** adj outspoken, straightforward; **söz dinlemek** v listen to; **söz dinlememek** v disobey; **söz etmek** v refer; **söz vermek** v promise; **sözünü kesmek** v

interrupt; **sözünü kesmek** v
break in (on), disrupt
sözcü [søzdʒy] **(sözcüler)** n
spokesperson, *(erkek)*
spokesman, *(kadın)*
spokeswoman
sözcük [søzdʒyk] n word; **sözcük
dağarcığı** n vocabulary; **sözcük
grubu** n phrase
sözlü [søzly] adj oral ▷ n oral
sözlük [søzlyk] n dictionary;
günlük ifadeler sözlüğü n
phrasebook
spagetti [spagetti] n spaghetti
spatül [spatyl] n spatula
sperm [sperm] n sperm
spesifik [spesifik] adj specific
spor [spor] n sport; **kano sporu** n
canoeing; **kayma sporu** n skiing;
kış sporları npl winter sports;
kürek sporu n rowing; **lastik
spor ayakkabısı** npl trainers;
spor ayakkabısı npl sneakers;
spor giysisi n sportswear; **yelken
sporu** n sailing; **Buralarda sport
tesisi var mı?** What sports
facilities are there?; **Hangi spor
gösterisine gidebiliriz?** Which
sporting events can we go to?
sporcu [spordʒu] **(sporcular)** n
(erkek) sportsman; **kadın sporcu**
n sportswoman
sporsever [sporsever] adj sporty
spot [spot] n **spot lambası** n
spotlight
stadyum [stadjum]
(stadyumlar) n stadium;
Stadyuma nasıl gidebiliriz? How
do we get to the stadium?
standart [standart] adj standard

▷ n standard; **yaşam standardı** n
standard of living; **Standart bir
kabin bileti** a standard-class
cabin
statüko [statyko] n status quo
steno [steno] n shorthand
stepne [stepne] n spare tyre, spare
wheel
stereo [stereo] n stereo; **Arabada
stereo var mı?** Is there a stereo in
the car?; **Stereo var mı?** Does it
have a stereo?
steril [steril] adj sterile
sterilze [sterilze] v **sterilize
etmek** v sterilize
sterlin [sterlin] n sterling; **pound
sterlin** *(İngiliz para birimi)* n
pound sterling
steroid [steroid] n steroid
stil [stil] n style
stilist [stilist] n stylist
stok [stok] n stock
stoklamak [stoklamak] v stock
strateji [stratexi] n strategy
stratejik [stratexik] adj strategic
stres [stres] n strain, stress
striptizci [striptizdʒi] n stripper
stüdyo [stydjo] n studio; **stüdyo
daire** n studio flat
su [su] n water; **deniz suyu** n sea
water; **içme suyu** n drinking
water; **maden suyu** n mineral
water; **meyve suyu** n fruit juice,
juice; **portakal suyu** n orange
juice; **sığ suda çıplak ayak
yürümek** v paddle; **sıcak su
torbası** n hot-water bottle; **su
baskınına uğramak** vi flood; **su
basmak** vt/vi flood; **su basması** n
flooding; **su birikintisi** n puddle;

su deposu n reservoir; **su geçirmez** adj waterproof; **su geçirmez parka** n cagoule; **su kaplumbağası** n turtle; **su kayağı** n water-skiing; **su keleri** m newt; **su samuru** n otter; **su teresi** n watercress; **suda boğulmak** v drown; **suda pişirilmiş** (yumurta, balık) adj poached (simmered gently); **sulu çamur** n slush; **sulu kar** n sleet; **sulu sepken yağmak** v sleet; **Bir bardak su** a glass of water; **Bir şişe maden suyu** a bottle of mineral water, a bottle of sparkling mineral water; **Bir şişe su** a bottle of still mineral water; **Bir sürahi su** a jug of water; **Biraz daha su getirir misiniz?** Please bring more water; **Burada su kayağı yapmak mümkün mü?** Is it possible to go water-skiing here?; **Sıcak su nasıl çalışıyor?** How does the water heater work?; **Sıcak su yok** There is no hot water; **Suyu kontrol eder misiniz lütfen?** Can you check the water, please?; **Suyun derinliği ne kadar?** How deep is the water?

sualtı [sualtə] adv underwater

suç [sutʃ] n blame, crime; **internet suçu** n cybercrime; **suç ortağı** n accomplice

suçiçeği [sutʃitʃeji:] n chickenpox

suçlama [sutʃlama] n accusation, charge (accusation)

suçlamak [sutʃlamak] v accuse, blame, charge (accuse)

suçlu [sutʃlu] adj criminal, guilty ▷ n criminal

suçluluk [sutʃluluk] n guilt

Sudan [sudan] adj Sudanese ▷ n Sudan

Sudanlı [sudanlə] n Sudanese

suit [suit] n suite

sulamak [sulamak] v water; **bahçe sulama bidonu** n watering can

sulandırılmış [sulandərəlməʃ] adj diluted

sulandırmak [sulandərmak] v dilute

sulh [sulh] n peace; **sulh hakimi** n magistrate

sulu [sulu] adj **sulu hamur** n batter; **sulu kabarcık** n blister

suluboya [suluboja] n watercolour

sunak [sunak] n altar

sunma [sunma] n presentation

sunucu [sunudʒu] n (bilişim) server (computer), (oyun, film, gösteri) compere, (radyo, TV) presenter; **haber sunucusu** n newsreader

surat [surat] n face; **suratı asık** adj sulky; **suratını asmak** v sulk

Suriye [surije] adj Syrian ▷ n Syria

Suriyeli [surijeli] n Syrian

susmak [susmak] v shut up

susturucu [susturudʒu] n silencer

susuz [susuz] adj dehydrated, thirsty; **Susadım** I'm thirsty

susuzluk [susuzluk] n thirst

Suudi [suudi] adj Saudi ▷ n Saudi

Suudi Arabistan [suudiarabistan] adj Saudi Arabia, Saudi Arabian

Suudi Arabistanlı [suudiarabistanlə] n Saudi Arabian

sübvansiyon [sybvansijon] *n* subsidy

süet [syet] *n* suede

sülün [sylyn] *n* pheasant

sümbül [symbyl] *n* hyacinth

sümüklüböcek [symyklybødʒek] *n* **kabuksuz sümüklüböcek** *n* slug

sünger [synger] *n (banyo)* sponge *(for washing)*

süper [syper] *adj* super

süpermarket [sypermarket] *n* supermarket; **Süpermarket arıyorum** I need to find a supermarket

süprüntü [syprynty] *adj* rubbish

süpürge [sypyrge] *n* broom; **elektrik süpürgesi** *n* Hoover®, vacuum cleaner; **süpürge otu** *n* heather

süpürgelik [sypyrgelik] *n* skirting board

süpürmek [sypyrmek] *v* sweep, *(elektrikli süpürgeyle)* hoover

sürahi [syrahi] *n* carafe, jug; **Bir sürahi beyaz şarap** a carafe of white wine; **Bir sürahi kırmızı şarap** a carafe of red wine; **Bir sürahi su** a jug of water; **Kendi şarabınızdan bir sürahi** a carafe of the house wine

sürat [syrat] *n* speed; **sürat motoru** *n* speedboat

sürdürmek [syrdyrmek] *v* keep up, maintain ▷ *vi* continue

süre [syre] *n* duration; **deneme süresi** *n* trial period; **uzatma süresi** *n* injury time

sürekli [syrekli] *adv* constantly

süresince [syresindʒe] *prep* during

sürgü [syrgy] *n* bolt

sürgün [syrgyn] *n (başka bir yere)* exile

sürmek [syrmek] *v* last, *(otomobil)* drive; **bisiklet sürmek** *v* cycle; **iz sürmek** *v* retrace; **izini sürmek** *v* track down; **tarla sürmek** *vt* plough

sürpriz [syrpriz] *n* surprise

sürtmek [syrtmek] *v* rub

sürü [syry] *n* flock, herd; **sürüden ayrılmış** *n* stray

sürücü [syrydʒy] *n* driver, motorist; **öğrenci sürücü** *n* learner driver; **disk sürücü** *n* disk drive; **sürücü ehliyeti** *n* driving licence; **taksi sürücüsü** *n* taxi driver

sürüklemek [syryklemek] *vt* drag

sürüklenmek [syryklenmek] *vi (sularla)* drift

sürükleyici [syryklejidʒi] *adj* gripping

sürüngen [syryngen] *n* reptile

süs [sys] *n* ornament; **şekerli kek süsü** *n* frosting; **pastanın üzerindeki şekerli süsleme** *n* icing; **toz süsleme şekeri** *n* icing sugar

süslemek [syslemek] *v* decorate; **elişiyle süslemek** *v* embroider

süslenmek [syslenmek] *v* dress up

süt [syt] *n* milk; **bebek sütü** *n* baby milk; **süt ürünleri** *n* dairy products; **sütlü çikolata** *n* milk chocolate; **sütle yapılmış** *n* dairy produce; **sütsüz kahve** *n* black coffee; **UHT süt** *n* UHT milk; **yağı alınmış süt** *n* skimmed milk;

yarım yağlı süt *n* semi-skimmed
milk; **Bu pastörize edilmemiş
sütten mi yapıldı?** Is it made with
unpasteurised milk?; **sütü ayrı
getirin** with the milk separate;
Süt içer misiniz? Do you drink
milk?; **Taze sütünüz var mı?**
Have you got real milk?
sütun [sytun] *n* column, pillar
sütyen [sytjen] *n* bra
süyek [syjek] *n* splint
süzgeç [syzgetʃ] *n* colander
süzmek [syzmek] *v* filter
Swaziland [svaziland] *n*
Swaziland

şafak [ʃafak] *n* dawn
şaheser [ʃaheser] *n* masterpiece
şahit [ʃahit] *n* witness; **yalancı
şahitlik** *n* perjury; **Yehovanın
Şahitleri** *n* Jehovah's Witness
şahmat [ʃahmat] *n* stalemate
şair [ʃair] *n* poet
şaka [ʃaka] *n* joke; **kaba şaka** *n*
prank; **şaka yapmak** *v* joke
şal [ʃal] *n* shawl
şalgam [ʃalgam] *n* turnip; **sarı
şalgam** *n* swede
şalter [ʃalter] *n* switch; **şalter
açmak** *v* switch on
şalvar [ʃalvar] *n* **şalvar biçimi** *adj*
baggy
şamandıra [ʃamandəra] *n* buoy
şamata [ʃamata] *n* din
şamdan [ʃamdan] *n* candlestick
şampanya [ʃampanja] *n*
champagne
şampiyon [ʃampijon] *n* champion

şampiyona [ʃampijona] *n* championship

şampuan [ʃampuan] *n* shampoo; **Şampuan satıyor musunuz?** Do you sell shampoo?

şans [ʃans] *n* luck

şanslı [ʃanslə] *adj* fortunate, lucky

şanssız [ʃanssəz] *adj* unlucky

şantaj [ʃantaʒ] *n* blackmail; **şantaj yapmak** *n* blackmail

şapel [ʃapel] *n* chapel

şapka [ʃapka] *n* hat

şaplak [ʃaplak] *n, v* **şaplak atmak** *v* spank

şarap [ʃarap] *n* wine; **elma şarabı** *n* cider; **ev şarabı** *n* house wine; **kırmızı şarap** *n* red wine; **şarap kadehi** *n* wineglass; **şarap listesi** *n* wine list; **pembe şarap** *n* rosé; **porto şarabı** *n* port *(wine)*; **yemeklik şarap** *n* table wine; **İyi bir beyaz şarap tavsiye edebilir misiniz?** Can you recommend a good white wine?; **İyi bir kırmızı şarap tavsiye edebilir misiniz?** Can you recommend a good red wine?; **İyi bir şarap tavsiye edebilir misiniz?** Can you recommend a good wine?; **İyi bir roze şarap tavsiye edebilir misiniz?** Can you recommend a good rosé wine?; **Bir şişe beyaz şarap** a bottle of white wine; **Bir şişe kırmızı şarap** a bottle of red wine; **Bir şişe kendi şarabınızdan** a bottle of the house wine; **Bir sürahi beyaz şarap** a carafe of white wine; **Bir sürahi kırmızı şarap** a carafe of red wine; **Bu şarap**

soğutulmamış This wine is not chilled; **Hiç şarap içmem** I never drink wine; **Kendi şarabınızdan bir sürahi** a carafe of the house wine; **Şarap lekesi** This stain is wine; **Şarap listesi lütfen** The wine list, please; **Şarap soğutulmuş mu?** Is the wine chilled?

şarj [ʃarʒ] *n* charge *(electricity)*; **şarj aleti** *n* charger; **şarj etmek** *(elektrik)* *v* charge *(electricity)*; **Şarj etmiyor** It's not charging, It's not holding its charge

şarjör [ʃarʒør] *n* magazine *(ammunition)*

şarkı [ʃarkə] *n* song; **çocuk şarkıları** *n* nursery rhyme; **şarkı söyleme** *n* singing; **şarkı söylemek** *v* sing; **Noel şarkısı** *n* carol

şarkıcı [ʃarkədʒə] *n* singer

şarküteri [ʃarkyteri] *n* delicatessen

şart [ʃart] *n* **şartlı tahliye** *n* parole

şaşı [ʃaʃə] *n* **şaşı bakmak** *v* squint

şaşırmış [ʃaʃərməʃ] *adj* astonished, bewildered, surprised

şaşırtıcı [ʃaʃərtədʒə] *adj* astonishing, puzzling, surprising; **şaşırtıcı bir şekilde** *adv* surprisingly

şaşırtmak [ʃaʃərtmak] *v* amaze, astonish

şaşkın [ʃaʃkən] *adj* amazed, baffled; **şaşkına dönmüş** *adj* stunned

şayet [ʃajet] *conj* whether

şef [ʃef] *n* chief; **orkestra şefi** *n* conductor

şefkatli [ʃefkatli] *adj* caring
şeftali [ʃeftali] *n* peach
şehir [ʃehir] *n* city, town; **şehir merkezi** *n* town centre; **şehir planlama** *n* town planning; **Bu şehre özgü bir şey istiyorum** Have you anything typical of this town?; **Şehir merkezinden ne kadar uzaktayız?** How far are we from the town centre?; **Şehir merkezine en kolay nasıl gidebilirim?** What's the best way to get to the city centre?
şehit [ʃehit] *n* martyr
şehvet [ʃehvet] *n* lust
şeker [ʃeker] *n* sugar, sweet; **şeker hastalığı** *n* diabetes; **şeker hastası** *n* diabetic; **şekerli kek süsü** *n* frosting; **nane şekeri** *n* peppermint; **pastanın üzerindeki şekerli süsleme** *n* icing; **toz süsleme şekeri** *n* icing sugar
şekersiz [ʃekersiz] *adj* no sugar, sugar-free
şekil [ʃekil] *n* figure, shape; **ağır bir şekilde** *adv* heavily; **özenli bir şekilde** *adv* cautiously; **etkili bir şekilde** *adv* effectively; **kötü bir şekilde** *adv* badly
şelale [ʃelale] *n* waterfall
şempanze [ʃempanze] *n* chimpanzee
şemsiye [ʃemsije] *n* umbrella
şen [ʃen] *adj* happy; **şen şakrak** *adj* merry
şenlik [ʃenlik] *n* festivity; **şenlik ateşi** *n* bonfire
şerefe [ʃerefe] *excl* cheers!
şeri [ʃeri] *n* sherry; **Bir sek şeri**

lütfen A dry sherry, please
şerit [ʃerit] *n* strip, stripe, tape; **çift-şeritli yol** *n* dual carriageway; **şerit metre** *n* tape measure; **şeritli yaya geçidi** *n* zebra crossing
şey [ʃej] *n* thing; **önemsiz şey** *n* trifle; **bir şey** *pron* something; **herhangi bir şey** *pron* anything; **hiçbir şey** *n* nothing
şeytan [ʃejtan] *n* devil
şezlong [ʃezlong] *n* deckchair
şık [ʃək] *adj* smart
şımartılmış [ʃəmartəlməʃ] *adj* spoilt
şınav [ʃənav] *n, v* **şınav çekmek** *n* press-up
şırınga [ʃərənga] *n* syringe
şiddet [ʃiddet] *n* violence; **şiddet uygulayan** *adj* violent; **şiddetle vurmak** *v* bash; **şiddetli rüzgar** *n* gale
şiddetli [ʃiddetli] *adj* harsh
şifre [ʃifre] *n* code, password; **kredi kartı şifresi** *npl* PIN
Şii [ʃii] *adj* Shiite
şiir [ʃiir] *n* poem, poetry
şikayet [ʃikajet] *n* complaint, grouse *(complaint)*; **Bir şikayette bulunmak istiyorum** I'd like to make a complaint
Şili [ʃili] *adj* Chilean ▷ *n* Chile
Şilili [ʃilili] *n* Chilean
şimdi [ʃiːmdi] *adv* now; **Şimdi kendinizi nasıl hissediyorsunuz?** How are you feeling now?; **Şimdi mi ödeyeceğim, sonra mı?** Do I pay now or later?
şimşek [ʃimʃek] *n* lightning
şirket [ʃirket] *n* company; **şirket**

arabası *n* company car; **şirket evliliği** *n* merger; **şirketiçi network** *n* intranet; **Şirket hakkında bilgi alabilir miyim?** I would like some information about the company; **Şirketimle ilgili bilgiler** Here's some information about my company

şiş [ʃiʃ] *adj* swollen ▷ *n* spit; **örgü şişi** *n* knitting needle; **kebap şişi** *n* skewer; **yangılı ayak şişi** *n* bunion

şişe [ʃiʃe] *n* bottle; **şişe açacağı** *n* bottle-opener; **şişe geri dönüşüm kutusu** *n* bottle bank; **Bir şişe beyaz şarap** a bottle of white wine; **Bir şişe daha getirir misiniz?** Please bring another bottle; **Bir şişe içki deklare etmek istiyorum** I have a bottle of spirits to declare; **Bir şişe kırmızı şarap** a bottle of red wine; **Bir şişe kendi şarabınızdan** a bottle of the house wine; **Bir şişe maden suyu** a bottle of mineral water, a bottle of sparkling mineral water; **Bir şişe su** a bottle of still mineral water

şişirilebilir [ʃiʃirilebilir] *adj* inflatable

şişirmek [ʃiʃirmek] *v* pump up

şişko [ʃiʃko] *adj* gross *(fat)*

şişman [ʃiʃman] *adj* fat

şizofren [ʃizofren] *adj* schizophrenic

şnorkel [ʃnorkel] *n* snorkel; **Şnorkelle dalmak istiyorum** I'd like to go snorkelling

şoför [ʃofør] *n* chauffeur; **kamyon şoförü** *n* lorry driver, truck driver

şok [ʃok] *n* shock; **şok geçirmek** *v* shock

şort [ʃort] *npl* shorts, *(erkek iç çamaşırı)* underpants; **bokser şort** *npl* boxer shorts; **yüzücü şortu** *npl* swimming trunks, trunks

şoven [ʃoven] *n* chauvinist

şömine [ʃømine] *n* fireplace; **şömine rafı** *n* mantelpiece

şöyle [ʃøjle] *adv* thus; **şöyle böyle** *adv* so-so

şu [ʃu] *adj* that; **şu an** *n* present *(time being)*; **şu anda** *adv* currently, presently; **Şu ne kadar?** How much does that cost?

Şubat [ʃubat] *n* February

şunlar [ʃunlar] *adj* those ▷ *pron* those

şunu [ʃunu] *pron* that

şurup [ʃurup] *n* syrup; **öksürük şurubu** *n* cough mixture

t

taahhüt [taahhyt] *n* contract, obligation; **iadeli taahhütlü** *n* recorded delivery; **iadeli taahhütlü ne kadar sürer?** How long will it take by registered post?

tabak [tabak] *n* plate; **fincan tabağı** *n* saucer; **servis tabağı** *n* dish *(plate)*

tabaka [tabaka] *n* layer; **ozon tabakası** *n* ozone layer

taban [taban] *n* **taban tepmek** *n* tramp *(long walk)*; **veri tabanı** *n* database

tabanca [tabandʒa] *n* **kısa kabzalı tabanca** *n* pistol

tabela [tabela] *n* sign; **yol tabelası** *n* signpost

tablet [tablet] *n* tablet *(medicine, computer)*

tablo [taplo] *n (grafik)* table *(chart)*; **gösterge tablosu** *n* dashboard

tabu [tabu] *adj* taboo ▷ *n* taboo

tabure [tabure] *n* stool

tabut [tabut] *n* coffin

Tacikistan [tadʒikistan] *n* Tajikistan

taciz [tadʒiz] *n* abuse, harassment; **çocuk tacizi** *n* child abuse

taç [tatʃ] *n* crown; **taç çizgisi** *n* touchline

tahıl [tahəl] *n* **tahıl gevreği** *n* cereal; **tahıl tanesi** *n* grain

Tahiti [tahiti] *n* Tahiti

tahliye [tahlije] *n* evacuation; **şartlı tahliye** *n* parole; **tahliye etmek** *v* vacate

tahmin [tahmin] *n* estimate, guess, *(hava, borsa vb)* forecast; **hava tahmini** *n* weather forecast; **tahmin edilebilir** *adj* predictable; **tahminde bulunmak** *v* estimate; **Hava tahmini nasıl?** What's the weather forecast?

tahribat [tahribat] *n* ruin

tahrip [tahrip] *n* destruction; **tahrip etmek** *n* vandalize

taht [taht] *n* throne

tahta [tahta] *n (ağaç)* wood *(material)*, *(okul)* board *(go aboard)*, *(okul)* board *(wood)*; **ütü tahtası** *n* ironing board; **beyaz yazı tahtası** *n* whiteboard; **ilan tahtası** *n* bulletin board, notice board; **sörf tahtası** *n* surfboard

tahterevalli [tahterevalli] *n* seesaw

takdim [takdim] *n* introduction, presentation; **takdim etmek** *v* present

takılmak [takəlmak] *v* **peşine takılmak** *v* pursue

takılmış [takəlməʃ] *adj* stuck; **Takıldı** It's stuck

takım [takəm] *n* kit; **bando takımı** *n* brass band; **takım elbise** *n* suit; **tamir takımı** *n* repair kit; **yatak takımı** *n* bedclothes, bedding; **Tamir takımı alabilir miyim?** Can I have a repair kit?; **Tamir takımınız var mı?** Do you have a repair kit?

takıntı [takəntə] *n* obsession

takıntılı [takəntələ] *adj* obsessed

takip [takip] *n* chase; **takibi bırakmak** *v* unfollow; **takip etmek** *v (computer)* follow

taklit [taklit] *n* copy *(reproduction)*, imitation; **taklit etmek** *v* imitate, mimic

takma [takma] *adj* false; **takma ad** *n* alias, nickname, pseudonym; **takma dişler** *npl* dentures

takmak [takmak] **birine takmak** *v* pick on

taksi [taksi] *n* cab, minicab, taxi; **taksi sırası** *n* taxi rank; **taksi sürücüsü** *n* taxi driver; **Bagajımı takside bıraktım** I left my bags in the taxi; **Bana bir taksi gerek** I need a taxi; **Birlikte bir taksi tutabiliriz** We could share a taxi; **Bu otele taksi ne kadar?** How much is the taxi fare to this hotel?; **Havaalanına taksi ne kadar?** How much is the taxi to the airport?; **Kente taksi ne kadar?** How much is the taxi fare into town?; **Nereden taksi bulabilirim?** Where can I get a taxi?; **Taksi durağı nerede?** Where is the taxi stand?; **Valizlerimi taksiye çıkarır mısınız lütfen?** Please take my luggage to a taxi

taksimetre [taksimetre] *n* **Taksimetre bozuk** The meter is broken; **Taksimetrenin gösterdiğinden daha fazla** It's more than on the meter; **Taksimetreniz var mı?** Do you have a meter?

taksit [taksit] *n* instalment

taktik [taktik] *npl* tactics

takunya [takunja] *n* clog

takvim [takvim] *n* calendar

takviye [takvije] *n* reinforcement; **takviye kablosu** *npl* jump leads

talan [talan] *n* **talan olmuş** shambles

talaş [talaʃ] *n* sawdust

talep [talep] *n* claim, demand; **talep etmek** *v* claim, demand

talihsizlik [talihsizlik] *n* misfortune

talimat [talimat] *n* **talimat vermek** *v* instruct

talimatlar [talimatlar] *npl* directions, instructions

talk [talk] *v* **talk pudrası** *n* talcum powder

tam [tam] *adj* exact, precise, sheer, *(bütün)* total; **tam gün** *adv* full-time; **tam olarak** *adv* exactly, fully, precisely

Tamam [tamam] OK!

tamamen [tamamen] *adv* completely, totally

tamir [tamir] *n* repair; **tamir takımı** *n* repair kit; **Bunu nerede tamir ettirebilirim?** Where can I get this repaired?; **Bunu tamir edebilir misiniz?** Can you repair this?; **Saatimi tamir edebilir misiniz?** Can you repair my watch?; **Tamir edebilir misiniz?** Can you repair it?; **Tamir etmek ne kadar sürer?** How long will it take to repair?; **Tamir ettirmeye değer mi?** Is it worth repairing?; **Tamir kaça malolacak?** How much will the repairs cost?; **Tamir takımı alabilir miyim?** Can I have a repair kit?; **Tamir takımınız var mı?** Do you have a repair kit?

tamirci [tamirdʒi] n (otomobil) mechanic; **Tamirci gönderebilir misiniz?** Can you send a mechanic?

tampon [tampon] n tampon, (oto) bumper

tandem [tandem] n **tandem bisiklet** n tandem

tane [tane] n piece; **kar tanesi** n snowflake; **tahıl tanesi** n grain

tanı [tanə] n diagnosis

tanık [tanək] n witness; **Tanıklık eder misiniz?** Can you be a witness for me?

tanım [tanəm] n definition

tanımak [tanəmak] v know, recognize

tanımlamak [tanəmlamak] v define

tanınabilir [tanənabilir] adj recognizable

tanınmış [tanənməʃ] adj renowned, well-known

tanışmak [tanəʃmak] vt meet; **Tanıştığımıza memnun oldum** Pleased to meet you

tanıtım [tanətəm] n promotion, publicity; **tanıtımını yapmak** v promote

tanıtma [tanətma] n

introduction; **tanıtma broşürü** n prospectus

tanıtmak [tanətmak] v introduce

tank [taŋ] n tank (large container), (ordu) tank (combat vehicle)

tanker [taŋer] n tanker

tanrı [tanrə] n god; **tanrı tanımaz** n atheist

tansiyon [tansijon] n blood pressure

Tanzanya [tanzanja] adj Tanzanian ▷ n Tanzania

Tanzanyalı [tanzanjalə] n Tanzanian

tapınak [tapənak] n temple; **Tapınak halka açık mı?** Is the temple open to the public?; **Tapınak ne zaman açık?** When is the temple open?

tapmak [tapmak] v adore

taraf [taraf] n side

tarafından [tarafəndan] prep by

tarafsız [tarafsəz] adj neutral ▷ n neutral

taraftar [taraftar] n supporter

tarak [tarak] n comb; **deniz tarağı** n scallop

tarama [tarama] n (bilgisayar) scan

taramak [taramak] v comb, (bilgisayar) scan

tarayıcı [tarajədʒə] n (internet) browser, (scanner) scanner; **internet tarayıcı** n web browser

tarçın [tartʃən] n cinnamon

tarhun [tarhun] n tarragon

tarım [tarəm] n agriculture

tarımsal [tarəmsal] adj agricultural

tarif [tarif] n account (report), recipe

tarife [tarife] n timetable,
schedule; **gümrük tarifesi** n
tariff; **tarifeli uçuş** n scheduled
flight; **tarifesiz uçuş** n charter
flight; **Bir tarife alabilir miyim,
lütfen?** Can I have a timetable,
please?; **Günlük tarifeniz nedir?**
What are your rates per day?;
Haftalık tarifeniz nedir? What
are your rates per week?; **Ucuz
tarifeli uçuşunuz var mı?** Are
there any cheap flights?

tarih [tari:h] n (geçmiş, ders)
history, (takvim) date; **son
kullanım tarihi** n best-before
date, expiry date; **son satış tarihi**
n sell-by date; **son teslim tarihi** n
deadline; **tarih öncesi** adj
prehistoric; **Bugün ayın kaçı?**
What is the date?; **Bugünün
tarihi nedir?** What is today's date?

tarihçi [tarihtʃi] n historian

tarihi [ta:rihi:] adj historical

tarla [tarla] n field; **tarla sürmek**
vt plough

tartışma [tarteʃma] n argument,
row (argument), (fikir) debate

tartışmak [tarteʃmak] v argue,
quarrel, row (to argue), (fikir)
debate

tartışmalı [tarteʃmalə] adj
controversial

tartışmasız [tarteʃmasəz] adj
undisputed

tarz [tarz] n style; **Yepyeni bir
tarz istiyorum** I want a
completely new style

tas [tas] n cup

tasalanmak [tasalanmak] vt
worry

tasarımcı [tasarəmdʒə] n
designer

tasarlamak [tasarlamak] v
design, devise

tasavvur [tasavvur] n
imagination, concept, idea;
tasavvur etmek v fancy, imagine

tasfiye [tasfije] n **tasfiye
memuru** n receiver (person)

taslak [taslak] n draft

taslamak [taslamak] v **patronluk
taslamak** v boss around

Tasmanya [tasmanja] n Tasmania

taş [taʃ] n stone; **çakıl taşı** n
pebble; **kaldırım taşı** n kerb;
kireç taşı n limestone; **mezar
taşı** n gravestone; **safra kesesi
taşı** n gallstone; **taş ocağı** n
quarry

taşıma [taʃəma] n removal,
transport; **toplu taşıma** n public
transport

taşımak [taʃəmak] v bear,
transport ▷ vt carry

taşınabilir [taʃənabilir] adj
portable, removable; **taşınabilir
ev** n mobile home

taşınmak [taʃənmak] v move in;
taşınma kamyonu n removal van

taşıt [taʃət] n vehicle; **yıllık taşıt
testi** n MOT

taşıyıcı [taʃəjədʒə] n carrier;
taşıyıcı anne n surrogate mother;
taşıyıcı bant n conveyor belt

taşmak [taʃmak] v boil over

tat [tat] n taste; **tatsız tuzsuz** adj
tasteless; **Bunun tadı pek iyi
değil** It doesn't taste very nice

tatarcık [tatardʒək] n midge

tatil [tatil] n holiday; **aktivite**

tatili n activity holiday; **paket tatil** n package holiday; **resmi tatil günü** n public holiday; **sömestr tatili** n half-term; **tatil evi** n holiday home; **tatil yeri** n resort; **yaz tatili** npl summer holidays; **İyi tatiller!** Enjoy your holiday!; **Burada tatildeyim** I'm here on holiday, I'm on holiday here

tatlandırıcı [tatlandərədʒə] n sweetener; **Tatlandırıcınız var mı?** Do you have any sweetener?

tatlı [tatlə] adj sweet (taste), (hoş) sweet (pleasing) ▷ n dessert ▷ npl afters; **tatlı kaşığı** n dessert spoon; **Tatlı menüsü lütfen** The dessert menu, please; **Tatlı rica ediyoruz** We'd like a dessert

tatlılar [tatlələr] npl sweets

tatlısu [tatləsu] adj **tatlısu balığı** n freshwater fish

tatmak [tatmak] v taste

tatmin [tatmin] n satisfaction; **tatmin edici** adj rewarding, satisfactory; **tatmin edici olmayan** adj disappointing, unsatisfactory; **tatmin olmuş** adj satisfied

tatsız [tatsəz] adj grim

tava [tava] n pan; **kızartma tavası** n frying pan

tavan [tavan] n ceiling; **açılır tavan** n sunroof; **tavan arası** n loft

tavır [tavər] n attitude, manner

tavsiye [tavsije] n recommendation; **tavsiye etmek** v advise, recommend; **Ne tavsiye edersiniz?** What do you recommend?

tavşan [tavʃan] n rabbit; **tavşan uykusu** n snooze; **yabani tavşan** n hare

tavuk, horoz [tavuk, horoz] n hen, chicken; **orman tavuğu** n grouse (game bird)

tavus [tavus] n **tavus kuşu** n peacock

tay [taj] n foal

tayfa [tajfa] n crew

Tayland [tajland] n Thailand

Taylandca [tajlanddʒa] n (dil) Thai (language)

Taylandlı [tajlandlə] n (kişi) Thai (person)

Tayvan [tajvan] adj Taiwanese ▷ n Taiwan

Tayvanlı [tajvanlə] n Taiwanese

taze [taze] adj fresh; **taze soğan** n spring onion; **Balıklarınız taze mi, dondurulmuş mu?** Is the fish fresh or frozen?; **Sebzeleriniz taze mi, dondurulmuş mu?** Are the vegetables fresh or frozen?; **Taze kahveniz var mı?** Have you got fresh coffee?

tazminat [tazminat] n compensation

tebeşir [tebeʃir] n chalk

tebrik [tebrik] interj **tebrik kartı** n greetings card

tebrikler [tebrikler] npl congratulations

tecavüz [tedʒavyz] n (cinsel) rape (sexual attack); **tecavüz etmek** v rape; **Tecavüze uğradım** I've been raped

tecavüzcü [tedʒavyzdʒy] n rapist

tedavi [tedavi] n cure; **tedavi etmek** vt cure

tedbir [tedbir] *n* measure, step;
sıkı tedbirler almak *v* crack down
on
tedbirli [tedbirli] *adj* cautious
tefsir [tefsir] *n* interpretation;
tefsir etmek *v* interpret
teğmen [te:men] *n (subay/polis)*
lieutenant
tehdit [tehdit] *n* threat; **tehdit
edici** *adj* threatening; **tehdit
etmek** *v* threaten
tehlike [tehlike] *n* danger; **tehlike
uyarı ışığı** *npl* hazard warning
lights; **tehlikeye atmak** *v*
endanger; **Çığ tehlikesi var mı?**
Is there a danger of avalanches?
tehlikeli [tehlikeli] *adj* dangerous
tek [tek] *adj* only, single; **tek
başına** *n* solo; **tek gidiş bileti** *n*
one-way ticket; **tek kişilik oda** *n*
single room; **tek kullanımlık** *adj*
disposable; **tek yatak** *n* single
bed; **tek yataklı oda** *n* single; **tek
yön bilet** *n* single ticket; **Tek gidiş
bilet ne kadar?** How much is a
single ticket?; **Tek kişilik bir oda
ayırtmak istiyorum** I want to
reserve a single room; **Tek kişilik
bir oda istiyorum** I'd like to book
a single room
tekdüze [tekdyze] *adj*
monotonous
tekel [tekel] *n* monopoly
tekerlek [tekerlek] *n* wheel; **üç
tekerlekli bisiklet** *n* tricycle;
tekerlekli sandalye *n* wheelchair;
Tekerlekler kilitleniyor The
wheels lock; **Tekerleklerin
havası ne kadar olmalı?** What
should the tyre pressure be?

tekil [tekil] *n* singular
tekinsiz [tekinsiz] *adj* uncanny
tekler [tekler] *npl (spor)* singles
teklif [teklif] *n* bid, offer; **teklif
etmek** *v* offer
teklifsiz [teklifsiz] *adj* informal
tekme [tekme] *n* kick
tekmelemek [tekmelemek] *vt*
kick
tekne [tekne] *n* boat; **balıkçı
teknesi** *n* fishing boat; **gemi
teknesi** *n* hull; **kürek teknesi** *n*
rowing boat
teknik [teknik] *adj* technical ▷ *n*
technique; **teknik bilgi** *n*
know-how
teknisyen [teknisjen] *n*
technician; **motor teknisyeni** *n*
motor mechanic
tekno [tekno] *n* techno
teknoloji [teknoloʒi] *n* technology
Teknoloji [teknoloʒi] *n*
Enformasyon Teknolojisi *n* IT
teknolojik [teknoloʒik] *adj*
technological
tekrar [tekrar] *n* repeat; **Tekrar
eder misiniz lütfen?** Could you
repeat that, please?
tekrarlamak [tekrarlamak] *v*
repeat
tekrarlayan [tekrarlajan] *adj*
repetitive
tekstil [tekstil] *n* textile
tel [tel] *n* wire; **dikenli tel** *n* barbed
wire; **gelin teli** *n* tinsel; **jant teli** *n*
spoke; **tel zımba** *n* stapler; **zımba
teli** *n* staple *(wire)*
telaffuz [telaffuz] *n*
pronunciation; **telaffuz etmek** *v*
pronounce, spell

telafi [telafi] *n* compensation;
telafi etmek *v* compensate
telaş [telaʃ] *n* rush; **telaş etmek** *vi*
rush
telaşla [telaʃla] *adv* hastily
teleferik [teleferik] *n* cable car,
chairlift, ski lift
telefon [telefon] *n* phone,
telephone; **akıllı telefon** *n* smart
phone; **ankesörlü telefon** *n*
payphone; **cep telefonu** *n* mobile
phone; **fotoğraflı telefon** *n*
camera phone; **kapı telefonu** *n*
entry phone; **kartlı telefon** *n*
cardphone; **telefon etmek** *v*
phone; **telefon faturası** *n* phone
bill; **telefon görüşmesi** *n*
phonecall; **telefon kartı** *n*
phonecard, top-up card; **telefon
kodu** *n* dialling code; **telefon
kulübesi** *n* call box, phonebox;
telefon numarası *n* phone
number; **telefon rehberi** *n*
telephone directory; **telefon
sinyali** *n* dialling tone; **telefonla
aramak** *v* ring up; **telefonla satış**
npl telesales; **telefonu kapatmak**
v hang up; **video telefon** *n*
videophone; **... a telefon ne
kadar?** How much is it to
telephone...?; **Acil bir telefon
görüşmesi yapmam gerek** I need
to make an urgent telephone call;
**Bir telefon görüşmesi yapmam
gerek** I must make a phone call;
**Buradan telefon edebilir
miyim?** Can I phone from here?;
**Cep telefonumu nerede şarj
edebilirim** Where can I charge my
mobile phone?; **Nereden telefon**

edebilirim? Where can I make a
phone call?; **Telefon etmek
istiyorum** I want to make a phone
call; **Telefon kartı satıyor
musunuz?** Do you sell phone
cards?; **Telefon numaranızı
alabilir miyim?** Can I have your
phone number?; **Telefon
numarası nedir?** What's the
telephone number?; **Telefonla
sorunum var** I'm having trouble
with the phone; **Telefonunuzu
kullanabilir miyim lütfen?** Can I
use your phone, please?;
**Telefonunuzu kullanabilir
miyim?** May I use your phone?;
**Uluslararası telefon kartı
satıyor musunuz?** Do you sell
international phone cards?;
**Yirmibeş euroluk telefon kartı
rica ediyorum** I'd like a
twenty-five euro phone card
telekomünikasyon
[telekomynikasjon] *npl*
telecommunications
telesekreter [telesekreter] *n*
answering machine,
answerphone
teleskop [teleskop] *n* telescope
televizyon [televizjon] *n*
television, telly; **dijital televizyon**
n digital television; **renkli
televizyon** *n* colour television;
televizyon dizisi *n* soap opera;
Televizyon nerede? Where is the
television?; **Televizyon odası var
mı?** Is there a television lounge?
telgraf [telgraf] *n* telegram; **Bir
telgraf çekmek istiyorum** I want
to send a telegram; **Buradan**

telgraf çekebilir miyim? Can I send a telegram from here?; **Nereden telgraf çekebilirim?** Where can I send a telegram from?

telif [telif] n **telif hakkı** n copyright

telsiz [telsiz] adj cordless ▷ n walkie-talkie

tema [tema] n topic

temas [temas] n contact; **temas kurmak** v contact; **temassız** adj contactless; **Sizinle nasıl temas kurabilirim?** Where can I contact you?

tembel [tembel] adj lazy

temel [temel] adj basic, main; **temel ürün** n staple (commodity); **temel bilgiler** npl basics

temiz [temiz] adj clean; **temiz ve tertipli** adj neat; **Temiz bir çatal alabilir miyim lütfen?** Could I have a clean fork please?; **Temiz bir bardak alabilir miyim lütfen?** Can I have a clean glass, please?; **Temiz bir kaşık alabilir miyim lütfen?** Could I have a clean spoon, please?

temizleme [temizleme] n cleaning

temizlemek [temizlemek] vt clean; **kar temizleme aracı** n snowplough; **kuru temizleme** n dry-cleaning; **silip temizlemek** v wipe up; **yüz temizleme losyonu** n cleansing lotion

temizleyici [temizlejidʒi] n cleanser

temizlik [temizlik] n cleanliness; **bahar temizliği** n spring-cleaning

temizlikçi [temizliktʃi] n cleaner,

cleaning lady; **Temizlikçi kaçta geliyor?** When does the cleaner come?

Temmuz [temmuz] n July

temsil [temsil] n representation; **temsil eden** adj representative; **temsil etmek** v represent

temsilci [temsildʒi] n agent, rep

ten [ten] n complexion; **bronzlaşmış ten** n tan

tencere [tendʒere] n pot; **saplı tencere** n saucepan

teneke [teneke] n tin; **çöp tenekesi** n bin; **teneke kutu** n canister

tenis [tenis] n tennis; **masa tenisi** n table tennis; **tenis kortu** n tennis court; **tenis oyuncusu** n tennis player; **tenis raketi** n tennis racket; **Nerede tenis oynayabilirim?** Where can I play tennis?; **Tenis kortu kiralamak kaça?** How much is it to hire a tennis court?; **Tenis oynamak istiyoruz** We'd like to play tennis

tenkit [teɲit] n (davranış) criticism

tenör [tenør] n tenor

tente [tente] n tarpaulin

tepe [tepe] n top, (coğrafya) hill; **kilise kulesinin sivri tepesi** n spire; **kum tepesi** n sand dune; **tepelere tırmanma** n hill-walking; **Tepelere yürüyüşe çıkmak isterim** I'd like to go hill walking

tepede [tepede] adj top

tepki [tepki] n reaction; **tepki göstermek** v react

tepmek [tepmek] v to kick; **geri tepmek** v backfire; **taban tepmek** n tramp (long walk)

tepsi [tepsi] n tray

ter [ter] n sweat; **ter önleyici deodorant** n antiperspirant

terapi [terapi] n therapy

teras [teras] n patio, terrace; **Terasta yiyebilir miyim?** Can I eat on the terrace?

terazi [terazi] npl scales

Terazi [terazi] n **Terazi burcu** n Libra

tercih [terdʒih] n preference; **tercih etmek** v prefer

tercihen [terdʒihen] adv preferably

tercüman [terdʒyman] n translator

tercüme [terdʒyme] n translation; **tercüme etmek** v translate

tere [tere] n cress; **su teresi** n watercress

tereyağı [tereja:ə] n butter

terim [terim] n term (description)

teriyer [terijer] n terrier

terketmek [terketmek] v abandon

terleme [terleme] n perspiration

terlemek [terlemek] v sweat

terli [terli] adj sweaty

terlik [terlik] n slipper

terminal [terminal] n terminal; **otobüs terminali** n bus station

termometre [termometre] n thermometer

termos [termos] n Thermos®

termostat [termostat] n thermostat

terörist [terörist] n terrorist; **terörist saldırı** n terrorist attack

terörizm [terörizm] n terrorism

ters [ters] adj inverted; **ters tırnak**

işareti npl inverted commas

tersane [tersane] n shipyard

terslik [terslik] n mishap

tertip [tertip] n arrangement; **temiz ve tertipli** adj neat

terzi [terzi] n tailor

tesis [tesis] n plant (site/equipment)

teslim [teslim] n delivery; **son teslim tarihi** n deadline; **teslim etmek** vt deliver; **teslim olmak** v surrender

teslimat [teslimat] n delivery

test [test] n test; **kan testi** n blood test; **Pap smear testi** n smear test; **yıllık taşıt testi** n MOT

testere [testere] n saw

teşekkür [teʃekkyr] n **teşekkür ederim** thank you ▷ v **teşekkür etmek** v thank; **İçmiyorum, sağolun** I'm not drinking, thank you; **İyiyim, teşekkür ederim** Fine, thanks; **Çok teşekkürler** Thank you very much; **Beni davet ettiğiniz için çok teşekkürler** It's very kind of you to invite me; **Bizi davet ettiğiniz için çok teşekkürler** It's very kind of you to invite us

teşekkürler [teʃekkyrler] excl thanks!, thank you!

teşvik [teʃvik] n incentive

tetanoz [tetanoz] n tetanus; **Tetanoz aşısı yaptırmam gerek** I need a tetanus shot

teveccüh [tevedʒdʒyh] n concern

teyit [tejit] n confirmation

teyze [tejze] n auntie, aunt (mother's sister)

tezahürat [tezahyrat] n cheer;

tezahürat yapmak v cheer
tezgah [tezgah] n stall
tezgahlar [tezgahlar] npl stands
tezgahtar [tezgahtar] n sales
assistant
Thai [thai] adj Thai
tıbbi [təbbi] adj medical
tığ [təɣ] n **tığ gibi** adj slender
tık [tək] n click
tıkabasa [təkabasa] n **tıkabasa**
doldurmak vi cram; **tıkabasa**
dolu adj crammed
tıkaç [təkatʃ] n plug; **kulak tıkacı**
npl earplugs
tıkalı [təkalə] adj blocked
tıkamak [təkamak] v obstruct
tıkanıklık [təkanəklək] n
blockage, congestion
tıkanmak [təkanmak] vi choke
tıkırdamak [təkərdamak] v tick
tıklamak [təklamak] v click
tıknaz [təknaz] adj plump
tıp [təp] n medical
tırmanma [tərmanma] n (kaya)
rock climbing
tırmanmak [tərmanmak] v
climb, mount; **tepelere**
tırmanma n hill-walking;
Tırmanmaya gitmek isterdim I'd
like to go climbing
tırmık [tərmək] n rake
tırnak [tərnak] n fingernail; **çift**
tırnak npl quotation marks;
tırnak cilası n nail varnish; **tırnak**
fırçası n nailbrush; **tırnak makası**
n nail scissors; **tırnak törpüsü** n
nailfile; **ters tırnak işareti** npl
inverted commas
tırtıl [tərtəl] n caterpillar
Tibet [tibet] adj Tibetan ▷ n Tibet

Tibetçe [tibettʃe] n (dil) Tibetan
(language)
Tibetli [tibetli] n (kişi) Tibetan
(person)
ticaret [tidʒaret] n business,
trade; **ticaret bankası** n
merchant bank
tifo [tifo] n typhoid
tiksinmek [tiksinmek] v loathe
tiksinmiş [tiksinmiʃ] adj
disgusted
tilki [tilki] n fox
timsah [timsah] n alligator,
crocodile
tip [tip] n type
tipik [tipik] adj typical
tirbuşon [tirbuʃon] n corkscrew
tire [tire] n hyphen
tişört [tiʃørt] n tee-shirt, T-shirt;
pamuklu kalın tişört n
sweatshirt
titremek [titremek] v shiver,
tremble; **korkarak titremek** v
shudder
tiyatro [tijatro] n theatre;
Tiyatroda ne var? What's on at
the theatre?
Togo [togo] n Togo
tohum [tohum] n seed
toka [toka] n clasp; **kemer tokası**
n buckle; **saç tokası** n hairgrip
tokat [tokat] v **tokat atmak** v
smack
tokatlamak [tokatlamak] v slap
tokmak [tokmak] n (kapı,
çekmece) knob
tokyo [tokjo] n (terlik) flip-flops
tombola [tombola] n bingo
tombul [tombul] adj chubby
tomruk [tomruk] n log

tomurcuk [tomurdʒuk] *n* blossom

ton [ton] *n (ağırlık)* ton; **çalma tonu** *n* ringtone; **ton balığı** *n* tuna

Tonga [tonga] *n* Tonga

tonik [tonik] *n* tonic; **Ben bir cin tonik alayım lütfen** I'll have a gin and tonic, please

top [top] *n* ball; **badminton topu** *n* shuttlecock; **derli toplu** *(düzenli)* neatly, *(tertipli)* tidy; **havan topu** *n* mortar *(military)*; **kar topu** *n* snowball

topal [topal] *adj* lame

topallamak [topallamak] *v* limp

toparlamak [toparlamak] *v* round up; **toparlayıp kaldırmak** *v* put away

toparlanmak [toparlanmak] *v* get over

toplam [toplam] *n* sum, total

toplamak [toplamak] *v* *(matematik)* add up, *(ortalığı)* clear up, *(ortalığı)* tidy ▷ *vt (çiçek vb)* pick, *(para, pul vb)* collect; **derleyip toplamak** *v* tidy up

toplanmak [toplanmak] *vi* meet ▷ *vt* gather

toplantı [toplantə] *n* meeting; **basın toplantısı** *n* press conference; **danslı toplantı** *n* dancing; **... ile bir toplantı ayarlamak istiyordum** I'd like to arrange a meeting with...

toplu [toplu] *n* **toplu iğne** *n* pin; **toplu taşıma** *n* public transport

topluluk [topluluk] *n* a lot, assembly, community

toplum [toplum] *n* society

toplumbilim [toplumbilim] *n* sociology

toplumcu [toplumdʒu] *adj* communist ▷ *n* communist

toprak [toprak] *n* soil; **toprak kayması** *n* landslide; **toprak sahibi** *n* landowner

toptan [toptan] *n* wholesale

topuk [topuk] *n* heel; **yüksek topuklar** *npl* high heels; **yüksek topuklu** *adj* high-heeled

torba [torba] *n* bag; **alışveriş torbası** *n* carrier bag; **naylon torba** *n* plastic bag, polythene bag; **sıcak su torbası** *n* hot-water bottle; **sidik torbası** *n* bladder; **torba çay** *n* tea bag; **Bir torba daha alabilir miyim lütfen?** Can I have an extra bag, please?; **Torba istemem, sağolun** I don't need a bag, thanks; **Torbanız var mı?** Can I have a bag, please?

torbacık [torbadʒək] *n* sachet

tornavida [tornavida] *n* screwdriver

torpido [torpido] *n* **torpido gözü** *n* glove compartment

torun [torun] *n* grandchild; **erkek torun** *n* grandson; **kız torun** *n* granddaughter

torunlar [torunlar] *npl* grandchildren

tost [tost] *n* toast *(culin)*

toyota [tojota] *n* **Toyota parçaları var mı?** Do you have parts for a Toyota?

toz [toz] *n* dust, powder; **çamaşır tozu** *n* washing powder; **çiçek tozu** *n* pollen; **kabartma tozu** *n* baking powder; **kırmızı toz biber** *n* paprika; **sabun tozu** *n* soap powder; **toz almak** *vt* dust;

toz süsleme şekeri *n* icing sugar; **Çamaşır tozunuz var mı?** Do you have washing powder?

tozlu [tozlu] *adj* dusty

tozluk [tozluk] *npl* leggings

tökezlemek [tøkezlemek] *v* stumble, trip (up)

tören [tøren] *n* ceremony; **ödül töreni** *n* prize-giving; **tören alayı** *n* parade

törpü [tørpy] *n* **tırnak törpüsü** *n* nailfile

törpülemek [tørpylemek] *v* file (smoothing)

trabzan [trabzan] *n* banister

trafik [trafik] *n* traffic; **hava trafik kontrolörü** *n* air-traffic controller; **sağdan trafik** *n* right-hand drive; **soldan trafik** *n* left-hand drive; **trafik ışıkları** *npl* traffic lights; **trafik işareti** *n* road sign; **trafik kuralları** *n* Highway Code; **trafik magandalığı** *n* road rage; **trafik memuru** *n* traffic warden; **trafik sıkışıklığı** *n* traffic jam; **Otoyolda trafik yoğun mu?** Is the traffic heavy on the motorway?; **Yoğun trafikten kaçabileceğim bir güzergah var mı?** Is there a route that avoids the traffic?

trajedi [traʒedi] *n* tragedy

trajik [traʒik] *adj* tragic

traktör [traktør] *n* tractor

tramplen [tramplen] *n* diving board, trampoline

tramvay [tramvaj] *n* tram

transfer [transfer] *n* transfer; **Bankamdan para transferi yapmak istiyorum** I would like to transfer some money from my

bank in...; **Hesabımdan para transferi yapmak istiyorum** I would like to transfer some money from my account; **Transfer ücreti var mı?** Is there a transfer charge?; **Transfer ne kadar sürer?** How long will it take to transfer?

transistör [transistør] *v* transistor

transit [transit] *n* transit; **transit yolcu salonu** *n* transit lounge

transparan [transparan] *adj* see-through

transvestit [transvestit] *n* transvestite

traş [traʃ] *n* **asker traşı** *n* crew cut; **traş bıçağı** *n* razor, razor blade; **traş köpüğü** *n* shaving foam; **traş kremi** *n* shaving cream; **traş losyonu** *n* aftershave; **traş makinesi** *n* shaver; **traş olmak** *v* shave; **Traş makinem için priz nerede?** Where is the socket for my electric razor?

traşsız [traʃsəz] *adj* unshaven

travmatik [travmatik] *adj* traumatic

tren [tren] *n* train; **her gün işe trenle giden kimse** *n* commuter; **tren abonmanı** *n* railcard; **tren istasyonu** *n* railway station; **... tren saatleri nedir?** What times are the trains to...?; **... treni bu mu?** Is this the train for...?; **... treni hangi platformdan kalkıyor?** Which platform does the train for... leave from?; **... treni hangi sıklıkta geliyor?** How frequent are the trains to...?; **... treni ne zaman?** What time is the train to ...?; **... trenine nereden binebilirim?** Where can I get a train to ...?; **... treninin kalkacağı platform burası mı?** Is this the right platform for the train to...?; **... a bir sonraki tren kaçta?** When is the next train to ...?; **... a ilk tren kaçta?** When is the first train to ...?; **... a son tren kaçta?** When is the last train to ...?; **Bir sonraki tren lütfen** The next available train, please; **Bu tren... da duruyor mu?** Does the train stop at ...?; **Direk tren mi?** Is it a direct train?; **Tren gecikmeli mi?** Is the train running late?; **Tren hangi platformdan kalkıyor?** Which platform does the train leave from?; **Tren kaçta geliyor?** When is the train due?; **Tren kaçta kalkacak?** What time does the train leave?; **Tren on dakika rötarlı** The train is running ten minutes late; **Tren saatinde mi kalkacak?** Is the train on time?; **Trende restoran var mı?** Is there a buffet car on the train?; **Trende tekerlekli sandalye girişi var mı?** Is the train wheelchair-accessible?; **Trenimi kaçırdım** I've missed my train; **Ucuz tren tarifesi var mı?** Are there any cheap train fares?

trend [trend] v **trend olmak** v trend

Trinidad ve Tobago [trinidadvetobago] n Trinidad and Tobago

troley [trolej] n **Valizler için troley var mı?** Are there any luggage trolleys?

trolley [trollej] n **bagaj trolleyi** n luggage trolley

trombon [trombon] n trombone

tropik [tropik] adj tropical

tsunami [tsunami] n tsunami

tuğla [tu:la] n brick

tuhaf [tuhaf] adj peculiar

tulum [tulum] n dungarees ▷ npl (giysi) overalls; **uyku tulumu** n sleeping bag

Tunus [tunus] adj Tunisian ▷ n Tunisia

Tunuslu [tunuslu] n Tunisian

tur [tur] n (gezi) tour; **paket tur** n package tour; **rehberli tur** n guided tour; **tur operatörü** n tour operator; **tur otobüsü** n coach (vehicle); **tur rehberi** n tour guide; **tura çıkmak** v tour; **Kent turunuz var mı?** Are there any sightseeing tours of the town?; **Rehberli tur kaçta başlıyor?** What time does the guided tour begin?; **Tur ne kadar sürüyor?** How long does the tour take?; **Tur otobüsü ne zaman kalkıyor?** When is the bus tour of the town?; **Tur saat... da başlıyor** The tour starts at about...; **Turdan çok zevk aldım** I enjoyed the tour

turba [turba] n peat

turist [turist] n tourist; **Buraya turist olarak geldim** I'm here as a tourist

turizm [turizm] n tourism; **turizm bürosu** n tourist office

turna [turna] n crane (bird)

turnike [turnike] n turnstile; **bilet turnikesi** n ticket barrier

turnuva [turnuva] n tournament

turp [turp] *n* **kırmızı turp** *n* radish

turta [turta] *n* flan, tart; **elmalı turta** *n* apple pie

tuş [tuʃ] *n (bilgisayar/piyano)* key *(music/computer)*

tuşlamak [tuʃlamak] *v (telefon)* dial

tutarlı [tutarlə] *adj* consistent

tutarsız [tutarsəz] *adj* inconsistent

tutkal [tutkal] *n* glue

tutku [tutku] *n* passion

tutmak [tutmak] *vt* hold, keep; **dışarda tutmak** *v* keep out; **dışında tutmak** *v* exclude; **göz önünde tutarak** *prep* considering; **uçak tutması** *n* airsick

tutuklama [tutuklama] *n* arrest

tutuklamak [tutuklamak] *v* arrest

tutumlu [tutumlu] *adj* thrifty

tutunmak [tutunmak] *v* hold on

tutya [tutja] *n* pewter

tuvalet [tuvalet] *n* lavatory, loo, toilet; **erkekler tuvaleti** *n* gents'; **kadınlar tuvaleti** *n* ladies'; **tuvalet çantası** *n* sponge bag, toilet bag; **tuvalet kağıdı** *n* toilet paper, toilet roll; **tuvalet masası** *n* dressing table; **Özürlüler için tuvaletiniz var mı?** Are there any accessible toilets?; **Burada tuvalet var mı?** Is there a toilet on board?; **Tuvalet kağıdı yok** There is no toilet paper; **Tuvaleti kullanabilir miyim?** Can I use the toilet?; **Tuvaletin sifonu çalışmıyor** The toilet won't flush; **Tuvaletler nerede?** Where are the toilets?

tuz [tuz] *n* salt; **tatsız tuzsuz** *adj* tasteless; **tuzlanıp tütsülenmiş ringa balığı** *n* kipper; **tuzlu ve baharatlı** *adj* savoury; **Tuzu uzatır mısınız lütfen?** Pass the salt, please

tuzak [tuzak] *n* ambush, trap

tuzlu [tuzlu] *adj* saltwater, salty

tüberküloz [tyberkyloz] *n* tuberculosis, TB

tüfek [tyfek] *n* rifle; **makineli tüfek** *n* machine gun

tükenmek [tykenmek] *v* **soyu tükenmiş** *adj* extinct

tükenmez [tykenmez] *adj* **tükenmez kalem** *n* Biro®, ballpoint pen

tükenmiş [tykenmiʃ] *adj* exhausted

tüketici [tyketidʒi] *n* consumer

tükürmek [tykyrmek] *v* spit

tükürük [tykyryk] *n* saliva

tül [tyl] *n* net

tümsekli [tymsekli] *adj* bumpy

tünel [tynel] *n* tunnel

tüp [typ] *n* tube; **deney tüpü** *n* test tube; **tüp gaz** *n* camping gas

tür [tyr] *n* kind, species

türbe [tyrbe] *n* tomb

Türk [tyrk] *adj* Turkish ▷ *n* Turk

Türkçe [tyrktʃe] *n* Turkish

Türkiye [tyrkije] *n* Turkey

türkuvaz [tyrkuvaz] *adj* **türkuvaz renkli** *adj* turquoise

tüten [tyten] *n* smoking

tütsü [tytsy] *n* smoke; **tuzlanıp tütsülenmiş ringa balığı** *n* kipper

tütsülenmiş [tytsylenmiʃ] *adj* smoked

tütün [tytyn] *n* tobacco

tütüncü [tytyndʒy] *n*
tobacconist's
tüy [tyj] *n* feather; **tüyler**
ürpertici *adj* gruesome
tüyler [tyjler] *n* **diken diken**
olmuş tüyler *mpl* goose pimples
TV [tv] *n* TV; **plazma TV** *n* plasma
TV
tweet [tweet] *n* tweet; **tweet**
atmak *v* tweet

ucuz [udʒuz] *adj* cheap; **ucuz**
sezon *n* low season; **Daha ucuz**
bir şey istiyorum I want
something cheaper; **Daha ucuz**
bir şeyiniz var mı? Do you have
anything cheaper?; **En ucuz bilet**
olsun lütfen I'd like the cheapest
option; **Ucuz tarifeli uçuşunuz**
var mı? Are there any cheap
flights?; **Ucuz tren tarifesi var**
mı? Are there any cheap train fares?
uç [utʃ] *n (kalem/dil)* tip *(end of*
object); **aşırı uçta** *n* extremist;
parmaklarının ucunda yürüme
n tiptoe; **uç uç böceği** *n* ladybird;
ucu ucuna *adv* barely
uçak [utʃak] *n* aircraft, plane
(aeroplane); **uçak pisti** *n* runway;
uçak postası *n* airmail; **uçak**
tutması *n* jet lag; **uçak tutması** *n*
airsick; **Uçağım... da kalkıyor**
My plane leaves at...

uçmak [utʃmak] *vi* fly; **havaya uçmak** *vi* blow; **planörle uçma** *n* gliding; **uçup gitmek** *v* fly away

uçuk [utʃuk] *n (sağlık)* cold sore

uçurmak [utʃurmak] *v* fly, ascend; **havaya uçurmak** *v* blow up

uçurtma [utʃurtma] *n* kite

uçuş [utʃuʃ] *n* flight; **tarifeli uçuş** *n* scheduled flight; **tarifesiz uçuş** *n* charter flight; **uçuş bekleme salonu** *n* departure lounge; **uçuş hostesi** *n* flight attendant; **Uçuşumu değiştirmek istiyorum** I'd like to change my flight; **Uçuşumu iptal ettirmek istiyorum** I'd like to cancel my flight; **Uçuşunuz gecikmeli** The flight has been delayed

U-dönüşü [udønyʃy] *n* U-turn

ufak [ufak] *adj* minor, tiny; **birine ufak bir armağan alma** *n* treat; **ufak karides** *n* shrimp; **ufak sorun** *n* hitch

UFO [ufo] *abbr* UFO

ufuk [ufuk] *n* horizon

Uganda [uganda] *adj* Ugandan ▷ *n* Uganda

Ugandalı [ugandalə] *n* Ugandan

uğraş [u:raʃ] *n* pastime

uğraşmak [u:raʃmak] *v* struggle

uğurlamak [u:urlamak] *v* send off

uğursuz [u:ursuz] *adj* sinister

UHT [uha:te:] *n* **UHT süt** *n* UHT milk

Ukrayna [ukrajna] *adj* Ukrainian ▷ *n* Ukraine

Ukraynaca [ukrajnadʒa] *n (dil)* Ukrainian *(language)*

Ukraynalı [ukrajnalə] *n (kişi)* Ukrainian *(person)*

ulak [ulak] *n* messenger

ulaşmak [ulaʃmak] *vt* reach

ultimatom [ultimatom] *n* ultimatum

ultrason [ultrason] *n* ultrasound

ulumak [ulumak] *v* howl

ulus [ulus] *n* nation, nationality; **çok uluslu** *n* multinational

ulusal [ulusal] *adj* national

ulusalcı [ulusaldʒə] *n* nationalist

ulusalcılık [ulusaldʒələk] *n* nationalism

uluslararası [uluslararasə] *adj* international; **Bir uluslararası telefon kartı lütfen** An international phone card, please; **Buradan uluslararası görüşme yapabilir miyim?** Can I phone internationally from here?; **Nereden uluslararası telefon görüşmesi yapabilirim?** Where can I make an international phone call?

ummak [ummak] *v* expect

Umman [umman] *n* Oman

umulmadık [umulmadək] *adj* unexpected

umursamaz [umursamaz] *adj* casual

umut [umut] *n* hope; **umut etmek** *v* hope

umutla [umutla] *adv* hopefully

umutlu [umutlu] *adj* hopeful

umutsuz [umutsuz] *adj* desperate, hopeless

umutsuzca [umutsuzdʒa] *adv* desperately

umutsuzluk [umutsuzluk] *n* despair

un [un] n flour; **kepekli undan yapılmış** adj wholemeal; **un kurabiyesi hamuru** n shortcrust pastry

unutmak [unutmak] v forget

unutulmaz [unutulmaz] adj unforgettable

unutulmuş [unutulmuʃ] adj forgotten

ur [ur] n tumour

uranyum [uranjum] n uranium

URL [ure:le:] n URL

Uruguay [uruguaj] adj Uruguayan ▷ n Uruguay

Uruguaylı [uruguajlə] n Uruguayan

USB [uesbe:] adj **USB bellek** n USB stick

uskumru [uskumru] n mackerel

usta [usta] adj skilful; **usta işi** adj ingenious

utanç [utantʃ] npl shame; **utanç verici** adj disgraceful

utangaç [utangatʃ] adj shy

utanmış [utanməʃ] adj embarrassed

uyanık [ujanək] adj alert, awake

uyanmak [ujanmak] v awake, wake up

uyarı [ujarə] n warning; **tehlike uyarı ışığı** npl hazard warning lights; **uyarı çağrısı** n alarm call

uyarlamak [ujarlamak] n adapt; **ihtiyaca uyarlanmış** adj customized

uyarmak [ujarmak] v alert, warn

uydu [ujdu] n satellite; **uydu çanak** n satellite dish

uydurmak [ujdurmak] vi fit ▷ vt match; **Olmadı** It doesn't fit me

uyduruk [ujduruk] adj fake

uygarlık [ujgarlək] n civilization

uygulama [ujgulama] n app

uygulamak [ujgulamak] v carry out

uygulanabilir [ujgulanabilir] adj feasible

uygun [ujgun] adj appropriate, available, convenient, decent, fit, suitable; **haklı olarak** adv rightly; **modaya uygun** adj fashionable, trendy; **uygun adım yürümek** v march; **uygun olmayan** adj unsuitable

uygunluk [ujgunluk] n availability

uyku [ujku] n sleep; **tavşan uykusu** n snooze; **uyku hapı** n sleeping pill; **uyku tulumu** n sleeping bag; **uykuda yürüme** v sleepwalk; **uykusunu almak** v have a lie-in, lie in; **uykuyu uzatmak** v snooze; **Uyuyamıyorum** I can't sleep

uykuda [ujkuda] adj asleep

uykulu [ujkulu] adj drowsy, sleepy

uykusuzluk [ujkusuzluk] n insomnia

uyma [ujma] n fit

uymak [ujmak] v suit ▷ vi fit in

uysal [ujsal] adj easy-going

uyumak [ujumak] v sleep; **Uyuyamıyorum** I can't sleep

uyumlu [ujumlu] adj compatible, matching

uyun adım yürüyüş [ujunadəmjyryjyʃ] n march

uyuşturucu [ujuʃturudʒu] n

uyuşturucu bağımlısı *n* drug addict; **uyuşturucu satıcısı** *n* drug dealer

uyuşuk [ujuʃuk] *adj* numb

uyuyakalmak [ujujakalmak] *v* doze off, oversleep, sleep in

uzak [uzak] *adj* distant, far, remote; **uzaktan kumandalı** *adj* radio-controlled; **uzaktan yakından** *adv* remotely; **Banka buraya ne kadar uzakta?** How far is the bank?; **Oldukça uzak** It's quite far; **Plajdan ne kadar uzaktayız?** How far are we from the beach?; **Uzak değil** It's not far; **Uzak mı?** Is it far?; **Uzak Doğu** *n* Far East

uzaklık [uzaklək] *n* distance; **mil hesabıyla uzaklık** *n* mileage

uzakta [uzakta] *adv* away, far

uzatma [uzatma] *n* extension; **uzatma kablosu** *n* extension cable; **uzatma süresi** *n* injury time

uzay [uzaj] *n* space; **uzay aracı** *n* spacecraft

uzman [uzman] *n* expert, specialist; **ayak uzmanı** *n* chiropodist; **doğa bilimleri uzmanı** *n* naturalist

uzmanlaşmak [uzmanlaʃmak] *v* specialize

uzmanlık [uzmanlək] *n* speciality

uzun [uzun] *adj* long; **daha uzun** *adv* longer; **uzun atlama** *n* jump, long jump; **uzun boylu** *adj* tall; **Çok uzun zamandır bekliyoruz** We've been waiting for a very long time

uzunca [uzundʒa] *adv* long

uzunluk [uzunluk] *n* length; **Bu uzunlukta olsun** This length, please

uzun uzadıya [uzunuzadəja] *adv* extensively

ü

ücret [ydʒret] *n* fee, wage;
öğretim ücreti *npl* tuition fees;
ücreti ödenmemiş *adj* unpaid;
banka ücretleri *npl* bank charges;
giriş ücreti *n* admission charge,
entrance fee; **posta ücreti** *n*
postage; **servis ücreti** *n* cover
charge, service charge; **Yer
ayırtmak için ücret ödemek
gerekiyor mu?** Is there a booking
fee to pay?
ücretli [ydʒretli] *adj* paid; **düşük
ücretli** *adj* underpaid
üç [ytʃ] *number* three; **üç boyutlu**
adj three-dimensional; **üç katı** *adj*
treble, triple; **üç tekerlekli
bisiklet** *n* tricycle; **Üç çocuğum
var** I have three children; **Üç Ekim
Pazar** It's Sunday the third of
October; **Üç numaralı pompa
lütfen** Pump number three,
please; **Bu akşam için üç kişilik**

bir masa ayırtmak istiyordum
I'd like to book a table for three
people for tonight; **saat üçte** at
three o'clock
üçgen [ytʃgen] *n* triangle
üçüncü [ytʃyndʒy] *adj* third ▷ *n*
third; **üçüncü kişi sorumluluk
sigortası** *n* third-party insurance;
üçüncü olarak *adv* thirdly;
Üçüncü Dünya *n* Third World
üçüzler [ytʃyzler] *npl* triplets
üflemek [yflemek] *v* blow;
üfleme cihazı *n* Breathalyser®
ülke [ylke] *n* country; **ülke içi** *adj*
domestic; **gelişmekte olan ülke**
n developing country; **Ülkenin
haritasını nereden alabilirim?**
Where can I buy a map of the
country?; **Körfez Ülkeleri** *npl*
Gulf States
ümit [ymit] *n* hope, expectation;
ümit veren *adj* promising
ün [yn] *n* fame, reputation
üniforma [yniforma] *n* uniform;
okul üniforması *n* school
uniform
ünite [ynite] *n* unit
üniversite [yniversite] *n* uni,
university; **üniversite mezunu** *n*
graduate, undergraduate
ünlem [ynlem] *n* **ünlem işareti** *n*
exclamation mark
ünlü [ynly] *adj* famous ▷ *n*
celebrity, (*gramer*) vowel
ünsüz [ynsyz] *n* (*gramer*)
consonant
Ürdün [yrdyn] *adj* Jordanian ▷ *n*
Jordan
Ürdünlü [yrdynly] *n* Jordanian
üreme [yreme] *n* reproduction

üretici [yretidʒi] *n* manufacturer, producer
üretim [yretim] *n* production
üretmek [yretmek] *v* manufacture
ürkünç [yrkyntʃ] *adj* frightening
ürkütücü [yrkytydʒy] *adj* alarming, spooky
ürün [yryn] *n* crop, product; **ürün sağlamak** *v* yield; **deniz ürünü** *n* seafood; **kabuklu deniz ürünü** *n* shellfish; **süt ürünleri** *n* dairy products; **temel ürün** *n* staple *(commodity)*
üst [yst] *adj* upper, *(rütbe)* senior ▷ *n (kalite/rütbe)* superior; **üst katta** *adv* upstairs; **üstü açılır araba** *n* convertible; **üstü kapalı yük aracı** *n* van; **üstünü çıkarmak** *v* take off
üste [yste] *n* **üstesinden gelmek** *v* tackle
üstelik [ystelik] *adv* besides
üstün [ystyn] *adj* superior
üstünde [ystynde] *prep* over
üstünlük [ystynlyk] *n* advantage
ütü [yty] *n* **ütü tahtası** *n* ironing board; **Ütüye ihtiyacım var** I need an iron; **Bunu nerede ütületebilirim?** Where can I get this ironed?
ütüleme [ytyleme] *n* ironing
ütülemek [ytylemek] *v* iron
üvey [yvej] *n* **üvey anne** *n* stepmother; **üvey baba** *n* stepfather; **üvey erkek kardeş** *n* stepbrother; **üvey kız evlat** *n* stepdaughter; **üvey kızkardeş** *n* stepsister; **üvey oğul** *n* stepson
üye [yje] *n* member; **belediye**

meclis üyesi *n* councillor; **Üye olmak gerekiyor mu?** Do you have to be a member?; **Üye olmam gerekiyor mu?** Do I have to be a member?
üyelik [yjelik] *n* membership; **üyelik kartı** *n* membership card
üzere [yzere] *conj* **Görüşmek üzere** See you soon
üzerinde [yzerinde] *prep* above
üzgün [yzgyn] *adj* sad
üzüm [yzym] *n* grape; **bektaşi üzümü** *n* gooseberry; **kuru üzüm** *n* raisin, sultana; **kırmızı Frenk üzümü** *n* redcurrant

V

vaaz [vaaz] n sermon

vade [vade] prep **vadesi geçmiş borç** npl arrears

vadi [vadi] n valley

vaftiz [vaftiz] n christening; **vaftiz çocuğu** n godchild; **vaftiz kızı** n goddaughter; **vaftiz oğlu** n godson

vagon [vagon] n carriage, (oto) estate car; **kuşetli vagon** n sleeping car; **yemek vagonu** n dining car; **yemekli vagon** n buffet car; **Otuz numaralı vagon nerede?** Where is carriage number thirty?

vaha [vaha] **(vahalar)** n oasis

vahşi [vahʃi] adj brutal; **vahşi doğa** n wildlife

vaiz [vaiz] n minister (clergy)

vaka [vaka] n case

vakıflar [vakəflar] npl foundations

vakit [vakit] n time; **boş vakit** n

leisure; **hali vakti yerinde** adj well-off; **Çok güzel vakit geçiriyoruz** We are having a nice time

vakumlamak [vakumlamak] v vacuum

vakumlanmış [vakumlanməʃ] adj airtight

valiz [valiz] n suitcase; **Valizim hasar görmüş** My suitcase has arrived damaged

vals [vals] n waltz; **vals yapmak** v waltz

vampir [vampir] n vampire

vandal [vandal] n vandal

vandalizm [vandalizm] n vandalism

vanilya [vanilja] n vanilla

vantilatör [vantilatør] n fan; **Odada vantilatör var mı?** Does the room have a fan?

vapur [vapur] n **... a bir sonraki vapur kaçta?** When is the next sailing to...?; **... a son vapur kaçta?** When is the last sailing to...?; **... a vapur var mı?** Is there a ferry to...?; **İlk vapur kaçta?** When is the first boat?; **Son vapur kaçta?** When is the last boat?; **Vapur kaçta hareket ediyor?** When do we sail?; **Vapur nereden kalkıyor?** Where does the boat leave from?

var [var] adj present; **var olmak** v exist

varış [varəʃ] n arrival

varis [varis] n heir, (kadın) heiress

varlık [varlək] n asset, assets, presence, (zenginlik) wealth

varmak [varmak] v arrive; **farkına varmak** v notice, realize

varsayım [varsajəm] n supposition; **varsayımda bulunmak** v speculate

varsaymak [varsajmak] v assume, suppose

varsıl [varsəl] adj wealthy

vasıta [vasəta] **vasıta ile çarpmak** vi crash

vasiyet [vasijet] n will (document)

vatandaş [vatandaʃ] n citizen; **yaşlı vatandaş** n senior citizen

vatandaşlık [vatandaʃlək] n citizenship

Vatikan [vatikan] n Vatican

vazgeçilmez [vazgetʃilmez] adj indispensable

vazgeçmek [vazgetʃmek] v give up, waive

vazo [vazo] n vase

vb [vb] abbr (kısaltma) etc

ve [ve] conj and

veda [veda] n farewell, goodbye; **bekarlığa veda partisi** (erkek) n stag night

vegan [vegan] n vegan; **Bu yemek veganlara uygun mu?** Is this suitable for vegans?; **Vegan yemeğiniz var mı?** Do you have any vegan dishes?

vejetaryen [veʒetarjen] adj vegetarian ▷ n vegetarian; **Bu yemek vejetaryenlere uygun mu?** Is this suitable for vegetarians?; **Vejetaryenim** I'm vegetarian; **Buralarda vejetaryen restoranlar var mı?** Are there any vegetarian restaurants here?; **Vejetaryen**

yemekleriniz var mı? Do you have any vegetarian dishes?

vekalet [vekalet] **vekalet etmek** v substitute

vekaleten [vekaleten] adj acting

velet [velet] n brat

Venezuela [venezuela] adj Venezuelan ▷ n Venezuela

Venezuelalı [venezuelalə] n Venezuelan

veranda [veranda] n porch

vergi [vergi] n tax; **gelir vergisi** n income tax; **vergi geliri** n revenue; **vergi iadesi** n tax return; **vergi yükümlüsü** n tax payer; **yol vergisi** n road tax

veri [veri] npl data; **veri tabanı** n database

verici [veridʒi] n donor; **cesaret verici** adj encouraging; **dehşet verici** adj horrifying; **endişe verici** adj worrying; **heyecan verici** adj exciting, thrilling; **keyif verici** adj delightful; **utanç verici** adj disgraceful

verimlilik [verimlilik] n productivity

verimsiz [verimsiz] adj infertile

vermek [vermek] v hand ▷ vt give; **ödün vermek** v compromise; **ödünç vermek** v lend, loan; **bahşiş vermek** vt tip (reward); **bilgi vermek** v inform; **ders vermek** v lecture; **fiyat vermek** (açık arttırmada) vi bid (at auction); **güven vermek** v reassure; **güvence vermek** v assure; **geri vermek** v give back; **hayret verici** adj amazing; **hesap vermek** v account for; **izin**

vermek n allow, let, permit; **karar vermek** v decide; **komut vermek** v order *(command)*; **nefes vermek** v breathe out; **not vermek** v mark *(grade)*; **oy vermek** v vote; **rapor vermek** v report; **rüşvet vermek** v bribe; **söz vermek** v promise; **talimat vermek** v instruct; **tepki vermek** v respond; **yanıt vermek** v answer; **yanlış hüküm vermek** v misjudge; **yetki vermek** v authorize; **zarar vermek** v damage, harm; **Bahşiş vermek adet midir?** Is it usual to give a tip?

versiyon [versijon] n version

vestiyer [vestijer] n cloakroom

veteriner [veteriner] n vet

veto [veto] n veto

veznedar [veznedar] n treasurer

vızıldamak [vəzəldamak] v hum

vicdan [vidʒdan] n conscience; **vicdan azabı** n remorse

vicdanlı [vidʒdanlə] adj conscientious

vida [vida] n screw; **vida somunu** n nut *(device)*; **Vida gevşemiş** The screw has come loose

video [video] n video; **video blogu** n vlog; **video blog yazarı** n vlogger; **video kamera** n camcorder; **video kamerası** n video camera; **video telefon** n videophone

Vietnam [vietnam] adj Vietnamese ▷ n Vietnam

Vietnamca [vietnamdʒa] n *(dil)* Vietnamese *(language)*

Vietnamlı [vietnamlə] n *(kişi)* Vietnamese *(person)*

villa [villa] n villa; **Bir villa kiralamak istiyorum** I'd like to rent a villa

vinç [vintʃ] n crane *(for lifting)*

viraj [viraʒ] n bend

viral [viral] adj viral; **viral olmak** v to go viral

virgül [virgyl] n comma; **noktalı virgül** n semicolon

virüs [virys] n virus

viski [viski] n whisky; **malt viskisi** n malt whisky; **bir viski soda** a whisky and soda; **Ben viski alayım** I'll have a whisky

vişne [viʃne] n vişne çürüğü **renginde** adj maroon

vitamin [vitamin] n vitamin

vites [vites] n gear; **vites kolu** n gear lever, gear stick, gearshift; **vites kutusu** n gear box; **Bisiklet vitesli mi?** Does the bike have gears?; **Vites çalışmıyor/Vitesler çalışmıyor** The gears don't work

vitray [vitraj] n stained glass

vitrin [vitrin] n shop window; **vitrin mankeni** n dummy

viyola [vijola] n viola

viyolonsel [vijolonsel] n cello

vize [vize] n visa; **Giriş vizem var** I have an entry visa; **Vizem burada** Here is my visa

vizon [vizon] n mink

voleybol [volejbol] n volleyball

volkan [volkan] **(volkanlar)** n volcano

volt [volt] n volt

voltaj [voltaʒ] n voltage; **Voltaj ne kadar?** What's the voltage?

votka [votka] n vodka

vurgulamak [vurgulamak] v

emphasize, highlight, stress

vurmak [vurmak] *v* knock, ram, thump, *(sineklik gibi yassı bir şeyle)* swat ▷ *vt* hit, strike; **ayağını yere vurmak** *v* stamp; **şiddetle vurmak** *v* bash

vurmalı [vurmalə] *n (müzik)* percussion

vuruş [vuruʃ] *n* knock, *(topa sopayla)* bat *(with ball)*; **başlama vuruşu** *n* kick-off; **başlama vuruşu yapmak** *v* kick off; **hafif vuruş** *n* tap

vücut [vydʒut] *n* body; **vücut geliştirme** *n* bodybuilding

waffle [vaffle] *n* waffle
webmaster [vebmaster] *n* webmaster
wifi [vifi] *n* WiFi

y

Yağ lekesi This stain is oil
yağlamak [ja:lamak] v oil
yağlı [ja:lə] *adj* greasy
yağmak [ja:mak] v rain; **dolu yağmak** v hail; **kar yağmak** v snow; **sulu sepken yağmak** v sleet; **yağmur yağmak** v rain
yağmur [ja:mur] *n* rain; **asit yağmuru** *n* acid rain; **yağmur ormanı** *n* rainforest; **yağmura dayanıklı** *adj* showerproof; **yağmurlama cihazı** *n* sprinkler; **Sizce yağmur yağacak mı?** Do you think it's going to rain?; **Yağmur yağıyor** It's raining
yağmurlu [ja:murlu] *adj* rainy
yağmurluk [ja:murluk] *n* mac, raincoat
Yahudi [jahudi] *adj* Jewish ▷ *n* Jew
yaka [jaka] *n* collar; **polo yakalı kazak** *n* polo-necked sweater
yakalamak [jakalamak] v seize ▷ *vt* catch
yakın [jakən] *adj* close, close by, intimate, near, nearby ▷ *adv* close; **en yakın akraba** *n* next-of-kin; **uzaktan yakından** *adv* remotely; **yakın dost** *n* pal; **Çok yakın** It's very near; **Buraya en yakın metro istasyonu nerede?** Where is the nearest tube station?; **Buraya en yakın otobüs durağı nerede?** Where is the nearest bus stop?; **Buraya yakın bir golf sahası var mı?** Is there a public golf course near here?; **Buraya yakın sakin bir kumsal var mı?** Is there a quiet beach near here?; **En yakın bisiklet tamircisi nerede?** Where is the nearest bike repair

ya [ja] *conj* either... or, or
yabancı [jabandʒə] *adj* foreign ▷ *n* alien, foreigner, stranger
yaban gelinciği [jabangelindʒə] *n* ferret
yabani [jabani] *adj* wild; **yabani havuç** *n* parsnip; **yabani ot** *n* weed; **yabani ot öldürücü** *n* weedkiller; **yabani tavşan** *n* hare
yaban mersini [jabanmersini] *n* blueberry; **kırmızı yaban mersini** *n* cranberry
yabanturpu [jabanturpu] *n* horseradish
ya da [jada] *adv* alternatively
yağ [ja:] *n* fat, grease, oil; **güneş yağı** *n* suntan oil; **yağ çubuğu** *n* dipstick; **yağı alınmış süt** *n* skimmed milk; **yarım yağlı süt** *n* semi-skimmed milk; **zeytin yağı** *n* olive oil; **Yağ ikaz ışığı yanıyor** The oil warning light won't go off;

shop?; **En yakın dağ kulübesi nerede?** Where is the nearest mountain hut?; **En yakın dağ kurtarma ekibi nerede?** Where is the nearest mountain rescue service post?; **En yakın eczane nerede?** Where is the nearest chemist?; **En yakın fotoğraf malzemeleri satan dükkan nerede?** Where is the nearest shop which sells photographic equipment?; **En yakın gazete satan dükkan nerede?** Where is the nearest shop which sells newspapers?; **En yakın metro istasyonu nerede?** Where is the nearest tube station?; **En yakın metro istasyonuna nasıl gidebilirim?** How do I get to the nearest tube station?; **Pul satan en yakın yer nerede?** Where is the nearest shop which sells stamps?; **Yakınlarda bir banka var mı?** Is there a bank nearby?

yakından [jakəndan] adv closely

yakınında [jakənənda] adv around, near

yakınlarda [jakənlarda] adv nearby

yakınlık [jakənlək] n proximity

yakınmak [jakənmak] v complain

yakışıklı [jakəʃəklə] adj good-looking, handsome

yakıt [jakət] n fuel; **yakıt ikmali yapmak** v refuel

yaklaşık [jaklaʃək] adj approximate ▷ adv about; **yaklaşık olarak** adv approximately

yaklaşmak [jaklaʃmak] v approach

yakmak [jakmak] v (ışık) light ▷ vt (ateşte) burn

yalak [jalak] n trough

yalamak [jalamak] v lick

yalan [jalan] n lie; **yalan söylemek** v lie

yalancı [jalandʒə] n liar; **yalancı şahitlik** n perjury

yaldız [jaldəz] n **kalay yaldızı** n tinfoil

yalı [jalə] adj **yalı çapkını** n kingfisher

yalıtım [jalətəm] n insulation

yalnız [jalnəz] adj alone, lonely, lonesome; **yalnız ebeveyn** n single parent

yalnızca [jalnəzdʒa] adv exclusively, only

yalnızlık [jalnəzlək] n loneliness

yama [jama] n patch

yamalı [jamalə] adj patched

yan [jan] n (destek) subsidiary; **yan ayna** n wing mirror; **yan etki** n side effect; **yan lambalar** n sidelight; **yan sokak** n side street; **yana doğru** adv sideways; **yanından geçmek** v go past

yanak [janak] n cheek

yangı [jangə] n inflammation

yangın [jangən] n fire; **yangın alarmı** n fire alarm; **yangın çıkışı** n fire escape; **yangın söndürücü** n fire extinguisher; **Yangın var!** Fire!

yanıcı [janədʒə] adj flammable

yanık [janək] n burn; **güneş yanığı** adj sunburn, sunburnt

yanılsama [janəlsama] n illusion

yanıltıcı [janəltədʒə] adj confusing, misleading

yanıltmak [janəltmak] v deceive
yanında [janənda] prep beside, next to
yanıt [janət] n answer, reply, response; **yanıt vermek** v answer; **Yanıtınızı bana mesajla geçer misiniz?** Can you text me your answer?
yanıtlamak [janətlamak] v reply
yankesicilik [jaŋesidʒilik] n pickpocket
yankı [jaŋə] n echo
yanlı [janlə] adj biased
yanlış [janləʃ] adj incorrect, wrong ▷ adv wrong ▷ n error; **yanlış alarm** n false alarm; **yanlış anlama** n misunderstanding; **yanlış anlamak** v misunderstand; **yanlış hüküm vermek** v misjudge; **yanlış numara** n wrong number; **yanlış yere koymak** v mislay; **Sanırım yanlış para üstü verdiniz** I think you've given me the wrong change; **Yanlış şerittesiniz** You are in the wrong lane; **Yanlış numara** You have the wrong number
yanlışlıkla [janləʃləkla] adv mistakenly
yanmak [janmak] v burn; **yanıp kül olmak** v burn down
yansıma [jansəma] n reflection
yansıtmak [jansətmak] v reflect
yansız [jansəz] adj impartial, impersonal
yapabilmek [japabilmek] **yapabilir almak** v to be able
yapamamak [japamamak] adj unable to
yapay [japaj] adj artificial, superficial

yapboz [jabboz] n jigsaw
yapı [japə] n building, construction, structure
yapıcı [japədʒə] adj constructive ▷ n maker
yapılmış [japəlməʃ] adj done; **sütle yapılmış** n dairy produce
yapım [japəm] n make; **el yapımı** adj handmade; **ev yapımı** adj home-made; **gemi yapımı** n shipbuilding; **yol yapım çalışması** npl roadworks
yapışkan [japəʃkan] adj sticky
yapışmak [japəʃmak] vi stick
yapıştırmak [japəʃtərmak] v glue
yapmak [japmak] v construct, make ▷ vt do; **alıntı yapmak** v quote; **ızgara yapmak** v grill; **başlama vuruşu yapmak** v kick off; **baskı yapmak** v lean on, pressure; **baskın yapmak** v raid; **blöf yapmak** v bluff; **düşük yapmak** n miscarriage; **değişiklik yapmak** v modify; **dedikodu yapmak** v gossip; **diyet yapmak** v diet; **ekonomi yapmak** v economize; **elle yapmak** v handle; **görüşme yapmak** v interview; **gösteriş yapmak** v show off; **giriş yapmak** v check in; **grev yapmak** vi strike (suspend work); **hata yapmak** v mistake, slip up; **hız yapmak** v speeding; **işbirliği yapmak** v collaborate; **iniş yapmak** vi land; **kaçakçılık yapmak** v smuggle; **kamp yapmak** v camp; **karalama yapmak** v sketch; **karşılıklı yapmak** v exchange; **şaka yapmak** v joke; **şantaj yapmak** n

blackmail; **manikür yapmak** n
manicure; **modelini yapmak** v
model; **otostop yapma** n
hitchhiking; **para iadesi yapmak**
v refund; **paten yapma** n skating;
paten yapmak v skate; **pratik
yapmak** v practise; **reklam
yapmak** v advertise; **sayı
yapmak** v score; **sörf yapma** n
surfing; **sörf yapmak** v surf;
skateboard yapma n
skateboarding; **tanıtımını
yapmak** v promote; **tezahürat
yapmak** v cheer; **vals yapmak** v
waltz; **yapmak zorunda olmak** v
have to; **yatırım yapmak** v invest;
yayın yapmak v broadcast;
yeniden yapmak v rebuild, redo;
yorum yapmak v comment
yaprak [japrak] n leaf; **defne
yaprağı** n bay leaf
yapraklar [japraklar] npl leaves
yaptırmak [japtərmak] **kayıt
yaptırmak** v register
yara [jara] n injury, scar, sore,
wound, (ülser) ulcer; **yara bandı** n
Elastoplast®, plaster (for wound)
yaradılış [jaradələʃ] n creation
yaralamak [jaralamak] v injure,
wound
yaralanmış [jaralanməʃ] adj
injured
yaramaz [jaramaz] adj (çocuk vb)
mischievous, (çocuk vb) naughty
yaramazlık [jaramazlək] n
mischief
yarar [jarar] n benefit; **yarar
sağlamak** v benefit
yararlı [jararlə] adj useful
yararsız [jararsəz] adj useless

yarasa [jarasa] n bat (mammal)
yaratıcı [jaratədʒə] adj creative;
gerginlik yaratıcı adj stressful
yaratık [jaratək] n creature
yaratmak [jaratmak] v create,
produce
yarda [jarda] n yard
(measurement)
yardım [jardəm] n aid, assistance,
favour, help; **ilk yardım** n first aid;
ilk yardım çantası n first-aid kit;
yardım derneği n charity;
yardım derneği dükkanı n
charity shop; **yardım etmek** vt
help; **yardım hattı** n helpline;
yoksulluk yardımı n dole;
**Binmeme yardım eder misiniz
lütfen?** Can you help me get on,
please?; **Valizleri taşımama
yardım eder misiniz lütfen?** Can
you help me with my luggage,
please?; **Yardım çağırın, çabuk!**
Fetch help quickly!; **Yardım
edebilir misiniz lütfen?** Can you
help me, please?; **Yardıma
ihtiyacım var** I need assistance;
Yardımcı olabilir misiniz? Can
you help me?
yardımcı [jardəmdʒə] adj
associate, helpful; **müdür
yardımcısı** n deputy head; **papaz
yardımcısı** n vicar; **yardımcı
öğretmen** n classroom assistant;
yardımcı olmayan adj unhelpful
yargıç [jargətʃ] n judge
yargılamak [jargəlamak] v judge
yarı [jarə] n **yarı fiyatı/yarı
fiyatına** adv half-price; **yarı
yarıya** adv fifty-fifty, half; **yarı
yolda** halfway

yarım [jarəm] *adj* half ▷ *n* half; **yarı final** *n* semifinal; **yarım daire** *n* semicircle; **yarım gün** *adv* part-time; **yarım peruk** *n* toupee; **yarım saat** *n* half-hour; **yarım yağlı süt** *n* semi-skimmed milk

yarımada [jarəmada] *n* peninsula

yarın [ja:rən] *adv* tomorrow; **Sizi yarın arayabilir miyim?** May I call you tomorrow?; **yarın öğleden sonra** tomorrow afternoon; **yarın gece** tomorrow night; **yarın sabah** tomorrow morning; **Yarın açık mı?** Is it open tomorrow?; **Yarın ayrılıyorum** I'm leaving tomorrow; **Yarın bir şeyler yapmak ister misiniz?** Would you like to do something tomorrow?; **Yarın sabah boşum** I'm free tomorrow morning; **Yarın tekrar arayacağım** I'll call back tomorrow

yarış [jarəʃ] *n* race *(contest)*; **at yarışı** *n* horse racing; **oto yarışı** *n* motor racing; **yarış arabası** *n* racing car; **yarış atı** *n* racehorse; **yarış parkuru** *n* racecourse; **yarış pisti** *n* racetrack; **At yarışı görmek isterdim** I'd like to see a horse race

yarışçı [jarəʃtʃə] *n* racer, *(otomobil)* racing driver

yarışma [jarəʃma] *n* competition, contest; **bilgi yarışması** *n* quiz

yarışmacı [jarəʃmadʒə] *n* competitor, contestant, runner

yarışmak [jarəʃmak] *v* compete ▷ *vi* race

yasa [jasa] *n* bill *(legislation)*, law

yasadışı [jasadəʃə] *adj* illegal

yasak [jasak] *adj* forbidden ▷ *n* ban

yasaklamak [jasaklamak] *v* ban, forbid, prohibit

yasaklanmış [jasaklanməʃ] *adj* banned, prohibited

yasal [jasal] *adj* legal

yasalar [jasalar] *n* constitution

yaslamak [jaslamak] *v* lean

yaslanır [jaslanər] *adj* reclining

yastık [jastək] *n* cushion, pillow; **hava yastığı** *n* airbag; **yastık kılıfı** *n* pillowcase

yaş [jaʃ] *n (yıl)* age; **orta yaşlı** *adj* middle-aged; **yaş sınırı** *n* age limit; **yaşça en büyük** *adj* eldest; **yaşça küçük** *adj* junior; **yaşlı vatandaş** *n* senior citizen; **yirmi yaş dişi** *n* wisdom tooth

yaşam [jaʃam] *n* life; **özel yaşam** *n* privacy; **sağlıklı yaşam** *n* keep-fit; **yaşam öyküsü** *n* biography; **yaşam biçimi** *n* lifestyle; **yaşam kavgası** *n* survival; **yaşam sigortası** *n* life insurance; **yaşam standardı** *n* standard of living; **yaşama bakış** *n* outlook

yaşamak [jaʃamak] *v* live; **beraber yaşamak** *v* live together

yaşlı [jaʃlə] *adj* aged, old; **daha yaşlı** *adj* elder

yaşlılar [jaʃləlar] *adj* elderly

yaşlılık [jaʃlələk] *n* geriatric

yat [jat] *n (tekne)* yacht; **yat limanı** *n* marina

yatak [jatak] *n* bed, *(döşek)* mattress; **çift kişilik yatak** *n* double bed; **çift yatak** *npl* twin beds; **çift yataklı oda** *n* twin room, twin-bedded room; **battal**

boy yatak *n* king-size bed; **deniz yatağı** *n* Lilo®; **güneşlenme yatağı** *n* sunbed; **tek yatak** *n* single bed; **yatak örtüsü** *n* bedspread; **yatak çarşafı** *n* bed linen; **yatak odası** *n* bedroom; **yatak takımı** *n* bedclothes, bedding; **yatak ve kahvaltı** *n* bed and breakfast; **İki yataklı bir oda rica ediyorum** I'd like a room with twin beds; **Çift yataklı bir oda rica ediyorum** I'd like a room with a double bed; **Tek bir yatak rica ediyorum** I'd like a dorm bed; **Yatak çok rahatsız** The bed is uncomfortable; **Yatakta mı kalmam gerekiyor?** Do I have to stay in bed?

yatakhane [jatakhane] *n* dormitory

yatay [jataj] *adj* horizontal, level

yatık [jatək] *n* **geriye yatık çizgi** *n* backslash

yatırım [jatərəm] *n* investment; **yatırım yapmak** *v* invest

yatırımcı [jatərəmdʒə] *n* investor

yatıştırıcı [jatəʃtərədʒə] *n* sedative

yatmak [jatmak] *v* lie, lie down; **önüne gelenle yatmak** *v* sleep around; **birlikte yatmak** *v* sleep together; **yatma zamanı** *n* bedtime

yavaş [javaʃ] *adj* slow; **yavaş yavaş kaynatmak** *v* simmer; **Bağlantı çok yavaş** The connection seems very slow; **Biraz daha yavaş konuşabilir misiniz lütfen?** Could you speak more slowly, please?

yavaşça [javaʃtʃa] *adv* slowly

yavaşlamak [javaʃlamak] *v* slow down

yavru [javru] *n (aslan/ayı)* cub; **kedi yavrusu** *n* kitten; **yavru köpek** *n* puppy; **yeni doğmuş yavrular** *n* litter *(offspring)*

yay [jaj] *n* bow *(weapon)*, spring *(coil)*

Yay [jaj] *n* **Yay burcu** *n* Sagittarius

yaya [jaja] *n* pedestrian; **ışıklı yaya geçidi** *n* pelican crossing; **şeritli yaya geçidi** *n* zebra crossing; **yaya geçidi** *n* pedestrian crossing; **yayalara ayrılmış** *adj* pedestrianized; **yayalara özel bölge** *n* pedestrian precinct

yaygara [jajgara] *n* fuss

yaygaracı [jajgaradʒə] *adj* fussy

yaygın [jajgən] *adj* widespread; **yaygın bir şekilde** *adv* largely

yayılım [jajələm] *n* spread

yayılmak [jajəlmak] *v* spread out

yayımlama [jajəmlama] *n* publication

yayımlamak [jajəmlamak] *v* publish

yayın [jajən] *n* broadcast, feed; **kablolu yayın** *n* cable television; **yayın akışı** *n* stream; **yayın aktarmak** *v* stream; **yayın yapmak** *v* broadcast

yayınevi [jajənevi] *n* publisher

yayıntı [jajəntə] *n* clutter

yaymak [jajmak] *vt* spread

yaz [jaz] *n (mevsim)* summer; **yaz sezonu** *n* summertime; **yaz tatili** *npl* summer holidays; **yaz boyunca** during the summer;

yazın in summer; **yazdan önce**
before summer; **yazdan sonra**
after summer

yazar [jazar] **(kadın yazar)** n
author, writer; **oyun yazarı** n
playwright; **yazar kasa** n till

yazı [jazə] n writing; **anma yazısı**
(ölünün ardından) n obituary;
beyaz yazı tahtası n whiteboard;
el yazısı n handwriting; **kazılmış**
yazı n inscription; **yazı kağıdı** n
writing paper

yazıcı [jazədʒə] n printer
(machine); **CD yazıcı** n CD burner;
DVD yazıcı n DVD burner; **Renkli**
yazıcı var mı? Is there a colour
printer?

yazık [jazək] n pity, shame; **ne**
yazık ki adv unfortunately

yazılım [jazələm] n software

yazım [jazəm] n spelling; **yazım**
denetimi n spellchecker

yazın [jazən] in summer

yazışma [jazəʃma] n
correspondence

yazlık [jazlək] n **yazlık iş** n holiday
job

yazma [jazma] adv **okuma**
yazması olmayan adj illiterate

yazmak [jazmak] v write, write
down, *(daktilo/bilgisayar)* type;
blog yazmak v blog; **ilaç yazmak**
v prescribe

yedek [jedek] adj spare ▷ n backup,
reserve *(retention)*, substitute;
yedek öğretmen n supply
teacher; **yedek oda** n spare room;
yedek parça n spare part; **Yedek**
çarşaf takımı var mı? Is there any
spare bedding?

yedi [jedi] *number* seven

yedinci [jedindʒi] adj seventh ▷ n
seventh

yeğen [je:en] n *(erkek)* nephew,
(kız) niece

Yehova [jehova] n **Yehovanın**
Şahitleri n Jehovah's Witness

yelek [jelek] n waistcoat;
cankurtaran yeleği n life jacket

yelken [jelken] n sail; **yelken**
sporu n sailing

yelkenli [jelkenli] n sailing boat

yemek [jemek] n dish *(food)* ▷ vt
eat; **akşam yemeği** n dinner; **ana**
yemek n main course; **artık**
yemek npl leftovers; **öğle yemeği**
n lunch; **ön yemek** n starter;
darbe yemek vi strike; **hafif**
akşam yemeği n supper; **hazır**
yemek n ready-cooked,
takeaway; **paket yemek** n packed
lunch; **yemek öncesi içki** n
aperitif; **yemek kitabı** n
cookbook, cookery book; **yemek**
molası n lunch break; **yemek**
salonu n dining room; **yemek**
vagonu n dining car; **yemek**
zamanı n dinner time, lunchtime,
mealtime; **yemekli parti** n dinner
party; **yemekli vagon** n buffet
car; **yemeklik şarap** n table wine;
İçinde nişasta olmayan
yemeğiniz var mı? Do you have
gluten-free dishes?; **Bir şey**
yemek ister misiniz? Would you
like something to eat?; **Bu yemeği**
nasıl pişiriyorsunuz? How do you
cook this dish?; **Bu yemeğin**
içinde ne var? What is in this
dish?; **Bu yemeğin yanında ne**

veriyorsunuz? How is this dish served?; **Feribotta yemek satan bir yer var mı?** Is there somewhere to eat on the boat?; **Günün yemeği ne?** What is the dish of the day?; **Helal yemeğiniz var mı?** Do you have halal dishes?; **Koşer yemeğiniz var mı?** Do you have kosher dishes?; **Ne yemek istersiniz?** What would you like to eat?; **Vegan yemeğiniz var mı?** Do you have any vegan dishes?; **Vejetaryen yemekleriniz var mı?** Do you have any vegetarian dishes?; **Yöresel bir yemek tavsiye edebilir misiniz?** Can you recommend a local dish?; **Yemek yediniz mi?** Have you eaten?

Yemen [jemen] n Yemen

yemin [jemin] n oath

yengeç [jengetʃ] n crab

Yengeç [jengetʃ] n **Yengeç Burcu** n Cancer (horoscope)

yeni [jeni] adj new, recent; **yeni başlayan** n beginner; **yeni doğan** adj newborn; **yeni doğmuş yavrular** n litter (offspring); **yeni gelen** n newcomer; **yeni yürümeye başlayan çocuk** n toddler; **yeniden çekim** n remake; **yeniden badana yapmak** v redecorate; **yeniden bir araya gelme** n reunion; **yeniden düzenlemek** v reorganize; **yeniden ele almak** vt reconsider; **yeniden evlenmek / yeniden gösterim** remarry; **yeniden göstermek** v replay; **yeniden kullanmak** v reuse; **yeniden sınava girmek** v resit;

yeniden yapılandırma v restructure; **yeniden yapmak** v rebuild, redo; **Yeni bir akü gerekiyor** I need a new battery; **Yepyeni bir tarz istiyorum** I want a completely new style; **Yeni Yıl** n New Year

yenilebilir [jenilebilir] adj edible

yenilemek [jenilemek] n makeover ▷ v renew, renovate

yenilenebilir [jenilenebilir] adj renewable

yenilgi [jenilgi] n defeat; **yenilgiyi kabullenmek** v give in

yenilik [jenilik] n innovation

yenilikçi [jeniliktʃi] adj innovative

yenilmez [jenilmez] adj unbeatable

yenilmiş [jenilmiʃ] n loser

Yeni Zelanda [jenizelanda] n New Zealand; **Yeni Zelandalı** n New Zealander

yenmek [jenmek] v beat (outdo), conquer, defeat, triumph

yepyeni [jepjeni] adj brand-new

yer [jer] n floor, ground, location, place, spot, venue; **ayağını yere vurmak** v stamp; **başka bir yerde** adv elsewhere; **bir yerde** adv someplace, somewhere; **doğum yeri** n birthplace, place of birth; **güzel manzaralı yer** n beauty spot; **gezinti yeri** n promenade; **gidilecek yer** n destination; **her yerde** adv everywhere; **herhangi bir yer** adv anywhere; **hiçbir yerde** adv nowhere; **kalacak yer** n accommodation; **kamp yeri** n campsite; **kapalı yer korkusu olan** adj claustrophobic; **pazar**

yeri n marketplace; **tatil yeri** n resort; **yanlış yere koymak** v mislay; **yer değiştirme** n shift; **yer değiştirmek** v shift; **yer muşambası** n lino; **yere sermek** v knock out; **yerin altında** adv underground; **yerini alma** n replacement; **yerini almak** v replace; **Burada dalınacak en iyi yer neresi?** Where is the best place to dive?; **Gidilecek iyi bir yer biliyor musunuz?** Do you know a good place to go?

yeraltı [jeraltə] n **yeraltı harekatı** n underground

yerden [jerden] n **yerden almak** v pick up

yerel [jerel] adj local; **Yerel bitkileri ve ağaçları görmek isterdik** We'd like to see local plants and trees; **Yerel müzisyenleri dinleyebileceğimiz bir yer var mı?** Where can we hear local musicians play?; **Yerel yürüyüşler için rehberiniz var mı?** Do you have a guide to local walks?; **Yerel yemeğiniz nedir?** What's the local speciality?; **Yerel yemeğiniz var mı?** Is there a local speciality?

yerfıstığı [jerfəstəə] n peanut

yerine [jerine] adv instead ▷ prep instead of

yerküre [jerkyre] n globe

yerleşmek [jerleʃmek] v settle down

yerleştirme [jerleʃtirme] n placement

yerleştirmek [jerleʃtirmek] vt place

yerli [jerli] adj native

yeryüzü [jerjyzy] n earth

yeşil [jeʃil] adj green (colour) ▷ n green; **yeşil limon** n lime (fruit); **yeşil salata** n green salad

Yeşilaycı [jeʃilajdʒə] adj teetotal

yetenek [jetenek] n ability, talent

yetenekli [jetenekli] adj gifted, talented

yeteneksiz [jeteneksiz] adj incompetent

yeter [jeter] adv **yeter ki** conj provided, providing; **Bu kadar yeter, sağolun** That's enough, thank you

yeterli [jeterli] adj sufficient

yetersiz [jetersiz] adj inadequate, inefficient, insufficient, skimpy; **yetersiz beslenme** n malnutrition

yetişkin [jetiʃkin] n adult; **yetişkin eğitimi** n adult education

yetişmek [jetiʃmek] v catch up

yetiştirilme [jetiʃtirilme] n upbringing

yetiştirmek [jetiʃtirmek] v bring up, (hayvan) breed

yetki [jetki] n authority; **yetki vermek** v authorize

yetkilendirmek [jetkilendirmek] v delegate

yetkili [jetkili] adj official

yetkin [jetkin] adj competent

yetmiş [jetmiʃ] number seventy

yığılmak [jəəlmak] n pile-up

yığın [jəən] n heap, pile, stack; **saman yığını** n haystack

yıkamak [jəkamak] v wash; **bulaşık yıkama** n washing-up; **bulaşık yıkamak** v wash up;

oto yıkama n car wash; **Arabayı yıkamak istiyorum** I would like to wash the car; **Yıkama makinesi nasıl çalışıyor?** How do I use the car wash?

yıkanabilir [jəkanabilir] adj machinede yıkanabilir n machine washable; **Bu yıkanabilir mi?** Is it washable?

yıkıcı [jəkədʒə] adj devastating

yıkmak [jəkmak] v demolish, pull down

yıl [jəl] n year; **akademik yıl** n academic year; **artık yıl** n leap year; **her yıl** adv annually, yearly; **mali yıl** n financial year, fiscal year; **on yıl** n decade; **yıllık taşıt testi** n MOT; **yüzüncü yıl** n centenary; **bu yıl** this year; **geçen yıl** last year; **gelecek yıl** next year; **Mutlu Yıllar!** Happy New Year!; **Yeni Yıl** n New Year

yılan [jəlan] n snake; **çıngıraklı yılan** n rattlesnake; **yılan balığı** n eel

yıldız [jəldəz] n (gök) star (sky), (kişi) star (person); **film yıldızı** n film star; **kuyruklu yıldız** n comet; **yıldız falı** n horoscope; **yıldız koymak** v star

yıl dönümü [jəldønymy] n anniversary

yıllık [jəllək] adj annual, yearly

yırtıcı [jərtədʒə] n **yırtıcı kuş** n bird of prey

yırtık [jərtək] n tear (split)

yırtmak [jərtmak] v rip up, tear, tear up ▷ vt rip

yine [jine] adv again; **yine de** adv yet (nevertheless)

yinelenen [jinelenen] adj recurring

yirmi [jirmi] number twenty; **yirmi yaş dişi** n wisdom tooth; **Her yirmi dakikada bir otobüs var** The bus runs every twenty minutes

yirminci [jirmindʒi] adj twentieth

yiyecek [jijedʒek] n food; **doğal yiyecek** npl wholefoods; **yiyecek maddeleri** npl groceries; **Yiyecek satıyor musunuz?** Do you have food?

yoga [joga] n yoga

yoğun [jou:n] adj intense, intensive; **yoğun bakım ünitesi** n intensive care unit

yoğunlaşma [jou:nlaʃma] n concentration

yoğunlaşmak [jou:nlaʃmak] v concentrate

yoğunluk [jou:nluk] n density

yoğurt [jou:rt] n yoghurt

yok [jok] adj absent ▷ adv not; **yok etmek** v destroy; **yok olmak** v vanish

yoklama [joklama] n roll call; **kamuoyu yoklaması** n opinion poll, poll

yoklamak [joklamak] v search, inspect; **elle yoklamak** v grope

yokluk [jokluk] n (devam) absence, (eksiklik) shortage

yoksa [joksa] conj otherwise

yoksul [joksul] adj hard up, poor

yoksulluk [joksulluk] n poverty; **yoksulluk yardımı** n dole

yokuş [jokuʃ] n slope; **yokuş yukarı** adv uphill

yol [jol] n road, way ▷ npl means;

çevre yolu n bypass, ring road; **çift-şeritli yol** n dual carriageway; **bağlantı yolu** n slip road; **bisiklet yolu** n cycle path; **bisiklet yolu** n cycle lane; **dar yol** n lane; **engebeli yol** n track; **kestirme yol** n shortcut; **yarı yolda** halfway ▷ v **yol açmak** v cause; **yol çukuru** n pothole; **yol göstermek** vt lead; **yol haritası** n road map; **yol kenarında geçici park yeri** n layby; **yol tabelası** n signpost; **yol vergisi** n road tax; **yol yapım çalışması** npl roadworks; **yola çıkmak** v go away, start off; **yola koyulmak** v set off; **yoluna koymak** v settle; **... yol haritası istiyorum** I need a road map of...; **... a gitmek için hangi yoldan gitmem gerek?** Which road do I take for...?; **Bu yolda hız limiti nedir?** What is the speed limit on this road?; **Yol hakkı sizin değildi** It wasn't your right of way; **Yol ne zaman açılır?** When will the road be clear?; **Yol vermedi** She didn't give way; **Yollar buzlu mu?** Are the roads icy?
yolcu [joldʒu] n fare, passenger; **büyük yolcu gemisi** n liner; **transit yolcu salonu** n transit lounge
yolcular [joldʒular] npl traveller
yolculuk [joldʒuluk] n (kısa) trip, (otomobil) drive; **gemiyle yolculuk etmek** n sail; **gidiş dönüş yolculuk** n round trip; **İyi yolculuklar!** Have a good trip!
yoldaş [joldaʃ] n companion
yoluyla [jolujla] prep past, via

yorgan [jorgan] n duvet, quilt
yorgun [jorgun] adj tired; **Biraz yorgunum** I'm a little tired; **Yorgunum** I'm tired
yorucu [jorudʒu] adj tiring
yorum [jorum] n comment, commentary; **yorum yapmak** v comment
yorumcu [jorumdʒu] n commentator
yosun [josun] n moss, seaweed
yozlaşma [jozlaʃma] n corruption
yozlaşmış [jozlaʃməʃ] adj corrupt
yön [jøn] n direction; **çok yönlü** n versatile; **doğu yönünde** adj eastbound; **ilgisini başka yöne çekmek** v distract; **mecburi yön** (trafik) n diversion; **saat yönünde** adv clockwise; **saatin aksi yönünde** adv anticlockwise; **tek yön bilet** n single ticket
yönetici [jønetidʒi] n executive
yönetim [jønetim] n administration, management, steering; **yönetim merkezi** n head office; **yönetimi ele almak** v take over
yönetmek [jønetmek] vt direct
yönetmelik [jønetmelik] n regulation
yöntem [jøntem] n method
yöre [jøre] n **Bu yöreye özgü bir şey denemek istiyorum lütfen** I'd like to try something local, please; **Bu yöreye özgü bir şey istiyorum** Do you have anything typical of this region?; **Yöreye özgü bir şey ısmarlamak istiyorum** I'd like to order something local; **Yöresel bir**

yemek tavsiye edebilir misiniz?
Can you recommend a local dish?
yukarı [jukarə] *adv* up; **yokuş
yukarı** *adv* uphill; **yukarıya doğru**
adv upwards
yukarıya [jukarəja] *adv* up
yulaf [julaf] *npl* oats; **yulaf
ezmesi** *n* oatmeal, porridge
yumruk [jumruk] *n* fist, punch
(blow)
yumruklamak [jumruklamak] *v*
punch
yumurta [jumurta] *n* egg;
haşlanmış yumurta *n* boiled egg;
karıştırılmış yumurta *npl*
scrambled eggs; **Paskalya
yumurtası** *n* Easter egg;
yumurta akı *n* egg white;
yumurta kabı *n* eggcup;
yumurta sarısı *n* egg yolk;
yumurtanın sarısı *n* yolk; **İçinde
yumurta olmayan bir yemek
yapabilir misiniz?** Could you
prepare a meal without eggs?;
Çiğ yumurta yiyemiyorum
I can't eat raw eggs
yumurtalık [jumurtalək] *n*
(sağlık) ovary
yumuşak [jumuʃak] *adj* tender ▷ *n*
soft
yumuşatıcı [jumuʃatədʒə] *n*
Yumuşatıcı satıyor musunuz?
Do you sell conditioner?;
Yumuşatıcınız var mı? Do you
have softener?
Yunan [junan] *adj* Greek
Yunanca [junandʒa] *n (dil)* Greek
(language)
Yunanistan [junanistan] *n*
Greece

Yunanlı [junanlə] *n (kişi)* Greek
(person)
yunus [junus] *n* dolphin
yurtdışı [jurddəʃə] *adv* abroad
yurtsever [jurtsever] *adj* patriotic
yusufçuk [jusuftʃuk] *n* dragonfly
yutma [jutma] *n* swallow
yutmak [jutmak] *vt* swallow
yutulmak [jutulmak] *vi* swallow
yuva [juva] *n* nest
yuvar [juvar] *n* **hamur yuvarı** *n*
dumpling
yuvarlak [juvarlak] *adj* round;
yuvarlak ekmek *n* bread roll
yuvarlanma [juvarlanma] *n* roll
yuvarlanmak [juvarlanmak] *vi*
roll
yük [jyk] *n* burden, load, pack;
ağır yük taşıma aracı *n* HGV;
yük arabası *n* lorry
yükleme [jykleme] *n* shipment
yüklemek [jyklemek] *v* load,
upload
yüklenici [jyklenidʒi] *n* contractor
yüksek [jyksek] *adj* high; **Çin'de
yüksek memur** *n* mandarin
(official); **yüksek atlama** *n* high
jump; **yüksek dozda** *n* overdose;
yüksek eğitim *n* higher
education; **yüksek maaşlı** *adj*
well-paid; **yüksek okul** *n* college;
yüksek sesle *adv* aloud, loudly;
yüksek sesle okumak *v* read out;
yüksek topuklar *npl* high heels;
yüksek topuklu *adj* high-heeled;
Sele çok yüksek The seat is too
high
yükseklik [jykseklik] *n* altitude,
height; **yükseklik korkusu** *n*
vertigo

yüksekte [jyksekte] *adv* high
yükselmek [jykselmek] *v* go up;
ani yükselme *n* surge
yükseltici [jykseltidʒi] *n* amplifier
yüküm [jykym] *n* **vergi**
yükümlüsü *n* tax payer
yün [jyn] *n* wool
yünlü [jynly] *adj* woollen
yünlüler [jynlyler] *npl* woollens
yürek [jyrek] *n* **iyi yüreklilik** *n*
kindness
yüreklendirme [jyreklendirme]
n encouragement
yüreklendirmek
[jyreklendirmek] *v* boost,
encourage
yürekli [jyrekli] *adj* courageous
yürüme [jyryme] *n* walking
yürümek [jyrymek] *v* walk;
ayaklarını sürüyerek yürümek *v*
shuffle; **parmaklarının ucunda**
yürüme *n* tiptoe; **uygun adım**
yürümek *v* march; **uykuda**
yürüme *v* sleepwalk; **yürüyen**
merdiven *n* escalator
yürürlük [jyryrlyk] *n*
yürürlükten kaldırma *n* abolition
yürüteç [jyrytetʃ] *n* Zimmer®
frame
yürüyüş [jyryjyʃ] *n* hiking, stroll,
walk; **yürüyüşe çıkma** *n* hike;
zahmetli yürüyüş *n* trek;
zahmetli bir yürüyüşe çıkmak *v*
trek; **Civarda ilginç yürüyüş**
yerleri var mı? Are there any
interesting walks nearby?;
Rehberli yürüyüş var mı? Are
there any guided walks?; **Tepelere**
yürüyüşe çıkmak isterim I'd like
to go hill walking; **Yürüyüş kaç**

kilometre? How many kilometres
is the walk?; **Yerel yürüyüşler**
için rehberiniz var mı? Do you
have a guide to local walks?
yüz [jyz] *adj* facial ▷ *n* face ▷ *number*
(sayı) hundred; **yüz bakımı** *n*
facial; **yüz havlusu** *n* face cloth ▷ *v*
yüz kızarması *n* flush; **yüz**
temizleme losyonu *n* cleansing
lotion; **yüzü kızarmak** *v* flush; **İki**
yüz... rica ediyorum I'd like two
hundred...; **İki yüz iki numaralı**
odanın anahtarı lütfen the key
for room number two hundred
and two; **Beş yüz... rica**
ediyorum I'd like five hundred...;
Yüz... lık... almak istiyorum I'd
like to change one hundred...
into...
yüzde [jyzde] *adv* per cent ▷ *n*
percentage
yüzdürmek [jyzdyrmek] *vi* float
yüzey [jyzej] *n* surface
yüzgeç [jyzgetʃ] *npl* flippers
yüzkızartıcı [jyzkəzartədʒə] *adj*
shocking
yüzme [jyzme] *n* swimming;
Yüzme havuzu nerede? Where is
the public swimming pool?;
Yüzme havuzunuz var mı? Is
there a swimming pool?
yüzmek [jyzmek] *v* bathe ▷ *vt*
swim; **sırtüstü yüzme** *n*
backstroke; **yüzme havuzu** *n*
swimming pool; **Burada güvenle**
yüzmek mümkün mü? Is it safe
to swim here?; **Burada**
yüzülebilir mi? Can you swim
here?; **Nerede yüzebilirim?**
Where can I go swimming?;

Yüzme havuzu var mı? Is there a swimming pool?; **Yüzmeye gidelim** Let's go swimming

yüzücü [jyzydʒy] n swimmer; **yüzücü şortu** npl swimming trunks, trunks

yüzük [jyzyk] n ring, (nikah) wedding ring; **nişan yüzüğü** n engagement ring

yüzüncü [jyzyndʒy] num **yüzüncü yıl** n centenary

yüzyıl [jyzjəl] n century

Z

zafer [zafer] n glory, triumph, victory

zahmet [zahmet] n trouble, difficulty; **zahmet etmek** v bother; **zahmetli yürüyüş** n trek

zahmetli [zahmetli] adj demanding

zaman [zaman] n time, (gramer) tense; **boş zaman** n spare time; **en kısa zamanda** adv asap; **her zaman** adv always; **kısa zamanda** adv shortly, soon; **ne zaman/ne zaman ki** conj when; **o zamandan beri** adv since; **son zamanlarda** adv lately, recently; **yatma zamanı** n bedtime; **yemek zamanı** n dinner time, lunchtime, mealtime; **zaman dilimi** n time zone; **... a ne zaman varırız?** What time do we get to...?; **Çok uzun zamandır bekliyoruz** We've been waiting for a very long time;

Gitme zamanı geldi mi? Is it time to go?; **Kenti gezecek kadar zamanımız var mı?** Do we have time to visit the town?; **Ne zaman kalkıyor?** What time does it leave?; **Otobüs ne zaman geliyor?** What time does the bus arrive?; **Otobüs ne zaman kalkacak?** What time does the bus leave?

zamanında [zamanənda] adj on time, punctual

zambak [zambak] n lily

Zambiya [zambija] adj Zambian ▷ n Zambia

Zambiyalı [zambijalə] n Zambian

zamir [zamir] n pronoun

zanaat [zanaat] n craft

zanaatkâr [zanaatka:r] n craftsman

zanlı [zanlə] n culprit, suspect

zaptetmek [zaptetmek] v capture

zar [zar] **(zarlar)** n (kumar) dice; **kulak zarı** n eardrum

zarar [zarar] n damage; **zarar vermek** v damage, harm; **zararını karşılamak** v reimburse

zararlı [zararlə] adj harmful

zararsız [zararsəz] adj harmless

zarf [zarf] n envelope

zarif [zarif] adj elegant, graceful

zaten [zaten] adv already

zatürre [zatyrre] n pneumonia

zayıf [zajəf] adj (ışık, ses vb) faint, (karakter) weak

zayıflık [zajəflək] n weakness

zayiat [zajiat] n casualty

zebra [zebra] n zebra

zehir [zehir] n poison, venom; **böcek zehiri** n pesticide; **gıda**

zehirlenmesi n food poisoning

zehirlemek [zehirlemek] v poison; **kan zehirlenmesi** n blood poisoning

zehirli [zehirli] adj poisonous, toxic

zeka [zekja:] n intelligence, wisdom

zeki [zeki] adj clever, intelligent

zemin [zemin] n ground, earth; **zemin kat** n ground floor; **Zemin katta yatak odası var mı?** Do you have any bedrooms on the ground floor?

zencefil [zendʒefil] n ginger

zengin [zengin] adj rich; **zengin pinti** n miser

zevk [zevk] n pleasure; **Sizinle tanışmak bir zevk** It was a pleasure to meet you

zevkli [zevkli] adj enjoyable

zeytin [zejtin] n olive; **zeytin ağacı** n olive tree; **zeytin yağı** n olive oil

zımba [zəmba] n, adj **tel zımba** n stapler; **zımba teli** n staple (wire)

zımbalamak [zəmbalamak] v staple

zımpara [zəmpara] n sandpaper

zırh [zərh] n armour

zırhlı [zərhlə] adj **muharebe zırhlısı** n battleship

zıt [zət] n contrary

zihin [zihin] n mind

zihniyet [zihnijet] n mentality

zil [zil] n (kapı, okul) bell ▷ npl (müzik) cymbals; **kapı zili** n doorbell

Zimbabwe [zimbabve] adj Zimbabwean ▷ n Zimbabwe

Zimbabweli [zimbabveli] *n*
Zimbabwean
zincir [zindʒir] *n* chain; **Kar zinciri
almam gerekiyor mu?** Do I need
snow chains?
zindan [zindan] *n* dungeon
zirve [zirve] *n* peak, summit
ziyaret [zijaret] *n* visit; **ziyaret
etmek** *v* visit; **ziyaret saatleri** *npl*
visiting hours; **Ziyaret saatleri
nedir?** When are visiting hours?
ziyaretçi [zijarettʃi] *n* visitor;
ziyaretçi merkezi *n* visitor centre
zonklamak [zoŋlamak] *v* throb
zoom mercek [zoommerdʒek] *n*
zoom merceği *n* zoom lens
zor [zor] *adj* hard (*difficult*) ▷ *adv*
hard
zorba [zorba] *n* bully; **zorbalık
etmek** *v* bully
zorlama [zorlama] *adj* strained
zorlamak [zorlamak] *v* force
zorlayıcı [zorlajədʒə] *adj*
challenging, drastic
zorluk [zorluk] *n* complication
zorunlu [zorunlu] *adj* essential
zulüm [zulym] *n* cruelty
züğürt [zy:yrt] *adj* broke
züppe [zyppe] *n* snob
zürafa [zyrafa] *n* giraffe

Turkish Grammar

1 Word formation

Turkish is an agglutinative language. This means that words and grammatical features are built up by adding a suffix at the end where separate words might be used in English. For example *hand* is **el** and *hands* is **eller**; *my hands* is **ellerim** and so on.

An important feature of Turkish is vowel harmony and you need to know about it in order to form plurals and other grammatical features correctly, such as different tenses and suffixes.

1.1 Vowel harmony

Any of the eight Turkish vowels may appear in the first syllable of a word, but each vowel is conditioned by the vowel immediately preceding it, according to vowel harmony rules. These rules are explained below.

Front vowels (**e, i, ö, ü**) must be followed by front vowels, and back vowels (**a, ı, o, u**) must be followed by back vowels.

otel	**otele**	
the hotel	*to the hotel*	
ev	**evimiz**	
a house	*our house*	
okul	**okuldan**	**okula**
school	*from the school*	*to the school*

Unrounded vowels (**a, e, i, ı**), must be followed by unrounded vowels.

deniz	**denizde**
the sea	*in the sea*
baktılar	
they had a look	

Rounded vowels (**o, ö, u, ü**) must be followed by rounded vowels.

yağmur
the rain

yağmur<u>lu</u>
rainy

gül<u>üyor</u>
he is laughing

Final vowel in the root	Vowel in the suffix
a, ı	a, ı
e, i	e, i
o, u	a, u
ö, ü	e, ü

1.2 Word order

The basic word order in a Turkish sentence is: subject-object-verb e.g. *I a book read*. Adjectives and adverbs come directly in front of the elements which they describe.

<u>Küçük</u> çocuk keki yedi.
The little child ate the cake.

Çocuk <u>küçük</u> keki yedi.
The child ate the little cake.

2 Verbs

The infinitive of a verb is the form normally used for referring to the verb and it is the one you find in a dictionary. In English, the infinitive has *to* in front of it; in Turkish, you attach the suffix **-mek** or **-mak** to the verb root to form the infinitive. To form different tenses, various verb suffixes are added to the root of the verb after removing the **-mek** or **-mak** ending.

içmek	**iç-iyor-um**
to drink	*I am drinking*

iç-ti-m	**iç-ece-ğim**
I have drunk	*I will drink*

The verb is normally a single word in Turkish and basically consists of two, sometimes three elements.

1. There is a verb root:

oku
read

2. There is a tense suffix and a personal ending added after the root:

oku<u>dum</u>
I read

-du is a tense suffix used in the Simple Past Tense and **-m** is a personal ending meaning *I*.

3. If the verb is transitive then there must be an object which precedes the verb. The object is a noun:

Ben <u>mektubu</u> okudum.
I read the letter.

2.1 Verb tenses

There are five different tenses in Turkish. They are formed by adding the tense suffix to the root of the verb and are followed by a personal suffix, which shows the subject of the sentence. Because of these different personal suffixes, there is usually no need in Turkish for separate personal pronouns like **ben**, **sen**, **o**, **biz**, **siz**, **onlar**.

Personal Pronouns	Personal Pronouns in Turkish	Personal Suffixes
I	ben	(y)im, -(y)ım, -(y)um, (y)üm
you	sen	-sin, -sın, -sun, -sün
he/she/it	o	-dir, -dır, -dur, -dür
we	biz	(y)iz, -(y)ız, -(y)uz, (y)üz
you	siz	siniz, -sınız, -sunuz, sünüz
they	onlar	-dirler, -dırlar, -durlar, -dürler

In colloquial, spoken Turkish, the third person singular **o** doesn't usually take a personal suffix. However, this is used in formal, written Turkish.

okuyor<u>um</u>	**okuyor**	**okuyor<u>uz</u>**
I am reading	*he/she is reading*	*we are reading*

The essential information on tenses is given below, but the main thing to remember is this: the form in which a verb appears in a dictionary may be very different from the one it takes when used in context. The parts to look for are the root, which tells you what the action is and the personal suffix, which tells you who is doing the action. Remember: if the subject is in the third person singular **o** (*he,she,it*), there will be no personal suffix.

2.2 Simple Present Tense

If the verb root ends with a vowel, you add **-r** after it. This is then followed by a personal suffix.

oku<u>r</u>um	**iste<u>r</u>**
I read	*he wants*

If the verb root ends with a consonant, you add **-er** or **-ir**. This is then followed by a personal suffix.

O çikolata sever.
She loves chocolate.

Onlar çok çalışırlar.
They work very hard.

2.3 Present Continuous Tense

The suffix **-iyor** is added to the verb root and is followed by a personal suffix.

Ben Fransızca öğreniyorum.
I am learning French.

If the verb root ends with a vowel the **-i** is dropped.

Biz kitap okuyoruz.
We are reading a book.

2.4 Simple Past Tense

The suffix **-di** is added to the verb root and is followed by a personal suffix. The simple past tense suffix has eight variants which change according to vowel harmony and consonant changes: **-di, -dı, -du, -dü, ti, -tı, -tu, -tü**.

Bu sabah iki kilometre koştum.
I ran two kilometres this morning.

Onlar buraya geldiler.
They came here.

2.5 Future Tense

If the verb root ends with a consonant, the suffix **-ecek** or **-acak**, is added to it. If the verb root ends with a vowel, the suffix **-yecek** or **-yacak** is added to it.

Yarın onlar bize gelecekler.
They will visit us tomorrow.

O bu magazini sonra okuyacak.
She will read this magazine later.

6

2.6 Story Past Tense

You use this tense when you talk about a past action that you have heard about from another source. This tense may be translated into English with expressions like *supposedly*, *apparently* or *they say*. The suffix **-miş** changes to **-mış**, **-muş** or **müş**, according to the vowel harmony rules.

> **Dün gece çok geç yatmışlar.**
> *They apparently went to bed very late last night.*

> **Ders çalışırken uyumuşum.**
> *Apparently I fell asleep while studying.*

3 Negatives

The predicate of a sentence says something about the subject. If it is an adjective or a noun phrase, it forms part of what is known as a non-verbal sentence.

> **Biz çok yorgunuz.**
> *We are very tired.*

> **O bir öğretmen.**
> *She is a teacher.*

The predicate can also be a verb, and so forms part of what is known as a verbal sentence.

> **Biz gazeteyi okuduk.**
> *We read the newspaper.*

The negative of non-verbal sentences is formed with the word **değil**, pronounced as **deil**. **Değil** follows the noun or adjective as a separate word, and personal endings are attached to it.

> **Ben yorgun değilim.**
> *I am not tired.*

> **Otel pahalı değil.**
> *The hotel is not expensive.*

The negative of verbal sentences is not formed with **değil** but with the suffix **-me**, which follows the verb root and precedes the tense. The negative suffix **-me** changes to **-ma**, **-mi**, **-mı**, **-mu**, or **-mü** in line with vowel harmony.

git<u>me</u>dim	oku<u>ma</u>dım	gel<u>me</u>diniz
I didn't go	*I didn't read*	*you didn't come*

3.1 Yes/No questions

The particle **-mi** is used for asking yes-or-no questions. It follows the word to which it applies, normally the predicate. It changes to **-mu**, **-mı**, or **-mü** in line with vowel harmony.

If the predicate is a verb, **-mi** follows the verb form and this stands alone at the end of the sentence as a separate word.

Geldi <u>mi</u>?	Onu gördünüz <u>mü</u>?
Did he come?	*Did you see him?*

If the predicate is non-verbal, **-mi** follows it as a separate word but precedes the personal ending; the ending is then attached to **-mi** and continues to be affected by vowel harmony.

Aç <u>mı</u>sınız?	İstanbul güzel <u>mi</u>?
Are you hungry?	*Is Istanbul beautiful?*

If **değil** is present, **-mi** follows **değil** and the personal ending is attached to **-mi** at the end of the sentence.

Doktor değil <u>mi</u>siniz?
Aren't you a doctor?

İyi değil <u>mi</u>sin?
Aren't you well?

4 Nouns

There is no gender distinction in Turkish i.e. no masculine or feminine nouns. There is also no distinction between *he*, *she* and *it* and no word for *the* (the definite article). For example **çanta** could mean *bag*, *the bag* or *a bag*, depending on the context. For *a* (the indefinite article) you use the same word as *one*.

<u>bir</u> kahve
one or *a coffee*

<u>bir</u> elma
an/one apple

<u>bir</u> ev
a/one house

4.1 Plurals

The suffix **-ler** or **-lar** is used to form plurals. If the last vowel in the main part of the word is a front vowel (**e, i, ö, ü**), it is followed by the plural suffix **-ler**.

ev
house

ev<u>ler</u>
houses

göz
eye

göz<u>ler</u>
eyes

gül
rose

gül<u>ler</u>
roses

If the last vowel in the main part of the word is a back vowel (**a, ı, o, u**), it is followed by the plural suffix **-lar**.

kapı
door

kapı<u>lar</u>
doors

soru
question

soru<u>lar</u>
questions

halı
carpet

halı<u>lar</u>
carpets

5 Pronouns

Personal pronouns

The Turkish personal pronouns are as follows.

Personal pronouns	
ben	*I*
sen	*you*
o	*he, she, it*
biz	*we*
siz	*you*
onlar	*they*

There are two words for *you* in Turkish. The difference between them is similar to that between French **tu** and **vous** or German **du** and **Sie**: **sen** along with the corresponding personal ending -**sın** is used for close friends, relatives and children; **siz** along with the corresponding ending -**siniz**, is formal and used for more distant acquaintances, superiors, strangers and people to whom one wishes to be polite. Remember that you will see Turkish personal pronouns in many different forms depending on the grammar of the sentence e.g. *they* could appear as **onlar**, **onları**, **onlara**, **onlarda**.

The most common use of the genitive forms is to show possession, and the possessive suffix for each person is different. The genitive form of the pronouns and the possessive suffixes are shown in the table below.

Personal Pronouns	Genitive Case	Possessive Suffixes
ben(*I*)	benim(*my*)	-im, -ım, -um, -üm
sen(*you*)	senin(*your*)	-sin, -sın, -sun, -sün
o(*he/she/it*)	onun(*her/his/its*)	-si, -sı, -su, -sü
biz(*we*)	bizim(*our*)	-miz, -mız, -muz, -müz
siz(*you*)	sizin(*your*)	-siniz, -sınız, -sunuz, -sünüz
onlar(*they*)	onların(*their*)	-leri, -ları

benim arabam	**onun** kızı
my car	*her/his daughter*

sizin işiniz	**onların** evleri
your job	*their houses*

6 Adjectives

Adjectives usually come directly before the noun. However, if **bir** (*one/a/an*) appears before the noun then the adjective precedes **bir**.

eski kitap	**eski bir** kitap
the old book	*an old book*

Some adjectives can be used as nouns, as shown in the examples below.

Eski ucuz, **yeni** pahalı.
The old one is cheap, the new one is expensive.

Küçük hoştur.
The little one (the young child) is pleasant.

The comparative form of adjectives is basically formed by adding the word **daha** before the adjective. In Turkish there are no special adjective forms to express the English comparatives *more* and *-er* as in *better* or *more beautiful*. Similarly, there are no special adjective forms to express the English superlatives *most* and *-est* as in *best* or *most beautiful*. The superlative form is formed by adding **-en** before the adjective.

daha pahalı	**daha** güzel
more expensive	*more beautiful*

daha iyi	**daha** ucuz
better	*cheaper*

en pahalı	**en** güzel
the most expensive	*the most beautiful*

en iyi	**en** ucuz
the best	*the cheapest*

7 Useful endings

Here are some of the most important endings in Turkish. You must remember that there is an apostrophe before the ending of all proper nouns e.g. **İstanbul'a**, not **İstanbula**.

7.1 With

The suffix **-li** is added to nouns to form adjectives meaning *having* or *with*. It has four variations in accordance with vowel harmony: **-li** (for front, unrounded vowels), **-lı** (for back, unrounded vowels), **-lü** (for front, rounded vowels) and **-lu** (for back, rounded vowels).

şeker	**şekerli**
sugar	*with sugar*
hız	**hızlı**
speed	*speedy*
süt	**sütlü**
milk	*with milk*
limon	**limonlu**
lemon	*with lemon*

It is used with colours to mean *in this colour* and with flavours to mean *in this flavour*.

kırmızılı kadın	**çikolatalı dondurma**
woman in red	*chocolate ice cream*

It is also used to indicate where a person is from.

İstanbullu
from Istanbul

7.2 Without

The suffix **-siz** is the opposite of **-li**: it is added to nouns to form adjectives meaning *without* or *not having*.

şeker	**şeker<u>siz</u>**
sugar	*without sugar*
akıl	**akıl<u>sız</u>**
intellect	*not intelligent*
süt	**süt<u>süz</u>**
milk	*without milk*
limon	**limon<u>suz</u>**
lemon	*without lemon*

7.3 In, At, On

The suffix **-de** (*in*, *at* or *on*) is used to show where something happens or where something is located. The suffix **-da** is used for back vowels and **-de** for front vowels. When the word ends with the consonant **f, s, t, k, ç, ş, h** or **p** the suffix **-da** turns into **-ta** and **-de** turns into **-te**. Please see the table below for these consonants.

Locational Suffix	Consonants	Suffix
a-ı-o-u = -da e-i-ö-ü = -de	f s t k ç ş h p	-ta -te

masa	**masa<u>da</u>**
table	*on the table*
ev	**ev<u>de</u>**
house	*at home*

dolap	**dolapta**
cupboard	*in the cupboard*
iş	**işte**
work	*at work*

Personal pronouns and demonstratives can also take these suffixes.

ben	**bende**
I	*on me, in me*

In the above example, *on me* has the sense of *I have got it* e.g. *it is in my pocket.*

7.4 To

The suffix **-(y)e** (front vowel) or **-(y)a** (back vowel) normally corresponds to the English words *to* and *for*. It indicates the place or the person toward which/whom movement is directed. When the word ends with a vowel, the buffer letter **-y** is added before the vowel.

masa	**masaya**
table	*to the table*
ofis	**ofise**
office	*to the office*
Londra'ya	
to London	

Personal pronouns and demonstratives can also take this suffix.

ben	**bana**
I	*to me*
sen	**sana**
you	*to you*

o	**ona**
he/she/it	*to him/her*

biz	**bize**
we	*to us*

7.5 From

The suffix **-den** (front vowel) or **-dan** (back vowel) corresponds to the English word *from*. It indicates the place or the person from which/whom the movement or action proceeds. When the word ends with the consonants **f, s, t, k, ç, ş, h** or **p**, the suffixes **-dan** and **-den** turn into **-tan** and **-ten**.

masa	**masadan**
table	*from the table*

ev	**evden**
house	*from home*

Londra'dan	**kasaptan**
from London	*from the butcher*

Murat'tan	
from Murat	

Personal pronouns and demonstratives can also take this suffix.

ben	**benden**
I	*from me*

sen	**senden**
you	*from you*

o	**ondan**
he/she/it	*from him/her*

onlar	**onlardan**
they	*from them*

bundan	**şundan**
from this	*from that*

Some Turkish verbs take this suffix automatically. These are intransitive verbs that do not take a direct object but may appear with a noun. They are: **korkmak** (*to be afraid of*), **nefret etmek** (*to hate*) and **vazgeçmek** (*to give up*).

Fatma kedi<u>den</u> korkar.
Fatma is afraid of a cat.

John tiyatro<u>dan</u> nefret eder.
John hates the theatre.

Mary sigara<u>dan</u> vazgeçemez.
Mary cannot give up cigarettes.

With the verb **yapmak** (*to make*) this suffix may be used to indicate the material from which something is made.

tahta<u>dan</u> bir masa yaptım.
I made a table out of/from wood.

The same suffix can be used to mean *since*, *before*, and *after*.

Sabah<u>tan</u> beri konuşuyorlar.
They had been talking since the morning.

Kahvaltı<u>dan</u> önce koşar.
She runs before breakfast.

Kahvaltı<u>dan</u> sonra işe gider.
She goes to work after breakfast.

İngilizce Dilbilgisi

1 Fiiller

Fiiler cümle içersinde bir iş, bir oluş, bir eylem hakkında konuşmamızı sağlayan sözcüklerdir; yapmak, etmek, olmak eylemlerini anlatırlar. Farklı türde kullanılan fiiler, aşağıda açıklanmıştır.

Geçişli fiiller (**Transitive Verbs**) bir eylemi, bir hareketi belirten ve nesne alan fiillerdir. Yükleme sorulan 'neyi' sorusuna yanıt verirler. Başka bir tanımlama ile nesne alan fiillere geçişli fiiler denir.

> **He described the house.**
> *O evi tarif etti.*

> **She visited her parents.**
> *O ebeveynlerini ziyaret etti.*

Eğer cümlede dolaysız bir nesne yoksa, fiil geçişli değildir.

> **The man broke.**
> *Adam kırdı (cümle eksik).*

> **The man dropped the glass.**
> *Adam bardağı düşürdü (cümle tam).*

Geçişsiz fiiller (**Intransitive Verbs**) bir eylemi, bir hareketi belirtmelerine rağmen dolaylı nesne almazlar. Yükleme sorulan 'neyi' sorusu yanıtsız kalır.

> **She fell.**
> *O düştü.*

Bazı fiiler ise, hem geçişli hem de geçişsiz olabilirler.

> **She laughed.**
> *Güldü (geçişsiz).*

> **She laughed at me.**
> *O bana güldü (geçişli).*

Düzenli Fiiller (**Regular Verbs**) belli bir kurala göre çekimlenirler.

to like
sevmek, beğenmek

I like	you like	she/he/it likes
severim	*seversin*	*sever*

we like	you like	they like
severiz	*seversiniz*	*severler*

Düzenli fiiller (**Regular Verbs**) cümlede kullanılan zamire göre değişmezler ancak 3. tekil şahıslarda (**he, she, it**), **-s** ya da **-es** takısı alırlar. İngilizcede fiillerin üç hali bulunur: i yalın hali yani *Mastar halidir* buna İngilizcede **Infinitive Verbs** denir; bu sözcüklerin sözlükte bulundukları halleridir. İkinci hali, *di'li geçmiş* (**simple past**) halidir. Üçüncü hali, *geçmiş zaman* (**past participle**) halidir. Düzenli fiillerde 2. ve 3. şekli oluşturmak için sadece köke **-ed** veya **-d** eklerini eklemek yeterlidir.

Türkçesi	Birinci yalın hali (Infinitive)	İkinci Hali (Simple Past)	Üçüncü Hali (Past Participle)
sevmek	to like	liked	liked
konuşmak	to talk	talked	talked
yürümek	to walk	walked	walked
çalışmak	to work	worked	worked
öğrenmek	to learn	learned	learned
bakmak	to look	looked	looked

Birçok fiil yukarıdaki tabloda gösterilen kurallara uymaz ve bu fiilere Düzensiz (kuralsız) Fiiler (**Irregular Verbs**) denir. Bu fiilerin 2. ve 3. hallerinin oluşumda bazen belli bir kalıp izlense de, çoğunlukla farklılıklar görülür. Düzensiz fiileri öğrenmenin en iyi yolu ise, ikinci ve üçüncü hallerini ezberlemektir.

Türkçesi	Birinci yalın hall (Infinitive)	İkinci Hali (Simple Past)	Üçüncü Hali (Past Participle)
içmek	to drink	drank	drunk
üflemek	to blow	blew	blown
olmak	to become	became	become
başlamak	to begin	began	begun
getirmek	to bring	brought	brought
söylemek	to say	said	said

1.1 Yardımcı Fiiler

Cümle içersinde ana fiil ile beraber kullanılan ve yalnız başlarına kullanıldıklarında bir anlamları olmayan *Yardımcı Fiillerin* (**Auxiliary Verbs**) cümledeki işlevi, ana fiil hakkında zaman, şahıs ve anlam bakımından bilgi vermektir. Her cümlede ana fiil ile beraber yardımcı fiil göremezsiniz.

İngilizcede üç farklı yardımcı fiil bulunur: **to be** – **to do** – **to have**.

<u>to be</u> Yardımcı Fiili

Türkçede bunların tam karşılığı yoktur. Türkçede yüklemin sonuna getirilen şahıs ve zaman ekleri, İngilizce'deki **to be** fiilinin karşılığıdır. Zamana ve zamire göre değişir:

being, been, am, are, is, was, were vb. Türkçedeki kelime karşılığı her ne kadar *olmak* ise de, tam karşılığı cins isimlerin sonuna gelen şahıs ekleridir: *(y)im -sin -dir -(y)iz -siniz -dirler*.

Cümle İçinde Kısaltılarak Kullanılabilirler. **I am = I'm, You are = You're, He is = He's, She is = She's, It is = It's, We are = We're, They are = They're**

Geçmiş Zaman Hali **was** ve **were** şeklindedir. **Was, am** ve **is** yardımcı fiillerinin geçmiş zaman halidir; **were** ise **are** yardımcı fiilinin, geçmiş zaman halidir. **was** tekil öznelerle, **were** ise çoğul öznelerle kullanılır.

> He <u>was</u> young.   She <u>was</u> his wife.
> *O gençti.*   *Onun karısıydı (artık değil).*

to have Yardımcı Fiili

Sahiplik (iyelik) anlamı bildirir. Üçüncü tekil şahıslarda **has** şeklini alır.

> **She <u>has</u> a nice car.**
> *Güzel bir arabası var.*

İkinci ve Üçüncü Hali **had** şeklini alır.

> **They <u>had</u> a big house.**
> *Büyük bir evleri vardı. (Büyük bir eve sahiptiler).*

to do Yardımcı Fiili

İngilizcede bu yardımcı fiile *destekleyici yardımcı fiil* (**supporting auxiliary verbs**) de denilir. Üçüncü tekil şahısta **-es** takısı alır.

Soru Cümlelerinin çoğu **do** fiiliyle yapılır.

> **<u>Do</u> you like oranges?**
> *Portakal sever misin?*

Cümleyi Olumsuz Yapar. İkinci Hali **did** şeklini alır.

> **<u>Didn't</u> you watch the news?**
> *Haberleri izlemedin mi?*

1.2 İngilizce Deyimler

Deyimler, ana fiilin zarfla, edatla ya da her ikisi ile birleşmesi sonucu oluşur.

Zarflarla bir araya gelerek:

> **to give in**
> *boyun eğmek, teslim olmak*

> **to take off**
> *terk etmek, kalkışa geçmek*

to pick on
Birisine takmak, kancayı takmak

to get at
Biri ile ya da birşeyle uğraşmak

Bazen de hem zarf hem de edat ile birleşerek:

to put up with
tahamül etmek

to get out of
yan çizmek

Bu kelimeler ayrı ayrı kullanıldıklarında tamamen farklı bir anlam oluştururlar.

1.3 Zamanlar

İngilizcede Zamanları **Present Tense** (*Şimdiki Zaman*), **Past Tense** (*Geçmiş Zaman*) ve **Future Tense** (*Gelecek Zaman*) olmak üzere üç ana grupta incelesek, belli başlı ana zamanların tümünü aşağıdaki tabloda toparlayabiliriz.

	Şimdiki Zamanlar (Present Tenses)	Geçmiş Zamanlar (Past Tenses)	Gelecek Zamanlar (Future Tenses)
Basit Zamanlar (Simple Tenses)	I swim	I swam	I shall swim
Süregelen Zamanlar (Continuous Tenses)	I am swimming	I was swimming	I shall be swimming
Tamamlanmış Zamanlar (Perfect Tenses)	I have been swimming	I had swum	I shall have swum
Geçmişte Süregelmiş ve Tamamlanmış Zamanlar (Perfect Continuous Tenses)	I have been swimming	I had been swimming	I shall have been swimming

Tabloda bulunan cümlelerin ana fiil ve yardımcı fiilerine dikkat ediniz.

2   İsimler

Kişiler, hayvanlar, yer, nesne, olay, nitelik, etkinlik ve soyut fikirleri adlandıran sözcüklerdir.

Özel İsimler: Bunlar kişi ve kurumların isimleridir. John Lennon, İngiltere, Milli Eğitim Bakanlığı.

Cins İsimler: Özel isimlerin dışında kalan isimlerdir. Cins isimler farklı gruplara ayrılırlar.

Soyut İsimler. Beş duyu ile algılanamayan kavramları ifade eden isimlerdir.

air	**time**
hava	*zaman*
honesty	**idea**
dürüstlük	*fikir*

Somut İsimler: Beş duyu ile algıladığımız kavramlara verilen isimlerdir.

dog	**stone**
köpek	*taş*

Birleşik İsimler: İki ya da daha fazla ismin bir araya gelmesi ile türetilen isimlerdir.

teapot (tea-pot)
çaydanlık

armchair (arm+chair)
koltuk

2.1 Sayılabilen ve Sayılamayan İsimler

Sayılabilen isimler, isimlerinden de anlaşılacağı gibi sayılabilirler: **one cat** (*bir kedi*), **two cats** (*iki kedi*), **three cats** (*üç kedi*). Tekil ya da çoğul halde bulunurlar, eğer tekil halde kullanılıyorlarsa, **a**, **an** ya da **the** *belirleyicileri* (**articles**) ile beraber kullanılmalıdırlar.

Fetch a chair for Alan.
Alan'a bir sandalye getirin.

Dogs ran wild in the streets.
Köpekler caddelerde vahşi bir halde koştular.

The dog is sleeping.
Köpek uyuyor.

Sayılamayan isimler genellikle yalın halde kullanılırlar, **a** ya da **an** *belirleyicileri* (**articles**) almazlar.

Sadie asked me for some advice.
Sadie benden bazı tavsiyelerde bulunmamı istedi.

Anna gave us some more information about her work.
Anna bize işi hakkında biraz bilgi verdi.

Ölçülebilen ve tartılabilen ama sayılamıyan isimlere ise *grup isimler* (**mass/uncountable nouns**) denilir. Bunlar da önlerine **a ya da an** gibi*belirleyicileri* **articles** almazlar.

Meat is usually more expensive than cheese.
Et genellikle peynirden daha pahalıdır.

Sugar is quite cheap.
Şeker oldukça ucuz.

2.2 İsimlerin Tekil ve Çoğul Halleri

İsimleri tekilden(**singular**), çoğula (**plural**) dönüştürmede en yaygın kural, tekil ismin sonuna **-s** harfini eklemektir.

cat	cats
kedi	*kediler*

İsimler **ch, sh, s, x** ya da **z** ile bitiyorsa, sonuna **-es** eklenerek çoğul yapılırlar.

box	boxes
kutu	*kutular*

church	churches
kilise	kiliseler

Tekil isim **-y** harfi ile bitiyorsa(**-by, -dy, -ty**) **-y** kaldırılır ve **-ies** eklenir.

city	cities
şehir	şehirler

Sonu **-f** yada **-fe** ile biten isimlerde **f** yerine **ve** konulur, **-es** ya da **-s** eklenerek çoğul haline getirilir.

knife	knives
bıçak	bıçaklar

Bazı isimlerin tekili de çoğulu da aynıdır.

sheep	fish
koyun koyunlar	balık, balıklar

Bazı isimlerin, tekil ve çoğul halleri farklı yazılır.

man	men
adam	adamlar

woman	women
kadın	kadınlar

child	children
çocuk	çocuklar

Tek bir nesneye ait olan ama iki bölümden veya iki ayrı parçadan oluşan ve Türkçede tekil olarak geçen bazı isimler, İngilizcede her zaman çoğul halde kullanılır. Sonlarındaki **-s** ya da **-es** çoğul ekine dikkat ediniz!

trousers	scissors
pantalon	makas

shorts	glasses
şort	gözlük

2.3 Adların Cinsiyeti

İngilizce'de birçok ad, belirtiği ismin dişi veya erkek oluşuna göre, farklılık gösterir.

actor	*aktör(erkek oyuncu)*
actress	*aktör(bayan)*
waiter	*garson(erkek)*
waitress	*garson(bayan)*

3 Zamirler

Zamirler isimlerin yerini tutan sözcüklerdir. Zamirleri, aynı ismi ya da aynı şahsı cümle içersinde tekrar etmemek için kullanırız.

Şahıs Zamirleri: Cümle içersinde yalın halde bulunurlar ve özne görevi yaparlar. **I** (*ben*) **you** (*sen*), **he, /she, / it** (*o*), **we** (*biz*), **you** (*siz*), **they** (*onlar*).

Cümle içersinde nesne görevi de yaparlar. **me** (*bana*), **you** (*sana*), **his/her** (*ona*), **us** (*bize*), **you** (*size*), **them** (*onlara*).

Dönüşlü Ve Vurgulayıcı Zamirler: Öznenin yaptığı eylemi tekrar o özneye döndürürler yani özne ile nesne aynı kişilerdir. Türkçedeki *kendi kendime* (**myself**), *kendikendine* (**herself**) sözcükleri gibi.

I did this myself.
Bunu kendi kendime yaptım.

She is talking to herself.
O kendi kendine konuşuyor.

İyelik Zamirleri: **mine** (*benimki*), **yours** (*seninki*), **his/hers/its** (*onunki*), **ours** (*bizimki*), **yours** (*sizinki*), **theirs** (*onlarinki*). Bunlar herhangi bir ismi nitelemezler ve başlarına kullanılırlar.

That book is mine.
Şu kitap benimkidir.

Give it back, it is mine.
Onu geri ver, o benim.

İşaret Zamirleri. Varlıkların yerini gösteren **this** (*bu*), **that** (*şu*), **these** (*bunlar*), **those** (*şunlar*) sözcükleridir.

This is David's, **that** is Robert's.
Bu David'in ki, şu Robert'in kidir.

These are nice, where did you find them?
Bunlar çok hoş. Bunlari nereden aldınız?

Soru Zamirleri. Bu zamirler **who, whom, whose, which, what** olup, her zaman fiillerden önce soru oluşturmada kullanılır.

What would you like for lunch?
Öğlen yemeğine ne istersiniz?

Who is responsible?
Kim sorumlu?

Belirsiz Zamirler: Şahıs Zamirleri kullanılamayan durumlarda, genel olarak bir kişi ya da kişilerden bahsedildiğinde belirsiz zamirler kullanılır.

Neither wanted to give in and apologize.
Hiçbiri boyun eğmedi ve özür diledi.

4 Sıfatlar

Sıfatlar isimleri niteleyen sözcüklerdir ve Türkçede olduğu gibi isimlerden önce gelerek ismi şekil, renk, sayı ve koku bakımından nitelerler.

their television
onların televizyonu

their new, wide-screen television
onların yeni, geniş-ekran televizyonu

the fat, black-and-white cat
şişman ve siyah-beyaz kedi

4.1 Karşılaştırma Sıfatları

Türkçede *daha* ile ifade edilen ve iki kişi ya da nesne arasında göreceli üstünlüğü belirten sıfatlardır ve İngilizcede **comparative adjectives** olarak bilinirler. İkiden fazla kişi veya nesne arasında e*n iyi, en üstün, en*... gibi özellikleri gösteren üstünlük sıfatları da, İngilizcede **superlative adjectives** olarak bilinirler.

Yapılan karşılaştırma iki nesne arasında oluyorsa, Türkçede *daha* kelimesi, İngilizcede ise, sıfatlardan önce **more** kelimesi ya da sıfattan sonra **-er** son eki kullanılır. Bu tamamen hece sayısına göre yapılır.

Yapılan karşılaştırma ikiden fazla nesne arasında oluyorsa, Türkçede **en** kelimesi, İngilizcede ise, sıfatlardan önce **most** kelimesi ya da sıfatlardan sonra **-est** son eki kullanılır. Bu yine tamamen hece sayısına göre yapılır ve sıfattan önce mutlaka **the** belirleyicisi **article** getirilir.

Tek heceli sıfatlara **-er (comparative)** ya da **-est (superlative)** son eki getirilir.

	Comparative	Superlative
bright	brighter	the brightest
long	longer	the longest
sharp	sharper	the sharpest

Tek heceli ve **-e** harfi ile biten sıfatlara sadece **-r (comparative)** ya da **-st (superlative)** son eki gelir. Eğer sıfat **-y** harfi ile bitiyorsa, genellikle **-y** harfi **-i** harfi ile değiştirilir ve **-er (comparative)** ya da **-est (superlative)** son eki alır. Tek heceli sıfatın sonunda bir sesli ve bir sessiz harf varsa, son harf eklerden önce tekrarlanır.

	Comparative	Superlative
wise	wiser	the wisest
pretty	prettier	the prettiest
big	bigger	the biggest

İki veya daha fazla heceli sıfatlardan önce **more (comparative)** ya da **the most (superlative)** gelir.

	Comparative	Superlative
beautiful	more beautiful	the most beautiful
colourful	more colourful	the most colourful
fortunate	more fortunate	the most fortunate

İngilizcedeki **irregular adjectives** (*düzensiz sıfatlar*), yukarıda sözü edilen kurallardan farklı olarak, aşağıdaki gibi kullanılır. Bunları öğrenmenin en iyi yolu ise, **comparative** ve **superlative** hallerini ezberlemektir.

	Comparative	Superlative
good	better	the best
bad	worse	the worst
much	more	the most
little	less	the least
far	further/farther	the furthest

5 Zarflar

Sıfatlar nasıl isimleri niteliyorlarsa, zarflar da sıfatları nitelerler. İngilizcede zarflar isimler dışında, cümlede bulunan diğer zarfları, edat cümleciklerini, isimleri, tam cümleleri ve sayıları da nitelerler.

Pek çok zarf, sıfatlara **-ly** eklenerek türetilir.
slow (*yavaş*) **slowly** (*yavaşça*), **clever** (*akıllı*) **cleverly** (*akıllıca*).

Sonları **-ble** ile biten sıfatlarda, önce **-e** harfi düşer, ondan sonra **-ly** eki gelir.
sensible (*hassas*) **sensibly** (*duyarlı olarak*), **suitable** (*uygun*) **suitably** (*uygunca, uygun bir şekilde*), **true** (*gerçek*) **truly** (*gerçekten*).

-y ile biten sıfatlarda **-y** harfi düşer, ve **-ily** eklenerek zarf türetilir.
happy (*mutlu*) **happily** (*mutlu bir şekilde*), **greedy** (*aç gözlü, hırslı*) **greedily** (*aç gözlüce, hırslıca*).

Bazı zarflar, sıfatlarla tamamen aynı yazılırlar. Bu tür kelimlerin zarf mı, yoksa sıfat mı olduğunu anlamak için birlikte kullanılan diğer sözcüklere bakmak gerekir. Eğer isimden önce geliyorsa, bu bir sıfattır.

a <u>short</u> way   **a <u>long</u> lecture**
Kestirme yol   *Uzun ders*

Ama eğer bir fiil ya da sıfattan önce geliyorsa, o zaman bu bir zarftır.

A lesson was cut <u>short</u>.
Ders kısa kesildi (zarf değil).

We meet <u>late</u> at night.
Biz gece geç vakit buluştuk (zarf).

Cümle başı zarfları: İsminden anlaşılacağı gibi cümlenin başında kullanılırlar.

<u>Actually</u>, I don't mind.
Gerçekten, bence fark etmez.

<u>Hopefully</u>, I will see you.
Umarım, sizi göreceğim.

Derece Zarfları: Cümlede sıfattan ya da cümledeki diğer zarflardan önce gelirler.

She seems <u>rather</u> nice.
O oldukça hoş görünüyor (İyi birisine benziyor).

Chris is a <u>very</u> good tennis player.
Chris çok iyi bir tenis oyuncusudur.

5.1 Karşılaştırma zarfları

Sıfatlarda olduğu gibi zarflarda da **comparative** (*karşılaştırma*) ve **superlative** (*üstünlük durumu*) vardır. Bunların sıfatlardan farklı olarak, Türkçede *daha* edatıyla ifade edilen ve iki kişi ya da nesne arasında göreceli üstünlüğü gösteren karşılaştırma zarfı **comparative** olarak genellikle sadece **more**, ikiden fazla kişi veya nesne arasında *en üstünlük* derecesini gösteren **superlative** zarflar da ise genellikle sadece **most** sözcükleri ile beraber kullanılır.

Could you speak <u>more</u> slowly, please?
Daha yavaş konuşabilir misiniz, lütfen?

Mrs.Kay's class behaved <u>(the) most</u> sensibly.
Kay Hanımın sınıfı en akıllı bir şekilde hareket etti.

5.2 Bağlaç Zarfları

Bu zarflar iki cümleyi birbirine bağlar ve onları birleştirirler.
However (*Mamafih, ancak, halbuki*), **Still** (*hala, yine de*),
Therefore (*bu nedenle, bundan dolayı*), **Thus** (*Böylece, bundan dolayı*).

6 Edatlar

Türkçedeki ismin -*de hali (bulunma)*, -*den hali (ayrılma)*, -*i hali*, -*e hali (yönelme)* gibi isimlere gelen hal ekleri İngilizcede **Prepositions** denilen edatlarla sağlanır. Edatlar, İngilizcede nesnelerden önce gelerek fiil, özne ve nesne arasında bağlantı kurarlar. Edatların cümle içerisinde tek başlarına herhangi bir anlamları ya da görevleri yoktur.

about (*hakkında, yaklaşık*)
    We talked <u>about</u> our jobs.
    İşimiz hakkında konuştuk.

after (-*den sonra, ardından*)
    <u>after</u> dinner   **<u>after</u> one o'clock**
    yemekten sonra   *saat birden sonra*

at (-*de/da, -e/a*)
    <u>at</u> one o'clock   **Look <u>at</u> me!**   **<u>at</u> home**
    saat birde   *bana bak!*   *evde*

before (-*den önce*)
    <u>before</u> Ankara   **<u>before</u> one o'clock**
    Ankara'dan önce   *saat birden önce*

between (*arasında*)
> **between** you and me
> *senin ve benim aramda*

from (*-den/dan*)
> **from Izmir**
> *İzmir'den*

in (*-de/da, -in içinde*)
> **in** Ankara   **in** the room
> *Ankara'da*   *odada*

into (*-in içine doğru, -e doğru*)
> Get **into** the car.
> *Arabaya gir.*

of (*-ın/in*)
> at the front **of** the house
> *evin önünde*

on (*-in üzerinde*)
> The cat is **on** the sofa.
> *Kedi koltuğun üzerindedir.*

over (*üzerinde- arada boşluk olacak şekilde*)
> The plane is flying **over** the city.
> *Uçak şehrin üzerinde uçuyor.*

to (*-e/a, -e doğru*)
> **to** London   I am going **to** London.
> *Londra'ya*   *Ben Londra'ya gidiyorum.*

under (*-in altında*)
> The dog is **under** the table.
> *Köpek masanın altında.*

with (*ile*)
> Come **with** me.   Water **with** ice.
> *Buzlu su.*   *Benimle gel.*

without (*-siz, -sız*)
> **without** him   **without** milk
> *Onsuz*   *sütsüz*

English–Turkish

İngilizce–Türkçe

a

a [eɪ] *art* bir
abandon [ə'bændən] *v* terketmek
abbey ['æbɪ] *n* manastır
abbreviation [ə,briːvɪ'eɪʃən] *n* kısaltma
abdomen ['æbdəmən; æb'dəʊ-] *n* karın
abduct [æb'dʌkt] *v* kaçırmak *(birini)*
ability [ə'bɪlɪtɪ] *n* yetenek
able ['eɪbəl] *adj* muktedir
abnormal [æb'nɔːməl] *adj* anormal
abolish [ə'bɒlɪʃ] *v* feshetmek
abolition [,æbə'lɪʃən] *n* yürürlükten kaldırma
abortion [ə'bɔːʃən] *n* kürtaj
about [ə'baʊt] *adv* yaklaşık ▷ *prep* hakkında; **Do you have any leaflets about…?**… hakkında broşürünüz var mı?
above [ə'bʌv] *prep* üzerinde

abroad [ə'brɔːd] *adv* yurtdışı
abrupt [ə'brʌpt] *adj* ani
abruptly [ə'brʌptlɪ] *adv* aniden
abscess ['æbsɛs; -sɪs] *n* apse; **I have an abscess** Burası apse yaptı
absence ['æbsəns] *n* yokluk *(devam)*
absent ['æbsənt] *adj* yok
absent-minded [,æbsən't'maɪndɪd] *adj* dalgın
absolutely [,æbsə'luːtlɪ] *adv* kesinlikle
abstract ['æbstrækt] *adj* soyut
absurd [əb'sɜːd] *adj* saçma
Abu Dhabi ['æbuː 'dɑːbɪ] *n* Abu Dabi
abuse [ə'bjuːs] *n* taciz ▷ [ə'bjuːz] *v* kötüye kullanmak; **child abuse** *n* çocuk tacizi
abusive [ə'bjuːsɪv] *adj* hakaretamiz
academic [,ækə'dɛmɪk] *adj* akademik; **academic year** *n* akademik yıl
academy [ə'kædəmɪ] *n* akademi
accelerate [æk'sɛlə,reɪt] *v* hızlanmak
acceleration [æk,sɛlə'reɪʃən] *n* hızlanma
accelerator [æk'sɛlə,reɪtə] *n* gaz pedalı
accept [ək'sɛpt] *v* kabul etmek
acceptable [ək'sɛptəbəl] *adj* kabul edilebilir
access ['æksɛs] *n* giriş *(geçiş)* ▷ *v* erişmek; **Do you provide access for people with disabilities?** Özürlüler için girişiniz var mı?

accessible [ək'sɛsəbᵊl] *adj* erişilebilir

accessory [ək'sɛsərı] *n* aksesuar

accident ['æksıdənt] *n* kaza; **accident & emergency department** *n* kaza & acil servis; **accident insurance** *n* kaza sigortası; **by accident** *adv* kazara; **I'd like to arrange personal accident insurance** Bireysel kaza sigortası yaptırmak istiyorum; **I've had an accident** Kaza geçirdim; **There's been an accident!** Bir kaza oldu!; **What do I do if I have an accident?** Kaza geçirirsem ne yapmam gerekiyor?

accidental [ˌæksı'dɛntᵊl] *adj* kaza sonucu

accidentally [ˌæksı'dɛntəlı] *adv* kazara

accommodate [ə'kɒməˌdeɪt] *v* barındırmak

accommodation [əˌkɒmə'deɪʃən] *n* kalacak yer

accompany [ə'kʌmpənı; ə'kʌmpnı] *v* eşlik etmek *(yanında gitmek)*

accomplice [ə'kɒmplıs; ə'kʌm-] *n* suç ortağı

according [ə'kɔːdıŋ] *prep* **according to** *prep* göre

accordingly [ə'kɔːdıŋlı] *adv* bundan dolayı

accordion [ə'kɔːdıən] *n* akordiyon

account [ə'kaunt] *n (in bank)* hesap *(banka)*, *(report)* tarif; **account number** *n* hesap numarası; **bank account** *n* banka hesabı; **current account** *n* cari hesap; **joint account** *n* ortak hesap

accountable [ə'kauntəbᵊl] *adj* sorumlu

accountancy [ə'kauntənsı] *n* muhasebecilik

accountant [ə'kauntənt] *n* muhasebeci

account for [ə'kaunt fɔː] *v* hesap vermek

accuracy ['ækjurəsı] *n* doğruluk

accurate ['ækjərıt] *adj* doğru *(söz, eylem, sonuç)*

accurately ['ækjərıtlı] *adv* doğru olarak

accusation [ˌækju'zeɪʃən] *n* suçlama

accuse [ə'kjuːz] *v* suçlamak

accused [ə'kjuːzd] *n* sanık

ace [eɪs] *n* as *(oyun, spor)*

ache [eɪk] *n* ağrı ▷ *v* ağrımak

achieve [ə'tʃiːv] *v* başarmak

achievement [ə'tʃiːvmənt] *n* başarı

acid ['æsıd] *n* asit; **acid rain** *n* asit yağmuru

acknowledgement [ək'nɒlıdʒmənt] *n* ikrar

acne ['æknı] *n* sivilce

acorn ['eɪkɔːn] *n* meşe palamudu

acoustic [ə'kuːstık] *adj* akustik

acrobat ['ækrəˌbæt] *n* akrobat

acronym ['ækrənım] *n* kısaltma

across [ə'krɒs] *prep* karşıya

act [ækt] *n* hareket ▷ *v* davranmak *(hareket)*

acting ['æktıŋ] *adj* vekaleten ▷ *n* oyunculuk

action ['ækʃən] *n* eylem

active ['æktıv] *adj* aktif

activity [æk'tıvıtı] *n* etkinlik; **activity holiday** *n* aktivite tatili;

Do you have activities for children? Çocuklar için etkinlikleriniz var mı?

actor ['æktə] *n* aktör

actress ['æktrɪs] *n* kadın oyuncu

actual ['æktʃʊəl] *adj* gerçek

actually ['æktʃʊəlɪ] *adv* aslında

acupuncture ['ækjʊˌpʌŋktʃə] *n* akupunktur

ad [æd] *abbr* reklam; **small ads** *npl* küçük ilanlar

AD [eɪ diː] *abbr* MS

adapt [əˈdæpt] *v* uyarlamak

adaptor [əˈdæptə] *n* adaptör

add [æd] *v* eklemek

addict ['ædɪkt] *n* bağımlı; **drug addict** *n* uyuşturucu bağımlısı

addicted [əˈdɪktɪd] *adj* bağımlı

additional [əˈdɪʃənᵊl] *adj* ek

additive ['ædɪtɪv] *n* katkı maddesi

address [əˈdrɛs] *n (location)* adres, *(speech)* hitap; **address book** *n* adres defteri; **home address** *n* ev adresi; **web address** *n* internet adresi; **My email address is…** E-posta adresim…; **Please send my mail on to this address** Mektuplarımı şu adrese gönderin lütfen; **The website address is…** İnternet adresi…; **What is your email address?** E-posta adresiniz nedir?; **Will you write down the address, please?** Adresi yazar mısınız lütfen?

add up [æd ʌp] *v* toplamak *(matematik)*

adjacent [əˈdʒeɪsᵊnt] *adj* bitişik

adjective ['ædʒɪktɪv] *n* sıfat

adjust [əˈdʒʌst] *v* ayarlamak

adjustable [əˈdʒʌstəbᵊl] *adj* ayarlanabilir

adjustment [əˈdʒʌstmənt] *n* ayarlama

administration [ədˌmɪnɪˈstreɪʃən] *n* yönetim

administrative [ədˈmɪnɪˌstrətɪv] *adj* idari

admiration [ˌædməˈreɪʃən] *n* hayranlık

admire [ədˈmaɪə] *v* hayranlık duymak

admission [ədˈmɪʃən] *n* kabul; **admission charge** *n* giriş ücreti

admit [ədˈmɪt] *v (allow in)* içeri almak, *(confess)* kabul etmek *(itiraf)*

admittance [ədˈmɪtᵊns] *n* giriş hakkı

adolescence [ˌædəˈlɛsəns] *n* ergenlik

adolescent [ˌædəˈlɛsᵊnt] *n* ergen

adopt [əˈdɒpt] *v* evlat edinmek

adopted [əˈdɒptɪd] *adj* evlat edinilmiş

adoption [əˈdɒpʃən] *n* evlat edinme

adore [əˈdɔː] *v* tapmak

Adriatic [ˌeɪdrɪˈætɪk] *adj* Adriyatik

Adriatic Sea [ˌeɪdrɪˈætɪk siː] *n* Adriyatik Denizi

adult ['ædʌlt; əˈdʌlt] *n* yetişkin; **adult education** *n* yetişkin eğitimi

advance [ədˈvɑːns] *n* ilerleme ▷ *v* ilerlemek; **advance booking** *n* önceden rezervasyon

advanced [ədˈvɑːnst] *adj* ileri

advantage [ədˈvɑːntɪdʒ] *n* üstünlük

advent ['ædvɛnt; -vənt] n Noel öncesi

adventure [əd'vɛntʃə] n macera

adventurous [əd'vɛntʃərəs] adj maceraperest

adverb ['ædˌvɜ:b] n belirteç

adversary ['ædvəsərɪ] n rakip

advert ['ædvɜ:t] n reklam

advertise ['ædvəˌtaɪz] v reklam yapmak

advertisement [əd'vɜ:tɪsmənt; -tɪz-] n reklam

advertising ['ædvəˌtaɪzɪŋ] n reklamcılık

advice [əd'vaɪs] n öğüt

advisable [əd'vaɪzəbªl] adj akıllıca

advise [əd'vaɪz] v tavsiye etmek

aerial ['ɛərɪəl] n anten

aerobics [ɛə'rəʊbɪks] npl aerobik

aerosol ['ɛərəˌsɒl] n aerosol

affair [ə'fɛə] n olay

affect [ə'fɛkt] v etkilemek (bir sonuç yaratarak)

affectionate [ə'fɛkʃənɪt] adj sevecen

afford [ə'fɔ:d] v gücü yetmek

affordable [ə'fɔ:dəbªl] adj keseye uygun

Afghan ['æfgæn; -gən] adj Afgan ▷ n Afgan

Afghanistan [æf'gænɪˌstɑ:n; -ˌstæn] n Afganistan

afraid [ə'freɪd] adj korkmuş

Africa ['æfrɪkə] n Afrika; **North Africa** n Kuzey Afrika; **South Africa** n Güney Afrika

African ['æfrɪkən] adj Afrikalı ▷ n Afrikalı; **Central African Republic** n Orta Afrika Cumhuriyeti; **North African** n Kuzey Afrika, Kuzey Afrikalı; **South African** n Güney Afrika, Güney Afrikalı

Afrikaans [ˌæfrɪ'kɑ:ns; -'kɑ:nz] n Afrikaanca

Afrikaner [afri'kɑ:nə; ˌæfrɪ'kɑ:nə] n Afrikaner

after ['ɑ:ftə] conj sonra; **after eight o'clock** saat sekizden sonra; **the week after next** bir sonraki hafta

afternoon [ˌɑ:ftə'nu:n] n öğleden sonra; **in the afternoon** öğleden sonra; **tomorrow afternoon** yarın öğleden sonra

afters ['ɑ:ftəz] npl tatlı

aftershave ['ɑ:ftəˌʃeɪv] n traş losyonu

afterwards ['ɑ:ftəwədz] adv sonra

again [ə'gɛn; ə'geɪn] adv yine

against [ə'gɛnst; ə'geɪnst] prep karşı

age [eɪdʒ] n yaş (yıl); **age limit** n yaş sınırı; **Middle Ages** npl Orta Çağ

aged ['eɪdʒɪd] adj yaşlı

agency ['eɪdʒənsɪ] n ajans; **travel agency** n seyahat acentası

agenda [ə'dʒɛndə] n gündem

agent ['eɪdʒənt] n temsilci; **estate agent** n emlakçı; **travel agent** n seyahat acentası (kişi)

aggressive [ə'grɛsɪv] adj saldırgan

AGM [eɪ dʒi: ɛm] abbr Yıllık Genel cunta

ago [ə'gəʊ] adv **a month ago** bir ay önce; **a week ago** bir hafta önce

agony ['ægənɪ] n ıstırap

agree [ə'gri:] v aynı fikirde olmak

agreed [ə'gri:d] adj mutabık

agreement [ə'gri:mənt] n anlaşma

agricultural ['ægrɪ,kʌltʃərəl] *adj* tarımsal

agriculture ['ægrɪ,kʌltʃə] *n* tarım

ahead [ə'hɛd] *adv* önde

aid [eɪd] *n* yardım; **first aid** *n* ilk yardım; **first-aid kit** *n* ilk yardım çantası; **hearing aid** *n* işitme cihazı

AIDS [eɪdz] *n* AIDS

aim [eɪm] *n* hedef ▷ *v* hedeflemek

air [ɛə] *n* hava; **air hostess** *n* hostes; **air-traffic controller** *n* hava trafik kontrolörü; **Air Force** *n* Hava Kuvvetleri; **Can you check the air, please?** Tekerleklerin havasını kontrol eder misiniz lütfen?; **How long will it take by air?** Hava postası ile ne kadar zamanda gider?

airbag [ɛəbæg] *n* hava yastığı

air-conditioned [ɛəkən'dɪʃənd] *adj* havalandırmalı

air conditioning [ɛə kən'dɪʃənɪŋ] *n* havalandırma

aircraft ['ɛə,krɑːft] *n* uçak

airline ['ɛə,laɪn] *n* havayolu

airmail ['ɛə,meɪl] *n* uçak postası

airport ['ɛə,pɔːt] *n* hava alanı; **airport bus** *n* hava alanı otobüsü

airsick ['ɛə,sɪk] *adj* uçak tutması

airspace ['ɛə,speɪs] *n* hava sahası

airtight ['ɛə,taɪt] *adj* vakumlanmış

aisle [aɪl] *n* koridor; **I'd like an aisle seat** Koltuğum koridor tarafında olsun

alarm [ə'lɑːm] *n* alarm; **alarm call** *n* uyarı çağrısı; **alarm clock** *n* çalar saat; **false alarm** *n* yanlış alarm; **fire alarm** *n* yangın alarmı; **smoke alarm** *n* duman alarmı

alarming [ə'lɑːmɪŋ] *adj* ürkütücü

Albania [æl'beɪnɪə] *n* Arnavutluk

Albanian [æl'beɪnɪən] *adj* Arnavut ▷ *n (language)* Arnavutça (dil), *(person)* Arnavut (kişi)

album ['ælbəm] *n* albüm *(müzik, fotoğraf)*; **photo album** *n* fotoğraf albümü

alcohol ['ælkə,hɒl] *n* alkol; **Does that contain alcohol?** Bunda alkol var mı?

alcohol-free ['ælkə,hɒlfriː] *adj* alkolsüz

alcoholic [,ælkə'hɒlɪk] *adj* alkollü ▷ *n* alkolik

alert [ə'lɜːt] *adj* uyanık ▷ *v* uyarmak

Algeria [æl'dʒɪərɪə] *n* Cezayir

Algerian [æl'dʒɪərɪən] *adj* Cezayir ▷ *n* Cezayirli

alias ['eɪlɪəs] *adv* takma ad ▷ *prep* diğer adıyla

alibi ['ælɪ,baɪ] *n* özür

alien ['eɪljən; 'eɪlɪən] *n* yabancı

alive [ə'laɪv] *adj* canlı *(hayatta)*

all [ɔːl] *adj* bütün *(hepsi)* ▷ *pron* hepsi; **We'd like to see nobody but us all day!** Bütün gün hiç kimseyi değil, sadece kendimizi görmek isterdik!

Allah ['ælə] *n* Allah

allegation [,ælɪ'geɪʃən] *n* iddia

alleged [ə'lɛdʒd] *adj* iddia edilen

allergic [ə'lɜːdʒɪk] *adj* alerjik

allergy ['ælədʒɪ] *n* alerji; **peanut allergy** *n* fıstık alerjisi

alley ['ælɪ] *n* dar sokak

alliance [ə'laɪəns] *n* ittifak

alligator ['ælɪ,geɪtə] *n* timsah

allow [ə'laʊ] *v* izin vermek

all right [ɔːl raɪt] *adv* iyi

ally ['ælaɪ; ə'laɪ] *n* müttefik

almond ['ɑːmənd] *n* badem

almost ['ɔːlməʊst] *adv* neredeyse;
It's almost half past two Saat
neredeyse iki buçuk

alone [ə'ləʊn] *adj* yalnız

along [ə'lɒŋ] *prep* boyunca

aloud [ə'laʊd] *adv* yüksek sesle

alphabet ['ælfəˌbɛt] *n* alfabe

Alps [ælps] *npl* Alper

already [ɔːl'rɛdɪ] *adv* zaten

alright [ɔːl'raɪt] *adv* **Are you
alright?** İyi misiniz?

also ['ɔːlsəʊ] *adv* dahi *(o da)*

altar ['ɔːltə] *n* sunak

alter ['ɔːltə] *v* değiştirmek

alternate [ɔːl'tɜːnɪt] *adj* karşılıklı

alternative [ɔːl'tɜːnətɪv] *adj*
alternatif ▷ *n* seçenek

alternatively [ɔːl'tɜːnətɪvlɪ] *adv*
ya da

although [ɔːl'ðəʊ] *conj* rağmen

altitude ['æltɪˌtjuːd] *n* yükseklik

altogether [ˌɔːltə'gɛðə;
'ɔːltəˌgɛðə] *adv* hep birlikte

aluminium [ˌæljʊ'mɪnɪəm] *n*
alüminyum

always ['ɔːlweɪz; -wɪz] *adv* her
zaman

a.m. [eɪɛm] *abbr* öğleden önce

amateur ['æmətə; -tʃə; -ˌtjʊə;
ˌæmə'tɜː] *n* amatör

amaze [ə'meɪz] *v* şaşırtmak

amazed [ə'meɪzd] *adj* şaşkın

amazing [ə'meɪzɪŋ] *adj* hayret
verici

ambassador [æm'bæsədə] *n*
büyükelçi

amber ['æmbə] *n* kehribar

ambition [æm'bɪʃən] *n* hırs

ambitious [æm'bɪʃəs] *adj* hırslı

ambulance ['æmbjʊləns] *n*
cankurtaran *(tıp)*

ambush ['æmbʊʃ] *n* tuzak

amenities [ə'miːnɪtɪz] *npl*
olanaklar

America [ə'mɛrɪkə] *n* Amerika;
Central America *n* Orta Amerika;
North America *n* Kuzey Amerika;
South America *n* Güney Amerika

American [ə'mɛrɪkən] *adj*
Amerikan ▷ *n* Amerikalı; **American
football** *n* Amerikan futbolu;
North American *n* Kuzey
Amerika, Kuzey Amerikalı; **South
American** *n* Güney Amerika,
Güney Amerikalı

ammunition [ˌæmjʊ'nɪʃən] *n*
cephane

among [ə'mʌŋ] *prep* arasında

amount [ə'maʊnt] *n* miktar; **I
have the allowed amount of
tobacco to declare** İzin verilen
miktarda sigara deklare etmek
istiyorum

amp [æmp] *n* amper

amplifier ['æmplɪˌfaɪə] *n*
yükseltici

amuse [ə'mjuːz] *v* eğlendirmek
(şakayla); **amusement arcade** *n*
oyun salonu

an [ɑːn] *art* bir

anaemic [ə'niːmɪk] *adj* kansız

anaesthetic [ˌænɪs'θɛtɪk] *n*
anestetik; **general anaesthetic** *n*
genel anestezi; **local anaesthetic**
n lokal anestezi

analyse ['ænəˌlaɪz] *v* çözümlemek

analysis [ə'nælɪsɪs] *n* çözümleme

ancestor ['ænsɛstə] n ata

anchor ['æŋkə] n çapa

anchovy ['æntʃəvɪ] n ançuez

ancient ['eɪnʃənt] adj eski

and [ænd; ənd; ən] conj ve

Andes ['ændiːz] npl And Dağları

Andorra [æn'dɔːrə] n Andora

angel ['eɪndʒəl] n melek

anger ['æŋgə] n öfke

angina [æn'dʒaɪnə] n anjin

angle ['æŋgəl] n açı; **right angle** n
dik açı

angler ['æŋglə] n olta balıkçısı

angling ['æŋglɪŋ] n olta balıkçılığı

Angola [æŋ'gəʊlə] n Angola

Angolan [æŋ'gəʊlən] adj Angola
▷ n Angolalı

angry ['æŋgrɪ] adj kızgın

animal ['ænɪməl] n hayvan

aniseed ['ænɪˌsiːd] n anason

ankle ['æŋkəl] n ayak bileği

anniversary [ˌænɪ'vɜːsərɪ] n yıl
dönümü; **wedding anniversary** n
evlilik yıldönümü

announce [ə'naʊns] v duyurmak

announcement [ə'naʊnsmənt]
n duyuru

annoy [ə'nɔɪ] v sinirini bozmak

annoying [ə'nɔɪɪŋ] adj sinir
bozucu

annual ['ænjʊəl] adj yıllık

annually ['ænjʊəlɪ] adv her yıl

anonymous [ə'nɒnɪməs] adj adsız

anorak ['ænəˌræk] n anorak

anorexia [ˌænɒ'rɛksɪə] n anoreksi

anorexic [ˌænɒ'rɛksɪk] adj
anoreksik

another [ə'nʌðə] adj diğer

answer ['ɑːnsə] n yanıt ▷ v
yanıt vermek

answerphone ['ɑːnsəfəʊn] n
telesekreter

ant [ænt] n karınca

antagonize [æn'tægəˌnaɪz] v
düşmanlığını kazanmak

Antarctic [ænt'ɑːktɪk] **the
Antarctic** n Güney Kutbu

Antarctica [ænt'ɑːktɪkə] n Güney
Kutbu

antelope ['æntɪˌləʊp] n antilop

antenatal [ˌæntɪ'neɪtəl] adj
doğum öncesi

anthem ['ænθəm] n marş

anthropology [ˌænθrə'pɒlədʒɪ] n
insan bilimi

antibiotic [ˌæntɪbaɪ'ɒtɪk] n
antibiyotik

antibody ['æntɪˌbɒdɪ] n antikor

anticlockwise [ˌæntɪ'klɒkˌwaɪz]
adv saatin aksi yönünde

antidepressant [ˌæntɪdɪ'prɛsənt]
n antidepresan

antidote ['æntɪˌdəʊt] n panzehir

antifreeze ['æntɪˌfriːz] n antifriz

antihistamine [ˌæntɪ'hɪstəˌmiːn;
-mɪn] n antihistamin

antiperspirant
[ˌæntɪ'pɜːspərənt] n ter önleyici
deodorant

antique [æn'tiːk] n antika;
antique shop n antikacı dukkanı

antiseptic [ˌæntɪ'sɛptɪk] n
antiseptik

antivirus ['æntɪˌvaɪrəs] n antivirüs

anxiety [æŋ'zaɪɪtɪ] n endişe

any ['ɛnɪ] pron her, herhangi

anybody ['ɛnɪˌbɒdɪ; -bədɪ] pron
herhangi biri

anyhow ['ɛnɪˌhaʊ] adv her
halükarda

anyone ['ɛnɪ,wʌn; -wən] *pron* herhangi biri

anything ['ɛnɪ,θɪŋ] *pron* herhangi bir şey

anyway ['ɛnɪ,weɪ] *adv* neyse

anywhere ['ɛnɪ,wɛə] *adv* herhangi bir yer

apart [ə'pɑːt] *adv* ayrı

apart from [ə'pɑːt frɒm] *prep* dışında *(ondan ayrı olarak)*

apartment [ə'pɑːtmənt] *n* apartman dairesi; **We're looking for an apartment** Bir apartman dairesi bakıyorduk; **We've booked an apartment in the name of...** ...adına bir apartman dairesi ayırtmıştık

aperitif [ɑː,pɛrɪ'tiːf] *n* yemek öncesi içki

aperture ['æpətʃə] *n* açıklık *(aralık)*

apologize [ə'pɒlə,dʒaɪz] *v* özür dilemek

apology [ə'pɒlədʒɪ] *n* özür

apostrophe [ə'pɒstrəfɪ] *n* kesme imi

app [æp] *n* uygulama

appalling [ə'pɔːlɪŋ] *adj* korkunç

apparatus [,æpə'reɪtəs; -'rɑːtəs; 'æpə,reɪtəs] *n* aygıt

apparent [ə'pærənt; ə'pɛər-] *adj* görünür

apparently [ə'pærəntlɪ; ə'pɛər-] *adv* açıkça

appeal [ə'piːl] *n* rica ▷ *v* rica etmek

appear [ə'pɪə] *v* görünmek

appearance [ə'pɪərəns] *n* görünüş

appendicitis [ə,pɛndɪ'saɪtɪs] *n* apandisit

appetite ['æpɪ,taɪt] *n* iştah

applaud [ə'plɔːd] *v* alkışlamak

applause [ə'plɔːz] *n* alkış

apple ['æpəl] *n* elma; **apple pie** *n* elmalı turta

appliance [ə'plaɪəns] *n* cihaz

applicant ['æplɪkənt] *n* başvurucu

application [,æplɪ'keɪʃən] *n* başvuru; **application form** *n* başvuru formu

apply [ə'plaɪ] *v* kullanmak

appoint [ə'pɔɪnt] *v* atamak

appointment [ə'pɔɪntmənt] *n* randevu; **Can I have an appointment with the doctor?** Doktordan randevu alabilir miyim?; **Do you have an appointment?** Randevunuz var mıydı?; **I have an appointment with...…** ile randevum vardı; **I'd like to make an appointment** Randevu almak istiyorum

appreciate [ə'priːʃɪ,eɪt; -sɪ-] *v* paha biçmek

apprehensive [,æprɪ'hɛnsɪv] *adj* endişeli

apprentice [ə'prɛntɪs] *n* çırak

approach [ə'prəʊtʃ] *v* yaklaşmak

appropriate [ə'prəʊprɪɪt] *adj* uygun

approval [ə'pruːvəl] *n* onay

approve [ə'pruːv] *v* onaylamak

approximate [ə'prɒksɪmɪt] *adj* yaklaşık

approximately [ə'prɒksɪmɪtlɪ] *adv* yaklaşık olarak

apricot ['eɪprɪ,kɒt] *n* kayısı

April ['eɪprəl] *n* Nisan; **April Fools' Day** *n* 1 Nisan Şakası

apron ['eɪprən] *n* önlük

aquarium [ə'kwɛərɪəm] n
akvaryum

Aquarius [ə'kwɛərɪəs] n Kova
burcu

Arab ['ærəb] adj Arap ▷ n Arap;
United Arab Emirates npl Birleşik
Arap Emirlikleri

Arabic ['ærəbɪk] adj Arap ▷ n Arapça

arbitration [ˌɑːbɪ'treɪʃən] n
hakem aracılığıyla çözümleme

arch [ɑːtʃ] n kemer

archaeologist [ˌɑːkɪ'ɒlədʒɪst] n
arkeolog

archaeology [ˌɑːkɪ'ɒlədʒɪ] n
arkeoloji

archbishop ['ɑːtʃ'bɪʃəp] n
başpiskopos

architect ['ɑːkɪˌtɛkt] n mimar

architecture ['ɑːkɪˌtɛktʃə] n
mimarlık

archive ['ɑːkaɪv] n arşiv

Arctic ['ɑːktɪk] **Arctic Circle** n
Kuzey Buzul Kuşağı; **Arctic Ocean**
n Kuzey Okyanusu; **the Arctic** n
Kuzey Kutbu

area ['ɛərɪə] n alan (ölçü birimi);
service area n konaklama alanı

Argentina [ˌɑːdʒən'tiːnə] n
Arjantin

Argentinian [ˌɑːdʒən'tɪnɪən] adj
Arjantin ▷ n (person) Arjantinli (kişi)

argue ['ɑːgjuː] v tartışmak

argument ['ɑːgjʊmənt] n
tartışma

Aries ['ɛəriːz] n Koç burcu

arm [ɑːm] n kol; **I can't move my
arm** Kolumu oynatamıyorum

armchair ['ɑːmˌtʃɛə] n koltuk

armed [ɑːmd] adj silahlı

Armenia [ɑː'miːnɪə] n Ermenistan

Armenian [ɑː'miːnɪən] adj Ermeni
▷ n (language) Ermenice (dil),
(person) Ermeni (kişi)

armour ['ɑːmə] n zırh

armpit ['ɑːmˌpɪt] n koltukaltı

army ['ɑːmɪ] n ordu

aroma [ə'rəumə] n koku

aromatherapy [əˌrəumə'θɛrəpɪ]
n aromaterapi

around [ə'raund] adv yakınında
▷ prep etrafında

arrange [ə'reɪndʒ] v düzenlemek
(toplantı)

arrangement [ə'reɪndʒmənt] n
düzenleme (aranjman)

arrears [ə'rɪəz] npl vadesi geçmiş
borç

arrest [ə'rɛst] n tutuklama ▷ v
tutuklamak

arrival [ə'raɪvəl] n varış

arrive [ə'raɪv] v varmak

arrogant ['ærəgənt] adj kendini
beğenmiş

arrow ['ærəu] n ok

arson ['ɑːsən] n kundaklama

art [ɑːt] n sanat; **art gallery** n
sanat galerisi; **art school** n sanat
okulu; **work of art** n sanat eseri

artery ['ɑːtərɪ] n atardamar

arthritis [ɑː'θraɪtɪs] n mafsal
iltihabı

artichoke ['ɑːtɪˌtʃəuk] n enginar

article ['ɑːtɪkəl] n makale

artificial [ˌɑːtɪ'fɪʃəl] adj yapay

artist ['ɑːtɪst] n sanatçı

artistic [ɑː'tɪstɪk] adj sanatsal

as [əz] adv gibi ▷ conj iken ▷ prep
kadar; **How much should I give
as a tip?** Ne kadar bahşiş
vermem gerek?

asap [eɪsæp] *abbr* en kısa zamanda

ascent [ə'sɛnt] *n* **When is the last ascent?** En son çıkış kaçta?

ashamed [ə'ʃeɪmd] *adj* mahcup

ashore [ə'ʃɔː] *adv* **Can we go ashore now?** Kıyıya çıkabilir miyiz?

ashtray ['æʃtreɪ] *n* küllük

Asia ['eɪʃə; 'eɪʒə] *n* Asya

Asian ['eɪʃən; 'eɪʒən] *adj* Asya ▷ *n* Asyalı

Asiatic [ˌeɪʃɪ'ætɪk; -zɪ-] *adj* Asyalı

ask [ɑːsk] *v* sormak

ask for [ɑːsk fɔː] *v* aramak

asleep [ə'sliːp] *adj* uykuda

asparagus [ə'spærəgəs] *n* kuşkonmaz

aspect ['æspɛkt] *n* bakış açısı

aspirin ['æsprɪn] *n* aspirin; **I can't take aspirin** Aspirin alamıyorum; **I'd like some aspirin** Aspirin rica ediyorum

assembly [ə'sɛmblɪ] *n* topluluk

asset ['æsɛt] *n* varlık; **assets** *npl* varlık

assignment [ə'saɪnmənt] *n* görev *(ödev vb)*

assistance [ə'sɪstəns] *n* yardım; **I need assistance** Yardıma ihtiyacım var

assistant [ə'sɪstənt] *n* asistan; **personal assistant** *n* kişisel asistan; **sales assistant** *n* tezgahtar; **shop assistant** *n* satış elemanı

associate [ə'səʊʃɪɪt] *adj* yardımcı ▷ [ə'səʊʃɪɪt]*n* iş arkadaşı

association [əˌsəʊsɪ'eɪʃən; -ʃɪ-] *n* birlik *(dernek)*

assortment [ə'sɔːtmənt] *n* çeşit

assume [ə'sjuːm] *v* varsaymak

assure [ə'ʃʊə] *v* güvence vermek

asthma ['æsmə] *n* astım

astonish [ə'stɒnɪʃ] *v* şaşırtmak

astonished [ə'stɒnɪʃt] *adj* şaşırmış

astonishing [ə'stɒnɪʃɪŋ] *adj* şaşırtıcı

astrology [ə'strɒlədʒɪ] *n* astroloji

astronaut ['æstrənɔːt] *n* astronot

astronomy [ə'strɒnəmɪ] *n* astronomi

asylum [ə'saɪləm] *n* sığınma; **asylum seeker** *n* sığınmacı

at [æt] *prep* de, da *(konum)*; **at least** *adv* en azından

atheist ['eɪθɪˌɪst] *n* tanrı tanımaz

athlete ['æθliːt] *n* atlet

athletic [æθ'lɛtɪk] *adj* atletik

athletics [æθ'lɛtɪks] *npl* atletizm

Atlantic [ət'læntɪk] *n* Atlantik

atlas ['ætləs] *n* atlas

atmosphere ['ætməsˌfɪə] *n* atmosfer

atom ['ætəm] *n* atom; **atom bomb** *n* atom bombası

atomic [ə'tɒmɪk] *adj* nükleer

attach [ə'tætʃ] *v* bağlamak

attached [ə'tætʃt] *adj* ekli

attachment [ə'tætʃmənt] *n* ek

attack [ə'tæk] *n* saldırı ▷ *v* saldırmak; **heart attack** *n* kalp krizi; **terrorist attack** *n* terörist saldırı; **I've been attacked** Saldırıya uğradım

attempt [ə'tɛmpt] *n* girişim ▷ *v* kalkışmak

attend [ə'tɛnd] *v* katılmak

attendance [ə'tɛndəns] *n* katılım

attendant [ə'tɛndənt] *n* **flight attendant** *n* uçuş hostesi

attention [əˈtɛnʃən] n dikkat

attic [ˈætɪk] n tavanarası

attitude [ˈætɪˌtjuːd] n tavır

attorney [əˈtɜːnɪ] n avukat

attract [əˈtrækt] v çekmek

attraction [əˈtrækʃən] n çekim

attractive [əˈtræktɪv] adj çekici; **You are very attractive** Çok çekicisiniz

aubergine [ˈəʊbəʒiːn] n patlıcan

auburn [ˈɔːbən] adj kumral

auction [ˈɔːkʃən] n açık arttırma

audience [ˈɔːdɪəns] n dinleyiciler

audit [ˈɔːdɪt] n hesap denetimi ▷ v hesapları denetlemek

audition [ɔːˈdɪʃən] n ses sınavı

auditor [ˈɔːdɪtə] n denetçi (maliye)

August [ˈɔːɡəst] n Ağustos

aunt [ɑːnt] n (maternal aunt) teyze

auntie [ˈɑːntɪ] n teyze

au pair [əʊ ˈpɛə; o pɛr] n au-pair

austerity [ɒˈstɛrɪtɪ] n darlık

Australasia [ˌɒstrəˈleɪzɪə] n Avustralasya

Australia [ɒˈstreɪlɪə] n Avustralya

Australian [ɒˈstreɪlɪən] adj Avustralyalı ▷ n Avustralyalı

Austria [ˈɒstrɪə] n Avusturya

Austrian [ˈɒstrɪən] adj Avusturya ▷ n Avusturyalı

authentic [ɔːˈθɛntɪk] adj özgün

author, authoress [ˈɔːθə, ˈɔːθəˌrɛs] n yazar

authorize [ˈɔːθəˌraɪz] v yetki vermek

autobiography [ˌɔːtəʊbaɪˈɒɡrəfɪ; ˌɔːtəbaɪ-] n özyaşam öyküsü

autograph [ˈɔːtəˌɡrɑːf; -ˌɡræf] n imza

automatic [ˌɔːtəˈmætɪk] adj otomatik; **An automatic, please** Otomatik olsun lütfen; **Is it an automatic car?** Bu araba otomatik mi?

automatically [ˌɔːtəˈmætɪklɪ] adv otomatik olarak

autonomous [ɔːˈtɒnəməs] adj özerk

autonomy [ɔːˈtɒnəmɪ] n özerklik

autumn [ˈɔːtəm] n sonbahar

availability [əˈveɪləbɪlɪtɪ] n uygunluk

available [əˈveɪləbəl] adj uygun

avalanche [ˈævəˌlɑːntʃ] n çığ

avenue [ˈævɪˌnjuː] n bulvar

average [ˈævərɪdʒ; ˈævrɪdʒ] adj ortalama ▷ n ortalama

avocado, avocados [ˌævəˈkɑːdəʊ, ˌævəˈkɑːdəʊs] n avokado

avoid [əˈvɔɪd] v kaçmak

awake [əˈweɪk] adj uyanık ▷ v uyanmak

award [əˈwɔːd] n ödül

aware [əˈwɛə] adj farkında

away [əˈweɪ] adv uzakta; **away match** n rakip sahada maç

awful [ˈɔːfʊl] adj berbat; **What awful weather!** Hava çok berbat!

awfully [ˈɔːfəlɪ; ˈɔːflɪ] adv son derece

awkward [ˈɔːkwəd] adj beceriksiz

axe [æks] n balta

axle [ˈæksəl] n dingil

Azerbaijan [ˌæzəbaɪˈdʒɑːn] n Azerbaycan

Azerbaijani [ˌæzəbaɪˈdʒɑːnɪ] adj Azerbaycan ▷ n Azerbaycanlı

b

B&B [bi: ænd bi:] *n* Yatak ve Kahvaltı

BA [bɑ:] *abbr* lisans derecesi *(edebiyat)*

baby ['beɪbɪ] *n* bebek; **baby milk** *n* bebek sütü; **baby wipe** *n* ıslak bebek mendili; **baby's bottle** *n* biberon; **Are there facilities for parents with babies?** Bebekli aileler için kolaylıklarınız var mı?

babysit ['beɪbɪsɪt] *v* bebek bakmak

babysitter ['beɪbɪsɪtə] *n* bebek bakıcısı

babysitting ['beɪbɪsɪtɪŋ] *n* bebek bakma

bachelor ['bætʃələ; 'bætʃlə] *n* bekar

back [bæk] *adj* arka ▷ *adv* arkada ▷ *n* sırt ▷ *v* geri çekilmek; **back pain** *n* sırt ağrısı; **I've got a bad back** Sırtım tutuldu

backache ['bæk,eɪk] *n* sırt ağrısı

backbone ['bæk,bəʊn] *n* omurga

backfire [,bæk'faɪə] *v* geri tepmek

background ['bæk,graʊnd] *n* arka plan

backing ['bækɪŋ] *n* destekleme

back out [bæk aʊt] *v* geri kalmak

backpack ['bæk,pæk] *n* sırt çantası

backpacker ['bæk,pækə] *n* sırt çantasıyla dolaşan gezgin

backpacking ['bæk,pækɪŋ] *n* sırt çantasıyla gezme

backside [,bæk'saɪd] *n* kıç

backslash ['bæk,slæʃ] *n* geriye yatık çizgi

backstroke ['bæk,strəʊk] *n* sırtüstü yüzme

back up [bæk ʌp] *v* destek olmak

backup [bæk,ʌp] *n* yedek

backwards ['bækwədz] *adv* geriye doğru

bacon ['beɪkən] *n* domuz pastırması

bacteria [bæk'tɪərɪə] *npl* bakteri

bad [bæd] *adj* kötü; **It's a bad line** Çok kötü bir hat

badge [bædʒ] *n* kimlik kartı

badger ['bædʒə] *n* porsuk

badly ['bædlɪ] *adv* kötü bir şekilde

badminton ['bædmɪntən] *n* badminton

bad-tempered [bæd'tɛmpəd] *adj* huysuz

baffled ['bæfˀld] *adj* şaşkın

bag [bæg] *n* torba; **bum bag** *n* bel çantası; **carrier bag** *n* alışveriş torbası; **overnight bag** *n* gecelik seyahat çantası; **plastic bag** *n* naylon torba; **polythene bag** *n* naylon torba; **shopping bag** *n* alışveriş çantası; **sleeping bag** *n* uyku tulumu; **tea bag** *n* torba çay; **toilet bag** *n* tuvalet çantası; **Can I have a bag, please?** Torbanız var mı?; **I don't need a bag, thanks** Torba istemem, sağolun

baggage ['bægɪdʒ] *n* bagaj; **baggage allowance** *n* bagaj limiti; **baggage reclaim** *n* bagaj alım; **excess baggage** *n* fazla bagaj; **What is the baggage allowance?** Bagaj limiti ne kadar?

baggy ['bægɪ] *adj* şalvar biçimi

bagpipes ['bæg,paɪps] *npl* gayda

Bahamas [bə'hɑːməz] *npl* Bahama Adaları

Bahrain [bɑː'reɪn] *n* Bahreyn

bail [beɪl] *n* kefalet

bake [beɪk] *v* fırında pişirmek

baked [beɪkt] *adj* fırında pişirilmiş; **baked potato** *n* kumpir

baker ['beɪkə] *n* fırıncı

bakery ['beɪkərɪ] *n* ekmekçi *(fırın)*

baking ['beɪkɪŋ] *n* fırında pişirme; **baking powder** *n* kabartma tozu

balance ['bæləns] *n* denge *(fizik)*; **balance sheet** *n* bilanço; **bank balance** *n* bakiye

balanced ['bælənst] *adj* dengeli

balcony ['bælkənɪ] *n* balkon; **Do you have a room with a balcony?** Balkonlu odanız var mı?

bald [bɔːld] *adj* kel

Balkan ['bɔːlkən] *adj* Balkan

ball [bɔːl] *n (dance)* balo, *(toy)* oyuncak top

ballerina [,bælə'riːnə] *n* balerin

ballet ['bæleɪ; bæ'leɪ] *n* bale; **ballet dancer** *n* balet; **ballet shoes** *npl* bale patiği; **Where can I**

buy tickets for the ballet? Baleye nereden bilet alabilirim?

balloon [bə'luːn] *n* balon

bamboo [bæm'buː] *n* bambu

ban [bæn] *n* yasak ▷ *v* yasaklamak

banana [bə'nɑːnə] *n* muz

band [bænd] *n (musical group)* orkestra, *(strip)* bant; **brass band** *n* bando takımı; **elastic band** *n* lastik bant; **rubber band** *n* elastik band

bandage ['bændɪdʒ] *n* bandaj ▷ *v* sarmak

bang [bæŋ] *n* patlama sesi ▷ *v* patlamak *(ses çıkararak)*

Bangladesh [,bɑːŋglə'dɛʃ; ,bæŋ-] *n* Bengaldeş

Bangladeshi [,bɑːŋglə'dɛʃɪ; ,bæŋ-] *adj* Bengaldeş ile ilgili ▷ *n* Bengaldeşli

banister ['bænɪstə] *n* trabzan

banjo ['bændʒəʊ] *n* banço

bank [bæŋk] *n (finance)* banka, *(ridge)* ırmak kıyısı; **bank account** *n* banka hesabı; **bank balance** *n* bakiye; **bank charges** *npl* banka ücretleri; **bank holiday** *n* İngiltere'de bankaların kapalı olduğu tatil günü; **bank statement** *n* hesap özeti; **bottle bank** *n* şişe geri dönüşüm kutusu; **merchant bank** *n* ticaret bankası; **How far is the bank?** Banka buraya ne kadar uzakta?; **I would like to transfer some money from my bank in...** Bankamdan para transferi yapmak istiyorum; **Is the bank open today?** Banka bugün açık mı?; **Is there a bank here?** Burada banka var mı?;

When does the bank close?
Banka ne zaman kapanıyor?

banker ['bæŋkə] n bankacı

banknote ['bæŋk,nəʊt] n banknot

bankrupt ['bæŋkrʌpt; -rəpt] adj
müflis

banned [bænd] adj yasaklanmış

Baptist ['bæptɪst] n Baptist

bar [bɑ:] n (alcohol) bar, (strip)
çubuk; **snack bar** n snack bar;
Where is the bar? Bar ne tarafta?;
Where is there a nice bar? İyi bir
bar biliyor musunuz?

Barbados [bɑ:'beɪdəʊs; -dəʊz;
-dɒs] n Barbados

barbaric [bɑ:'bærɪk] adj barbar

barbecue ['bɑ:bɪ,kju:] n barbekü;
Where is the barbecue area?
Barbekü kısmı nerede?

barber ['bɑ:bə] n berber

bare [bɛə] adj çıplak ▷ v açığa
çıkarmak

barefoot ['bɛə,fʊt] adj çıplak ayak
▷ adv çıplak ayakla

barely ['bɛəlɪ] adv ucu ucuna

bargain ['bɑ:gɪn] n pazarlık

barge [bɑ:dʒ] n mavna

bark [bɑ:k] v havlamak

barley ['bɑ:lɪ] n arpa

barmaid ['bɑ:,meɪd] n kadın
barmen

barman, barmen ['bɑ:mən,
'bɑ:mɛn] n barmen

barn [bɑ:n] n samanlık

barrel ['bærəl] n fıçı

barrier ['bærɪə] n bariyer; **ticket
barrier** n bilet turnikesi

bartender ['bɑ:,tɛndə] n barmen

base [beɪs] n ana

baseball ['beɪs,bɔ:l] n beyzbol;

baseball cap n beyzbol kepi

based [beɪst] adj dayanan

basement ['beɪsmənt] n bodrum

bash [bæʃ] n darbe ▷ v şiddetle
vurmak

basic ['beɪsɪk] adj temel

basically ['beɪsɪklɪ] adv aslında

basics ['beɪsɪks] npl temel bilgiler

basil ['bæzəl] n fesleğen

basin ['beɪsən] n leğen

basis ['beɪsɪs] n anafikir

basket ['bɑ:skɪt] n sepet;
wastepaper basket n çöp sepeti

basketball ['bɑ:skɪt,bɔ:l] n
basketbol

Basque [bæsk; bɑ:sk] adj Bask ▷ n
(language) Bask dili, (person) Basklı
(kişi)

bass [beɪs] n bas; **bass drum** n bas
davul; **double bass** n kontrabas

bassoon [bə'su:n] n fagot

bat [bæt] n (mammal) yarasa, (with
ball) vuruş (topa sopayla)

bath [bɑ:θ] n banyo; **bubble bath** n
köpüklü banyo

bathe [beɪð] v yüzmek

bathrobe ['bɑ:θ,rəʊb] n bornoz

bathroom ['bɑ:θ,ru:m; -,rʊm] n
banyo; **Are there support
railings in the bathroom?**
Banyoda tutunma rayı var mı?;
**Does the room have a private
bathroom?** Odada banyo var mı?;
The bathroom is flooded Banyo
taşıyor

baths [bɑ:θz] npl hamam

bathtub ['bɑ:θ,tʌb] n küvet

batter ['bætə] n sulu hamur

battery ['bætərɪ] n pil; **Do you
have any batteries?** Pil satıyor

musunuz?; **Do you have batteries for this camera?** Bu makineye uygun pil var mı?

battle ['bætᵊl] *n* muharebe

battleship ['bætᵊlˌʃɪp] *n* muharebe zırhlısı

bay [beɪ] *n* körfez; **bay leaf** *n* defne yaprağı

BC [bi: si:] *abbr* İÖ

be [bi:; bɪ] *v* olmak

beach [bi:tʃ] *n* kumsal

bead [bi:d] *n* boncuk

beak [bi:k] *n* gaga

beam [bi:m] *n* ışın

bean [bi:n] *n* fasulye; **broad bean** *n* bakla *(sebze)*; **coffee bean** *n* kahve çekirdeği; **French beans** *npl* çalı fasulyesi; **runner bean** *n* çalı fasulyesi

beansprout ['bi:nsprautʊ] *n* **beansprouts** *npl* fasulye filizi

bear [bɛə] *n* ayı ▷ *v* taşımak; **polar bear** *n* kutup ayısı; **teddy bear** *n* oyuncak ayı

beard [bɪəd] *n* sakal

bearded [bɪədɪd] *adj* sakallı

bear up [bɛə ʌp] *v* dayanmak

beat [bi:t] *n* ritim ▷ *v (outdo)* yenmek, *(strike)* dövmek

beautiful ['bju:tɪfʊl] *adj* güzel

beautifully ['bju:tɪflɪ] *adv* hoşça

beauty ['bju:tɪ] *n* güzellik; **beauty salon** *n* güzellik salonu; **beauty spot** *n* güzel manzaralı yer

beaver ['bi:və] *n* kunduz

because [bɪ'kɒz; -'kəz] *conj* çünkü

become [bɪ'kʌm] *v* olmak

bed [bɛd] *n* yatak; **bed and breakfast** *n* yatak ve kahvaltı; **bunk beds** *npl* ranza; **camp bed** *n* portatif karyola; **double bed** *n* çift kişilik yatak; **king-size bed** *n* battal boy yatak; **single bed** *n* tek yatak; **sofa bed** *n* çek-yat; **twin beds** *npl* çift yatak; **Do I have to stay in bed?** Yatakta mı kalmam gerekiyor?; **I'd like a dorm bed** Tek bir yatak rica ediyorum; **The bed is uncomfortable** Yatak çok rahatsız

bedclothes ['bɛdˌkləʊðz] *npl* yatak takımı

bedding ['bɛdɪŋ] *n* yatak takımı

bedroom ['bɛdˌru:m; -ˌrʊm] *n* yatak odası; **Do you have any bedrooms on the ground floor?** Zemin katta yatak odası var mı?

bedsit ['bɛdˌsɪt] *n* kiralık oda

bedspread ['bɛdˌsprɛd] *n* yatak örtüsü

bedtime ['bɛdˌtaɪm] *n* yatma zamanı

bee [bi:] *n* arı

beech [bi:tʃ] *n* **beech (tree)** *n* kayın ağacı

beef [bi:f] *n* sığır eti

beefburger ['bi:fˌbɜ:gə] *n* hamburger

beer [bɪə] *n* bira; **another beer, please** Bir bira daha lütfen; **A draught beer, please** Bir çekme bira lütfen

beetle ['bi:tᵊl] *n* böcek

beetroot ['bi:tˌru:t] *n* pancar

before [bɪ'fɔ:] *adv* önceden ▷ *conj* önce ▷ *prep* önünde; **before five o'clock** saat beşten önce; **Do we have to clean the house before we leave?** Ayrılmadan önce evi temizlememiz gerekiyor mu?;

the day before yesterday önceki gün; **the week before last** bundan bir hafta önce

beforehand [bɪ'fɔː,hænd] adv daha önceden

beg [bɛg] v dilenmek

beggar ['bɛgə] n dilenci

begin [bɪ'gɪn] v başlamak

beginner [bɪ'gɪnə] n yeni başlayan

beginning [bɪ'gɪnɪŋ] n başlangıç

behave [bɪ'heɪv] v davranmak (tavır)

behaviour [bɪ'heɪvjə] n davranış

behind [bɪ'haɪnd] adv arkasında ▷ n arka ▷ prep arkada; **lag behind** v geride kalmak

beige [beɪʒ] adj bej

Beijing ['beɪ'dʒɪŋ] n Pekin

Belarus ['bɛlə,rʌs; -,rʊs] n beyaz rusya

Belarussian [,bɛləʊ'rʌʃən; ,bjɛl-] adj Belarus ▷ n (language) Belarusca, (person) Belaruslu

Belgian ['bɛldʒən] adj Belçika ▷ n Belçikalı

Belgium ['bɛldʒəm] n Belçika

belief [bɪ'liːf] n inanç

believe [bɪ'liːv] vi inandırmak ▷ vt inanmak

bell [bɛl] n zil (kapı, okul)

belly ['bɛlɪ] n göbek; **belly button** n göbek (deliği)

belong [bɪ'lɒŋ] v ait olmak; **belong to** v ait olmak

belongings [bɪ'lɒŋɪŋz] npl eşya

below [bɪ'ləʊ] adv altında ▷ prep altında

belt [bɛlt] n kemer; **conveyor belt** n taşıyıcı bant; **money belt** n bel

çantası; **safety belt** n emniyet kemeri

bench [bɛntʃ] n bank

bend [bɛnd] n viraj ▷ v kıvrılmak; **bend down** v eğilmek (kıvrılarak); **bend over** v eğilmek (ayak uçlarına doğru)

beneath [bɪ'niːθ] prep altında

benefit ['bɛnɪfɪt] n yarar ▷ v yarar sağlamak

bent [bɛnt] adj (dishonest) namussuz, (not straight) bükülmüş

beret ['bɛreɪ] n bere (giyim)

berry ['bɛrɪ] n çalı meyvesi

berth [bɜːθ] n ranza

beside [bɪ'saɪd] prep yanında

besides [bɪ'saɪdz] adv üstelik

best [bɛst] adj en iyi ▷ adv en iyisi; **best man** n sağdıç

bestseller [,bɛst'sɛlə] n çoksatar

bet [bɛt] n bahis ▷ v bahse girmek

betray [bɪ'treɪ] v ihanet etmek

better ['bɛtə] adj daha iyi ▷ adv daha iyisi

betting [bɛtɪŋ] n bahse girme; **betting shop** n bahis bayii

between [bɪ'twiːn] prep arasında

bewildered [bɪ'wɪldəd] adj şaşırmış

beyond [bɪ'jɒnd] prep ötesinde

biased ['baɪəst] adj yanlı

bib [bɪb] n mama önlüğü

Bible ['baɪbəl] n İncil

bicarbonate [baɪ'kɑːbənɪt; -,neɪt] n **bicarbonate of soda** n karbonat

bicycle ['baɪsɪkəl] n bisiklet; **bicycle pump** n bisiklet pompası

bid [bɪd] n teklif ▷ v (at auction) fiyat vermek (açık arttırmada)

bifocals [baɪ'fəʊkəlz] npl çift odaklı gözlük

big [bɪg] *adj* büyük; **It's too big**
Çok büyük; **The house is quite
big** Ev oldukça büyük
bigger [bɪgə] *adj* daha büyük; **Do
you have a bigger one?** Daha
büyük bir odanız var mı?
bigheaded ['bɪg,hɛdɪd] *adj* kendini
beğenmiş
bike [baɪk] *n* bisiklet; **mountain
bike** *n* dağ bisikleti; **Can I keep
my bike here?** Bisikletimi buraya
bırakabilir miyim?; **Does the bike
have brakes?** Bisikletin frenleri
var mı?; **Does the bike have
gears?** Bisiklet vitesli mi?; **I want
to hire a bike** Bisiklet kiralamak
istiyorum; **Where can I hire a
bike?** Nereden bisiklet
kiralayabilirim?; **Where is the
nearest bike repair shop?** En
yakın bisiklet tamircisi nerede?
bikini [bɪ'ki:nɪ] *n* bikini
bilingual [baɪ'lɪŋgwəl] *adj* iki
dilli
bill [bɪl] *n* *(account)* hesap,
(legislation) yasa; **phone bill** *n*
telefon faturası; **Can I have an
itemized bill?** Ayrıntılı hesap
alabilir miyim?; **The bill is wrong**
Hesapta bir yanlışlık var
billiards ['bɪljədz] *npl* bilardo
billion ['bɪljən] *n* milyar
bin [bɪn] *n* çöp tenekesi; **litter bin**
n çöp kutusu
binding ['baɪndɪŋ] *n* **Can you
adjust my bindings, please?**
Bağlarımı ayarlar mısınız lütfen?;
**Can you tighten my bindings,
please?** Bağlarımı sıkılar mısınız
lütfen?

bingo ['bɪŋgəʊ] *n* tombola
binoculars [bɪ'nɒkjʊləz; baɪ-] *npl*
dürbün
biochemistry [,baɪəʊ'kɛmɪstrɪ] *n*
biyokimya
biodegradable
[,baɪəʊdɪ'greɪdəbᵊl] *adj*
biyo-çözünür
biography [baɪ'ɒgrəfɪ] *n* yaşam
öyküsü
biological [,baɪə'lɒdʒɪkᵊl] *adj*
biyolojik
biology [baɪ'ɒlədʒɪ] *n* biyoloji
biometric [,baɪəʊ'mɛtrɪk] *adj*
biyometrik
birch [bɜːtʃ] *n* huş ağacı
bird [bɜːd] *n* kuş; **bird flu** *n* kuş
gribi; **bird of prey** *n* yırtıcı kuş
birdwatching [bɜːdwɒtʃɪŋ] *n* kuş
gözleme
Biro® ['baɪrəʊ] *n* tükenmez kalem
birth [bɜːθ] *n* doğum; **birth
certificate** *n* nüfus cüzdanı; **birth
control** *n* doğum kontrolü; **place
of birth** *n* doğum yeri
birthday ['bɜːθ,deɪ] *n* doğum günü
birthplace ['bɜːθ,pleɪs] *n* doğum
yeri
biscuit ['bɪskɪt] *n* bisküvi
bishop ['bɪʃəp] *n* piskopos
bit [bɪt] *n* parça
bitch [bɪtʃ] *n* kancık
bite [baɪt] *n* ısırma ▷ *v* ısırmak
bitter ['bɪtə] *adj* acı *(tat)*
black [blæk] *adj* siyah; **black ice** *n*
gizli buz; **in black and white**
Siyah beyaz
blackberry ['blækbərɪ] *n*
böğürtlen
blackbird ['blæk,bɜːd] *n* karatavuk

blackboard ['blæk,bɔ:d] *n*
karatahta

blackcurrant [,blæk'kʌrənt] *n*
kuşüzümü

blackmail ['blæk,meɪl] *n* şantaj ▷ *v*
şantaj yapmak

blackout ['blækaʊt] *n* karartma

bladder ['blædə] *n* sidik torbası;
gall bladder *n* safra kesesi

blade [bleɪd] *n* bıçak; **razor blade**
n traş bıçağı; **shoulder blade** *n*
kürek kemiği

blame [bleɪm] *n* suç ▷ *v* suçlamak

blank [blæŋk] *adj* boş *(kağıt, zihin)*
▷ *n* boşluk *(yazı, zihin)*; **blank
cheque** *n* açık çek

blanket ['blæŋkɪt] *n* battaniye;
electric blanket *n* elektrikli
battaniye; **Please bring me an
extra blanket** Bana bir battaniye
daha getirir misiniz lütfen?; **We
need more blankets** Daha fazla
battaniyeye ihtiyacımız var

blast [blɑ:st] *n* patlama

blatant ['bleɪtᵊnt] *adj* apaçık

blaze [bleɪz] *n* parlak alev

blazer ['bleɪzə] *n* blazer

bleach [bli:tʃ] *n* ağartıcı

bleached [bli:tʃt] *adj* ağartılmış

bleak [bli:k] *adj* rüzgara açık

bleed [bli:d] *v* kanamak

bleeper ['bli:pə] *n* çağrı cihazı

blender ['blɛndə] *n* mikser

bless [blɛs] *v* kutsamak

blind [blaɪnd] *adj* kör ▷ *n* jaluzi;
Venetian blind *n* jaluzi; **I'm blind**
Körüm

blindfold ['blaɪnd,fəʊld] *n* göz
bağı ▷ *v* gözlerini bağlamak

blink [blɪŋk] *v* göz kırpmak

bliss [blɪs] *n* mutluluk

blister ['blɪstə] *n* sulu kabarcık

blizzard ['blɪzəd] *n* kar fırtınası

block [blɒk] *n (buildings)* blok
(bina), *(obstruction)* engel, *(solid
piece)* blok ▷ *v* bloke etmek

blockage ['blɒkɪdʒ] *n* tıkanıklık

blocked [blɒkt] *adj* tıkalı

blog [blɒg] *n* blog ▷ *v* blog yazmak

blogger ['blɒgə] *n* blog yazarı

blogpost ['blɒg,pəʊst] *n* blog yazısı

bloke [bləʊk] *n* herif

blonde [blɒnd] *adj* sarışın

blood [blʌd] *n* kan; **blood group** *n*
kan grubu; **blood poisoning** *n*
kan zehirlenmesi; **blood pressure**
n tansiyon; **blood sports** *n* hayvan
dövüşleri; **blood test** *n* kan testi;
blood transfusion *n* kan nakli;
My blood group is O positive
Kan grubum O pozitif; **This stain
is blood** Kan lekesi

bloody ['blʌdɪ] *adj* kanlı

blossom ['blɒsəm] *n* tomurcuk ▷ *v*
çiçek açmak

blouse [blaʊz] *n* bluz

blow [bləʊ] *n* esinti ▷ *v* havaya
uçmak

blow-dry [bləʊdraɪ] *n* fön

blow up [bləʊ ʌp] *v* havaya uçurmak

blue [blu:] *adj* mavi

blueberry ['blu:bərɪ; -brɪ] *n* yaban
mersini

blues [blu:z] *npl* melankoli

bluff [blʌf] *n* blöf ▷ *v* blöf yapmak

blunder ['blʌndə] *n* gaf

blunt [blʌnt] *adj* kör *(bıçak/makas)*

blush [blʌʃ] *v* kızarmak

blusher ['blʌʃə] *n* allık

board [bɔ:d] *n (meeting)* kurul,

(wood) tahta *(okul)* ▷ v *(go aboard)* tahta *(okul)*; **board game** n aile oyunları; **boarding card** n biniş kartı; **boarding pass** n biniş kartı; **boarding school** n yatılı okul; **bulletin board** n ilan tahtası; **diving board** n tramplen; **draining board** n damlalıklı eviye; **half board** n kahvaltı ve akşam yemeği dahil; **ironing board** n ütü tahtası; **notice board** n ilan tahtası; **skirting board** n süpürgelik

boarder ['bɔːdə] n yatılı öğrenci

boast [bəʊst] v böbürlenmek

boat [bəʊt] n tekne; **fishing boat** n balıkçı teknesi; **rowing boat** n kürek teknesi; **sailing boat** n yelkenli; **Are there any boat trips on the river?** Nehirde tekne turu var mı?

body ['bɒdɪ] n beden

bodybuilding ['bɒdɪˌbɪldɪŋ] n vücut geliştirme

bodyguard ['bɒdɪˌɡɑːd] n özel koruma

bog [bɒɡ] n bataklık

boil [bɔɪl] vi pişirmek ▷ vt kaynatmak

boiled [bɔɪld] adj kaynamış; **boiled egg** n haşlanmış yumurta

boiler ['bɔɪlə] n kazan

boiling ['bɔɪlɪŋ] adj kaynar

boil over [bɔɪl 'əʊvə] v taşmak

Bolivia [bə'lɪvɪə] n Bolivya

Bolivian [bə'lɪvɪən] adj Bolivya ▷ n Bolivyalı

bolt [bəʊlt] n sürgü

bomb [bɒm] n bomba ▷ v bombalamak; **atom bomb** n atom bombası

bombing ['bɒmɪŋ] n bombalama

bond [bɒnd] n bağ

bone [bəʊn] n kemik; **bone dry** adj kupkuru

bonfire ['bɒnˌfaɪə] n şenlik ateşi

bonnet ['bɒnɪt] n *(car)* motor kapağı

bonus ['bəʊnəs] n prim

book [bʊk] n kitap ▷ v rezerve etmek; **address book** n adres defteri

bookcase ['bʊkˌkeɪs] n kitaplık

booking ['bʊkɪŋ] n rezervasyon; **advance booking** n önceden rezervasyon; **booking office** n bilet gişesi; **Can I change my booking?** Rezervasyonumu değiştirebilir miyim?; **I want to cancel my booking** Rezervasyonumu iptal ettirmek istiyorum

booklet ['bʊklɪt] n kitapçık

bookmark ['bʊkˌmɑːk] n kitap ayracı

bookshelf ['bʊkˌʃelf] n kitap rafı

bookshop ['bʊkˌʃɒp] n kitapçı

boost [buːst] v yüreklendirmek

boot [buːt] n çizme *(ayakkabı)*

booze [buːz] n içki

border ['bɔːdə] n sınır

bore [bɔː] v *(be dull)* can sıkmak, *(drill)* delmek

bored [bɔːd] adj canı sıkılmış

boredom ['bɔːdəm] n can sıkıntısı

boring ['bɔːrɪŋ] adj sıkıcı

born [bɔːn] adj doğmuş

borrow ['bɒrəʊ] v ödünç almak

Bosnia ['bɒznɪə] n Bosna; **Bosnia and Herzegovina** n Bosna-Hersek

Bosnian [ˈbɒznɪən] *adj* Bosna ▷ *n*
(person) Bosnalı *(kişi)*
boss [bɒs] *n* patron
boss around [bɒs əˈraʊnd] *v*
patronluk taslamak
bossy [ˈbɒsɪ] *adj* buyurgan
both [bəʊθ] *adj* her iki ▷ *pron* her
ikisi de
bother [ˈbɒðə] *v* zahmet etmek
Botswana [bʊˈtʃwɑːnə;
bʊtˈswɑːnə; bɒt-] *n* Botsvana
bottle [ˈbɒtˀl] *n* şişe; **baby's bottle**
n biberon; **bottle bank** *n* şişe geri
dönüşüm kutusu; **hot-water
bottle** *n* sıcak su torbası; **a bottle
of mineral water** Bir şişe maden
suyu; **a bottle of red wine** Bir şişe
kırmızı şarap; **Please bring
another bottle** Bir şişe daha
getirir misiniz?
bottle-opener [ˈbɒtˀlˈəʊpənə] *n*
şişe açacağı
bottom [ˈbɒtəm] *adj* en alt ▷ *n* dip
bought [bɔːt] *adj* satın alınmış
bounce [baʊns] *v* avara etmek
bouncer [ˈbaʊnsə] *n* fedai
boundary [ˈbaʊndərɪ; -drɪ] *n* sınır
bouquet [ˈbuːkeɪ] *n* buket
bow *n* [bəʊ] *(weapon)* yay ▷ *v* [baʊ]
baş eğmek
bowels [ˈbaʊəlz] *npl* bağırsaklar
bowl [bəʊl] *n* kase
bowling [ˈbəʊlɪŋ] *n* bowling;
bowling alley *n* bowling salonu;
tenpin bowling *n* bovling
bow tie [bəʊ] *n* papyon kravat
box [bɒks] *n* boks; **box office** *n*
bilet gişesi; **call box** *n* telefon
kulübesi; **fuse box** *n* sigorta
kutusu; **gear box** *n* vites kutusu

boxer [ˈbɒksə] *n* boksör; **boxer
shorts** *npl* bokser şort
boxing [ˈbɒksɪŋ] *n* boks
boy [bɔɪ] *n* oğlan çocuğu
boyfriend [ˈbɔɪˌfrɛnd] *n* erkek
arkadaş; **I have a boyfriend** Erkek
arkadaşım var
bra [brɑː] *n* sütyen
brace [breɪs] *n (fastening)* destek
(bağ, kuşak vb)
bracelet [ˈbreɪslɪt] *n* kolçak
braces [ˈbreɪsɪz] *npl* pantolon
askıları
brackets [ˈbrækɪts] *npl* köşeli
parantezler
brain [breɪn] *n* beyin
brainy [ˈbreɪnɪ] *adj* akıllı
brake [breɪk] *n* fren ▷ *v* frenlemek;
brake light *n* fren lambası; **Does
the bike have back-pedal
brakes?** Bisikletin geri frenleri var
mı?; **The brakes don't work**
Frenler çalışmıyor
bran [bræn] *n* kepek
branch [brɑːntʃ] *n* dal *(ağaç vb)*
brand [brænd] *n* marka; **brand
name** *n* marka
brand-new [brændˈnjuː] *adj*
yepyeni
brandy [ˈbrændɪ] *n* brendi; **I'll
have a brandy** Ben brendi alayım
brass [brɑːs] *n* pirinç *(metal)*;
brass band *n* bando takımı
brat [bræt] *n* velet
brave [breɪv] *adj* cesur
bravery [ˈbreɪvərɪ] *n* cesaret
Brazil [brəˈzɪl] *n* Brezilya
Brazilian [brəˈzɪljən] *adj* Brezilya
▷ *n* Brezilyalı
bread [brɛd] *n* ekmek; **bread roll** *n*

yuvarlak ekmek; **brown bread** n esmer ekmek; **Please bring more bread** Biraz daha ekmek getirir misiniz?; **Would you like some bread?** Biraz daha ekmek ister misiniz?

bread bin [brɛdbɪn] n ekmek kutusu

breadcrumbs ['brɛdˌkrʌmz] npl ekmek kırıntısı

break [breɪk] n kırık ▷ v kırmak; **lunch break** n yemek molası

break down [breɪk daʊn] v bozmak

breakdown ['breɪkdaʊn] n arıza; **breakdown truck** n çekici; **breakdown van** n kurtarma aracı; **nervous breakdown** n sinir krizi

breakfast ['brɛkfəst] n kahvaltı; **bed and breakfast** n yatak ve kahvaltı; **continental breakfast** n çörek ve kahve ya da çaydan oluşan kahvaltı; **Can I have breakfast in my room?** Odamda kahvaltı edebilir miyim?; **Is breakfast included?** Kahvaltı dahil mi?; **with breakfast** kahvaltı dahil; **without breakfast** kahvaltı hariç; **What time is breakfast?** Kahvaltı kaçta?; **What would you like for breakfast?** Kahvaltıda ne yemek istersiniz?

break in [breɪk ɪn] v terbiye etmek; **break in (on)** v sözünü kesmek

break-in [breɪkɪn] n hırsızlık

break up [breɪk ʌp] v kırmak

breast [brɛst] n göğüs

breast-feed ['brɛstˌfiːd] v emzirmek

breaststroke ['brɛstˌstrəʊk] n kurbağalama (yüzme)

breath [brɛθ] n nefes

Breathalyser® ['brɛθəˌlaɪzə] n üfleme cihazı

breathe [briːð] v nefes almak

breathe in [briːð ɪn] v nefes almak

breathe out [briːð aʊt] v nefes vermek

breathing ['briːðɪŋ] n nefes alma

breed [briːd] n cins (hayvan) ▷ v yetiştirmek (hayvan)

breeze [briːz] n hafif rüzgar

brewery ['brʊərɪ] n bira fabrikası

bribe [braɪb] v rüşvet vermek

bribery ['braɪbərɪ] n rüşvet

brick [brɪk] n tuğla

bricklayer ['brɪkˌleɪə] n duvarcı

bride [braɪd] n gelin (damadın eşi)

bridegroom ['braɪdˌgruːm; -ˌgrʊm] n damat (gelinin kocası)

bridesmaid ['braɪdzˌmeɪd] n nedime

bridge [brɪdʒ] n köprü; **suspension bridge** n asma köprü

brief [briːf] adj kısa

briefcase ['briːfˌkeɪs] n evrak çantası

briefing ['briːfɪŋ] n brifing

briefly ['briːflɪ] adv kısaca

briefs [briːfs] npl külot

bright [braɪt] adj parlak

brilliant ['brɪljənt] adj pırıl pırıl

bring [brɪŋ] v getirmek

bring back [brɪŋ bæk] v geri getirmek

bring forward [brɪŋ 'fɔːwəd] v öncelik getirmek

bring up [brɪŋ ʌp] v yetiştirmek

Britain ['brɪtᵊn] n İngiltere

British ['brɪtɪʃ] adj İngiliz ▷ n İngiliz

broad [brɔːd] adj geniş *(yayvan)*

broadband ['brɔːdˌbænd] n geniş bant

broadcast ['brɔːdˌkɑːst] n yayın ▷ v yayın yapmak

broad-minded [brɔːd'maɪndɪd] adj açık fikirli

broccoli ['brɒkəlɪ] n brokoli

brochure ['brəʊʃjʊə; -ʃə] n broşür

broke [brəʊk] adj züğürt

broken ['brəʊkən] adj kırık; **broken down** adj kırık

broker ['brəʊkə] n komisyoncu

bronchitis [brɒŋ'kaɪtɪs] n bronşit

bronze [brɒnz] n bronz

brooch [brəʊtʃ] n broş

broom [bruːm; brʊm] n süpürge

broth [brɒθ] n et ya da sebze suyuna çorba

brother ['brʌðə] n erkek kardeş

brother-in-law ['brʌðə ɪn lɔː] n kayın birader

brown [braʊn] adj kahverengi; **brown bread** n esmer ekmek; **brown rice** n esmer pirinç

browse [braʊz] v göz atmak

browser ['braʊzə] n tarayıcı *(internet)*

bruise [bruːz] n bere *(tıp)*

brush [brʌʃ] n fırça ▷ v fırçalamak

Brussels sprouts ['brʌsᵊlz spraʊts] npl Brüksel lahanası

brutal ['bruːtᵊl] adj vahşi

bubble ['bʌbᵊl] n kabarcık; **bubble bath** n köpüklü banyo; **bubble gum** n balonlu çiklet

bucket ['bʌkɪt] n kova

buckle ['bʌkᵊl] n kemer tokası

Buddha ['bʊdə] n Buda

Buddhism ['bʊdɪzəm] n Budizm

Buddhist ['bʊdɪst] adj Budist ▷ n Budist

budgerigar ['bʌdʒərɪˌɡɑː] n muhabbet kuşu

budget ['bʌdʒɪt] n bütçe

budgie ['bʌdʒɪ] n muhabbet kuşu

buffalo ['bʌfəˌləʊ] n manda

buffet ['bʊfeɪ] n açık büfe; **buffet car** n yemekli vagon

bug [bʌɡ] n böcek; **There are bugs in my room** Odamda böcek var

bugged ['bʌɡd] adj gizli dinleme cihazı yerleştirilmiş

buggy ['bʌɡɪ] n at arabası

build [bɪld] v inşa etmek

builder ['bɪldə] n inşaatçı

building ['bɪldɪŋ] n yapı; **building site** n inşaat alanı

bulb [bʌlb] n *(electricity)* ampul *(elektrik)*, *(plant)* soğan *(bitki)*

Bulgaria [bʌl'ɡɛərɪə; bʊl-] n Bulgaristan

Bulgarian [bʌl'ɡɛərɪən; bʊl-] adj Bulgar ▷ n *(language)* Bulgarca *(dil)*, *(person)* Bulgar *(kişi)*

bulimia [bjuː'lɪmɪə] n bulimia

bull [bʊl] n boğa

bulldozer ['bʊlˌdəʊzə] n buldozer

bullet ['bʊlɪt] n kurşun *(silah)*

bully ['bʊlɪ] n zorba ▷ v zorbalık etmek

bum [bʌm] n kıç; **bum bag** n bel çantası

bumblebee ['bʌmbᵊlˌbiː] n hezen arısı

bump [bʌmp] n çarpma; **bump into** v kazara çarpmak

bumper ['bʌmpə] n tampon (oto)
bumpy ['bʌmpɪ] adj tümsekli
bun [bʌn] n çörek
bunch [bʌntʃ] n demet
bungalow ['bʌŋgələʊ] n bungalov
bungee jumping ['bʌndʒɪ] n bungee jumping
bunion ['bʌnjən] n yangılı ayak şişi
bunk [bʌŋk] n ranza; **bunk beds** npl ranza
buoy [bɔɪ; 'buːɪ] n şamandıra
burden ['bɜːdən] n yük
bureaucracy [bjʊəˈrɒkrəsɪ] n bürokrasi
bureau de change ['bjʊərəʊ də 'ʃɒnʒ] n **bureau de change** n döviz bürosu; **I need to find a bureau de change** Döviz bürosu arıyorum; **Is there a bureau de change here?** Burada döviz bürosu var mı?; **When is the bureau de change open?** Döviz bürosu ne zaman açılıyor?
burger ['bɜːgə] n burger
burglar ['bɜːglə] n hırsız; **burglar alarm** n hırsız alarmı
burglary ['bɜːglərɪ] n hırsızlık
burgle ['bɜːgəl] v soymak
Burma ['bɜːmə] n Burma
Burmese [bɜːˈmiːz] adj Burma ▷ n (language) Burma dili (dil), (person) Burmalı (kişi)
burn [bɜːn] n yanık ▷ v yakmak (ateşte)
burn down [bɜːn daʊn] v yanıp kül olmak
burp [bɜːp] n geğirme ▷ v geğirmek
burst [bɜːst] v patlamak (delinerek)
bury ['bɛrɪ] v gömmek
bus [bʌs] n otobüs; **airport bus** n hava alanı otobüsü; **bus station** n otobüs terminali; **bus stop** n otobüs durağı; **bus ticket** n otobüs bileti; **Does this bus go to...?** Bu otobüs... a gider mi?; **Excuse me, which bus goes to...?** Affedersiniz,... a hangi otobüs gidiyor?; **How often are the buses to...?** ... otobüsü ne kadarda bir geliyor?; **Is there a bus to the airport?** Havaalanına otobüs var mı?; **What time does the bus leave?** Otobüs ne zaman kalkacak?; **What time is the last bus?** Son otobüs kaçta?; **When is the next bus to...?** ... a bir sonraki otobüs kaçta?; **Where can I buy a bus card?** Nereden otobüs kartı alabilirim?; **Where can I get a bus to...?** ... otobüsüne nereden binebilirim?; **Where is the bus station?** Otobüs terminali nerede?
bush [bʊʃ] n (shrub) çalı, (thicket) çalılık
business ['bɪznɪs] n ticaret; **business class** n hizmet sınıfı; **business trip** n iş seyahati; **show business** n eğlence sanayii
businessman, businessmen ['bɪznɪsˌmæn; -mən, 'bɪznɪsˌmɛn] n iş adamı
businesswoman, businesswomen ['bɪznɪsˌwʊmən, 'bɪznɪsˌwɪmɪn] n iş kadını
busker ['bʌskə] n sokak çalgıcısı
bust [bʌst] n göğüs
busy ['bɪzɪ] adj meşgul; **busy signal** n meşgul sinyali; **Sorry, I'm busy**

Kusura bakmayın, meşgulüm

but [bʌt] *conj* fakat

butcher [ˈbʊtʃə] *n* kasap

butcher's [ˈbʊtʃəz] *n* kasap

butter [ˈbʌtə] *n* tereyağı; **peanut butter** *n* fıstık ezmesi

buttercup [ˈbʌtəˌkʌp] *n* düğün çiçeği

butterfly [ˈbʌtəˌflaɪ] *n* kelebek *(hayvan)*

buttocks [ˈbʌtəkz] *npl* kalça

button [ˈbʌtᵊn] *n* düğme *(giysi, elektrik)*; **belly button** *n* göbek *(deliği)*; **Which button do I press?** Hangi düğmeye basacağım?

buy [baɪ] *v* satın almak

buyer [ˈbaɪə] *n* alıcı

buyout [ˈbaɪˌaʊt] *n* satın alma *(şirket)*

by [baɪ] *prep* tarafından

bye [baɪ] *excl* hoşçakal!

bye-bye [baɪbaɪ] *excl* hoşçakal!

bypass [ˈbaɪˌpɑːs] *n* çevre yolu

C

cab [kæb] *n* taksi

cabbage [ˈkæbɪdʒ] *n* lahana

cabin [ˈkæbɪn] *n* kabin, kulübe; **cabin crew** *n* kabin mürettebatı; **a first class cabin** Birinci sınıf bir kabin; **a standard class cabin** Standart bir kabin bileti; **Where is cabin number five?** Beş numaralı kabin nerede?

cabinet [ˈkæbɪnɪt] *n* kabine

cable [ˈkeɪbᵊl] *n* kablo; **cable car** *n* teleferik; **cable television** *n* kablolu yayın

cactus [ˈkæktəs] *n* kaktüs

cadet [kəˈdɛt] *n* askeri öğrenci

café [ˈkæfeɪ; ˈkæfɪ] *n* kafe; **internet café** *n* internet kafe; **Are there any internet cafés here?** Buralarda internet kafe var mı?

cafeteria [ˌkæfɪˈtɪərɪə] *n* kafeterya

caffeine [ˈkæfiːn; ˈkæfɪˌiːn] *n* kafein

cage [keɪdʒ] n kafes
cagoule [kə'guːl] n su geçirmez parka
cake [keɪk] n kek
calcium ['kælsɪəm] n kalsiyum
calculate ['kælkjʊ‚leɪt] v hesaplamak
calculation [‚kælkjʊ'leɪʃən] n hesaplama
calculator ['kælkjʊ‚leɪtə] n hesap makinesi; **pocket calculator** n cep hesap makinesi
calendar ['kælɪndə] n takvim
calf, calves [kɑːf, kɑːvz] n dana
call [kɔːl] n çağrı ▷ v aramak; **alarm call** n uyarı çağrısı; **call box** n telefon kulübesi; **call centre** n çağrı merkezi; **roll call** n yoklama
call back [kɔːl bæk] v geri aramak
call for [kɔːl fɔː] v icap ettirmek
call off [kɔːl ɒf] v iptal etmek
calm [kɑːm] adj sakin
calm down [kɑːm daʊn] v sakinleşmek
calorie ['kælərɪ] n kalori
Cambodia [kæm'bəʊdɪə] n Kamboçya
Cambodian [kæm'bəʊdɪən] adj Kamboçya ▷ n (person) Kamboçyalı (kişi)
camcorder ['kæm‚kɔːdə] n video kamera
camel ['kæməl] n deve
camera ['kæmərə; 'kæmrə] n fotoğraf makinesi; **camera phone** n fotoğraflı telefon; **digital camera** n dijital fotoğraf makinesi; **video camera** n video kamerası

cameraman, cameramen ['kæmərə‚mæn; 'kæmrə-, 'kæmərə‚mɛn] n kameraman
Cameroon [‚kæmə'ruːn; 'kæmə‚ruːn] n Kamerun
camp [kæmp] n kamp ▷ v kamp yapmak; **camp bed** n portatif karyola
campaign [kæm'peɪn] n kampanya
camper ['kæmpə] n kampçı, karavan
camping ['kæmpɪŋ] n kamping; **camping gas** n tüp gaz
campsite ['kæmp‚saɪt] n kamp yeri; **Is there a campsite here?** Buralarda bir kamp yeri var mı?
campus ['kæmpəs] n kampüs
can [kæn] n pet ▷ v yapabilmek; **watering can** n bahçe sulama bidonu
Canada ['kænədə] n Kanada
Canadian [kə'neɪdɪən] adj Kanada ▷ n Kanadalı
canal [kə'næl] n kanal
Canaries [kə'nɛərɪːz] npl Kanarya Adaları
canary [kə'nɛərɪ] n kanarya
cancel ['kænsəl] v iptal etmek
cancellation [‚kænsɪ'leɪʃən] n iptal
cancer ['kænsə] n (illness) kanser (hastalık)
Cancer ['kænsə] n (horoscope) Yengeç Burcu
candidate ['kændɪ‚deɪt; -dɪt] n aday
candle ['kændəl] n mum
candlestick ['kændəl‚stɪk] n şamdan

candyfloss ['kændɪˌflɒs] n pamuk helva

canister ['kænɪstə] n teneke kutu

cannabis ['kænəbɪs] n esrar (bitki)

canned [kænd] adj kutulanmış

canoe [kə'nu:] n kano

canoeing [kə'nu:ɪŋ] n kano sporu; **Where can we go canoeing?** Kano sporu nerede yapabiliriz?

can-opener ['kæn'əʊpənə] n kutu açacağı

canteen [kæn'ti:n] n kantin

canter ['kæntə] v eşkin gitmek

canvas ['kænvəs] n kaput bezi

canvass ['kænvəs] v oy propagandası yapmak

cap [kæp] n kep; **baseball cap** n beyzbol kepi

capable ['keɪpəbəl] adj muktedir

capacity [kə'pæsɪtɪ] n kapasite

capital ['kæpɪtəl] n başkent

capitalism ['kæpɪtəˌlɪzəm] n kapitalizm

Capricorn ['kæprɪˌkɔːn] n Oğlak burcu

capsize [kæp'saɪz] v alabora olmak

capsule ['kæpsjuːl] n kapsül

captain ['kæptɪn] n kaptan

caption ['kæpʃən] n başlık

capture ['kæptʃə] v zaptetmek

car [kɑː] n araba; **buffet car** n yemekli vagon; **cable car** n teleferik; **car hire** n araba kiralama; **car park** n otopark; **car rental** n oto kiralama; **car wash** n oto yıkama; **company car** n şirket arabası; **dining car** n yemek vagonu; **estate car** n vagon (oto); **hired car** n kiralık araba; **patrol car** n devriye arabası; **racing car** n yarış arabası; **rental car** n kiralık araba; **saloon car** n sedan araba; **sleeping car** n kuşetli vagon; **Can you take me by car?** Beni arabayla alabilir misiniz?; **Do I have to return the car here?** Arabayı buraya mı geri getirmem gerekiyor; **I want to hire a car** Araba kiralamak istiyorum; **I've crashed my car** Arabamı çarptım; **My car has been broken into** Arabamı soydular; **When will the car be ready?** Araba ne zaman hazır olur?; **Where can I park the car?** Arabamı nereye park edebilirim?

carafe [kə'ræf; -'rɑːf] n sürahi; **a carafe of the house wine** Kendi şarabınızdan bir sürahi

caramel ['kærəməl; -ˌmɛl] n karamelâ

carat ['kærət] n kırat

caravan ['kærəˌvæn] n karavan; **caravan site** n karavan kampı; **Can we park our caravan here?** Karavanımızı buraya park edebilir miyiz?; **We'd like a site for a caravan** Karavanımızla kamp edebileceğimiz bir yer arıyoruz

carbohydrate [ˌkɑːbəʊ'haɪdreɪt] n karbonhidrat

carbon ['kɑːbən] n karbon; **carbon footprint** n karbon ayak izi

carburettor [ˌkɑːbjʊ'rɛtə; 'kɑːbjʊˌrɛtə; -bə-] n karbüratör

card [kɑːd] n kart; **boarding card** n biniş kartı; **credit card** n kredi kartı; **debit card** n banka kartı; **greetings card** n tebrik kartı;

ID card *abbr* kimlik kartı;
membership card *n* üyelik kartı;
playing card *n* oyun kartı; **report
card** *n* karne; **top-up card** *n*
telefon kartı; **A memory card for
this digital camera, please** Bu
dijital kameraya hafıza kartı almak
istiyorum lütfen; **Can I have your
card?** Kartınızı alabilir miyim?;
Can I use my card to get cash?
Nakit almak için kartımı
kullanabilir miyim?; **Do you sell
phone cards?** Telefon kartı
satıyor musunuz?; **Do you take
credit cards?** Kredi kartı kabul
ediyor musunuz?; **Do you take
debit cards?** Banka kartı kabul
ediyor musunuz?; **I need to
cancel my card** Kartımı iptal
ettirmek istiyorum; **My card has
been stolen** Kartım çalındı;
Where can I post these cards?
Bu kartları nereden
postalayabilirim?
cardboard ['kɑːdˌbɔːd] *n* mukavva
cardigan ['kɑːdɪgən] *n* hırka
cardphone ['kɑːdfəʊn] *n* kartlı
telefon
care [kɛə] *n* bakım *(hasta vb)* ▷ *v*
bakmak *(hasta vb)*; **intensive
care unit** *n* yoğun bakım ünitesi
career [kə'rɪə] *n* kariyer
careful ['kɛəfʊl] *adj* dikkatli
carefully ['kɛəfʊlɪ] *adv* dikkatli
careless ['kɛəlɪs] *adj* dikkatsiz
caretaker ['kɛəˌteɪkə] *n* bakıcı
(apartman, ev)
car-ferry ['kɑːfɛrɪ] *n* arabalı
feribot
cargo ['kɑːgəʊ] *n* kargo

Caribbean [ˌkærɪ'biːən;
kə'rɪbɪən] *adj* Karayip ▷ *n* Karayip
denizi
caring ['kɛərɪŋ] *adj* şefkatli
carnation [kɑː'neɪʃən] *n* karanfil
(çiçek)
carnival ['kɑːnɪvᵊl] *n* karnaval
carol ['kærəl] *n* Noel şarkısı
carpenter ['kɑːpɪntə] *n* marangoz
carpentry ['kɑːpɪntrɪ] *n*
marangozluk
carpet ['kɑːpɪt] *n* halı; **fitted
carpet** *n* duvardan duvara halı
carriage ['kærɪdʒ] *n* vagon; **Where
is carriage number thirty?** Otuz
numaralı vagon nerede?
carriageway ['kærɪdʒˌweɪ] *n* **dual
carriageway** *n* çift-şeritli yol
carrot ['kærət] *n* havuç
carry ['kærɪ] *v* taşımak
carrycot ['kærɪˌkɒt] *n* portbebe
carry on ['kærɪ ɒn] *v* devam
etmek
carry out ['kærɪ aʊt] *v* uygulamak
cart [kɑːt] *n* at arabası
carton ['kɑːtᵊn] *n* karton kutu
cartoon [kɑː'tuːn] *n* karikatür
cartridge ['kɑːtrɪdʒ] *n* fişek *(silah)*
carve [kɑːv] *v* oymak *(ağaç)*
case [keɪs] *n* vaka; **pencil case** *n*
kalemlik
cash [kæʃ] *n* nakit; **cash dispenser**
n bankamatik; **cash register** *n*
yazar kasa; **Can I get a cash
advance with my credit card?**
Kredi kartıma nakit ödeme alabilir
miyim?; **Do you offer a discount
for cash?** Nakit ödemelere indirim
yapıyor musunuz?; **I don't have
any cash** Üzerimde nakit yok

cashew ['kæʃuː; kæ'ʃuː] n Hint fıstığı

cashier [kæ'ʃɪə] n kasiyer

cashmere ['kæʃmɪə] n kaşmir

casino [kə'siːnəʊ] n kumarhane

casserole ['kæsəˌrəʊl] n güveç

cassette [kæ'sɛt] n kaset

cast [kɑːst] n oyuncu kadrosu

castle ['kɑːsᵊl] n kale (şato vb)

casual ['kæʒjʊəl] adj umursamaz

casually ['kæʒjʊəlɪ] adv gelişigüzel

casualty ['kæʒjʊəltɪ] n zayiat

cat [kæt] n kedi

catalogue ['kætəˌlɒg] n katalog; **I'd like a catalogue** Katalog istiyorum

cataract ['kætəˌrækt] n (eye) katarakt, (waterfall) çağlayan

catarrh [kə'tɑː] n akıntı (nezle)

catastrophe [kə'tæstrəfɪ] n felaket (doğal afet)

catch [kætʃ] v yakalamak

catching ['kætʃɪŋ] adj bulaşıcı

catch up [kætʃ ʌp] v yetişmek

category ['kætɪgərɪ] n kategori

catering ['keɪtərɪŋ] n catering

caterpillar ['kætəˌpɪlə] n tırtıl

cathedral [kə'θiːdrəl] n katedral; **When is the cathedral open?** Katedral ne zaman açık?

Catholic ['kæθəlɪk; 'kæθlɪk] adj Katolik ▷ n Katolik; **Roman Catholic** n Roma Katoliği, Roma Katolik

cattle ['kætᵊl] npl davar

Caucasus ['kɔːkəsəs] n Kafkas

cauliflower ['kɒlɪˌflaʊə] n karnabahar

cause [kɔːz] n (ideals) amaç, (reason) neden ▷ v yol açmak

caution ['kɔːʃən] n önlem

cautious ['kɔːʃəs] adj tedbirli

cautiously ['kɔːʃəslɪ] adv özenli bir şekilde

cave [keɪv] n mağara

CCTV [siː siː tiː viː] abbr Kapalı Devre Televizyon Sistemi

CD [siː diː] n CD; **CD burner** n CD yazıcı; **CD player** n CD çalar; **Can I make CDs at this computer?** Bu bilgisayarda CD yapabilir miyim?; **When will the CD be ready?** CD ne zaman hazır olur?

CD-ROM [-'rɒm] n CD-ROM

ceasefire ['siːsˌfaɪə] n ateşkes

ceiling ['siːlɪŋ] n tavan

celebrate ['sɛlɪˌbreɪt] v kutlamak

celebration ['sɛlɪˌbreɪʃən] n kutlama

celebrity [sɪ'lɛbrɪtɪ] n ünlü

celery ['sɛlərɪ] n kereviz sapı

cell [sɛl] n hücre

cellar ['sɛlə] n mahzen

cello ['tʃɛləʊ] n viyolonsel

cement [sɪ'mɛnt] n çimento

cemetery ['sɛmɪtrɪ] n mezarlık

census ['sɛnsəs] n nüfus sayımı

cent [sɛnt] n sent (para birimi)

centenary [sɛn'tiːnərɪ] n yüzüncü yıl

centimetre ['sɛntɪˌmiːtə] n santimetre

central ['sɛntrəl] adj merkezi; **central heating** n merkezi ısıtma; **Central America** n Orta Amerika

centre ['sɛntə] n merkez; **call centre** n çağrı merkezi; **city centre** n kent merkezi; **job centre** n iş bulma kurumu; **leisure centre** n eğlence merkezi;

shopping centre n alışveriş merkezi; **town centre** n şehir merkezi; **visitor centre** n ziyaretçi merkezi; **How do I get to the centre of…?** … merkezine nasıl gidebilirim?

century ['sɛntʃərɪ] n yüzyıl

CEO [siː iː əʊ] abbr CEO

ceramic [sɪ'ræmɪk] adj seramik

cereal ['sɪərɪəl] n tahıl gevreği

ceremony ['sɛrɪmənɪ] n tören

certain ['sɜːtⁿn] adj kesin

certainly ['sɜːtⁿnlɪ] adv kesinlikle

certainty ['sɜːtⁿntɪ] n kesinlik

certificate [sə'tɪfɪkɪt] n sertifika; **birth certificate** n nüfus cüzdanı; **marriage certificate** n evlilik cüzdanı; **medical certificate** n sağlık belgesi

Chad [tʃæd] n Çad

chain [tʃeɪn] n zincir; **Do I need snow chains?** Kar zinciri almam gerekiyor mu?

chair [tʃeə] n (furniture) sandalye; **easy chair** n koltuk; **rocking chair** n sallanan sandalye; **Do you have a high chair?** Mama sandalyeniz var mı?

chairlift ['tʃeə͵lɪft] n teleferik; **When does the first chairlift go?** İlk teleferik kaçta?

chairman, chairmen ['tʃeəmən, 'tʃeəmɛn] n başkan

chalk [tʃɔːk] n tebeşir

challenge ['tʃælɪndʒ] n meydan okuma ▷ v meydan okumak

challenging ['tʃælɪndʒɪŋ] adj zorlayıcı

chambermaid ['tʃeɪmbə͵meɪd] n oda görevlisi

champagne [ʃæm'peɪn] n şampanya

champion ['tʃæmpɪən] n şampiyon

championship ['tʃæmpɪən͵ʃɪp] n şampiyona

chance [tʃɑːns] n gelişigüzel; **by chance** adv kazara

change [tʃeɪndʒ] n değişim ▷ vi değiştirmek; **changing room** n soyunma odası (spor); **I want to change my ticket** Biletimi değiştirmek istiyorum; **I want to change some… into…** …larımı… la değiştirmek istiyorum; **I'd like to change my flight** Uçuşumu değiştirmek istiyorum

changeable ['tʃeɪndʒəbⁿl] adj değiştirilebilir

channel ['tʃænⁿl] n kanal

chaos ['keɪɒs] n kargaşa

chaotic ['keɪ'ɒtɪk] adj karmakarışık

chap [tʃæp] n ahpap

chapel ['tʃæpⁿl] n şapel

chapter ['tʃæptə] n bölüm (kitap)

character ['kærɪktə] n karakter

characteristic [͵kærɪktə'rɪstɪk] n karakteristik

charcoal ['tʃɑː͵kəʊl] n odun kömürü

charge [tʃɑːdʒ] n (accusation) suçlama, (electricity) şarj, (price) fiyat biçmek ▷ v (accuse) suçlamak, (electricity) şarj etmek (elektrik), (price) fiyat biçmek; **admission charge** n giriş ücreti; **cover charge** n servis ücreti; **service charge** n servis ücreti; **Where can I charge my mobile phone?** Cep telefonumu nerede şarj edebilirim

charger [ˈtʃɑːdʒə] n şarj aleti

charity [ˈtʃærɪtɪ] n yardım derneği; **charity shop** n yardım derneği dükkanı

charm [tʃɑːm] n çekim

charming [ˈtʃɑːmɪŋ] adj sevimli

chart [tʃɑːt] n harita; **pie chart** n dilimli grafik

chase [tʃeɪs] n takip ▷ v takip etmek

chat [tʃæt] n sohbet ▷ v sohbet etmek; **chat show** n sohbet programı

chatroom [ˈtʃætˌruːm; -ˌrʊm] n sohbet odası

chauffeur [ˈʃəʊfə; ʃəʊˈfɜː] n şoför

chauvinist [ˈʃəʊvɪˌnɪst] n şoven

cheap [tʃiːp] adj ucuz; **Do you have anything cheaper?** Daha ucuz bir şeyiniz var mı?; **I'd like the cheapest option** En ucuz bilet olsun lütfen

cheat [tʃiːt] n dolandırıcı ▷ v dolandırmak

Chechnya [ˈtʃetʃnjə] n Çeçenistan

check [tʃek] n denetim ▷ v denetlemek (kontrol)

checked [tʃekt] adj kareli

check in [tʃek ɪn] v giriş yapmak

check-in [tʃekɪn] n giriş (havaalanı)

check out [tʃek aʊt] v çıkış yapmak

checkout [ˈtʃekaʊt] n çıkış

check-up [tʃekʌp] n revizyon

cheek [tʃiːk] n yanak

cheekbone [ˈtʃiːkˌbəʊn] n elmacık kemiği

cheeky [ˈtʃiːkɪ] adj arsız

cheer [tʃɪə] n tezahürat ▷ v tezahürat yapmak

cheerful [ˈtʃɪəfʊl] adj neşeli

cheerio [ˌtʃɪərɪˈəʊ] excl sağlıcakla!

cheers [tʃɪəz] excl şerefe!

cheese [tʃiːz] n peynir; **cottage cheese** n süzme peynir

chef [ʃef] n aşçıbaşı

chemical [ˈkemɪkəl] n kimyasal

chemist [ˈkemɪst] n eczacı; **chemist('s)** n eczane

chemistry [ˈkemɪstrɪ] n kimya

cheque [tʃek] n çek; **blank cheque** n açık çek; **traveller's cheque** n seyahat çeki; **Can I change my traveller's cheques here?** Seyahat çeklerimi burada bozdurabilir miyim?; **I want to change these traveller's cheques** Bu seyahat çeklerini bozdurmak istiyorum; **Someone's stolen my traveller's cheques** Biri seyahat çeklerimi çaldı

chequebook [ˈtʃekˌbʊk] n çek defteri

cherry [ˈtʃerɪ] n kiraz

chess [tʃes] n satranç

chest [tʃest] n (body part) göğüs, (storage) sandık; **chest of drawers** n komodin

chestnut [ˈtʃesˌnʌt] n kestane

chew [tʃuː] v çiğnemek; **chewing gum** n çiklet

chick [tʃɪk] n civciv

chicken [ˈtʃɪkɪn] n tavuk

chickenpox [ˈtʃɪkɪnˌpɒks] n suçiçeği

chickpea [ˈtʃɪkˌpiː] n nohut

chief [tʃiːf] adj baş ▷ n şef

child, children [tʃaɪld, ˈtʃɪldrən] n çocuk; **child abuse** n çocuk

tacizi; **I need someone to look after the children tonight** Bu akşam çocuklara bakacak birine ihtiyacım var; **I'd like a child seat for a two-year-old child** İki yaşında bir çocuk için çocuk koltuğu istiyorum; **I'm looking for a present for a child** Bir çocuk için armağan almak istiyordum
childcare ['tʃaɪld,kɛə] n çocuk bakımı
childhood ['tʃaɪldhʊd] n çocukluk
childish ['tʃaɪldɪʃ] adj çocukça
childminder ['tʃaɪld,maɪndə] n çocuk bakıcısı
Chile ['tʃɪlɪ] n Şili
Chilean ['tʃɪlɪən] adj Şili ▷ n Şilili
chill [tʃɪl] v soğutmak
chilli ['tʃɪlɪ] n acı (biber)
chilly ['tʃɪlɪ] adj soğuk
chimney ['tʃɪmnɪ] n baca
chimpanzee [,tʃɪmpæn'ziː] n şempanze
chin [tʃɪn] n çene
china ['tʃaɪnə] n porselen
China ['tʃaɪnə] n Çin
Chinese [tʃaɪ'niːz] adj Çin ▷ n (language) Çince (dil), (person) Çinli (kişi)
chip [tʃɪp] n (electronic) çip (elektronik), (small piece) parça; **silicon chip** n silikon çip
chips [tʃɪps] npl patates kızartması
chiropodist [kɪ'rɒpədɪst] n ayak uzmanı
chisel ['tʃɪzəl] n keski
chives [tʃaɪvz] npl Frenk soğanı
chlorine ['klɔːriːn] n klor
chocolate ['tʃɒkəlɪt; 'tʃɒklɪt; -lət] n çikolata; **milk chocolate** n sütlü

çikolata; **plain chocolate** n sade çikolata
choice [tʃɔɪs] n seçim
choir [kwaɪə] n koro
choke [tʃəʊk] v tıkanmak
cholesterol [kə'lɛstə,rɒl] n kolesterol
choose [tʃuːz] v seçmek
chop [tʃɒp] n doğrama ▷ v doğramak (et, sebze); **pork chop** n domuz pirzolası
chopsticks ['tʃɒpstɪks] npl Çin çubuğu
chosen ['tʃəʊzən] adj seçilmiş
Christ [kraɪst] n İsa
christening ['krɪsənɪŋ] n vaftiz
Christian ['krɪstʃən] adj Hristiyan ▷ n Hristiyan; **Christian name** n ön adı
Christianity [,krɪstɪ'ænɪtɪ] n Hristiyanlık
Christmas ['krɪsməs] n Noel; **Christmas card** n Noel kartı; **Christmas Eve** n Noel arifesi; **Christmas tree** n Noel ağacı; **Merry Christmas!** Mutlu Noeller!
chrome [krəʊm] n krom kaplı
chronic ['krɒnɪk] adj kronik
chrysanthemum [krɪ'sænθəməm] n kasımpatı
chubby ['tʃʌbɪ] adj tombul
chunk [tʃʌŋk] n parça
church [tʃɜːtʃ] n kilise; **Can we visit the church?** Kiliseyi gezebilir miyiz?
cider ['saɪdə] n elma şarabı
cigar [sɪ'gɑː] n puro
cigarette [,sɪgə'rɛt] n sigara; **cigarette lighter** n çakmak
cinema ['sɪnɪmə] n sinema;

What's on at the cinema?
Sinemada ne oynuyor?

cinnamon ['sɪnəmən] n tarçın

circle ['sɜːkəl] n daire; **Arctic Circle**
n Kuzey Buzul Kuşağı

circuit ['sɜːkɪt] n devre

circular ['sɜːkjʊlə] adj dairesel

circulation [ˌsɜːkjʊ'leɪʃən] n kan
dolaşımı

circumstances ['sɜːkəmstənsɪz]
npl koşullar

circus ['sɜːkəs] n sirk

citizen ['sɪtɪzᵊn] n vatandaş;
senior citizen n yaşlı vatandaş

citizenship ['sɪtɪzən,ʃɪp] n
vatandaşlık

city ['sɪtɪ] n şehir; **city centre** n
kent merkezi

civilian [sɪ'vɪljən] adj sivil ▷ n sivil

civilization [ˌsɪvɪlaɪ'zeɪʃən] n
uygarlık

claim [kleɪm] n talep ▷ v talep
etmek; **claim form** n istek formu

clap [klæp] v alkışlanmak

clarify ['klærɪ,faɪ] v açıklık
kazandırmak

clarinet [ˌklærɪ'nɛt] n klarnet

clash [klæʃ] v çatışmak

clasp [klɑːsp] n toka

class [klɑːs] n sınıf; **business class**
n hizmet sınıfı; **economy class** n
ikinci sınıf; **second class** n ikinci
sınıf; **a first-class cabin** Birinci
sınıf bir kabin; **a first-class return
to...** ... a birinci sınıf bir gidiş
dönüş bilet; **I would like to travel
first class** Birinci sınıf seyahat
etmek istiyorum

classic ['klæsɪk] adj klasik ▷ n klasik

classical ['klæsɪkᵊl] adj klasik

classmate ['klɑːs,meɪt] n sınıf
arkadaşı

classroom ['klɑːs,ruːm; -,rʊm] n
sınıf; **classroom assistant** n
yardımcı öğretmen

clause [klɔːz] n madde (yasa vb)

claustrophobic [ˌklɔːstrə'fəʊbɪk;
ˌklɒs-] adj kapalı yer korkusu olan

claw [klɔː] n pençe

clay [kleɪ] n kil

clean [kliːn] adj temiz ▷ v
temizlemek; **Can you clean the
room, please?** Odamı temizler
misiniz lütfen; **I need this
dry-cleaned** Bunu kuru
temizleyiciye vermek istiyorum;
**I'd like to get these things
cleaned** Bunları temizletmek
istiyorum; **The room isn't clean**
Oda temizlenmemiş; **Where can I
get this cleaned?** Bunu nerede
temizletebilirim?

cleaner ['kliːnə] n temizlikçi;
When does the cleaner come?
Temizlikçi kaçta geliyor?

cleaning ['kliːnɪŋ] n temizleme;
cleaning lady n temizlikçi

cleanser ['klɛnzə] n temizleyici

clear [klɪə] adj açık (hava vb)

clearly ['klɪəlɪ] adv açıkça

clear off [klɪə ɒf] v ayak altından
çekilmek

clear up [klɪə ʌp] v toplamak
(ortalığı)

clementine ['klɛmən,tiːn; -,taɪn]
n mandalina

clever ['klɛvə] adj zeki

click [klɪk] n tık ▷ v tıklamak

client ['klaɪənt] n müşteri

cliff [klɪf] n kayalık

climate ['klaɪmɪt] n iklim; **climate change** n iklim değişikliği

climb [klaɪm] v tırmanmak

climber ['klaɪmə] n dağcı (tırmanıcı)

climbing ['klaɪmɪŋ] n dağcılık (tırmanıcılık)

clinic ['klɪnɪk] n poliklinik

clip [klɪp] n klips

clippers ['klɪpəz] npl makas (tırnak/saç/tel/çalı)

cloakroom ['kləʊkˌruːm; -ˌrʊm] n vestiyer

clock [klɒk] n saat (genelde); **alarm clock** n çalar saat; **before five o'clock** saat beşten önce; **It's two o'clock** Saat iki

clockwise ['klɒkˌwaɪz] adv saat yönünde

clog [klɒg] n takunya

clone [kləʊn] n klon ▷ v klonlamak

close adj [kləʊs] yakın ▷ adv [kləʊs] yakın ▷ v [kləʊz] kapatmak; **close by** adj yakın; **closing time** n kapanış saati

closed [kləʊzd] adj kapalı

closely [kləʊslɪ] adv yakından

closure ['kləʊʒə] n kapanış

cloth [klɒθ] n kumaş

clothes [kləʊðz] npl giysiler; **clothes line** n çamaşır ipi; **clothes peg** n çamaşır mandalı; **My clothes are damp** Giysilerim ıslak

clothing ['kləʊðɪŋ] n giyim

cloud [klaʊd] n bulut

cloudy ['klaʊdɪ] adj bulutlu; **It's cloudy** Hava bulutlu

clove [kləʊv] n karanfil (baharat)

clown [klaʊn] n palyaço

club [klʌb] n (group) klüp, (weapon) sopa (silah); **golf club** n (stick) golf sopası, (society) golf klübü; **Do they hire out golf clubs?** Golf sopaları kiralıyorlar mı?

club together [klʌb təˈgɛðə] v paylaşmak (iş/masraf)

clue [kluː] n delil

clumsy ['klʌmzɪ] adj sakar

clutch [klʌtʃ] n debriyaj

clutter ['klʌtə] n yayıntı

coach [kəʊtʃ] n (trainer) koç (spor), (vehicle) tur otobüsü

coal [kəʊl] n kömür

coarse [kɔːs] adj kaba (kumaş, sakal vb)

coast [kəʊst] n kıyı

coastguard ['kəʊstˌgɑːd] n sahil koruma görevlisi

coat [kəʊt] n kaban; **fur coat** n kürk (giysi)

coathanger ['kəʊtˌhæŋə] n elbise askısı

cobweb ['kɒbˌwɛb] n örümcek ağı

cocaine [kəˈkeɪn] n kokain

cock [kɒk] n horoz

cockerel ['kɒkərəl; 'kɒkrəl] n horoz

cockpit ['kɒkˌpɪt] n kokpit

cockroach ['kɒkˌrəʊtʃ] n hamam böceği

cocktail ['kɒkˌteɪl] n kokteyl; **Do you sell cocktails?** Kokteyl yapıyor musunuz?

cocoa ['kəʊkəʊ] n kakao

coconut ['kəʊkəˌnʌt] n Hindistan cevizi

cod [kɒd] n morina balığı

code [kəʊd] n şifre; **dialling code** n telefon kodu; **Highway Code** n trafik kuralları

coeliac ['siːlɪˌæk] *adj* karın boşluğu ile ilgili

coffee ['kɒfɪ] *n* kahve; **black coffee** *n* sütsüz kahve; **coffee bean** *n* kahve çekirdeği; **decaffeinated coffee** *n* kafeinsiz kahve; **A white coffee, please** Sütlü kahve lütfen; **Could we have another cup of coffee, please?** Bir fincan kahve daha alabilir miyiz?; **Have you got fresh coffee?** Taze kahveniz var mı?

coffeepot ['kɒfɪˌpɒt] *n* cezve

coffin ['kɒfɪn] *n* tabut

coin [kɔɪn] *n* madeni para

coincide [ˌkəʊɪn'saɪd] *v* çakışmak

coincidence [kəʊ'ɪnsɪdəns] *n* rastlantı

Coke® [kəʊk] *n* Kola

colander ['kɒləndə; 'kʌl-] *n* süzgeç

cold [kəʊld] *adj* soğuk ▷ *n* soğuk; **cold sore** *n* uçuk *(sağlık)*; **I have a cold** Soğuk algınlığım var; **I'd like something for a cold** Soğuk algınlığı için bir şey rica ediyorum; **The food is too cold** Yemek çok soğuk; **The room is too cold** Oda çok soğuk; **Will it be cold tonight?** Bu gece hava soğuk mu olacak?

coleslaw ['kəʊlˌslɔː] *n* lahana salatası

collaborate [kə'læbəˌreɪt] *v* işbirliği yapmak

collapse [kə'læps] *v* çökmek

collar ['kɒlə] *n* yaka

collarbone ['kɒləˌbəʊn] *n* köprücük kemiği

colleague ['kɒliːg] *n* meslekdaş

collect [kə'lɛkt] *v* toplamak *(para, pul vb)*

collection [kə'lɛkʃən] *n* koleksiyon

collective [kə'lɛktɪv] *adj* kolektif ▷ *n* kolektif

collector [kə'lɛktə] *n* kolleksiyoncu; **ticket collector** *n* biletçi

college ['kɒlɪdʒ] *n* yüksek okul

collide [kə'laɪd] *v* çarpışmak

collie ['kɒlɪ] *n* İskoç çoban köpeği

colliery ['kɒljərɪ] *n* kömür ocağı

collision [kə'lɪʒən] *n* çarpışma

Colombia [kə'lɒmbɪə] *n* Kolombiya

Colombian [kə'lɒmbɪən] *adj* Kolombiya ▷ *n* Kolombiyalı

colon ['kəʊlən] *n* iki nokta üst üste

colonel ['kɜːnəl] *n* albay

colour ['kʌlə] *n* renk; **A colour film, please** Renkli film istiyorum lütfen; **in colour** Renkli; **I'd like a colour photocopy of this, please** Bunun renkli fotokopisini istiyorum lütfen

colour-blind ['kʌlə'blaɪnd] *adj* renk körü

colourful ['kʌləfʊl] *adj* renkli

colouring ['kʌlərɪŋ] *n* boyama

column ['kɒləm] *n* sütun

coma ['kəʊmə] *n* koma

comb [kəʊm] *n* tarak ▷ *v* taramak

combination [ˌkɒmbɪ'neɪʃən] *n* birleştirme

combine [kəm'baɪn] *v* birleştirmek

come [kʌm] *v* gelmek

come back [kʌm bæk] *v* geri gelmek

comedian [kə'mi:dɪən] n
komedyen
come down [kʌm daʊn] v aşağıya
inmek
comedy ['kɒmɪdɪ] n komedi
come from [kʌm frəm] v gelmek
come in [kʌm ɪn] v girmek
(içeriye)
come off [kʌm ɒf] v **The handle
has come off** Kolu çıktı
come out [kʌm aʊt] v çıkmak
come round [kʌm raʊnd] v
kendine gelmek
comet ['kɒmɪt] n kuyruklu yıldız
come up [kʌm ʌp] v gündeme
gelmek
comfortable ['kʌmftəbəl;
'kʌmfətəbəl] adj rahat
comic ['kɒmɪk] n komik; **comic
book** n mizah dergisi; **comic strip**
n çizgi öykü
coming ['kʌmɪŋ] adj gelecek
comma ['kɒmə] n virgül; **inverted
commas** npl ters tırnak işareti
command [kə'mɑ:nd] n emir
comment ['kɒmɛnt] n yorum ▷ v
yorum yapmak
commentary ['kɒməntərɪ; -trɪ] n
yorum
commentator ['kɒmən,teɪtə] n
yorumcu
commercial [kə'mɜ:ʃəl] n reklam;
commercial break n reklam arası
commission [kə'mɪʃən] n
komisyon; **Do you charge
commission?** Komisyon alıyor
musunuz?; **What's the
commission?** Komisyon ne
kadar?
commit [kə'mɪt] v işlemek

committee [kə'mɪtɪ] n komite
common ['kɒmən] adj müşterek;
common sense n sağduyu
communicate [kə'mju:nɪ,keɪt] v
iletişim kurmak
communication
[kə,mju:nɪ'keɪʃən] n iletişim
communion [kə'mju:njən] n
ortak görüş
communism ['kɒmjʊ,nɪzəm] n
komünizm
communist ['kɒmjʊnɪst] adj
toplumcu ▷ n toplumcu
community [kə'mju:nɪtɪ] n
topluluk
commute [kə'mju:t] v her gün işi
ile evi arasında gidip gelmek
commuter [kə'mju:tə] n her gün
işe trenle giden kimse
compact ['kəm'pækt] adj sımsıkı
paketlenmiş; **compact disc** n
kompakt disk
companion [kəm'pænjən] n
yoldaş
company ['kʌmpənɪ] n şirket;
company car n şirket arabası
comparable ['kɒmpərəbəl] adj
kıyaslanabilir
comparatively [kəm'pærətɪvlɪ]
adv göreceli olarak
compare [kəm'pɛə] v kıyaslamak
comparison [kəm'pærɪsən] n
kıyaslama
compartment [kəm'pɑ:tmənt] n
kompartıman
compass ['kʌmpəs] n pusula
compatible [kəm'pætəbəl] adj
uyumlu
compensate ['kɒmpɛn,seɪt] v
telafi etmek

compensation [ˌkɒmpɛnˈseɪʃən] *n* tazminat

compere [ˈkɒmpɛə] *n* sunucu *(oyun, film, gösteri)*

compete [kəmˈpiːt] *v* yarışmak

competent [ˈkɒmpɪtənt] *adj* yetkin

competition [ˌkɒmpɪˈtɪʃən] *n* yarışma

competitive [kəmˈpɛtɪtɪv] *adj* rekabete açık

competitor [kəmˈpɛtɪtə] *n* yarışmacı

complain [kəmˈpleɪn] *v* yakınmak

complaint [kəmˈpleɪnt] *n* şikayet; **I'd like to make a complaint** Bir şikayette bulunmak istiyorum

complementary [ˌkɒmplɪˈmɛntərɪ; -trɪ] *adj* bütünleyici

complete [kəmˈpliːt] *adj* bütün

completely [kəmˈpliːtlɪ] *adv* tamamen

complex [ˈkɒmplɛks] *adj* komplike ▷ *n* kompleks

complexion [kəmˈplɛkʃən] *n* ten

complicated [ˈkɒmplɪˌkeɪtɪd] *adj* komplike

complication [ˌkɒmplɪˈkeɪʃən] *n* zorluk

compliment *n* [ˈkɒmplɪmənt] kompliman ▷ *v* [ˈkɒmplɪˌmɛnt] iltifat etmek

complimentary [ˌkɒmplɪˈmɛntərɪ; -trɪ] *adj* övücü

component [kəmˈpəʊnənt] *adj* bileşen ▷ *n* bileşen

composer [kəmˈpəʊzə] *n* besteci

composition [ˌkɒmpəˈzɪʃən] *n* beste

comprehension [ˌkɒmprɪˈhɛnʃən] *n* anlama

comprehensive [ˌkɒmprɪˈhɛnsɪv] *adj* kapsamlı

compromise [ˈkɒmprəˌmaɪz] *n* ödün ▷ *v* ödün vermek

compulsory [kəmˈpʌlsərɪ] *adj* metazori

computer [kəmˈpjuːtə] *n* bilgisayar; **computer game** *n* bilgisayar oyunu; **computer science** *n* bilgisayar bilimi; **May I use your computer?** Bilgisayarınızı kullanabilir miyim?; **Where is the computer room?** Bilgisayar odası nerede?

computing [kəmˈpjuːtɪŋ] *n* bilgisayar çalışması

concentrate [ˈkɒnsənˌtreɪt] *v* yoğunlaşmak

concentration [ˌkɒnsənˈtreɪʃən] *n* yoğunlaşma

concern [kənˈsɜːn] *n* teveccüh

concerned [kənˈsɜːnd] *adj* ilgili

concerning [kənˈsɜːnɪŋ] *prep* ilgili

concert [ˈkɒnsɜːt; -sət] *n* konser; **Are there any good concerts on?** İyi konserler var mı?; **What's on tonight at the concert hall?** Konser salonunda bu gece ne var?; **Where can I buy tickets for the concert?** Konser biletlerini nereden alabilirim?

concerto, concerti [kənˈtʃɛətəʊ, kənˈtʃɛətɪ] *n* konçerto

concession [kənˈsɛʃən] *n* ayrıcalık

concise [kənˈsaɪs] *adj* kısa ve öz

conclude [kənˈkluːd] *v* son vermek

conclusion [kənˈkluːʒən] *n* sonuç

concrete ['kɒnkriːt] n beton

concussion [kən'kʌʃən] n sarsıntı

condemn [kən'dɛm] v kınamak

condensation [ˌkɒndɛn'seɪʃən] n buğu

condition [kən'dɪʃən] n koşul

conditional [kən'dɪʃənᵊl] adj koşullu

conditioner [kən'dɪʃənə] n saç kremi

condom ['kɒndɒm; 'kɒndəm] n prezervatif

conduct [kən'dʌkt] v rehberlik etmek

conductor [kən'dʌktə] n orkestra şefi; **bus conductor** n biletçi

cone [kəʊn] n koni

conference ['kɒnfərəns; -frəns] n konferans; **press conference** n basın toplantısı; **Please take me to the conference centre** Konferans merkezine lütfen

confess [kən'fɛs] v itiraf etmek

confession [kən'fɛʃən] n itiraf

confetti [kən'fɛtɪ] npl konfeti

confidence ['kɒnfɪdəns] n (secret) sır, (self-assurance) özgüven, (trust) güven

confident ['kɒnfɪdənt] adj kendine güvenen

confidential [ˌkɒnfɪ'dɛnʃəl] adj gizli

confirm [kən'fɜːm] v doğrulamak

confirmation [ˌkɒnfə'meɪʃən] n teyit

confiscate ['kɒnfɪˌskeɪt] v elkoymak

conflict ['kɒnflɪkt] n çatışma

confuse [kən'fjuːz] v karıştırmak (fikir)

confused [kən'fjuːzd] adj kafası karışık

confusing [kən'fjuːzɪŋ] adj yanıltıcı

confusion [kən'fjuːʒən] n karışıklık

congestion [kən'dʒɛstʃən] n tıkanıklık

Congo ['kɒŋgəʊ] n Kongo

congratulate [kən'grætjʊˌleɪt] v kutlamak

congratulations [kənˌgrætjʊ'leɪʃənz] npl tebrikler

conifer ['kəʊnɪfə; 'kɒn-] n kozalak

conjugation [ˌkɒndʒʊ'geɪʃən] n birleşme

conjunction [kən'dʒʌŋkʃən] n bağlantı

conjurer ['kʌndʒərə] n illüzyonist

connect [kə'nɛkt] v bağlamak (kablo)

connection [kə'nɛkʃən] n bağlantı; **I've missed my connection** Bağlantı uçağımı kaçırdım; **Is there an internet connection in the room?** Odada internet bağlantısı var mı?; **The connection seems very slow** Bağlantı çok yavaş

conquer ['kɒŋkə] v yenmek

conscience ['kɒnʃəns] n vicdan

conscientious [ˌkɒnʃɪ'ɛnʃəs] adj vicdanlı

conscious ['kɒnʃəs] adj bilinçli

consciousness ['kɒnʃəsnɪs] n bilinçlilik

consecutive [kən'sɛkjʊtɪv] adj ardı ardına

consensus [kən'sɛnsəs] n oy birliği

consequence ['kɒnsɪkwəns] n
sonuç

consequently ['kɒnsɪkwəntlɪ]
adv nitekim

conservation [ˌkɒnsə'veɪʃən] n
koruma

conservative [kən'sɜːvətɪv] adj
muhafazakâr

conservatory [kən'sɜːvətrɪ] n
limonluk

consider [kən'sɪdə] v hesaba
katmak

considerate [kən'sɪdərɪt] adj
düşünceli (özenli)

considering [kən'sɪdərɪŋ] prep
göz önünde tutarak

consist [kən'sɪst] v **consist of** v
oluşmak

consistent [kən'sɪstənt] adj tutarlı

consonant ['kɒnsənənt] n ünsüz
(gramer)

conspiracy [kən'spɪrəsɪ] n
komplo

constant ['kɒnstənt] adj sabit
(değişmez)

constantly ['kɒnstəntlɪ] adv
sürekli

constipated ['kɒnstɪˌpeɪtɪd] adj
kabız; **I'm constipated** Kabızlık
çekiyorum

constituency [kən'stɪtjʊənsɪ] n
seçmen bölgesi

constitution [ˌkɒnstɪ'tjuːʃən] n
yasalar

construct [kən'strʌkt] v yapmak

construction [kən'strʌkʃən] n
yapı

constructive [kən'strʌktɪv] adj
yapıcı

consul ['kɒnsəl] n konsolos

consulate ['kɒnsjʊlɪt] n
konsolosluk

consult [kən'sʌlt] v danışmak

consultant [kən'sʌltənt] n
(adviser) danışman

consumer [kən'sjuːmə] n tüketici

contact n ['kɒntækt] temas ▷ v
[kən'tækt] temas kurmak;
contact lenses npl kontakt lens;
Where can I contact you? Sizinle
nasıl temas kurabilirim?; **Who do
we contact if there are
problems?** Bir sorun çıkarsa
kiminle temas kuracağız?

contactless ['kɒntæktlɪs] adj
temassız

contagious [kən'teɪdʒəs] adj
bulaşıcı

contain [kən'teɪn] v içermek

container [kən'teɪnə] n kap

contemporary [kən'tɛmprərɪ]
adj çağdaş

contempt [kən'tɛmpt] n hor
görme

content ['kɒntɛnt] n muhteviyat;
contents (list) npl muhteviyat

contest ['kɒntɛst] n yarışma

contestant [kən'tɛstənt] n
yarışmacı

context ['kɒntɛkst] n içerik

continent ['kɒntɪnənt] n kıta

continual [kən'tɪnjʊəl] adj daimi

continually [kən'tɪnjʊəlɪ] adv
daimi

continue [kən'tɪnjuː] vi
sürdürmek ▷ vt devam etmek

continuous [kən'tɪnjʊəs] adj
kesintisiz

contraception [ˌkɒntrə'sɛpʃən] n
doğum kontrolü

contraceptive [ˌkɒntrə'sɛptɪv] n
doğum kontrol hapı

contract ['kɒntrækt] n kontrat

contractor ['kɒntræktə;
kən'træk-] n yüklenici

contradict [ˌkɒntrə'dɪkt] v
çelişmek

contradiction [ˌkɒntrə'dɪkʃən] n
çelişki

contrary ['kɒntrərɪ] n zıt

contrast ['kɒntrɑːst] n karşıtlık

contribute [kən'trɪbjuːt] v
katkıda bulunmak

contribution [ˌkɒntrɪ'bjuːʃən] n
katkı

control [kən'trəʊl] n kontrol ▷ v
idare etmek; **birth control** n
doğum kontrolü; **passport
control** n pasaport kontrol;
remote control n uazaktan
kumanda

controller [kən'trəʊlə] n
air-traffic controller n hava
trafik kontrolörü

controversial ['kɒntrə'vɜːʃəl] adj
tartışmalı

convenient [kən'viːnɪənt] adj
uygun

convent ['kɒnvənt] n manastır

conventional [kən'vɛnʃənˀl] adj
konvensiyonel (alışılmış)

conversation [ˌkɒnvə'seɪʃən] n
konuşma

convert [kən'vɜːt] v değiştirmek
(dönüştürmek); **catalytic
converter** n katalitik konvertör

convertible [kən'vɜːtəbˀl] adj
konvertibl ▷ n üstü açılır araba

convict [kən'vɪkt] v hükümlü

convince [kən'vɪns] v inandırmak

convincing [kən'vɪnsɪŋ] adj
inandırıcı

convoy ['kɒnvɔɪ] n konvoy

cook [kʊk] n ahçı ▷ v pişirmek

cookbook ['kʊkˌbʊk] n yemek
kitabı

cooker ['kʊkə] n ocak (fırın vb);
gas cooker n gazlı ocak

cookery ['kʊkərɪ] n aşçılık;
cookery book n yemek kitabı

cooking ['kʊkɪŋ] n pişirme

cool [kuːl] adj (cold) serin, (stylish)
havalı

cooperation [kəʊˌɒpə'reɪʃən] n
işbirliği

cop [kɒp] n aynasız

cope [kəʊp] v **cope (with)** v başa
çıkmak

copper ['kɒpə] n bakır

copy ['kɒpɪ] n (reproduction) taklit,
(written text) kopya (nüsha) ▷ v
kopyalamak

copyright ['kɒpɪˌraɪt] n telif hakkı

coral ['kɒrəl] n mercan

cord [kɔːd] n **spinal cord** n omurilik

cordless ['kɔːdlɪs] adj telsiz

corduroy ['kɔːdəˌrɔɪ; ˌkɔːdə'rɔɪ] n
fitilli kadife

core [kɔː] n çekirdekli kısım
(meyve)

coriander [ˌkɒrɪ'ændə] n kişniş

cork [kɔːk] n mantar (eşya)

corkscrew ['kɔːkˌskruː] n tirbuşon

corn [kɔːn] n mısır (sebze)

corner ['kɔːnə] n köşe; **It's on the
corner** Köşede; **It's round the
corner** Köşeyi dönünce

cornet ['kɔːnɪt] n kornet

cornflakes ['kɔːnˌfleɪks] npl
mısır gevreği

cornflour ['kɔːnˌflauə] n mısır
nişastası

corporal ['kɔːpərəl; -prəl] n
onbaşı

corpse [kɔːps] n ceset

correct [kə'rɛkt] adj doğru (işlem,
hareket) ▷ v düzeltmek (hata,
yanlış)

correction [kə'rɛkʃən] n düzelti

correctly [kə'rɛktlı] adv doğru
olarak

correspondence
[ˌkɒrɪ'spɒndəns] n yazışma

correspondent [ˌkɒrɪ'spɒndənt]
n muhabir

corridor ['kɒrɪˌdɔː] n koridor

corrupt [kə'rʌpt] adj yozlaşmış

corruption [kə'rʌpʃən] n
yozlaşma

cosmetics [kɒz'mɛtɪks] npl
makyaj malzemesi

cost [kɒst] n eder ▷ v mal olmak;
cost of living n hayat pahalılığı

Costa Rica ['kɒstə 'riːkə] n Kosta
Rika

costume ['kɒstjuːm] n kostüm;
swimming costume n mayo

cosy ['kəuzı] adj rahat

cot [kɒt] n bebek karyolası

cottage ['kɒtɪdʒ] n kulübe;
cottage cheese n süzme peynir

cotton ['kɒtˀn] n pamuk (bitki);
cotton bud n kulak çubuğu;
cotton wool n pamuk

couch [kautʃ] n kanepe

couchette [kuː'ʃɛt] n kuşet

cough [kɒf] n öksürük ▷ v
öksürmek; **cough mixture** n
öksürük şurubu

council ['kaunsəl] n meclis

(belediye vb); **council house** n
sosyal konut

councillor ['kaunsələ] n belediye
meclis üyesi

count [kaunt] v saymak

counter ['kauntə] n kontuar

count on [kaunt ɒn] v güvenmek

country ['kʌntrı] n ülke;
developing country n gelişmekte
olan ülke

countryside ['kʌntrɪˌsaɪd] n kırsal
bölge

couple ['kʌpˀl] n çift

courage ['kʌrɪdʒ] n cesaret

courageous [kə'reɪdʒəs] adj
yürekli

courgette [kuə'ʒɛt] n kabak

courier ['kuərɪə] n kurye; **I want
to send this by courier** Kuryeyle
göndermek istiyorum

course [kɔːs] n kurs; **golf course** n
golf sahası; **main course** n ana
yemek; **refresher course** n bilgi
tazeleme eğitimi; **training course**
n eğitim kursu

court [kɔːt] n mahkeme; **tennis
court** n tenis kortu

courtyard ['kɔːtˌjɑːd] n avlu

cousin ['kʌzˀn] n kuzen

cover ['kʌvə] n örtü ▷ v örtmek;
cover charge n servis ücreti

cow [kau] n inek

coward ['kauəd] n korkak

cowardly ['kauədlı] adj korkakça

cowboy ['kauˌbɔɪ] n kovboy

crab [kræb] n yengeç

crack [kræk] n (cocaine) krek
(kokain), (fracture) çatlak ▷ v
çatlatmak; **crack down on** v sıkı
tedbirler almak

cracked [krækt] adj çatlak
cracker ['krækə] n kraker
cradle ['kreɪdəl] n beşik
craft [krɑːft] n zanaat
craftsman ['krɑːftsmən] n zanaatkâr
cram [kræm] v tıkabasa doldurmak
crammed [kræmd] adj tıkabasa dolu
cranberry ['krænbəri; -bri] n kırmızı yaban mersini
crane [kreɪn] n (bird) turna, (for lifting) vinç
crash [kræʃ] n araba kazası ▷ vi çarpışmak (araçla) ▷ vt vasıta ile çarpmak
crawl [krɔːl] v emeklemek
crayfish ['kreɪˌfɪʃ] n kerevit
crayon ['kreɪən; -ɒn] n mum boya
crazy ['kreɪzɪ] adj çılgın
cream [kriːm] adj krem renkli ▷ n krem, krema; **ice cream** n dondurma; **shaving cream** n traş kremi; **whipped cream** n köpük krema
crease [kriːs] n kırışıklık
creased [kriːst] adj kırışık
create [kriːˈeɪt] v yaratmak
creation [kriːˈeɪʃən] n yaradılış
creative [kriːˈeɪtɪv] adj yaratıcı
creature ['kriːtʃə] n yaratık
crêche [kreʃ] n kreş
credentials [krɪˈdɛnʃəlz] npl itimatname
credible ['krɛdɪbəl] adj inandırıcı
credit ['krɛdɪt] n kredi; **credit card** n kredi kartı; **Can I pay by credit card?** Kredi kartıyla ödeme yapabilir miyim?; **Do you take**

credit cards? Kredi kartı kabul ediyor musunuz?
crematorium, crematoria [ˌkrɛməˈtɔːrɪəm, ˌkrɛməˈtɔːrɪə] n krematoryum
cress [krɛs] n tere
crew [kruː] n tayfa; **crew cut** n asker traşı
cricket ['krɪkɪt] n (game) kriket, (insect) cırcır böceği
crime [kraɪm] n suç
criminal ['krɪmɪnəl] adj suçlu ▷ n suçlu
crisis ['kraɪsɪs] n kriz
crisp [krɪsp] adj gevrek (çıtır çıtır)
crisps [krɪsps] npl cips
crispy ['krɪspɪ] adj gevrek
criterion, criteria [kraɪˈtɪərɪən, kraɪˈtɪərɪə] n kriter
critic ['krɪtɪk] n eleştirmen
critical ['krɪtɪkəl] adj kritik
criticism ['krɪtɪˌsɪzəm] n tenkit (davranış)
criticize ['krɪtɪˌsaɪz] v eleştirmek
Croatia [krəʊˈeɪʃə] n Hırvatistan
Croatian [krəʊˈeɪʃən] adj Hırvat ▷ n (language) Hırvatça (dil), (person) Hırvat (kişi)
crochet ['krəʊʃeɪ; -ʃɪ] v kroşe yapmak
crockery ['krɒkərɪ] n **We need more crockery** Daha fazla tabak çanağa ihtiyacımız var
crocodile ['krɒkəˌdaɪl] n timsah
crocus ['krəʊkəs] n çiğdem (çiçek)
crook [krʊk] n düzenbaz, (swindler) düzenbaz
crop [krɒp] n ürün
cross [krɒs] adj öfkeli ▷ n çapraz ▷ v karşıdan karşıya geçmek;

Red Cross n Kızılhaç

cross-country ['krɒs'kʌntrɪ] n arazide

crossing ['krɒsɪŋ] n geçit; **level crossing** n hemzemin geçit; **pedestrian crossing** n yaya geçidi; **pelican crossing** n ışıklı yaya geçidi; **zebra crossing** n şeritli yaya geçidi

cross out [krɒs aʊt] v silmek *(silip çıkarmak)*

crossroads ['krɒs,rəʊdz] n dört yol ağzı

crossword ['krɒs,wɜːd] n bulmaca

crouch down [kraʊtʃ daʊn] v çömelmek

crow [krəʊ] n karga

crowd [kraʊd] n kalabalık

crowded [kraʊdɪd] adj kalabalık

crowdfunding ['kraʊd,fʌndɪŋ] n kitle fonlaması

crown [kraʊn] n taç

crucial ['kruːʃəl] adj önemli

crucifix ['kruːsɪfɪks] n krüsifi

crude [kruːd] adj kaba *(iş vb)*

cruel ['kruːəl] adj gaddar

cruelty ['kruːəltɪ] n zulüm

cruise [kruːz] n gemi gezisi

crumb [krʌm] n ekmek kırıntısı

crush [krʌʃ] v ezmek *(sıkıştırarak)*

crutch [krʌtʃ] n koltuk değneği

cry [kraɪ] n ağlamak ▷ v ağlamak

crystal ['krɪstəl] n kristal

cub [kʌb] n yavru *(aslan/ayı)*

Cuba ['kjuːbə] n Küba

Cuban ['kjuːbən] adj Küba ▷ n Kübalı

cube [kjuːb] n küp; **ice cube** n küp buz; **stock cube** n bulyon

cubic ['kjuːbɪk] adj kübik

cuckoo ['kʊkuː] n guguk kuşu

cucumber ['kjuː,kʌmbə] n salatalık

cuddle ['kʌdəl] n kucaklama ▷ v kucaklamak

cue [kjuː] n *(billiards)* ıstaka

cufflinks ['kʌflɪŋks] npl kol düğmeleri

culprit ['kʌlprɪt] n zanlı

cultural ['kʌltʃərəl] adj kültürel

culture ['kʌltʃə] n kültür

cumin ['kʌmɪn] n kimyon

cunning ['kʌnɪŋ] adj kurnaz

cup [kʌp] n tas; **World Cup** n Dünya Kupası

cupboard ['kʌbəd] n dolap *(mobilya)*

curb [kɜːb] n hakimiyet

cure [kjʊə] n tedavi ▷ v tedavi etmek

curfew ['kɜːfjuː] n karartma

curious ['kjʊərɪəs] adj meraklı

curl [kɜːl] n bukle *(saç)*

curler ['kɜːlə] n bigudi

curly ['kɜːlɪ] adj kıvırcık; **My hair is naturally curly** Saçım doğuştan kıvırcık

currant ['kʌrənt] n kuşüzümü

currency ['kʌrənsɪ] n kur *(para)*

current ['kʌrənt] adj güncel ▷ n *(electricity)* akım, *(flow)* akış; **current account** n cari hesap; **current affairs** npl güncel haberler

currently ['kʌrəntlɪ] adv şu anda

curriculum [kə'rɪkjʊləm] n müfredat; **curriculum vitae** n özgeçmiş

curry ['kʌrɪ] n köri; **curry powder** n köri baharatı

curse [kɜːs] n küfür

cursor ['kɜːsə] n imleç
curtain ['kɜːtᵊn] n perde
cushion ['kʊʃən] n yastık
custard ['kʌstəd] n krema
custody ['kʌstədɪ] n koruma altına alma
custom ['kʌstəm] n adet (gelenek)
customer ['kʌstəmə] n müşteri
customized ['kʌstəˌmaɪzd] adj ihtiyaca uyarlanmış
customs ['kʌstəmz] npl gümrük; **customs officer** n gümrük memuru
cut [kʌt] n kesme ▷ v kesmek; **crew cut** n asker traşı; **power cut** n elektrik kesintisi; **Don't cut too much off** Çok kesmeyin
cutback ['kʌtˌbæk] n azaltma
cut down [kʌt daʊn] v kesmek
cute [kjuːt] adj sevimli
cutlery ['kʌtlərɪ] n çatal, bıçak, kaşık
cutlet ['kʌtlɪt] n pirzola
cut off [kʌt ɒf] v kesmek
cutting ['kʌtɪŋ] n gazete kesiği
cut up [kʌt ʌp] v makaslamak
CV [siː viː] abbr CV
cyberbullying ['saɪbəˌbʊliɪŋ] n siber zorbalık
cybercafé ['saɪbəˌkæfeɪ; -ˌkæfɪ] n siber kafe
cybercrime ['saɪbəˌkraɪm] n internet suçu
cycle ['saɪkᵊl] n (bike) bisiklete binme, (recurring period) döngü ▷ v bisiklet sürmek; **cycle lane** n bisiklet yolu; **cycle path** n bisiklet yolu
cycling ['saɪklɪŋ] n bisiklete binme; **Let's go cycling** Bisiklete binmeye gidelim; **We would like**

to go cycling Bisiklete binmek istiyoruz
cyclist ['saɪklɪst] n bisikletçi
cyclone ['saɪkləʊn] n siklon
cylinder ['sɪlɪndə] n silindir
cymbals ['sɪmbᵊlz] npl zil (müzik)
Cypriot ['sɪprɪət] adj Kıbrıs ▷ n (person) Kıbrıslı (kişi)
Cyprus ['saɪprəs] n kıbrıs
cyst [sɪst] n kist
cystitis [sɪ'staɪtɪs] n sistit
Czech [tʃɛk] adj Çek ▷ n (language) Çek dili (dil), (person) Çek (kişi); **Czech Republic** n Çek Cumhuriyeti

d

Dans etmek istiyorum; **Would you like to dance?** Dans etmek ister misiniz?

dancer ['dɑːnsə] n dansçı

dancing ['dɑːnsɪŋ] n danslı toplantı; **ballroom dancing** n salon dansı

dandelion ['dændɪˌlaɪən] n kara hindiba

dandruff ['dændrəf] n kepek (saç)

Dane [deɪn] n Danimarkalı

danger ['deɪndʒə] n tehlike; **Is there a danger of avalanches?** Çığ tehlikesi var mı?

dangerous ['deɪndʒərəs] adj tehlikeli

Danish ['deɪnɪʃ] adj Danimarka ▷ n (language) Danimarka dili (dil)

dare [dɛə] v cüret etmek

daring ['dɛərɪŋ] adj cesur

dark [dɑːk] adj karanlık ▷ n karanlık; **It's dark** Karanlık

darkness ['dɑːknɪs] n karanlık

darling ['dɑːlɪŋ] n sevgilim

dart [dɑːt] n dart oku

darts [dɑːts] npl dart oyunu

dash [dæʃ] v hızla koşmak

dashboard ['dæʃbɔːd] n gösterge tablosu

dashcam ['dæʃkæm] n araç içi kamera

data ['deɪtə; 'dɑːtə] npl veri

database ['deɪtəˌbeɪs] n veri tabanı

date [deɪt] n tarih (takvim); **best-before date** n son kullanım tarihi; **expiry date** n son kullanım tarihi; **sell-by date** n son satış tarihi; **What is today's date?** Bugünün tarihi nedir?

daughter ['dɔːtə] n kız evlat

dad [dæd] n baba

daddy ['dædɪ] n babacığım

daffodil ['dæfədɪl] n nergiz

daft [dɑːft] adj saf

daily ['deɪlɪ] adj günlük ▷ adv her gün

dairy ['dɛərɪ] n mandıra; **dairy produce** n sütle yapılmış; **dairy products** npl süt ürünleri

daisy ['deɪzɪ] n papatya

dam [dæm] n baraj

damage ['dæmɪdʒ] n zarar ▷ v zarar vermek

damaged ['dæmɪdʒd] adj **My luggage has been damaged** Bagajım hasar görmüş; **My suitcase has arrived damaged** Valizim hasar görmüş

damn [dæm] adj lanet

damp [dæmp] adj nemli

dance [dɑːns] n dans ▷ v dans etmek; **I don't really dance** Dans etmem pek; **I feel like dancing**

daughter-in-law ['dɔ:tə ɪn lɔ:]
(**daughters-in-law**) n gelin
dawn [dɔ:n] n şafak
day [deɪ] n gün; **day return** n
günlük bilet; **Valentine's Day** n
Sevgililer Günü; **Do you run day
trips to…?**… a günlük turunuz var
mı?; **I want to hire a car for five
days** Beş günlüğüne bir araba
kiralamak istiyorum; **Is the
museum open every day?** Müze
her gün açık mı?; **the day after
tomorrow** öbür gün; **the day
before yesterday** önceki gün;
What a lovely day! Harika bir
gün!; **What are your rates per
day?** Günlük tarifeniz nedir?;
What day is it today? Bugün
günlerden ne?; **What is the dish
of the day?** Günün yemeği ne?
daytime ['deɪˌtaɪm] n gündüz
dead [dɛd] adj ölü ▷ adv ölü; **dead
end** n çıkmaz sokak
deadline ['dɛdˌlaɪn] n son teslim
tarihi
deaf [dɛf] adj sağır; **I'm deaf**
Sağırım
deafening ['dɛfᵊnɪŋ] adj sağır edici
deal [di:l] n anlaşma
dealer ['di:lə] n satıcı; **drug dealer**
n uyuşturucu satıcısı
deal with [di:l wɪð] v halletmek
dear [dɪə] adj (expensive) pahalı,
(loved) sevgili
death [dɛθ] n ölüm
debate [dɪ'beɪt] n tartışma (fikir)
▷ v tartışmak (fikir)
debit ['dɛbɪt] n hesabından çekilen
para ▷ v birinin hesabına borç
kaydetmek; **debit card** n banka

kartı; **direct debit** n otomatik
ödeme
debt [dɛt] n borç
decade ['dɛkeɪd; dɪ'keɪd] n on yıl
decaffeinated [dɪ'kæfɪˌneɪtɪd]
adj kafeinsiz; **decaffeinated
coffee** n kafeinsiz kahve
decay [dɪ'keɪ] v çürümek
deceive [dɪ'si:v] v yanıltmak
December [dɪ'sɛmbə] n Aralık
(ay); **on Friday the thirty first of
December** Otuz bir Aralık Cuma
günü
decent ['di:sᵊnt] adj uygun
decide [dɪ'saɪd] v karar vermek
decimal ['dɛsɪməl] adj onluk
decision [dɪ'sɪʒən] n karar
decisive [dɪ'saɪsɪv] adj belirleyici
deck [dɛk] n güverte; **Can we go
out on deck?** Güverteye çıkabilir
miyiz?; **How do I get to the car
deck?** Araba güvertesine nasıl
gidebilirim?
deckchair ['dɛkˌtʃɛə] n şezlong
declare [dɪ'klɛə] v deklare etmek;
**I have a bottle of spirits to
declare** Bir şişe içki deklare etmek
istiyorum; **I have the allowed
amount of alcohol to declare**
İzin verilen miktarda içki deklare
etmek istiyorum
decorate ['dɛkəˌreɪt] v dekore
etmek
decorator ['dɛkəˌreɪtə] n
dekoratör
decrease n [di:kri:s] azalma
▷ v [dɪ'kri:s] azalmak
dedicated ['dɛdɪˌkeɪtɪd] adj
adanmış
dedication [ˌdɛdɪ'keɪʃən] n ithaf

deduct [dɪ'dʌkt] v çıkarmak (*matematik*)

deep [di:p] *adj* derin

deep-fry [di:pfraɪ] v kızartma

deeply ['di:plɪ] *adv* derinden

deer [dɪə] geyik

defeat [dɪ'fi:t] n yenilgi ▷ v yenmek

defect [dɪ'fɛkt] n kusur

defence [dɪ'fɛns] n savunma

defend [dɪ'fɛnd] v korumak

defendant [dɪ'fɛndənt] n davalı

defender [dɪ'fɛndə] n savunucu

deficit ['dɛfɪsɪt; dɪ'fɪsɪt] n açık (*finans*)

define [dɪ'faɪn] v tanımlamak

definite ['dɛfɪnɪt] *adj* kesin

definitely ['dɛfɪnɪtlɪ] *adv* kesinlikle

definition [ˌdɛfɪ'nɪʃən] n tanım

degree [dɪ'gri:] n derece (*sıcaklık*); **degree centigrade** n Santigrat derece; **degree Celsius** n Santigrat derece; **degree Fahrenheit** n Fahrenheit derece

dehydrated [di:'haɪdreɪtɪd] *adj* susuz

de-icer [di:'aɪsə] n buz çözücü

delay [dɪ'leɪ] n gecikme ▷ v gecikmek

delayed [dɪ'leɪd] *adj* gecikmeli; **The flight has been delayed** Uçuşunuz gecikmeli

delegate n ['dɛlɪˌgɪt] delege ▷ v ['dɛlɪˌgeɪt] yetkilendirmek

delete [dɪ'li:t] v silmek

deliberate [dɪ'lɪbərɪt] *adj* kasıtlı

deliberately [dɪ'lɪbərətlɪ] *adv* kasıtlı olarak

delicate ['dɛlɪkɪt] *adj* hassas

delicatessen [ˌdɛlɪkə'tɛsˀn] n şarküteri

delicious [dɪ'lɪʃəs] *adj* lezzetli

delight [dɪ'laɪt] n haz

delighted [dɪ'laɪtɪd] *adj* hoşnut

delightful [dɪ'laɪtfʊl] *adj* keyif verici

deliver [dɪ'lɪvə] v teslim etmek

delivery [dɪ'lɪvərɪ] n teslimat; **recorded delivery** n iadeli taahhütlü

demand [dɪ'mɑ:nd] n talep ▷ v talep etmek

demanding [dɪ'mɑ:ndɪŋ] *adj* zahmetli

demo, demos ['dɛməʊ, 'dɛməʊz] n demo

democracy [dɪ'mɒkrəsɪ] n demokrasi

democratic [ˌdɛmə'krætɪk] *adj* demokratik

demolish [dɪ'mɒlɪʃ] v yıkmak

demonstrate ['dɛmənˌstreɪt] v bulgularla kanıtlamak

demonstration [ˌdɛmən'streɪʃən] n gösteri (*politik*)

demonstrator ['dɛmənˌstreɪtə] n gösterici

denim ['dɛnɪm] n blucin kumaşı

denims ['dɛnɪmz] *npl* blucin

Denmark ['dɛnmɑ:k] n Danimarka

dense [dɛns] *adj* sık (*orman*)

density ['dɛnsɪtɪ] n yoğunluk

dent [dɛnt] n göçük ▷ v göçürmek

dental ['dɛntˀl] *adj* diş; **dental floss** n diş ipi; **I don't know if I have dental insurance** Diş sigortam var mı bilmiyorum?

dentist ['dɛntɪst] n dişçi; **I need a dentist** Dişçiye ihtiyacım var

dentures ['dɛntʃəz] npl takma
dişler; **Can you repair my
dentures?** Takma dişlerimi
onarabilir misiniz?

deny [dɪ'naɪ] v inkar etmek

deodorant [di:'əʊdərənt] n
deodoran

depart [dɪ'pɑːt] v bir yerden
hareket etmek

department [dɪ'pɑːtmənt] n
bölüm (idari); **accident &
emergency department** n kaza
& acil servis; **department store** n
büyük mağaza; **Where is the
lingerie department?** İç
çamaşırları bölümü ne tarafta?

departure [dɪ'pɑːtʃə] n kalkış;
departure lounge n uçuş
bekleme salonu

depend [dɪ'pɛnd] v güvenine bağlı
olmak

deport [dɪ'pɔːt] v sınır dışı etmek

deposit [dɪ'pɒzɪt] n depozito

depressed [dɪ'prɛst] adj canı
sıkkın

depressing [dɪ'prɛsɪŋ] adj iç
karartıcı

depression [dɪ'prɛʃən] n
depresyon

depth [dɛpθ] n derinlik

descend [dɪ'sɛnd] v inmek
(alçalmak)

describe [dɪ'skraɪb] v betimlemek

description [dɪ'skrɪpʃən] n
betimleme

desert ['dɛzət] n çöl; **desert island**
n ıssız ada

deserve [dɪ'zɜːv] v hak etmek

design [dɪ'zaɪn] n dizayn ▷ v
tasarlamak

designer [dɪ'zaɪnə] n tasarımcı;
interior designer n iç mimar

desire [dɪ'zaɪə] n arzu ▷ v arzu etmek

desk [dɛsk] n sıra (okul); **enquiry
desk** n danışma

despair [dɪ'spɛə] n umutsuzluk

desperate ['dɛspərɪt; -prɪt] adj
umutsuz

desperately ['dɛspərɪtlɪ] adv
umutsuzca

despise [dɪ'spaɪz] v hor görmek

despite [dɪ'spaɪt] prep karşın

dessert [dɪ'zɜːt] n tatlı; **dessert
spoon** n tatlı kaşığı; **The dessert
menu, please** Tatlı menüsü
lütfen; **We'd like a dessert** Tatlı
rica ediyoruz

destination [ˌdɛstɪ'neɪʃən] n
gidilecek yer

destiny ['dɛstɪnɪ] n kader

destroy [dɪ'strɔɪ] v yok etmek

destruction [dɪ'strʌkʃən] n imha

detail ['diːteɪl] n ayrıntı

detailed ['diːteɪld] adj ayrıntılı

detective [dɪ'tɛktɪv] n dedektif

detention [dɪ'tɛnʃən] n gözaltına
alma

detergent [dɪ'tɜːdʒənt] n deterjan

deteriorate [dɪ'tɪərɪəˌreɪt] v
kötülemek

determined [dɪ'tɜːmɪnd] adj
kararlı

detour ['diːtʊə] n güzergah
değiştirme

devaluation [diːˌvæljuː'eɪʃən] n
devalüasyon

devastated ['dɛvəˌsteɪtɪd] adj
mahvolmuş

devastating ['dɛvəˌsteɪtɪŋ]
adj yıkıcı

develop [dɪˈvɛləp] vi geliştirmek
(büyüme) ▷ vt gelişmek;
developing country n gelişmekte
olan ülke
development [dɪˈvɛləpmənt] n
gelişme (büyüme)
device [dɪˈvaɪs] n araç
devil [ˈdɛvᵊl] n şeytan
devise [dɪˈvaɪz] v tasarlamak
devoted [dɪˈvəʊtɪd] adj özverili
diabetes [ˌdaɪəˈbiːtɪs; -tiːz] n
şeker hastalığı
diabetic [ˌdaɪəˈbɛtɪk] adj diyabetik
▷ n şeker hastası
diagnosis [ˌdaɪəɡˈnəʊsɪs] n tanı
diagonal [daɪˈæɡənᵊl] adj
diyagonal
diagram [ˈdaɪəˌɡræm] n diyagram
dial [ˈdaɪəl; daɪl] v tuşlamak
(telefon); **dialling code** n telefon
kodu; **dialling tone** n telefon
sinyali
dialect [ˈdaɪəˌlɛkt] n diyalekt
dialogue [ˈdaɪəˌlɒɡ] n diyalog
diameter [daɪˈæmɪtə] n çap
diamond [ˈdaɪəmənd] n elmas
diarrhoea [ˌdaɪəˈrɪə] n ishal
diary [ˈdaɪərɪ] n günlük
dice, die [daɪs, daɪ] npl zar (kumar)
dictation [dɪkˈteɪʃən] n dikte
dictator [dɪkˈteɪtə] n diktatör
dictionary [ˈdɪkʃənərɪ; -ʃənrɪ] n
sözlük
die [daɪ] v ölmek
diesel [ˈdiːzᵊl] n dizel; **... worth of
diesel, please** ...lık dizel lütfen
diet [ˈdaɪət] n diyet ▷ v diyet
yapmak
difference [ˈdɪfərəns; ˈdɪfrəns]
n fark

different [ˈdɪfərənt; ˈdɪfrənt] adj
farklı; **I would like something
different** Farklı bir şey istiyordum
difficult [ˈdɪfɪkᵊlt] adj güç (zor)
difficulty [ˈdɪfɪkᵊltɪ] n güçlük
dig [dɪɡ] v kazmak
digest [dɪˈdʒɛst; daɪ-] v sindirmek
digestion [dɪˈdʒɛstʃən; daɪ-] n
sindirim
digger [ˈdɪɡə] n ekskavatör
digital [ˈdɪdʒɪtᵊl] adj dijital; **digital
camera** n dijital fotoğraf
makinesi; **digital radio** n dijital
radyo; **digital television** n dijital
televizyon; **digital watch** n dijital
saat
dignity [ˈdɪɡnɪtɪ] n haysiyet
dilemma [dɪˈlɛmə; daɪ-] n ikilem
dilute [daɪˈluːt] v sulandırmak
diluted [daɪˈluːtɪd] adj
sulandırılmış
dim [dɪm] adj loş
dimension [dɪˈmɛnʃən] n ebat
diminish [dɪˈmɪnɪʃ] v azaltmak
din [dɪn] n şamata
diner [ˈdaɪnə] n lokanta müşterisi
dinghy [ˈdɪŋɪ] n küçük sandal
dinner [ˈdɪnə] n akşam yemeği;
dinner jacket n smokin; **dinner
party** n yemekli parti; **dinner
time** n yemek zamanı; **What time
is dinner?** Akşam yemeği kaçta?;
**Would you like to go out for
dinner?** Benimle akşam yemeğine
çıkmak ister misiniz?
dinosaur [ˈdaɪnəˌsɔː] n dinozor
dip [dɪp] n (food/sauce) ezme
(yiyecek) ▷ v daldırmak
diploma [dɪˈpləʊmə] n diploma
diplomat [ˈdɪpləˌmæt] n diplomat

diplomatic [ˌdɪplə'mætɪk] *adj*
diplomatik

dipstick ['dɪpˌstɪk] *n* yağ çubuğu

direct [dɪ'rɛkt; daɪ-] *adj* kestirme
▷ *v* yönetmek; **direct debit** *n*
otomatik ödeme

direction [dɪ'rɛkʃən; daɪ-] *n* yön

directions [dɪ'rɛkʃənz; daɪ-] *npl*
talimatlar

directly [dɪ'rɛktlɪ; daɪ-] *adv*
doğrudan doğruya

director [dɪ'rɛktə; daɪ-] *n* direktör;
managing director *n* genel
müdür

directory [dɪ'rɛktərɪ; -trɪ; daɪ-] *n*
telefon rehberi; **directory
enquiries** *npl* bilinmeyen
numaralar; **telephone directory**
n telefon rehberi

dirt [dɜːt] *n* kir

dirty ['dɜːtɪ] *adj* kirli; **My sheets
are dirty** Çarşaflarım kirli

disability [ˌdɪsə'bɪlɪtɪ] *n* sakatlık

disabled [dɪ'seɪbᵊld] *adj* engelli,
özürlü

disadvantage [ˌdɪsəd'vɑːntɪdʒ] *n*
dezavantaj

disagree [ˌdɪsə'griː] *v* görüşe
katılmamak

disagreement [ˌdɪsə'griːmənt] *n*
anlaşmazlık

disappear [ˌdɪsə'pɪə] *v* gözden
kaybolmak

disappearance [ˌdɪsə'pɪərəns] *n*
gözden kaybolma

disappoint [ˌdɪsə'pɔɪnt] *v* hayal
kırıklığına uğratmak

disappointed [ˌdɪsə'pɔɪntɪd] *adj*
hayal kırıklığına uğramış

disappointing [ˌdɪsə'pɔɪntɪŋ] *adj*
tatmin edici olmayan

disappointment
[ˌdɪsə'pɔɪntmənt] *n* düş kırıklığı

disaster [dɪ'zɑːstə] *n* felaket

disastrous [dɪ'zɑːstrəs] *adj*
korkunç

disc [dɪsk] *n* disk; **compact disc** *n*
kompakt disk; **disc jockey** *n*
disk jokey; **slipped disc** *n* disk
kayması

discharge [dɪs'tʃɑːdʒ] *v* **When
will I be discharged?** Ne zaman
çıkacağım?

discipline ['dɪsɪplɪn] *n* disiplin

disclose [dɪs'kləʊz] *v* ortaya
çıkarmak

disco ['dɪskəʊ] *n* disko

disconnect [ˌdɪskə'nɛkt] *v*
kesilmek *(bağlantı)*

discount ['dɪskaʊnt] *n* indirim;
student discount *n* öğrenci
indirimi; **Do you offer a discount
for cash?** Nakit ödemelere indirim
yapıyor musunuz?

discourage [dɪs'kʌrɪdʒ] *v*
cesaretini kırmak

discover [dɪ'skʌvə] *v* keşfetmek

discretion [dɪ'skrɛʃən] *n* sağduyu

discrimination
[dɪˌskrɪmɪ'neɪʃən] *n* ayrımcılık

discuss [dɪ'skʌs] *v* görüşmek

discussion [dɪ'skʌʃən] *n*
münazara

disease [dɪ'ziːz] *n* illet;
Alzheimer's disease *n* Alzheimer
hastalığı

disgraceful [dɪs'greɪsfʊl] *adj*
utanç verici

disguise [dɪs'gaɪz] *v* kılık
değiştirmek

disgusted [dɪsˈɡʌstɪd] *adj*
tiksinmiş

disgusting [dɪsˈɡʌstɪŋ] *adj* iğrenç

dish [dɪʃ] *n (food)* yemek, *(plate)*
servis tabağı; **dish towel** *n*
kurulama havlusu; **satellite dish**
n uydu çanak; **soap dish** *n*
sabunluk; **Can you recommend a
local dish?** Yöresel bir yemek
tavsiye edebilir misiniz?; **Do you
have any vegetarian dishes?**
Vejetaryen yemekleriniz var mı?;
**Which dishes have no meat /
fish?** İçinde et / balık olmayan ne
yemekleriniz var mı?

dishcloth [ˈdɪʃˌklɒθ] *n* kurulama
bezi

dishonest [dɪsˈɒnɪst] *adj* dürüst
olmayan

dishwasher [ˈdɪʃˌwɒʃə] *n* bulaşık
makinesi

disinfectant [ˌdɪsɪnˈfɛktənt] *n*
dezenfektan

disk [dɪsk] *n* disk; **disk drive** *n* disk
sürücü

diskette [dɪsˈkɛt] *n* disket

dislike [dɪsˈlaɪk] *v* hoşlanmamak

dismal [ˈdɪzməl] *adj* iç karartıcı

dismiss [dɪsˈmɪs] *v* işten
çıkarmak

disobedient [ˌdɪsəˈbiːdɪənt] *adj*
asi

disobey [ˌdɪsəˈbeɪ] *v* söz
dinlememek

dispenser [dɪˈspɛnsə] *n* dağıtıcı;
cash dispenser *n* bankamatik

display [dɪˈspleɪ] *n* sergileme ▷ *v*
sergilemek

disposable [dɪˈspəʊzəbᵊl] *adj* tek
kullanımlık

disqualify [dɪsˈkwɒlɪˌfaɪ] *v*
diskalifiye etmek

disrupt [dɪsˈrʌpt] *v* sözünü
kesmek

dissatisfied [dɪsˈsætɪsˌfaɪd] *adj*
hoşnutsuz

dissolve [dɪˈzɒlv] *v* erimek

distance [ˈdɪstəns] *n* uzaklık

distant [ˈdɪstənt] *adj* uzak

distillery [dɪˈstɪlərɪ] *n* damıtımevi

distinction [dɪˈstɪŋkʃən] *n* fark
gözetme

distinctive [dɪˈstɪŋktɪv] *adj*
belirgin

distinguish [dɪˈstɪŋgwɪʃ] *v* ayırt
etmek

distract [dɪˈstrækt] *v* ilgisini başka
yöne çekmek

distribute [dɪˈstrɪbjuːt] *v*
dağıtmak

distributor [dɪˈstrɪbjʊtə] *n*
distribütör

district [ˈdɪstrɪkt] *n* bölge

disturb [dɪˈstɜːb] *v* rahatsız etmek

ditch [dɪtʃ] *n* hendek ▷ *v*
sepetlemek

dive [daɪv] *n* dalış ▷ *v* dalmak *(deniz
vb)*; **I'd like to go diving** Dalmak
istiyorum

diver [ˈdaɪvə] *n* dalgıç

diversion [daɪˈvɜːʃən] *n* mecburi
yön *(trafik)*

divide [dɪˈvaɪd] *v* bölmek

diving [ˈdaɪvɪŋ] *n* dalma *(denize)*;
diving board *n* tramplen; **scuba
diving** *n* tüplü dalış

division [dɪˈvɪʒən] *n* bölme

divorce [dɪˈvɔːs] *n* boşanma ▷ *v*
boşanma

divorced [dɪˈvɔːst] *adj* boşanmış

DIY [di: aɪ waɪ] *abbr* kendin-yap
dizzy ['dɪzɪ] *adj* başı dönmüş
DJ [di: dʒeɪ] *abbr* DJ
DNA [di: ɛn eɪ] *n* DNA
do [dʊ] *v* yapmak; **What would you like to do today?** Bugün ne yapmak istersiniz?
dock [dɒk] *n* dok
doctor ['dɒktə] *n* doktor; **Call a doctor!** Bir doktor çağırın; **I need a doctor** Bana bir doktor gerek; **Is there a doctor who speaks English?** İngilizce bilen bir doktor var mı?; **Please call the emergency doctor** Nöbetçi doktoru çağırın lütfen
document ['dɒkjʊmənt] *n* belge; **I want to copy this document** Bu belgenin fotokopisini çektirmek istiyorum
documentary [ˌdɒkjʊ'mɛntərɪ; -trɪ] *n* belgesel
documentation [ˌdɒkjʊmɛn'teɪʃən] *n* belgeleme
documents [ˌdɒkjʊmɛnts] *npl* belgeler
dodge [dɒdʒ] *v* kenara kaçmak
dog [dɒɡ] *n* köpek; **guide dog** *n* rehber köpek; **hot dog** *n* sosisli sandviç
dole [dəʊl] *n* yoksulluk yardımı
doll [dɒl] *n* oyuncak bebek
dollar ['dɒlə] *n* dolar; **Do you take dollars?** Dolar kabul ediyor musunuz?
dolphin ['dɒlfɪn] *n* yunus
domestic [də'mɛstɪk] *adj* ülke içi
Dominican Republic [də'mɪnɪkən rɪ'pʌblɪk] *n* Dominik Cumhuriyeti

domino ['dɒmɪˌnəʊ] *n* domino
dominoes ['dɒmɪˌnəʊz] *npl* domino oyunu
donate [dəʊ'neɪt] *v* bağışlamak
done [dʌn] *adj* yapılmış
donkey ['dɒŋkɪ] *n* eşek
donor ['dəʊnə] *n* verici
door [dɔː] *n* kapı; **door handle** *n* kapı kolu; **Keep the door locked** Kapınızı kilitleyin; **The door handle has come off** Kapının kolu çıktı; **The door won't close** Kapı kapanmıyor; **The door won't lock** Kapı kilitlenmiyor; **The door won't open** Kapı açılmıyor; **Which is the key for the front door?** Hangisi ön kapının anahtarı?
doorbell ['dɔːˌbɛl] *n* kapı zili
doorman, doormen ['dɔːˌmæn; -mən, 'dɔːˌmɛn] *n* kapıcı
doorstep ['dɔːˌstɛp] *n* kapı eşiği
dorm [dɔːm] *n* **Do you have any single sex dorms?** Yalnızca kadınlar/erkekler için yeriniz var mı?
dormitory ['dɔːmɪtərɪ; -trɪ] *n* yatakhane
dose [dəʊs] *n* doz
dot [dɒt] *n* nokta (şekil)
double ['dʌbəl] *adj* çift ▷ *v* iki katına çıkmak; **double bass** *n* kontrabas; **double bed** *n* çift kişilik yatak; **double glazing** *n* çift cam; **double room** *n* iki kişilik oda
doubt [daʊt] *n* kuşku ▷ *v* kuşku duymak
doubtful ['daʊtfʊl] *adj* kuşkulu
dough [dəʊ] *n* hamur
doughnut ['dəʊnʌt] *n* donut®

do up [dʊ ʌp] v sarmak

dove [dʌv] n beyaz güvercin

do without [dʊ wɪ'ðaʊt] v onsuz yapmak

down [daʊn] adv aşağıda

download ['daʊn‚ləʊd] n indirme *(bilgisayar)* ▷ v indirmek *(bilgisayar)*

downpour ['daʊn‚pɔː] n sağanak

downstairs ['daʊn'stɛəz] adj alt kat ▷ adv alt katta

downtown ['daʊn'taʊn] adv kent merkezinde

doze [dəʊz] v kestirmek

dozen ['dʌzən] n düzine

doze off [dəʊz ɒf] v uyuyakalmak

drab [dræb] adj sıkıcı

draft [drɑːft] n taslak

drag [dræg] v sürüklemek

dragon ['drægən] n ejderha

dragonfly ['drægən‚flaɪ] n yusufçuk

drain [dreɪn] n atık borusu ▷ v atık boşaltmak; **draining board** n damlalıklı eviye

drainpipe ['dreɪn‚paɪp] n atık borusu

drama ['drɑːmə] n dram

dramatic [drə'mætɪk] adj dramatik

drastic ['dræstɪk] adj zorlayıcı

draught [drɑːft] n cereyan

draughts [drɑːfts] npl dama oyunu

draw [drɔː] n *(lottery)* kura, *(tie)* çekiliş ▷ v *(equal with)* berabere kalmak, *(sketch)* çizmek *(resim)*

drawback ['drɔː‚bæk] n engel

drawer ['drɔːə] n çekmece

drawers [drɔːz] n **chest of drawers** n komodin

drawing ['drɔːɪŋ] n çizim

drawing pin ['drɔːɪŋ pɪn] n **drawing pin** n raptiye

dreadful ['drɛdfʊl] adj korkunç

dream [driːm] n düş *(rüya)* ▷ v düş görmek

drench [drɛntʃ] v sırılsıklam etmek

dress [drɛs] n giysi *(elbise)* ▷ v giyinmek; **evening dress** n gece elbisesi; **wedding dress** n gelinlik; **Is there a dress code?** Giysi kuralı var mı?

dressed [drɛst] adj giyinik

dresser ['drɛsə] n mutfak dolabı

dressing ['drɛsɪŋ] n **salad dressing** n salata sosu

dressing gown ['drɛsɪŋ gaʊn] n sabahlık

dressing table ['drɛsɪŋ 'teɪbəl] n tuvalet masası

dress up [drɛs ʌp] v süslenmek

dried [draɪd] adj kuru

drift [drɪft] n birikinti ▷ v sürüklenmek *(sularla)*

drill [drɪl] n matkap ▷ v delmek *(matkapla)*; **pneumatic drill** n pnömatik matkap

drink [drɪŋk] n içecek ▷ v içmek; **binge drinking** n ölçüsüz içme; **drinking water** n içme suyu; **soft drink** n içecek; **What would you like to drink?** Ne içmek istersiniz?; **Would you like a drink?** Bir şey içmek ister misiniz?

drink-driving ['drɪŋk'draɪvɪŋ] n içkili araba kullanma

drip [drɪp] n damla ▷ v damlamak

drive [draɪv] n yolculuk *(otomobil)*

▷ v sürmek *(otomobil)*; **driving
instructor** n direksiyon
öğretmeni; **four-wheel drive** n
dört çekerli; **left-hand drive** n
soldan trafik; **right-hand drive** n
sağdan trafik

driver ['draɪvə] n sürücü; **learner
driver** n öğrenci sürücü; **lorry
driver** n kamyon şoförü; **racing
driver** n yarışçı *(otomobil)*; **truck
driver** n kamyon şoförü

driveway ['draɪvˌweɪ] n kişinin
evinin önündeki özel yol

driving lesson ['draɪvɪŋ 'lɛsᵊn] n
direksiyon dersi

driving licence ['draɪvɪŋ 'laɪsəns]
n sürücü ehliyeti; **Here is my
driving licence** İşte ehliyetim;
**I don't have my driving licence
on me** Ehliyetim üzerimde değil;
My driving licence number is…
Ehliyet numaram…

driving test ['draɪvɪŋ 'tɛst] n
direksiyon sınavı

drizzle ['drɪzᵊl] n çisenti

drop [drɒp] n damla ▷ v düşürmek;
eye drops npl göz damlası

drought [draʊt] n kuraklık

drown [draʊn] v suda boğulmak

drowsy ['draʊzɪ] adj uykulu

drug [drʌg] n ilaç; **drug addict** n
uyuşturucu bağımlısı; **drug dealer**
n uyuşturucu satıcısı

drum [drʌm] n davul

drummer ['drʌmə] n davulcu

drunk [drʌŋk] adj sarhoş ▷ n
sarhoş

dry [draɪ] adj kuru ▷ v kurutmak;
bone dry adj kupkuru; **I have dry
hair** Saçım kuru

dry-cleaner's ['draɪ'kli:nəz] n
kuru temizleyici

dry-cleaning ['draɪ'kli:nɪŋ] n
kuru temizleme

dryer ['draɪə] n kurutucu; **spin
dryer** n çamaşır kurutma
makinesi; **tumble dryer** n
çamaşır kurutma makinesi

dual ['dju:əl] adj **dual
carriageway** n çift-şeritli yol

dubbed [dʌbt] adj altyazılı

dubious ['dju:bɪəs] adj kuşkulu

duck [dʌk] n ördek

due [dju:] adj olması beklenen

due to [dju: tʊ] prep dolayı

dull [dʌl] adj fersiz

dumb [dʌm] adj dilsiz

dummy ['dʌmɪ] n vitrin mankeni

dump [dʌmp] n çöplük ▷ v atmak;
rubbish dump n çöp döküm
alanı

dumpling ['dʌmplɪŋ] n hamur
yuvarı

dune [dju:n] n **sand dune** n kum
tepesi

dungarees [ˌdʌŋgə'ri:z] npl tulum

dungeon ['dʌndʒən] n zindan

duration [djʊ'reɪʃən] n süre

during ['djʊərɪŋ] prep süresince

dusk [dʌsk] n alacakaranlık

dust [dʌst] n toz ▷ v toz almak

dustbin ['dʌstˌbɪn] n çöp sepeti

dustman, dustmen ['dʌstmən,
'dʌstmɛn] n çöpçü

dustpan ['dʌstˌpæn] n faraş

dusty ['dʌstɪ] adj tozlu

Dutch [dʌtʃ] adj Hollanda'ya ait ▷ n
Hollandalı

Dutchman, Dutchmen
['dʌtʃmən, 'dʌtʃmɛn] n Hollandalı

Dutchwoman, Dutchwomen
[ˌdʌtʃwʊmən, ˈdʌtʃˌwɪmɪn] *n*
Hollandalı
duty [ˈdjuːtɪ] *n* görev; **(customs)**
duty *n* gümrük
duty-free [ˈdjuːtɪˈfriː] *adj*
duty-free ▷ *n* duty-free
duvet [ˈduːveɪ] *n* yorgan
DVD [diː viː diː] *n* DVD; **DVD**
burner *n* DVD yazıcı; **DVD player**
n DVD oynatıcı
dwarf, dwarves [dwɔːf, dwɔːvz]
n cüce
dye [daɪ] *n* boya *(giysi)* ▷ *v*
boyamak; **Can you dye my hair,**
please? Saçımı boyar mısınız
lütfen?
dynamic [daɪˈnæmɪk] *adj* dinamik
dyslexia [dɪsˈlɛksɪə] *n* disleksi
dyslexic [dɪsˈlɛksɪk] *adj* disleksik

e

each [iːtʃ] *adj* her bir ▷ *pron* her bir
eagle [ˈiːgəl] *n* kartal
ear [ɪə] *n* kulak
earache [ˈɪərˌeɪk] *n* kulak ağrısı
eardrum [ˈɪəˌdrʌm] *n* kulak zarı
earlier [ˈɜːlɪə] *adv* daha önce
early [ˈɜːlɪ] *adj* erken ▷ *adv* erken;
We arrived early/late Erken/
geç geldik
earn [ɜːn] *v* kazanmak
earnings [ˈɜːnɪŋz] *npl* gelir *(aylık*
kazanç)
earphones [ˈɪəˌfəʊnz] *npl* kulaklık
earplugs [ˈɪəˌplʌgz] *npl* kulak tıkacı
earring [ˈɪəˌrɪŋ] *n* küpe
earth [ɜːθ] *n* yeryüzü
earthquake [ˈɜːθˌkweɪk] *n* deprem
easily [ˈiːzɪlɪ] *adv* kolaylıkla
east [iːst] *adj* doğu ▷ *adv*
doğusunda ▷ *n* doğu; **Far East** *n*
Uzak Doğu; **Middle East** *n*
Orta Doğu

eastbound ['i:st̩baʊnd] *adj* doğu yönünde

Easter ['i:stə] *n* Paskalya; **Easter egg** *n* Paskalya yumurtası

eastern ['i:stən] *adj* doğu

easy ['i:zɪ] *adj* kolay; **easy chair** *n* koltuk

easy-going ['i:zɪ'gəʊɪŋ] *adj* uysal

eat [i:t] *v* yemek; **Have you eaten?** Yemek yediniz mi?; **Is there somewhere to eat on the boat?** Feribotta yemek satan bir yer var mı?; **What would you like to eat?** Ne yemek istersiniz?; **Would you like something to eat?** Bir şey yemek ister misiniz?

e-book ['i:'bʊk] *n* digital not defteri

eccentric [ɪk'sɛntrɪk] *adj* eksantrik

echo ['ɛkəʊ] *n* yankı

e-cigarette ['i:sɪgəˈrɛt] *n* elektronik sigara

ecofriendly ['i:kəʊˌfrɛndlɪ] *adj* çevre dostu

ecological [ˌi:kəˈlɒdʒɪkəl] *adj* ekolojik

ecology [ɪ'kɒlədʒɪ] *n* çevrebilim

e-commerce ['i:kɒmɜ:s] *n* e-ticaret

economic [ˌi:kəˈnɒmɪk; ˌɛkə-] *adj* ekonomi

economical [ˌi:kəˈnɒmɪkəl; ˌɛkə-] *adj* ekonomik

economics [ˌi:kəˈnɒmɪks; ˌɛkə-] *npl* ekonomi

economist [ɪ'kɒnəmɪst] *n* ekonomist

economize [ɪ'kɒnəˌmaɪz] *v* ekonomi yapmak

economy [ɪ'kɒnəmɪ] *n* ekonomi; **economy class** *n* ikinci sınıf

ecstasy ['ɛkstəsɪ] *n* coşku

Ecuador ['ɛkwədɔ:] *n* Ekvador

eczema ['ɛksɪmə; ɪg'zi:mə] *n* egzema

edge [ɛdʒ] *n* sınır

edgy ['ɛdʒɪ] *adj* gergin *(sinirli)*

edible ['ɛdɪbəl] *adj* yenilebilir

edition [ɪ'dɪʃən] *n* baskı *(gazete, dergi)*

editor ['ɛdɪtə] *n* editör

educated ['ɛdjʊˌkeɪtɪd] *adj* eğitimli

education [ˌɛdjʊ'keɪʃən] *n* eğitim *(okul)*; **adult education** *n* yetişkin eğitimi; **higher education** *n* yüksek eğitim

educational [ˌɛdjʊ'keɪʃənəl] *adj* eğitimsel

eel [i:l] *n* yılan balığı

effect [ɪ'fɛkt] *n* etki; **side effect** *n* yan etki

effective [ɪ'fɛktɪv] *adj* etkili

effectively [ɪ'fɛktɪvlɪ] *adv* etkili bir şekilde

efficient [ɪ'fɪʃənt] *adj* etkin *(nüfuzlu)*

efficiently [ɪ'fɪʃəntlɪ] *adv* etkili bir biçimde

effort ['ɛfət] *n* çaba

e.g. [i: dʒi:] *abbr* örneğin

egg [ɛg] *n* yumurta; **boiled egg** *n* haşlanmış yumurta; **egg white** *n* yumurta akı; **egg yolk** *n* yumurta sarısı; **Easter egg** *n* Paskalya yumurtası; **scrambled eggs** *npl* karıştırılmış yumurta; **Could you prepare a meal without eggs?** İçinde yumurta olmayan bir yemek yapabilir misiniz?; **I can't eat raw eggs** Çiğ yumurta yiyemiyorum

eggcup ['εg,kʌp] n yumurta kabı

Egypt ['i:dʒɪpt] n Mısır *(ülke)*

Egyptian [ɪ'dʒɪpʃən] adj Mısır ▷ n Mısırlı

eight [eɪt] *number* sekiz; **two for the eight o'clock showing** Sekiz matinesine iki bilet lütfen

eighteen ['eɪ'ti:n] *number* onsekiz

eighteenth ['eɪ'ti:nθ] adj onsekizinci

eighth [eɪtθ] adj sekizinci ▷ n sekizinci

eighty ['eɪtɪ] *number* seksen

Eire ['εərə] n İrlanda

either ['aɪðə; 'i:ðə] conj *(... or)* ya o, ya bu ▷ pron biri; **either... or** conj ya

elastic [ɪ'læstɪk] n lastik; **elastic band** n lastik bant

Elastoplast® [ɪ'læstə,plɑ:st] n yara bandı

elbow ['εlbəʊ] n dirsek

elder ['εldə] adj daha yaşlı

elderly ['εldəlɪ] adj yaşlılar

eldest ['εldɪst] adj yaşça en büyük

elect [ɪ'lεkt] v seçmek

election [ɪ'lεkʃən] n seçim; **general election** n genel seçim

electorate [ɪ'lεktərɪt] n seçmen bölgesi

electric [ɪ'lεktrɪk] adj elektrikli; **electric blanket** n elektrikli battaniye; **electric shock** n elektrik çarpması

electrical [ɪ'lεktrɪkəl] adj elektrikli

electrician [ɪlεk'trɪʃən; ,i:lεk-] n elektrikçi

electricity [ɪlεk'trɪsɪtɪ; ,i:lεk-] n elektrik; **Do we have to pay extra for electricity?** Elektrik için ayrıca para ödememiz gerekiyor mu?; **Is the cost of electricity included?** Elektrik ücrete dahil mi?; **There is no electricity** Elektrik yok; **Where is the electricity meter?** Elektrik sayacı nerede?

electronic [ɪlεk'trɒnɪk; ,i:lεk-] adj elektronik

electronics [ɪlεk'trɒnɪks; ,i:lεk-] npl elektronik bilimi

elegant ['εlɪgənt] adj zarif

element ['εlɪmənt] n bileşen

elephant ['εlɪfənt] n fil

eleven [ɪ'lεvən] *number* onbir

eleventh [ɪ'lεvənθ] adj onbirinci

eliminate [ɪ'lɪmɪ,neɪt] v gidermek

elm [εlm] n karaağaç

else [εls] adj diğer

elsewhere [,εls'wεə] adv başka bir yerde

email ['i:meɪl] n e-posta ▷ vt *(a person)* e-posta atmak; **email address** n e-posta adresi; **Can I have your email?** E-postanızı alabilir miyim?; **Can I send an email?** E-posta gönderebilir miyim?; **Did you get my email?** E-postamı aldınız mı?; **Do you have an email?** E-postanız var mı?; **My email address is...** E-posta adresim...; **What is your email address?** E-posta adresiniz nedir?

embankment [ɪm'bæŋkmənt] n bent

embarrassed [,ɪm'bærəst] adj utanmış

embarrassing [ɪm'bærəsɪŋ] adj nahoş

embassy ['εmbəsɪ] n elçilik

embroider [ɪmˈbrɔɪdə] v elişiyle süslemek

embroidery [ɪmˈbrɔɪdərɪ] n nakış

emergency [ɪˈmɜːdʒənsɪ] n acil durum; **accident & emergency department** n kaza & acil servis; **emergency exit** n acil çıkış kapısı; **emergency landing** n acil iniş

emigrate [ˈemɪˌɡreɪt] v göç etmek

emoji [ɪˈməʊdʒɪ] n emoji

emotion [ɪˈməʊʃən] n duygu

emotional [ɪˈməʊʃənᵊl] adj duygusal

emperor, empress [ˈempərə, ˈemprɪs] n imparator

emphasize [ˈemfəˌsaɪz] v vurgulamak

empire [ˈempaɪə] n imparatorluk

employ [ɪmˈplɔɪ] v işe almak

employee [emˈplɔɪiː, ˌemplɔɪˈiː] n işçi

employer [ɪmˈplɔɪə] n işveren

employment [ɪmˈplɔɪmənt] n işe alma

empty [ˈemptɪ] adj boş (mekan) ▷ v boşaltmak

enamel [ɪˈnæməl] n emaye

encourage [ɪnˈkʌrɪdʒ] v yüreklendirmek

encouragement [ɪnˈkʌrɪdʒmənt] n yüreklendirme

encouraging [ɪnˈkʌrɪdʒɪŋ] adj cesaret verici

encyclopaedia [enˌsaɪkləʊˈpiːdɪə] n ansiklopedi

end [end] n son ▷ v sonlandırmak; **dead end** n çıkmaz sokak; **at the end of June** Haziran sonunda; **Is this the end of the queue?** Kuyruğun sonu burası mı?

endanger [ɪnˈdeɪndʒə] v tehlikeye atmak

ending [ˈendɪŋ] n son

endless [ˈendlɪs] adj sonsuz

enemy [ˈenəmɪ] n düşman

energetic [ˌenəˈdʒetɪk] adj enerji dolu

energy [ˈenədʒɪ] n enerji

engaged [ɪnˈɡeɪdʒd] adj nişanlı; **engaged tone** n meşgul sinyali; **I'm engaged** Nişanlıyım

engagement [ɪnˈɡeɪdʒmənt] n randevu; **engagement ring** n nişan yüzüğü

engine [ˈendʒɪn] n makine; **search engine** n arama motoru

engineer [ˌendʒɪˈnɪə] n mühendis

engineering [ˌendʒɪˈnɪərɪŋ] n mühendislik

England [ˈɪŋɡlənd] n İngiltere

English [ˈɪŋɡlɪʃ] adj İngiliz ▷ n İngilizce; **Do you speak English?** İngilizce biliyor musunuz?; **Does anyone speak English?** İngilizce bilen biri var mı?; **I don't speak English** İngilizce bilmiyorum; **I speak very little English** Çok az İngilizce konuşabiliyorum

Englishman, Englishmen [ˈɪŋɡlɪʃmən, ˈɪŋɡlɪʃmen] n İngiliz

Englishwoman, Englishwomen [ˈɪŋɡlɪʃˌwʊmən, ˈɪŋɡlɪʃˌwɪmɪn] n İngiliz kadın

engrave [ɪnˈɡreɪv] v kazımak

enjoy [ɪnˈdʒɔɪ] v hoşlanmak

enjoyable [ɪnˈdʒɔɪəbᵊl] adj zevkli

enlargement [ɪnˈlɑːdʒmənt] n büyütme

enormous [ɪˈnɔːməs] adj muazzam

enough [ɪˈnʌf] adj kâfi ▷ pron kâfi

enquire [ɪn'kwaɪə] v araştırmak

enquiry [ɪn'kwaɪərɪ] n araştırma; **enquiry desk** n danışma

ensure [ɛn'ʃʊə; -'ʃɔː] v garantiye almak

enter ['ɛntə] v girmek (bir yere)

entertain [ˌɛntə'teɪn] v eğlendirmek

entertainer [ˌɛntə'teɪnə] n eğlence düzenleyen

entertaining [ˌɛntə'teɪnɪŋ] adj eğlendirici

entertainment [ˌɛntə'teɪnmənt] n eğlence

enthusiasm [ɪn'θjuːzɪˌæzəm] n heves

enthusiastic [ɪnˌθjuːzɪ'æstɪk] adj hevesli

entire [ɪn'taɪə] adj bütün (tamamı)

entirely [ɪn'taɪəlɪ] adv bütünüyle

entrance ['ɛntrəns] n giriş (kapı); **entrance fee** n giriş ücreti; **Where is the wheelchair-accessible entrance?** Tekerlekli sandalye girişi nerede?

entry ['ɛntrɪ] n giriş; **entry phone** n kapı telefonu

envelope ['ɛnvəˌləʊp; 'ɒn-] n zarf

envious ['ɛnvɪəs] adj kıskanç

environment [ɪn'vaɪrənmənt] n çevre

environmental [ɪnˌvaɪrən'mɛntəl] adj çevresel; **environmentally friendly** adj çevre dostu

envy ['ɛnvɪ] n haset ▷ v hasetlenmek

epidemic [ˌɛpɪ'dɛmɪk] n salgın

epileptic [ˌɛpɪ'lɛptɪk] **epileptic seizure** n sara nöbeti

episode ['ɛpɪˌsəʊd] n bölüm (dizi)

equal ['iːkwəl] adj eşit ▷ v eşitlemek

equality [ɪ'kwɒlɪtɪ] n eşitlik (siyasi)

equalize ['iːkwəˌlaɪz] v eşitlemek

equation [ɪ'kweɪʒən; -ʃən] n eşitlik (matematik)

equator [ɪ'kweɪtə] n ekvator

Equatorial Guinea [ˌɛkwə'tɔːrɪəl 'gɪnɪ] n Ekvator Ginesi

equipment [ɪ'kwɪpmənt] n donanım

equipped [ɪ'kwɪpt] adj donanımlı

equivalent [ɪ'kwɪvələnt] n denk (eşit)

erase [ɪ'reɪz] v silmek

e-reader ['iːˌriːdə] n elektronik kitap okuyucu

Eritrea [ˌɛrɪ'treɪə] n Eritre

erotic [ɪ'rɒtɪk] adj erotik

error ['ɛrə] n yanlış

escalator ['ɛskəˌleɪtə] n yürüyen merdiven

escape [ɪ'skeɪp] n kaçış ▷ v kaçmak; **fire escape** n yangın çıkışı

escort [ɪs'kɔːt] v eşlik etmek (refakat)

especially [ɪ'spɛʃəlɪ] adv özellikle

espionage ['ɛspɪəˌnɑːʒ; ˌɛspɪə'nɑːʒ; 'ɛspɪənɪdʒ] n casusluk

essay ['ɛseɪ] n deneme

essential [ɪ'sɛnʃəl] adj zorunlu

estate [ɪ'steɪt] n malikane; **estate agent** n emlakçı; **estate car** n vagon (oto)

estimate n ['ɛstɪmɪt] tahmin ▷ v ['ɛstɪˌmeɪt] tahminde bulunmak

Estonia [ɛ'stəʊnɪə] n Estonya

Estonian [ɛ'stəʊnɪən] *adj* Estonya
▷ *n (language)* Estonya dili *(dil)*,
(person) Estonyalı *(kişi)*

etc [ɪt 'sɛtrə] *abbr vb (kısaltma)*

eternal [ɪ'tɜːn³l] *adj* sonsuz

eternity [ɪ'tɜːnɪtɪ] *n* sonsuz

ethical ['ɛθɪk³l] *adj* ahlaki

Ethiopia [,iː'θɪ'əʊpɪə] *n* Etyopya

Ethiopian [,iː'θɪ'əʊpɪən] *adj*
Etyopya ▷ *n* Etyopyalı

ethnic ['ɛθnɪk] *adj* etnik

e-ticket ['iː'tɪkɪt] *n* e-bilet

EU [iː juː] *abbr* AB

euro ['jʊərəʊ] *n* avro

Europe ['jʊərəp] *n* Avrupa

European [,jʊərə'pɪən] *adj* Avrupa
▷ *n* Avrupalı; **European Union** *n*
Avrupa Birliği

evacuate [ɪ'vækjʊˌeɪt] *v*
boşaltmak *(bina)*

eve [iːv] *n* arife

even ['iːv³n] *adj* düz *(düzgün)* ▷ *adv*
hatta

evening ['iːvnɪŋ] *n* akşam;
evening class *n* akşam okulu;
evening dress *n* gece elbisesi;
Good evening İyi akşamlar; **in
the evening** akşam; **The table is
booked for nine o'clock this
evening** Masa bu akşam saat
dokuz için rezerve edildi; **What
are you doing this evening?** Bu
akşam ne yapıyorsunuz?; **What is
there to do in the evenings?**
Burada akşamları yapılabilecek ne
var?

event [ɪ'vɛnt] *n* olay

eventful [ɪ'vɛntfʊl] *adj* olaylı

eventually [ɪ'vɛntʃʊəlɪ] *adv*
sonuçta

ever ['ɛvə] *adv* hiç; **Have you ever
been to…?** … a hiç gittiniz mi?

every ['ɛvrɪ] *adj* her; **The bus runs
every twenty minutes** Her yirmi
dakikada bir otobüs var

everybody ['ɛvrɪˌbɒdɪ] *pron*
herkes

everyone ['ɛvrɪˌwʌn; -wən] *pron*
herkes

everything ['ɛvrɪθɪŋ] *pron* herşey

everywhere ['ɛvrɪˌwɛə] *adv* her
yerde

evidence ['ɛvɪdəns] *n* kanıt

evil ['iːv³l] *adj* kötücül

evolution [,iːvə'luːʃən] *n* evrim

ewe [juː] *n* koyun *(dişi)*

exact [ɪg'zækt] *adj* tam

exactly [ɪg'zæktlɪ] *adv* tam olarak

exaggerate [ɪg'zædʒəˌreɪt] *v*
abartmak

exaggeration [ɪg'zædʒəˌreɪʃən] *n*
abartı

exam [ɪg'zæm] *n* sınav

examination [ɪgˌzæmɪ'neɪʃən] *n*
(medical) sınav, *(school)* sınav

examine [ɪg'zæmɪn] *v* incelemek

examiner [ɪg'zæmɪnə] *n* sınav
görevlisi

example [ɪg'zaːmp³l] *n* örnek

excellent ['ɛksələnt] *adj*
mükemmel; **The lunch was
excellent** Yemek mükemmeldi

except [ɪk'sɛpt] *prep* hariç

exception [ɪk'sɛpʃən] *n* dışında
(haricinde)

exceptional [ɪk'sɛpʃən³l] *adj*
müstesna

excessive [ɪk'sɛsɪv] *adj* aşırı

exchange [ɪks'tʃeɪndʒ] *v* karşılıklı
yapmak; **exchange rate** *n* döviz

kuru; **rate of exchange** n döviz kuru; **stock exchange** n borsa

excited [ɪkˈsaɪtɪd] adj heyecanlı

exciting [ɪkˈsaɪtɪŋ] adj heyecan verici

exclude [ɪkˈskluːd] v dışında tutmak

excluding [ɪkˈskluːdɪŋ] prep dışında (onu hariç tutarak)

exclusively [ɪkˈskluːsɪvlɪ] adv yalnızca

excuse n [ɪkˈskjuːs] özür ▷ v [ɪkˈskjuːz] özür beyan etmek

execute [ˈɛksɪˌkjuːt] v idam etmek

execution [ˌɛksɪˈkjuːʃən] n idam

executive [ɪgˈzɛkjʊtɪv] n yönetici

exercise [ˈɛksəˌsaɪz] n egzersiz

exhaust [ɪgˈzɔːst] n **The exhaust is broken** Egzos patladı

exhausted [ɪgˈzɔːstɪd] adj tükenmiş

exhibition [ˌɛksɪˈbɪʃən] n sergi

ex-husband [ɛksˈhʌzbənd] n eski koca

exile [ˈɛgzaɪl; ˈɛksaɪl] n sürgün (başka bir yere)

exist [ɪgˈzɪst] v var olmak

exit [ˈɛgzɪt; ˈɛksɪt] n çıkış; **emergency exit** n acil çıkış kapısı; **Which exit for...?** ... çıkışı nerede?

exotic [ɪgˈzɒtɪk] adj egzotik

expect [ɪkˈspɛkt] v ummak

expedition [ˌɛkspɪˈdɪʃən] n keşif gezisi

expel [ɪkˈspɛl] v kovmak

expenditure [ɪkˈspɛndɪtʃə] n harcamalar

expenses [ɪkˈspɛnsɪz] npl masraflar

expensive [ɪkˈspɛnsɪv] adj pahalı;

It's quite expensive Çok pahalı; **It's too expensive for me** Benim için çok pahalı

experience [ɪkˈspɪərɪəns] n deneyim; **work experience** n iş deneyimi

experienced [ɪkˈspɪərɪənst] adj deneyimli

experiment [ɪkˈspɛrɪmənt] n deney

expert [ˈɛkspɜːt] n uzman

expire [ɪkˈspaɪə] v sona erdirme

explain [ɪkˈspleɪn] v açıklamak

explanation [ˌɛkspləˈneɪʃən] n açıklama (izah)

explode [ɪkˈspləʊd] v patlamak (havaya uçarak)

exploit [ɪkˈsplɔɪt] v sömürmek

exploitation [ˌɛksplɔɪˈteɪʃən] n sömürü

explore [ɪkˈsplɔː] v araştırmak

explorer [ɪkˈsplɔːrə] n kaşif

explosion [ɪkˈspləʊʒən] n patlama

explosive [ɪkˈspləʊsɪv] n patlayıcı madde

export n [ˈɛkspɔːt] ihracat ▷ v [ɪkˈspɔːt] ihraç etmek

express [ɪkˈsprɛs] v ifade etmek

expression [ɪkˈsprɛʃən] n anlatım

extension [ɪkˈstɛnʃən] n uzatma; **extension cable** n uzatma kablosu

extensive [ɪkˈstɛnsɪv] adj geniş (ferah, yaygın)

extensively [ɪkˈstɛnsɪvlɪ] adv uzun uzadıya

extent [ɪkˈstɛnt] n boyut

exterior [ɪkˈstɪərɪə] adj dış (yapı vb)

external [ɪkˈstɜːnəl] adj dış (harici)

extinct [ɪk'stɪŋkt] *adj* soyu tükenmiş

extinguisher [ɪk'stɪŋgwɪʃə] *n* söndürücü *(yangın)*

extortionate [ɪk'stɔːʃənɪt] *adj* ölçüsüz

extra ['ɛkstrə] *adj* ilave *(fazladan)* ▷ *adv* ilaveten

extraordinary [ɪk'strɔːdᵊnrɪ; -dᵊnərɪ] *adj* olağanüstü

extravagant [ɪk'strævɪgənt] *adj* savruk

extreme [ɪk'striːm] *adj* aşırı

extremely [ɪk'striːmlɪ] *adv* aşırı derecede

extremism [ɪk'striːmɪzəm] *n* aşırıcılık

extremist [ɪk'striːmɪst] *n* aşırı uçta

ex-wife [ɛks'waɪf] *n* eski karı

eye [aɪ] *n* göz; **eye drops** *npl* göz damlası; **eye shadow** *n* göz farı; **I have something in my eye** Gözüme bir şey kaçtı; **My eyes are sore** Gözlerim yanıyor

eyebrow ['aɪ,braʊ] *n* kaş

eyelash ['aɪ,læʃ] *n* kirpik

eyelid ['aɪ,lɪd] *n* göz kapağı

eyeliner ['aɪ,laɪnə] *n* rimel

eyesight ['aɪ,saɪt] *n* görme yetisi

f

fabric ['fæbrɪk] *n* kumaş

fabulous ['fæbjʊləs] *adj* inanılmaz

face [feɪs] *n* yüz ▷ *v* bakmak *(karşılıklı)*; **face cloth** *n* yüz havlusu

facial ['feɪʃəl] *adj* yüz ▷ *n* yüz bakımı

facilities [fə'sɪlɪtɪz] *npl* kolaylıklar; **Do you have facilities for children?** Çocuklar için kolaylıklarınız neler?; **What facilities do you have for people with disabilities?** Özürlüler için kolaylıklarınız nelerdir?

fact [fækt] *n* gerçek *(bilgi)*

factory ['fæktərɪ] *n* fabrika; **I work in a factory** Bir fabrikada çalışıyorum

fade [feɪd] *v* solmak

fag [fæg] *n* sigara *(argo)*

fail [feɪl] *v* başarısız olmak

failure ['feɪljə] *n* başarısızlık

faint [feɪnt] *adj* zayıf *(ışık, ses vb)* ▷ *v* bayılmak

fair [fɛə] *adj (light colour)* açık renk *(ten/saç)*, *(reasonable)* adil ▷ *n* fuar

fairground ['fɛəˌɡraʊnd] *n* fuar alanı

fairly ['fɛəlɪ] *adv* oldukça

fairness ['fɛənɪs] *n* dürüstlük

fairy ['fɛərɪ] *n* peri

fairytale ['fɛərɪˌteɪl] *n* peri masalı

faith [feɪθ] *n* inanç

faithful ['feɪθfʊl] *adj* sadık

faithfully ['feɪθfʊlɪ] *adv* sadakatle

fake [feɪk] *adj* uyduruk ▷ *n* sahte

fall [fɔːl] *n* düşüş ▷ *v* düşmek

fall down [fɔːl daʊn] *v* düşmek

fall for [fɔːl fɔː] *v* cazibesine kapılmak

fall out [fɔːl aʊt] *v* sıradan çıkmak

false [fɔːls] *adj* düzmece; **false alarm** *n* yanlış alarm

fame [feɪm] *n* ün

familiar [fəˈmɪlɪə] *adj* bildik

family ['fæmɪlɪ; 'fæmlɪ] *n* aile; **I want to reserve a family room** Aile odası ayırtmak istiyorum; **I'd like to book a family room** Aile odası istiyorum; **I'm here with my family** Ailemle geldim

famine ['fæmɪn] *n* kıtlık

famous ['feɪməs] *adj* ünlü

fan [fæn] *n* vantilatör; **fan belt** *n* soğutucu kayışı; **Does the room have a fan?** Odada vantilatör var mı?

fanatic [fəˈnætɪk] *n* fanatik

fancy ['fænsɪ] *v* tasavvur etmek; **fancy dress** *n* balo kostümü

fantastic [fænˈtæstɪk] *adj* harika

FAQ [ɛf eɪ kjuː] *abbr* sık sorulan sorular

far [fɑː] *adj* uzak ▷ *adv* uzakta; **Far East** *n* Uzak Doğu; **How far are we from the beach?** Plajdan ne kadar uzaktayız?; **How far are we from the bus station?** Otobüs terminaline ne kadar uzaktayız?; **How far is it?** Ne kadar uzak?; **How far is the bank?** Banka buraya ne kadar uzakta?; **Is it far?** Uzak mı?; **It's not far** Uzak değil; **It's quite far** Oldukça uzak

fare [fɛə] *n* yolcu

farewell [ˌfɛəˈwɛl] *excl* elveda!

farm [fɑːm] *n* çiftlik

farmer ['fɑːmə] *n* çiftçi

farmhouse ['fɑːmˌhaʊs] *n* çiftlik evi

farming ['fɑːmɪŋ] *n* çiftçilik

Faroe Islands ['fɛərəʊ 'aɪləndz] *npl* Faroe Adaları

fascinating ['fæsɪˌneɪtɪŋ] *adj* büyüleyici

fashion ['fæʃən] *n* moda

fashionable ['fæʃənəbʰl] *adj* modaya uygun

fast [fɑːst] *adj* hızlı ▷ *adv* hızlı; **He was driving too fast** Çok hızlı gidiyordu

fat [fæt] *adj* şişman ▷ *n* yağ

fatal ['feɪtʰl] *adj* ölümcül

fate [feɪt] *n* kader

father ['fɑːðə] *n* baba

father-in-law ['fɑːðə ɪn lɔː] (**fathers-in-law**) *n* kayınpeder

fault [fɔːlt] *n (defect)* hata, *(mistake)* hata; **It wasn't my fault** Hata bende değildi

faulty ['fɔːltɪ] *adj* hatalı

fauna ['fɔːnə] *npl* hayvanat

favour ['feɪvə] *n* yardım

favourite ['feɪvərɪt; 'feɪvrɪt] *adj*
gözde ▷ *n* gözde

fax [fæks] *n* faks ▷ *v* fakslamak; **Do
you have a fax?** Faksınız var mı?;
How much is it to send a fax?
Faks göndermek ne kadar?; **I
want to send a fax** Faks çekmek
istiyorum; **Is there a fax machine
I can use?** Kullanabileceğim bir
faks makinesi var mı?; **Please
resend your fax** Faksınızı bir
daha gönderin; **There is a
problem with your fax**
Faksınızda bir sorun var; **What is
the fax number?** Faks numarası
nedir?

fear [fɪə] *n* korku ▷ *v* korkmak

feasible ['fiːzəbəl] *adj* uygulanabilir

feather ['fɛðə] *n* tüy

feature ['fiːtʃə] *n* özellik

February ['fɛbrʊərɪ] *n* Şubat

fed up [fɛd ʌp] *adj* bıkmış

fee [fiː] *n* ücret; **entrance fee** *n*
giriş ücreti; **tuition fees** *npl*
öğretim ücreti; **Is there a
booking fee to pay?** Yer ayırtmak
için ücret ödemek gerekiyor mu?

feed [fiːd] *v* beslemek ▷ *n* yayın

feedback ['fiːdˌbæk] *n* geribildirim

feel [fiːl] *v* hissetmek

feeling ['fiːlɪŋ] *n* his

feet [fiːt] *npl* ayaklar; **My feet are
sore** Ayaklarım ağrıyor

felt [fɛlt] *n* keçe

female ['fiːmeɪl] *adj* kadın ▷ *n*
kadın

feminine ['fɛmɪnɪn] *adj* kadınsı

feminist ['fɛmɪnɪst] *n* feminist

fence [fɛns] *n* çit (tahta, tel örgü)

fennel ['fɛnəl] *n* rezene

fern [fɜːn] *n* eğrelti otu

ferret ['fɛrɪt] *n* yaban gelinciği

ferry ['fɛrɪ] *n* feribot; **Where do
we catch the ferry to...?**
... feribotuna nereden binebiliriz?

fertile ['fɜːtaɪl] *adj* doğurgan

fertilizer ['fɜːtɪˌlaɪzə] *n* gübre

festival ['fɛstɪvəl] *n* festival

fetch [fɛtʃ] *v* getirmek

fever ['fiːvə] *n* ateş (sağlık); **hay
fever** *n* saman nezlesi; **He has a
fever** Ateşi çok yüksek

few [fjuː] *adj* birkaç ▷ *pron* birkaç

fewer [fjuːə] *adj* daha az (sayıca)

fiancé [fɪˈɒnseɪ] *n* nişanlı (erkek)

fiancée [fɪˈɒnseɪ] *n* nişanlı
(kadın)

fibre ['faɪbə] *n* fibre

fibreglass ['faɪbəˌglɑːs] *n* cam
yünü

fiction ['fɪkʃən] *n* kurgu; **science
fiction** *n* bilim kurgu

field [fiːld] *n* tarla; **playing field** *n*
oyun alanı

fierce [fɪəs] *adj* azgın

fifteen ['fɪf'tiːn] *number* onbeş

fifteenth ['fɪf'tiːnθ] *adj* onbeşinci

fifth [fɪfθ] *adj* beşinci

fifty ['fɪftɪ] *number* elli

fifty-fifty ['fɪftɪ'fɪftɪ] *adj* yarı
yarıya ▷ *adv* yarı yarıya

fig [fɪg] *n* incir

fight [faɪt] *n* dövüş ▷ *v* savaşmak

fighting [faɪtɪŋ] *n* dövüşme

figure ['fɪgə; 'fɪgjər] *n* şekil

figure out ['fɪgə aʊt] *v* çözmek

Fiji ['fiːdʒiː; fiːˈdʒiː] *n* Fiji

file [faɪl] *n* (folder) dosya, (tool)
eğe ▷ *v* (folder) dosyalamak,
(smoothing) törpülemek

Filipino, Filipina [ˌfɪlɪ'piːnəʊ, ˌfɪlɪ'piːna] *adj* Filipinli ▷ *n* Filipinli

fill [fɪl] *v* doldurmak *(içini)*

fillet ['fɪlɪt] *n* fileto ▷ *v* fileto kesmek

fill in [fɪl ɪn] *v* doldurmak

fill up [fɪl ʌp] *v* doldurmak *(benzin deposu)*

film [fɪlm] *n* film *(fotoğraf vb)*; **film star** *n* film yıldızı; **horror film** *n* korku filmi; **Are there any films in English?** İngilizce film var mı?; **Can I film here?** Burada film çekebilir miyim?; **Can you develop this film, please?** Bu filmi banyo edebilir misiniz lütfen?; **The film has jammed** Film takıldı; **When does the film start?** Film kaçta başlıyor; **Where can we go to see a film?** Film görmek için nereye gidebiliriz?; **Which film is on at the cinema?** Sinemada hangi film oynuyor?

filter ['fɪltə] *n* filtre ▷ *v* süzmek

filthy ['fɪlθɪ] *adj* iğrenç

final ['faɪnᵊl] *adj* son ▷ *n* final

finalize ['faɪnəˌlaɪz] *v* sonlandırmak

finally ['faɪnəlɪ] *adv* sonunda

finance [fɪ'næns; 'faɪnæns] *n* finans ▷ *v* finanse etmek

financial [fɪ'nænʃəl; faɪ-] *adj* mali; **financial year** *n* mali yıl

find [faɪnd] *v* bulmak *(aradığı bir şeyi)*

find out [faɪnd aʊt] *v* bulmak *(keşfetmek)*

fine [faɪn] *adj* çok iyi ▷ *adv* pekala ▷ *n* ceza; **How much is the fine?** Ceza ne kadar?; **Where do I pay the fine?** Cezayı nereye yatıracağım?

finger ['fɪŋgə] *n* parmak; **index finger** *n* işaret parmağı

fingernail ['fɪŋgəˌneɪl] *n* tırnak

fingerprint ['fɪŋgəˌprɪnt] *n* parmak izi

finish ['fɪnɪʃ] *n* son ▷ *v* bitmek *(son bulmak)*

finished ['fɪnɪʃt] *adj* hazır

Finland ['fɪnlənd] *n* Finlandiya

Finn ['fɪn] *n* Fin

Finnish ['fɪnɪʃ] *adj* Fin ▷ *n* Finli

fir [fɜː] *n* **fir (tree)** *n* köknar ağacı

fire [faɪə] *n* yangın; **fire alarm** *n* yangın alarmı; **fire brigade** *n* itfaiye; **fire escape** *n* yangın çıkışı; **fire extinguisher** *n* yangın söndürücü; **Fire!** Yangın var!

firefighter ['faɪəˌfaɪtə] *n* itfaiye eri

fireman, firemen ['faɪəmən, 'faɪəmɛn] *n* itfaiyeci

fireplace ['faɪəˌpleɪs] *n* şömine

firewall ['faɪəˌwɔːl] *n* güvenlik duvarı

fireworks ['faɪəˌwɜːks] *npl* havai fişek gösterileri

firm [fɜːm] *adj* sıkı ▷ *n* firma

first [fɜːst] *adj* ilk ▷ *adv* ilkin ▷ *n* ilk; **first aid** *n* ilk yardım; **first name** *n* ön ad; **This is my first trip to...** Bu benim... a ilk gelişim; **When is the first bus to...?** ... a ilk otobüs kaçta?

first-class ['fɜːst'klɑːs] *adj* birinci sınıf

firstly ['fɜːstlɪ] *adv* öncelikle

fiscal ['fɪskᵊl] *adj* mali; **fiscal year** *n* mali yıl

fish [fɪʃ] *n* balık ▷ *v* balık avlamak;

freshwater fish *n* tatlısu balığı;
Am I allowed to fish here?
Burada balık avlayabilir miyim?;
Can we fish here? Burada balık
avlanabilir mi?; **Could you
prepare a meal without fish?**
İçinde balık olmayan bir yemek
yapabilir misiniz?; **I don't eat fish**
Balık yemiyorum; **I'll have the
fish** Balık alayım; **Is the fish fresh
or frozen?** Balıklarınız taze mi,
dondurulmuş mu?; **Is this cooked
in fish stock?** Bu yemekte balık
suyu var mı?; **What fish dishes do
you have?** Balıklardan ne var?;
Where can I go fishing? Nerede
balık tutabilirim?

fisherman, fishermen
['fɪʃəmən, 'fɪʃəmɛn] *n* balıkçı

fishing ['fɪʃɪŋ] *n* balık avlamak;
fishing boat *n* balıkçı teknesi;
fishing rod *n* olta; **fishing tackle**
n olta

fishmonger ['fɪʃˌmʌŋgə] *n* balıkçı
(dükkan)

fist [fɪst] *n* yumruk

fit [fɪt] *adj* uygun ▷ *n* uyma ▷ *v*
uydurmak; **fitted kitchen** *n* hazır
mutfak; **fitted sheet** *n* fitted
çarşaf; **fitting room** *n* soyunma
odası *(mağaza)*

fit in [fɪt ɪn] *v* uymak

five [faɪv] *number* beş

fix [fɪks] *v* sabitlemek

fixed [fɪkst] *adj* sabitlenmiş

fizzy ['fɪzɪ] *adj* köpüklü

flabby ['flæbɪ] *adj* gevşek *(sarkmış
karın vb)*

flag [flæg] *n* bayrak

flame [fleɪm] *n* alev

flamingo [flə'mɪŋgəʊ] *n*
flamingo

flammable ['flæməbᵊl] *adj* yanıcı

flan [flæn] *n* turta

flannel ['flænᵊl] *n* fanila

flap [flæp] *v* kanat çırpmak

flash [flæʃ] *n* flaş ▷ *v* parlamak;
The flash is not working Flaş
çalışmıyor

flashlight ['flæʃˌlaɪt] *n* fener

flask [flɑːsk] *n* cep matarası

flat [flæt] *adj* düz *(yassı)* ▷ *n*
apartman dairesi; **studio flat** *n*
stüdyo daire

flat-screen ['flætˌskriːn] *adj* düz
ekran

flatter ['flætə] *v* pohpohlamak

flattered ['flætəd] *adj*
pohpohlanmış

flavour ['fleɪvə] *n* lezzet

flavouring ['fleɪvərɪŋ] *n* lezzet
katıcı

flaw [flɔː] *n* kusur

flea [fliː] *n* pire; **flea market** *n* bit
pazarı

flee [fliː] *v* kaçmak

fleece [fliːs] *n* post

fleet [fliːt] *n* filo

flex [flɛks] *n* kablo

flexible ['flɛksɪbᵊl] *adj* esnek

flexitime ['flɛksɪˌtaɪm] *n* esnek
çalışma saati

flight [flaɪt] *n* uçuş; **charter flight**
n tarifesiz uçuş; **flight attendant**
n uçuş hostesi; **scheduled flight** *n*
tarifeli uçuş; **Are there any cheap
flights?** Ucuz tarifeli uçuşunuz
var mı?; **I'd like to cancel my
flight** Uçuşumu iptal ettirmek
istiyorum; **I'd like to change my**

flight Uçuşumu değiştirmek istiyorum; **The flight has been delayed** Uçuşunuz gecikmeli; **Which gate for the flight to...?** ... uçağı hangi uçuş kapısında?

fling [flɪŋ] v savurmak

flip-flops ['flɪp'flɒpz] npl tokyo (terlik)

flippers ['flɪpəz] npl yüzgeç

flirt [flɜːt] n flört ▷ v flört etmek

float [fləʊt] n sal ▷ v yüzdürmek

flock [flɒk] n sürü

flood [flʌd] n sel ▷ vi su baskınına uğramak ▷ vt/vi su basmak

flooding ['flʌdɪŋ] n su basması

floodlight ['flʌd,laɪt] n projektör ışığı

floor [flɔː] n yer; **ground floor** n zemin kat

flop [flɒp] n fiyasko

floppy ['flɒpɪ] adj **floppy disk** n disket

flora ['flɔːrə] npl flora

florist ['flɒrɪst] n çiçekçi

flour ['flaʊə] n un

flow [fləʊ] v akmak

flower ['flaʊə] n çiçek ▷ v çiçek açmak

flu [fluː] n grip; **bird flu** n kuş gribi; **I had flu recently** Yakınlarda grip atlattım; **I've got flu** Grip geçiriyorum

fluent ['fluːənt] adj akıcı

fluorescent [ˌfluəˈrɛsᵊnt] adj floresan

flush [flʌʃ] n yüz kızarması ▷ v yüzü kızarmak

flute [fluːt] n flüt

fly [flaɪ] n sinek ▷ v uçmak

fly away [flaɪ ə'weɪ] v uçup gitmek

foal [fəʊl] n tay

foam [fəʊm] n **shaving foam** n traş köpüğü

focus ['fəʊkəs] n odak ▷ v odaklanmak

foetus ['fiːtəs] n cenin

fog [fɒg] n sis; **fog light** n sis lambası

foggy ['fɒgɪ] adj sisli

foil [fɔɪl] n folyo

fold [fəʊld] n kat (giysi, kağıt vb) ▷ v katlamak

folder ['fəʊldə] n dosya

folding [fəʊldɪŋ] adj katlanır

folklore ['fəʊk,lɔː] n folklor

follow ['fɒləʊ] v izlemek, (social media) takip et

following ['fɒləʊɪŋ] adj izleyen

food [fuːd] n yiyecek; **food poisoning** n gıda zehirlenmesi; **food processor** n mutfak robotu; **Do you have food?** Yiyecek satıyor musunuz?

fool [fuːl] n ahmak ▷ v kandırmak

foot, feet [fʊt, fiːt] n ayak; **My feet are a size six** Ayakkabı numaram altı

football ['fʊt,bɔːl] n futbol; **American football** n Amerikan futbolu; **football match** n futbol maçı; **football player** n futbolcu; **I'd like to see a football match** Futbol maçı görmek isterdim; **Let's play football** Futbol oynayalım

footballer ['fʊt,bɔːlə] n futbolcu

footpath ['fʊt,pɑːθ] n patika

footprint ['fʊt,prɪnt] n ayakizi

footstep ['fʊt,stɛp] n adım

for [fɔː; fə] prep için; **I want to hire**

a car for the weekend Hafta sonu için bir araba kiralamak istiyorum; **I'd like to book a table for four people for tonight at eight o'clock** Bu akşam saat sekiz için dört kişilik bir masa ayırtmak istiyordum; **I'd like two tickets for tonight** Bu akşam için iki bilet almak istiyorum

forbid [fə'bɪd] v yasaklamak

forbidden [fə'bɪdᵊn] adj yasak

force [fɔːs] n güç (kuvvet) ▷ v zorlamak; **Air Force** n Hava Kuvvetleri

forecast ['fɔːˌkɑːst] n tahmin (hava, borsa vb); **What's the weather forecast?** Hava tahmini nasıl?

foreground ['fɔːˌgraʊnd] n ön plan

forehead ['fɒrɪd; 'fɔːˌhɛd] n alın

foreign ['fɒrɪn] adj yabancı

foreigner ['fɒrɪnə] n yabancı

foresee [fɔː'siː] v öngörmek

forest ['fɒrɪst] n orman

forever [fɔː'rɛvə; fə-] adv ebediyen

forge [fɔːdʒ] v demir dövmek

forgery ['fɔːdʒərɪ] n sahte

forget [fə'gɛt] v unutmak

forgive [fə'gɪv] v bağışlamak

forgotten [fə'gɒtᵊn] adj unutulmuş

fork [fɔːk] n çatal; **Could I have a clean fork please?** Temiz bir çatal alabilir miyim lütfen?

form [fɔːm] n form; **application form** n başvuru formu; **order form** n sipariş formu

formal ['fɔːməl] adj resmi

formality [fɔː'mælɪtɪ] n formalite

format ['fɔːmæt] n format ▷ v formatlamak

former ['fɔːmə] adj eski (önceki)

formerly ['fɔːməlɪ] adv önceki

formula ['fɔːmjʊlə] n formül

fort [fɔːt] n hisar

fortnight ['fɔːtˌnaɪt] n iki hafta

fortunate ['fɔːtʃənɪt] adj şanslı

fortunately ['fɔːtʃənɪtlɪ] adv neyse ki

fortune ['fɔːtʃən] n servet

forty ['fɔːtɪ] number kırk

forum ['fɔːrəm] n forum

forward ['fɔːwəd] adv ileriye ▷ v iletlemek; **forward slash** n eğik çizgi; **lean forward** v öne eğilmek

foster ['fɒstə] v koruyucu aile olmak; **foster child** n koruyucu aile bakımındaki çocuk

foul [faʊl] adj kirli ▷ n faul

foundations [faʊn'deɪʃənz] npl vakıflar

fountain ['faʊntɪn] n çeşme; **fountain pen** n dolmakalem

four [fɔː] number dört

fourteen ['fɔː'tiːn] number ondört

fourteenth ['fɔː'tiːnθ] adj ondördüncü

fourth [fɔːθ] adj dördüncü

fox [fɒks] n tilki

fracture ['fræktʃə] n kırık

fragile ['frædʒaɪl] adj kırılgan

frail [freɪl] adj hastalıklı

frame [freɪm] n çerçeve; **picture frame** n resim çerçevesi; **Zimmer® frame** n yürüteç

France [frɑːns] n Fransa

frankly ['fræŋklɪ] adv içtenlikle

frantic ['fræntɪk] adj çılgın

fraud [frɔːd] n dolandırıcılık (sahte para vb)

freckles ['frɛkəlz] npl çiller

free [friː] adj (no cost) bedava, (no restraint) özgür ▷ v özgürlüğünü kavratmak; **free kick** n frikik

freedom ['friːdəm] n özgürlük

freelance ['friːˌlɑːns] adj bağımsız ▷ adv bağımsız olarak

freeze [friːz] v dondurmak

freezer ['friːzə] n dondurucu (derin)

freezing ['friːzɪŋ] adj dondurucu (çok soğuk)

freight [freɪt] n nakliye

French [frɛntʃ] adj Fransız ▷ n Fransız; **French beans** npl çalı fasulyesi; **French horn** n korno

Frenchman, Frenchmen ['frɛntʃmən, 'frɛntʃmɛn] n Fransız erkek

Frenchwoman, Frenchwomen ['frɛntʃwʊmən, 'frɛntʃwɪmɪn] n Fransız kadın

frequency ['friːkwənsɪ] n sıklık

frequent ['friːkwənt] adj sık; **How frequent are the buses to...?** ... otobüsü ne sıklıkta geliyor?

fresh [frɛʃ] adj taze

freshen up ['frɛʃən ʌp] v ferahlamak

fret [frɛt] v endişe etmek

Friday ['fraɪdɪ] n Cuma; **Good Friday** n Kutsal Cuma; **on Friday the thirty first of December** Otuz bir Aralık Cuma günü; **on Friday** Cuma günü

fridge [frɪdʒ] n buzdolabı

fried [fraɪd] adj kızarmış

friend [frɛnd] n arkadaş ▷ v arkadaş; **I'm here with my**

friends Arkadaşlarımla geldim

friendly ['frɛndlɪ] adj dostça

friendship ['frɛndʃɪp] n dostluk

fright [fraɪt] n korku

frighten ['fraɪtən] v korkutmak

frightened ['fraɪtənd] adj korkmuş

frightening ['fraɪtənɪŋ] adj ürkünç

fringe [frɪndʒ] n kahkül

frog [frɒg] n kurbağa

from [frɒm; frəm] prep den, dan; **How far are we from the beach?** Plajdan ne kadar uzaktayız?

front [frʌnt] adj ön ▷ n ön

frontier ['frʌntɪə; frʌn'tɪə] n cephe

frost [frɒst] n don (hava)

frosting ['frɒstɪŋ] n şekerli kek süsü

frosty ['frɒstɪ] adj buzlu

frown [fraʊn] v kaşlarını çatmak

frozen ['frəʊzən] adj donmuş

fruit [fruːt] n (botany) meyve, (collectively) meyve; **fruit juice** n meyve suyu; **fruit machine** n slot makinesi; **fruit salad** n meyve salatası; **passion fruit** n çarkıfelek meyvası

frustrated [frʌ'streɪtɪd] adj engellenmiş

fry [fraɪ] v kızartmak; **frying pan** n kızartma tavası

fuel [fjʊəl] n yakıt

fulfil [fʊl'fɪl] v gerçekleştirmek

full [fʊl] adj dolu; **full moon** n dolunay; **full stop** n nokta (gramer)

full-time ['fʊlˌtaɪm] adj tam gün ▷ adv tam gün

fully ['fʊlɪ] *adv* tam olarak

fumes [fjuːmz] *npl* duman *(pis kokulu)*; **exhaust fumes** *npl* egzos gazı

fun [fʌn] *adj* eğlendirici ▷ *n* eğlence

funds [fʌndz] *npl* parasal kaynak

funeral ['fjuːnərəl] *n* cenaze; **funeral parlour** *n* cenazenin gömülmeye ya da yakılmaya hazırlandığı oda

funfair ['fʌnˌfɛə] *n* lunapark

funnel ['fʌnəl] *n* huni

funny ['fʌnɪ] *adj* komik

fur [fɜː] *n* kürk; **fur coat** *n* kürk *(giysi)*

furious ['fjʊərɪəs] *adj* öfkeden çıldırmış

furnished ['fɜːnɪʃt] *adj* mobilyalı

furniture ['fɜːnɪtʃə] *n* mobilya

further ['fɜːðə] *adj* daha ileri ▷ *adv* daha ileriye; **further education** *n* ileri eğitim

fuse [fjuːz] *n* sigorta *(elektrik)*; **fuse box** *n* sigorta kutusu; **A fuse has blown** Sigorta attı; **Can you mend a fuse?** Sigortayı tamir eder misiniz?

fuss [fʌs] *n* yaygara

fussy ['fʌsɪ] *adj* yaygaracı

future ['fjuːtʃə] *adj* gelecek ▷ *n* gelecek

g

Gabon [gəˈbɒn] *n* Gabon

gain [geɪn] *n* kazanç ▷ *v* kazanmak

gale [geɪl] *n* şiddetli rüzgar

gallery ['gælərɪ] *n* galeri; **art gallery** *n* sanat galerisi

gallop ['gæləp] *n* dörtnala gidiş ▷ *v* dörtnala koşmak

gallstone ['gɔːlˌstəʊn] *n* safra kesesi taşı

Gambia ['gæmbɪə] *n* Gambiya

gamble ['gæmbəl] *v* kumar oynamak

gambler ['gæmblə] *n* kumarcı

gambling ['gæmblɪŋ] *n* kumar

game [geɪm] *n* oyun; **board game** *n* aile oyunları; **games console** *n* oyun konsolu; **Can I play video games?** Oyun oynayabilir miyim?

gang [gæŋ] *n* çete

gangster ['gæŋstə] *n* gangster

gap [gæp] *n* gedik *(yer)*

garage ['gærɑːʒ; -rɪdʒ] *n* garaj;

Which is the key for the garage?
Hangisi garaj anahtarı?

garbage ['gɑːbɪdʒ] n çöp

garden ['gɑːdᵊn] n bahçe; **garden centre** n bahçe merkezi; **Can we visit the gardens?** Bahçeleri gezebilir miyiz?

gardener ['gɑːdnə] n bahçıvan

gardening ['gɑːdᵊnɪŋ] n bahçecilik

garlic ['gɑːlɪk] n sarımsak; **Is there any garlic in it?** Bunda sarımsak var mı?

garment ['gɑːmənt] n giysi *(kıyafet)*

gas [gæs] n gaz; **gas cooker** n gazlı ocak; **natural gas** n doğal gaz; **I can smell gas** Gaz kokusu alıyorum; **Where is the gas meter?** Gaz sayacı nerede?

gasket ['gæskɪt] n conta

gate [geɪt] n kapı; **Please go to gate...** ... numaralı kapıya gidiniz; **Which gate for the flight to...?** ... uçağı hangi uçuş kapısında?

gateau, gateaux ['gætəʊ, 'gætəʊz] n kremalı pasta

gather ['gæðə] v toplanmak

gauge [geɪdʒ] n ölçek ▷ v ölçmek

gaze [geɪz] v gözünü dikmek

gear [gɪə] n *(equipment)* vites, *(mechanism)* dişli; **gear lever** n vites kolu; **gear stick** n vites kolu; **Does the bike have gears?** Bisiklet vitesli mi?; **The gears don't work** Vitesler çalışmıyor

gearbox ['gɪəbɒks] n vites kutusu

gearshift ['gɪəʃɪft] n vites kolu

gel [dʒɛl] n jöle *(saç)*; **hair gel** n saç jölesi

gem [dʒɛm] n mücevher

Gemini ['dʒɛmɪˌnaɪ; -ˌniː] n İkizler burcu

gender ['dʒɛndə] n cinsiyet

gene [dʒiːn] n gen

general ['dʒɛnərəl; 'dʒɛnrəl] adj genel ▷ n genel; **general anaesthetic** n genel anestezi; **general election** n genel seçim; **general knowledge** n genel kültür

generalize ['dʒɛnrəˌlaɪz] v genellemek

generally ['dʒɛnrəlɪ] adv genellikle

generation [ˌdʒɛnə'reɪʃən] n kuşak *(jenerasyon)*

generator ['dʒɛnəˌreɪtə] n jeneratör

generosity [ˌdʒɛnə'rɒsɪtɪ] n cömertlik

generous ['dʒɛnərəs; 'dʒɛnrəs] adj cömert

genetic [dʒɪ'nɛtɪk] adj genetik

genetically-modified [dʒɪ'nɛtɪklɪ'mɒdɪˌfaɪd] adj genetik olarak değiştirilmiş

genetics [dʒɪ'nɛtɪks] n genetik bilimi

genius ['dʒiːnɪəs; -njəs] n dahi *(zeki)*

gentle ['dʒɛntᵊl] adj kibar

gentleman, gentlemen ['dʒɛntᵊlmən, 'dʒɛntᵊlmɛn] n centilmen

gently ['dʒɛntlɪ] adv kibarca

gents' [dʒɛnts] n erkekler tuvaleti; **Where is the gents?** Erkekler tuvaleti nerede?

genuine ['dʒɛnjʊɪn] adj gerçek *(mücevher)*

geography [dʒɪ'ɒgrəfɪ] n coğrafya

geology [dʒɪ'ɒlədʒɪ] n jeoloji

Georgia ['dʒɔːdʒə] n (country) Gürcistan, (US state) Georgia (Amerikan eyaleti)

Georgian ['dʒɔːdʒən] adj Georgia'ya ait ▷ n (inhabitant of Georgia) Gürcü

geranium [dʒɪ'reɪnɪəm] n sardunya

gerbil ['dʒɜːbɪl] n çöl faresi

geriatric [,dʒerɪ'ætrɪk] adj yaşlılar ▷ n yaşlılık

germ [dʒɜːm] n mikrop

German ['dʒɜːmən] adj Alman ▷ n (language) Almanca (dil), (person) Alman; **German measles** n kızamıkçık

Germany ['dʒɜːmənɪ] n Almanya

gesture ['dʒestʃə] n jest

get [ɡet] v almak, (to a place) almak

get away [ɡet ə'weɪ] v sıvışmak

get back [ɡet bæk] v geri getirmek

get in [ɡet ɪn] v mekana girmek

get into [ɡet 'ɪntə] v girmek

get off [ɡet ɒf] v inmek

get on [ɡet ɒn] v binmek

get out [ɡet aʊt] v çıkmak

get over [ɡet 'əʊvə] v toparlanmak

get together [ɡet tə'ɡeðə] v bir araya gelmek

get up [ɡet ʌp] v kalkmak

Ghana ['ɡɑːnə] n Gana

Ghanaian [ɡɑː'neɪən] adj Gana ▷ n Ganalı

ghost [ɡəʊst] n hayalet

giant ['dʒaɪənt] adj dev gibi ▷ n dev

gift [ɡɪft] n armağan; **gift shop** n hediye dükkanı; **gift voucher** n hediye çeki; **This is a gift for you** Bu armağan sizin için

gifted ['ɡɪftɪd] adj yetenekli

gigantic [dʒaɪ'ɡæntɪk] adj devasa

giggle ['ɡɪɡəl] v kıkırdamak

gin [dʒɪn] n cin (alkol); **I'll have a gin and tonic, please** Ben bir cin tonik alayım lütfen

ginger ['dʒɪndʒə] adj kızılımsı sarı saçlı ▷ n zencefil

giraffe [dʒɪ'rɑːf; -'ræf] n zürafa

girl [ɡɜːl] n kız

girlfriend ['ɡɜːl,frend] n kız arkadaş; **I have a girlfriend** Kız arkadaşım var

give [ɡɪv] v vermek

give back [ɡɪv bæk] v geri vermek

give in [ɡɪv ɪn] v yenilgiyi kabullenmek

give out [ɡɪv aʊt] v dağıtmak (vermek)

give up [ɡɪv ʌp] v vazgeçmek

glacier ['ɡlæsɪə; 'ɡleɪs-] n buzul

glad [ɡlæd] adj memnun

glamorous ['ɡlæmərəs] adj göz kamaştırıcı

glance [ɡlɑːns] n bakış ▷ v gözatmak

gland [ɡlænd] n beze

glare [ɡleə] v öfkeyle bakmak

glaring ['ɡleərɪŋ] adj bariz

glass [ɡlɑːs] n cam, (vessel) cam bardak; **magnifying glass** n büyüteç; **stained glass** n vitray

glasses ['ɡlɑːsɪz] npl gözlük; **Can you repair my glasses?** Gözlüklerimi tamir edebilir misiniz?

glazing ['ɡleɪzɪŋ] n **double glazing** n çift cam

glider ['ɡlaɪdə] n planör

gliding ['ɡlaɪdɪŋ] n planörle uçma

global ['gləʊbᵊl] *adj* küresel; **global warming** *n* küresel ısınma

globalization [ˌgləʊbᵊlaɪ'zeɪʃən] *n* küreselleşme

globe [gləʊb] *n* yerküre

gloomy ['glu:mɪ] *adj* kasvetli

glorious ['glɔ:rɪəs] *adj* görkemli

glory ['glɔ:rɪ] *n* zafer

glove [glʌv] *n* eldiven; **glove compartment** *n* torpido gözü; **oven glove** *n* fırın eldiveni; **rubber gloves** *npl* lastik eldiven

glucose ['glu:kəʊz; -kəʊs] *n* glükoz

glue [glu:] *n* tutkal ▷ *v* yapıştırmak

gluten ['glu:tᵊn] *n* glüten

GM [dʒi: ɛm] *abbr* GM

go [gəʊ] *v* gitmek; **I'd like to go home** Eve gitmek istiyorum; **I'm going to...** ... a gitmek istiyorum; **We'd like to go to...** ... a gitmek istiyorduk

go after [gəʊ 'ɑ:ftə] *v* çabalamak

go ahead [gəʊ ə'hɛd] *v* önden gitmek

goal [gəʊl] *n* gol

goalkeeper ['gəʊlˌki:pə] *n* kaleci

goat [gəʊt] *n* keçi

go away [gəʊ ə'weɪ] *v* yola çıkmak

go back [gəʊ bæk] *v* dönmek

go by [gəʊ baɪ] *v* geçmek

god [gɒd] *n* tanrı

godchild, godchildren ['gɒdˌtʃaɪld, 'gɒdˌtʃɪldrən] *n* vaftiz çocuğu

goddaughter ['gɒdˌdɔ:tə] *n* vaftiz kızı

godfather ['gɒdˌfɑ:ðə] *n (baptism)* isim babası *(vaftiz)*, *(criminal leader)* baba *(mafya)*

godmother ['gɒdˌmʌðə] *n* isim annesi

go down [gəʊ daʊn] *v* azalmak

godson ['gɒdˌsʌn] *n* vaftiz oğlu

goggles ['gɒgᵊlz] *npl* koruma gözlüğü

go in [gəʊ ɪn] *v* girmek *(içeriye)*

gold [gəʊld] *n* altın *(metal)*

golden ['gəʊldən] *adj* altın *(metal)*

goldfish ['gəʊldˌfɪʃ] *n* Japon balığı

gold-plated ['gəʊld'pleɪtɪd] *adj* altın kaplama

golf [gɒlf] *n* golf; **golf club** *n (stick)* golf sopası, *(society)* golf klübü; **golf course** *n* golf sahası; **Do they hire out golf clubs?** Golf sopaları kiralıyorlar mı?; **Is there a public golf course near here?** Buraya yakın bir golf sahası var mı?; **Where can I play golf?** Nerede golf oynayabilirim?

gone [gɒn] *adj* geçmiş

good [gʊd] *adj* iyi

goodbye [ˌgʊd'baɪ] *excl* hoşçakal!

good-looking ['gʊd'lʊkɪŋ] *adj* yakışıklı

good-natured ['gʊd'neɪtʃəd] *adj* iyi huylu

goods [gʊdz] *npl* mallar

go off [gəʊ ɒf] *v* kapamak

go on [gəʊ ɒn] *v* devam etmek

goose, geese [gu:s, gi:s] *n* kaz; **goose pimples** *npl* diken diken olmuş tüyler

gooseberry ['gʊzbərɪ; -brɪ] *n* bektaşi üzümü

go out [gəʊ aʊt] *v* dışarı çıkmak

go past [gəʊ pɑ:st] *v* yanından geçmek

gorgeous ['gɔːdʒəs] *adj* çok güzel

gorilla [gə'rɪlə] *n* goril

go round [gəʊ raʊnd] *v* idare etmek

gospel ['gɒspəl] *n* incil

gossip ['gɒsɪp] *n* dedikodu ▷ *v* dedikodu yapmak

go through [gəʊ θruː] *v* geçirmek

go up [gəʊ ʌp] *v* yükselmek

government ['gʌvənmənt; 'gʌvəmənt] *n* hükümet

gown [gaʊn] *n* **dressing gown** *n* sabahlık

GP [dʒiː piː] *abbr* pratisyen hekim

GPS [dʒiː piː ɛs] *abbr* GPS sistemi

grab [græb] *v* kavramak

graceful ['greɪsfʊl] *adj* zarif

grade [greɪd] *n* derece *(düzey)*

gradual ['grædjʊəl] *adj* derece derece

gradually ['grædjʊəlɪ] *adv* adım adım

graduate ['grædjʊɪt] *n* üniversite mezunu

graduation [ˌgrædjʊ'eɪʃən] *n* mezuniyet

graffiti, graffito [græ'fiːtiː, græ'fiːtəʊ] *npl* grafiti

grain [greɪn] *n* tahıl tanesi

grammar ['græmə] *n* gramer

grammatical [grə'mætɪkəl] *adj* gramatik

gramme [græm] *n* gram

grand [grænd] *adj* gösterişli

grandchild ['grænˌtʃaɪld] *n* torun; **grandchildren** *npl* torunlar

granddad ['grænˌdæd] *n* dede

granddaughter ['grænˌdɔːtə] *n* kız torun

grandfather ['grænˌfɑːðə] *n* dede

grandma ['grænˌmɑː] *n* nine

grandmother ['grænˌmʌðə] *n* büyükanne

grandpa ['grænˌpɑː] *n* dede

grandparents ['grænˌpɛərəntz] *npl* büyükanne ve büyükbaba

grandson ['grænsʌn; 'grænd-] *n* erkek torun

granite ['grænɪt] *n* granit

granny ['grænɪ] *n* nine

grant [grɑːnt] *n* fon *(destek)*

grape [greɪp] *n* üzüm

grapefruit ['greɪpˌfruːt] *n* greyfurt

graph [grɑːf; græf] *n* grafik

graphics ['græfɪks] *npl* grafik

grasp [grɑːsp] *v* kavramak

grass [grɑːs] *n* *(informer)* muhbir, *(marijuana)* ot *(esrar)*, *(plant)* ot

grasshopper ['grɑːsˌhɒpə] *n* çekirge

grate [greɪt] *v* rendelemek

grateful ['greɪtfʊl] *adj* müteşekkir

grave [greɪv] *n* mezar

gravel ['grævəl] *n* çakıl

gravestone ['greɪvˌstəʊn] *n* mezar taşı

graveyard ['greɪvˌjɑːd] *n* mezarlık

gravy ['greɪvɪ] *n* et sosu

grease [griːs] *n* yağ

greasy ['griːzɪ; -sɪ] *adj* yağlı

great [greɪt] *adj* büyük *(müthiş)*

Great Britain ['greɪt 'brɪtən] *n* İngiltere

great-grandfather ['greɪt'grænˌfɑːðə] *n* dedenin babası

great-grandmother ['greɪt'grænˌmʌðə] *n* ninenin annesi

Greece [griːs] *n* Yunanistan

greedy ['gri:dɪ] *adj* açgözlü

Greek [gri:k] *adj* Yunan ▷ *n* *(language)* Yunanca *(dil)*, *(person)* Yunanlı *(kişi)*

green [gri:n] *adj* *(colour)* yeşil, *(inexperienced)* acemi ▷ *n* yeşil; **green salad** *n* yeşil salata

greengrocer's ['gri:n,grəʊsəz] *n* manav

greenhouse ['gri:n,haʊs] *n* sera

Greenland ['gri:nlənd] *n* Grönland

greet [gri:t] *v* selamlamak

greeting ['gri:tɪŋ] *n* selamlaşma; **greetings card** *n* tebrik kartı

grey [greɪ] *adj* gri

grey-haired [,greɪ'hɛəd] *adj* beyaz saçlı

grid [grɪd] *n* ızgara

grief [gri:f] *n* keder

grill [grɪl] *n* ızgara ▷ *v* ızgara yapmak

grilled [grɪld] *adj* ızgarada

grim [grɪm] *adj* tatsız

grin [grɪn] *n* sırıtış ▷ *v* sırıtmak

grind [graɪnd] *v* öğütmek

grip [grɪp] *v* sımsıkı kavramak

gripping [grɪpɪŋ] *adj* sürükleyici

grit [grɪt] *n* kum

groan [grəʊn] *v* inlemek

grocer ['grəʊsə] *n* bakkal

groceries ['grəʊsərɪz] *npl* yiyecek maddeleri

grocer's ['grəʊsəz] *n* bakkal *(dükkan)*

groom [gru:m; grʊm] *n* seyis, *(bridegroom)* damat *(gelinin kocası)*

grope [grəʊp] *v* elle yoklamak

gross [grəʊs] *adj* *(fat)* şişko, *(income etc.)* hantal

grossly [grəʊslɪ] *adv* kabaca

ground [graʊnd] *n* yer ▷ *v* yere indirmek; **ground floor** *n* zemin kat

group [gru:p] *n* grup; **Are there any reductions for groups?** Grup indirimi var mı?

grouse [graʊs] *n* *(complaint)* şikayet, *(game bird)* orman tavuğu

grow [grəʊ] *vi* büyümek ▷ *vt* bitki yetiştirmek

growl [graʊl] *v* hırlamak

grown-up [grəʊnʌp] *n* erişkin

growth [grəʊθ] *n* büyüme

grow up [grəʊ ʌp] *v* büyümek

grub [grʌb] *n* kurtçuk

grudge [grʌdʒ] *n* kin

gruesome ['gru:səm] *adj* tüyler ürpertici

grumpy ['grʌmpɪ] *adj* huysuz

guarantee [,gærən'ti:] *n* garanti ▷ *v* garanti etmek; **It's still under guarantee** Hala garantisi var

guard [gɑ:d] *n* nöbetçi ▷ *v* korumak; **security guard** *n* güvenlik görevlisi

Guatemala [,gwɑ:tə'mɑ:lə] *n* Guatemala

guess [gɛs] *n* tahmin ▷ *v* sezmek

guest [gɛst] *n* konuk

guesthouse ['gɛst,haʊs] *n* konukevi

guide [gaɪd] *n* rehber *(turizm)* ▷ *v* rehber *(turizm)*; **guide dog** *n* rehber köpek; **guided tour** *n* rehberli tur; **tour guide** *n* tur rehberi; **Can you guide me, please?** Bana rehberlik eder misiniz lütfen; **Do you have a guide to local walks?** Yerel

yürüyüşler için rehberiniz var mı?;
I have a guide dog Rehber
köpeğim var; **Is there a guide
who speaks English?** İngilizce
konuşan bir rehber var mı?

guidebook ['gaɪdˌbʊk] n rehber
(kılavuz)

guilt [gɪlt] n suçluluk

guilty ['gɪltɪ] adj suçlu

Guinea ['gɪnɪ] n Gine; **guinea pig** n
(for experiment) kobay, (rodent)
kobay faresi

guitar [gɪ'tɑː] n gitar

gum [gʌm] n sakız; **chewing gum**
n çiklet

gun [gʌn] n silah; **machine gun** n
makineli tüfek

gust [gʌst] n ani rüzgar

gut [gʌt] n bağırsak

guy [gaɪ] n adam

Guyana [gaɪ'ænə] n Güyan

gym [dʒɪm] n jimnastik salonu

gymnast ['dʒɪmnæst] n
jimnastikçi

gymnastics [dʒɪm'næstɪks] npl
jimnastik

gynaecologist [ˌgaɪnɪ'kɒlədʒɪst]
n jinekolog

gypsy ['dʒɪpsɪ] n çingene

habit ['hæbɪt] n alışkanlık

hack [hæk] v doğramak

hacker ['hækə] n hacker

haddock ['hædək] n mezgit balığı

haemorrhoids ['hɛməˌrɔɪdz] npl
hemoroid

haggle ['hægəl] v pazarlık etmek

hail [heɪl] n dolu (hava) ▷ v dolu
yağmak

hair [hɛə] n saç; **hair gel** n saç
jölesi; **hair spray** n saç spreyi; **Can
you dye my hair, please?** Saçımı
boyar mısınız lütfen?; **Can you
straighten my hair?** Saçımı
düzleştirebilir misiniz?; **I have
greasy hair** Saçım yağlı; **I need
a hair dryer** Saç kurutma
makinesine ihtiyacım var; **My hair
is naturally straight** Saçım
doğuştan düz; **My hair is permed**
Saçım permalı; **What do you
recommend for my hair?** Saçıma

ne tavsiye edersiniz?

hairband ['hɛəˌbænd] n saç bandı

hairbrush ['hɛəˌbrʌʃ] n saç fırçası

haircut ['hɛəˌkʌt] n saç kestirme

hairdo ['hɛəˌduː] n saç modeli

hairdresser ['hɛəˌdrɛsə] n kuaför

hairdresser's ['hɛəˌdrɛsəz] n kuaför

hairdryer ['hɛəˌdraɪə] n saç kurutma makinesi

hairgrip ['hɛəˌɡrɪp] n saç tokası

hairstyle ['hɛəˌstaɪl] n saç modeli

hairy ['hɛərɪ] adj kıllı

Haiti ['heɪtɪ; hɑːˈiːtɪ] n Haiti

half [hɑːf] adj yarım ▷ adv yarı yarıya ▷ n yarım; **half board** n kahvaltı ve akşam yemeği dahil

half-hour ['hɑːfˌaʊə] n yarım saat

half-price ['hɑːfˌpraɪs] adj yarı fiyatı ▷ adv yarı fiyatına

half-term ['hɑːfˌtɜːm] n sömestr tatili

half-time ['hɑːfˌtaɪm] n devre arası

halfway [ˌhɑːfˈweɪ] adv yarı yolda

hall [hɔːl] n salon; **town hall** n belediye binası

hallway ['hɔːlˌweɪ] n antre

halt [hɔːlt] n duraksama

ham [hæm] n jambon

hamburger ['hæmˌbɜːɡə] n hamburger

hammer ['hæmə] n çekiç

hammock ['hæmək] n hamak

hamster ['hæmstə] n hamster

hand [hænd] n el ▷ v vermek; **hand luggage** n el bagajı; **Where can I wash my hands?** Ellerimi nerede yıkayabilirim?

handbag ['hændˌbæɡ] n çanta

handball ['hændˌbɔːl] n hentbol

handbook ['hændˌbʊk] n referans kitabı

handbrake ['hændˌbreɪk] n el freni

handcuffs ['hændˌkʌfs] npl kelepçe

handicap ['hændɪˌkæp] n handikap

handkerchief ['hæŋkətʃɪf; -tʃiːf] n mendil

handle ['hændəl] n kol ▷ v elle yapmak; **The door handle has come off** Kapının kolu çıktı

handlebars ['hændəlˌbɑːz] npl gidon

handmade [ˌhændˈmeɪd] adj el yapımı; **Is this handmade?** Bu el yapımı mı?

hands-free ['hændzˌfriː] adj handsfree; **hands-free kit** n handsfree set

handsome ['hændsəm] adj yakışıklı

handwriting ['hændˌraɪtɪŋ] n el yazısı

handy ['hændɪ] adj el altında

hang [hæŋ] vi asılmak ▷ vt asmak

hanger ['hæŋə] n askı

hang-gliding ['hæŋˈɡlaɪdɪŋ] n hang-gliding; **I'd like to go hang-gliding** Hang-gliding yapmak isterdim

hang on [hæŋ ɒn] v sabretmek

hangover ['hæŋˌəʊvə] n akşamdan kalma

hang up [hæŋ ʌp] v telefonu kapatmak

hankie ['hæŋkɪ] n mendil
happen ['hæpⁿn] v olmak
happily ['hæpɪlɪ] adv seve seve
happiness ['hæpɪnɪs] n mutluluk
happy ['hæpɪ] adj mutlu; **Happy New Year!** Mutlu Yıllar!
harassment ['hærəsmənt] n taciz
harbour ['hɑːbə] n liman
hard [hɑːd] adj (difficult) zor, (firm, rigid) sert ▷ adv zor; **hard disk** n bilgisayar hafızası; **hard shoulder** n dönemeç
hardboard ['hɑːdˌbɔːd] n mukavva
hardly ['hɑːdlɪ] adv güçlükle
hard up [hɑːd ʌp] adj yoksul
hardware ['hɑːdˌwɛə] n hırdavat
hare [hɛə] n yabani tavşan
harm [hɑːm] v zarar vermek
harmful ['hɑːmfʊl] adj zararlı
harmless ['hɑːmlɪs] adj zararsız
harp [hɑːp] n harp (müzik)
harsh [hɑːʃ] adj şiddetli
harvest ['hɑːvɪst] n hasat ▷ v hasat kaldırmak
hastily [heɪstɪlɪ] adv telaşla
hat [hæt] n şapka
hatchback ['hætʃˌbæk] n hatchback
hate [heɪt] v nefret etmek
hatred ['heɪtrɪd] n nefret
haunted ['hɔːntɪd] adj perili
have [hæv] v sahip olmak
have to [hæv tʊ] v yapmak zorunda olmak
hawthorn ['hɔːˌθɔːn] n akdiken
hay [heɪ] n saman; **hay fever** n saman nezlesi
haystack ['heɪˌstæk] n saman yığını

hazelnut ['heɪzⁿlˌnʌt] n fındık
he [hiː] pron o (erkek)
head [hɛd] n (body part) baş (vücut), (principal) baş (yönetim) ▷ v başı çekmek; **deputy head** n müdür yardımcısı; **head office** n yönetim merkezi
headache ['hɛdˌeɪk] n baş ağrısı; **I'd like something for a headache** Baş ağrısı için bir şey rica ediyorum
headlamp ['hɛdˌlæmp] n ön lamba
headlight ['hɛdˌlaɪt] n ön lamba
headline ['hɛdˌlaɪn] n başlık (haber)
headphones ['hɛdˌfəʊnz] npl kulaklık; **Does it have headphones?** Kulaklık var mı?
headquarters [ˌhɛd'kwɔːtəz] npl merkez
headroom ['hɛdˌrʊm; -ˌruːm] n boşluk payı (tavanda)
headscarf, headscarves ['hɛdˌskɑːf, 'hɛdˌskɑːvz] n eşarp
headteacher ['hɛdˌtiːtʃə] n müdür
heal [hiːl] v iyileşmek
health [hɛlθ] n sağlık; **I don't have health insurance** Sağlık sigortam yok; **I have private health insurance** Özel sağlık sigortam var
healthy ['hɛlθɪ] adj sağlıklı
heap [hiːp] n yığın
hear [hɪə] v işitmek
hearing ['hɪərɪŋ] n işitme; **hearing aid** n işitme cihazı
heart [hɑːt] n kalp; **heart attack** n kalp krizi; **I have a heart condition** Kalp hastasıyım

heartbroken ['hɑ:t,brəʊkən] *adj* kalbi kırık

heartburn ['hɑ:t,bɜ:n] *n* mide ekşimesi

heat [hi:t] *n* ısı ▷ *v* ısıtmak

heater ['hi:tə] *n* ısıtıcı

heather ['hɛðə] *n* süpürge otu

heating ['hi:tɪŋ] *n* ısıtma; **central heating** *n* merkezi ısıtma

heat up [hi:t ʌp] *v* kızışmak

heaven ['hɛvᵊn] *n* cennet

heavily ['hɛvɪlɪ] *adv* ağır bir şekilde

heavy ['hɛvɪ] *adj* ağır; **This is too heavy** Bu çok ağır

hedge [hɛdʒ] *n* çit *(çalılık)*

hedgehog ['hɛdʒ,hɒg] *n* kirpi

heel [hi:l] *n* topuk; **high heels** *npl* yüksek topuklar

height [haɪt] *n* yükseklik

heir [ɛə] *n* varis

heiress ['ɛərɪs] *n* varis *(kadın)*

helicopter ['hɛlɪ,kɒptə] *n* helikopter

hell [hɛl] *n* cehennem

hello [hɛ'ləʊ] *excl* merhaba!

helmet ['hɛlmɪt] *n* kask *(motosiklet)*; **Can I have a helmet?** Kask alabilir miyim?

help [hɛlp] *n* yardım ▷ *v* yardım etmek; **Can you help me?** Yardımcı olabilir misiniz?; **Fetch help quickly!** Yardım çağırın, çabuk!

helpful ['hɛlpfʊl] *adj* yardımcı

helpline ['hɛlp,laɪn] *n* yardım hattı

hen [hɛn] *n* tavuk; **hen night** *n* kına gecesi

hepatitis [,hɛpə'taɪtɪs] *n* karaciğer iltihabı

her [hɜ:; hə; ə] *pron* onu, ona *(kadın)*

herbs [hɜ:bz] *npl* kokulu otlar

herd [hɜ:d] *n* sürü

here [hɪə] *adv* burada

hereditary [hɪ'rɛdɪtərɪ; -trɪ] *adj* kalıtsal

heritage ['hɛrɪtɪdʒ] *n* miras

hernia ['hɜ:nɪə] *n* fıtık

hero ['hɪərəʊ] *n* kahraman

heroin ['hɛrəʊɪn] *n* eroin

heroine ['hɛrəʊɪn] *n* kadın kahraman

heron ['hɛrən] *n* balıkçıl kuşu

herring ['hɛrɪŋ] *n* ringa balığı

hers [hɜ:z] *pron* onunki *(kadın)*

herself [hə'sɛlf] *pron* kendisi *(kadın)*

hesitate ['hɛzɪ,teɪt] *v* duraksamak

heterosexual [,hɛtərəʊ'sɛksjʊəl] *adj* heteroseksüel

HGV [eɪtʃ dʒi: vi:] *abbr* ağır yük taşıma aracı

hi [haɪ] *excl* selam!

hiccups ['hɪkʌps] *npl* hıçkırık

hidden ['hɪdᵊn] *adj* saklı

hide [haɪd] *vi* saklamak

hide-and-seek [,haɪdænd'si:k] *n* saklambaç

hideous ['hɪdɪəs] *adj* itici

hifi ['haɪ'faɪ] *n* hi-fi

high [haɪ] *adj* yüksek ▷ *adv* yüksekte; **high heels** *npl* yüksek topuklar; **high jump** *n* yüksek atlama; **high season** *n* pahalı sezon; **How high is it?** Yüksekliği ne kadar?

highchair ['haɪ,tʃɛə] *n* bebe sandalyesi

high-heeled ['haɪ,hi:ld] *adj* yüksek topuklu

highlight ['haɪˌlaɪt] n önemli olay
▷ v vurgulamak

highlighter ['haɪˌlaɪtə] n marker

high-rise ['haɪˌraɪz] n gökdelen

hijack ['haɪˌdʒæk] v gaspetmek

hijacker ['haɪˌdʒækə] n korsan
(uçak/hava)

hike [haɪk] n yürüyüşe çıkma

hiking [haɪkɪŋ] n yürüyüş

hilarious [hɪ'lɛərɪəs] adj çok
komik

hill [hɪl] n tepe (coğrafya); **I'd like
to go hill walking** Tepelere
yürüyüşe çıkmak isterim

hill-walking ['hɪlˌwɔːkɪŋ] n
tepelere tırmanma

him [hɪm; ɪm] pron onu, ona
(erkek)

himself [hɪm'sɛlf; ɪm'sɛlf] pron
kendisi (erkek)

Hindu ['hɪnduː; hɪn'duː] adj Hindu
▷ n Hindu

Hinduism ['hɪnduˌɪzəm] n
Hinduizm

hinge [hɪndʒ] n menteşe

hint [hɪnt] n ima ▷ v imada
bulunmak

hip [hɪp] n kalça

hippie ['hɪpɪ] n hippi

hippo ['hɪpəʊ] n hipopotam

hippopotamus, hippopotami
[ˌhɪpə'pɒtəməs, ˌhɪpə'pɒtəmaɪ] n
hipopotam

hire ['haɪə] n kiralama ▷ v
kiralamak; **car hire** n araba
kiralama; **hire car** n kiralık araba;
**How much is it to hire a tennis
court?** Tenis kortu kiralamak
kaça?; **I want to hire a bike**
Bisiklet kiralamak istiyorum;

I want to hire a car for five days
Beş günlüğüne bir araba
kiralamak istiyorum; **I'd like to
hire...** ... kiralamak istiyorum

his [hɪz; ɪz] adj onun (erkek) ▷ pron
onun (erkek)

historian [hɪ'stɔːrɪən] n tarihçi

historical [hɪ'stɒrɪkəl] adj tarihi

history ['hɪstərɪ; 'hɪstrɪ] n tarih
(geçmiş, ders)

hit [hɪt] n çarpma ▷ v vurmak

hitch [hɪtʃ] n ufak sorun

hitchhike ['hɪtʃˌhaɪk] v otostop

hitchhiker ['hɪtʃˌhaɪkə] n
otostopçu

hitchhiking ['hɪtʃˌhaɪkɪŋ] n
otostop yapma

HIV-negative [eɪtʃ aɪ viː 'nɛgətɪv]
adj HIV'li olmayan

HIV-positive [eɪtʃ aɪ viː 'pɒzɪtɪv]
adj HIV'li

hobby ['hɒbɪ] n hobi

hockey ['hɒkɪ] n hokey; **ice
hockey** n buz hokeyi

hold [həʊld] v tutmak

holdall ['həʊldˌɔːl] n sırt çantası

hold on [həʊld ɒn] v tutunmak

hold up [həʊld ʌp] v kaldırmak

hold-up [həʊldʌp] n soygun

hole [həʊl] n delik (çorap, duvar
vb); **I have a hole in my shoe**
Ayakkabımda delik var

holiday ['hɒlɪˌdeɪ; -dɪ] n tatil;
activity holiday n aktivite tatili;
bank holiday n İngiltere'de
bankaların kapalı olduğu tatil
günü; **holiday home** n tatil evi;
holiday job n yazlık iş; **package
holiday** n paket tatil; **public
holiday** n resmi tatil günü;

Enjoy your holiday! İyi tatiller!; **I'm here on holiday** Burada tatildeyim

Holland ['hɒlənd] *n* Hollanda

hollow ['hɒləʊ] *adj* oyuk

holly ['hɒlɪ] *n* çoban püskülü

holy ['həʊlɪ] *adj* kutsal

home [həʊm] *adv* evde ▷ *n* ev; **home address** *n* ev adresi; **home match** *n* kendi sahasında maç; **home page** *n* açılış sayfası; **mobile home** *n* taşınabilir ev; **nursing home** *n* huzurevi *(yaşlılar için)*; **stately home** *n* malikane; **I'd like to go home** Eve gitmek istiyorum; **Please come home by 11p.m.** Akşam saat on bire kadar evde olun lütfen; **When do you go home?** Eve ne zaman gideceksiniz?; **Would you like to phone home?** Evi aramak ister misiniz?

homeland ['həʊm,lænd] *n* anavatan

homeless ['həʊmlɪs] *adj* evsiz

home-made ['həʊm'meɪd] *adj* ev yapımı

homeopathic [,həʊmɪ'ɒpæθɪk] *adj* homeopatik

homeopathy [,həʊmɪ'ɒpəθɪ] *n* homeopati

homesick ['həʊm,sɪk] *adj* sıla acısı çeken

homework ['həʊm,wɜːk] *n* ev ödevi

Honduras [hɒn'djʊərəs] *n* Honduras

honest ['ɒnɪst] *adj* dürüst

honestly ['ɒnɪstlɪ] *adv* dürüstçe

honesty ['ɒnɪstɪ] *n* dürüstlük

honey ['hʌnɪ] *n* bal

honeymoon ['hʌnɪ,muːn] *n* balayı; **We are on our honeymoon** Balayındayız

honeysuckle ['hʌnɪ,sʌkəl] *n* hanımeli

honour ['ɒnə] *n* onur *(şeref)*

hood [hʊd] *n* kapüşon

hook [hʊk] *n* kanca

hooray [huː'reɪ] *excl* hurra!

Hoover® ['huːvə] *n* elektrik süpürgesi; **hoover** *v* süpürmek *(elektrikli süpürgeyle)*

hope [həʊp] *n* umut ▷ *v* umut etmek

hopeful ['həʊpfʊl] *adj* umutlu

hopefully ['həʊpfʊlɪ] *adv* umutla

hopeless ['həʊplɪs] *adj* umutsuz

horizon [hə'raɪzən] *n* ufuk

horizontal [,hɒrɪ'zɒntəl] *adj* yatay

hormone ['hɔːməʊn] *n* hormon

horn [hɔːn] *n* boynuz; **French horn** *n* korno

horoscope ['hɒrə,skəʊp] *n* yıldız falı

horrendous [hɒ'rɛndəs] *adj* korkunç

horrible ['hɒrəbəl] *adj* korkunç

horrifying ['hɒrɪ,faɪɪŋ] *adj* dehşet verici

horror ['hɒrə] *n* dehşet; **horror film** *n* korku filmi

horse [hɔːs] *n* at *(hayvan)*; **horse racing** *n* at yarışı; **horse riding** *n* binicilik; **rocking horse** *n* sallanan at; **Can we go horse riding?** Ata binebilir miyiz?; **I'd like to see a horse race** At yarışı görmek isterdim; **Let's go horse riding** Ata binmeye gidelim

horseradish ['hɔːsˌrædɪʃ] *n* yabanturpu

horseshoe ['hɔːsˌʃuː] *n* at nalı

hose [həʊz] *n* hortum

hosepipe ['həʊzˌpaɪp] *n* hortum

hospital ['hɒspɪtᵊl] *n* hastane; **maternity hospital** *n* doğum hastanesi; **How do I get to the hospital?** Hastaneye nasıl gidebilirim?; **I work in a hospital** Hastanede çalışıyorum; **We must get him to hospital** Hastaneye götürmemiz gerek; **Where is the hospital?** Hastane nerede?; **Will he have to go to hospital?** Hastaneye gitmesi gerekiyor mu?

hospitality [ˌhɒspɪ'tælɪtɪ] *n* konukseverlik

host [həʊst] *n (entertains)* ev sahibi, *(multitude)* kalabalık

hostage ['hɒstɪdʒ] *n* rehine

hostel ['hɒstᵊl] *n* öğrenci yurdu

hostess ['həʊstɪs] *n* **air hostess** *n* hostes

hostile ['hɒstaɪl] *adj* düşmanca

hot [hɒt] *adj* sıcak; **hot dog** *n* sosisli sandviç; **I'm too hot** Çok sıcakladım; **It's very hot** Çok sıcak; **The food is too hot** Yemek çok sıcak; **The room is too hot** Oda çok sıcak

hotel [həʊ'tɛl] *n* otel; **Can you book me into a hotel?** Bana bir otelde yer ayırtabilir misiniz?; **Can you recommend a hotel?** Bir otel tavsiye edebilir misiniz?; **He runs the hotel** Oteli yönetiyor; **I'm staying at a hotel** Otelde kalıyorum; **Is your hotel accessible to wheelchairs?** Otelinizde tekerlekli sandalye girişi var mı?; **We're looking for a hotel** Bir otel arıyoruz; **What's the best way to get to this hotel?** Şu otele en kolay nasıl gidebilirim?

hour [aʊə] *n* saat *(zaman)*; **office hours** *npl* çalışma saatleri; **opening hours** *npl* açılış saatleri; **peak hours** *npl* sıkışık saat; **rush hour** *n* sıkışık saatler; **visiting hours** *npl* ziyaret saatleri; **How much is it per hour?** Saati ne kadar?; **The journey takes two hours** Yolculuk iki saat sürüyor; **When are visiting hours?** Ziyaret saatleri nedir?

hourly ['aʊəlɪ] *adj* saat başı ▷ *adv* saat başı

house [haʊs] *n* ev; **council house** *n* sosyal konut; **detached house** *n* müstakil ev; **semi-detached house** *n* bitişik nizam ev; **Do we have to clean the house before we leave?** Ayrılmadan önce evi temizlememiz gerekiyor mu?

household ['haʊsˌhəʊld] *n* hane halkı

housewife, housewives ['haʊsˌwaɪf, 'haʊsˌwaɪvz] *n* evkadını

housework ['haʊsˌwɜːk] *n* ev işi

hovercraft ['hɒvəˌkrɑːft] *n* hoverkraft

how [haʊ] *adv* nasıl; **Do you know how to do this?** Bunun nasıl yapıldığını biliyor musunuz?; **How are you?** Nasılsınız?; **How do I get to…?** … na nasıl gidebilirim?; **How does this work?** Bu nasıl çalışıyor?

however [haʊ'ɛvə] *adv* ancak
howl [haʊl] *v* ulumak
HQ [eɪtʃ kjuː] *abbr* genel merkez
hubcap ['hʌbˌkæp] *n* jant kapağı
hug [hʌg] *n* kucaklama ▷ *v*
kucaklamak
huge [hjuːdʒ] *adj* kocaman
hull [hʌl] *n* gemi teknesi
hum [hʌm] *v* vızıldamak
human ['hjuːmən] *adj* insan;
human being *n* insanoğlu;
human rights *npl* insan hakları
humanitarian
[hjuːˌmænɪ'tɛərɪən] *adj* hümanist
humble ['hʌmbəl] *adj* alçak
gönüllü
humid ['hjuːmɪd] *adj* nemli
humidity [hjuː'mɪdɪtɪ] *n* nem
humorous ['hjuːmərəs] *adj*
nükteli
humour ['hjuːmə] *n* mizah;
sense of humour *n* mizah
duygusu
hundred ['hʌndrəd] *number* yüz
(sayı); **I'd like five hundred...**
Beş yüz... rica ediyorum; **the key
for room number two hundred
and two** İki yüz iki numaralı
odanın anahtarı lütfen
Hungarian [hʌŋ'gɛərɪən] *adj*
Macar ▷ *n* Macar
Hungary ['hʌŋgərɪ] *n* Macaristan
hunger ['hʌŋgə] *n* açlık
hungry ['hʌŋgrɪ] *adj* aç *(karın)*;
I'm hungry Açım; **I'm not
hungry** Aç değilim
hunt [hʌnt] *n* avlamak ▷ *v* avlamak
hunter ['hʌntə] *n* avcı
hunting ['hʌntɪŋ] *n* av
hurdle ['hɜːdəl] *n* engel

hurricane ['hʌrɪkən; -keɪn] *n*
kasırga
hurry ['hʌrɪ] *n* acele ▷ *v* acele
etmek; **I'm in a hurry** Acelem var
hurry up ['hʌrɪ ʌp] *v* acele etmek
hurt [hɜːt] *adj* incinmiş ▷ *v* incitmek
husband ['hʌzbənd] *n* koca *(eş)*
hut [hʌt] *n* baraka
hyacinth ['haɪəsɪnθ] *n* sümbül
hydrogen ['haɪdrɪdʒən] *n* hidrojen
hygiene ['haɪdʒiːn] *n* hijyen
hymn [hɪm] *n* ilahi
hypermarket ['haɪpəˌmɑːkɪt] *n*
hipermarket
hyphen ['haɪfən] *n* tire

I [aɪ] *pron* ben *(kişi)*
ice [aɪs] *n* buz; **black ice** *n* gizli buz;
ice cube *n* küp buz; **ice hockey** *n*
buz hokeyi; **ice lolly** *n* çubuk buz;
ice rink *n* buz pateni sahası; **With
ice, please** buzlu lütfen
iceberg ['aɪsbɜːg] *n* buzdağı
icebox ['aɪsˌbɒks] *n* buz kutusu
ice cream ['aɪs 'kriːm] *n* **ice
cream** *n* dondurma; **I'd like an ice
cream** Ben dondurma alayım
Iceland ['aɪslənd] *n* İzlanda
Icelandic [aɪs'lændɪk] *adj* İzlanda
▷ *n* İzlandalı
ice-skating ['aɪsˌskeɪtɪŋ] *n* buz
pateni
icing ['aɪsɪŋ] *n* pastanın üzerindeki
şekerli süsleme; **icing sugar** *n* toz
süsleme şekeri
icon ['aɪkɒn] *n* ikon
icy ['aɪsɪ] *adj* buzlu; **Are the roads
icy?** Yollar buzlu mu?

idea [aɪ'dɪə] *n* fikir *(düşünce)*
ideal [aɪ'dɪəl] *adj* ideal
ideally [aɪ'dɪəlɪ] *adv* en iyi şekilde
identical [aɪ'dɛntɪkəl] *adj* özdeş
identification [aɪˌdɛntɪfɪ'keɪʃən]
n kimlik
identify [aɪ'dɛntɪˌfaɪ] *v* kimlik
belirlemek
identity [aɪ'dɛntɪtɪ] *n* kimlik;
identity card *n* kimlik kartı;
identity theft *n* kimlik hırsızlığı
ideology [ˌaɪdɪ'ɒlədʒɪ] *n* ideoloji
idiot ['ɪdɪət] *n* salak
idiotic [ˌɪdɪ'ɒtɪk] *adj* salakça
idle ['aɪdəl] *adj* boş *(insan)*
i.e. [aɪ iː] *abbr* örneğin
if [ɪf] *conj* eğer
ignition [ɪg'nɪʃən] *n* ateşleme
ignorance ['ɪgnərəns] *n* cehalet
ignorant ['ɪgnərənt] *adj* cahil
ignore [ɪg'nɔː] *v* reddeylemek
ill [ɪl] *adj* hasta; **My child is ill**
Çocuğum hasta
illegal [ɪ'liːgəl] *adj* yasadışı
illegible [ɪ'lɛdʒɪbəl] *adj* okunaksız
illiterate [ɪ'lɪtərɪt] *adj* okuma
yazması olmayan
illness ['ɪlnɪs] *n* hastalık
ill-treat [ɪl'triːt] *v* kötü muamele
etmek
illusion [ɪ'luːʒən] *n* yanılsama
illustration [ˌɪlə'streɪʃən] *n*
resimleme *(kitabı)*
image ['ɪmɪdʒ] *n* imge
imaginary [ɪ'mædʒɪnərɪ; -dʒɪnrɪ]
adj hayali
imagination [ɪˌmædʒɪ'neɪʃən] *n*
hayal
imagine [ɪ'mædʒɪn] *v* tasavvur
etmek

imitate ['ɪmɪˌteɪt] v taklit etmek

imitation [ˌɪmɪ'teɪʃən] n taklit

immature [ˌɪmə'tjʊə; -'tʃʊə] adj gelişmemiş

immediate [ɪ'mi:dɪət] adj acil

immediately [ɪ'mi:dɪətlɪ] adv anında

immigrant ['ɪmɪɡrənt] n göçmen

immigration [ˌɪmɪ'ɡreɪʃən] n göçme

immoral [ɪ'mɒrəl] adj ahlak dışı

impact ['ɪmpækt] n etki (sonuç)

impartial [ɪm'pɑ:ʃəl] adj yansız

impatience [ɪm'peɪʃəns] n sabırsızlık

impatient [ɪm'peɪʃənt] adj sabırsız

impatiently [ɪm'peɪʃəntlɪ] adv sabırsızlıkla

impersonal [ɪm'pɜ:sənəl] adj yansız

import n ['ɪmpɔ:t] ithal ▷ v [ɪm'pɔ:t] ithal etmek

importance [ɪm'pɔ:təns] n önem

important [ɪm'pɔ:tənt] adj önemli

impossible [ɪm'pɒsəbəl] adj imkansız

impractical [ɪm'præktɪkəl] adj pratik olmayan

impress [ɪm'prɛs] v etkilemek (iz bırakmak)

impressed [ɪm'prɛst] adj etkilenmiş

impression [ɪm'prɛʃən] n izlenim

impressive [ɪm'prɛsɪv] adj etkileyici

improve [ɪm'pru:v] v geliştirmek

improvement [ɪm'pru:vmənt] n gelişme (iyileşme)

in [ɪn] prep içinde

inaccurate [ɪn'ækjʊrɪt] adj doğru olmayan

inadequate [ɪn'ædɪkwɪt] adj yetersiz

inadvertently [ˌɪnəd'vɜ:təntlɪ] adv kasıtsız olarak

inbox ['ɪnbɒks] n gelen kutusu

incentive [ɪn'sɛntɪv] n teşvik

inch [ɪntʃ] n inç

incident ['ɪnsɪdənt] n olay

include [ɪn'klu:d] v dahil etmek

included [ɪn'klu:dɪd] adj dahil; **Is breakfast included?** Kahvaltı dahil mi?; **Is fully comprehensive insurance included in the price?** Fiyata tam kapsamlı sigorta dahil mi?; **Is service included?** Servis dahil mi?; **Is the cost of electricity included?** Elektrik ücrete dahil mi?; **Is VAT included?** KDV dahil mi?; **What is included in the price?** Fiyata neler dahil?

including [ɪn'klu:dɪŋ] prep dahil

inclusive [ɪn'klu:sɪv] adj kapsamlı

income ['ɪnkʌm; 'ɪnkəm] n gelir (maaş); **income tax** n gelir vergisi

incompetent [ɪn'kɒmpɪtənt] adj yeteneksiz

incomplete [ˌɪnkəm'pli:t] adj eksik

inconsistent [ˌɪnkən'sɪstənt] adj tutarsız

inconvenience [ˌɪnkən'vi:njəns; -'vi:nɪəns] n rahatsızlık

inconvenient [ˌɪnkən'vi:njənt; -'vi:nɪənt] adj rahatsız

incorrect [ˌɪnkə'rɛkt] adj yanlış

increase ['ɪnkri:s] n artış ▷ [ɪn'kri:s] v artmak

increasingly [ɪn'kri:sɪŋlɪ] adv gitgide artarak

incredible [ɪnˈkrɛdəbəl] *adj*
inanılmaz

indecisive [ˌɪndɪˈsaɪsɪv] *adj*
kararsız

indeed [ɪnˈdiːd] *adv* gerçekten

independence [ˌɪndɪˈpɛndəns] *n*
bağımsızlık

independent [ˌɪndɪˈpɛndənt] *adj*
bağımsız

index [ˈɪndɛks] *n (list)* indeks,
(numerical scale) dizin *(sayısal)*;
index finger *n* işaret parmağı

India [ˈɪndɪə] *n* Hindistan

Indian [ˈɪndɪən] *adj* Hint ▷ *n* Hintli;
Indian Ocean *n* Hint Okyanusu

indicate [ˈɪndɪˌkeɪt] *v* işaretlemek

indicator [ˈɪndɪˌkeɪtə] *n* gösterge

indigestion [ˌɪndɪˈdʒɛstʃən] *n*
hazımsızlık

indirect [ˌɪndɪˈrɛkt] *adj* dolaylı

indispensable [ˌɪndɪˈspɛnsəbəl]
adj vazgeçilmez

individual [ˌɪndɪˈvɪdjʊəl] *adj*
birey

Indonesia [ˌɪndəʊˈniːzɪə] *n*
Endonezya

Indonesian [ˌɪndəʊˈniːzɪən] *adj*
Endonezya ▷ *n (person)*
Endonezyalı

indoor [ˈɪnˌdɔː] *adj* kapalı alan

indoors [ˌɪnˈdɔːz] *adv* içeride

industrial [ɪnˈdʌstrɪəl] *adj*
endüstriyel; **industrial estate** *n*
sanayi sitesi

industry [ˈɪndəstrɪ] *n* endüstri

inefficient [ˌɪnɪˈfɪʃənt] *adj* yetersiz

inevitable [ɪnˈɛvɪtəbəl] *adj*
kaçınılmaz

inexpensive [ˌɪnɪkˈspɛnsɪv] *adj*
pahalı olmayan

inexperienced [ˌɪnɪkˈspɪərɪənst]
adj deneyimsiz

infantry [ˈɪnfəntrɪ] *n* piyade

infection [ɪnˈfɛkʃən] *n* enfeksiyon

infectious [ɪnˈfɛkʃəs] *adj* bulaşıcı;
Is it infectious? Bulaşıcı mı?

inferior [ɪnˈfɪərɪə] *adj* aşağı
(durum) ▷ *n* ast

infertile [ɪnˈfɜːtaɪl] *adj* verimsiz

infinitive [ɪnˈfɪnɪtɪv] *n* sonsuz

infirmary [ɪnˈfɜːmərɪ] *n* revir

inflamed [ɪnˈfleɪmd] *adj* kızgın

inflammation [ˌɪnfləˈmeɪʃən] *n*
yangı

inflatable [ɪnˈfleɪtəbəl] *adj*
şişirilebilir

inflation [ɪnˈfleɪʃən] *n* enflasyon

inflexible [ɪnˈflɛksəbəl] *adj* esnek
olmayan

influence [ˈɪnflʊəns] *n* etki
(nüfuz) ▷ *v* etkilemek

influenza [ˌɪnflʊˈɛnzə] *n* grip

inform [ɪnˈfɔːm] *v* bilgi vermek

informal [ɪnˈfɔːməl] *adj* teklifsiz

information [ˌɪnfəˈmeɪʃən] *n*
bilgi; **information office** *n*
enformasyon bürosu; **Here's
some information about my
company** Şirketimle ilgili bilgiler;
**I'd like some information
about...** ... hakkında bilgi
istiyordum

informative [ɪnˈfɔːmətɪv] *adj*
bilgilendirici

infrastructure [ˈɪnfrəˌstrʌktʃə] *n*
altyapı

infuriating [ɪnˈfjʊərɪeɪtɪŋ] *adj*
çileden çıkaran

ingenious [ɪnˈdʒiːnjəs; -nɪəs] *adj*
usta işi

ingredient [ɪnˈgriːdɪənt] n
malzeme

inhabitant [ɪnˈhæbɪtənt] n sakin
(konut)

inhaler [ɪnˈheɪlə] n inhalasyon
cihazı

inherit [ɪnˈhɛrɪt] v miras almak

inheritance [ɪnˈhɛrɪtəns] n miras

inhibition [ˌɪnɪˈbɪʃən; ˌɪnhɪ-] n
ketlenme

initial [ɪˈnɪʃəl] adj başlangıç *(ilk)* ▷ v
adının ön harflerini yazmak

initially [ɪˈnɪʃəlɪ] adv başlangıçta

initials [ɪˈnɪʃəlz] npl adın baş
harfleri

initiative [ɪˈnɪʃɪətɪv] n girişim
(inisiyatif)

inject [ɪnˈdʒɛkt] v enjekte etmek

injection [ɪnˈdʒɛkʃən] n enjeksiyon

injure [ˈɪndʒə] v yaralamak

injured [ˈɪndʒəd] adj yaralanmış

injury [ˈɪndʒərɪ] n yara; **injury
time** n uzatma süresi

injustice [ɪnˈdʒʌstɪs] n adaletsizlik

ink [ɪŋk] n mürekkep

in-laws [ɪnlɔːz] npl eşinin ailesi

inmate [ˈɪnˌmeɪt] n hükümlü

inn [ɪn] n han

inner [ˈɪnə] adj iç; **inner tube** n iç
lastik

innocent [ˈɪnəsənt] adj masum

innovation [ˌɪnəˈveɪʃən] n yenilik

innovative [ˈɪnəveɪtɪv] adj
yenilikçi

inquest [ˈɪnˌkwɛst] n soruşturma

inquire [ɪnˈkwaɪə] v soruşturmak

inquiry [ɪnˈkwaɪərɪ] n soru;
inquiries office n danışma bürosu

inquisitive [ɪnˈkwɪzɪtɪv] adj
meraklı

insane [ɪnˈseɪn] adj deli

inscription [ɪnˈskrɪpʃən] n
kazılmış yazı

insect [ˈɪnsɛkt] n böcek; **insect
repellent** n böcek ilacı; **stick
insect** n sopa çekirgesi; **Do you
have insect repellent?** Böcek
ilacınız var mı?

insecure [ˌɪnsɪˈkjʊə] adj güvensiz

insensitive [ɪnˈsɛnsɪtɪv] adj
duyarsız

inside adv [ˌɪnˈsaɪd] içeride ▷ n
[ˈɪnˈsaɪd] içerisi ▷ prep içeride

insincere [ˌɪnsɪnˈsɪə] adj
samimiyetsiz

insist [ɪnˈsɪst] v ısrar etmek

insomnia [ɪnˈsɒmnɪə] n
uykusuzluk

inspect [ɪnˈspɛkt] v denetlemek
(teftiş)

inspector [ɪnˈspɛktə] n denetçi
(müfettiş); **ticket inspector** n
bilet kontrolörü

instability [ˌɪnstəˈbɪlɪtɪ] n
dengesizlik

instalment [ɪnˈstɔːlmənt] n taksit

instance [ˈɪnstəns] n örnek

instant [ˈɪnstənt] adj derhal

instantly [ˈɪnstəntlɪ] adv derhal

instead [ɪnˈstɛd] adv yerine;
instead of prep yerine

instinct [ˈɪnstɪŋkt] n içgüdü

institute [ˈɪnstɪˌtjuːt] n enstitü

institution [ˌɪnstɪˈtjuːʃən] n
kurum *(enstitü)*

instruct [ɪnˈstrʌkt] v talimat
vermek

instructions [ɪnˈstrʌkʃənz] npl
talimatlar

instructor [ɪnˈstrʌktə] n

öğretmen; **driving instructor** *n* direksiyon öğretmeni

instrument ['ɪnstrəmənt] *n* alet; **musical instrument** *n* müzik aleti

insufficient [ˌɪnsə'fɪʃənt] *adj* yetersiz

insulation [ˌɪnsjʊ'leɪʃən] *n* yalıtım

insulin ['ɪnsjʊlɪn] *n* ensülin

insult *n* ['ɪnsʌlt] hakaret ▷ *v* [ɪn'sʌlt] onur kırmak

insurance [ɪn'ʃʊərəns; -'ʃɔː-] *n* sigorta *(poliçe)*; **accident insurance** *n* kaza sigortası; **car insurance** *n* araba sigortası; **insurance certificate** *n* sigorta belgesi; **insurance policy** *n* sigorta poliçesi; **life insurance** *n* yaşam sigortası; **third-party insurance** *n* üçüncü kişi sorumluluk sigortası; **travel insurance** *n* seyahat sigortası; **Can I see your insurance certificate please?** Sigorta belgenizi görebilir miyim lütfen?; **Do you have insurance?** Sigortanız var mı?; **Give me your insurance details, please** Sigorta bilgilerinizi verin lütfen; **Here are my insurance details** İşte sigorta bilgilerim; **How much extra is comprehensive insurance cover?** Tam kapsamlı sigorta için ne kadar ekstra ödemem gerekiyor?; **I don't have dental insurance** Diş sigortam yok; **I don't have health insurance** Sağlık sigortam yok; **I have insurance** Sigortalıyım; **I'd like to arrange personal**

accident insurance Bireysel kaza sigortası yaptırmak istiyorum; **Is fully comprehensive insurance included in the price?** Fiyata tam kapsamlı sigorta dahil mi?

insure [ɪn'ʃʊə; -'ʃɔː] *v* sigortalamak

insured [ɪn'ʃʊəd; -'ʃɔːd] *adj* sigortalı

intact [ɪn'tækt] *adj* bütün *(bölünmemiş)*

intellectual [ˌɪntɪ'lɛktʃʊəl] *adj* entellektüel ▷ *n* entellektüel

intelligence [ɪn'tɛlɪdʒəns] *n* zeka

intelligent [ɪn'tɛlɪdʒənt] *adj* zeki

intend [ɪn'tɛnd] *v* **intend to** *v* niyetlenmek

intense [ɪn'tɛns] *adj* yoğun

intensive [ɪn'tɛnsɪv] *adj* yoğun; **intensive care unit** *n* yoğun bakım ünitesi

intention [ɪn'tɛnʃən] *n* niyet

intentional [ɪn'tɛnʃənəl] *adj* kasıtlı

intercom ['ɪntəˌkɒm] *n* interkom

interest ['ɪntrɪst; -tərɪst] *n* *(curiosity)* ilgi *(merak)*, *(income)* faiz ▷ *v* ilgilenmek; **interest rate** *n* faiz oranı

interested ['ɪntrɪstɪd; -tərɪs-] *adj* ilgili

interesting ['ɪntrɪstɪŋ; -tərɪs-] *adj* ilgi çekici

interior [ɪn'tɪərɪə] *n* iç; **interior designer** *n* iç mimar

intermediate [ˌɪntə'miːdɪɪt] *adj* orta

internal [ɪn'tɜːnəl] *adj* iç *(organ vb)*

international [ˌɪntə'næʃənəl] *adj* uluslararası; **Where can I make an international phone call?**

Nereden uluslararası telefon
görüşmesi yapabilirim?

internet ['ıntənɛt] *n* internet;
internet café *n* internet kafe;
internet user *n* internet
kullanıcısı; **Are there any
internet cafés here?** Buralarda
internet kafe var mı?; **Does the
room have wireless internet
access?** Odada kablosuz internet
bağlantısı var mı?; **Is there an
internet connection in the
room?** Odada internet bağlantısı
var mı?

interpret [ın'tɜːprıt] *v* tefsir etmek

interpreter [ın'tɜːprıtə] *n*
mütercim

interrogate [ın'tɛrəˌgeıt] *v*
sorgulamak

interrupt [ˌıntə'rʌpt] *v* sözünü
kesmek

interruption [ˌıntə'rʌpʃən] *n*
müdahale

interval ['ıntəvəl] *n* ara *(konser,
tiyatro)*

interview ['ıntəˌvjuː] *n* görüşme
▷ *v* görüşme yapmak

interviewer ['ıntəˌvjuːə] *n*
görüşmeci

intimate ['ıntımıt] *adj* yakın

intimidate [ın'tımıˌdeıt] *v* gözünü
korkutmak

into ['ıntuː; 'ıntə] *prep* içeri; **bump
into** *v* kazara çarpmak

intolerant [ın'tɒlərənt] *adj*
hoşgörüsüz

intranet ['ıntrəˌnɛt] *n* şirketiçi
network

introduce [ˌıntrə'djuːs] *v*
tanıtmak

introduction [ˌıntrə'dʌkʃən] *n*
tanıtma

intruder [ın'truːdə] *n* davetsiz
misafir

intuition [ˌıntjʊ'ıʃən] *n* önsezi

invade [ın'veıd] *v* akın etmek

invalid ['ınvəˌliːd] *n* sakat

invent [ın'vɛnt] *v* icat etmek

invention [ın'vɛnʃən] *n* icat

inventor [ın'vɛntə] *n* mucit

inventory ['ınvəntərı; -trı] *n*
envanter

invest [ın'vɛst] *v* yatırım yapmak

investigation [ınˌvɛstı'geıʃən] *n*
soruşturma

investment [ın'vɛstmənt] *n*
yatırım

investor [ın'vɛstə] *n* yatırımcı

invigilator [ın'vıdʒıˌleıtə] *n* sınav
gözcüsü

invisible [ın'vızəbəl] *adj* görünmez

invitation [ˌınvı'teıʃən] *n* davet

invite [ın'vaıt] *v* davet etmek

invoice ['ınvɔıs] *n* fatura ▷ *v*
faturalamak

involve [ın'vɒlv] *v* dahil etmek

iPod® ['aıˌpɒd] *n* iPod®

IQ [aı kjuː] *abbr* IQ

Iran [ı'rɑːn] *n* İran

Iranian [ı'reınıən] *adj* İran ▷ *n*
(person) İranlı *(kişi)*

Iraq [ı'rɑːk] *n* Irak

Iraqi [ı'rɑːkı] *adj* Irak ▷ *n* Iraklı

Ireland ['aıələnd] *n* İrlanda;
Northern Ireland *n* Kuzey
İrlanda

iris ['aırıs] *n* iris

Irish ['aırıʃ] *adj* İrlanda ▷ *n* İrlandalı

Irishman, Irishmen ['aırıʃmən,
'aırıʃmɛn] *n* İrlandalı *(erkek)*

Irishwoman, Irishwomen
['aɪrɪʃwʊmən, 'aɪrɪʃwɪmɪn] *n*
İrlandalı *(kadın)*

iron ['aɪən] *n* demir ▷ *v* ütülemek

ironic [aɪ'rɒnɪk] *adj* alaycı

ironing ['aɪənɪŋ] *n* ütüleme;
ironing board *n* ütü tahtası

ironmonger's ['aɪən,mʌŋgəz] *n*
demirci dükkanı

irony ['aɪrənɪ] *n* ince alay

irregular [ɪ'rɛgjʊlə] *adj* düzensiz

irrelevant [ɪ'rɛləvənt] *adj* alakasız

irresponsible [,ɪrɪ'spɒnsəbᵊl] *adj*
sorumsuz

irritable ['ɪrɪtəbᵊl] *adj* çabuk kızan

irritating ['ɪrɪ,teɪtɪŋ] *adj* sinir
bozucu

Islam ['ɪzlɑːm] *n* Müslümanlık

Islamic ['ɪzləmɪk] *adj* İslami

island ['aɪlənd] *n* ada; **desert
island** *n* ıssız ada

isolated ['aɪsə,leɪtɪd] *adj*
soyutlanmış

ISP [aɪ ɛs piː] *abbr* İSS

Israel ['ɪzreɪəl; -rɪəl] *n* İsrail

Israeli [ɪz'reɪlɪ] *adj* İsrail ▷ *n* İsrailli

issue ['ɪʃjuː] *n* mesele ▷ *v*
kamuoyuna açıklamak

it [ɪt] *pron* o *(eşya/hayvan)*; **I can't
read it** Okuyamıyorum; **Is it safe
for children?** Çocuklara verilebilir
mi?; **It hurts** Acıyor; **It won't turn
on** Açılmıyor; **It's ten to two** Saat
ikiye on var

IT [aɪ tiː] *abbr* Enformasyon
Teknolojisi

Italian [ɪ'tæljən] *adj* İtalyan ▷ *n
(language)* İtalyanca *(dil), (person)*
İtalyan *(kişi)*

Italy ['ɪtəlɪ] *n* İtalya

itch [ɪtʃ] *v* kaşınmak

itchy [ɪtʃɪ] *adj* kaşıntılı

item ['aɪtəm] *n* madde *(dizi)*

itinerary [aɪ'tɪnərərɪ; ɪ-] *n*
güzergah

its [ɪts] *adj* onun

itself [ɪt'sɛlf] *pron* kendisi

ivory ['aɪvərɪ; -vrɪ] *n* fildişi

ivy ['aɪvɪ] *n* sarmaşık

J

jab [dʒæb] n aşı (tıp)
jack [dʒæk] n kriko
jacket ['dʒækɪt] n ceket; **dinner jacket** n smokin; **jacket potato** n kumpir; **life jacket** n cankurtaran yeleği
jackpot ['dʒækˌpɒt] n jackpot
jail [dʒeɪl] n hapishane ▷ v hapse atmak
jam [dʒæm] n reçel; **jam jar** n reçel kavanozu; **traffic jam** n trafik sıkışıklığı
Jamaican [dʒə'meɪkən] adj Jamaika ▷ n Jamaikalı
jammed [dʒæmd] adj sıkışmış
janitor ['dʒænɪtə] n bina sorumlusu
January ['dʒænjʊərɪ] n Ocak (ay)
Japan [dʒə'pæn] n Japonya
Japanese [ˌdʒæpə'niːz] adj Japon ▷ n (language) Japonca (dil), (person) Japon (kişi)

jar [dʒɑː] n kavanoz; **jam jar** n reçel kavanozu
jaundice ['dʒɔːndɪs] n sarılık
javelin ['dʒævlɪn] n mızrak
jaw [dʒɔː] n çene
jazz [dʒæz] n caz
jealous ['dʒɛləs] adj kıskanç
jeans [dʒiːnz] npl blucin
jelly ['dʒɛlɪ] n jöle (tatlı)
jellyfish ['dʒɛlɪˌfɪʃ] n deniz anası; **Are there jellyfish here?** Burada deniz anası var mı?
jersey ['dʒɜːzɪ] n kazak
Jesus ['dʒiːzəs] n İsa
jet [dʒɛt] n jet; **jet lag** n uçak tutması; **jumbo jet** n jumbo jet
jetty ['dʒɛtɪ] n rıhtım
Jew [dʒuː] n Yahudi
jewel ['dʒuːəl] n mücevher
jeweller ['dʒuːələ] n kuyumcu
jeweller's ['dʒuːələz] n kuyumcu dükkanı
jewellery ['dʒuːəlrɪ] n mücevherat
Jewish ['dʒuːɪʃ] adj Yahudi
jigsaw ['dʒɪgˌsɔː] n yapboz
job [dʒɒb] n iş; **job centre** n iş bulma kurumu
jobless ['dʒɒblɪs] adj işsiz
jockey ['dʒɒkɪ] n jokey
jog [dʒɒg] v jogging yapmak
jogging ['dʒɒgɪŋ] n jogging
join [dʒɔɪn] v birleştirmek, katılmak
joiner ['dʒɔɪnə] n doğramacı
joint [dʒɔɪnt] adj ortak ▷ n (junction) bağlantı, (meat) kemikli et; **joint account** n ortak hesap
joke [dʒəʊk] n şaka ▷ v şaka yapmak
jolly ['dʒɒlɪ] adj neşeli
Jordan ['dʒɔːdən] n Ürdün

Jordanian [dʒɔː'deɪnɪən] *adj*
Ürdün ▷ *n* Ürdünlü
jot down [dʒɒt daʊn] *v* not almak
jotter ['dʒɒtə] *n* not defteri
journalism ['dʒɜː'nᵊˌlɪzəm] *n*
gazetecilik
journalist ['dʒɜː'nᵊlɪst] *n* gazeteci
journey ['dʒɜːnɪ] *n* seyahat
joy [dʒɔɪ] *n* neşe
joystick ['dʒɔɪˌstɪk] *n* joystick
judge [dʒʌdʒ] *n* yargıç ▷ *v*
yargılamak
judo ['dʒuːdəʊ] *n* judo
jug [dʒʌg] *n* sürahi; **a jug of water**
Bir sürahi su
juggler ['dʒʌglə] *n* hokkabaz
juice [dʒuːs] *n* meyve suyu; **orange**
juice *n* portakal suyu
July [dʒuː'laɪ; dʒə-; dʒʊ-] *n*
Temmuz
jump [dʒʌmp] *n* uzun atlama ▷ *v*
atlamak; **high jump** *n* yüksek
atlama; **jump leads** *npl* takviye
kablosu; **long jump** *n* uzun atlama
jumper ['dʒʌmpə] *n* kazak
jumping ['dʒʌmpɪŋ] *n*
show-jumping *n* engel atlama
junction ['dʒʌŋkʃən] *n* kavşak;
Go right at the next junction
Bir sonraki kavşaktan sağa
dönün
June [dʒuːn] *n* Haziran; **at the**
beginning of June Haziran
başında; **at the end of June**
Haziran sonunda; **for the whole**
of June bütün Haziran boyunca;
It's Monday the fifteenth of
June On beş Haziran Pazartesi
jungle ['dʒʌŋgᵊl] *n* orman
junior ['dʒuːnjə] *adj* yaşça küçük

junk [dʒʌŋk] *n* pılı pırtı; **junk mail** *n*
istenmeyen posta
jury ['dʒʊərɪ] *n* jüri
just [dʒʌst] *adv* henüz
justice ['dʒʌstɪs] *n* adalet
justify ['dʒʌstɪˌfaɪ] *v* haklılığını
göstermek

K

kangaroo [ˌkæŋɡəˈruː] *n* kanguru
karaoke [ˌkɑːrəˈəʊkɪ] *n* karaoke
karate [kəˈrɑːtɪ] *n* karate
Kazakhstan [ˌkɑːzɑːkˈstæn; -ˈstɑːn] *n* Kazakistan
kebab [kəˈbæb] *n* kebap
keen [kiːn] *adj* istekli
keep [kiːp] *v* bırakmak, tutmak
keep-fit [ˈkiːpˌfɪt] *n* sağlıklı yaşam
keep out [kiːp aʊt] *v* dışarda tutmak
keep up [kiːp ʌp] *v* sürdürmek; **keep up with** *v* uygun adım yürümek
kennel [ˈkɛnᵊl] *n* köpek kulübesi
Kenya [ˈkɛnjə; ˈkiːnjə] *n* Kenya
Kenyan [ˈkɛnjən; ˈkiːnjən] *adj* Kenya ▷ *n* Kenyalı
kerb [kɜːb] *n* kaldırım taşı
kerosene [ˈkɛrəˌsiːn] *n* gazyağı
ketchup [ˈkɛtʃəp] *n* ketçap
kettle [ˈkɛtᵊl] *n* çaydanlık

key [kiː] *n (for lock)* anahtar *(kilit)*, *(music/computer)* tuş *(bilgisayar/ piyano)*; **car keys** *npl* araba anahtarları; **Can I have a key?** Anahtar alabilir miyim?; **I left the keys in the car** Anahtarları arabada bıraktım; **I'm having trouble with the key** Anahtarla sorunum var; **I've forgotten the key** Anahtarımı unuttum; **the key for room number two hundred and two** İki yüz iki numaralı odanın anahtarı lütfen; **The key doesn't work** Anahtar uymuyor; **We need a second key** Yedek bir anahtar istiyoruz; **What's this key for?** Bu anahtar nerenin?; **Where do we get the key…?** Anahtarı nereden alacağız?; **Where do we hand in the key when we're leaving?** Ayrılırken anahtarı nereye bırakacağız?; **Which is the key for the back door?** Hangisi arka kapının anahtarı?; **Which is the key for this door?** Bu kapının anahtarı hangisi?
keyboard [ˈkiːˌbɔːd] *n* klavye
keyring [ˈkiːˌrɪŋ] *n* anahtarlık
kick [kɪk] *n* tekme ▷ *v* tekmelemek
kick off [kɪk ɒf] *v* başlama vuruşu yapmak
kick-off [kɪkɒf] *n* başlama vuruşu
kid [kɪd] *n* çocuk ▷ *v* dalga geçmek
kidnap [ˈkɪdnæp] *v* kaçırmak *(adam)*
kidney [ˈkɪdnɪ] *n* böbrek
kill [kɪl] *v* öldürmek
killer [ˈkɪlə] *n* katil
kilo [ˈkiːləʊ] *n* kilo

kilometre [kɪ'lɒmɪtə; 'kɪlə,miːtə]
 n kilometre
kilt [kɪlt] n kilt
kind [kaɪnd] adj iyi kalpli ▷ n tür
kindly ['kaɪndlɪ] adv iyilikle
kindness ['kaɪndnɪs] n iyi
 yüreklilik
king [kɪŋ] n kral
kingdom ['kɪŋdəm] n krallık
kingfisher ['kɪŋ,fɪʃə] n yalı çapkını
kiosk ['kiːɒsk] n büfe (dükkan)
kipper ['kɪpə] n tuzlanıp
 tütsülenmiş ringa balığı
kiss [kɪs] n öpücük ▷ v öpmek
kit [kɪt] n takım; **hands-free kit** n
 handsfree set; **repair kit** n tamir
 takımı; **Can I have a repair kit?**
 Tamir takımı alabilir miyim?
kitchen ['kɪtʃɪn] n mutfak; **fitted
 kitchen** n hazır mutfak
kite [kəɪt] n uçurtma
kitten ['kɪtᵊn] n kedi yavrusu
kiwi ['kiːwiː] n kivi (kuş)
knee [niː] n diz
kneecap ['niː,kæp] n dizkapağı
kneel [niːl] v diz çökmek
kneel down [niːl daʊn] v diz
 çökmek
knickers ['nɪkəz] npl külot (kadın)
knife [naɪf] n bıçak
knit [nɪt] v örmek
knitting ['nɪtɪŋ] n örgü; **knitting
 needle** n örgü şişi
knob [nɒb] n tokmak (kapı,
 çekmece)
knock [nɒk] n vuruş ▷ v vurmak,
 (on the door etc.) kapıyı çalmak
knock down [nɒk daʊn] v
 devirmek (düşürmek)
knock out [nɒk aʊt] v yere sermek

knot [nɒt] n düğüm
know [nəʊ] v bilmek, tanımak
know-all ['nəʊ,ɔːl] n bilgiç
know-how ['nəʊ,haʊ] n teknik
 bilgi
knowledge ['nɒlɪdʒ] n bilgi
knowledgeable ['nɒlɪdʒəbᵊl] adj
 bilgili
known [nəʊn] adj bilinen
Koran [kɔː'rɑːn] n Kuran
Korea [kə'riːə] n Kore; **North
 Korea** n Kuzey Kore; **South Korea**
 n Güney Kore
Korean [kə'riːən] adj Kore ▷ n
 (language) Korece (dil), (person)
 Koreli (kişi)
kosher ['kəʊʃə] adj kaşer
Kosovo ['kɔsɔvɔ; 'kɒsəvəʊ] n
 Kosova
Kuwait [kʊ'weɪt] n Kuveyt
Kuwaiti [kʊ'weɪtɪ] adj Kuveyt ▷ n
 Kuveytli
Kyrgyzstan ['kɪəgɪz,stɑːn;
 -,stæn] n Kırgızistan

lab [læb] n laboratuvar
label ['leɪbəl] n etiket *(fiyat vb)*
laboratory [lə'bɒrətərɪ; -trɪ; 'læbrəˌtɔːrɪ] n laboratuvar; **language laboratory** n dil laboratuvarı
labour ['leɪbə] n emek
labourer ['leɪbərə] n işçi
lace [leɪs] n dantel
lack [læk] n eksiklik
lacquer ['lækə] n lake
lad [læd] n delikanlı
ladder ['lædə] n taşınır merdiven
ladies ['leɪdɪz] n **ladies'** n kadınlar tuvaleti; **Where is the ladies?** Bayanlar tuvaleti nerede?
ladle ['leɪdəl] n kepçe *(mutfak)*
lady ['leɪdɪ] n leydi
ladybird ['leɪdɪˌbɜːd] n uç uç böceği
lager ['lɑːgə] n hafif bira
lagoon [lə'guːn] n lagün

laid-back ['leɪdbæk] adj rahat
lake [leɪk] n göl
lamb [læm] n kuzu
lame [leɪm] adj topal
lamp [læmp] n lamba; **bedside lamp** n başucu lambası; **The lamp is not working** Lamba çalışmıyor
lamppost ['læmpˌpəʊst] n lamba direği
lampshade ['læmpˌʃeɪd] n abajur
land [lænd] n kara *(coğrafya)* ▷ v iniş yapmak
landing ['lændɪŋ] n merdiven başı
landlady ['lændˌleɪdɪ] n ev sahibesi
landlord ['lændˌlɔːd] n ev sahibi
landmark ['lændˌmɑːk] n sınır işareti
landowner ['lændˌəʊnə] n toprak sahibi
landscape ['lændˌskeɪp] n manzara
landslide ['lændˌslaɪd] n toprak kayması
lane [leɪn] n dar yol, *(driving)* patika; **cycle lane** n bisiklet yolu
language ['læŋgwɪdʒ] n dil *(lisan)*; **language laboratory** n dil laboratuvarı; **language school** n dil okulu; **sign language** n işaret dili; **What languages do you speak?** Hangi dilleri konuşabiliyorsunuz?
lanky ['læŋkɪ] adj sırık gibi
Laos [laʊz; laʊs] n Laos
lap [læp] n kucak
laptop ['læpˌtɒp] n dizüstü bilgisayarı; **Can I use my own laptop here?** Burada dizüstü bilgisayarımı kullanabilir miyim?

larder ['lɑːdə] n kiler

large [lɑːdʒ] adj büyük (iri); **Do you have a large?** Büyük beden var mı?; **Do you have an extra large?** Ekstra büyük beden var mı?

largely ['lɑːdʒlɪ] adv yaygın bir şekilde

laryngitis [ˌlærɪnˈdʒaɪtɪs] n larenjit

laser ['leɪzə] n lazer

lass [læs] n genç kız

last [lɑːst] adj son ▷ adv sonda ▷ v sürmek; **When does the last chair-lift go?** Son teleferik kaçta?; **When is the last bus to...?**... a son otobüs kaçta?

lastly ['lɑːstlɪ] adv son olarak

late [leɪt] adj (dead) eski (ölmüş), (delayed) gecikmeli ▷ adv geç; **Is the train running late?** Tren gecikmeli mi?; **It's too late** Çok geç

lately ['leɪtlɪ] adv son zamanlarda

later ['leɪtə] adv daha sonra; **Can you try again later?** Daha sonra tekrar arayabilir misiniz; **Shall I come back later?** Daha sonra tekrar geleyim mi?

Latin ['lætɪn] n Latin

Latin America ['lætɪn əˈmɛrɪkə] n Latin Amerika

Latin American ['lætɪn əˈmɛrɪkən] adj Latin Amerika

latitude ['lætɪˌtjuːd] n enlem

Latvia ['lætvɪə] n Latviya

Latvian ['lætvɪən] adj Latviya ▷ n (language) Letonca (dil), (person) Letonyalı (kişi)

laugh [lɑːf] n gülüş ▷ v kahkahayla gülmek

laughter ['lɑːftə] n kahkaha

launch [lɔːntʃ] v başlatmak, denize indirmek

Launderette® [ˌlɔːndəˈrɛt; lɔːnˈdrɛt] n çamaşırhane; **Is there a launderette near here?** Buralarda bir çamaşırhane var mı?

laundry ['lɔːndrɪ] n çamaşır

lava ['lɑːvə] n lav

lavatory ['lævətərɪ; -trɪ] n tuvalet

lavender ['lævəndə] n lavanta

law [lɔː] n yasa; **law school** n hukuk fakültesi

lawn [lɔːn] n çim alan

lawnmower ['lɔːnˌməʊə] n çim biçme makinesi

lawyer ['lɔːjə; 'lɔɪə] n avukat

laxative ['læksətɪv] n müshil

lay [leɪ] v koymak

layby ['leɪˌbaɪ] n yol kenarında geçici park yeri

layer ['leɪə] n katman; **ozone layer** n ozon tabakası

lay off [leɪ ɒf] v işten çıkarmak

layout ['leɪˌaʊt] n düzenleme (masa vb)

lazy ['leɪzɪ] adj tembel

lead¹ [liːd] n (in play/film) başrol (oyun/film), (position) ana ▷ v yol göstermek; **jump leads** npl takviye kablosu; **lead singer** n as solist

lead² [lɛd] n (metal) kurşun (metal)

leader ['liːdə] n lider

lead-free [ˌlɛdˈfriː] adj kurşunsuz

leaf [liːf] n yaprak; **bay leaf** n defne yaprağı

leaflet ['liːflɪt] n broşür; **Do you have a leaflet in English?** İngilizce broşürünüz var mı?;

Do you have any leaflets about...?... hakkında broşürünüz var mı?; **Do you have any leaflets?** Broşürünüz var mı?

league [li:g] n lig

leak [li:k] n sızıntı ▷ v sızdırmak; **There is a leak in the radiator** Radyatör sızıntı yapıyor

lean [li:n] v yaslamak; **lean forward** v öne eğilmek

lean on [li:n ɒn] v baskı yapmak

lean out [li:n aʊt] v dışarıya sarkmak

leap [li:p] v sıçramak; **leap year** n artık yıl

learn [lɜ:n] v öğrenmek

learner ['lɜ:nə] n öğrenci; **learner driver** n öğrenci sürücü

lease [li:s] n kira sözleşmesi ▷ v kiralamak

least [li:st] adj en az; **at least** adv en azından

leather ['lɛðə] n deri (hayvan, giysi vb)

leave [li:v] n izin (işten izne ayrılmak) ▷ v ayrılmak, biryerden ayrılmak; **maternity leave** n doğum izni; **paternity leave** n babalık izni; **sick leave** n hastalık izni

leave out [li:v aʊt] v çıkarmak

leaves [li:vz] npl yapraklar

Lebanese [ˌlɛbə'ni:z] adj Lübnan'a ait ▷ n Lübnanlı

Lebanon ['lɛbənən] n Lübnan

lecture ['lɛktʃə] n ders ▷ v ders vermek

lecturer ['lɛktʃərə] n okutman

leek [li:k] n pırasa

left [lɛft] adj sol ▷ adv soldaki ▷ n

sol; **Go left at the next junction** Bir sonraki kavşaktan sola dönün; **Turn left** Sola dönün

left-hand [ˌlɛft'hænd] adj sol; **left-hand drive** n soldan trafik

left-handed [ˌlɛft'hændɪd] adj solak

left-luggage [ˌlɛft'lʌgɪdʒ] n emanet bagaj; **left-luggage locker** n bagaj emanet dolabı; **left-luggage office** n emanet bagaj bürosu

leftovers ['lɛftˌəʊvəz] npl artık yemek

left-wing [ˌlɛftˌwɪŋ] adj sol (politika)

leg [lɛg] n bacak

legal ['li:gəl] adj yasal

legend ['lɛdʒənd] n efsane

leggings ['lɛgɪŋz] npl tozluk

legible ['lɛdʒəbəl] adj okunaklı

legislation [ˌlɛdʒɪs'leɪʃən] n mevzuat

leisure ['lɛʒə; 'li:ʒər] n boş vakit; **leisure centre** n eğlence merkezi

lemon ['lɛmən] n limon; **with lemon** limonlu

lemonade [ˌlɛmə'neɪd] n limonata

lend [lɛnd] v ödünç vermek

length [lɛŋkθ; lɛŋθ] n uzunluk

lens [lɛnz] n lens; **contact lenses** npl kontakt lens; **zoom lens** n zoom merceği; **cleansing solution for contact lenses** Lens solüsyonu; **I wear contact lenses** Lens takıyorum

Lent [lɛnt] n 40 günlük Paskalya dönemi

lentils ['lɛntɪlz] npl mercimek

Leo ['li:əʊ] n Aslan burcu

leopard ['lɛpəd] *n* leopar
leotard ['lɪəˌtɑːd] *n* leotard
less [lɛs] *adv* daha az *(miktar olarak)* ▷ *pron* daha az
lesson ['lɛsᵊn] *n* ders *(sınıf)*; **driving lesson** *n* direksiyon dersi; **Can we take lessons?** Ders alabilir miyiz?; **Do you give lessons?** Ders veriyor musunuz?; **Do you organise skiing lessons?** Kayak dersleri veriyor musunuz?; **Do you organise snowboarding lessons?** Snowboarding dersleri veriyor musunuz?
let [lɛt] *v* izin vermek
let down [lɛt daʊn] *v* hayal kırıklığına uğratmak
let in [lɛt ɪn] *v* içeriye almak
letter ['lɛtə] *n (a, b, c)* harf, *(message)* mektup
letterbox ['lɛtəˌbɒks] *n* posta kutusu
lettuce ['lɛtɪs] *n* marul
leukaemia [luːˈkiːmɪə] *n* lösemi
level ['lɛvᵊl] *adj* yatay ▷ *n* düzey; **level crossing** *n* hemzemin geçit; **sea level** *n* deniz seviyesi
lever ['liːvə] *n* kol
liar ['laɪə] *n* yalancı
liberal ['lɪbərəl; 'lɪbrəl] *adj* açık görüşlü
liberation [ˌlɪbəˈreɪʃən] *n* önyargılardan arındırma
Liberia [laɪˈbɪərɪə] *n* Liberya
Liberian [laɪˈbɪərɪən] *adj* Liberya ▷ *n* Liberyalı
Libra ['liːbrə] *n* Terazi burcu
librarian [laɪˈbrɛərɪən] *n* kütüphaneci
library ['laɪbrərɪ] *n* kütüphane

Libya ['lɪbɪə] *n* Libya
Libyan ['lɪbɪən] *adj* Libya ▷ *n* Libyalı
lice [laɪs] *npl* bit *(saç)*
licence ['laɪsəns] *n* ehliyet; **driving licence** *n* sürücü ehliyeti; **I don't have my driving licence on me** Ehliyetim üzerimde değil; **My driving licence number is...** Ehliyet numaram...
lick [lɪk] *v* yalamak
lid [lɪd] *n* kapak
lie [laɪ] *n* yalan ▷ *v* yalan söylemek, yatmak
Liechtenstein ['lɪktənˌstaɪn; 'lɪçtənʃtaɪn] *n* Lihtenştayn
lie down [laɪ daʊn] *v* yatmak
lie in [laɪ ɪn] *v* uykusunu almak
lie-in [laɪɪn] *n* **have a lie-in** *v* uykusunu almak
lieutenant [lɛfˈtɛnənt; luːˈtɛnənt] *n* teğmen *(subay/polis)*
life [laɪf] *n* yaşam; **life insurance** *n* yaşam sigortası; **life jacket** *n* cankurtaran yeleği
lifebelt ['laɪfˌbɛlt] *n* cankurtaran simidi
lifeboat ['laɪfˌbəʊt] *n* cankurtaran sandalı
lifeguard ['laɪfˌgɑːd] *n* cankurtaran *(sahil)*; **Get the lifeguard!** Cankurtaran çağırın!; **Is there a lifeguard?** Cankurtaran var mı?
life-saving ['laɪfˌseɪvɪŋ] *adj* can kurtaran
lifestyle ['laɪfˌstaɪl] *n* yaşam biçimi
lift [lɪft] *n (free ride)* birini arabayla evine bırakma, *(up/down)* kaldırma/indirme ▷ *v* kaldırmak

(yukarıya); **ski lift** *n* teleferik

light [laɪt] *adj (not dark)* açık *(renk)*, *(not heavy)* hafif ▷ *n* ışık ▷ *v* yakmak *(ışık)*; **brake light** *n* fren lambası; **hazard warning lights** *npl* tehlike uyarı ışığı; **light bulb** *n* ampul; **pilot light** *n* kontrol lambası; **traffic lights** *npl* trafik ışıkları

lighter ['laɪtə] *n* çakmak

lighthouse ['laɪtˌhaʊs] *n* deniz feneri

lighting ['laɪtɪŋ] *n* ışıklandırma

lightning ['laɪtnɪŋ] *n* şimşek

like [laɪk] *prep* gibi ▷ *v* sevmek

likely ['laɪklɪ] *adj* olası

lilac ['laɪlək] *adj* leylak renkli ▷ *n* leylak

Lilo® ['laɪləʊ] *n* deniz yatağı

lily ['lɪlɪ] *n* zambak; **lily of the valley** *n* inci çiçeği

lime [laɪm] *n (compound)* kireç, *(fruit)* yeşil limon

limestone ['laɪmˌstəʊn] *n* kireç taşı

limit ['lɪmɪt] *n* sınır; **age limit** *n* yaş sınırı; **speed limit** *n* hız sınırı

limousine ['lɪməˌziːn; ˌlɪmə'ziːn] *n* limuzin

limp [lɪmp] *v* topallamak

line [laɪn] *n* çizgi; **washing line** *n* çamaşır ipi

linen ['lɪnɪn] *n* keten *(kumaş)*; **bed linen** *n* yatak çarşafı

liner ['laɪnə] *n* büyük yolcu gemisi

lingerie ['lænʒərɪ] *n* iç çamaşırı

linguist ['lɪŋgwɪst] *n* dilbilimci

linguistic [lɪŋ'gwɪstɪk] *adj* dilbilim

lining ['laɪnɪŋ] *n* astar *(kumaş)*

link [lɪŋk] *n* halka *(zincir)*; **link (up)** *v* birleştirmek *(parçaları)*

lino ['laɪnəʊ] *n* yer muşambası

lion ['laɪən] *n* aslan

lioness ['laɪənɪs] *n* aslan *(dişi)*

lip [lɪp] *n* dudak; **lip salve** *n* dudak kremi

lip-read ['lɪpˌriːd] *v* dudak okuma

lipstick ['lɪpˌstɪk] *n* ruj

liqueur [lɪ'kjʊə; likœr] *n* likör; **What liqueurs do you have?** Likör olarak neleriniz var?

liquid ['lɪkwɪd] *n* sıvı; **washing-up liquid** *n* bulaşık deterjanı

liquidizer ['lɪkwɪˌdaɪzə] *n* mikser

list [lɪst] *n* liste ▷ *v* listelemek; **mailing list** *n* adres listesi; **price list** *n* fiyat listesi; **waiting list** *n* bekleme listesi; **wine list** *n* şarap listesi; **The wine list, please** Şarap listesi lütfen

listen ['lɪsᵊn] *v* dinlemek; **listen to** *v* söz dinlemek

listener ['lɪsnə] *n* dinleyici

literally ['lɪtərəlɪ] *adv* harfi harfine

literature ['lɪtərɪtʃə; 'lɪtrɪ-] *n* edebiyat

Lithuania [ˌlɪθjʊ'eɪnɪə] *n* Litvanya

Lithuanian [ˌlɪθjʊ'eɪnɪən] *adj* Litvanya ▷ *n (language)* Litvanca *(dil)*, *(person)* Litvanyalı *(kişi)*

litre ['liːtə] *n* litre

litter ['lɪtə] *n (offspring)* yeni doğmuş yavrular, *(rubbish)* çöp; **litter bin** *n* çöp kutusu

little ['lɪtᵊl] *adj* küçük

live¹ [lɪv] *v* yaşamak

live² [laɪv] *adj* canlı *(yaşayan)*; **Where can we hear live music?** Canlı müzik dinleyebileceğimiz bir yer var mı?

lively ['laɪvlɪ] *adj* enerjik

live on [lɪv ɒn] v geçinmek
liver ['lɪvə] n karaciğer
live together [lɪv] v beraber yaşamak
living ['lɪvɪŋ] n canlı (yaşayan); **cost of living** n hayat pahalılığı; **living room** n oturma odası; **standard of living** n yaşam standardı
lizard ['lɪzəd] n kertenkele
load [ləʊd] n yük ▷ v yüklemek
loaf, loaves [ləʊf, ləʊvz] n somun (ekmek)
loan [ləʊn] n kredi ▷ v ödünç vermek
loathe [ləʊð] v tiksinmek
lobby ['lɒbɪ] n **I'll meet you in the lobby** Lobide buluşuruz
lobster ['lɒbstə] n ıstakoz
local ['ləʊkəl] adj yerel; **local anaesthetic** n lokal anestezi; **We'd like to see local plants and trees** Yerel bitkileri ve ağaçları görmek isterdik; **What's the local speciality?** Yerel yemeğiniz nedir?
location [ləʊ'keɪʃən] n yer; **My location is...** Yerim tam olarak...
lock [lɒk] n (door) kilit, (hair) bukle (saç) ▷ v kilitlemek; **The door won't lock** Kapı kilitlenmiyor; **The lock is broken** Kilit kırılmış; **The wheels lock** Tekerlekler kilitleniyor
locker ['lɒkə] n kilitli dolap; **left-luggage locker** n bagaj emanet dolabı
locket ['lɒkɪt] n madalyon
lock out [lɒk aʊt] v kilitlmek
locksmith ['lɒk‚smɪθ] n çilingir

lodger ['lɒdʒə] n pansiyoner
loft [lɒft] n tavan arası
log [lɒg] n tomruk
logical ['lɒdʒɪkəl] adj mantıklı
log in [lɒg ɪn] v oturum açmak
logo ['ləʊgəʊ; 'lɒg-] n logo
log off [lɒg ɒf] v oturum kapatmak
log on [lɒg ɒn] v oturum açmak
log out [lɒg aʊt] v oturum kapatmak
lollipop ['lɒlɪ‚pɒp] n lolipop
lolly ['lɒlɪ] n lolipop
London ['lʌndən] n Londra
loneliness ['ləʊnlɪnɪs] n yalnızlık
lonely ['ləʊnlɪ] adj yalnız
lonesome ['ləʊnsəm] adj yalnız
long [lɒŋ] adj uzun ▷ adv uzunca ▷ v özlemek; **long jump** n uzun atlama
longer [lɒŋə] adv daha uzun
longitude ['lɒndʒɪ‚tjuːd; 'lɒŋg-] n boylam
loo [luː] n tuvalet
look [lʊk] n bakış ▷ v gözünü dikmek; **look at** v gözünü dikmek
look after [lʊk ɑːftə] v bakmak
look for [lʊk fɔː] v aramak
look round [lʊk raʊnd] v bakınmak
look up [lʊk ʌp] v aramak
loose [luːs] adj gevşek (düğüm vb)
lorry ['lɒrɪ] n yük arabası; **lorry driver** n kamyon şoförü
lose [luːz] vi kaybolmak ▷ vt kaybetmek
loser ['luːzə] n yenilmiş
loss [lɒs] n kayıp
lost [lɒst] adj kayıp; **lost-property office** n kayıp eşya bürosu

lost-and-found ['lɒstænd'faʊnd] n kaybolup bulunmuş

lot [lɒt] n **a lot** n topluluk

lotion ['ləʊʃən] n losyon; **after sun lotion** n güneş sonrası krem; **cleansing lotion** n yüz temizleme losyonu; **suntan lotion** n bronzlaşma losyonu

lottery ['lɒtərɪ] n piyango

loud [laʊd] adj gürültülü; **It's too loud** Çok gürültülü

loudly ['laʊdlɪ] adv yüksek sesle

loudspeaker [ˌlaʊd'spiːkə] n hoparlör

lounge [laʊndʒ] n salon; **departure lounge** n uçuş bekleme salonu; **transit lounge** n transit yolcu salonu; **Could we have coffee in the lounge?** Salonda kahve içebilir miyiz?

lousy ['laʊzɪ] adj alçak

love [lʌv] n sevgi/aşk ▷ v sevmek

lovely ['lʌvlɪ] adj hoş

lover ['lʌvə] n aşık

low [ləʊ] adj aşağı (konum) ▷ adv aşağı (konum); **low season** n ucuz sezon

low-alcohol ['ləʊˌælkəˌhɒl] adj düşük alkollü

lower ['ləʊə] adj daha aşağı ▷ v düşürmek

low-fat ['ləʊˌfæt] adj az-yağlı

loyalty ['lɔɪəltɪ] n sadakat

luck [lʌk] n şans

luckily ['lʌkɪlɪ] adv neyse ki

lucky ['lʌkɪ] adj şanslı

lucrative ['luːkrətɪv] adj kazançlı

luggage ['lʌgɪdʒ] n bagaj; **hand luggage** n el bagajı; **luggage rack** n port bagaj; **luggage trolley** n

bagaj trolleyi; **Can I insure my luggage?** Bagajımı sigorta ettirebilir miyim?; **My luggage has been damaged** Bagajım hasar görmüş; **My luggage has been lost** Bagajım kaybolmuş; **My luggage hasn't arrived** Bagajım çıkmadı; **Where do I check in my luggage?** Bagajlarımı nerede check-in yaptırabilirim; **Where is the luggage for the flight from...?** ... uçağının bagajları nerede?

lukewarm [ˌluːk'wɔːm] adj ılık

lullaby ['lʌləˌbaɪ] n ninni

lump [lʌmp] n iri parça

lunatic ['luː'nætɪk] n (inf!) kaçık

lunch [lʌntʃ] n öğle yemeği; **lunch break** n yemek molası; **packed lunch** n paket yemek

lunchtime ['lʌntʃˌtaɪm] n yemek zamanı

lung [lʌŋ] n akciğer

lush [lʌʃ] adj özlü

lust [lʌst] n şehvet

Luxembourg ['lʌksəmˌbɜːg] n Lüksemburg

luxurious [lʌg'zjʊərɪəs] adj lüks

luxury ['lʌkʃərɪ] n lüks

lyrics ['lɪrɪks] npl güfte

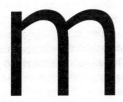

m

mac [mæk] *abbr* yağmurluk
macaroni [,mækə'rəʊnɪ] *npl*
makarna
machine [mə'ʃiːn] *n* makine;
answering machine *n*
telesekreter; **machine gun** *n*
makineli tüfek; **machine**
washable *adj* makinede
yıkanabilir; **sewing machine** *n*
dikiş makinesi; **slot machine** *n*
jetonlu makine; **ticket machine** *n*
bilet otomatı; **vending machine**
n otomatik satış makinesi;
washing machine *n* çamaşır
makinesi; **Can I use my card with**
this cash machine? Bu kartı bu
makinede kullanabilir miyim?;
How does the washing machine
work? Çamaşır makinesi nasıl
çalışıyor?; **Is there a fax machine**
I can use? Kullanabileceğim bir
faks makinesi var mı?; **The cash**
machine swallowed my card
Makine kartımı yuttu; **Where are**
the washing machines? Çamaşır
makineleri nerede?
machinery [mə'ʃiːnərɪ] *n*
mekanizma
mackerel ['mækrəl] *n* uskumru
mad [mæd] *adj (angry)* çılgın,
(insane) kaçık
Madagascar [,mædə'gæskə] *n*
Madagaskar
madam ['mædəm] *n* madam
madly ['mædlɪ] *adv* çılgınca
madman ['mædmən] *n* manyak
madness ['mædnɪs] *n* çılgınlık
magazine [,mægə'ziːn] *n*
(ammunition) şarjör, *(periodical)*
dergi; **Where can I buy a**
magazine? Dergi nereden
alabilirim?
maggot ['mægət] *n* larva
magic ['mædʒɪk] *adj* büyülü ▷ *n*
büyü
magical ['mædʒɪkəl] *adj* sihirli
magician [mə'dʒɪʃən] *n* sihirbaz
magistrate ['mædʒɪ,streɪt;
-strɪt] *n* sulh hakimi
magnet ['mægnɪt] *n* mıknatıs
magnetic [mæg'nɛtɪk] *adj*
mıknatıslı
magnificent [mæg'nɪfɪsᵊnt] *adj*
harika
magpie ['mæg,paɪ] *n* saksağan
mahogany [mə'hɒgənɪ] *n*
maun
maid [meɪd] *n* hizmetçi kadın
maiden ['meɪdᵊn] *n* **maiden**
name *n* kızlık soyadı
mail [meɪl] *n* posta ▷ *v* postalamak;
junk mail *n* istenmeyen posta

mailbox ['meɪl,bɒks] n posta kutusu

mailing list ['meɪlɪŋ 'lɪst] n adres listesi

main [meɪn] adj temel; **main course** n ana yemek; **main road** n anayol

mainland ['meɪnlənd] n anakara

mainly ['meɪnlɪ] adv başlıca

maintain [meɪn'teɪn] v sürdürmek

maintenance ['meɪntɪnəns] n bakım (araba vb)

maize [meɪz] n mısır

majesty ['mædʒɪstɪ] n görkem

major ['meɪdʒə] adj büyük

majority [mə'dʒɒrɪtɪ] n büyük çoğunluk

make [meɪk] v yapmak

makeover ['meɪk,əʊvə] n yenileme

maker ['meɪkə] n yapıcı

make up [meɪk ʌp] v oluşturmak

make-up ['meɪkʌp] n makyaj

malaria [mə'lɛərɪə] n sıtma

Malawi [mə'lɑːwɪ] n Malawi

Malaysia [mə'leɪzɪə] n Malezya

Malaysian [mə'leɪzɪən] adj Malezya ▷ n Malezyalı

male [meɪl] adj erkek ▷ n erkek

malicious [mə'lɪʃəs] adj kötü niyetli

malignant [mə'lɪgnənt] adj kötücül

malnutrition [,mælnjuː'trɪʃən] n yetersiz beslenme

Malta ['mɔːltə] n Malta

Maltese [mɔːl'tiːz] adj Malta ▷ n (language) Malta dili (dil), (person) Maltalı (kişi)

mammal ['mæməl] n memeli

mammoth ['mæməθ] adj devasa ▷ n mamut

man, men [mæn, mɛn] n erkek; **best man** n sağdıç

manage ['mænɪdʒ] v becermek

manageable ['mænɪdʒəbəl] adj üstesinden gelinebilir

management ['mænɪdʒmənt] n yönetim

manager ['mænɪdʒə] n müdür; **I'd like to speak to the manager, please** Müdürle konuşmak istiyorum lütfen

manageress [,mænɪdʒə'rɛs; 'mænɪdʒə,rɛs] n müdür (kadın)

mandarin ['mændərɪn] n (fruit) mandalina, (official) Çin'de yüksek memur

mangetout ['mɑ̃ʒ'tuː] n mangetout

mango ['mæŋgəʊ] n mango

mania ['meɪnɪə] n çılgınlık

maniac ['meɪnɪˌæk] n manyak

manicure ['mænɪˌkjʊə] n manikür ▷ v manikür yapmak

manipulate [mə'nɪpjʊˌleɪt] v idare etmek

mankind [,mæn'kaɪnd] n insanlık

man-made ['mæn,meɪd] adj insan yapısı

manner ['mænə] n tavır

manners ['mænəz] npl görgü

manpower ['mæn,paʊə] n insan gücü

mansion ['mænʃən] n konak

mantelpiece ['mæntəl,piːs] n şömine rafı

manual ['mænjʊəl] n kullanım kılavuzu

manufacture [ˌmænjʊˈfæktʃə] v
üretmek

manufacturer [ˌmænjʊˈfæktʃərə]
n üretici

manure [məˈnjʊə] n gübre

manuscript [ˈmænjʊˌskrɪpt] n
elyazması

many [ˈmɛnɪ] adj çok ▷ pron çok

Maori [ˈmaʊrɪ] adj Maori ▷ n
(language) Maori dili (dil), (person)
Maori (kişi)

map [mæp] n harita; **road map** n
yol haritası; **street map** n sokak
haritası; **Can I have a map?** Harita
alabilir miyim?; **Can you show me
where it is on the map?** Haritada
yerini gösterebilir misiniz?; **Do you
have a map of the ski runs?**
Kayak güzergahlarının haritası var
mı?; **Do you have a map of the
tube?** Metro haritası var mı?;
Have you got a map of...? ...
haritası var mı?; **I need a road
map of...** ... yol haritası istiyorum;
**Is there a cycle map of this
area?** Bu bölgenin bisiklet haritası
var mı?; **Where can I buy a map
of the area?** Bölgenin haritasını
nereden alabilirim?

maple [ˈmeɪpᵊl] n akçaağaç

marathon [ˈmærəθən] n
maraton

marble [ˈmɑːbᵊl] n mermer

march [mɑːtʃ] n uyun adım
yürüyüş ▷ v uygun adım yürümek

March [mɑːtʃ] n Mart

mare [mɛə] n kısrak

margarine [ˌmɑːdʒəˈriːn; ˌmɑːgə-]
n margarin

margin [ˈmɑːdʒɪn] n sınır

marigold [ˈmærɪˌgəʊld] n kadife
çiçeği

marijuana [ˌmærɪˈhwɑːnə] n Hint
keneviri (yaprakları esrar olarak
kullanılır)

marina [məˈriːnə] n yat limanı

marinade n [ˌmærɪˈneɪd] terbiye
sosu ▷ v [ˈmærɪˌneɪd] terbiye
sosuna yatırmak

marital [ˈmærɪtᵊl] adj **marital
status** n medeni hal

maritime [ˈmærɪˌtaɪm] adj
denizcilikle ilgili

marjoram [ˈmɑːdʒərəm] n
mercanköşk

mark [mɑːk] n işaret ▷ v (grade) not
vermek, (make sign) işaretlemek;
exclamation mark n ünlem
işareti; **question mark** n soru
işareti; **quotation marks** npl çift
tırnak

market [ˈmɑːkɪt] n pazar (piyasa);
market research n pazar
araştırması; **stock market** n
borsa; **When is the market on?**
Hangi günler pazar kuruluyor?

marketing [ˈmɑːkɪtɪŋ] n
pazarlama

marketplace [ˈmɑːkɪtˌpleɪs] n
pazar yeri

marmalade [ˈmɑːməˌleɪd] n
marmelat

maroon [məˈruːn] adj vişne
çürüğü renginde

marriage [ˈmærɪdʒ] n evlilik;
marriage certificate n evlilik
cüzdanı

married [ˈmærɪd] adj evli; **I'm
married** Evliyim

marrow [ˈmærəʊ] n ilik (anatomi)

marry ['mærɪ] v evlenmek

marsh [mɑːʃ] n bataklık

martyr ['mɑːtə] n şehit

marvellous ['mɑːvˀləs] adj harika

Marxism ['mɑːksɪzəm] n Marksizm

marzipan ['mɑːzɪˌpæn] n badem ezmesi

mascara [mæ'skɑːrə] n rimel

masculine ['mæskjʊlɪn] adj erkeksi

mask [mɑːsk] n maske

masked [mɑːskt] adj maskeli

mass [mæs] n (amount) kütle, (church) ayin (kilise); **When is mass?** Ayin ne zaman?

massacre ['mæsəkə] n katliam

massage ['mæsɑːʒ; -sɑːdʒ] n masaj

massive ['mæsɪv] adj masif

mast [mɑːst] n direk (kale, gemi)

master ['mɑːstə] n bey ▷ v üstesinden gelmek

masterpiece ['mɑːstəˌpiːs] n şaheser

mat [mæt] n paspas (ayak silme); **mouse mat** n fare pedi

match [mætʃ] n (partnership) denk (uygun), (sport) maç ▷ v uydurmak; **away match** n rakip sahada maç; **home match** n kendi sahasında maç; **I'd like to see a football match** Futbol maçı görmek isterdim

matching [mætʃɪŋ] adj uyumlu

mate [meɪt] n ahbap

material [mə'tɪərɪəl] n malzeme

maternal [mə'tɜːnˀl] adj annelik

mathematical [ˌmæθə'mætɪkˀl; ˌmæθ'mæt-] adj matematiksel

mathematics [ˌmæθə'mætɪks; ˌmæθ'mæt-] npl matematik

maths [mæθs] npl matematik

matter ['mætə] n madde (fizik) ▷ v önemli olmak

mattress ['mætrɪs] n yatak (döşek)

mature [mə'tjʊə; -'tʃʊə] adj olgun (kişi); **mature student** n olgun öğrenci

Mauritania [ˌmɒrɪ'teɪnɪə] n Moritanya

Mauritius [mə'rɪʃəs] n Mauritius Adası

mauve [məʊv] adj pembemsi leylak rengi

maximum ['mæksɪməm] adj en fazla ▷ n maksimum

May [meɪ] n Mayıs

maybe ['meɪˌbiː] adv belki

mayonnaise [ˌmeɪə'neɪz] n mayonez

mayor, mayoress [mɛə, 'mɛərɪs] n belediye başkanı

maze [meɪz] n labirent

me [miː] pron ben (kişi)

meadow ['mɛdəʊ] n çayır

meal [miːl] n öğün

mealtime ['miːlˌtaɪm] n yemek zamanı

mean [miːn] adj eli sıkı ▷ v kastetmek

meaning ['miːnɪŋ] n anlam

means [miːnz] npl yol

meantime ['miːnˌtaɪm] adv bu arada

meanwhile ['miːnˌwaɪl] adv o sırada

measles ['miːzəlz] npl kızamık; **German measles** n kızamıkçık;

I had measles recently
Yakınlarda kızamık geçirdim
measure ['mɛʒə] v ölçmek; **tape measure** n şerit metre
measurements ['mɛʒəmənts] npl ölçüler
meat [miːt] n et *(yiyecek)*; **red meat** n kırmızı et; **Do you eat meat?** Et yiyor musunuz?; **I don't eat meat** Et yemiyorum; **I don't eat red meat** Kırmızı et yemiyorum; **I don't like meat** Et sevmem; **The meat is cold** Et soğuk; **This meat is off** Et bozulmuş
meatball ['miːt,bɔːl] n köfte
Mecca ['mɛkə] n Mekke
mechanic [mɪ'kænɪk] n tamirci *(otomobil)*; **Can you send a mechanic?** Tamirci gönderebilir misiniz?
mechanical [mɪ'kænɪkəl] adj mekanik
mechanism ['mɛkə,nɪzəm] n mekanizma
medal ['mɛdəl] n madalya
medallion [mɪ'dæljən] n madalyon
media ['miːdɪə] npl medya
mediaeval [,mɛdɪ'iːvəl] adj ortaçağ
medical ['mɛdɪkəl] adj tıbbi ▷ n tıp; **medical certificate** n sağlık belgesi
medication [,mɛdɪ'keɪʃən] n **I'm on this medication** Bu ilacı kullanıyorum
medicine ['mɛdɪsɪn; 'mɛdsɪn] n ilaç
meditation [,mɛdɪ'teɪʃən] n meditasyon

Mediterranean [,mɛdɪtə'reɪnɪən] adj Akdeniz ▷ n Akdeniz
medium ['miːdɪəm] adj *(between extremes)* ılımlı
medium-sized ['miːdɪəm,saɪzd] adj orta boy
meet [miːt] vi toplanmak ▷ vt tanışmak; **It was a pleasure to meet you** Sizinle tanışmak bir zevk
meeting ['miːtɪŋ] n buluşma
meet up [miːt ʌp] v buluşmak
mega ['mɛgə] adj mega
melody ['mɛlədɪ] n melodi
melon ['mɛlən] n kavun
melt [mɛlt] vi eritmek
member ['mɛmbə] n üye
membership ['mɛmbə,ʃɪp] n üyelik; **membership card** n üyelik kartı
meme [miːm] n meme
memento [mɪ'mɛntəʊ] n hatıra
memo ['mɛməʊ; 'miːməʊ] n kısa not
memorial [mɪ'mɔːrɪəl] n anıt
memorize ['mɛmə,raɪz] v ezberlemek
memory ['mɛmərɪ] n bellek; **memory card** n hafıza kartı
mend [mɛnd] v onarmak
meningitis [,mɛnɪn'dʒaɪtɪs] n menenjit
menopause ['mɛnəʊ,pɔːz] n menopoz
menstruation [,mɛnstrʊ'eɪʃən] n regl
mental ['mɛntəl] adj akıl
mentality [mɛn'tælɪtɪ] n zihniyet
mention ['mɛnʃən] v bahsetmek

menu ['mɛnjuː] n mönü; **set menu** n fiks mönü
mercury ['mɜːkjʊrɪ] n cıva
mercy ['mɜːsɪ] n merhamet
mere [mɪə] adj sadece
merge [mɜːdʒ] v kaynaştırmak
merger ['mɜːdʒə] n şirket evliliği
meringue [məˈræŋ] n beze (tatlı)
mermaid ['mɜːˌmeɪd] n deniz kızı
merry ['mɛrɪ] adj şen şakrak
merry-go-round ['mɛrɪgəʊˈraʊnd] n atlıkarınca
mess [mɛs] n dağınıklık
mess about [mɛs əˈbaʊt] v boş durmak
message ['mɛsɪdʒ] n mesaj; **text message** n mesaj; **Are there any messages for me?** Bana mesaj var mı?; **Can I leave a message with his secretary?** Sekreterine mesaj bırakabilir miyim?; **Can I leave a message?** Mesaj bırakabilir miyim?
messenger ['mɛsɪndʒə] n ulak
mess up [mɛs ʌp] v berbat etmek
messy ['mɛsɪ] adj kirli
metabolism [mɪˈtæbəˌlɪzəm] n metabolizma
metal ['mɛtˀl] n metal
meteorite ['miːtɪəˌraɪt] n göktaşı
meter ['miːtə] n sayaç; **parking meter** n otopark ödeme cihazı
method ['mɛθəd] n yöntem
Methodist ['mɛθədɪst] adj Methodist mezhebine ait
metre ['miːtə] n metre
metric ['mɛtrɪk] adj metrik
Mexican ['mɛksɪkən] adj Meksika'ya ait ▷ n Meksikalı
Mexico ['mɛksɪˌkəʊ] n Meksika

microchip ['maɪkrəʊˌtʃɪp] n mikroçip
microphone ['maɪkrəˌfəʊn] n mikrofon; **Does it have a microphone?** Mikrofon var mı?
microscope ['maɪkrəˌskəʊp] n mikroskop
mid [mɪd] adj orta
midday ['mɪdˌdeɪ] n öğle; **It's twelve midday** Saat öğlen on iki
middle ['mɪdˀl] n orta; **Middle Ages** npl Orta Çağ; **Middle East** n Orta Doğu
middle-aged ['mɪdˀlˌeɪdʒɪd] adj orta yaşlı
middle-class ['mɪdˀlˌklɑːs] adj orta sınıf
midge [mɪdʒ] n tatarcık
midnight ['mɪdˌnaɪt] n geceyarısı; **at midnight** Geceyarısı
midwife, midwives ['mɪdˌwaɪf, 'mɪdˌwaɪvz] n ebe
migraine ['miːgreɪn; 'maɪ-] n migren
migrant ['maɪgrənt] adj göçmen ▷ n göçmen
migration [maɪˈgreɪʃən] n göç
mike [maɪk] n mikrofon
mild [maɪld] adj ılımlı
mile [maɪl] n mil
mileage ['maɪlɪdʒ] n mil hesabıyla uzaklık
mileometer [maɪˈlɒmɪtə] n mil ölçer
military ['mɪlɪtərɪ; -trɪ] adj askeri
milk [mɪlk] n süt ▷ v sağmak; **baby milk** n bebek sütü; **milk chocolate** n sütlü çikolata; **semi-skimmed milk** n yarım yağlı süt; **skimmed milk** n yağı alınmış

süt; **UHT milk** n UHT süt; **Do you drink milk?** Süt içer misiniz?; **Have you got real milk?** Taze sütünüz var mı?; **Is it made with unpasteurised milk?** Bu pastörize edilmemiş sütten mi yapıldı?; **with the milk separate** sütü ayrı getirin

milkshake ['mɪlkˌʃeɪk] n milkshake

mill [mɪl] n değirmen

millennium [mɪ'lenɪəm] n milenyum

millimetre ['mɪlɪˌmiːtə] n milimetre

million ['mɪljən] n milyon

millionaire [ˌmɪljə'neə] n milyoner

mimic ['mɪmɪk] v taklit etmek

mince [mɪns] v kıyma

mind [maɪnd] n zihin ⊳ v aldırmak

mine [maɪn] n maden ocağı ⊳ pron benim

miner ['maɪnə] n madenci

mineral ['mɪnərəl; 'mɪnrəl] adj madensel ⊳ n maden; **mineral water** n maden suyu; **a bottle of sparkling mineral water** Bir şişe maden suyu

miniature ['mɪnɪtʃə] adj minyatür ⊳ n minyatür

minibar ['mɪnɪˌbɑː] n minibar

minibus ['mɪnɪˌbʌs] n minibüs

minicab ['mɪnɪˌkæb] n taksi

minimal ['mɪnɪməl] adj en düşük

minimize ['mɪnɪˌmaɪz] v en aza indirgemek

minimum ['mɪnɪməm] adj en az ⊳ n en az

mining ['maɪnɪŋ] n madencilik

miniskirt ['mɪnɪˌskɜːt] n mini etek

minister ['mɪnɪstə] n (clergy) vaiz, (government) bakan (hükümet); **prime minister** n başbakan

ministry ['mɪnɪstrɪ] n (government) bakanlık, (religion) papazlık

mink [mɪŋk] n vizon

minor ['maɪnə] adj ufak ⊳ n küçük

minority [maɪ'nɒrɪtɪ; mɪ-] n azınlık

mint [mɪnt] n (coins) darphane, (herb/sweet) nane (bitki/şeker)

minus ['maɪnəs] prep eksi

minute adj [maɪ'njuːt] küçük ⊳ n ['mɪnɪt] dakika; **Could you watch my bag for a minute, please?** Bir dakikalığına çantama göz kulak olur musunuz lütfen?; **We are ten minutes late** On dakika geciktik

miracle ['mɪrək^əl] n mucize

mirror ['mɪrə] n ayna; **rear-view mirror** n arka ayna; **wing mirror** n yan ayna

misbehave [ˌmɪsbɪ'heɪv] v yaramazlık yapmak

miscarriage [mɪs'kærɪdʒ] n düşük yapmak

miscellaneous [ˌmɪsə'leɪnɪəs] adj çeşitli

mischief ['mɪstʃɪf] n yaramazlık

mischievous ['mɪstʃɪvəs] adj yaramaz (çocuk vb)

miser ['maɪzə] n zengin pinti

miserable ['mɪzərəb^əl; 'mɪzrə-] adj kepaze

misery ['mɪzərɪ] n sefalet

misfortune [mɪs'fɔːtʃən] n talihsizlik

mishap ['mɪshæp] n terslik

misjudge [ˌmɪsˈdʒʌdʒ] v yanlış hüküm vermek

mislay [mɪsˈleɪ] v yanlış yere koymak

misleading [mɪsˈliːdɪŋ] adj yanıltıcı

misprint [ˈmɪsˌprɪnt] n baskı hatası

miss [mɪs] v kaçırmak (treni, otobüsü)

Miss [mɪs] n Bayan (evlenmemiş kadınlara hitap şekli)

missile [ˈmɪsaɪl] n füze

missing [ˈmɪsɪŋ] adj kayıp; **My child is missing** Çocuğum kayıp

missionary [ˈmɪʃənərɪ] n misyoner

mist [mɪst] n sis

mistake [mɪˈsteɪk] n hata ▷ v hata yapmak

mistaken [mɪˈsteɪkən] adj hatalı

mistakenly [mɪˈsteɪkənlɪ] adv yanlışlıkla

mistletoe [ˈmɪsəlˌtəʊ] n ökseotu

mistress [ˈmɪstrɪs] n metres

misty [ˈmɪstɪ] adj sisli

misunderstand [ˌmɪsʌndəˈstænd] v yanlış anlamak

misunderstanding [ˌmɪsʌndəˈstændɪŋ] n yanlış anlama; **There's been a misunderstanding** Bir yanlış anlama var

mitten [ˈmɪtən] n parmaksız eldiven

mix [mɪks] n karışık (şeker/çiçek) ▷ v karıştırmak (nesne)

mixed [mɪkst] adj karışık; **mixed salad** n karışık salata

mixer [ˈmɪksə] n mikser

mixture [ˈmɪkstʃə] n karışım

mix up [mɪks ʌp] v karıştırmak (salata, baharat vb)

mix-up [mɪksʌp] n karışıklık

MMS [ɛm ɛm ɛs] abbr MMS

moan [məʊn] v inlemek

moat [məʊt] n hendek

mobile [ˈməʊbaɪl] adj mobil; **mobile home** n taşınabilir ev; **mobile number** n cep numarası; **mobile phone** n cep telefonu

mock [mɒk] adj deneme sınavı ▷ v alay etmek

mod cons [ˈmɒd kɒnz] npl konfor ve rahatlık

model [ˈmɒdəl] adj örnek ▷ n model ▷ v modelini yapmak

modem [ˈməʊdɛm] n modem

moderate [ˈmɒdərɪt] adj ılımlı

moderation [ˌmɒdəˈreɪʃən] n ılımlılık

modern [ˈmɒdən] adj modern; **modern languages** npl modern diller

modernize [ˈmɒdəˌnaɪz] v modernize etmek

modest [ˈmɒdɪst] adj alçak gönüllü

modification [ˌmɒdɪfɪˈkeɪʃən] n değişiklik

modify [ˈmɒdɪˌfaɪ] v değişiklik yapmak

module [ˈmɒdjuːl] n modül

moist [mɔɪst] adj ıslak

moisture [ˈmɔɪstʃə] n nem

moisturizer [ˈmɔɪstʃəˌraɪzə] n nemlendirici

Moldova [mɒlˈdəʊvə] n Moldova

Moldovan [mɒlˈdəʊvən] adj

Moldova ▷ n Moldovalı
mole [məʊl] n *(infiltrator)* köstebek *(casus)*, *(mammal)* köstebek *(hayvan)*, *(skin)* ben *(cilt)*
molecule ['mɒlɪˌkjuːl] n molekül.
moment ['məʊmənt] n an
momentarily ['məʊməntərəlɪ; -trɪlɪ] adv bir anlığına
momentary ['məʊməntərɪ; -trɪ] adj bir anlık
momentous [məʊ'mɛntəs] adj çok önemli
Monaco ['mɒnəˌkəʊ; mə'nɑːkəʊ] n Monako
monarch ['mɒnək] n kral
monarchy ['mɒnəkɪ] n kraliyet
monastery ['mɒnəstərɪ; -strɪ] n manastır; **Is the monastery open to the public?** Manastır halka açık mı?
Monday ['mʌndɪ] n Pazartesi; **It's Monday the fifteenth of June** On beş Haziran Pazartesi; **on Monday** Pazartesi günü
monetary ['mʌnɪtərɪ; -trɪ] adj parasal
money ['mʌnɪ] n para; **money belt** n bel çantası; **pocket money** n cep harçlığı; **Can I have my money back?** Paramı geri alabilir miyim?; **Can you arrange to have some money sent over urgently?** Bana acilen para gönderilmesini ayarlayabilir misiniz?; **I have no money** Hiç param yok; **I have run out of money** Param bitti; **I would like to transfer some money from my account** Hesabımdan para transferi yapmak istiyorum

Mongolia [mɒŋ'gəʊlɪə] n Moğolistan
Mongolian [mɒŋ'gəʊlɪən] adj Moğol ▷ n *(language)* Moğolca *(dil)*, *(person)* Mongolistanlı *(kişi)*
mongrel ['mʌŋgrəl] n melez
monitor ['mɒnɪtə] n gözcü
monk [mʌŋk] n keşiş
monkey ['mʌŋkɪ] n maymun
monopoly [mə'nɒpəlɪ] n tekel
monotonous [mə'nɒtənəs] adj tekdüze
monsoon [mɒn'suːn] n muson
monster ['mɒnstə] n canavar
month [mʌnθ] n ay *(zaman)*; **a month ago** bir ay önce; **in a month's time** bir ay sonra
monthly ['mʌnθlɪ] adj aylık *(zaman)*
monument ['mɒnjʊmənt] n anıt
mood [muːd] n ruh durumu
moody ['muːdɪ] adj bedbin
moon [muːn] n ay *(uydu)*; **full moon** n dolunay
moor [mʊə; mɔː] n bozkır ▷ v bağlamak *(tekne)*
mop [mɒp] n paspas *(yer silme)*
moped ['məʊpɛd] n moped; **I want to hire a moped** Moped kiralamak istiyorum
mop up [mɒp ʌp] v paspaslamak
moral ['mɒrəl] adj ahlaki ▷ n ders *(ahlaki)*
morale [mɒ'rɑːl] n moral
morals ['mɒrəlz] npl ahlak kuralları
more [mɔː] adj daha fazla ▷ adv daha ▷ pron fazla; **Could you speak more slowly, please?** Biraz daha yavaş konuşabilir

misiniz lütfen?; **Please bring more bread** Biraz daha ekmek getirir misiniz?; **We need more blankets** Daha fazla battaniyeye ihtiyacımız var

morgue [mɔːg] n morg

morning ['mɔːnɪŋ] n sabah; **morning sickness** n hamilelik bulantısı; **in the morning** sabah; **I will be leaving tomorrow morning at ten a.m.** Yarın sabah onda ayrılıyorum; **I've been sick since this morning** Bu sabahtan beri kusuyorum; **Is the museum open in the morning?** Müze sabahları açık mı?; **this morning** bu sabah; **tomorrow morning** yarın sabah

Moroccan [mə'rɒkən] adj Fas ▷ n Faslı

Morocco [mə'rɒkəʊ] n Fas

morphine ['mɔːfiːn] n morfin

Morse [mɔːs] n Morse (alfabe)

mortar ['mɔːtə] n (military) havan topu, (plaster) harç

mortgage ['mɔːgɪdʒ] n konut kredisi ▷ v ipotek etmek

mosaic [mə'zeɪɪk] n mozaik

Moslem ['mɒzləm] adj Müslüman ▷ n Müslüman

mosque [mɒsk] n cami; **Where is there a mosque?** Cami nerede var?

mosquito [mə'skiːtəʊ] n sivrisinek

moss [mɒs] n yosun

most [məʊst] adj en çok ▷ adv (superlative) en çok ▷ n (majority) çok

mostly ['məʊstlɪ] adv çoğunlukla

MOT [ɛm əʊ tiː] abbr yıllık taşıt testi

motel [məʊ'tɛl] n motel

moth [mɒθ] n güve

mother ['mʌðə] n anne; **mother tongue** n anadil; **surrogate mother** n taşıyıcı anne

mother-in-law ['mʌðə ɪn lɔː] (**mothers-in-law**) n kayınvalide

motionless ['məʊʃənlɪs] adj hareketsiz

motivated ['məʊtɪˌveɪtɪd] adj motive olmuş

motivation [ˌməʊtɪ'veɪʃən] n motivasyon

motive ['məʊtɪv] n sebep

motor ['məʊtə] n motor; **motor mechanic** n motor teknisyeni; **motor racing** n oto yarışı

motorbike ['məʊtəˌbaɪk] n motosiklet; **I want to hire a motorbike** Motosiklet kiralamak istiyorum

motorboat ['məʊtəˌbəʊt] n deniz motoru

motorcycle ['məʊtəˌsaɪkəl] n motosiklet

motorcyclist ['məʊtəˌsaɪklɪst] n motosikletçi

motorist ['məʊtərɪst] n sürücü

motorway ['məʊtəˌweɪ] n otoyol; **How do I get to the motorway?** Otoyola nereden gidebilirim?; **Is there a toll on this motorway?** Bu otoyol ücretli mi?

mould [məʊld] n (fungus) küf, (shape) kalıp (pasta, jöle, briket vb)

mouldy ['məʊldɪ] adj küflü

mount [maʊnt] v tırmanmak

mountain ['maʊntɪn] n dağ;

mountain bike n dağ bisikleti; **Where is the nearest mountain rescue service post?** En yakın dağ kurtarma ekibi nerede?

mountaineer [ˌmaʊntɪˈnɪə] n dağcı

mountaineering [ˌmaʊntɪˈnɪərɪŋ] n dağcılık

mountainous [ˈmaʊntɪnəs] adj dağlık

mount up [maʊnt ʌp] v birikmek

mourning [ˈmɔːnɪŋ] n matem

mouse, mice [maʊs, maɪs] n fare; **mouse mat** n fare pedi

mousse [muːs] n köpük krema

moustache [məˈstɑːʃ] n bıyık

mouth [maʊθ] n ağız; **mouth organ** n armonika

mouthwash [ˈmaʊθˌwɒʃ] n gargara

move [muːv] n hareket ▷ vi kımıldamak ▷ vt kımıldatmak

move back [muːv bæk] v geri gitmek

move forward [muːv fɔːwəd] v ileri gitmek

move in [muːv ɪn] v taşınmak

movement [ˈmuːvmənt] n hareket

movie [ˈmuːvɪ] n film (sinema)

moving [ˈmuːvɪŋ] adj dokunaklı (sahne, film)

mow [məʊ] v biçmek

mower [ˈmaʊə] n çim biçme makinesi

Mozambique [ˌməʊzəmˈbiːk] n Mozambik

mph [maɪlz pə aʊə] abbr mil/saat

Mr [ˈmɪstə] n Bay

Mrs [ˈmɪsɪz] n Bayan (hanım)

Ms [mɪz; məs] n Bayan (evli olup olmadığını belirtmeyenler için)

MS [ɛm ɛs] abbr MS (hastalık)

much [mʌtʃ] adj fazla ▷ adv fazla, (graded) çokça; **There's too much... in it** Çok fazla... koymuşsunuz

mud [mʌd] n çamur

muddle [ˈmʌdəl] n kargaşa

muddy [ˈmʌdɪ] adj çamurlu

mudguard [ˈmʌdˌgɑːd] n çamurluk

muesli [ˈmjuːzlɪ] n müsli

muffler [ˈmʌflə] n atkı (giysi)

mug [mʌg] n kupa (kahve) ▷ v saldırmak

mugger [ˈmʌgə] n kapkaççı

mugging [mʌgɪŋ] n kapkaççılık

mule [mjuːl] n katır

multinational [ˌmʌltɪˈnæʃənəl] adj çok uluslu ▷ n çok uluslu

multiple [ˈmʌltɪpəl] adj **multiple sclerosis** n multipl skleroz

multiplication [ˌmʌltɪplɪˈkeɪʃən] n çarpma işlemi

multiply [ˈmʌltɪˌplaɪ] v çarpmak (matematik)

mum [mʌm] n anne

mummy [ˈmʌmɪ] n (body) mumya, (mother) annecim

mumps [mʌmps] n kabakulak

murder [ˈmɜːdə] n cinayet ▷ v katletmek

murderer [ˈmɜːdərə] n katil

muscle [ˈmʌsəl] n kas

muscular [ˈmʌskjʊlə] adj kas

museum [mjuːˈzɪəm] n müze; **Is the museum open every day?** Müze her gün açık mı?; **When is the museum open?** Müze ne zaman açık?

mushroom ['mʌʃruːm; -rʊm] *n*
mantar *(botanik)*

music ['mjuːzɪk] *n* müzik; **folk**
music *n* halk müziği; **music**
centre *n* müzik seti; **Where can**
we hear live music? Canlı müzik
dinleyebileceğimiz bir yer var mı?

musical ['mjuːzɪkᵊl] *adj* müzik ▷ *n*
müzikal; **musical instrument** *n*
müzik aleti

musician [mjuː'zɪʃən] *n* müzisyen;
Where can we hear local
musicians play? Yerel
müzisyenleri dinleyebileceğimiz
bir yer var mı?

Muslim ['mʊzlɪm; 'mʌz-] *adj*
Müslüman ▷ *n* Müslüman

mussel ['mʌsᵊl] *n* midye

must [mʌst] *v* gereğinde olmak

mustard ['mʌstəd] *n* hardal

mutter ['mʌtə] *v* mırıldanmak

mutton ['mʌtᵊn] *n* koyun eti

mutual ['mjuːtʃʊəl] *adj* karşılıklı

my [maɪ] *pron* benim

Myanmar ['maɪænmɑː;
'mjænmɑː] *n* Myanmar

myself [maɪ'sɛlf] *pron* kendim

mysterious [mɪ'stɪərɪəs] *adj*
gizemli

mystery ['mɪstərɪ] *n* gizem

myth [mɪθ] *n* efsane

mythology [mɪ'θɒlədʒɪ] *n*
mitoloji

naff [næf] *adj* salaş

nag [næg] *v* dırdır etmek

nail [neɪl] *n* çivi; **nail polish** *n* oje;
nail scissors *npl* tırnak makası;
nail varnish *n* tırnak cilası; **nail**
varnish remover *n* oje çıkarıcı

nailbrush ['neɪlˌbrʌʃ] *n* tırnak
fırçası

nailfile ['neɪlˌfaɪl] *n* tırnak törpüsü

naive [nɑː'iːv; naɪ'iːv] *adj* saf

naked ['neɪkɪd] *adj* çıplak

name [neɪm] *n* ad *(kişi)*; **brand**
name *n* marka; **first name** *n* ön
ad; **maiden name** *n* kızlık soyadı;
I booked a room in the name
of... ... adına yer ayırtmıştım; **My**
name is... Benim adım...; **What's**
your name? Adınız ne?

nanny ['nænɪ] *n* çocuk bakıcısı

nap [næp] *n* kestirme *(uyku)*

napkin ['næpkɪn] *n* peçete

nappy ['næpɪ] *n* bebek bezi

narrow ['nærəʊ] adj dar
narrow-minded
['nærəʊ'maɪndɪd] adj dar görüşlü
nasty ['nɑːstɪ] adj berbat
nation ['neɪʃən] n ulus; **United
Nations** n Birleşmiş Milletler
national ['næʃən⁹l] adj ulusal;
national anthem n milli marş;
national park n milli park
nationalism ['næʃənə̩lɪzəm;
'næʃnə-] n ulusalcılık
nationalist ['næʃənəlɪst] n
ulusalcı
nationality [ˌnæʃə'nælɪtɪ] n ulus
nationalize ['næʃənəˌlaɪz;
'næʃnə-] v kamulaştırmak
native ['neɪtɪv] adj yerli; **native
speaker** n anadilini konuşan
NATO ['neɪtəʊ] abbr NATO
natural ['nætʃrəl; -tʃərəl] adj
doğal; **natural gas** n doğal gaz;
natural resources npl doğal
kaynaklar
naturalist ['nætʃrəlɪst; -tʃərəl-] n
doğa bilimleri uzmanı
naturally ['nætʃrəlɪ; -tʃərə-] adv
doğal olarak
nature ['neɪtʃə] n doğa
naughty ['nɔːtɪ] adj yaramaz
(çocuk vb)
nausea ['nɔːzɪə; -sɪə] n bulantı
naval ['neɪv⁹l] adj deniz (askeri)
navel ['neɪv⁹l] n göbek
navy ['neɪvɪ] n donanma (deniz)
navy-blue ['neɪvɪ'bluː] adj lacivert
NB [ɛn biː] abbr (notabene)
dikkatinize
near [nɪə] adj yakın ▷ adv yakınında
▷ prep bitişiğinde; **How do I get
to the nearest tube station?**

En yakın metro istasyonuna nasıl
gidebilirim?; **It's very near** Çok
yakın; **Where is the nearest bus
stop?** Buraya en yakın otobüs
durağı nerede?
nearby adj ['nɪəˌbaɪ] yakın ▷ adv
[ˌnɪə'baɪ] yakınlarda; **Is there a
bank nearby?** Yakınlarda bir
banka var mı?
nearly ['nɪəlɪ] adv hemen hemen
near-sighted [ˌnɪə'saɪtɪd] adj
miyop
neat [niːt] adj temiz ve tertipli
neatly [niːtlɪ] adv derli toplu
(düzenli)
necessarily ['nɛsɪsərɪlɪ;
ˌnɛsɪ'sɛrɪlɪ] adv kaçınılmaz bir
şekilde
necessary ['nɛsɪsərɪ] adj gerekli
necessity [nɪ'sɛsɪtɪ] n gereklilik
neck [nɛk] n boyun
necklace ['nɛklɪs] n kolye
nectarine ['nɛktərɪn] n nektarin
need [niːd] n ihtiyaç ▷ v gerek
duymak
needle ['niːd⁹l] n iğne; **knitting
needle** n örgü şişi
negative ['nɛgətɪv] adj olumsuz
▷ n olumsuz
neglect [nɪ'glɛkt] n ihmal ▷ v ihmal
etmek
neglected [nɪ'glɛktɪd] adj ihmal
edilmiş
negligee ['nɛglɪˌʒeɪ] n gecelik
(hafif)
negotiate [nɪ'gəʊʃɪˌeɪt] v görüşmek
negotiations [nɪˌgəʊʃɪ'eɪʃənz] npl
görüşmeler
negotiator [nɪ'gəʊʃɪˌeɪtə] n
görüşmeci

neighbour ['neɪbə] n komşu
neighbourhood ['neɪbəˌhʊd] n
mahalle
neither ['naɪðə; 'niːðə] adv hiçbiri
▷ conj ne ▷ pron hiçbir
neon ['niːɒn] n neon
Nepal [nɪ'pɔːl] n Nepal
nephew ['nɛvjuː; 'nɛf-] n yeğen
(erkek)
nerve [nɜːv] n (boldness) cüret,
(anat) sinir (anatomi)
nerve-racking ['nɜːv'rækɪŋ] adj
sinir bozucu
nervous ['nɜːvəs] adj sinirli;
nervous breakdown n sinir krizi
nest [nɛst] n yuva
net [nɛt] n tül
Net [nɛt] n İnternet
netball ['nɛtˌbɔːl] n netbol
Netherlands ['nɛðələndz] npl
Hollanda
nettle ['nɛtəl] n ısırgan
network ['nɛtˌwɜːk] n ağ
(bilişim)
neurotic [njʊ'rɒtɪk] adj nörotik
neutral ['njuːtrəl] adj tarafsız ▷ n
tarafsız
never ['nɛvə] adv asla
nevertheless [ˌnɛvəðə'lɛs] adv
bununla birlikte
new [njuː] adj yeni; **New Year** n
Yeni Yıl; **New Zealand** n Yeni
Zelanda; **New Zealander** n Yeni
Zelandalı
newborn ['njuːˌbɔːn] adj yeni
doğan
newcomer ['njuːˌkʌmə] n yeni
gelen
news [njuːz] npl haberler; **When is
the news?** Haberler kaçta?

newsagent ['njuːzˌeɪdʒənt] n
gazete bayii
newspaper ['njuːzˌpeɪpə] n
gazete; **Do you have
newspapers?** Gazete satıyor
musunuz?; **I would like a
newspaper** Gazete almak
istiyorum; **Where can I buy a
newspaper?** Gazete nereden
alabilirim?; **Where is the nearest
shop which sells newspapers?**
En yakın gazete satan dükkan
nerede?
newsreader ['njuːzˌriːdə] n haber
sunucusu
newt [njuːt] n su keleri
next [nɛkst] adj gelecek ▷ adv bir
sonraki; **next to** prep yanında; **the
week after next** bir sonraki
hafta; **What is the next stop?** Bir
sonraki durak neresi?; **When is
the next bus to…?**… a bir sonraki
otobüs kaçta?
next-of-kin ['nɛkstɒv'kɪn] n en
yakın akraba
Nicaragua [ˌnɪkə'rægjʊə;
nika'raɣwa] n Nicaragua
Nicaraguan [ˌnɪkə'rægjʊən;
-gwən] adj Nikaragua ▷ n
Nikaragualı
nice [naɪs] adj hoş
nickname ['nɪkˌneɪm] n takma ad
nicotine ['nɪkəˌtiːn] n nikotin
niece [niːs] n yeğen (kız)
Niger ['naɪdʒɪər] n Nijer
Nigeria [naɪ'dʒɪərɪə] n Nijerya
Nigerian [naɪ'dʒɪərɪən] adj Nijerya
▷ n Nijeryalı
night [naɪt] n gece; **hen night** n
kına gecesi; **night school** n gece

okulu; **stag night** n bekarlığa veda
partisi *(erkek)*; **at night** gece;
Good night İyi geceler; **How
much is it per night?** Odanın
geceliği ne kadar?; **I want to stay
an extra night** Bir gece daha
kalmak istiyorum; **I'd like to stay
for two nights** İki gece kalmak
istiyorum; **last night** dün gece;
tomorrow night yarın gece

nightclub ['naɪtˌklʌb] n gece
kulübü

nightdress ['naɪtˌdrɛs] n gecelik

nightie ['naɪtɪ] n gecelik

nightlife ['naɪtˌlaɪf] n gece hayatı

nightmare ['naɪtˌmɛə] n
karabasan

nightshift ['naɪtˌʃɪft] n gece
nöbeti

nil [nɪl] n sıfır

nine [naɪn] *number* dokuz

nineteen [ˌnaɪn'tiːn] *number*
ondokuz

nineteenth [ˌnaɪn'tiːnθ] *adj*
ondokuzuncu

ninety ['naɪntɪ] *number* doksan

ninth [naɪnθ] *adj* dokuzuncu ▷ n
dokuzda bir

nitrogen ['naɪtrədʒən] n
nitrojen

no [nəʊ] *pron* hiç; **no!** *excl* hayır;
no one *pron* hiç kimse; **I have no
money** Hiç param yok

nobody ['nəʊbədɪ] *pron* hiç kimse;
**We'd like to see nobody but us
all day!** Bütün gün hiç kimseyi
değil, sadece kendimizi görmek
isterdik!

nod [nɒd] v başıyla onaylamak

noise [nɔɪz] n gürültü; **I can't**

sleep for the noise Gürültüden
uyuyamıyorum

noisy ['nɔɪzɪ] *adj* gürültülü; **It's
noisy** Çok gürültülü; **The room is
too noisy** Bu oda çok gürültülü

nominate ['nɒmɪˌneɪt] v aday
göstermek

nomination [ˌnɒmɪ'neɪʃən] n
adaylık

none [nʌn] *pron* hiçbiri

nonsense ['nɒnsəns] n saçma

non-smoker [nɒn'sməʊkə] n
sigara içmeyen

non-smoking [nɒn'sməʊkɪŋ] *adj*
sigara içilmeyen; **I want to book
a seat in a non-smoking
compartment** Sigara içilmeyen
kompartmanda yer ayırtmak
istiyorum

non-stop ['nɒn'stɒp] *adv* hiç
durmadan

noodles ['nuːdᵊlz] *npl* noodle

noon [nuːn] n öğle

nor [nɔː; nə] *conj* ne de

normal ['nɔːmᵊl] *adj* normal; **How
long will it take by normal post?**
Normal postayla ne kadar sürer?

normally ['nɔːməlɪ] *adv* normalde

north [nɔːθ] *adj* kuzey ▷ *adv*
kuzeyde ▷ n kuzey; **North Africa** n
Kuzey Afrika; **North African** n
Kuzey Afrika, Kuzey Afrikalı;
North America n Kuzey Amerika;
North American n Kuzey
Amerika, Kuzey Amerikalı; **North
Korea** n Kuzey Kore; **North Pole** n
Kuzey Kutbu; **North Sea** n Kuzey
Denizi

northbound ['nɔːθˌbaʊnd] *adj*
kuzeye doğru

northeast [ˌnɔːθˈiːst; ˌnɔːrˈiːst] n
kuzeydoğu

northern [ˈnɔːðən] adj kuzey;
Northern Ireland n Kuzey İrlanda

northwest [ˌnɔːθˈwɛst; ˌnɔːrˈwɛst]
n kuzeybatı

Norway [ˈnɔːˌweɪ] n Norveç

Norwegian [nɔːˈwiːdʒən] adj
Norveç ▷ n (language) Norveççe
(dil), (person) Norveçli (kişi)

nose [nəʊz] n burun

nosebleed [ˈnəʊzˌbliːd] n burun
kanaması

nostril [ˈnɒstrɪl] n burun deliği

nosy [ˈnəʊzɪ] adj meraklı

not [nɒt] adv yok

note [nəʊt] n (banknote) banknot,
(message) not (mesaj), (music)
nota (müzik); **sick note** n hasta
belgesi

notebook [ˈnəʊtˌbʊk] n not
defteri

note down [nəʊt daʊn] v not
almak

notepad [ˈnəʊtˌpæd] n not defteri

notepaper [ˈnəʊtˌpeɪpə] n not
kağıdı

nothing [ˈnʌθɪŋ] pron hiçbir şey

notice [ˈnəʊtɪs] n (note) farkına
varma, (termination) mühlet ▷ v
farkına varmak; **notice board** n
ilan tahtası

noticeable [ˈnəʊtɪsəbəl] adj
dikkat çeken

notification [ˌnəʊtɪfɪˈkeɪʃən] n
bildirim

notify [ˈnəʊtɪˌfaɪ] v bildirimde
bulunmak

nought [nɔːt] n sıfır

noun [naʊn] n ad (gramer)

novel [ˈnɒvəl] n roman

novelist [ˈnɒvəlɪst] n romancı

November [nəʊˈvɛmbə] n Kasım
(ay)

now [naʊ] adv şimdi

nowadays [ˈnaʊəˌdeɪz] adv
bugünlerde

nowhere [ˈnəʊˌwɛə] adv hiçbir
yerde

nuclear [ˈnjuːklɪə] adj nükleer

nude [njuːd] adj çıplak ▷ n çıplak

nudist [ˈnjuːdɪst] n nüdist

nuisance [ˈnjuːsəns] n sıkıntı

numb [nʌm] adj uyuşuk

number [ˈnʌmbə] n sayı; **account
number** n hesap numarası;
mobile number n cep numarası;
number plate n plaka (otomobil);
phone number n telefon
numarası; **reference number** n
referans numarası; **room number**
n oda numarası; **wrong number** n
yanlış numara

numerous [ˈnjuːmərəs] adj
sayısız

nun [nʌn] n rahibe

nurse [nɜːs] n hemşire; **I'd like to
speak to a nurse** Hemşireyle
konuşmak istiyorum

nursery [ˈnɜːsrɪ] n çocuk odası;
nursery rhyme n çocuk şarkıları;
nursery school n kreş

nursing home [ˈnɜːsɪŋ həʊm] n
huzurevi (yaşlılar için)

nut [nʌt] n (device) vida somunu,
(food) fındık fıstık; **nut allergy** n
fıstık alerjisi; **Could you prepare a
meal without nuts?** İçinde fındık
fıstık olmayan bir yemek yapabilir
misiniz?

nutmeg ['nʌtmɛg] *n* küçük
Hindistan cevizi
nutrient ['njuːtrɪənt] *n* besleyici
(gıda)
nutrition [njuːˈtrɪʃən] *n* beslenme
nutritious [njuːˈtrɪʃəs] *adj*
besleyici
nutter ['nʌtə] *n* kaçık
nylon ['naɪlɒn] *n* naylon

oak [əʊk] *n* meşe
oar [ɔː] *n* kürek
oasis, oases [əʊˈeɪsɪs, əʊˈeɪsiːz] *n*
vaha
oath [əʊθ] *n* yemin
oatmeal ['əʊtˌmiːl] *n* yulaf ezmesi
oats [əʊts] *npl* yulaf
obedient [əˈbiːdɪənt] *adj* itaatkar
obese [əʊˈbiːs] *adj* obez
obey [əˈbeɪ] *v* boyun eğmek
obituary [əˈbɪtjʊərɪ] *n* anma yazısı
(ölünün ardından)
object ['ɒbdʒɪkt] *n* nesne
objection [əbˈdʒɛkʃən] *n* itiraz
objective [əbˈdʒɛktɪv] *n* amaç
oblong ['ɒbˌlɒŋ] *adj* dikdörtgen
şeklinde
obnoxious [əbˈnɒkʃəs] *adj* iğrenç
oboe ['əʊbəʊ] *n* obua
obscene [əbˈsiːn] *adj* açık saçık
observant [əbˈzɜːvənt] *adj*
gözlemci

observatory [əb'zɜːvətərɪ; -trɪ] *n*
gözlemevi

observe [əb'zɜːv] *v* gözlemlemek

observer [əb'zɜːvə] *n* gözlemci

obsessed [əb'sɛst] *adj* takıntılı

obsession [əb'sɛʃən] *n* takıntı

obsolete ['ɒbsəliːt; ˌɒbsə'liːt] *adj*
modası geçmiş

obstacle ['ɒbstəkəl] *n* engel

obstinate ['ɒbstɪnɪt] *adj* müzmin

obstruct [əb'strʌkt] *v* tıkamak

obtain [əb'teɪn] *v* elde etmek

obvious ['ɒbvɪəs] *adj* açık *(kavram)*

obviously ['ɒbvɪəslɪ] *adv* açıkçası

occasion [ə'keɪʒən] *n* fırsat
(durum)

occasional [ə'keɪʒənəl] *adj* arasıra

occasionally [ə'keɪʒənəlɪ] *adv*
arada sırada

occupation [ˌɒkjʊ'peɪʃən] *n*
(invasion) işgal, *(work)* meslek

occupy ['ɒkjʊˌpaɪ] *v* oturmak

occur [ə'kɜː] *v* meydana gelmek

occurrence [ə'kʌrəns] *n* olay

ocean ['əʊʃən] *n* okyanus; **Arctic
Ocean** *n* Kuzey Okyanusu; **Indian
Ocean** *n* Hint Okyanusu

Oceania [ˌəʊʃɪ'ɑːnɪə] *n* Okyanusya

o'clock [ə'klɒk] *adv* **after eight
o'clock** saat sekizden sonra; **at
three o'clock** saat üçte; **I'd like
to book a table for four people
for tonight at eight o'clock** Bu
akşam saat sekiz için dört kişilik
bir masa ayırtmak istiyordum;
It's one o'clock Saat bir;
It's six o'clock Saat altı

October [ɒk'təʊbə] *n* Ekim *(ay)*;
It's Sunday the third of October
Üç Ekim Pazar

octopus ['ɒktəpəs] *n* ahtapot

odd [ɒd] *adj* acaip

odour ['əʊdə] *n* koku

of [ɒv; əv] *prep* onun

off [ɒf] *adv* kapalı ▷ *prep* den, dan;
time off *n* izin *(işten alınan)*

offence [ə'fɛns] *n* saldırı

offend [ə'fɛnd] *v* gücendirmek

offensive [ə'fɛnsɪv] *adj* saldırgan

offer ['ɒfə] *n* teklif ▷ *v* teklif etmek;
special offer *n* indirimli fiyatla
sunulan eşya

office ['ɒfɪs] *n* büro; **booking
office** *n* bilet gişesi; **box office** *n*
bilet gişesi; **head office** *n* yönetim
merkezi; **information office** *n*
enformasyon bürosu;
left-luggage office *n* emanet
bagaj bürosu; **lost-property
office** *n* kayıp eşya bürosu; **office
hours** *npl* çalışma saatleri; **post
office** *n* postane; **registry office** *n*
evlendirme dairesi; **ticket office** *n*
bilet gişesi; **tourist office** *n* turizm
bürosu; **Do you have a press
office?** Basın büronuz var mı?;
How do I get to your office?
Büronuza nasıl gelebilirim?; **I work
in an office** Bir büroda
çalışıyorum

officer ['ɒfɪsə] *n* görevli memur
(polis/asker); **customs officer** *n*
gümrük memuru; **police officer** *n*
polis görevlisi; **prison officer** *n*
hapishane görevlisi

official [ə'fɪʃəl] *adj* yetkili

off-licence ['ɒfˌlaɪsəns] *n* içki
satan dükkan

off-peak ['ɒfˌpiːk] *adv* iş saatleri
dışında

off-season [ˈɒfˌsiːzᵊn] adj sezon dışı ▷ adv sezon dışında

offside [ˈɒfˈsaɪd] adj ofsayt

often [ˈɒfᵊn; ˈɒftᵊn] adv sıklıkla

oil [ɔɪl] n yağ ▷ v yağlamak; **olive oil** n zeytin yağı; **The oil warning light won't go off** Yağ ikaz ışığı yanıyor; **This stain is oil** Yağ lekesi

oil refinery [ɔɪl rɪˈfaɪnərɪ] n petrol rafinerisi

oil rig [ɔɪl rɪg] n petrol platformu

oil slick [ɔɪl slɪk] n petrol sızması

oil well [ɔɪl wɛl] n petrol kuyusu

ointment [ˈɔɪntmənt] n merhem

OK [ˌəʊˈkeɪ] excl OK!

okay [ˌəʊˈkeɪ] adj okey; **okay!** excl okey!

old [əʊld] adj yaşlı; **old-age pensioner** n emekli

old-fashioned [ˈəʊldˈfæʃənd] adj eski moda

olive [ˈɒlɪv] n zeytin; **olive oil** n zeytin yağı; **olive tree** n zeytin ağacı

Oman [əʊˈmɑːn] n Umman

omelette [ˈɒmlɪt] n omlet

on [ɒn] adv açık ▷ prep de, da; **on behalf of** namına; **on time** adj zamanında; **I don't have my driving licence on me** Ehliyetim üzerimde değil; **I'm here on holiday** Burada tatildeyim; **I'm on a diet** Rejimdeyim; **It's on the corner** Köşede; **Take the first turning on your right** Sağdan ilk sokağa dönün; **The drinks are on me** İçkiler benden; **What's on tonight at the cinema?** Bu gece sinemada ne var?; **Which film is on at the cinema?** Sinemada hangi film oynuyor?

once [wʌns] adv bir seferinde

one [wʌn] number bir ▷ pron bir; **no one** pron hiç kimse

one-off [wʌnɒf] n bir seferlik

onion [ˈʌnjən] n soğan; **spring onion** n taze soğan

online [ˈɒnˌlaɪn] adj çevirimiçi ▷ adv hatta (bilgisayar)

onlooker [ˈɒnˌlʊkə] n izleyici

only [ˈəʊnlɪ] adj tek ▷ adv yalnızca

open [ˈəʊpᵊn] adj açık (kapı, pencere vb) ▷ v açmak (kapı vb); **opening hours** npl açılış saatleri; **Are you open?** Açık mısınız?; **Is it open today?** Bugün açık mı?; **Is the castle open to the public?** Kale halka açık mı?; **Is the museum open in the afternoon?** Müze öğleden sonra açık mı?

opera [ˈɒpərə] n opera; **soap opera** n televizyon dizisi; **What's on tonight at the opera?** Bu gece operada ne var?

operate [ˈɒpəˌreɪt] v (to function) işlemek, (to perform surgery) ameliyat etmek

operating theatre [ˈɒpəˌreɪtɪŋ ˈθɪətə] n ameliyat odası

operation [ˌɒpəˈreɪʃən] n (surgery) ameliyat (tıp), (undertaking) operasyon

operator [ˈɒpəˌreɪtə] n operatör

opinion [əˈpɪnjən] n fikir (bir konuda); **opinion poll** n kamuoyu yoklaması; **public opinion** n kamuoyu

opponent [əˈpəʊnənt] n karşıt

opportunity [ˌɒpə'tjuːnɪtɪ] n
fırsat *(olanak)*

oppose [ə'pəʊz] v karşı çıkmak

opposed [ə'pəʊzd] adj karşı

opposing [ə'pəʊzɪŋ] adj karşı
çıkan

opposite ['ɒpəzɪt; -sɪt] adj karşıt
▷ adv karşılıklı ▷ prep karşısında

opposition [ˌɒpə'zɪʃən] n
muhalefet

optician [ɒp'tɪʃən] n gözlükçü

optimism ['ɒptɪˌmɪzəm] n
iyimserlik

optimist ['ɒptɪˌmɪst] n iyimser

optimistic [ɒptɪ'mɪstɪk] adj
iyimser

option ['ɒpʃən] n seçenek

optional ['ɒpʃənᵊl] adj isteğe bağlı

opt out [ɒpt aʊt] v çekilmek

or [ɔː] conj ya; **either... or** conj ya

oral ['ɔːrəl; 'ɒrəl] adj sözlü ▷ n sözlü

orange ['ɒrɪndʒ] adj portakal rengi
▷ n portakal; **orange juice** n
portakal suyu

orchard ['ɔːtʃəd] n meyve bahçesi

orchestra ['ɔːkɪstrə] n orkestra

orchid ['ɔːkɪd] n orkide

ordeal [ɔː'diːl] n çetin sınav

order ['ɔːdə] n emir, sıra ▷ v
(command) komut vermek,
(request) ısmarlamak; **order form**
n sipariş formu; **postal order** n
posta havalesi; **standing order** n
banka ödeme emri; **I'd like to
order something local** Yöreye
özgü bir şey ısmarlamak istiyorum

ordinary ['ɔːdᵊnrɪ] adj sıradan

oregano [ˌɒrɪ'gɑːnəʊ] n
mercanköşk *(yabani)*

organ ['ɔːgən] n *(body part)* organ,
(music) org; **mouth organ** n
armonika

organic [ɔː'gænɪk] adj organik

organism ['ɔːgəˌnɪzəm] n
organizma

organization [ˌɔːgənaɪ'zeɪʃən] n
organizasyon

organize ['ɔːgəˌnaɪz] v organize
etmek

organizer ['ɔːgəˌnaɪzə] n
personal organizer n kişisel
organizatör

orgasm ['ɔːgæzəm] n orgazm

Orient ['ɔːrɪənt] n Doğu

oriental [ˌɔːrɪ'ɛntᵊl] adj oryantal

origin ['ɒrɪdʒɪn] n kaynak *(çıkış
noktası)*

original [ə'rɪdʒɪnᵊl] adj özgün

originally [ə'rɪdʒɪnəlɪ] adv
başlangıç olarak

ornament ['ɔːnəmənt] n süs

orphan ['ɔːfən] n kimsesiz

ostrich ['ɒstrɪtʃ] n devekuşu

other ['ʌðə] adj diğer

otherwise ['ʌðəˌwaɪz] adv başka
türlü ▷ conj yoksa

otter ['ɒtə] n su samuru

ounce [aʊns] n ons

our [aʊə] adj bizim

ours [aʊəz] pron bizimki

ourselves [aʊə'sɛlvz] pron biz
(kendimiz)

out [aʊt] adj dış (iç karşıtı) ▷ adv
dışarıda; **He's out** Dışarıda

outbreak ['aʊtˌbreɪk] n ayaklanma

outcome ['aʊtˌkʌm] n sonuç

outdoor ['aʊt'dɔː] adj açık hava;
**What outdoor activities are
there?** Açık hava sporu olarak
ne yapabilirim?

outdoors [ˌaʊtˈdɔːz] adv açık havada

outfit [ˈaʊtˌfɪt] n kılık

outgoing [ˈaʊtˌgəʊɪŋ] adj dışa dönük

outing [ˈaʊtɪŋ] n dışarı çıkmak

outline [ˈaʊtˌlaɪn] n özet

outlook [ˈaʊtˌlʊk] n yaşama bakış

out-of-date [ˈaʊtʊvˈdeɪt] adj günü geçmiş

out-of-doors [ˈaʊtʊvˈdɔːz] adv açık havada

outrageous [aʊtˈreɪdʒəs] adj dehşet verici

outset [ˈaʊtˌsɛt] n başlangıç (çıkış)

outside adj [ˈaʊtˌsaɪd] dışarı ▷ adv [ˌaʊtˈsaɪd] dışarıda ▷ n [ˈaʊtˈsaɪd] dışarısı ▷ prep dışında; **I want to make an outside call, can I have a line?** Dışarıyı aramak istiyorum, hat bağlar mısınız?

outsize [ˈaʊtˌsaɪz] adj bedenine göre büyük

outskirts [ˈaʊtˌskɜːts] npl eteklerinde

outspoken [ˈaʊtˈspəʊkən] adj açık sözlü

outstanding [ˌaʊtˈstændɪŋ] adj mükemmel

oval [ˈəʊvəl] adj oval

ovary [ˈəʊvərɪ] n yumurtalık (sağlık)

oven [ˈʌvən] n fırın; **microwave oven** n mikrodalga fırın; **oven glove** n fırın eldiveni

ovenproof [ˈʌvənˌpruːf] adj ateşe dayanıklı

over [ˈəʊvə] adj bitmiş ▷ prep üstünde

overall [ˌəʊvərˈɔːl] adv kapsamlı

overalls [ˌəʊvəˈrɔːlz] npl tulum (giysi)

overcast [ˈəʊvəˌkɑːst] adj bulutlu

overcharge [ˌəʊvəˈtʃɑːdʒ] v fazla fiyat istemek

overcoat [ˈəʊvəˌkəʊt] n palto

overcome [ˌəʊvəˈkʌm] v üstesinden gelmek

overdone [ˌəʊvəˈdʌn] adj çok pişmiş

overdose [ˈəʊvəˌdəʊs] n yüksek dozda

overdraft [ˈəʊvəˌdrɑːft] n fazla para çekme

overdrawn [ˌəʊvəˈdrɔːn] adj hesabından fazla para çekmiş

overdue [ˌəʊvəˈdjuː] adj ödeme günü geçmiş

overestimate [ˌəʊvərˈɛstɪˌmeɪt] v gözünde büyütmek

overheads [ˈəʊvəˌhɛdz] npl işletme masrafları

overlook [ˌəʊvəˈlʊk] v gözden kaçırmak

overrule [ˌəʊvəˈruːl] v kararı bozmak

overseas [ˌəʊvəˈsiːz] adv denizaşırı

oversight [ˈəʊvəˌsaɪt] n (mistake) hata, (supervision) gözetim

oversleep [ˌəʊvəˈsliːp] v uyuyakalmak

overtake [ˌəʊvəˈteɪk] v sollamak

overtime [ˈəʊvəˌtaɪm] n fazla mesai

overweight [ˌəʊvəˈweɪt] adj aşırı kilolu

owe [əʊ] v borçlu olmak

owing to [ˈəʊɪŋ tuː] prep için

owl [aʊl] n baykuş

own [əʊn] adj kendi ▷ v sahip olmak

owner ['əʊnə] *n* sahip
own up [əʊn ʌp] *v* sahip çıkmak
oxygen ['ɒksɪdʒən] *n* oksijen
oyster ['ɔɪstə] *n* istridye
ozone ['əʊzəʊn; əʊ'zəʊn] *n* ozon;
  ozone layer *n* ozon tabakası

PA [piː eɪ] *abbr* kişisel asistan
pace [peɪs] *n* adım
pacemaker ['peɪsˌmeɪkə] *n* kalp
  pili
Pacific [pə'sɪfɪk] *n* Pasifik
pack [pæk] *n* yük ▷ *v* paketlemek
package ['pækɪdʒ] *n* paket;
  package holiday *n* paket tatil;
  package tour *n* paket tur
packaging ['pækɪdʒɪŋ] *n*
  paketleme
packed [pækt] *adj* paketlenmiş;
  packed lunch *n* paket yemek
packet ['pækɪt] *n* paket
pad [pæd] *n* ped
paddle ['pædᵊl] *n* kısa kürek ▷ *v* sığ
  suda çıplak ayak yürümek
padlock ['pædˌlɒk] *n* asma kilit
paedophile ['piːdəʊˌfaɪl] *n* pedofil
page [peɪdʒ] *n* sayfa ▷ *v* anons
  etmek; **home page** *n* açılış sayfası;
  Yellow Pages® *npl* Sarı Sayfalar

pager ['peɪdʒə] n çağrı cihazı

paid [peɪd] adj ücretli

pail [peɪl] n kova

pain [peɪn] n acı; **back pain** n sırt ağrısı

painful ['peɪnfʊl] adj acılı

painkiller ['peɪnˌkɪlə] n ağrı kesici

paint [peɪnt] n boya (yapı) ▷ v boyamak

paintbrush ['peɪntˌbrʌʃ] n boya fırçası

painter ['peɪntə] n ressam

painting ['peɪntɪŋ] n resim

pair [pɛə] n çift

Pakistan [ˌpɑːkɪˈstɑːn] n Pakistan

Pakistani [ˌpɑːkɪˈstɑːnɪ] adj Pakistan ▷ n Pakistanlı

pal [pæl] n yakın dost

palace ['pælɪs] n saray; **Is the palace open to the public?** Saray halka açık mı?; **When is the palace open?** Saray ne zaman açık?

pale [peɪl] adj soluk

Palestine ['pælɪˌstaɪn] n Filistin

Palestinian [ˌpælɪˈstɪnɪən] adj Filistin ▷ n Filistinli

palm [pɑːm] n (part of hand) avuçiçi, (tree) palmiye

pamphlet ['pæmflɪt] n broşür

pan [pæn] n tava; **frying pan** n kızartma tavası

Panama [ˌpænəˈmɑː; 'pænəˌmɑː] n Panama

pancake ['pænˌkeɪk] n krep (yiyecek)

panda ['pændə] n panda

panic ['pænɪk] n panik ▷ v paniğe kapılmak

panther ['pænθə] n panter

panties ['pæntɪz] npl külot

pantomime ['pæntəˌmaɪm] n pandomim

pants [pænts] npl külot

paper ['peɪpə] n kağıt; **paper round** n gazete dağıtım; **scrap paper** n karalama kağıdı; **toilet paper** n tuvalet kağıdı; **tracing paper** n aydınger kağıdı; **wrapping paper** n paket kağıdı; **writing paper** n yazı kağıdı

paperback ['peɪpəˌbæk] n ikinci baskı kitap

paperclip ['peɪpəˌklɪp] n ataş

paperweight ['peɪpəˌweɪt] n kağıt ağırlığı

paperwork ['peɪpəˌwɜːk] n evrak işi

paprika ['pæprɪkə; pæˈpriː-] n kırmızı toz biber

paracetamol [ˌpærəˈsiːtəˌmɒl; -ˈsɛtə-] n **I'd like some paracetamol** Parasetamol rica ediyorum

parachute ['pærəˌʃuːt] n paraşüt

parade [pəˈreɪd] n tören alayı

paradise ['pærəˌdaɪs] n cennet

paraffin ['pærəfɪn] n parafin

paragraph ['pærəˌɡrɑːf; -ˌɡræf] n paragraf

Paraguay ['pærəˌɡwaɪ] n Paraguay

Paraguayan [ˌpærəˈɡwaɪən] adj Paraguay ▷ n Paraguaylı

parallel ['pærəˌlɛl] adj paralel

paralysed ['pærəˌlaɪzd] adj felçli

paramedic [ˌpærəˈmedɪk] n paramedik

parcel ['pɑːsəl] n paket; **How much is it to send this parcel?**

Bu paket kaça gider?; **I'd like to send this parcel** Bu paketi postalamak istiyorum

pardon ['pɑ:dᵊn] *n* bağışlama

parent ['pɛərənt] *n* ebeveyn; **parents** *npl* ebeveynler; **single parent** *n* yalnız ebeveyn

parish ['pærɪʃ] *n* kilisenin dini bölgesi

park [pɑ:k] *n* park ▷ *v* park etmek; **car park** *n* otopark; **national park** *n* milli park; **theme park** *n* konulu eğlence parkı; **Can I park here?** Arabamı buraya park edebilir miyim?; **Can we park our caravan here?** Karavanımızı buraya park edebilir miyiz?; **How long can I park here?** Ne kadarlığına park edebilirim?; **Is there a car park near here?** Buralarda bir otopark var mı?; **Where can I park the car?** Arabamı nereye park edebilirim?

parking [pɑ:kɪŋ] *n* park etme; **parking meter** *n* otopark ödeme cihazı; **parking ticket** *n* otopark bileti

parliament ['pɑ:ləmənt] *n* parlamento

parole [pə'rəʊl] *n* şartlı tahliye

parrot ['pærət] *n* papağan

parsley ['pɑ:slɪ] *n* maydanoz

parsnip ['pɑ:snɪp] *n* yabani havuç

part [pɑ:t] *n* parça; **spare part** *n* yedek parça; **Do you have parts for a Toyota?** Toyota parçaları var mı?

partial ['pɑ:ʃəl] *adj* kısmi

participate [pɑ:'tɪsɪˌpeɪt] *v* katılmak

particular [pə'tɪkjʊlə] *adj* özellik

particularly [pə'tɪkjʊləlɪ] *adv* özellikle

parting ['pɑ:tɪŋ] *n* ayrılış

partly ['pɑ:tlɪ] *adv* kısmen

partner ['pɑ:tnə] *n* partner; **I have a partner** Partnerim var; **This is my partner** Bu partnerim

partridge ['pɑ:trɪdʒ] *n* keklik

part-time ['pɑ:tˌtaɪm] *adj* yarım gün ▷ *adv* yarım gün

part with [pɑ:t wɪð] *v* ayırılmak

party ['pɑ:tɪ] *n* (group) parti (grup), (social gathering) parti (sosyal etkinlik) ▷ *v* partiye katılmak; **dinner party** *n* yemekli parti; **search party** *n* arama ekibi

pass [pɑ:s] *n* (in mountains) geçit (dağ), (meets standard) geçer (standartlara uygun), (permit) paso ▷ *v* (an exam) sınavı kazanmak ▷ *vi* geçilmek ▷ *vt* geçmek; **boarding pass** *n* biniş kartı; **ski pass** *n* kayak izni

passage ['pæsɪdʒ] *n* (musical) parça (müzik), (route) geçit

passenger ['pæsɪndʒə] *n* yolcu

passion ['pæʃən] *n* tutku; **passion fruit** *n* çarkıfelek meyvası

passive ['pæsɪv] *adj* pasif

pass out [pɑ:s aʊt] *v* bayılmak

Passover ['pɑ:sˌəʊvə] *n* Musevilerin Fısıh Bayramı

passport ['pɑ:spɔ:t] *n* pasaport; **passport control** *n* pasaport kontrol; **Here is my passport** İşte pasaportum; **I've forgotten my passport** Pasaportumu unutmuşum; **I've lost my passport** Pasaportumu

kaybettim; **My passport has been stolen** Pasaportum çalındı; **Please give me my passport back** Pasaportumu alabilir miyim?; **The children are on this passport** Çocuklar bu pasaportta
password ['pɑːsˌwɜːd] n şifre
past [pɑːst] adj geçmiş ▷ n geçmiş ▷ prep yoluyla
pasta ['pæstə] n makarna; **I'd like pasta as a starter** Başlangıç olarak makarna alayım
paste [peɪst] n macun
pasteurized ['pæstəˌraɪzd] adj pastörize
pastime ['pɑːsˌtaɪm] n uğraş
pastry ['peɪstrɪ] n hamur; **puff pastry** n milföy hamuru; **shortcrust pastry** n un kurabiyesi hamuru
patch [pætʃ] n yama
patched [pætʃt] adj yamalı
path [pɑːθ] n patika; **cycle path** n bisiklet yolu; **Keep to the path** Patikadan ayrılmayın
pathetic [pə'θɛtɪk] adj acınası
patience ['peɪʃəns] n sabır
patient ['peɪʃənt] adj sabırlı ▷ n hasta
patio ['pætɪˌəʊ] n teras
patriotic ['pætrɪəˌtɪk] adj yurtsever
patrol [pə'trəʊl] n devriye; **patrol car** n devriye arabası
pattern ['pætən] n kalıp (dikiş)
pause [pɔːz] n duraklama
pavement ['peɪvmənt] n kaldırım
pavilion [pə'vɪljən] n sayvan
paw [pɔː] n pençe
pawnbroker ['pɔːnˌbrəʊkə] n rehinci

pay [peɪ] n maaş ▷ v ödemek; **sick pay** n hastalık ödentisi
payable ['peɪəbəl] adj ödenecek
pay back [peɪ bæk] v geri ödemek
payment ['peɪmənt] n ödeme
payphone ['peɪˌfəʊn] n ankesörlü telefon
PC [piː siː] n PC
PDF [piː diː ɛf] n PDF
peace [piːs] n barış
peaceful ['piːsfʊl] adj barışçıl
peach [piːtʃ] n şeftali
peacock ['piːˌkɒk] n tavus kuşu
peak [piːk] n zirve; **peak hours** npl sıkışık saat
peanut ['piːˌnʌt] n yerfıstığı; **peanut allergy** n fıstık alerjisi; **peanut butter** n fıstık ezmesi
pear [pɛə] n armut
pearl [pɜːl] n inci
peas [piːs] npl bezelye
peat [piːt] n turba
pebble ['pɛbəl] n çakıl taşı
peculiar [pɪ'kjuːlɪə] adj tuhaf
pedal ['pɛdəl] n pedal
pedestrian [pɪ'dɛstrɪən] n yaya; **pedestrian crossing** n yaya geçidi; **pedestrian precinct** n yayalara özel bölge
pedestrianized [pɪ'dɛstrɪəˌnaɪzd] adj yayalara ayrılmış
pedigree ['pɛdɪˌgriː] adj cins
peel [piːl] n meyva kabuğu ▷ v soymak (meyva, deri vb)
peg [pɛg] n kanca
Pekinese [ˌpiːkɪŋ'iːz] n Pekinez
pelican ['pɛlɪkən] n pelikan; **pelican crossing** n ışıklı yaya geçidi
pellet ['pɛlɪt] n metal çekirdek

pelvis ['pɛlvɪs] *n* leğen kemiği

pen [pɛn] *n* kalem; **ballpoint pen** *n* Tükenmez kalem; **felt-tip pen** *n* keçe kalem; **fountain pen** *n* dolmakalem; **Do you have a pen I could borrow?** Kaleminiz var mı?

penalize ['piːnəˌlaɪz] *v* cezalandırmak

penalty ['pɛnᵊltɪ] *n* penaltı

pencil ['pɛnsᵊl] *n* kurşun kalem; **pencil case** *n* kalemlik; **pencil sharpener** *n* kalem açacağı

pendant ['pɛndənt] *n* pandantif

penfriend ['pɛnˌfrɛnd] *n* kalem arkadaşı

penguin ['pɛŋgwɪn] *n* penguen

penicillin [ˌpɛnɪ'sɪlɪn] *n* penisilin

peninsula [pɪ'nɪnsjʊlə] *n* yarımada

penknife ['pɛnˌnaɪf] *n* çakı

penny ['pɛnɪ] *n* peni

pension ['pɛnʃən] *n* emekli maaşı

pensioner ['pɛnʃənə] *n* emekli; **old-age pensioner** *n* emekli

pentathlon [pɛn'tæθlən] *n* pentatlon

penultimate [pɪ'nʌltɪmɪt] *adj* sondan bir önceki

people ['piːpᵊl] *npl* insanlar

pepper ['pɛpə] *n* biber

peppermill ['pɛpəˌmɪl] *n* biberlik

peppermint ['pɛpəˌmɪnt] *n* nane şekeri

per [pɜː; pə] *prep* başına; **per cent** *adv* yüzde; **How much is it per person?** Kişi başına ne kadar?

percentage [pə'sɛntɪdʒ] *n* yüzde

percussion [pə'kʌʃən] *n* vurmalı *(müzik)*

perfect ['pɜːfɪkt] *adj* mükemmel

perfection [pə'fɛkʃən] *n* mükemmellik

perfectly ['pɜːfɪktlɪ] *adv* mükemmel bir şekilde

perform [pə'fɔːm] *v* performans göstermek

performance [pə'fɔːməns] *n* *(artistic)* sahne performansı, *(functioning)* performans

perfume ['pɜːfjuːm] *n* parfüm

perhaps [pə'hæps; præps] *adv* belki

period ['pɪərɪəd] *n* dönem; **trial period** *n* deneme süresi

perjury ['pɜːdʒərɪ] *n* yalancı şahitlik

perm [pɜːm] *n* perma

permanent ['pɜːmənənt] *adj* kalıcı

permanently ['pɜːmənəntlɪ] *adv* kalıcı bir şekilde

permission [pə'mɪʃən] *n* izin *(birine bir şey yapmak için verilen)*

permit *n* ['pɜːmɪt] izin ▷ *v* [pə'mɪt] izin vermek; **work permit** *n* çalışma izni; **Do you need a fishing permit?** Avlanma izin belgesi gerekiyor mu?

persecute ['pɜːsɪˌkjuːt] *v* eziyet etmek

persevere [ˌpɜːsɪ'vɪə] *v* azmetmek

Persian ['pɜːʃən] *adj* İranlı

persistent [pə'sɪstənt] *adj* ısrarlı

person ['pɜːsᵊn] *n* kişi; **How much is it per person?** Kişi başına ne kadar?

personal ['pɜːsənᵊl] *adj* kişisel; **personal assistant** *n* kişisel asistan; **personal organizer** *n* kişisel organizatör; **personal**

stereo n kişisel müzik çalar
personality [ˌpɜːsə'nælɪtɪ] n kişilik
personally ['pɜːsənəlɪ] adv kişisel olarak
personnel [ˌpɜːsə'nɛl] n personel
perspective [pə'spɛktɪv] n perspektif
perspiration [ˌpɜːspə'reɪʃən] n terleme
persuade [pə'sweɪd] v ikna etme
persuasive [pə'sweɪsɪv] adj ikna edici
Peru [pə'ruː] n Peru
Peruvian [pə'ruːvɪən] adj Peru ▷ n Perulu
pessimist ['pɛsɪˌmɪst] n kötümser
pessimistic ['pɛsɪˌmɪstɪk] adj kötümser
pest [pɛst] n baş belası
pester ['pɛstə] v musallat olmak
pesticide ['pɛstɪˌsaɪd] n böcek zehiri
pet [pɛt] n ev hayvanı
petition [pɪ'tɪʃən] n dilekçe
petrified ['pɛtrɪˌfaɪd] adj ödü kopmak
petrol ['pɛtrəl] n benzin; **petrol station** n benzin istasyonu; **petrol tank** n benzin deposu; **unleaded petrol** n kurşunsuz benzin; **I've run out of petrol** Benzinim bitti; **Is there a petrol station near here?** Buraya en yakın benzin istasyonu nerede?; **The petrol has run out** Benzin bitti
pewter ['pjuːtə] n tutya
pharmacist ['fɑːməsɪst] n eczacı
pharmacy ['fɑːməsɪ] n eczane;

Which pharmacy provides emergency service? Hangi eczane nöbetçi?
PhD [piː eɪtʃ diː] n doktora
pheasant ['fɛzᵊnt] n sülün
philosophy [fɪ'lɒsəfɪ] n felsefe
phobia ['fəʊbɪə] n fobi
phone [fəʊn] n telefon ▷ v telefon etmek; **camera phone** n fotoğraflı telefon; **entry phone** n kapı telefonu; **mobile phone** n cep telefonu; **phone back** v geri aramak; **phone bill** n telefon faturası; **phone number** n telefon numarası; **smart phone** n akıllı telefon; **Can I have your phone number?** Telefon numaranızı alabilir miyim?; **Can I phone from here?** Buradan telefon edebilir miyim?; **Can I use your phone, please?** Telefonunuzu kullanabilir miyim lütfen?; **Do you sell international phone cards?** Uluslararası telefon kartı satıyor musunuz?; **I must make a phone call** Bir telefon görüşmesi yapmam gerek; **I want to make a phone call** Telefon etmek istiyorum; **I'd like a twenty-five euro phone card** Yirmibeş euroluk telefon kartı rica ediyorum; **I'd like some coins for the phone, please** Telefon için bozuk para rica ediyorum; **I'm having trouble with the phone** Telefonla sorunum var; **May I use your phone?** Telefonunuzu kullanabilir miyim?; **Where can I charge my mobile phone?** Cep telefonumu nerede şarj edebilirim;

Where can I make a phone call?
Nereden telefon edebilirim?
phonebook ['fəʊn,bʊk] *n* telefon
rehberi
phonebox ['fəʊn,bɒks] *n* telefon
kulübesi
phonecall ['fəʊn,kɔːl] *n* telefon
görüşmesi
phonecard ['fəʊn,kɑːd] *n* telefon
kartı; **A phonecard, please** Bir
telefon kartı lütfen; **Where can I
buy a phonecard?** Nereden
telefon kartı alabilirim?
photo ['fəʊtəʊ] *n* fotoğraf; **photo
album** *n* fotoğraf albümü; **Can I
download photos to here?**
Fotoğraf indirebilir miyim?; **Can
you put these photos on CD,
please?** Bu fotoğrafları CD'ye
yükleybilir misiniz lütfen?; **How
much do the photos cost?**
Fotoğraflar kaça malolur?; **I'd like
the photos glossy** Fotoğrafları
parlak kağıda basın lütfen; **I'd like
the photos matt** Fotoğrafları
mat kağıda basın lütfen
photobomb ['fəʊtəʊ,bɒm] *v*
photobomb yapmak ▷ *n*
photobomb
photocopier ['fəʊtəʊ,kɒpɪə] *n*
fotokopi makinesi
photocopy ['fəʊtəʊ,kɒpɪ] *n*
fotokopi ▷ *v* fotokopisini çekmek;
**I'd like a photocopy of this,
please** Bunun fotokopisini
istiyorum lütfen; **Where can I get
some photocopying done?**
Nerede fotokopi çektirebilirim?
photograph ['fəʊtə,grɑːf; -,græf]
n fotoğraf ▷ *v* fotoğrafını çekmek

photographer [fə'tɒɡrəfə] *n*
fotoğrafçı
photography [fə'tɒɡrəfɪ] *n*
fotoğrafçılık
phrase [freɪz] *n* sözcük grubu
phrasebook ['freɪz,bʊk] *n* günlük
ifadeler sözlüğü
physical ['fɪzɪkᵊl] *adj* fiziksel ▷ *n*
fizik (görünüş)
physicist ['fɪzɪsɪst] *n* fizikçi
physics ['fɪzɪks] *npl* fizik
physiotherapist
[,fɪzɪəʊ'θɛrəpɪst] *n* fizyoterapist
physiotherapy [,fɪzɪəʊ'θɛrəpɪ] *n*
fizyoterapi
pianist ['pɪənɪst] *n* piyanist
piano [pɪ'ænəʊ] *n* piyano
pick [pɪk] *n* kazma ▷ *v* toplamak
(çiçek vb)
pick on [pɪk ɒn] *v* birine takmak
pick out [pɪk aʊt] *v* seçmek
pickpocket ['pɪk,pɒkɪt] *n*
yankesicilik
pick up [pɪk ʌp] *v* yerden almak
picnic ['pɪknɪk] *n* piknik
picture ['pɪktʃə] *n* resim; **picture
frame** *n* resim çerçevesi
picturesque [,pɪktʃə'rɛsk] *adj*
resmedilmeye değer
pie [paɪ] *n* börek; **apple pie** *n* elmalı
turta; **pie chart** *n* dilimli grafik
piece [piːs] *n* parça
pier [pɪə] *n* rıhtım
pierce [pɪəs] *v* delmek
pierced [pɪəst] *adj* delik (kulak vb)
piercing ['pɪəsɪŋ] *n* delici
pig [pɪɡ] *n* domuz; **guinea pig** *n*
(for experiment) kobay, (rodent)
kobay faresi
pigeon ['pɪdʒɪn] *n* güvercin

piggybank ['pɪgɪ,bæŋk] n kumbara
pigtail ['pɪg,teɪl] n saç örgüsü
pile [paɪl] n yığın
piles [paɪlz] npl basur
pile-up [paɪlʌp] n yığılmak
pilgrim ['pɪlgrɪm] n hacı
pilgrimage ['pɪlgrɪmɪdʒ] n hac
pill [pɪl] n hap; **sleeping pill** n uyku
hapı; **I'm not on the pill** Doğum
kontrol hapı kullanmıyorum; **I'm
on the pill** Doğum kontrol hapı
kullanıyorum
pillar ['pɪlə] n sütun
pillow ['pɪləʊ] n yastık
pillowcase ['pɪləʊ,keɪs] n yastık
kılıfı
pilot ['paɪlət] n pilot; **pilot light** n
kontrol lambası
pimple ['pɪmpəl] n sivilce
pin [pɪn] n toplu iğne; **drawing pin**
n raptiye; **rolling pin** n oklava;
safety pin n kilitli iğne
PIN [pɪn] npl kredi kartı şifresi
pinafore ['pɪnə,fɔ:] n önlük
pinch [pɪntʃ] v çimdiklemek
pine [paɪn] n çam
pineapple ['paɪn,æpəl] n ananas
pink [pɪŋk] adj pembe
pint [paɪnt] n pint (içki)
pip [pɪp] n çekirdek
pipe [paɪp] n boru; **exhaust pipe** n
egzos borusu
pipeline ['paɪp,laɪn] n boru hattı
pirate ['paɪrɪt] n korsan (deniz)
Pisces ['paɪsi:z; 'pɪ-] n Balık burcu
pistol ['pɪstəl] n kısa kabzalı
tabanca
piston ['pɪstən] n piston
pitch [pɪtʃ] n (sound) perde (ses),
(sport) saha (spor) ▷ v fırlatmak

pity ['pɪtɪ] n acıma (duygu) ▷ v
acımak
pixel ['pɪksəl] n piksel
pizza ['pi:tsə] n pizza
place [pleɪs] n yer ▷ v yerleştirmek;
place of birth n doğum yeri;
**Do you know a good place to
go?** Gidilecek iyi bir yer biliyor
musunuz?; **Where is the best
place to dive?** Burada dalınacak
en iyi yer neresi?
placement ['pleɪsmənt] n
yerleştirme
plain [pleɪn] adj düz (desensiz,
süssüz) ▷ n ova; **plain chocolate** n
sade çikolata
plait [plæt] n saç örgüsü
plan [plæn] n plan ▷ v planlamak;
street plan n sokak planı
plane [pleɪn] n (aeroplane) uçak,
(surface) düzlem, (tool) rende
planet ['plænɪt] n gezegen
planning ['plænɪŋ] n planlama
plant [plɑ:nt] n (site/equipment)
tesis, (vegetable organism) bitki ▷ v
dikmek (bitki); **plant pot** n çiçek
saksısı; **pot plant** n saksı çiçeği;
**We'd like to see local plants and
trees** Yerel bitkileri ve ağaçları
görmek isterdik
plaque [plæk; plɑ:k] n plaket
plaster ['plɑ:stə] n (for wall)
badana, (for wound) yara bandı;
I'd like some plasters Yara bandı
rica ediyorum
plastic ['plæstɪk; 'plɑ:s-] adj
plastik ▷ n plastik; **plastic bag** n
naylon torba; **plastic surgery** n
plastik cerrahi
plate [pleɪt] n tabak; **number**

plate n plaka *(otomobil)*
platform ['plætfɔːm] n platform;
Is this the right platform for the train to…? … treninin kalkacağı platform burası mı?; **Which platform does the train leave from?** Tren hangi platformdan kalkıyor?
platinum ['plætɪnəm] n platin
play [pleɪ] n oyun ▷ v *(in sport)* oynamak, *(music)* çalmak; **play truant** v okuldan kaçmak; **playing card** n oyun kartı; **playing field** n oyun alanı; **Can I play video games?** Oyun oynayabilir miyim?; **We'd like to play tennis** Tenis oynamak istiyoruz; **Where can we go to see a play?** Tiyatro oyunu görmek için nereye gidebiliriz?
player ['pleɪə] n *(instrumentalist)* müzisyen, *(of sport)* oyuncu *(spor)*; **CD player** n CD çalar; **MP3 player** n MP3 çalar; **MP4 player** n MP4 çalar
playful ['pleɪfʊl] adj oyuncu *(oyunbaz)*
playground ['pleɪ,graʊnd] n oyun alanı
playgroup ['pleɪ,gruːp] n çocuk oyun grubu
PlayStation® ['pleɪ,steɪʃən] n PlayStation®
playtime ['pleɪ,taɪm] n oyun saati
playwright ['pleɪ,raɪt] n oyun yazarı
pleasant ['plɛzənt] adj hoş
please [pliːz] excl lütfen
pleased [pliːzd] adj memnun; **Pleased to meet you**

Tanıştığımıza memnun oldum
pleasure ['plɛʒə] n zevk; **It was a pleasure to meet you** Sizinle tanışmak bir zevk; **It's been a pleasure working with you** Sizinle çalışmak bir zevkti
plenty ['plɛntɪ] n çok
pliers ['plaɪəz] npl pense
plot [plɒt] n *(piece of land)* arsa, *(secret plan)* komplo ▷ v *(conspire)* gizli plan
plough [plaʊ] n pulluk ▷ v tarla sürmek
plug [plʌg] n tıkaç; **spark plug** n buji
plughole ['plʌg,həʊl] n musluk deliği
plug in [plʌg ɪn] v elektriğe bağlamak
plum [plʌm] n erik
plumber ['plʌmə] n muslukçu
plumbing ['plʌmɪŋ] n musluk işleri
plump [plʌmp] adj tıknaz
plunge [plʌndʒ] v hızla atlamak
plural ['plʊərəl] n çoğul
plus [plʌs] prep ayrıca
plywood ['plaɪ,wʊd] n kontrplak
p.m. [piː ɛm] abbr öğleden sonra
pneumonia [njuːˈməʊnɪə] n zatürre
poached [pəʊtʃt] adj *(caught illegally)* kaçak avlanmış, *(simmered gently)* suda pişirilmiş *(yumurta, balık)*
pocket ['pɒkɪt] n cep; **pocket calculator** n cep hesap makinesi; **pocket money** n cep harçlığı
podcast ['pɒd,kɑːst] n podcast
poem ['pəʊɪm] n şiir

poet ['pəʊɪt] *n* şair

poetry ['pəʊɪtrɪ] *n* şiir

point [pɔɪnt] *n* nokta *(yer)* ▷ *v* göstermek

pointless ['pɔɪntlɪs] *adj* anlamsız

point out [pɔɪnt aʊt] *v* dikkatini çekmek

poison ['pɔɪzⁿn] *n* zehir ▷ *v* zehirlemek

poisonous ['pɔɪzənəs] *adj* zehirli

poke [pəʊk] *v* dürtmek

poker ['pəʊkə] *n* poker

Poland ['pəʊlənd] *n* Polonya

polar ['pəʊlə] *adj* kutup; **polar bear** *n* kutup ayısı

pole [pəʊl] *n* direk *(elektrik, telgraf)*; **North Pole** *n* Kuzey Kutbu; **pole vault** *n* sırıkla atlama; **South Pole** *n* Güney Kutbu; **tent pole** *n* çadır direği

police [pə'liːs] *n* polis; **police station** *n* polis istasyonu; **Call the police** Polis çağırın; **I need a police report for my insurance** Sigortam için polise bildirmemiz gerekiyor; **We will have to report it to the police** Polise haber vermemiz gerekiyor; **Where is the police station?** Polis karakolu nerede?

policeman, policemen [pə'liːsmən, pə'liːsmɛn] *n* erkek polis

police officer *n* polis görevlisi

policewoman, policewomen [pə'liːswʊmən, pə'liːswɪmɪn] *n* kadın polis

policy ['pɒlɪsɪ] *n* **insurance policy** *n* sigorta poliçesi

polio ['pəʊlɪəʊ] *n* çocuk felci

polish ['pɒlɪʃ] *n* cila ▷ *v* cilalamak; **nail polish** *n* oje; **shoe polish** *n* ayakkabı cilası

Polish ['pəʊlɪʃ] *adj* Polonya ▷ *n* Polonyalı

polite [pə'laɪt] *adj* kibar

politely [pə'laɪtlɪ] *adv* kibarca

politeness [pə'laɪtnɪs] *n* kibarlık

political [pə'lɪtɪkəl] *adj* politik

politician [ˌpɒlɪ'tɪʃən] *n* politikacı

politics ['pɒlɪtɪks] *npl* politika

poll [pəʊl] *n* kamuoyu yoklaması; **opinion poll** *n* kamuoyu yoklaması

pollen ['pɒlən] *n* çiçek tozu

pollute [pə'luːt] *v* kirletmek

polluted [pə'luːtɪd] *adj* kirlenmiş

pollution [pə'luːʃən] *n* kirlilik

Polynesia [ˌpɒlɪ'niːʒə; -ʒɪə] *n* Polonezya Adaları

Polynesian [ˌpɒlɪ'niːʒən; -ʒɪən] *adj* Polonezya ▷ *n (language)* Polonezce *(dil)*, *(person)* Polonezyalı *(kişi)*

pomegranate ['pɒmɪˌɡrænɪt; 'pɒmˌɡrænɪt] *n* nar

pond [pɒnd] *n* gölcük

pony ['pəʊnɪ] *n* midilli; **pony trekking** *n* midilliyle gezme

ponytail ['pəʊnɪˌteɪl] *n* atkuyruğu

poodle ['puːdəl] *n* kaniş

pool [puːl] *n (resources)* fon *(mali birikim)*, *(water)* havuz; **paddling pool** *n* sığ havuz; **swimming pool** *n* yüzme havuzu; **Is it an outdoor pool?** Açık yüzme havuzu mu?; **Is the pool heated?** Havuz ısıtılmış mı?; **Is there a children's pool?** Çocuk havuzu var mı?; **Is there a**

paddling pool for the children?
Çocuklar için yüzme havuzu var
mı?; **Is there a swimming pool?**
Yüzme havuzu var mı?

poor [pʊə; pɔ:] *adj* yoksul

poorly ['pʊəlɪ; 'pɔ:-] *adj* acemice

popcorn ['pɒp,kɔ:n] *n* patlamış
mısır

pope [pəʊp] *n* papa

poplar ['pɒplə] *n* kavak

poppy ['pɒpɪ] *n* gelincik *(çiçek)*

popular ['pɒpjʊlə] *adj* popüler

popularity ['pɒpjʊlærɪtɪ] *n*
popülerlik

population [,pɒpjʊ'leɪʃən] *n* nüfus

pop-up [pɒpʌp] *n* ortaya çıkmak

porch [pɔ:tʃ] *n* veranda

pork [pɔ:k] *n* domuz eti; **pork
chop** *n* domuz pirzolası; **I don't
eat pork** Domuz eti yemiyorum

porn [pɔ:n] *n (informal)* porno

pornographic [pɔ:'nɒgræfɪk] *adj*
pornografik

pornography [pɔ:'nɒgrəfɪ] *n*
pornografi

porridge ['pɒrɪdʒ] *n* yulaf ezmesi

port [pɔ:t] *n (ships)* liman, *(wine)*
porto şarabı

portable ['pɔ:təbəl] *adj* taşınabilir

porter ['pɔ:tə] *n* hamal

portfolio [pɔ:'fəʊlɪəʊ] *n* portföy

portion ['pɔ:ʃən] *n* parça

portrait ['pɔ:trɪt; -treɪt] *n* portre

Portugal ['pɔ:tjʊgəl] *n* Portekiz

Portuguese [,pɔ:tjʊ'gi:z] *adj*
Portekiz ▷ *n (language)* Portekizce
(dil), *(person)* Portekizli *(kişi)*

position [pə'zɪʃən] *n* pozisyon

positive ['pɒzɪtɪv] *adj* olumlu

possess [pə'zɛs] *v* sahip olmak

possession [pə'zɛʃən] *n* mülkiyet

possibility [,pɒsɪ'bɪlɪtɪ] *n* olasılık

possible ['pɒsɪbəl] *adj* olası

possibly ['pɒsɪblɪ] *adv* olasılıkla

post [pəʊst] *n (mail)* posta,
(position) görev *(pozisyon)*, *(stake)*
direk *(çit)* ▷ *v (mail)* postalamak,
(social media) paylaş; **post office** *n*
postane; **When does the post
office open?** Postane ne zaman
açılıyor?; **Where can I post these
cards?** Bu kartları nereden
postalayabilirim?

postage ['pəʊstɪdʒ] *n* posta
ücreti

postbox ['pəʊst,bɒks] *n* posta
kutusu

postcard ['pəʊst,kɑ:d] *n*
kartpostal; **Can I have stamps
for four postcards to...** Bu dört
kartpostal için pul alacaktım... a
gidecek; **Do you have any
postcards?** Kartpostal satıyor
musunuz?; **I'm looking for
postcards** Kartpostal
bakıyordum; **Where can I buy
some postcards?** Nereden
kartpostal alabilirim?

postcode ['pəʊst,kəʊd] *n* alan
kodu

poster ['pəʊstə] *n* poster

postgraduate [pəʊst'grædjʊɪt] *n*
üniversite sonrası eğitim yapan
öğrenci

postman, postmen ['pəʊstmən,
'pəʊstmɛn] *n* postacı

postmark ['pəʊst,mɑ:k] *n* posta
damgası

postpone [pəʊst'pəʊn; pə'spəʊn]
v ertelemek

postwoman, postwomen ['pəʊstwʊmən, 'pəʊstwɪmɪn] n kadın postacı

pot [pɒt] n tencere; **plant pot** n çiçek saksısı; **pot plant** n saksı çiçeği

potato, potatoes [pə'teɪtəʊ, pə'teɪtəʊz] n patates; **baked potato** n kumpir; **jacket potato** n kumpir; **mashed potatoes** npl patates püresi; **potato peeler** n patates soyucu

potential [pə'tɛnʃəl] adj potansiyel ▷ n potansiyel

pothole ['pɒt,həʊl] n yol çukuru

pottery ['pɒtərɪ] n çanak çömlek

potty ['pɒtɪ] n lazımlık

pound [paʊnd] n pound (İngiliz ağırlık birimi); **pound sterling** n pound sterlin (İngiliz para birimi)

pour [pɔː] v akmak

poverty ['pɒvətɪ] n yoksulluk

powder ['paʊdə] n toz; **baking powder** n kabartma tozu; **soap powder** n sabun tozu; **talcum powder** n talk pudrası; **washing powder** n çamaşır tozu; **Do you have washing powder?** Çamaşır tozunuz var mı?

power ['paʊə] n güç (erk); **power cut** n elektrik kesintisi; **solar power** n güneş enerjisi

powerful ['paʊəfʊl] adj güçlü

practical ['præktɪkəl] adj pratik

practically ['præktɪkəlɪ; -klɪ] adv pratik olarak

practice ['præktɪs] n pratik

practise ['præktɪs] v pratik yapmak

praise [preɪz] v övmek

pram [præm] n bebek arabası

prank [præŋk] n kaba şaka

prawn [prɔːn] n karides

pray [preɪ] v dua etmek

prayer [prɛə] n dua

precaution [prɪ'kɔːʃən] n önlem

preceding [prɪ'siːdɪŋ] adj önceki

precinct ['priːsɪŋkt] n bölge (kent); **pedestrian precinct** n yayalara özel bölge

precious ['prɛʃəs] adj değerli

precise [prɪ'saɪs] adj tam

precisely [prɪ'saɪslɪ] adv tam olarak

predecessor ['priːdɪˌsɛsə] n selef

predict [prɪ'dɪkt] v öngörmek

predictable [prɪ'dɪktəbəl] adj tahmin edilebilir

prefect ['priːfɛkt] n başkan (okul)

prefer [prɪ'fɜː] v tercih etmek

preferably ['prɛfərəblɪ; 'prɛfrəblɪ] adv tercihen

preference ['prɛfərəns; 'prɛfrəns] n tercih

pregnancy ['prɛgnənsɪ] n gebelik

pregnant ['prɛgnənt] adj gebe

prehistoric [ˌpriːhɪ'stɒrɪk] adj tarih öncesi

prejudice ['prɛdʒʊdɪs] n önyargı

prejudiced ['prɛdʒʊdɪst] adj önyargılı

premature [ˌprɛmə'tjʊə; 'prɛmətjʊə] adj erken

premiere ['prɛmɪˌɛə; 'prɛmɪə] n gala

premises ['prɛmɪsɪz] npl bina ve etrafındaki arazi

premonition [ˌprɛmə'nɪʃən] n kehanet

preoccupied [priː'ɒkjʊˌpaɪd] adj kafasını takmış

prepaid [priːˈpeɪd] adj önceden ödenmiş

preparation [ˌprɛpəˈreɪʃən] n hazırlık

prepare [prɪˈpɛə] v hazırlama

prepared [prɪˈpɛəd] adj hazırlanmış

Presbyterian [ˌprɛzbɪˈtɪərɪən] adj Presbiteryan ▷ n Presbiteryan

prescribe [prɪˈskraɪb] v ilaç yazmak

prescription [prɪˈskrɪpʃən] n reçete; **Where can I get this prescription made up?** Bu reçeteyi nerede yaptırabilirim

presence [ˈprɛzəns] n varlık

present adj [ˈprɛznt] var ▷ n [ˈprɛznt] (gift) armağan, (time being) şu an ▷ v [prɪˈzɛnt] takdim etmek; **I'm looking for a present for my husband** Eşime bir armağan almak istiyordum

presentation [ˌprɛzənˈteɪʃən] n sunma

presenter [prɪˈzɛntə] n sunucu (radyo, TV)

presently [ˈprɛzəntlɪ] adv şu anda

preservative [prɪˈzɜːvətɪv] n katkı maddesi

president [ˈprɛzɪdənt] n başkan (şirket)

press [prɛs] n pres ▷ v bastırmak; **press conference** n basın toplantısı

press-up [prɛsʌp] n şınav çekmek

pressure [ˈprɛʃə] n basınç ▷ v baskı yapmak; **blood pressure** n tansiyon

prestige [prɛˈstiːʒ] n prestij

prestigious [prɛˈstɪdʒəs] adj saygın

presumably [prɪˈzjuːməblɪ] adv olasılıkla

presume [prɪˈzjuːm] v farzetmek

pretend [prɪˈtɛnd] v yapar gibi görünmek

pretext [ˈpriːtɛkst] n bahane

prettily [ˈprɪtɪlɪ] adv hoş bir şekilde

pretty [ˈprɪtɪ] adj hoş ▷ adv bayağı (oldukça)

prevent [prɪˈvɛnt] v önlemek

prevention [prɪˈvɛnʃən] n önleme

previous [ˈpriːvɪəs] adj önceki

previously [ˈpriːvɪəslɪ] adv daha önceden

prey [preɪ] n ev

price [praɪs] n fiyat; **price list** n fiyat listesi; **retail price** n perakende fiyatı; **selling price** n satış fiyatı; **Does the price include boots?** Fiyata botlar da dahil mi?; **Please write down the price** Fiyatı yazar mısınız?; **What is included in the price?** Fiyata neler dahil?

prick [prɪk] v delmek (iğneyle)

pride [praɪd] n gurur

priest [priːst] n rahip

primarily [ˈpraɪmərəlɪ] adv başlıca

primary [ˈpraɪmərɪ] adj ilk; **primary school** n ilkokul

primitive [ˈprɪmɪtɪv] adj ilkel

primrose [ˈprɪmˌrəʊz] n çuha çiçeği

prince [prɪns] n prens

princess [prɪnˈsɛs] n prenses

principal [ˈprɪnsɪpəl] adj baş (tepede) ▷ n müdür

principle [ˈprɪnsɪpəl] n ilke

print [prɪnt] n baskı (matbaa) ▷ v basmak (matbaa)

printer ['prɪntə] n *(machine)* yazıcı, *(person)* matbaacı; **Is there a colour printer?** Renkli yazıcı var mı?

printout ['prɪntaʊt] n çıktı *(bilgisayar)*

priority [praɪ'ɒrɪtɪ] n öncelik

prison ['prɪzᵊn] n hapishane; **prison officer** n hapishane görevlisi

prisoner ['prɪzənə] n mahkum

privacy ['praɪvəsɪ; 'prɪvəsɪ] n özel yaşam

private ['praɪvɪt] adj özel; **private property** n özel mülk; **Can I speak to you in private?** Sizinle özel olarak konuşabilir miyim?

privatize ['praɪvɪˌtaɪz] v özelleştirmek

privilege ['prɪvɪlɪdʒ] n ayrıcalık

prize [praɪz] n ödül

prize-giving ['praɪzˌgɪvɪŋ] n ödül töreni

prizewinner ['praɪzˌwɪnə] n ödüllü

probability [ˌprɒbə'bɪlɪtɪ] n olasılık

probable ['prɒbəbᵊl] adj olası

probably ['prɒbəblɪ] adv olasılıkla

problem ['prɒbləm] n sorun; **No problem** Sorun değil; **There's a problem with the room** Odada bir sorun var; **Who do we contact if there are problems?** Bir sorun çıkarsa kiminle temas kuracağız?

proceedings [prə'siːdɪŋz] npl dava

proceeds ['prəʊsiːdz] npl gelir *(toplanan para)*

process ['prəʊsɛs] n işlem

procession [prə'sɛʃən] n alay *(tören/gelin)*

produce [prə'djuːs] v yaratmak

producer [prə'djuːsə] n üretici

product ['prɒdʌkt] n ürün

production [prə'dʌkʃən] n üretim

productivity [ˌprɒdʌk'tɪvɪtɪ] n verimlilik

profession [prə'fɛʃən] n meslek

professional [prə'fɛʃənᵊl] adj profesyonel ▷ n profesyonel

professionally [prə'fɛʃənəlɪ] adv profesyonelce

professor [prə'fɛsə] n profesör

profile ['prəʊfaɪl] n profil; **profile picture** n profil fotoğrafı

profit ['prɒfɪt] n kazanç

profitable ['prɒfɪtəbᵊl] adj kazançlı

program ['prəʊgræm] n program ▷ v programlamak

programme ['prəʊgræm] n program

programmer ['prəʊgræmə] n programcı

programming ['prəʊgræmɪŋ] n programlama

progress ['prəʊgrɛs] n ilerleme

prohibit [prə'hɪbɪt] v yasaklamak

prohibited [prə'hɪbɪtɪd] adj yasaklanmış

project ['prɒdʒɛkt] n proje

projector [prə'dʒɛktə] n projektör; **overhead projector** n projektör

promenade [ˌprɒmə'nɑːd] n gezinti yeri

promise ['prɒmɪs] n söz ▷ v söz vermek

promising ['prɒmɪsɪŋ] adj ümit veren

promote [prə'məʊt] v tanıtımını yapmak

promotion [prə'məʊʃən] n tanıtım

prompt [prɒmpt] adj çabuk

promptly [prɒmptlı] adv çabucak

pronoun ['prəʊˌnaʊn] n zamir

pronounce [prə'naʊns] v telaffuz etmek

pronunciation [prəˌnʌnsı'eıʃən] n telaffuz

proof [pruːf] n (evidence) kanıt, (for checking) deneme baskısı

propaganda [ˌprɒpə'gændə] n propaganda

proper ['prɒpə] adj doğru dürüst

properly ['prɒpəlı] adv doğru dürüst; **This isn't cooked properly** Bu doğru dürüst pişmemiş; **This part doesn't work properly** Bu kısım doğru dürüst çalışmıyor

property ['prɒpətı] n mülk; **private property** n özel mülk

proportion [prə'pɔːʃən] n oran

proportional [prə'pɔːʃənəl] adj orantılı

proposal [prə'pəʊzəl] n öneri

propose [prə'pəʊz] v önermek

prosecute ['prɒsıˌkjuːt] v kovuşturma açmak

prospect ['prɒspɛkt] n gelecek beklentisi

prospectus [prə'spɛktəs] n tanıtma broşürü

prosperity [prɒ'spɛrıtı] n gönenç

prostitute ['prɒstıˌtjuːt] n fahişe

protect [prə'tɛkt] v korumak

protection [prə'tɛkʃən] n koruma

protein ['prəʊtiːn] n protein

protest n ['prəʊtɛst] protesto ▷ v [prə'tɛst] protesto etmek

Protestant ['prɒtıstənt] adj Protestan ▷ n Protestan

proud [praʊd] adj gururlu

prove [pruːv] v kanıtlamak

proverb ['prɒvɜːb] n atasözü

provide [prə'vaıd] v sağlamak; **provide for** v geçimini sağlamak

provided [prə'vaıdıd] conj yeter ki

providing [prə'vaıdıŋ] conj yeter ki

provisional [prə'vıʒənəl] adj geçici (bir süreliğine)

proximity [prɒk'sımıtı] n yakınlık

prune [pruːn] n kuru erik

pry [praı] v gözetlemek

pseudonym ['sjuːdəˌnım] n takma ad

psychiatric [ˌsaıkı'ætrık] adj psikiyatrik

psychiatrist [saı'kaıətrıst] n psikiyatrist

psychological [ˌsaıkə'lɒdʒıkəl] adj psikolojik

psychologist [saı'kɒlədʒıst] n psikolog

psychology [saı'kɒlədʒı] n psikoloji

psychotherapy [ˌsaıkəʊ'θɛrəpı] n psikoterapi

PTO [piː tiː əʊ] abbr Lütfen Arka Sayfaya Bakınız

pub [pʌb] n birahane

public ['pʌblık] adj halk ▷ n halk; **public holiday** n resmi tatil günü; **public opinion** n kamuoyu; **public relations** npl halkla ilişkiler; **public school** n devlet koleji; **public transport** n toplu taşıma; **Is the castle open to the**

public? Kale halka açık mı?
publican ['pʌblɪkən] n bar
işletmecisi
publication [ˌpʌblɪ'keɪʃən] n
yayımlama
publish ['pʌblɪʃ] v yayımlamak
publisher ['pʌblɪʃə] n yayınevi
pudding ['pʊdɪŋ] n puding
puddle ['pʌdəl] n su birikintisi
Puerto Rico ['pwɜ:təʊ 'ri:kəʊ;
'pwɛə-] n Portoriko
pull [pʊl] v çekmek
pull down [pʊl daʊn] v yıkmak
pull out [pʊl aʊt] vi kenara
çekmek (araç)
pullover ['pʊlˌəʊvə] n kazak
pull up [pʊl ʌp] v kenara çekmek
(araç)
pulse [pʌls] n nabız
pulses [pʌlsɪz] npl bakliyat
pump [pʌmp] n pompa ▷ v
pompalamak; **bicycle pump** n
bisiklet pompası; **Do you have a
pump?** Bisiklet pompanız var mı?;
Pump number three, please Üç
numaralı pompa lütfen
pumpkin ['pʌmpkɪn] n balkabağı
pump up [pʌmp ʌp] v şişirmek
punch [pʌntʃ] n (blow) yumruk,
(hot drink) pançı ▷ v yumruklamak
punctual ['pʌŋktjʊəl] adj
zamanında
punctuation [ˌpʌŋktjʊ'eɪʃən] n
noktalama
puncture ['pʌŋktʃə] n patlak
punish ['pʌnɪʃ] v cezalandırmak
punishment ['pʌnɪʃmənt] n ceza;
capital punishment n idam
cezası; **corporal punishment** n
dayak cezası

punk [pʌŋk] n punkçu
pupil ['pju:pəl] n (eye) gözbebeği,
(learner) öğrenci
puppet ['pʌpɪt] n kukla
puppy ['pʌpɪ] n yavru köpek
purchase ['pɜ:tʃɪs] v satın almak
pure [pjʊə] adj saf
purple ['pɜ:pəl] adj mor
purpose ['pɜ:pəs] n maksat
purr [pɜ:] v mırıldanmak (kedi gibi)
purse [pɜ:s] n cüzdan (kadın)
pursue [pə'sju:] v peşine takılmak
pursuit [pə'sju:t] n kovalamaca
pus [pʌs] n irin
push [pʊʃ] v ittirmek
pushchair ['pʊʃtʃeə] n puset
push-up [pʊʃʌp] n pres (spor)
put [pʊt] v koymak; **I would like to
put my jewellery in the safe**
Mücevherlerimi kasaya koymak
istiyorum
put aside [pʊt ə'saɪd] v biriktirmek
put away [pʊt ə'weɪ] v toparlayıp
kaldırmak
put back [pʊt bæk] v geri koymak
put forward [pʊt fɔ:wəd] v ileriye
almak
put in [pʊt ɪn] v öncelik belirlemek
put off [pʊt ɒf] v ertelemek
put up [pʊt ʌp] v dikmek
puzzle ['pʌzəl] n bilmece
puzzled ['pʌzəld] adj kafası
karışmış
puzzling ['pʌzlɪŋ] adj şaşırtıcı
pyjamas [pə'dʒɑ:məz] npl pijama
pylon ['paɪlən] n elektrik direği
pyramid ['pɪrəmɪd] n piramit

q

Qatar [kæ'tɑː] n Katar

quail [kweɪl] n bıldırcın

quaint [kweɪnt] adj eski ve hoş

Quaker ['kweɪkə] n Quaker mezhebinden

qualification [ˌkwɒlɪfɪ'keɪʃən] n nitelik

qualified ['kwɒlɪˌfaɪd] adj nitelikli

qualify ['kwɒlɪˌfaɪ] v nitelemek

quality ['kwɒlɪtɪ] n kalite

quantify ['kwɒntɪˌfaɪ] v miktar belirtmek

quantity ['kwɒntɪtɪ] n miktar

quarantine ['kwɒrənˌtiːn] n karantina

quarrel ['kwɒrəl] n kavga ▷ v tartışmak

quarry ['kwɒrɪ] n taş ocağı

quarter ['kwɔːtə] n çeyrek; **quarter final** n çeyrek final; **It's quarter past two** Saat ikiyi çeyrek geçiyor;

It's quarter to two Saat ikiye çeyrek var

quartet [kwɔː'tɛt] n kuartet

quay [kiː] n iskele (deniz)

queen [kwiːn] n kraliçe

query ['kwɪərɪ] n soru ▷ v sorgulamak

question ['kwɛstʃən] n soru ▷ v sormak; **question mark** n soru işareti

questionnaire [ˌkwɛstʃə'nɛə; ˌkɛs-] n anket

queue [kjuː] n kuyruk (insan sırası) ▷ v kuyruğa girmek

quick [kwɪk] adj çabuk

quickly [kwɪklɪ] adv çabukça

quiet ['kwaɪət] adj sessiz; **I'd like a quiet room** Sessiz bir oda rica ediyorum

quietly ['kwaɪətlɪ] adv sessizce

quilt [kwɪlt] n yorgan

quit [kwɪt] v bırakmak

quite [kwaɪt] adv büsbütün, bütünüyle

quiz, quizzes [kwɪz, 'kwɪzɪz] n bilgi yarışması

quota ['kwəʊtə] n kota

quotation [kwəʊ'teɪʃən] n alıntı; **quotation marks** npl çift tırnak

quote [kwəʊt] n alıntı ▷ v alıntı yapmak

r

rabbi ['ræbaɪ] n haham
rabbit ['ræbɪt] n tavşan
rabies ['reɪbiːz] n kuduz
race [reɪs] n (contest) yarış, (origin) ırk ▷ v yarışmak; **I'd like to see a horse race** At yarışı görmek isterdim
racecourse ['reɪs,kɔːs] n yarış parkuru
racehorse ['reɪs,hɔːs] n yarış atı
racer ['reɪsə] n yarışçı
racetrack ['reɪs,træk] n yarış pisti
racial ['reɪʃəl] adj ırkla ilgili
racing ['reɪsɪŋ] n **horse racing** n at yarışı; **motor racing** n oto yarışı; **racing car** n yarış arabası; **racing driver** n yarışçı (otomobil)
racism ['reɪsɪzəm] n ırkçılık
racist ['reɪsɪst] adj ırkçı ▷ n ırkçı
rack [ræk] n askılık; **luggage rack** n port bagaj
racket ['rækɪt] n (racquet) raket;

tennis racket n tenis raketi; **Where can I hire a racket?** Raket nereden kiralayabilirim?
racoon [rə'kuːn] n rakun
racquet ['rækɪt] n raket
radar ['reɪdɑː] n radar
radiation [ˌreɪdɪ'eɪʃən] n radyasyon
radiator ['reɪdɪˌeɪtə] n radyatör; **There is a leak in the radiator** Radyatör sızıntı yapıyor
radio ['reɪdɪəʊ] n radyo; **digital radio** n dijital radyo; **radio station** n radyo istasyonu; **Can I switch the radio off?** Radyoyu kapatabilir miyim?; **Can I switch the radio on?** Radyoyu açabilir miyim?
radioactive [ˌreɪdɪəʊ'æktɪv] adj radyoaktif
radio-controlled ['reɪdɪəʊ'kən'trəʊld] adj uzaktan kumandalı
radish ['rædɪʃ] n kırmızı turp
raffle ['ræfəl] n çekiliş
raft [rɑːft] n sal
rag [ræg] n çaput
rage [reɪdʒ] n hiddet; **road rage** n trafik magandalığı
raid [reɪd] n baskın ▷ v baskın yapmak
rail [reɪl] n parmaklık, ray
railcard ['reɪlˌkɑːd] n tren abonmanı
railings ['reɪlɪŋz] npl parmaklık
railway ['reɪlˌweɪ] n demiryolu; **railway station** n tren istasyonu
rain [reɪn] n yağmur ▷ v yağmur yağmak; **acid rain** n asit yağmuru; **Do you think it's going to rain?**

Sizce yağmur yağacak mı?; **It's raining** Yağmur yağıyor

rainbow ['reɪnˌbəʊ] *n* gökkuşağı

raincoat ['reɪnˌkəʊt] *n* yağmurluk

rainforest ['reɪnˌfɒrɪst] *n* yağmur ormanı

rainy ['reɪnɪ] *adj* yağmurlu

raise [reɪz] *v* kabartmak

raisin ['reɪzᵊn] *n* kuru üzüm

rake [reɪk] *n* tırmık

rally ['rælɪ] *n* miting

ram [ræm] *n* koç ▷ *v* vurmak

Ramadan [ˌræmə'dɑːn] *n* Ramazan

rambler ['ræmblə] *n* avare

ramp [ræmp] *n* rampa

random ['rændəm] *adj* rastgele

range [reɪndʒ] *n (limits)* sınır, *(mountains)* sıradağ ▷ *v* çeşitlilik göstermek

rank [ræŋk] *n (line)* sıra *(taksi vb)*, *(status)* rütbe ▷ *v* sıralamak

ransom ['rænsəm] *n* fidye

rape [reɪp] *n (plant)* hardal otu, *(sexual attack)* tecavüz *(cinsel)* ▷ *v* tecavüz etmek; **I've been raped** Tecavüze uğradım

rapids ['ræpɪdz] *npl* çağlayanlar

rapist ['reɪpɪst] *n* tecavüzcü

rare [rɛə] *adj (uncommon)* az görülür, *(undercooked)* az pişmiş

rarely ['rɛəlɪ] *adv* nadiren

rash [ræʃ] *n* kızarıklık

raspberry ['rɑːzbərɪ; -brɪ] *n* ahududu

rat [ræt] *n* sıçan

rate [reɪt] *n* oran ▷ *v* oranlamak; **interest rate** *n* faiz oranı; **rate of exchange** *n* döviz kuru

rather ['rɑːðə] *adv* oldukça

ratio ['reɪʃɪˌəʊ] *n* oran

rational ['ræʃənᵊl] *adj* akıllıca

rattle ['rætᵊl] *n* çıngırak

rattlesnake ['rætᵊlˌsneɪk] *n* çıngıraklı yılan

rave [reɪv] *n* abuk sabuk konuşma ▷ *v* saçmalamak

raven ['reɪvᵊn] *n* kuzgunî

ravenous ['rævənəs] *adj* kurt gibi aç

ravine [rə'viːn] *n* koyak

raw [rɔː] *adj* çiğ *(pişmemiş)*

razor ['reɪzə] *n* traş bıçağı; **razor blade** *n* traş bıçağı

reach [riːtʃ] *v* ulaşmak

react [rɪ'ækt] *v* tepki göstermek

reaction [rɪ'ækʃən] *n* tepki

reactor [rɪ'æktə] *n* reaktör

read [riːd] *v* okumak

reader ['riːdə] *n* okuyucu

readily ['rɛdɪlɪ] *adv* hazır bir şekilde

reading ['riːdɪŋ] *n* okuma

read out [riːd] *v* yüksek sesle okumak

ready ['rɛdɪ] *adj* hazır; **Are you ready?** Hazır mısınız?; **I'm not ready** Hazır değilim; **I'm ready** Hazırım; **When will it be ready?** Ne zaman hazır olur?; **When will the car be ready?** Araba ne zaman hazır olur?

ready-cooked ['rɛdɪ'kʊkt] *adj* hazır yemek

real ['rɪəl] *adj* gerçek *(durum)*

realistic [ˌrɪə'lɪstɪk] *adj* gerçekçi

reality [rɪ'ælɪtɪ] *n* gerçeklik; **reality TV** *n* biri bizi gözetliyor; **virtual reality** *n* sanal gerçeklik

realize ['rɪəˌlaɪz] *v* farkına varmak

really ['rɪəlɪ] *adv* gerçekten
rear [rɪə] *adj* arka ▷ *n* arka;
  rear-view mirror *n* arka ayna
reason ['riːzᵊn] *n* mantık
reasonable ['riːzənəbᵊl] *adj*
  mantıklı
reasonably ['riːzənəblɪ] *adv* makul
reassure [ˌriːəˈʃʊə] *v* güven vermek
reassuring [ˌriːəˈʃʊərɪŋ] *adj* güven
  verici
rebate ['riːbeɪt] *n* para iadesi
rebellious [rɪˈbɛljəs] *adj* isyankar
rebuild [riːˈbɪld] *v* yeniden yapmak
receipt [rɪˈsiːt] *n* fiş; **I need a**
  receipt for the insurance Sigorta
  için fiş almam gerekiyor; **I need a**
  receipt, please Fiş istiyorum
  lütfen
receive [rɪˈsiːv] *v* almak
receiver [rɪˈsiːvə] *n (electronic)*
  alıcı, *(person)* tasfiye memuru
recent ['riːsᵊnt] *adj* yeni
recently ['riːsəntlɪ] *adv* son
  zamanlarda
reception [rɪˈsɛpʃən] *n* resepsiyon
receptionist [rɪˈsɛpʃənɪst] *n*
  resepsiyonist
recession [rɪˈsɛʃən] *n* durgunluk
  (piyasa)
recharge [riːˈtʃɑːdʒ] *v* yüklemek
  (pil vb)
recipe ['rɛsɪpɪ] *n* tarif
recipient [rɪˈsɪpɪənt] *n* alıcı *(kişi)*
reckon ['rɛkən] *v* hesaba katmak
reclining [rɪˈklaɪnɪŋ] *adj* yaslanır
recognizable ['rɛkəɡˌnaɪzəbᵊl] *adj*
  tanınabilir
recognize ['rɛkəɡˌnaɪz] *v* tanımak
recommend [ˌrɛkəˈmɛnd] *v*
  tavsiye etmek

recommendation
  [ˌrɛkəmɛnˈdeɪʃən] *n* öneri
reconsider [ˌriːkənˈsɪdə] *v* yeniden
  ele almak
record *n* ['rɛkɔːd] kayıt ▷ *v* [rɪˈkɔːd]
  kaydetmek
recorder [rɪˈkɔːdə] *n (music)* ses
  kayıt cihazı, *(scribe)* kayıt aleti
recording [rɪˈkɔːdɪŋ] *n* kayıt
recover [rɪˈkʌvə] *v* iyileşmek
recovery [rɪˈkʌvərɪ] *n* iyileşme
recruitment [rɪˈkruːtmənt] *n*
  eleman alma
rectangle ['rɛkˌtæŋɡᵊl] *n*
  dikdörtgen
rectangular [rɛkˈtæŋɡjʊlə] *adj*
  dikdörtgen biçiminde
rectify ['rɛktɪˌfaɪ] *v* düzeltmek
  (hatalı bir davranış)
recurring [rɪˈkʌrɪŋ] *adj*
  yinelenen
recycle [riːˈsaɪkᵊl] *v* geri
  dönüştürmek
recycling [riːˈsaɪklɪŋ] *n* geri
  dönüştürmek
red [rɛd] *adj* kırmızı; **red meat** *n*
  kırmızı et; **red wine** *n* kırmızı
  şarap; **Red Cross** *n* Kızılhaç; **Red**
  Sea *n* Kızıl Deniz; **a bottle of red**
  wine Bir şişe kırmızı şarap; **I don't**
  eat red meat Kırmızı et
  yemiyorum
redcurrant ['rɛdˈkʌrənt] *n* kırmızı
  Frenk üzümü
redecorate [riːˈdɛkəˌreɪt] *v*
  yeniden badana yapmak
red-haired ['rɛdˌhɛəd] *adj* kızıl
  saçlı
redhead ['rɛdˌhɛd] *n* kızıl saçlı
redo [riːˈduː] *v* yeniden yapmak

reduce [rɪ'dju:s] v azaltmak

reduction [rɪ'dʌkʃən] n indirim; **Are there any reductions for children?** Çocuklara indirim var mı?; **Are there any reductions for groups?** Grup indirimi var mı?; **Are there any reductions for senior citizens?** Yaşlılara indirim var mı?; **Is there a reduction for people with disabilities?** Özürlüler için indiriminiz var mı?; **Is there a reduction with this pass?** Bu kartla indirim alabilir miyim?

redundancy [rɪ'dʌndənsɪ] n işten çıkarma *(ihtiyaç fazlası olarak)*

redundant [rɪ'dʌndənt] adj işten çıkarılmış *(ihtiyaç fazlası olarak)*

reed [ri:d] n kamış

reel [ri:l; rɪəl] n makara

refer [rɪ'fɜ:] v söz etmek

referee [ˌrɛfə'ri:] n hakem

reference ['rɛfərəns; 'rɛfrəns] n gönderme *(kaynak)*; **reference number** n referans numarası

refill [ri:'fɪl] v doldurmaya devam etmek

refinery [rɪ'faɪnərɪ] n rafineri; **oil refinery** n petrol rafinerisi

reflect [rɪ'flɛkt] v yansıtmak

reflection [rɪ'flɛkʃən] n yansıma

reflex ['ri:flɛks] n refleks

refreshing [rɪ'frɛʃɪŋ] adj iç ferahlatıcı

refreshments [rɪ'frɛʃmənts] npl serinletici içecek

refrigerator [rɪ'frɪdʒəˌreɪtə] n buzdolabı

refuel [ri:'fju:əl] v yakıt ikmali yapmak

refuge ['rɛfju:dʒ] n sığınak

refugee [ˌrɛfʊ'dʒi:] n sığınmacı

refund n ['ri:ˌfʌnd] para iadesi ▷ v [rɪ'fʌnd] para iadesi yapmak

refusal [rɪ'fju:zəl] n red

refuse[1] [rɪ'fju:z] v reddetmek

refuse[2] ['rɛfju:s] n çöp

regain [rɪ'geɪn] v kendine gelmek

regard [rɪ'gɑ:d] n saygı ▷ v değerlendirmek

regarding [rɪ'gɑ:dɪŋ] prep ilgili olarak

regiment ['rɛdʒɪmənt] n alay *(askeri)*

region ['ri:dʒən] n bölge; **Where can I buy a map of the region?** Bu bölgenin haritasını nereden alabilirim?

regional ['ri:dʒənəl] adj bölgesel

register ['rɛdʒɪstə] n kayıt ▷ v kayıt yaptırmak; **cash register** n yazar kasa

registered ['rɛdʒɪstəd] adj kayıtlı

registration [ˌrɛdʒɪ'streɪʃən] n kayıt

regret [rɪ'grɛt] n pişmanlık ▷ v hayıflanmak

regular ['rɛgjʊlə] adj düzenli

regularly ['rɛgjʊləlɪ] adv düzenli olarak

regulation [ˌrɛgjʊ'leɪʃən] n düzeltme, yönetmelik

rehearsal [rɪ'hɜ:səl] n prova

rehearse [rɪ'hɜ:s] v denemek

reimburse [ˌri:ɪm'bɜ:s] v zararını karşılamak

reindeer ['reɪnˌdɪə] n ren geyiği

reins [reɪnz] npl dizgin *(at)*

reject [rɪ'dʒɛkt] v reddetmek

relapse ['riːˌlæps] n eski haline
dönmek

related [rɪ'leɪtɪd] adj akraba

relation [rɪ'leɪʃən] n ilişki; **public
relations** npl halkla ilişkiler

relationship [rɪ'leɪʃənˌʃɪp] n ilişki

relative ['rɛlətɪv] n göreceli

relatively ['rɛlətɪvlɪ] adv göreceli
olarak

relax [rɪ'læks] v gevşemek

relaxation [ˌriːlæk'seɪʃən] n
gevşeme

relaxed [rɪ'lækst] adj rahat

relaxing [rɪ'læksɪŋ] adj gevşetici

relay ['riːleɪ] n eski grubun yerini
alan yeni grup

release [rɪ'liːs] n serbest bırakma
▷ v serbest bırakmak

relegate ['rɛlɪˌgeɪt] v daha
önemsiz bir göreve kaydırmak

relevant ['rɛlɪvənt] adj ilişkin

reliable [rɪ'laɪəbəl] adj güvenilir

relief [rɪ'liːf] n iç rahatlığı

relieve [rɪ'liːv] v dindirmek (acı)

relieved [rɪ'liːvd] adj rahatlamış

religion [rɪ'lɪdʒən] n din

religious [rɪ'lɪdʒəs] adj dini

reluctant [rɪ'lʌktənt] adj gönülsüz

reluctantly [rɪ'lʌktəntlɪ] adv
gönülsüzce

rely [rɪ'laɪ] v **rely on** v güvenmek

remain [rɪ'meɪn] v kalmak

remaining [rɪ'meɪnɪŋ] adj kalan

remains [rɪ'meɪnz] npl kalıntı

remake ['riːˌmeɪk] n yeniden
çekim

remark [rɪ'mɑːk] n görüş (fikir)

remarkable [rɪ'mɑːkəbəl] adj
dikkate değer

remarkably [rɪ'mɑːkəblɪ] adv
dikkat çekecek derecede

remarry [riː'mærɪ] v yeniden
evlenmek

remedy ['rɛmɪdɪ] n ilaç

remember [rɪ'mɛmbə] v
hatırlamak

remind [rɪ'maɪnd] v hatırlatmak

reminder [rɪ'maɪndə] n hatırlatıcı

remorse [rɪ'mɔːs] n vicdan azabı

remote [rɪ'məʊt] adj uzak;
remote control n uazaktan
kumanda

remotely [rɪ'məʊtlɪ] adv uzaktan
yakından

removable [rɪ'muːvəbəl] adj
taşınabilir

removal [rɪ'muːvəl] n taşıma;
removal van n taşınma kamyonu

remove [rɪ'muːv] v kaldırmak

remover [rɪ'muːvə] n **nail-polish
remover** n oje çıkarıcı

rendezvous ['rɒndɪˌvuː] n
randevu

renew [rɪ'njuː] v yenilemek

renewable [rɪ'njuːəbəl] adj
yenilenebilir

renovate ['rɛnəˌveɪt] v yenilemek

renowned [rɪ'naʊnd] adj tanınmış

rent [rɛnt] n kira ▷ v kiralamak; **Do
you rent DVDs?** DVD kiralayabilir
miyim?; **I'd like to rent a room** Bir
oda kiralamak istiyorum

rental ['rɛntəl] n kira; **car rental** n
oto kiralama; **rental car** n kiralık
araba

reorganize [riːˈɔːgəˌnaɪz] v
yeniden düzenlemek

rep [rɛp] n temsilci

repair [rɪ'pɛə] n tamir ▷ v onarmak;
repair kit n tamir takımı; **Can you**

repair it? Tamir edebilir misiniz?;
Can you repair my watch?
Saatimi tamir edebilir misiniz?;
Can you repair this? Bunu tamir
edebilir misiniz?; **Do you have a
repair kit?** Tamir takımınız var
mı?; **How long will it take to
repair?** Tamir etmek ne kadar
sürer?; **How much will the
repairs cost?** Tamir kaça
malolacak?; **Where can I get this
repaired?** Bunu nerede tamir
ettirebilirim?; **Where is the
nearest bike repair shop?** En
yakın bisiklet tamircisi nerede?
repay [rɪ'peɪ] v geri ödemek
repayment [rɪ'peɪmənt] n geri
ödeme
repeat [rɪ'piːt] n tekrar ▷ v
tekrarlamak; **Could you repeat
that, please?** Tekrar eder misiniz
lütfen?
repeatedly [rɪ'piːtɪdlɪ] adv
defalarca
repellent [rɪ'pɛlənt] adj itici;
insect repellent n böcek ilacı
repercussions [ˌriːpə'kʌʃənz] npl
sonuçlar
repetitive [rɪ'pɛtɪtɪv] adj
tekrarlayan
replace [rɪ'pleɪs] v yerini almak
replacement [rɪ'pleɪsmənt] n
yerini alma
replay n ['riːˌpleɪ] yeniden
gösterim ▷ v [riː'pleɪ] yeniden
göstermek
replica ['rɛplɪkə] n kopya
(taklit)
reply [rɪ'plaɪ] n yanıt ▷ v
yanıtlamak

report [rɪ'pɔːt] n rapor ▷ v rapor
vermek; **report card** n karne
reporter [rɪ'pɔːtə] n muhabir
represent [ˌrɛprɪ'zɛnt] v temsil
etmek
representative [ˌrɛprɪ'zɛntətɪv]
adj temsil eden
reproduction [ˌriːprə'dʌkʃən] n
üreme
reptile ['rɛptaɪl] n sürüngen
republic [rɪ'pʌblɪk] n cumhuriyet
repulsive [rɪ'pʌlsɪv] adj iğrenç
reputable ['rɛpjʊtəbªl] adj
saygıdeğer
reputation [ˌrɛpjʊ'teɪʃən] n ün
request [rɪ'kwɛst] n rica ▷ v rica
etmek
require [rɪ'kwaɪə] v gerektirmek
requirement [rɪ'kwaɪəmənt] n
gereksinim
rescue ['rɛskjuː] n kurtarma ▷ v
kurtarmak; **Where is the nearest
mountain rescue service post?**
En yakın dağ kurtarma ekibi
nerede?
research [rɪ'sɜːtʃ; 'riːsɜːtʃ] n
araştırma; **market research** n
pazar araştırması
resemblance [rɪ'zɛmbləns] n
benzerlik
resemble [rɪ'zɛmbªl] v benzetmek
resent [rɪ'zɛnt] v nefret etmek
resentful [rɪ'zɛntfʊl] adj içerlemiş
reservation [ˌrɛzə'veɪʃən] n itiraz
reserve [rɪ'zɜːv] n (land) koruma
alanı, (retention) yedek ▷ v
saklamak (korumak)
reserved [rɪ'zɜːvd] adj ayrılmış
reservoir ['rɛzəˌvwɑː] n su deposu
resident ['rɛzɪdənt] n sakin (konut)

residential [ˌrɛzɪ'dɛnʃəl] *adj*
meskun

resign [rɪ'zaɪn] *v* istifa etmek

resin ['rɛzɪn] *n* reçine

resist [rɪ'zɪst] *v* direnmek

resistance [rɪ'zɪstəns] *n* direnme

resit [riː'sɪt] *v* yeniden sınava
girmek

resolution [ˌrɛzə'luːʃən] *n*
kararlılık

resort [rɪ'zɔːt] *n* tatil yeri; **resort
to** *v* başvurmak

resource [rɪ'zɔːs; -'sɔːs] *n* kaynak
(destek); **natural resources** *npl*
doğal kaynaklar

respect [rɪ'spɛkt] *n* saygı ▷ *v* saygı
duymak

respectable [rɪ'spɛktəbᵊl] *adj*
saygıdeğer

respectively [rɪ'spɛktɪvlɪ] *adv*
sırasıyla

respond [rɪ'spɒnd] *v* tepki vermek

response [rɪ'spɒns] *n* yanıt

responsibility [rɪˌspɒnsə'bɪlɪtɪ] *n*
sorumluluk

responsible [rɪ'spɒnsəbᵊl] *adj*
sorumlu

rest [rɛst] *n* dinlenme ▷ *v*
dinlenmek; **the rest** *n* dinlenme

restaurant ['rɛstəˌrɒŋ; 'rɛstrɒŋ;
-rɒnt] *n* restoran; **Are there any
vegetarian restaurants here?**
Buralarda vejetaryen restoranlar
var mı?

restful ['rɛstfʊl] *adj* dinlendirici

restless ['rɛstlɪs] *adj* huzursuz

restore [rɪ'stɔː] *v* restore etmek

restrict [rɪ'strɪkt] *v* sınırlamak

restructure [riː'strʌktʃə] *v*
yeniden yapılandırma

result [rɪ'zʌlt] *n* sonuç; **result in** *v*
sonucu olmak

resume [rɪ'zjuːm] *v* devam etmek

retail ['riːteɪl] *n* perakende ▷ *v*
perakende satmak; **retail price** *n*
perakende fiyatı

retailer ['riːteɪlə] *n* perakendeci

retire [rɪ'taɪə] *v* emekli olmak

retired [rɪ'taɪəd] *adj* emekli; **I'm
retired** Emekliyim

retirement [rɪ'taɪəmənt] *n*
emeklilik

retrace [rɪ'treɪs] *v* iz sürmek

return [rɪ'tɜːn] *n (coming back)* geri
dönüş, *(yield)* getiri ▷ *vi* geri
döndürmek ▷ *vt* geri dönmek; **day
return** *n* günlük bilet; **return
ticket** *n* gidiş-dönüş bilet; **tax
return** *n* vergi iadesi

reunion [riː'juːnjən] *n* yeniden bir
araya gelme

reuse [riː'juːz] *v* yeniden
kullanmak

reveal [rɪ'viːl] *v* ifşa etmek

revenge [rɪ'vɛndʒ] *n* intikam

revenue ['rɛvɪˌnjuː] *n* vergi geliri

reverse [rɪ'vɜːs] *n* geri dönme ▷ *v*
geri dönmek

review [rɪ'vjuː] *n* eleştiri *(kitap,
film vb)*

revise [rɪ'vaɪz] *v* gözden geçirmek
(yeniden)

revision [rɪ'vɪʒən] *n* revizyon

revive [rɪ'vaɪv] *v* canlandırmak

revolting [rɪ'vəʊltɪŋ] *adj* iğrenç

revolution [ˌrɛvə'luːʃən] *n* devrim

revolutionary [ˌrɛvə'luːʃənərɪ]
adj devrimci

revolver [rɪ'vɒlvə] *n* revolver

reward [rɪ'wɔːd] *n* ödül

rewarding [rɪˈwɔːdɪŋ] *adj* tatmin edici

rewind [riːˈwaɪnd] *v* geri sarmak

rheumatism [ˈruːmətɪzəm] *n* romatizma

rhubarb [ˈruːbɑːb] *n* ravent

rhyme [raɪm] *n* **nursery rhyme** *n* çocuk şarkıları

rhythm [ˈrɪðəm] *n* ritim

rib [rɪb] *n* kaburga

ribbon [ˈrɪbən] *n* kurdele

rice [raɪs] *n* pirinç *(yiyecek)*; **brown rice** *n* esmer pirinç

rich [rɪtʃ] *adj* zengin

ride [raɪd] *n* gezinti *(at/araba/bisiklet)* ▷ *v* binmek *(hayvana)*

rider [ˈraɪdə] *n* binici

ridiculous [rɪˈdɪkjʊləs] *adj* gülünç

riding [ˈraɪdɪŋ] *n* ata binme; **horse riding** *n* binicilik

rifle [ˈraɪfˀl] *n* tüfek

rig [rɪg] *n* petrol platformu; **oil rig** *n* petrol platformu

right [raɪt] *adj (correct)* doğru *(işlem, hareket)*, *(not left)* sağ *(yan, yön)* ▷ *adv* doğru olarak ▷ *n* hak; **civil rights** *npl* özlük hakları; **human rights** *npl* insan hakları; **right angle** *n* dik açı; **right of way** *n* geçiş hakkı; **Go right at the next junction** Bir sonraki kavşaktan sağa dönün; **It wasn't your right of way** Yol hakkı sizin değildi; **Turn right** Sağa dönün

right-hand [ˈraɪtˌhænd] *adj* sağ taraf; **right-hand drive** *n* sağdan trafik

right-handed [ˈraɪtˌhændɪd] *adj* sağ elini kullanan

rightly [ˈraɪtlɪ] *adv* haklı olarak

right-wing [ˈraɪtˌwɪŋ] *adj* sağ kanat

rim [rɪm] *n* ağız *(çaydanlık vb)*

ring [rɪŋ] *n* yüzük ▷ *v* çalmak *(zil/çan)*; **engagement ring** *n* nişan yüzüğü; **ring binder** *n* klasör; **ring road** *n* çevre yolu; **wedding ring** *n* yüzük *(nikah)*

ring back [rɪŋ bæk] *v* geri aramak

ringtone [ˈrɪŋˌtəʊn] *n* çalma tonu

ring up [rɪŋ ʌp] *v* telefonla aramak

rink [rɪŋk] *n* paten alanı; **ice rink** *n* buz pateni sahası; **skating rink** *n* paten alanı

rinse [rɪns] *n* durulama ▷ *v* durulamak

riot [ˈraɪət] *n* ayaklanma ▷ *v* başkaldırmak

rip [rɪp] *v* yırtmak

ripe [raɪp] *adj* olgun *(mevye)*

rip off [rɪp ɒf] *v* kazıklamak

rip-off [ˈrɪpɒf] *n* kazık *(pahalı)*

rip up [rɪp ʌp] *v* yırtmak

rise [raɪz] *n* doğrulma ▷ *v* doğrulmak

risk [rɪsk] *n* risk ▷ *vt* risk almak

risky [ˈrɪskɪ] *adj* riskli

ritual [ˈrɪtjʊəl] *adj* ayinsel ▷ *n* ayin *(tören)*

rival [ˈraɪvˀl] *adj* rakip ▷ *n* rakip

rivalry [ˈraɪvəlrɪ] *n* rekabet

river [ˈrɪvə] *n* nehir; **Can one swim in the river?** Nehirde yüzülebilir mi?

road [rəʊd] *n* yol; **main road** *n* anayol; **ring road** *n* çevre yolu; **road map** *n* yol haritası; **road rage** *n* trafik magandalığı; **road sign** *n* trafik işareti; **road tax** *n* yol vergisi; **slip road** *n* bağlantı yolu;

Are the roads icy? Yollar buzlu mu?; **Do you have a road map of this area?** Bu bölgenin karayolları haritası var mı?; **I need a road map of...** ... yol haritası istiyorum; **Is the road to... snowed up?** ... yolunda kar var mı?; **What is the speed limit on this road?** Bu yolda hız limiti nedir?; **When will the road be clear?** Yol ne zaman açılır?; **Which road do I take for...?** ... a gitmek için hangi yoldan gitmem gerek?

roadblock ['rəʊd,blɒk] n çevirme (trafik)

roadworks ['rəʊd,wɜːks] npl yol yapım çalışması

roast [rəʊst] adj kavrulmuş

rob [rɒb] v soymak

robber ['rɒbə] n soyguncu

robbery ['rɒbərɪ] n soygun

robin ['rɒbɪn] n kızılgerdan

robot ['rəʊbɒt] n robot

rock [rɒk] n kaya ▷ v sallamak; **rock climbing** n tırmanma (kaya)

rocket ['rɒkɪt] n roket

rod [rɒd] n çubuk (demir)

rodent ['rəʊdᵊnt] n kemirgen

role [rəʊl] n ödev

roll [rəʊl] n yuvarlanma ▷ v yuvarlanmak; **bread roll** n yuvarlak ekmek; **roll call** n yoklama

roller ['rəʊlə] n silindir

rollercoaster ['rəʊlə,kəʊstə] n rollercoaster

rollerskates ['rəʊlə,skeɪts] npl paten

rollerskating ['rəʊlə,skeɪtɪŋ] n patenle kaymak

Roman ['rəʊmən] adj Romen; **Roman Catholic** n Roma Katoliği, Roma Katolik

romance ['rəʊmæns] n aşk ilişkisi

Romanesque [,rəʊmə'nɛsk] adj Romanesk

Romania [rəʊ'meɪnɪə] n Romanya

Romanian [rəʊ'meɪnɪən] adj Romen ▷ n (language) Rumence (dil), (person) Rumen (kişi)

romantic [rəʊ'mæntɪk] adj romantik

roof [ruːf] n çatı

roof rack ['ruːf,ræk] n port bagaj

room [ruːm; rʊm] n oda; **changing room** n soyunma odası (spor); **dining room** n yemek salonu; **double room** n iki kişilik oda; **fitting room** n soyunma odası (mağaza); **living room** n oturma odası; **room number** n oda numarası; **room service** n oda servisi; **single room** n tek kişilik oda; **sitting room** n oturma odası; **spare room** n yedek oda; **twin room** n çift yataklı oda; **twin-bedded room** n çift yataklı oda; **utility room** n çamaşır odası; **waiting room** n bekleme odası; **Can I see the room?** Odayı görebilir miyim?; **Can I switch rooms?** Odamı değiştirebilir miyim?; **Can you clean the room, please?** Odamı temizler misiniz lütfen; **Do you have a room for tonight?** Bu gece için odanız var mı?; **Does the room have air conditioning?** Odada klima var mı?; **How much is the room?**

Oda ne kadar?; **I need a room with wheelchair access** Tekerlekli sandalye girişi olan bir oda istiyorum; **I want to reserve a double room** İki kişilik bir oda ayırtmak istiyorum; **I want to reserve a single room** Tek kişilik bir oda ayırtmak istiyorum; **I'd like a no smoking room** Sigara içilemeyen bir oda rica ediyorum; **I'd like a room with a view of the sea** Deniz manzaralı bir oda rica ediyorum; **I'd like to rent a room** Bir oda kiralamak istiyorum; **Please charge it to my room** Oda hesabıma yazın lütfen; **The room is dirty** Oda pis; **The room is too cold** Oda çok soğuk; **There's a problem with the room** Odada bir sorun var

roommate ['ruːmˌmeɪt; 'rʊm-] n oda arkadaşı

root [ruːt] n kök

rope [rəʊp] n ip

rope in [rəʊp ɪn] v inandırmak

rose [rəʊz] n gül

rosé ['rəʊzeɪ] n pembe şarap

rosemary ['rəʊzmərɪ] n biberiye

rot [rɒt] v çürümek

rotten ['rɒtᵊn] adj çürümüş

rough [rʌf] adj kaba *(aceleyle yapılmış)*

roughly ['rʌflɪ] adv kabaca

roulette [ruː'lɛt] n rulet

round [raʊnd] adj yuvarlak ▷ n *(circle)* halka (çember), *(series)* sıra *(oyun)* ▷ prep etrafını; **paper round** n gazete dağıtım; **round trip** n gidiş dönüş yolculuk; **Whose round is it?** İçki sırası kimde?

roundabout ['raʊndəˌbaʊt] n döner kavşak

round up [raʊnd ʌp] v toparlamak

route [ruːt] n güzergah; **Is there a route that avoids the traffic?** Yoğun trafikten kaçabileceğim bir güzergah var mı?

routine [ruː'tiːn] n sıradan

row[1] [rəʊ] n *(line)* sıra (dizi) ▷ v *(in boat)* kürek çekmek; **Where can we go rowing?** Kürek çekmek için nereye gidebiliriz?

row[2] [raʊ] n *(argument)* tartışma ▷ v *(to argue)* tartışmak

rowing [rəʊɪŋ] n kürek sporu; **rowing boat** n kürek teknesi

royal ['rɔɪəl] adj kraliyet

rub [rʌb] v sürtmek

rubber ['rʌbə] n lastik; **rubber band** n elastik band; **rubber gloves** npl lastik eldiven

rubbish ['rʌbɪʃ] adj süprüntü ▷ n çöp; **rubbish dump** n çöp döküm alanı

rucksack ['rʌkˌsæk] n sırt çantası

rude [ruːd] adj kaba *(davranış)*

rug [rʌg] n küçük halı

rugby ['rʌgbɪ] n rugbi

ruin ['ruːɪn] n tahribat ▷ v mahvetmek

rule [ruːl] n kural

rule out [ruːl aʊt] v hesaba katmamak

ruler ['ruːlə] n *(commander)* hükümdar, *(measure)* cetvel

rum [rʌm] n rom

rumour ['ruːmə] n söylenti

run [rʌn] n koşu ▷ vi koşturmak ▷ vt koşmak

run away [rʌn ə'weɪ] v kaçmak
(uzaklara)

runner ['rʌnə] n yarışmacı; **runner
bean** n çalı fasulyesi

runner-up ['rʌnəʌp] n ikinci
(yarışma)

running ['rʌnɪŋ] n koşma, koşu

run out of [rʌn aʊt ɒv] v bitmek
(tükenmek)

run over [rʌn 'əʊvə] v ezmek
(arabayla)

runway ['rʌnˌweɪ] n uçak pisti

rural ['rʊərəl] adj kırsal

rush [rʌʃ] n telaş ▷ v telaş etmek;
rush hour n sıkışık saatler

rusk [rʌsk] n bebe bisküvisi

Russia ['rʌʃə] n Rusya

Russian ['rʌʃən] adj Rus ▷ n
(language) Rusça (dil), (person)
Rus (kişi)

rust [rʌst] n pas (metal)

rusty ['rʌstɪ] adj paslı

ruthless ['ruːθlɪs] adj acımasız

rye [raɪ] n çavdar

S

Sabbath ['sæbəθ] n dinlenme
günü (Yahudiler için Cumartesi,
Hristiyanlar için Pazar)

sabotage ['sæbəˌtɑːʒ] n sabotaj
▷ v sabote etmek

sachet ['sæʃeɪ] n torbacık

sack [sæk] n (container) çuval,
(dismissal) işten atma ▷ v işten
atmak

sacred ['seɪkrɪd] adj kutsal

sacrifice ['sækrɪˌfaɪs] n feda
etmek

sad [sæd] adj üzgün

saddle ['sædəl] n semer

saddlebag ['sædəlˌbæg] n heybe

sadly [sædlɪ] adv acıklı bir şekilde

safari [sə'fɑːrɪ] n safari

safe [seɪf] adj güvenli ▷ n kasa;
I have some things in the safe
Kasada eşyalarım vardı; **I would
like to put my jewellery in the
safe** Mücevherlerimi kasaya

koymak istiyorum; **Put that in the safe, please** Bunu kasaya koyun lütfen

safety ['seɪftɪ] n güvenlik; **safety belt** n emniyet kemeri; **safety pin** n kilitli iğne

saffron ['sæfrən] n safran

Sagittarius [ˌsædʒɪ'tɛərɪəs] n Yay burcu

Sahara [sə'hɑːrə] n Sahra

sail [seɪl] n yelken ▷ v gemiyle yolculuk etmek

sailing ['seɪlɪŋ] n yelken sporu; **sailing boat** n yelkenli

sailor ['seɪlə] n bahriyeli

saint [seɪnt; sənt] n aziz

salad ['sæləd] n salata; **mixed salad** n karışık salata; **salad dressing** n salata sosu

salami [sə'lɑːmɪ] n salam

salary ['sælərɪ] n maaş

sale [seɪl] n satış; **sales assistant** n tezgahtar; **sales rep** n satış elemanı

salesman, salesmen ['seɪlzmən, 'seɪlzmɛn] n satıcı (erkek)

salesperson ['seɪlzpɜːsən] n satıcı

saleswoman, saleswomen ['seɪlzwʊmən, 'seɪlzwɪmɪn] n satıcı

saliva [sə'laɪvə] n tükürük

salmon ['sæmən] n som balığı

salon ['sælɒn] n **beauty salon** n güzellik salonu

saloon [sə'luːn] n salon; **saloon car** n sedan araba

salt [sɔːlt] n tuz; **Pass the salt, please** Tuzu uzatır mısınız lütfen?

saltwater ['sɔːltˌwɔːtə] adj tuzlu

salty ['sɔːltɪ] adj tuzlu; **The food is too salty** Yemek çok tuzlu

salute [sə'luːt] v selamlamak

salve [sælv] n **lip salve** n dudak kremi

same [seɪm] adj aynı; **I'll have the same** Bana da aynısından

sample ['sɑːmpəl] n örnek

sand [sænd] n kum; **sand dune** n kum tepesi

sandal ['sændəl] n sandalet

sandcastle [sændkɑːsəl] n kumdan kale

sandpaper ['sændˌpeɪpə] n zımpara

sandpit ['sændˌpɪt] n kum havuzu

sandstone ['sændˌstəʊn] n kumtaşı

sandwich ['sænwɪdʒ; -wɪtʃ] n sandviç; **What kind of sandwiches do you have?** Sandviç olarak ne var?

San Marino [ˌsæn mə'riːnəʊ] n San Marino

sapphire ['sæfaɪə] n safir

sarcastic [sɑː'kæstɪk] adj alaycı

sardine [sɑː'diːn] n sardalya

satchel ['sætʃəl] n omuz çantası

satellite ['sætəˌlaɪt] n uydu; **satellite dish** n uydu çanak

satisfaction [ˌsætɪs'fækʃən] n tatmin

satisfactory [ˌsætɪs'fæktərɪ; -trɪ] adj tatmin edici

satisfied ['sætɪsˌfaɪd] adj tatmin olmuş

sat nav ['sæt næv] n satnav

Saturday ['sætədɪ] n Cumartesi; **every Saturday** her Cumartesi; **last Saturday** geçen Cumartesi;

next Saturday önümüzdeki
Cumartesi; **on Saturday**
Cumartesi günü; **on Saturdays**
Cumartesileri; **this Saturday** bu
Cumartesi
sauce [sɔːs] n sos; **soy sauce** n
soya sosu; **tomato sauce** n
domates sosu
saucepan ['sɔːspən] n saplı
tencere
saucer ['sɔːsə] n fincan tabağı
Saudi ['sɔːdɪ; 'saʊ-] adj Suudi ▷ n
Suudi
Saudi Arabia ['sɔːdɪ; 'saʊ-] n
Suudi Arabistan
Saudi Arabian ['sɔːdɪ ə'reɪbɪən]
adj Suudi Arabistan ▷ n Suudi
Arabistanlı
sauna ['sɔːnə] n sauna
sausage ['sɒsɪdʒ] n sosis
save [seɪv] v kurtarmak
save up [seɪv ʌp] v biriktirmek
savings ['seɪvɪŋz] npl birikim
savoury ['seɪvərɪ] adj tuzlu ve
baharatlı
saw [sɔː] n testere
sawdust ['sɔːˌdʌst] n talaş
saxophone ['sæksəˌfəʊn] n
saksafon
say [seɪ] v söylemek
saying ['seɪɪŋ] n deyim
scaffolding ['skæfəldɪŋ] n iskele
(inşaat)
scale [skeɪl] n (measure) ölçü, (tiny
piece) pul (balık)
scales [skeɪlz] npl terazi
scallop ['skɒləp; 'skæl-] n deniz
tarağı
scam [skæm] n dolandırıcılık
(hileli iş)

scampi ['skæmpɪ] npl büyük
karides
scan [skæn] n tarama (bilgisayar)
▷ v taramak (bilgisayar)
scandal ['skændəl] n skandal
Scandinavia [ˌskændɪ'neɪvɪə] n
İskandinavya
Scandinavian [ˌskændɪ'neɪvɪən]
adj İskandinav
scanner ['skænə] n tarayıcı
(scanner)
scar [skɑː] n yara
scarce [skɛəs] adj kıt
scarcely ['skɛəslɪ] adv nadiren
scare [skɛə] n panik ▷ v korkutmak
scarecrow ['skɛəˌkrəʊ] n korkuluk
scared [skɛəd] adj korkmuş
scarf, scarves [skɑːf, skɑːvz] n
eşarp
scarlet ['skɑːlɪt] adj kan kırmızısı
scary ['skɛərɪ] adj korkutucu
scene [siːn] n sahne (olay, bölüm)
scenery ['siːnərɪ] n manzara
scent [sɛnt] n koku
sceptical ['skɛptɪkəl] adj kuşkulu
schedule ['ʃɛdjuːl; 'skɛdʒʊəl] n
program; **We are on schedule**
Programa uygun gidiyoruz; **We
are slightly behind schedule**
Programın gerisindeyiz
scheme [skiːm] n plan
schizophrenic [ˌskɪtsəʊ'frɛnɪk]
adj şizofren
scholarship ['skɒləʃɪp] n burs
school [skuːl] n okul; **art school** n
sanat okulu; **boarding school** n
yatılı okul; **elementary school** n
ilkokul; **infant school** n ana okulu;
language school n dil okulu; **law
school** n hukuk fakültesi; **night**

school n gece okulu; **nursery school** n kreş; **primary school** n ilkokul; **public school** n devlet koleji; **school uniform** n okul üniforması; **secondary school** n ortaokul

schoolbag ['sku:l̩bæg] n okul çantası

schoolbook ['sku:l̩bʊk] n ders kitabı

schoolboy ['sku:l̩bɔɪ] n erkek öğrenci

schoolchildren ['sku:l̩tʃɪldrən] n okul çocukları

schoolgirl ['sku:l̩gɜ:l] n kız öğrenci

schoolteacher ['sku:l̩ti:tʃə] n öğretmen

science ['saɪəns] n bilim; **science fiction** n bilim kurgu

scientific [ˌsaɪən'tɪfɪk] adj bilimsel

scientist ['saɪəntɪst] n bilim adamı

sci-fi ['saɪˌfaɪ] n sci-fi

scissors ['sɪzəz] npl makas; **nail scissors** npl tırnak makası

sclerosis [sklɪə'rəʊsɪs] n **multiple sclerosis** n multipl skleroz

scoff [skɒf] v alay etmek

scold [skəʊld] v azarlamak

scooter ['sku:tə] n skuter

score [skɔ:] n (game/match) sayı (maç/oyun), (of music) nota ▷ v sayı yapmak

Scorpio ['skɔ:pɪˌəʊ] n Akrep burcu

scorpion ['skɔ:pɪən] n akrep

Scot [skɒt] n İskoç

Scotland ['skɒtlənd] n İskoçya

Scots [skɒts] adj İskoç

Scotsman, Scotsmen ['skɒtsmən, 'skɒtsmɛn] n İskoç (erkek)

Scotswoman, Scotswomen ['skɒtsˌwʊmən, 'skɒtsˌwɪmɪn] n İskoç

Scottish ['skɒtɪʃ] adj İskoç

scout [skaʊt] n izci

scrap [skræp] n (dispute) kavga, (small piece) parça ▷ v atmak; **scrap paper** n karalama kağıdı

scrapbook ['skræpˌbʊk] n karalama defteri

scratch [skrætʃ] n çizme (boyasını vb) ▷ v çizmek (arabanın boyasını vb)

scream [skri:m] n çığlık ▷ v çığlık atmak

screen [skri:n] n ekran; **plasma screen** n plazma ekran

screen-saver ['skri:nseɪvə] n ekran koruyucusu

screw [skru:] n vida; **The screw has come loose** Vida gevşemiş

screwdriver ['skru:ˌdraɪvə] n tornavida

scribble ['skrɪbəl] v karalamak

scroll [skrəʊl] v ekranı kaydırma; **scroll down** v aşağı kaydır; **scroll up** v yukarı kaydır

scrub [skrʌb] v ovalamak

sculptor ['skʌlptə] n heykeltraş

sculpture ['skʌlptʃə] n heykel

sea [si:] n deniz (coğrafya); **North Sea** n Kuzey Denizi; **Red Sea** n Kızıl Deniz; **sea level** n deniz seviyesi; **sea water** n deniz suyu

seafood ['si:ˌfu:d] n deniz ürünü

seagull ['si:ˌgʌl] n martı

seal [si:l] n (animal) fok, (mark) mühür ▷ v mühürlemek

seam [si:m] n dikiş (giysinin)

seaman, seamen ['si:mən, 'si:mɛn] n denizci

search [sɜːtʃ] n arama ▷ v aramak; **search engine** n arama motoru; **search party** n arama ekibi

seashore ['siːˌʃɔː] n deniz kıyısı (sahil)

seasick ['siːˌsɪk] adj deniz tutmuş

seaside ['siːˌsaɪd] n deniz kıyısı

season ['siːzᵊn] n mevsim; **high season** n pahalı sezon; **low season** n ucuz sezon; **season ticket** n abonman kartı

seasonal ['siːzənˀl] adj mevsimlik

seasoning ['siːzənɪŋ] n çeşni

seat [siːt] n (constituency) koltuk (politika), (furniture) sandalye; **aisle seat** n koridor koltuğu; **window seat** n cam kenarı koltuğu; **Do you have a baby seat?** Bebek sandalyeniz var mı?; **I'd like a non-smoking seat** Sigara içilmeyen bölümde bir koltuk lütfen; **I'd like a seat in the smoking area** Sigara içilen bölümde bir koltuk lütfen; **Is this seat free?** Bu koltuk boş mu?

seatbelt ['siːtˌbɛlt] n emniyet kemeri

seaweed ['siːˌwiːd] n yosun

second ['sɛkənd] adj ikinci ▷ n ikinci; **second class** n ikinci sınıf

second-class ['sɛkəndˌklɑːs] adj ikinci sınıf

secondhand ['sɛkəndˌhænd] adj ikinci el

secondly ['sɛkəndlɪ] adv ikinci olarak

second-rate ['sɛkəndˌreɪt] adj ikinci kalite

secret ['siːkrɪt] adj gizli ▷ n sır; **secret service** n gizli servis

secretary ['sɛkrətrɪ] n sekreter

secretly ['siːkrɪtlɪ] adv gizlice

sect [sɛkt] n mezhep

section ['sɛkʃən] n bölüm (bina, konum)

sector ['sɛktə] n sektör

secure [sɪ'kjʊə] adj güvenli

security [sɪ'kjʊərɪtɪ] n güvenlik; **security guard** n güvenlik görevlisi; **social security** n sosyal güvenlik

sedative ['sɛdətɪv] n yatıştırıcı

see [siː] v görmek; **Where can we go to see a film?** Film görmek için nereye gidebiliriz?

seed [siːd] n tohum

seek [siːk] v aramak

seem [siːm] v görünmek

seesaw ['siːˌsɔː] n tahterevalli

see-through ['siːˌθruː] adj transparan

seize [siːz] v yakalamak

seizure ['siːʒə] n nöbet

seldom ['sɛldəm] adv nadiren

select [sɪ'lɛkt] v seçmek

selection [sɪ'lɛkʃən] n seçme

self-assured ['sɛlfə'ʃʊəd] adj kendine güvenen

self-catering ['sɛlfˌkeɪtərɪŋ] n self-catering

self-centred ['sɛlfˌsɛntəd] adj bencil

self-conscious ['sɛlfˌkɒnʃəs] adj içine kapanık

self-contained ['sɛlfˌkən'teɪnd] adj müstakil

self-control ['sɛlfˌkən'trəʊl] n özkontrol

self-defence ['sɛlfˌdɪ'fɛns] n özsavunma

self-discipline ['sɛlf‚dısıplın] *n*
özdisiplin

self-employed ['sɛlım'plɔıd] *adj*
serbest çalışan

selfie ['sɛlfı] *n* özçekim

selfish ['sɛlfıʃ] *adj* bencil

self-service ['sɛlf‚sɜːvıs] *adj*
selfservis

sell [sɛl] *v* satmak; **sell-by date** *n*
son satış tarihi; **selling price** *n*
satış fiyatı

sell off [sɛl ɒf] *v* elden çıkarmak

Sellotape® ['sɛlə‚teıp] *n* seloteyp

sell out [sɛl aʊt] *v* hepsini satmak

semester [sı'mɛstə] *n* sömestr

semi ['sɛmı] *n* bitişik nizam ev

semicircle ['sɛmı‚sɜːkᵊl] *n* yarım
daire

semicolon [‚sɛmı'kəʊlən] *n*
noktalı virgül

semifinal [‚sɛmı'faınᵊl] *n* yarı final

send [sɛnd] *v* göndermek; **I want
to send this by courier** Kuryeyle
göndermek istiyorum

send back [sɛnd bæk] *v* geri
göndermek

sender ['sɛndə] *n* gönderen

send off [sɛnd ɒf] *v* uğurlamak

send out [sɛnd aʊt] *v* göndermek

Senegal [‚sɛnı'gɔːl] *n* Senegal

Senegalese [‚sɛnıgə'liːz] *adj*
Senegal ▷ *n* Senegalli

senior ['siːnjə] *adj* üst *(rütbe)*;
senior citizen *n* yaşlı vatandaş

sensational [sɛn'seıʃənᵊl] *adj*
sansasyonel

sense [sɛns] *n* duyu; **sense of
humour** *n* mizah duygusu

senseless ['sɛnslıs] *adj* amaçsız

sensible ['sɛnsıbᵊl] *adj* sağduyulu

sensitive ['sɛnsıtıv] *adj* duyarlı

sensuous ['sɛnsjʊəs] *adj* duyarlı
(tensel)

sentence ['sɛntəns] *n*
(punishment) ceza, *(words)* cümle
▷ *v* mahkum etmek

sentimental [‚sɛntı'mɛntᵊl] *adj*
duygusal

separate *adj* ['sɛpərıt] ayrı ▷ *v*
['sɛpə‚reıt] ayırmak; **with the
milk separate** sütü ayrı getirin

separately ['sɛpərətlı] *adv* ayrı
olarak

separation [‚sɛpə'reıʃən] *n*
ayrılma

September [sɛp'tɛmbə] *n* Eylül

sequel ['siːkwəl] *n* devamı

sequence ['siːkwəns] *n* dizi

Serbia ['sɜːbıə] *n* Sırbistan

Serbian ['sɜːbıən] *adj* Sırp ▷ *n*
(language) Sırpça *(dil)*, *(person)* Sırp
(kişi)

sergeant ['sɑːdʒənt] *n* çavuş

serial ['sıərıəl] *n* seri

series ['sıəriːz; -rız] *n* dizi

serious ['sıərıəs] *adj* ciddi; **Is it
serious?** Ciddi bir şey mi?

seriously ['sıərıəslı] *adv* ciddiyetle

sermon ['sɜːmən] *n* vaaz

servant ['sɜːvᵊnt] *n* hizmetçi; **civil
servant** *n* hükümet görevlisi

serve [sɜːv] *n* servis atmak ▷ *v*
hizmet etmek

server ['sɜːvə] *n* *(computer)* sunucu
(bilişim), *(person)* hizmet eden

service ['sɜːvıs] *n* servis ▷ *v* hizmet
etmek; **room service** *n* oda
servisi; **secret service** *n* gizli
servis; **service area** *n* konaklama
alanı; **service charge** *n* servis

ücreti; **service station** n benzin istasyonu; **social services** npl sosyal hizmetler; **Call the breakdown service, please** Tamir servisini çağırabilir misiniz lütfen?; **I want to complain about the service** Servisten şikayetçiyim; **Is service included?** Servis dahil mi?; **Is there a child-minding service?** Çocuk bakıcı servisiniz var mı?; **Is there room service?** Oda servisi var mı?; **The service was terrible** Servis berbattı

serviceman, servicemen ['sɜːvɪsˌmæn; -mən, 'sɜːvɪsˌmɛn] n ordu mensubu (erkek)

servicewoman, servicewomen ['sɜːvɪsˌwumən, 'sɜːvɪsˌwimin] n ordu mensubu (kadın)

serviette [ˌsɜːvɪˈɛt] n kağıt peçete

session ['sɛʃən] n seans

set [sɛt] n ayarlama ▷ v ayarlamak

setback ['sɛtbæk] n engel

set off [sɛt ɒf] v yola koyulmak

set out [sɛt aut] v düzenlemek (masa, eşya vb)

settee [sɛˈtiː] n divan

settle ['sɛtəl] v yoluna koymak

settle down ['sɛtəl daun] v yerleşmek

seven ['sɛvən] number yedi

seventeen ['sɛvənˈtiːn] number onyedi

seventeenth ['sɛvənˈtiːnθ] adj onyedinci

seventh ['sɛvənθ] adj yedinci ▷ n yedinci

seventy ['sɛvəntɪ] number yetmiş

several ['sɛvrəl] adj birkaç ▷ pron birkaç

sew [səu] v dikmek

sewer ['suːə] n lağım borusu

sewing ['səuɪŋ] n dikiş (eylem); **sewing machine** n dikiş makinesi

sew up [səu ʌp] v dikmek (onarmak)

sex [sɛks] n cinsiyet (seks)

sexism ['sɛksɪzəm] n cinsiyet ayrımcılığı

sexist ['sɛksɪst] adj cinsiyet ayrımcılığı yapan

sexual ['sɛksjʊəl] adj cinsel; **sexual intercourse** n cinsel birleşim

sexuality [ˌsɛksjʊˈælɪtɪ] n seksilik

sexy ['sɛksɪ] adj seksi

shabby ['ʃæbɪ] adj eski püskü

shade [ʃeɪd] n gölge (tente, ağaç altı)

shadow ['ʃædəu] n gölge (birinin ya da bir şeyin); **eye shadow** n göz farı

shake [ʃeɪk] vi çalkalanmak ▷ vt çalkalamak

shaken ['ʃeɪkən] adj sarsılmış

shaky ['ʃeɪkɪ] adj bitkin

shallow ['ʃæləu] adj sığ

shambles ['ʃæmbəlz] npl talan olmuş

shame [ʃeɪm] n utanç

shampoo [ʃæmˈpuː] n şampuan

shape [ʃeɪp] n şekil

share [ʃeə] n pay ▷ v paylaşmak

shareholder ['ʃeəˌhəuldə] n hisse sahibi

share out [ʃeə aut] v paylaştırmak

shark [ʃɑːk] n köpek balığı

sharp [ʃɑːp] adj keskin

shave [ʃeɪv] v traş olmak; **shaving cream** n traş kremi; **shaving foam** n traş köpüğü

shaver ['ʃeɪvə] n traş makinesi

shawl [ʃɔːl] n şal

she [ʃiː] pron o (kadın)

shed [ʃɛd] n bahçe kulübesi

sheep [ʃiːp] n koyun

sheepdog ['ʃiːpˌdɒg] n çoban köğeği

sheepskin ['ʃiːpˌskɪn] n koyun postu

sheer [ʃɪə] adj tam

sheet [ʃiːt] n çarşaf; **balance sheet** n bilanço; **fitted sheet** n fitted çarşaf; **We need more sheets** Daha fazla çarşafa ihtiyacımız var

shelf, shelves [ʃɛlf, ʃɛlvz] n raf

shell [ʃɛl] n kabuk; **shell suit** n eşofman

shellfish ['ʃɛlˌfɪʃ] n kabuklu deniz ürünü

shelter ['ʃɛltə] n barınak

shepherd ['ʃɛpəd] n çoban

sherry ['ʃɛrɪ] n şeri

shield [ʃiːld] n kalkan

shift [ʃɪft] n yer değiştirme ▷ v yer değiştirmek

shifty ['ʃɪftɪ] adj kaypak

Shiite ['ʃiːaɪt] adj Şii

shin [ʃɪn] n kaval kemiği

shine [ʃaɪn] v parlamak

shiny ['ʃaɪnɪ] adj parlak

ship [ʃɪp] n gemi

shipbuilding ['ʃɪpˌbɪldɪŋ] n gemi yapımı

shipment ['ʃɪpmənt] n yükleme

shipwreck ['ʃɪpˌrɛk] n deniz kazası

shipwrecked ['ʃɪpˌrɛkt] adj deniz kazası geçirmiş

shipyard ['ʃɪpˌjɑːd] n tersane

shirt [ʃɜːt] n gömlek; **polo shirt** n polo gömlek

shiver ['ʃɪvə] v titremek

shock [ʃɒk] n şok ▷ v şok geçirmek; **electric shock** n elektrik çarpması

shocking ['ʃɒkɪŋ] adj yüzkızartıcı

shoe [ʃuː] n ayakkabı; **shoe polish** n ayakkabı cilası; **shoe shop** n ayakkabıcı; **Can you re-heel these shoes?** Ayakkabılarımın topuklarını değiştirebilir misiniz?; **Can you repair these shoes?** Bu ayakkabıları tamir edebilir misiniz?; **I have a hole in my shoe** Ayakkabımda delik var; **Which floor are shoes on?** Ayakkabılar hangi katta?

shoelace ['ʃuːˌleɪs] n ayakkabı bağı

shoot [ʃuːt] v ateş etmek

shooting ['ʃuːtɪŋ] n ateş etme

shop [ʃɒp] n dükkan/mağaza; **antique shop** n antikacı dükkanı; **gift shop** n hediye dükkanı; **shop assistant** n satış elemanı; **shop window** n vitrin

shopkeeper ['ʃɒpˌkiːpə] n bakkal

shoplifting ['ʃɒpˌlɪftɪŋ] n aşırma (dükkanda)

shopping ['ʃɒpɪŋ] n alışveriş; **shopping bag** n alışveriş çantası; **shopping centre** n alışveriş merkezi; **shopping trolley** n market arabası

shore [ʃɔː] n kıyı

short [ʃɔːt] adj kısa; **short story** n kısa öykü

shortage ['ʃɔːtɪdʒ] n yokluk (eksiklik)

shortcoming ['ʃɔːtˌkʌmɪŋ] n eksiklik

shortcut ['ʃɔːtˌkʌt] n kestirme yol

shortfall ['ʃɔːtˌfɔːl] n mali açıklık

shorthand ['ʃɔːtˌhænd] n steno

shortlist ['ʃɔːtˌlɪst] n ön eleme listesi

shortly ['ʃɔːtlɪ] adv kısa zamanda

shorts [ʃɔːts] npl şort

short-sighted ['ʃɔːt'saɪtɪd] adj miyop

short-sleeved ['ʃɔːtˌsliːvd] adj kısa kollu

shot [ʃɒt] n ateş

shotgun ['ʃɒtˌɡʌn] n kısa menzilli silah

shoulder ['ʃəʊldə] n omuz; **hard shoulder** n dönemeç; **shoulder blade** n kürek kemiği; **I've hurt my shoulder** Omuzumu incittim

shout [ʃaʊt] n bağırtı ▷ v bağırmak

shovel ['ʃʌvəl] n kürek

show [ʃəʊ] n gösteri (eğlence) ▷ v göstermek; **show business** n eğlence sanayii; **Where can we go to see a show?** Gösteri için nereye gidebiliriz?

shower ['ʃaʊə] n duş; **shower cap** n duş başlığı; **shower gel** n duş jeli; **Are there showers?** Burada duş var mı?; **The shower doesn't work** Duş çalışmıyor; **The shower is dirty** Duş kirli; **The showers are cold** Duş soğuk akıyor; **Where are the showers?** Duşlar nerede?

showerproof ['ʃaʊəˌpruːf] adj yağmura dayanıklı

showing ['ʃəʊɪŋ] n gösterim (film vb)

show off [ʃəʊ ɒf] v gösteriş yapmak

show-off [ʃəʊɒf] n gösteriş

show up [ʃəʊ ʌp] v ortaya çıkmak

shriek [ʃriːk] v feryat etmek

shrimp [ʃrɪmp] n ufak karides

shrine [ʃraɪn] n mabed

shrink [ʃrɪŋk] v kısalmak

shrub [ʃrʌb] n çalı

shrug [ʃrʌɡ] v omuz silkmek

shrunk [ʃrʌŋk] adj kısalmış

shudder ['ʃʌdə] v korkarak titremek

shuffle ['ʃʌfəl] v ayaklarını sürüyerek yürümek

shut [ʃʌt] v kapatmak

shut down [ʃʌt daʊn] v kapatmak

shutters ['ʃʌtəz] n kepenk

shuttle ['ʃʌtəl] n karşılıklı sefer yapan araç

shuttlecock ['ʃʌtəlˌkɒk] n badminton topu

shut up [ʃʌt ʌp] v susmak

shy [ʃaɪ] adj utangaç

Siberia [saɪ'bɪərɪə] n Siberya

siblings ['sɪblɪŋz] npl kardeşler

sick [sɪk] adj hasta; **sick leave** n hastalık izni; **sick note** n hasta belgesi; **sick pay** n hastalık ödentisi

sickening ['sɪkənɪŋ] adj mide bulandırıcı

sickness ['sɪknɪs] n hastalık; **morning sickness** n hamilelik bulantısı; **travel sickness** n araba tutması

side [saɪd] n taraf; **side effect** n yan etki; **side street** n yan sokak

sideboard ['saɪdˌbɔːd] n büfe (mobilya)

sidelight ['saɪdˌlaɪt] n yan lambalar

sideways ['saɪd,weɪz] *adv* yana
doğru

sieve [sɪv] *n* elek

sigh [saɪ] *n* iç çekme ▷ *v* iç geçirmek

sight [saɪt] *n* görüş *(göz)*

sightseeing ['saɪt,si:ɪŋ] *n* gezip
görme

sign [saɪn] *n* işaret ▷ *v* işaret
etmek; **road sign** *n* trafik işareti;
sign language *n* işaret dili; **I can't
find the at sign** at işaretini
bulamıyorum

signal ['sɪgnəl] *n* işaret ▷ *v* sinyal
vermek; **busy signal** *n* meşgul
sinyali

signature ['sɪgnɪtʃə] *n* imza

significance [sɪg'nɪfɪkəns] *n*
önem

significant [sɪg'nɪfɪkənt] *adj*
önemli

sign on [saɪn ɒn] *v* kaydolmak

signpost ['saɪn,pəʊst] *n* yol
tabelası

Sikh [si:k] *adj* Sikh ▷ *n* Sikh

silence ['saɪləns] *n* sessizlik

silencer ['saɪlənsə] *n* susturucu

silent ['saɪlənt] *adj* sessiz

silk [sɪlk] *n* ipek

silly ['sɪlɪ] *adj* aptalca

silver ['sɪlvə] *n* gümüş

similar ['sɪmɪlə] *adj* benzer

similarity ['sɪmɪ'lærɪtɪ] *n*
benzerlik

simmer ['sɪmə] *v* yavaş yavaş
kaynatmak

simple ['sɪmpəl] *adj* basit

simplify ['sɪmplɪ,faɪ] *v*
basitleştirmek

simply ['sɪmplɪ] *adv* basitçe

simultaneous [,sɪməl'teɪnɪəs;
,saɪməl'teɪnɪəs] *adj* aynı anda olan

simultaneously
[,sɪməl'teɪnɪəslɪ] *adv* aynı anda

sin [sɪn] *n* günah

since [sɪns] *adv* o zamandan beri
▷ *conj* den beri; **I've been sick
since Monday** Pazartesi'nden
beri kusuyorum

sincere [sɪn'sɪə] *adj* içten

sincerely [sɪn'sɪəlɪ] *adv* içtenlikle

sing [sɪŋ] *v* şarkı söylemek

singer ['sɪŋə] *n* şarkıcı; **lead singer**
n as solist

singing ['sɪŋɪŋ] *n* şarkı söyleme

single ['sɪŋgəl] *adj* tek ▷ *n* tek
yataklı oda; **single bed** *n* tek
yatak; **single parent** *n* yalnız
ebeveyn; **single room** *n* tek kişilik
oda; **single ticket** *n* tek yön bilet;
How much is a single ticket? Tek
gidiş bilet ne kadar?; **I want to
reserve a single room** Tek kişilik
bir oda ayırtmak istiyorum

singles ['sɪŋgəlz] *npl* tekler *(spor)*

singular ['sɪŋgjʊlə] *n* tekil

sinister ['sɪnɪstə] *adj* uğursuz

sink [sɪŋk] *n* lavabo ▷ *v* batmak

sinus ['saɪnəs] *n* sinüs

sir [sɜ:] *n* sör

siren ['saɪərən] *n* siren

sister ['sɪstə] *n* kızkardeş

sister-in-law ['sɪstə ɪn lɔ:] *n* elti

sit [sɪt] *v* oturmak

sitcom ['sɪt,kɒm] *n* sitkom

sit down [sɪt daʊn] *v* oturmak

site [saɪt] *n* alan *(yer)*; **building
site** *n* inşaat alanı; **caravan site** *n*
karavan kampı

situated ['sɪtjʊ,eɪtɪd] *adj*
konuşlanmış

situation [ˌsɪtjʊ'eɪʃən] *n* durum

six [sɪks] *number* altı; **It's six o'clock** Saat altı

sixteen ['sɪks'tiːn] *number* onaltı

sixteenth ['sɪks'tiːnθ] *adj* onaltıncı

sixth [sɪksθ] *adj* altıncı

sixty ['sɪkstɪ] *number* altmış

size [saɪz] *n* boyut

skate [skeɪt] *v* paten yapmak

skateboard ['skeɪtˌbɔːd] *n* skateboard; **I'd like to go skateboarding** Skateboarding yapmak isterdim

skateboarding ['skeɪtˌbɔːdɪŋ] *n* skateboard yapma

skates [skeɪts] *npl* patenler

skating ['skeɪtɪŋ] *n* paten yapma; **skating rink** *n* paten alanı

skeleton ['skɛlɪtən] *n* iskelet

sketch [skɛtʃ] *n* karalama ▷ *v* karalama yapmak

skewer ['skjʊə] *n* kebap şişi

ski [skiː] *n* kayak ▷ *v* kayak yapmak; **ski lift** *n* teleferik; **ski pass** *n* kayak izni; **Can we hire skis here?** Burada kayak kiralayabilir miyiz?; **Do you have a map of the ski runs?** Kayak güzergahlarının haritası var mı?; **How much is a ski pass?** Kayak kartı ne kadar?; **I want to hire ski poles** Kayak sopası kiralamak istiyorum; **I want to hire skis** Kayak kiralamak istiyorum; **I'd like a ski pass for a day** Bir günlük kayak kartı almak istiyorum; **Is there a ski school?** Burada kayak okulu var mı?; **Where can I buy a ski pass?** Kayak kartı nereden alabilirim?

skid [skɪd] *v* kaymak

skier ['skiːə] *n* kayakçı

skiing ['skiːɪŋ] *n* kayma sporu

skilful ['skɪlfʊl] *adj* becerikli

skill [skɪl] *n* beceri

skilled [skɪld] *adj* becerikli

skimpy ['skɪmpɪ] *adj* yetersiz

skin [skɪn] *n* cilt

skinhead ['skɪnˌhɛd] *n* dazlak kafa

skinny ['skɪnɪ] *adj* kürdan gibi

skin-tight ['skɪn'taɪt] *adj* daracık

skip [skɪp] *v* atlamak

skirt [skɜːt] *n* etek *(giysi)*

skive [skaɪv] *v* kaytarmak

skull [skʌl] *n* kafatası

sky [skaɪ] *n* gök

skyscraper ['skaɪˌskreɪpə] *n* gökdelen

slack [slæk] *adj* gevşek *(tavır)*

slam [slæm] *v* çarparak kapatmak

slang [slæŋ] *n* argo

slap [slæp] *v* tokatlamak

slash [slæʃ] *n* **forward slash** *n* eğik çizgi

slate [sleɪt] *n* arduvaz

slave [sleɪv] *n* köle ▷ *v* köle gibi çalışmak

sledge [slɛdʒ] *n* kızak; **Where can we go sledging?** Kızak kaymak için nereye gitmemiz gerek?

sledging ['slɛdʒɪŋ] *n* kızak kaymak

sleep [sliːp] *n* uyku ▷ *v* uyumak; **sleeping bag** *n* uyku tulumu; **sleeping car** *n* kuşetli vagon; **sleeping pill** *n* uyku hapı

sleep around [sliːp ə'raʊnd] *v* önüne gelenle yatmak

sleep in [sliːp ɪn] *v* uyuyakalmak

sleep together [sliːp tə'gɛðə] *v* birlikte yatmak

sleepwalk ['sliːp,wɔːk] v uykuda
yürüme
sleepy ['sliːpɪ] adj uykulu
sleet [sliːt] n sulu kar ▷ v sulu
sepken yağmak
sleeve [sliːv] n kol ağzı
sleeveless ['sliːvlɪs] adj kolsuz
(giysi)
slender ['slɛndə] adj tığ gibi
slice [slaɪs] n dilim ▷ v dilimlemek
slick [slɪk] n **oil slick** n petrol
sızması
slide [slaɪd] n kayma ▷ v kaymak
slight [slaɪt] adj az
slightly ['slaɪtlɪ] adv azıcık
slim [slɪm] adj ince (vücut vb)
sling [slɪŋ] n kol askısı (sağlık)
slip [slɪp] n (mistake) hata, (paper)
kağıt parçası, (underwear) iç
gömleği ▷ v kaymak; **slip road** n
bağlantı yolu; **slipped disc** n disk
kayması
slipper ['slɪpə] n terlik
slippery ['slɪpərɪ; -prɪ] adj kaygan
slip up [slɪp ʌp] v hata yapmak
slip-up [slɪpʌp] n hata
slope [sləʊp] n yokuş; **nursery
slope** n kayak alıştırma pisti
sloppy ['slɒpɪ] adj pasaklı
slot [slɒt] n boşluk (konum); **slot
machine** n jetonlu makine
Slovak ['sləʊvæk] adj Slovak ▷ n
(language) Slovakça (dil), (person)
Slovak (kişi)
Slovakia [sləʊ'vækɪə] n Slovakya
Slovenia [sləʊ'viːnɪə] n Slovenya
Slovenian [sləʊ'viːnɪən] adj
Slovenya ▷ n (language) Slovence
(dil), (person) Slovenyalı (kişi)
slow [sləʊ] adj yavaş; **The**

connection seems very slow
Bağlantı çok yavaş
slow down [sləʊ daʊn] v
yavaşlamak
slowly [sləʊlɪ] adv yavaşça
slug [slʌg] n kabuksuz
sümüklüböcek
slum [slʌm] n gecekondu
slush [slʌʃ] n sulu çamur
sly [slaɪ] adj kurnaz
smack [smæk] v tokat atmak
small [smɔːl] adj küçük; **small ads**
npl küçük ilanlar; **Do you have a
small?** Küçük beden var mı?; **Do
you have this in a smaller size?**
Bunun bir küçük bedeni var mı?;
It's too small Çok küçük; **The
room is too small** Bu oda çok
küçük
smart [smɑːt] adj şık; **smart
phone** n akıllı telefon
smash [smæʃ] v parçalamak
smashing ['smæʃɪŋ] adj harika
smell [smɛl] n koku ▷ vi kokmak
▷ vt koklamak; **I can smell gas**
Gaz kokusu alıyorum; **My room
smells of smoke** Odada duman
kokusu var; **There's a funny
smell** Garip bir koku var
smelly ['smɛlɪ] adj pis kokulu
smile [smaɪl] n gülümseme ▷ v
gülümsemek
smiley ['smaɪlɪ] n neşeli
smoke [sməʊk] n duman ▷ v sigara
içmek; **smoke alarm** n duman
alarmı; **My room smells of
smoke** Odada duman kokusu var
smoked ['sməʊkt] adj tütsülenmiş
smoker ['sməʊkə] n sigara içen
smoking ['sməʊkɪŋ] n tüten

smooth [smuːð] *adj* pürüzsüz

smoothie ['smuːðɪ] *n* smoothie

SMS [ɛs ɛm ɛs] *n* SMS

smudge [smʌdʒ] *n* leke

smug [smʌg] *adj* kendinden memnun

smuggle ['smʌgəl] *v* kaçakçılık yapmak

smuggler ['smʌglə] *n* kaçakçı

smuggling ['smʌglɪŋ] *n* kaçakçılık

snack [snæk] *n* atıştırma; **snack bar** *n* snack bar

snail [sneɪl] *n* salyangoz

snake [sneɪk] *n* yılan

snap [snæp] *v* kopmak

snapshot ['snæp,ʃɒt] *n* enstantane

snarl [snɑːl] *v* hırlamak

snatch [snætʃ] *v* kapmak

sneakers ['sniːkəz] *npl* spor ayakkabısı

sneeze [sniːz] *v* hapşırmak

sniff [snɪf] *v* burnunu çekmek

snigger ['snɪgə] *v* kıs kıs gülmek

snob [snɒb] *n* züppe

snooker ['snuːkə] *n* snooker

snooze [snuːz] *n* tavşan uykusu ▷ *v* uykuyu uzatmak

snore [snɔː] *v* horlamak

snorkel ['snɔːkəl] *n* şnorkel

snow [snəʊ] *n* kar ▷ *v* kar yağmak; **Do I need snow chains?** Kar zinciri almam gerekiyor mu?; **Do you think it will snow?** Kar yağacak mı dersiniz?; **It's snowing** Kar yağıyor; **The snow is very heavy** Kar çok şiddetli; **What are the snow conditions?** Kar durumu nasıl?; **What is the snow like?** Kar nasıl?

snowball ['snəʊ,bɔːl] *n* kar topu

snowboard ['snəʊ,bɔːd] *n* **I want to hire a snowboard** Snowboard kiralamak istiyorum

snowflake ['snəʊ,fleɪk] *n* kar tanesi

snowman ['snəʊ,mæn] *n* kardan adam

snowplough ['snəʊ,plaʊ] *n* kar temizleme aracı

snowstorm ['snəʊ,stɔːm] *n* kar fırtınası

so [səʊ] *adv* öyle, öylesine; **so (that)** *conj* öyle ki

soak [səʊk] *v* ıslatmak

soaked [səʊkt] *adj* ıslak

soap [səʊp] *n* sabun; **soap dish** *n* sabunluk; **soap opera** *n* televizyon dizisi; **soap powder** *n* sabun tozu; **There is no soap** Sabun yok

sob [sɒb] *v* hıçkırarak ağlamak

sober ['səʊbə] *adj* ayık

sociable ['səʊʃəbəl] *adj* sosyal

social ['səʊʃəl] *adj* sosyal; **social media** *n* sosyal medya; **social security** *n* sosyal güvenlik; **social services** *npl* sosyal hizmetler; **social worker** *n* sosyal hizmetler görevlisi

socialism ['səʊʃə,lɪzəm] *n* sosyalizm

socialist ['səʊʃəlɪst] *adj* sosyalist ▷ *n* sosyalist

society [sə'saɪətɪ] *n* toplum

sociology [,səʊsɪ'ɒlədʒɪ] *n* toplumbilim

sock [sɒk] *n* çorap

socket ['sɒkɪt] *n* priz; **Where is the socket for my electric razor?** Traş makinem için priz nerede?

sofa ['səʊfə] *n* kanepe *(koltuk)*; **sofa bed** *n* çek-yat

soft [sɒft] *adj* yumuşak; **soft drink** *n* içecek

softener ['sɒfᵊnə] *n* yumuşatıcı

software ['sɒft,wɛə] *n* yazılım

soggy ['sɒgɪ] *adj* ıslak

soil [sɔɪl] *n* toprak

solar ['səʊlə] *adj* güneş; **solar power** *n* güneş enerjisi; **solar system** *n* güneş sistemi

soldier ['səʊldʒə] *n* asker

sold out [səʊld aʊt] *adj* satılıp tükenmiş

solicitor [sə'lɪsɪtə] *n* hukuk danışmanı

solid ['sɒlɪd] *adj* katı *(maddenin hali)*

solo ['səʊləʊ] *n* tek başına

soloist ['səʊləʊɪst] *n* solist

soluble ['sɒljʊbᵊl] *adj* çözünür

solution [sə'luːʃən] *n* çözüm

solve [sɒlv] *v* çözmek

solvent ['sɒlvənt] *n* çözücü

Somali [səʊ'mɑːlɪ] *adj* Somali ▷ *n (language)* Somalice, *(person)* Somalili *(kişi)*

Somalia [səʊ'mɑːlɪə] *n* Somali

some [sʌm; səm] *adj* herhangi ▷ *pron* bazı, biraz; **Could you lend me some money?** Bana biraz borç verebilir misiniz?

somebody ['sʌmbədɪ] *pron* birisi

somehow ['sʌm,haʊ] *adv* nasılsa

someone ['sʌm,wʌn; -wən] *pron* birisi

someplace ['sʌm,pleɪs] *adv* bir yerde

something ['sʌmθɪŋ] *pron* bir şey; **I'd like to order something local** Yöreye özgü bir şey ısmarlamak istiyorum; **Would you like**

something to eat? Bir şey yemek ister misiniz?; **Would you like to do something tomorrow?** Yarın bir şeyler yapmak ister misiniz?

sometime ['sʌm,taɪm] *adv* bir ara

sometimes ['sʌm,taɪmz] *adv* bazen

somewhere ['sʌm,wɛə] *adv* bir yerde

son [sʌn] *n* oğul

song [sɒŋ] *n* şarkı

son-in-law [sʌn ɪn lɔː] **(sons-in-law)** *n* damat *(kızının kocası)*

soon [suːn] *adv* kısa zamanda; **as soon as possible** en kısa zamanda

sooner ['suːnə] *adv* daha erken

soot [sʊt] *n* kurum *(is)*

sophisticated [sə'fɪstɪ,keɪtɪd] *adj* sofistike

soppy ['sɒpɪ] *adj* aşırı duygusal

soprano [sə'prɑːnəʊ] *n* soprano

sorbet ['sɔːbeɪ; -bɪt] *n* sorbet

sorcerer ['sɔːsərə] *n* büyücü

sore [sɔː] *adj* ağrılı ▷ *n* yara; **cold sore** *n* uçuk *(sağlık)*

sorry ['sɒrɪ] *interj* **sorry!** *excl* affedersiniz!; **I'm sorry** Özür dilerim; **I'm sorry to trouble you** Rahatsız ettiğim için özür dilerim; **I'm very sorry, I didn't know the regulations** Özür dilerim, kuralları bilmiyordum; **Sorry we're late** Geciktiğimiz için özür dileriz; **Sorry, I didn't catch that** Pardon, anlayamadım; **Sorry, I'm not interested** Kusura bakmayın, ilgilenmiyorum

sort [sɔːt] *n* çeşit

sort out [sɔːt aʊt] v halletmek

SOS [ɛs əʊ ɛs] n SOS

so-so [səʊsəʊ] adv şöyle böyle

soul [səʊl] n ruh

sound [saʊnd] adj sağlam ▷ n ses

soundtrack [ˈsaʊndˌtræk] n film müziği

soup [suːp] n çorba; **What is the soup of the day?** Günün çorbası ne?

sour [ˈsaʊə] adj ekşi

south [saʊθ] adj güney ▷ adv güneyde ▷ n güney; **South Africa** n Güney Afrika; **South African** n Güney Afrika, Güney Afrikalı; **South America** n Güney Amerika; **South American** n Güney Amerika, Güney Amerikalı; **South Korea** n Güney Kore; **South Pole** n Güney Kutbu

southbound [ˈsaʊθˌbaʊnd] adj güneye giden

southeast [ˌsaʊθˈiːst; ˌsaʊˈiːst] n güneydoğu

southern [ˈsʌðən] adj güney

southwest [ˌsaʊθˈwɛst; ˌsaʊˈwɛst] n güneybatı

souvenir [ˌsuːvəˈnɪə; ˈsuːvəˌnɪə] n anmalık

soya [ˈsɔɪə] n soya

spa [spɑː] n ılıca

space [speɪs] n boşluk (mekan)

spacecraft [ˈspeɪsˌkrɑːft] n uzay aracı

spade [speɪd] n kürek

spaghetti [spəˈgɛtɪ] n spagetti

Spain [speɪn] n İspanya

spam [spæm] n istenmeyen e-mail

Spaniard [ˈspænjəd] n İspanyol

spaniel [ˈspænjəl] n cocker spaniel

Spanish [ˈspænɪʃ] adj İspanyol ▷ n İspanyol

spank [spæŋk] v şaplak atmak

spanner [ˈspænə] n İngiliz anahtarı

spare [spɛə] adj yedek ▷ v hayatını bağışlamak; **spare part** n yedek parça; **spare room** n yedek oda; **spare time** n boş zaman; **spare tyre** n stepne; **spare wheel** n stepne; **Is there any spare bedding?** Yedek çarşaf takımı var mı?

spark [spɑːk] n kıvılcım; **spark plug** n buji

sparrow [ˈspærəʊ] n serçe

spasm [ˈspæzəm] n kramp

spatula [ˈspætjʊlə] n spatül

speak [spiːk] v konuşmak; **I'd like to speak to…, please…** ile konuşmak istiyorum lütfen; **I'd like to speak to a doctor** Doktorla konuşmak istiyorum lütfen; **I'd like to speak to the manager, please** Müdürle konuşmak istiyorum lütfen

speaker [ˈspiːkə] n konuşmacı; **native speaker** n anadilini konuşan

speak up [spiːk ʌp] v açıkça fikrini söylemek

special [ˈspɛʃəl] adj özel; **special offer** n indirimli fiyatla sunulan eşya

specialist [ˈspɛʃəlɪst] n uzman

speciality [ˌspɛʃɪˈælɪtɪ] n uzmanlık

specialize [ˈspɛʃəˌlaɪz] v uzmanlaşmak

specially [ˈspɛʃəlɪ] adv özellikle

species [ˈspiːʃiːz; ˈspiːʃiˌiːz] n tür

specific [spɪ'sɪfɪk] *adj* spesifik
specifically [spɪ'sɪfɪklɪ] *adv* özellikle
specify ['spɛsɪ,faɪ] *v* belirtmek
specs [spɛks] *npl* özellikler
spectacles ['spɛktəkᵊlz] *npl* gözlük
spectacular [spɛk'tækjʊlə] *adj* görülmeye değer
spectator [spɛk'teɪtə] *n* izleyici
speculate ['spɛkjʊ,leɪt] *v* varsayımda bulunmak
speech [spi:tʃ] *n* konuşma
speechless ['spi:tʃlɪs] *adj* nutku tutulmuş
speed [spi:d] *n* hız; **speed limit** *n* hız sınırı; **What is the speed limit on this road?** Bu yolda hız limiti nedir?
speedboat ['spi:d,bəʊt] *n* sürat motoru
speeding ['spi:dɪŋ] *n* hız yapmak
speedometer [spɪ'dɒmɪtə] *n* hızölçer
speed up [spi:d ʌp] *v* hızlanmak
spell [spɛl] *n (magic)* büyü, *(time)* dönem *(belirli bir süre)* ▷ *v* telaffuz etmek
spellchecker ['spɛl,tʃɛkə] *n* yazım denetimi
spelling ['spɛlɪŋ] *n* heceleme
spend [spɛnd] *v* harcamak
sperm [spɜ:m] *n* sperm
spice [spaɪs] *n* baharat
spicy ['spaɪsɪ] *adj* acılı
spider ['spaɪdə] *n* örümcek
spill [spɪl] *v* dökmek
spinach ['spɪnɪdʒ; -ɪtʃ] *n* ıspanak
spine [spaɪn] *n* belkemiği
spinster ['spɪnstə] *n* kız kurusu

spire [spaɪə] *n* kilise kulesinin sivri tepesi
spirit ['spɪrɪt] *n* ruh
spirits ['spɪrɪts] *npl* alkollü içki
spiritual ['spɪrɪtjʊəl] *adj* manevi
spit [spɪt] *n* şiş ▷ *v* tükürmek
spite [spaɪt] *n* kincilik ▷ *v* kin gütmek
spiteful ['spaɪtfʊl] *adj* kinci
splash [splæʃ] *v* sıçratmak
splendid ['splɛndɪd] *adj* görkemli
splint [splɪnt] *n* süyek
splinter ['splɪntə] *n* kıymık
split [splɪt] *v* ayırmak
split up [splɪt ʌp] *v* ayrılmak
spoil [spɔɪl] *v* berbat etmek
spoilsport ['spɔɪl,spɔ:t] *n* oyunbozan
spoilt [spɔɪlt] *adj* şımartılmış
spoke [spəʊk] *n* jant teli
spokesman, spokesmen ['spəʊksmən, 'spəʊksmɛn] *n* sözcü *(erkek)*
spokesperson ['spəʊks,pɜːsən] *n* sözcü
spokeswoman, spokeswomen ['spəʊks,wʊmən, 'spəʊks,wɪmɪn] *n* sözcü *(kadın)*
sponge [spʌndʒ] *n (cake)* pandispanya, *(for washing)* sünger *(banyo)*; **sponge bag** *n* tuvalet çantası
sponsor ['spɒnsə] *n* finansör ▷ *v* finanse etmek
sponsorship ['spɒnsəʃɪp] *n* mali destek
spontaneous [spɒn'teɪnɪəs] *adj* kendiliğinden
spooky ['spu:kɪ] *adj* ürkütücü
spoon [spu:n] *n* kaşık; **Could I**

have a clean spoon, please?
Temiz bir kaşık alabilir miyim
lütfen?

spoonful ['spu:n,fʊl] *n* bir kaşık
dolusu

sport [spɔ:t] *n* spor; **winter sports**
npl kış sporları; **What sports
facilities are there?** Buralarda
sport tesisi var mı?; **Which
sporting events can we go to?**
Hangi spor gösterisine gidebiliriz?

sportsman, sportsmen
['spɔ:tsmən, 'spɔ:tsmɛn] *n*
sporcu *(erkek)*

sportswear ['spɔ:ts,wɛə] *n* spor
giysisi

sportswoman, sportswomen
['spɔ:ts,wʊmən, 'spɔ:ts,wımın] *n*
kadın sporcu

sporty ['spɔ:tı] *adj* sporsever

spot [spɒt] *n (blemish)* akne, *(place)*
yer ▷ *v* dikkat etmek

spotless ['spɒtlıs] *adj* pırıl pırıl

spotlight ['spɒt,laıt] *n* spot
lambası

spotty ['spɒtı] *adj* sivilceli

spouse [spaʊs] *n* eş *(karıkoca)*

sprain [spreın] *n* burkulma ▷ *v*
burkmak *(bilek)*

spray [spreı] *n* serpinti ▷ *v*
püskürtmek; **hair spray** *n* saç
spreyi

spread [sprɛd] *n* yayılım ▷ *v*
yaymak

spread out [sprɛd aʊt] *v* yayılmak

spreadsheet ['sprɛd,ʃi:t] *n* hesap
çizelgesi

spring [sprıŋ] *n (coil)* yay,
(season) ilkbahar; **spring onion** *n*
taze soğan

spring-cleaning ['sprıŋ,kli:nıŋ]
n bahar temizliği

springtime ['sprıŋ,taım] *n* bahar

sprinkler ['sprıŋklə] *n*
yağmurlama cihazı

sprint [sprınt] *n* kısa mesafe hız
koşusu ▷ *v* hızla koşmak

sprinter ['sprıntə] *n* kısa mesafe
koşucusu

spy [spaı] *n* casus ▷ *v* casusluk etmek

spying ['spaııŋ] *n* casusluk

squabble ['skwɒbəl] *v* ağız dalaşı

squander ['skwɒndə] *v* müsrüflük
etmek

square [skwɛə] *adj* kare ▷ *n* kare

squash [skwɒʃ] *n* ezme ▷ *v* ezmek

squeak [skwi:k] *v* cıyaklamak

squeeze [skwi:z] *v* sıkmak

squeeze in [skwi:z ın] *v* sıkışmak

squid [skwıd] *n* kalamar

squint [skwınt] *v* şaşı bakmak

squirrel ['skwırəl; 'skwɜ:rəl;
'skwʌr-] *n* sincap

Sri Lanka [,sri: 'læŋkə] *n* Sri Lanka

stab [stæb] *v* bıçaklamak

stability [stə'bılıtı] *n* denge
(durum)

stable ['steıbəl] *adj* dengede ▷ *n*
ahır

stack [stæk] *n* yığın

stadium, stadia ['steıdıəm,
'steıdıə] *n* stadyum; **How do we
get to the stadium?** Stadyuma
nasıl gidebiliriz?

staff [stɑ:f] *n (stick or rod)* sopa
(asa), *(workers)* eleman

staffroom ['stɑ:f,ru:m] *n*
öğretmen odası

stage [steıdʒ] *n* sahne
(tiyatro mekan)

stagger ['stægə] v sendelemek

stain [steɪn] n leke ▷ v lekelemek; **stain remover** n leke çıkarıcı; **Can you remove this stain?** Bu lekeyi çıkarabilir misiniz?; **This stain is coffee** Kahve lekesi; **This stain is wine** Şarap lekesi

staircase ['stɛəˌkeɪs] n merdiven

stairs [stɛəz] npl merdivenler

stale [steɪl] adj bayat

stalemate ['steɪlˌmeɪt] n şahmat

stall [stɔːl] n tezgah

stamina ['stæmɪnə] n dayanıklılık

stammer ['stæmə] v kekelemek

stamp [stæmp] n pul ▷ v ayağını yere vurmak; **Can I have stamps for four postcards to...** Bu dört kartpostal için pul alacaktım... a gidecek; **Do you sell stamps?** Pul satıyor musunuz?; **Where can I buy stamps?** Pul nereden alabilirim?; **Where is the nearest shop which sells stamps?** Pul satan en yakın yer nerede?

stand [stænd] v ayakta durmak

standard ['stændəd] adj standart ▷ n standart; **standard of living** n yaşam standardı

stand for [stænd fɔː] v anlamına gelmek

stand out [stænd aʊt] v kendini göstermek

standpoint ['stændˌpɔɪnt] n bakış noktası

stands ['stændz] npl tezgahlar

stand up [stænd ʌp] v ayağa kalkmak

staple ['steɪpəl] n (commodity) temel ürün, (wire) zımba teli ▷ v zımbalamak

stapler ['steɪplə] n tel zımba

star [stɑː] n (person) yıldız (kişi), (sky) yıldız (gök) ▷ v yıldız koymak; **film star** n film yıldızı

starch [stɑːtʃ] n nişasta

stare [stɛə] v boşluğa bakmak

stark [stɑːk] adj katı (durum)

start [stɑːt] n başlangıç (iş, yarış vb) ▷ vi başlatmak ▷ vt başlamak

starter ['stɑːtə] n ön yemek

startle ['stɑːtəl] v irkilmek

start off [stɑːt ɒf] v yola çıkmak

starve [stɑːv] v açlık çekmek

state [steɪt] n durum (ruhsal) ▷ v ifade etmek; **Gulf States** npl Körfez Ülkeleri

statement ['steɪtmənt] n açıklama (beyan); **bank statement** n hesap özeti

station ['steɪʃən] n istasyon; **bus station** n otobüs terminali; **metro station** n metro istasyonu; **petrol station** n benzin istasyonu; **police station** n polis istasyonu; **radio station** n radyo istasyonu; **railway station** n tren istasyonu; **service station** n benzin istasyonu; **tube station** n metro istasyonu; **Is there a petrol station near here?** Buraya en yakın benzin istasyonu nerede?; **Where is the nearest tube station?** Buraya en yakın metro istasyonu nerede?

stationer's ['steɪʃənəz] n kırtasiyeci

stationery ['steɪʃənərɪ] n kırtasiye

statistics [stə'tɪstɪks] npl sayımlama

statue ['stætjuː] n heykel

status ['steɪtəs] n **marital status**
n medeni hal

status quo ['steɪtəs kwəʊ] n
statüko

stay [steɪ] n kalış ▷ v kalmak;
I want to stay an extra night
Bir gece daha kalmak istiyorum;
**I want to stay from Monday
till Wednesday** Pazartesi'den
Çarşamba'ya kadar kalmak
istiyorum; **I'd like to stay for two
nights** İki gece kalmak istiyorum

stay in [steɪ ɪn] v evde kalmak

stay up [steɪ ʌp] v geç saatlere
kadar oturmak

steady ['stɛdɪ] adj sabit (dengeli)

steak [steɪk] n biftek; **rump steak**
n biftek

steal [stiːl] v çalmak

steam [stiːm] n buhar

steel [stiːl] n çelik; **stainless steel**
n paslanmaz çelik

steep [stiːp] adj dik (yokuş vb); **Is it
very steep?** Yokuş çok mu dik?

steeple ['stiːpᵊl] n kilise kulesi

steering ['stɪərɪŋ] n yönetim;
steering wheel n direksiyon

step [stɛp] n adım

stepbrother ['stɛpˌbrʌðə] n üvey
erkek kardeş

stepdaughter ['stɛpˌdɔːtə] n üvey
kız evlat

stepfather ['stɛpˌfɑːðə] n üvey
baba

stepladder ['stɛpˌlædə] n ayaklı
merdiven

stepmother ['stɛpˌmʌðə] n üvey
anne

stepsister ['stɛpˌsɪstə] n
üvey kızkardeş

stepson ['stɛpˌsʌn] n üvey oğul

stereo ['stɛrɪəʊ; 'stɪər-] n stereo;
personal stereo n kişisel müzik
çalar; **Is there a stereo in the
car?** Arabada stereo var mı?

stereotype ['stɛrɪəˌtaɪp; 'stɪər-] n
basmakalıp

sterile ['stɛraɪl] adj steril

sterilize ['stɛrɪˌlaɪz] v sterilize
etmek

sterling ['stɜːlɪŋ] n sterlin

steroid ['stɪərɔɪd; 'stɛr-] n steroid

stew [stjuː] n güveç

steward ['stjʊəd] n hostes

stick [stɪk] n sopa (çubuk) ▷ v
yapışmak; **stick insect** n sopa
çekirgesi; **walking stick** n baston

sticker ['stɪkə] n etiket (defter vb)

stick out [stɪk aʊt] v çıkarmak

sticky ['stɪkɪ] adj yapışkan

stiff [stɪf] adj katı (kumaş vb)

stifling ['staɪflɪŋ] adj boğucu

still [stɪl] adj durgun ▷ adv hala

sting [stɪŋ] n sokma (arı, böcek) ▷ v
sokmak (arı, böcek vb)

stingy ['stɪndʒɪ] adj ısırıcı

stink [stɪŋk] n leş gibi kokma ▷ v
kötü kokmak

stir [stɜː] v karıştırmak (çorba vb)

stitch [stɪtʃ] n dikiş (tıp, nakış vb)
▷ v dikmek (tıp, nakış vb)

stock [stɒk] n stok ▷ v stoklamak;
stock cube n bulyon; **stock
exchange** n borsa; **stock market**
n borsa

stockbroker ['stɒkˌbrəʊkə] n
borsacı

stockholder ['stɒkˌhəʊldə] n
hissedar

stocking ['stɒkɪŋ] n naylon çorap

stock up [stɒk ʌp] v **stock up on** v depoyu doldurmak

stomach ['stʌmək] n mide

stomachache ['stʌmək,eɪk] n mide ağrısı

stone [stəʊn] n taş

stool [stuːl] n tabure

stop [stɒp] n durdurma ▷ vi durdurmak ▷ vt bırakmak; **bus stop** n otobüs durağı; **full stop** n nokta (gramer)

stopover ['stɒp,əʊvə] n konaklama

stopwatch ['stɒp,wɒtʃ] n kronometre

storage ['stɔːrɪdʒ] n depo

store [stɔː] n depo ▷ v depolamak; **department store** n büyük mağaza

storm [stɔːm] n fırtına; **Do you think there will be a storm?** Fırtına çıkabilir mi?

stormy ['stɔːmɪ] adj fırtınalı

story ['stɔːrɪ] n öykü; **short story** n kısa öykü

stove [stəʊv] n soba

straight [streɪt] adj doğru (çizgi); **straight on** adv dosdoğru

straighteners ['streɪtᵊnəz] npl saç maşası

straightforward [,streɪt'fɔːwəd] adj açık sözlü

strain [streɪn] n stres ▷ v psikolojik anlamda germek

strained [streɪnd] adj zorlama

stranded ['strændɪd] adj kısılıp kalmak

strange [streɪndʒ] adj garip

stranger ['streɪndʒə] n yabancı

strangle ['stræŋgᵊl] v boğazlamak

strap [stræp] n kayış; **watch strap** n saat kayışı

strategic [strə'tiːdʒɪk] adj stratejik

strategy ['strætɪdʒɪ] n strateji

straw [strɔː] n saman

strawberry ['strɔːbərɪ; -brɪ] n çilek

stray [streɪ] n sürüden ayrılmış

stream [striːm] n dere ▷ v stream etmek

street [striːt] n cadde; **street map** n sokak haritası; **street plan** n sokak planı

streetlamp ['striːt,læmp] n sokak lambası

streetwise ['striːt,waɪz] adj sokaklarda büyümüş

strength [strɛŋθ] n güç (kuvvet)

strengthen ['strɛŋθən] v güçlendirmek

stress [strɛs] n stres ▷ v vurgulamak

stressed ['strɛst] adj gerilmiş

stressful ['strɛsfʊl] adj gerginlik yaratıcı

stretch [strɛtʃ] v esnetmek

stretcher ['strɛtʃə] n sedye

stretchy ['strɛtʃɪ] adj esnek (materyal)

strict [strɪkt] adj katı (kural vb)

strictly [strɪktlɪ] adv katı bir şekilde

strike [straɪk] n grev ▷ vi darbe yemek, (suspend work) grev yapmak ▷ vt vurmak; **because of a strike** grev vardı, o yüzden

striker ['straɪkə] n grevci

striking ['straɪkɪŋ] adj çarpıcı

string [strɪŋ] n ip

strip [strɪp] n şerit ▷ v soyunmak

stripe [straɪp] n şerit

striped [straɪpt] *adj* çizgili

stripper ['strɪpə] *n* striptizci

stripy ['straɪpɪ] *adj* çizgili

stroke [strəʊk] *n (apoplexy)* okşama, *(hit)* okşama ▷ *v* okşamak

stroll [strəʊl] *n* yürüyüş

strong [strɒŋ] *adj* güçlü

strongly [strɒŋlɪ] *adv* kuvvetli

structure ['strʌktʃə] *n* yapı

struggle ['strʌgəl] *v* uğraşmak

stub [stʌb] *n* izmarit *(sigara)*

stubborn ['stʌbən] *adj* inatçı

stub out [stʌb aʊt] *v* bastırarak söndürmek

stuck [stʌk] *adj* takılmış

stuck-up [stʌkʌp] *adj* kibirli

stud [stʌd] *n* kabara

student ['stjuːdənt] *n* öğrenci; **student discount** *n* öğrenci indirimi

studio ['stjuːdɪˌəʊ] *n* stüdyo; **studio flat** *n* stüdyo daire

study ['stʌdɪ] *v* çalışmak

stuff [stʌf] *n* madde

stuffy ['stʌfɪ] *adj* havasız

stumble ['stʌmbəl] *v* tökezlemek

stunned [stʌnd] *adj* şaşkına dönmüş

stunning ['stʌnɪŋ] *adj* göz kamaştırıcı

stunt [stʌnt] *n* dublör

stuntman, stuntmen ['stʌntmən, 'stʌntmɛn] *n* dublör

stupid ['stjuːpɪd] *adj* aptal

stutter ['stʌtə] *v* kekelemek

style [staɪl] *n* stil

styling ['staɪlɪŋ] *n* **Do you sell styling products?** Saç bakım ürünleri satıyor musunuz?

stylist ['staɪlɪst] *n* stilist

subject ['sʌbdʒɪkt] *n* konu

submarine ['sʌbməˌriːn; ˌsʌbmə'riːn] *n* denizaltı

subscription [səb'skrɪpʃən] *n* abonelik

subsidiary [səb'sɪdɪərɪ] *n* yan *(destek)*

subsidize ['sʌbsɪˌdaɪz] *v* mali destek sağlamak

subsidy ['sʌbsɪdɪ] *n* sübvansiyon

substance ['sʌbstəns] *n* madde

substitute ['sʌbstɪˌtjuːt] *n* yedek ▷ *v* vekalet etmek

subtitled ['sʌbˌtaɪtəld] *adj* altyazılı

subtitles ['sʌbˌtaɪtəlz] *npl* altyazı

subtle ['sʌtəl] *adj* belli belirsiz

subtract [səb'trækt] *v* çıkarma işlemi

suburb ['sʌbɜːb] *n* banliyö

suburban [sə'bɜːbən] *adj* banliyö

subway ['sʌbˌweɪ] *n* altgeçit

succeed [sək'siːd] *v* başarmak

success [sək'sɛs] *n* başarı

successful [sək'sɛsfʊl] *adj* başarılı

successfully [sək'sɛsfʊlɪ] *adv* başarıyla

successive [sək'sɛsɪv] *adj* ardıl

successor [sək'sɛsə] *n* halef

such [sʌtʃ] *adj* böyle ▷ *adv* böylesine

suck [sʌk] *v* emmek

Sudan [suː'dɑːn; -'dæn] *n* Sudan

Sudanese [ˌsuːdə'niːz] *adj* Sudan ▷ *n* Sudanlı

sudden ['sʌdən] *adj* ani

suddenly ['sʌdənlɪ] *adv* aniden

sue [sjuː; suː] *v* dava etmek

suede [sweɪd] *n* süet

suffer ['sʌfə] *v* acı çekmek

sufficient [sə'fɪʃənt] *adj* yeterli

suffocate ['sʌfəˌkeɪt] *v* boğmak

sugar ['ʃʊgə] n şeker; **icing sugar** n toz süsleme şekeri; **no sugar** şekersiz

sugar-free ['ʃʊgəfriː] adj şekersiz

suggest [sə'dʒɛst; səg'dʒɛst] v önermek

suggestion [sə'dʒɛstʃən] n öneri

suicide ['suːɪˌsaɪd; 'sjuː-] n intihar; **suicide bomber** n intihar bombacısı

suit [suːt; sjuːt] n takım elbise ▷ v uymak; **bathing suit** n mayo; **shell suit** n eşofman

suitable ['suːtəbᵊl; 'sjuːt-] adj uygun

suitcase ['suːtˌkeɪs; 'sjuːt-] n valiz

suite [swiːt] n suit

sulk [sʌlk] v suratını asmak

sulky ['sʌlkɪ] adj suratı asık

sultana [sʌl'tɑːnə] n kuru üzüm

sum [sʌm] n toplam

summarize ['sʌməˌraɪz] v özetlemek

summary ['sʌmərɪ] n özet

summer ['sʌmə] n yaz (mevsim); **summer holidays** npl yaz tatili; **after summer** yazdan sonra; **during the summer** yaz boyunca; **in summer** yazın

summertime ['sʌməˌtaɪm] n yaz sezonu

summit ['sʌmɪt] n zirve

sum up [sʌm ʌp] v özetlemek

sun [sʌn] n güneş

sunbathe ['sʌnˌbeɪð] v güneşte yanmak

sunbed ['sʌnˌbɛd] n güneşlenme yatağı

sunblock ['sʌnˌblɒk] n koruyucu güneş kremi

sunburn ['sʌnˌbɜːn] n güneş yanığı

sunburnt ['sʌnˌbɜːnt] adj güneş yanığı; **I am sunburnt** Güneş yanığım var

suncream ['sʌnˌkriːm] n güneş kremi

Sunday ['sʌndɪ] n Pazar; **Is the museum open on Sundays?** Müze Pazar günleri açık mı?; **on Sunday** Pazar günü

sunflower ['sʌnˌflaʊə] n ayçiçeği

sunglasses ['sʌnˌglɑːsɪz] npl güneş gözlüğü

sunlight ['sʌnlaɪt] n gün ışığı

sunny ['sʌnɪ] adj güneşli; **It's sunny** Hava güneşli

sunrise ['sʌnˌraɪz] n gün doğuşu

sunroof ['sʌnˌruːf] n açılır tavan

sunscreen ['sʌnˌskriːn] n güneşlik

sunset ['sʌnˌsɛt] n gün batımı

sunshine ['sʌnˌʃaɪn] n gün ışığı

sunstroke ['sʌnˌstrəʊk] n güneş çarpması

suntan ['sʌnˌtæn] n bronzlaşma; **suntan lotion** n bronzlaşma losyonu; **suntan oil** n güneş yağı

super ['suːpə] adj süper

superb [sʊ'pɜːb; sjuː-] adj muhteşem

superficial [ˌsuːpə'fɪʃəl] adj yapay

superior [suː'pɪərɪə] adj üstün ▷ n üst (kalite/rütbe)

supermarket ['suːpəˌmɑːkɪt] n süpermarket; **I need to find a supermarket** Süpermarket arıyorum

supernatural [ˌsuːpə'nætʃrəl; -'nætʃərəl] adj doğaüstü

superstitious [ˌsuːpə'stɪʃəs] adj batıl inançları olan

supervise ['suːpəˌvaɪz] v
denetlemek

supervisor ['suːpəˌvaɪzə] n
amir *(iş)*

supper ['sʌpə] n hafif akşam
yemeği

supplement ['sʌplɪmənt] n
ilave *(ek)*

supplier [sə'plaɪə] n satıcı

supplies [sə'plaɪz] npl erzak

supply [sə'plaɪ] n malzeme temin
etme ▷ v temin etmek; **supply
teacher** n yedek öğretmen

support [sə'pɔːt] n destek
(manevi) ▷ v desteklemek

supporter [sə'pɔːtə] n taraftar

suppose [sə'pəʊz] v varsaymak

supposedly [sə'pəʊzɪdlɪ] adv
varsayalım ki

supposing [sə'pəʊzɪŋ] conj
diyelim ki

surcharge ['sɜːˌtʃɑːdʒ] n fazla fiyat
isteme

sure [ʃʊə; ʃɔː] adj emin

surely ['ʃʊəlɪ; 'ʃɔː-] adv muhakkak

surf [sɜːf] n sörf ▷ v sörf yapmak;
Where can you go surfing? Sörf
için nereye gitmek gerek?

surface ['sɜːfɪs] n yüzey

surfboard ['sɜːfˌbɔːd] n sörf
tahtası

surfer ['sɜːfə] n sörfçü

surfing ['sɜːfɪŋ] n sörf yapma

surge [sɜːdʒ] n ani yükselme

surgeon ['sɜːdʒən] n cerrah

surgery ['sɜːdʒərɪ] n *(doctor's)*
klinik, *(operation)* ameliyat;
cosmetic surgery n kozmetik
cerrahi; **plastic surgery** n
plastik cerrahi

surname ['sɜːˌneɪm] n soyadı

surplus ['sɜːpləs] adj fazla ▷ n
fazlalık

surprise [sə'praɪz] n sürpriz

surprised [sə'praɪzd] adj şaşırmış

surprising [sə'praɪzɪŋ] adj
şaşırtıcı

surprisingly [sə'praɪzɪŋlɪ] adv
şaşırtıcı bir şekilde

surrender [sə'rɛndə] v teslim
olmak

surround [sə'raʊnd] v çevrelemek

surroundings [sə'raʊndɪŋz] npl
çevre

survey ['sɜːveɪ] n inceleme

surveyor [sɜː'veɪə] n denetçi

survival [sə'vaɪvəl] n yaşam
kavgası

survive [sə'vaɪv] v hayatta kalmak

survivor [sə'vaɪvə] n hayatta
kalan

suspect n ['sʌspɛkt] zanlı ▷ v
[sə'spɛkt] kuşkulanmak

suspend [sə'spɛnd] v askıya almak

suspenders [sə'spɛndəz] npl
jartiyer

suspense [sə'spɛns] n kuşku ve
gerilimli bekleyiş

suspension [sə'spɛnʃən] n askıya
alma; **suspension bridge** n aşma
köprü

suspicious [sə'spɪʃəs] adj kuşkulu

swallow ['swɒləʊ] n yutma ▷ vi
yutulmak ▷ vt yutmak

swamp [swɒmp] n bataklık

swan [swɒn] n kuğu

swap [swɒp] v değiştirmek

swat [swɒt] v vurmak *(sineklik gibi
yassı bir şeyle)*

sway [sweɪ] v salınmak

Swaziland ['swɑːzɪˌlænd] n
Swaziland

swear [swɛə] v küfretmek

swearword ['swɛəˌwɜːd] n küfür

sweat [swɛt] n ter ▷ v terlemek

sweater ['swɛtə] n kazak;
polo-necked sweater n polo
yakalı kazak

sweatshirt ['swɛtˌʃɜːt] n pamuklu
kalın tişört

sweaty ['swɛtɪ] adj terli

swede [swiːd] n sarı şalgam

Swede [swiːd] n İsveçli

Sweden ['swiːdən] n İsveç

Swedish ['swiːdɪʃ] adj İsveç ▷ n
İsveçli

sweep [swiːp] v süpürmek

sweet [swiːt] adj (pleasing) tatlı
(hoş), (taste) tatlı ▷ n şeker

sweetcorn ['swiːtˌkɔːn] n bebe
mısır

sweetener ['swiːtənə] n
tatlandırıcı; **Do you have any
sweetener?** Tatlandırıcınız var
mı?

sweets [swiːts] npl tatlılar

sweltering ['swɛltərɪŋ] adj
boğucu sıcak

swerve [swɜːv] v direksiyonu
kırmak

swim [swɪm] v yüzmek

swimmer ['swɪmə] n yüzücü

swimming ['swɪmɪŋ] n yüzme;
swimming costume n mayo;
swimming pool n yüzme havuzu;
swimming trunks npl yüzücü
şortu; **Is there a swimming pool?**
Yüzme havuzu var mı?; **Where is
the public swimming pool?**
Yüzme havuzu nerede?

swimsuit ['swɪmˌsuːt; -ˌsjuːt] n
mayo

swing [swɪŋ] n sallanma ▷ v
sallanmak

Swiss [swɪs] adj İsviçre ▷ n
İsviçreli

switch [swɪtʃ] n elektrik düğmesi
▷ v elektrik düğmesini çevirmek

switchboard ['swɪtʃˌbɔːd] n
santral

switch off [swɪtʃ ɒf] v elektriği
kapamak

switch on [swɪtʃ ɒn] v şalter
açmak

Switzerland ['swɪtsələnd] n
İsviçre

swollen ['swəʊlən] adj şiş

sword [sɔːd] n kılıç

swordfish ['sɔːdˌfɪʃ] n kılıç balığı

swot [swɒt] v ineklemek

syllable ['sɪləbəl] n hece

syllabus ['sɪləbəs] n müfredat

symbol ['sɪmbəl] n sembol

symmetrical [sɪ'mɛtrɪkəl] adj
simetrik

sympathetic [ˌsɪmpə'θɛtɪk] adj
anlayışlı

sympathize ['sɪmpəˌθaɪz] v
halden anlamak

sympathy ['sɪmpəθɪ] n halden
anlama

symphony ['sɪmfənɪ] n senfoni

symptom ['sɪmptəm] n belirti
(hastalık)

synagogue ['sɪnəˌgɒg] n sinagog;
Where is there a synagogue?
Sinagog nerede var?

syndrome ['sɪndrəʊm] n **Down's
syndrome** n Down sendromu

Syria ['sɪrɪə] n Suriye

Syrian ['sɪrɪən] *adj* Suriye ▷ *n*
Suriyeli
syringe ['sɪrɪndʒ; sɪ'rɪndʒ] *n*
şırınga
syrup ['sɪrəp] *n* şurup
system ['sɪstəm] *n* sistem;
immune system *n* bağışıklık
sistemi; **solar system** *n* güneş
sistemi; **systems analyst** *n*
sistem analizcisi
systematic [ˌsɪstɪ'mætɪk] *adj*
sistemli

table ['teɪbəl] *n (chart)* tablo *(grafik)*,
(furniture) masa; **bedside table** *n*
komodin; **coffee table** *n* sehpa;
dressing table *n* tuvalet masası;
table tennis *n* masa tenisi; **table
wine** *n* yemeklik şarap; **A table
for four people, please** Dört
kişilik bir masa lütfen; **I'd like to
book a table for three people
for tonight** Bu akşam için üç kişilik
bir masa ayırtmak istiyordum;
**I'd like to book a table for two
people for tomorrow night**
Yarın akşam için iki kişilik bir masa
ayırtmak istiyordum; **The table is
booked for nine o'clock this
evening** Masa bu akşam saat
dokuz için rezerve edildi
tablecloth ['teɪbəlˌklɒθ] *n* masa
örtüsü
tablespoon ['teɪbəlˌspuːn] *n*
çorba kaşığı

tablet ['tæblɪt] n (medicine) hap, (computer) tablet

taboo [tə'buː] adj tabu ▷ n tabu

tackle ['tækəl; 'teɪkəl] n palanga ▷ v üstesinden gelmek; **fishing tackle** n olta

tact [tækt] n incelik

tactful ['tæktfʊl] adj incelikli

tactics ['tæktɪks] npl taktik

tactless ['tæktlɪs] adj patavatsız

tadpole ['tæd.pəʊl] n iribaş

tag [tæg] n etiket (bilişim)

Tahiti [tə'hiːtɪ] n Tahiti

tail [teɪl] n kuyruk (hayvan vb)

tailor ['teɪlə] n terzi

Taiwan ['taɪ'wɑːn] n Tayvan

Taiwanese [.taɪwɑː'niːz] adj Tayvan ▷ n Tayvanlı

Tajikistan [tɑːˌdʒɪkɪ'stɑːn; -stæn] n Tacikistan

take [teɪk] v almak, (time) almak

take after [teɪk 'ɑːftə] v benzemek

take apart [teɪk ə'pɑːt] v sökmek (parçalarına ayırmak)

take away [teɪk ə'weɪ] v çıkarmak

takeaway ['teɪkəˌweɪ] n hazır yemek

take back [teɪk bæk] v geri almak

take off [teɪk ɒf] v üstünü çıkarmak

takeoff ['teɪkˌɒf] n kalkış (uçak)

take over [teɪk 'əʊvə] v yönetimi ele almak

takeover ['teɪkˌəʊvə] n devralma

takings ['teɪkɪŋz] npl hasılat

tale [teɪl] n hikaye

talent ['tælənt] n yetenek

talented ['tæləntɪd] adj yetenekli

talk [tɔːk] n konuşma ▷ v konuşmak; **talk to** v biriyle konuşmak

talkative ['tɔːkətɪv] adj konuşkan

tall [tɔːl] adj uzun boylu

tame [teɪm] adj evcil

tampon ['tæmpɒn] n tampon

tan [tæn] n bronzlaşmış ten

tandem ['tændəm] n tandem bisiklet

tangerine [.tændʒə'riːn] n mandalina

tank [tæŋk] n (combat vehicle) tank (ordu), (large container) tank; **petrol tank** n benzin deposu; **septic tank** n foseptik çukuru

tanker ['tæŋkə] n tanker

tanned [tænd] adj güneşte yanmış

tantrum ['tæntrəm] n öfke nöbeti

Tanzania [.tænzə'nɪə] n Tanzanya

Tanzanian [.tænzə'nɪən] adj Tanzanya ▷ n Tanzanyalı

tap [tæp] n hafif vuruş

tap-dancing ['tæp.dɑːnsɪŋ] n step dansı

tape [teɪp] n şerit ▷ v kaydetmek; **tape measure** n şerit metre; **tape recorder** n ses kayıt cihazı

target ['tɑːgɪt] n hedef

tariff ['tærɪf] n gümrük tarifesi

tarmac ['tɑːmæk] n asfalt

tarpaulin [tɑː'pɔːlɪn] n tente

tarragon ['tærəgən] n tarhun

tart [tɑːt] n turta

tartan ['tɑːtən] adj ekose

task [tɑːsk] n görev

Tasmania [tæz'meɪnɪə] n Tasmanya

taste [teɪst] n tat ▷ v tatmak

tasteful ['teɪstfʊl] adj lezzetli

tasteless ['teɪstlɪs] adj tatsız tuzsuz

tasty ['teɪstɪ] adj lezzetli

tattoo [tæ'tuː] n dövme

Taurus ['tɔːrəs] n Boğa burcu

tax [tæks] n vergi; **income tax** n gelir vergisi; **road tax** n yol vergisi; **tax payer** n vergi yükümlüsü; **tax return** n vergi iadesi

taxi ['tæksɪ] n taksi; **taxi driver** n taksi sürücüsü; **taxi rank** n taksi sırası; **How much is the taxi fare into town?** Kente taksi ne kadar?; **I left my bags in the taxi** Bagajımı takside bıraktım; **I need a taxi** Bana bir taksi gerek; **Where can I get a taxi?** Nereden taksi bulabilirim?; **Where is the taxi stand?** Taksi durağı nerede?

TB [tiː biː] n tüberküloz

tea [tiː] n çay; **herbal tea** n bitki çayı; **tea bag** n torba çay; **tea towel** n mutfak havlusu; **A tea, please** Bir çay lütfen; **Could we have another cup of tea, please?** Bir çay daha alabilir miyiz?

teach [tiːtʃ] v öğretmek

teacher ['tiːtʃə] n öğretmen; **supply teacher** n yedek öğretmen

teaching ['tiːtʃɪŋ] n öğretme

teacup ['tiːˌkʌp] n çay fincanı

team [tiːm] n ekip

teapot ['tiːˌpɒt] n çaydanlık

tear¹ [tɪə] n (from eye) gözyaşı

tear² [tɛə] n (split) yırtık ▷ v yırtmak; **tear up** v yırtmak

teargas ['tɪəˌgæs] n gözyaşı bombası

tease [tiːz] v kızdırmak

teaspoon ['tiːˌspuːn] n çay kaşığı

teatime ['tiːˌtaɪm] n çay saati

technical ['tɛknɪkəl] adj teknik

technician [tɛk'nɪʃən] n teknisyen

technique [tɛk'niːk] n teknik

techno ['tɛknəʊ] n tekno

technological [tɛk'nɒlədʒɪkəl] adj teknolojik

technology [tɛk'nɒlədʒɪ] n teknoloji

tee [tiː] n golf sopası

teenager ['tiːnˌeɪdʒə] n ergen

teens [tiːnz] npl ergenler

tee-shirt ['tiːˌʃɜːt] n tişört

teethe [tiːð] v diş çıkarmak

teetotal [tiː'təʊtəl] adj Yeşilaycı

telecommunications [ˌtɛlɪkəˌmjuːnɪ'keɪʃənz] npl telekomünikasyon

telegram ['tɛlɪˌgræm] n telgraf; **Can I send a telegram from here?** Buradan telgraf çekebilir miyim?

telephone ['tɛlɪˌfəʊn] n telefon; **telephone directory** n telefon rehberi; **How much is it to telephone...?**... a telefon ne kadar?; **I need to make an urgent telephone call** Acil bir telefon görüşmesi yapmam gerek; **What's the telephone number?** Telefon numarası nedir?

telesales ['tɛlɪˌseɪlz] npl telefonla satış

telescope ['tɛlɪˌskəʊp] n teleskop

television ['tɛlɪˌvɪʒən] n televizyon; **cable television** n kablolu yayın; **colour television** n renkli televizyon; **digital**

television n dijital televizyon; **Where is the television?** Televizyon nerede?

tell [tɛl] v anlatmak

teller ['tɛlə] n anlatıcı

tell off [tɛl ɒf] v azarlamak

telly ['tɛlɪ] n televizyon

temp [tɛmp] n geçici görevli

temper ['tɛmpə] n ruh hali

temperature ['tɛmprɪtʃə] n sıcaklık

temple ['tɛmpᵊl] n tapınak; **Is the temple open to the public?** Tapınak halka açık mı?; **When is the temple open?** Tapınak ne zaman açık?

temporary ['tɛmpərərɪ; 'tɛmprərɪ] adj geçici

tempt [tɛmpt] v kışkırtmak

temptation [tɛmp'teɪʃən] n ayartma

tempting ['tɛmptɪŋ] adj baştan çıkarıcı

ten [tɛn] number on; **It's ten o'clock** Saat on

tenant ['tɛnənt] n kiracı

tend [tɛnd] v eğilim göstermek

tendency ['tɛndənsɪ] n eğilim

tender ['tɛndə] adj yumuşak

tendon ['tɛndən] n kiriş (anatomi)

tennis ['tɛnɪs] n tenis; **table tennis** n masa tenisi; **tennis player** n tenis oyuncusu; **tennis racket** n tenis raketi; **How much is it to hire a tennis court?** Tenis kortu kiralamak kaça?; **Where can I play tennis?** Nerede tenis oynayabilirim?

tenor ['tɛnə] n tenör

tense [tɛns] adj gergin (huzursuz)

▷ n zaman (gramer)

tension ['tɛnʃən] n gerginlik

tent [tɛnt] n çadır; **tent peg** n çadır kazığı; **tent pole** n çadır direği; **We'd like a site for a tent** Bir çadır yeri istiyoruz

tenth [tɛnθ] adj onuncu ▷ n onuncu

term [tɜːm] n (description) terim, (division of year) dönem (akademik dönem)

terminal ['tɜːmɪnᵊl] adj ölümcül ▷ n terminal

terminally ['tɜːmɪnᵊlɪ] adv ölümcül

terrace ['tɛrəs] n teras; **Can I eat on the terrace?** Terasta yiyebilir miyim?

terraced ['tɛrəst] adj sıra evler

terrible ['tɛrəbᵊl] adj korkunç

terribly ['tɛrəblɪ] adv aşırı derecede

terrier ['tɛrɪə] n teriyer

terrific [tə'rɪfɪk] adj müthiş

terrified ['tɛrɪˌfaɪd] adj aşırı derecede korkmuş

terrify ['tɛrɪˌfaɪ] v dehşete düşürmek

territory ['tɛrɪtərɪ; -trɪ] n bölge (arazi)

terrorism ['tɛrəˌrɪzəm] n terörizm

terrorist ['tɛrərɪst] n terörist; **terrorist attack** n terörist saldırı

test [tɛst] n test ▷ v denemek; **driving test** n direksiyon sınavı; **smear test** n Pap smear testi; **test tube** n deney tüpü

testicle ['tɛstɪkᵊl] n haya (anatomi)

tetanus ['tɛtənəs] n tetanoz;

I need a tetanus shot Tetanoz aşısı yaptırmam gerek

text [tɛkst] n metin ▷ v mesaj atmak; **text message** n mesaj

textbook ['tɛkstˌbʊk] n ders kitabı

textile ['tɛkstaɪl] n tekstil

Thai [taɪ] adj Thai ▷ n *(language)* Taylandca *(dil)*, *(person)* Taylandlı *(kişi)*

Thailand ['taɪˌlænd] n Tayland

than [ðæn; ðən] conj den, dan; **It's more than on the meter** Taksimetrenin gösterdiğinden daha fazla

thank [θæŋk] v teşekkür etmek

thanks [θæŋks] excl teşekkürler!

that [ðæt; ðət] adj şu, bu ▷ conj ki ▷ pron şu, bu, şunu; **Does that contain alcohol?** Bunda alkol var mı?

thatched [θætʃt] adj saz ve saman çatılı

thaw [θɔː] v eritmek

the [ðə] def art bu, şu, o

theatre ['θɪətə] n tiyatro; **operating theatre** n ameliyat odası; **What's on at the theatre?** Tiyatroda ne var?

theft [θɛft] n hırsızlık; **identity theft** n kimlik hırsızlığı

their [ðɛə] pron onların

theirs [ðɛəz] pron onlarınki

them [ðɛm; ðəm] pron onları

theme [θiːm] n konu; **theme park** n konulu eğlence parkı

themselves [ðəm'sɛlvz] pron kendileri

then [ðɛn] adv öyleyse ▷ conj ondan sonra

theology [θɪ'ɒlədʒɪ] n din bilimi

theory ['θɪərɪ] n kuram

therapy ['θɛrəpɪ] n terapi

there [ðɛə] adv orada; **It's over there** Orada

therefore ['ðɛəˌfɔː] adv bu sebeple

thermometer [θə'mɒmɪtə] n termometre

Thermos® ['θɜːməs] n termos

thermostat ['θɜːməˌstæt] n termostat

these [ðiːz] adj bunların ▷ pron bunlar

they [ðeɪ] pron onlar

thick [θɪk] adj kalın

thickness ['θɪknɪs] n kalınlık

thief [θiːf] n hırsız

thigh [θaɪ] n but

thin [θɪn] adj ince

thing [θɪŋ] n şey

think [θɪŋk] v düşünmek

third [θɜːd] adj üçüncü ▷ n üçüncü; **third-party insurance** n üçüncü kişi sorumluluk sigortası; **Third World** n Üçüncü Dünya

thirdly ['θɜːdlɪ] adv üçüncü olarak

thirst [θɜːst] n susuzluk

thirsty ['θɜːstɪ] adj susuz

thirteen ['θɜː'tiːn] number onüç

thirteenth ['θɜː'tiːnθ] adj onüçüncü

thirty ['θɜːtɪ] number otuz

this [ðɪs] adj bu ▷ pron bu; **I'll have this** Bunu alayım; **This is your room** Odanız burası; **What is in this?** Bunun içinde ne var?

thistle ['θɪsəl] n deve dikeni

thorn [θɔːn] n diken

thorough ['θʌrə] adj baştanbaşa

thoroughly ['θʌrəlɪ] adv derinlemesine

those [ðəʊz] *adj* şunlar ▷ *pron*
şunlar

though [ðəʊ] *adv* gerçi ▷ *conj* her
ne kadar

thought [θɔːt] *n* düşünce

thoughtful ['θɔːtfʊl] *adj* düşünceli

thoughtless ['θɔːtlɪs] *adj*
düşüncesiz

thousand ['θaʊzənd] *number* bin
(sayı)

thousandth ['θaʊzənθ] *adj* bininci
▷ *n* bininci

thread [θrɛd] *n (in clothing)* iplik,
(social media) konu

threat [θrɛt] *n* tehdit

threaten ['θrɛtºn] *v* tehdit etmek

threatening ['θrɛtºnɪŋ] *adj* tehdit
edici

three [θriː] *number* üç; **It's three
o'clock** Saat üç

three-dimensional
[ˌθriːdɪ'mɛnʃənºl] *adj* üç boyutlu

thrifty ['θrɪftɪ] *adj* tutumlu

thrill [θrɪl] *n* heyecan

thrilled [θrɪld] *adj* çok sevinmiş

thriller ['θrɪlə] *n* polisiye

thrilling ['θrɪlɪŋ] *adj* heyecan verici

throat [θrəʊt] *n* boğaz

throb [θrɒb] *v* zonklamak

throne [θrəʊn] *n* taht

through [θruː] *prep* içinden

throughout [θruː'aʊt] *prep*
baştan başa

throw [θrəʊ] *v* atmak

throw away [θrəʊ ə'weɪ] *v* atmak

throw out [θrəʊ aʊt] *v* atmak

throw up [θrəʊ ʌp] *v* kusmak

thrush [θrʌʃ] *n* ardıç kuşu

thug [θʌg] *n* eşkiya

thumb [θʌm] *n* baş parmak

thumb tack ['θʌmˌtæk] *n* raptiye

thump [θʌmp] *v* vurmak

thunder ['θʌndə] *n* gök gürültüsü

thunderstorm ['θʌndəˌstɔːm] *n*
gök gürültülü fırtına

thundery ['θʌndərɪ] *adj* gök
gürültülü

Thursday ['θɜːzdɪ] *n* Perşembe;
on Thursday Perşembe günü

thyme [taɪm] *n* kekik

Tibet [tɪ'bɛt] *n* Tibet

Tibetan [tɪ'bɛtºn] *adj* Tibet ▷ *n*
(language) Tibetçe *(dil)*, *(person)*
Tibetli *(kişi)*

tick [tɪk] *n* im ▷ *v* tıkırdamak

ticket ['tɪkɪt] *n* bilet; **bus ticket** *n*
otobüs bileti; **one-way ticket** *n*
tek gidiş bileti; **parking ticket** *n*
otopark bileti; **return ticket** *n*
gidiş-dönüş bilet; **season ticket** *n*
abonman kartı; **single ticket** *n*
tek yön bilet; **stand-by ticket** *n*
beklemede bilet; **ticket barrier** *n*
bilet turnikesi; **ticket collector** *n*
biletçi; **ticket inspector** *n* bilet
kontrolörü; **ticket machine** *n*
bilet otomatı; **ticket office** *n* bilet
gişesi; **a child's ticket** Bir çocuk
bileti; **Can I buy the tickets here?**
Biletleri buradan alabilir miyim?;
Can you book the tickets for us?
Biletleri siz ayırtır mısınız lütfen?;
**Do I need to buy a car-parking
ticket?** Bilet almam gerekiyor
mu?; **Do you have multi-journey
tickets?** Birkaç seyahati içeren
bilet satıyor musunuz?; **How
much are the tickets?** Biletler ne
kadar?; **How much is a return
ticket?** Gidiş dönüş bilet ne

kadar?; **I want to upgrade my ticket** Biletimi birinci sınıfa çevirmek istiyorum; **I'd like two tickets for next Friday** Cuma günü için iki bilet almak istiyorum; **I'd like two tickets, please** İki bilet, lütfen; **I've lost my ticket** Biletimi kaybettim; **two return tickets to...** ... a gidiş dönüş iki bilet; **The ticket machine isn't working** Bilet makinası çalışmıyor; **Two tickets for tonight, please** Bu akşam için iki bilet lütfen; **Where can I buy tickets for the concert?** Konser biletlerini nereden alabilirim?; **Where can I get tickets?** Nereden bilet alabilirim?; **Where is the ticket machine?** Bilet makinası nerede?

tickle ['tɪkəl] v gıdıklamak
ticklish ['tɪklɪʃ] adj kolay gıdıklanan
tick off [tɪk ɒf] v payalamak
tide [taɪd] n gelgit
tidy ['taɪdɪ] adj derli toplu (tertipli) ▷ v toplamak (ortalığı)
tidy up ['taɪdɪ ʌp] v derleyip toplamak
tie [taɪ] n kravat ▷ v bağlamak; **bow tie** n papyon kravat
tie up [taɪ ʌp] v birini bağlamak
tiger ['taɪɡə] n kaplan
tight [taɪt] adj sıkı
tighten ['taɪtən] v sıkılamak
tights [taɪts] npl külotlu çorap
tile [taɪl] n fayans
tiled ['taɪld] adj fayans döşeli
till [tɪl] conj ...'e kadar (zaman) ▷ prep ...e kadar (yer) ▷ n yazar kasa

timber ['tɪmbə] n kereste
time [taɪm] n zaman; **closing time** n kapanış saati; **dinner time** n yemek zamanı; **on time** adj zamanında; **spare time** n boş zaman; **time off** n izin (işten alınan); **time zone** n zaman dilimi; **By what time?** En geç ne zaman?; **Is it time to go?** Gitme zamanı geldi mi?; **We've been waiting for a very long time** Çok uzun zamandır bekliyoruz; **What time do we get to...?** ... a ne zaman varırız?; **What time does it leave?** Ne zaman kalkıyor?; **What time does the bus arrive?** Otobüs ne zaman geliyor?; **What time does the bus leave?** Otobüs ne zaman kalkacak?; **What time is the train to...?** ... treni ne zaman?
time bomb ['taɪm ˌbɒm] n saatli bomba
timer ['taɪmə] n saat (fırın vb)
timeshare ['taɪmˌʃɛə] n devre mülk
timetable ['taɪmˌteɪbəl] n program
tin [tɪn] n teneke; **tin-opener** n kutu açacağı
tinfoil ['tɪnˌfɔɪl] n kalay yaldızı
tinned [tɪnd] adj kutulanmış konserve
tinsel ['tɪnsəl] n gelin teli
tinted ['tɪntɪd] adj boyalı
tiny ['taɪnɪ] adj ufak
tip [tɪp] n (end of object) uç (kalem/dil), (reward) bahşiş, (suggestion) öğüt ▷ v (incline) devirmek (dökmek), (reward) bahşiş vermek; **How much should I give as a tip?**

Ne kadar bahşiş vermem gerek?; **Is it usual to give a tip?** Bahşiş vermek adet midir?

tipsy ['tɪpsɪ] *adj* çakırkeyif

tiptoe ['tɪpˌtəʊ] *n* parmaklarının ucunda yürüme

tired ['taɪəd] *adj* yorgun; **I'm tired** Yorgunum

tiring ['taɪərɪŋ] *adj* yorucu

tissue ['tɪsjuː; 'tɪʃuː] *n (anatomy)* kağıt mendil, *(paper)* kağıt mendil

title ['taɪtᵊl] *n* başlık *(kitap, albüm vb)*

to [tuː; tʊ; tə] *prep* oraya, orada

toad [təʊd] *n* kara kurbağa

toadstool ['təʊdˌstuːl] *n* mantar *(botanik)*

toast [təʊst] *n (culin)* tost, *(tribute)* kadeh kaldırmak

toaster ['təʊstə] *n* ekmek kızartma makinesi

tobacco [tə'bækəʊ] *n* tütün

tobacconist's [tə'bækənɪsts] *n* tütüncü

tobogganing [tə'bɒgənɪŋ] *n* kızak kayma

today [tə'deɪ] *adv* bugün; **What day is it today?** Bugün günlerden ne?; **What is today's date?** Bugünün tarihi nedir?

toddler ['tɒdlə] *n* yeni yürümeye başlayan çocuk

toe [təʊ] *n* ayak parmağı

toffee ['tɒfɪ] *n* karamela

together [tə'gɛðə] *adv* birlikte; **All together, please** Hepsini birlikte yazın lütfen

Togo ['təʊgəʊ] *n* Togo

toilet ['tɔɪlɪt] *n* tuvalet; **toilet bag** *n* tuvalet çantası; **toilet paper** *n* tuvalet kağıdı; **toilet roll** *n* tuvalet kağıdı; **Are there any accessible toilets?** Özürlüler için tuvaletiniz var mı?; **Can I use the toilet?** Tuvaleti kullanabilir miyim?; **Is there a toilet on board?** Otobüste tuvalet var mı?; **The toilet won't flush** Tuvaletin sifonu çalışmıyor; **There is no toilet paper** Tuvalet kağıdı yok; **Where are the toilets?** Tuvaletler nerede?

toiletries ['tɔɪlɪtriːs] *npl* makyaj malzemeleri

token ['təʊkən] *n* nişan *(belirti)*

tolerant ['tɒlərənt] *adj* hoşgörülü

toll [təʊl] *n* çan sesi

tomato, tomatoes [tə'mɑːtəʊ, tə'mɑːtəʊz] *n* domates; **tomato sauce** *n* domates sosu

tomb [tuːm] *n* türbe

tomboy ['tɒmˌbɔɪ] *n* erkek Fatma

tomorrow [tə'mɒrəʊ] *adv* yarın; **Is it open tomorrow?** Yarın açık mı?; **tomorrow morning** yarın sabah

ton [tʌn] *n* ton *(ağırlık)*

tone [təʊn] *n* **dialling tone** *n* telefon sinyali; **engaged tone** *n* meşgul sinyali

Tonga ['tɒŋgə] *n* Tonga

tongue [tʌŋ] *n* dil *(anatomi)*; **mother tongue** *n* anadil

tonic ['tɒnɪk] *n* tonik

tonight [tə'naɪt] *adv* bu gece; **What's on tonight at the cinema?** Bu gece sinemada ne var?

tonsillitis [ˌtɒnsɪ'laɪtɪs] *n* bademcik iltihabı

tonsils ['tɒnsəlz] *npl* bademcikler

too [tuː] *adv* -de, -da *(kıyaslama)*, de, da *(kıyaslama)*

tool [tuːl] *n* araç *(mekanik)*

tooth, teeth ['tuːθ, tiːθ] *n* diş; **wisdom tooth** *n* yirmi yaş dişi; **I've broken a tooth** Dişim kırıldı; **This tooth hurts** Bu dişim ağrıyor

toothache ['tuːθˌeɪk] *n* diş ağrısı

toothbrush ['tuːθˌbrʌʃ] *n* diş fırçası

toothpaste ['tuːθˌpeɪst] *n* diş macunu

toothpick ['tuːθˌpɪk] *n* kürdan

top [tɒp] *adj* tepede ▷ *n* tepe

topic ['tɒpɪk] *n* tema

topical ['tɒpɪkᵊl] *adj* güncel *(haber vb)*

top-secret ['tɒp'siːkrɪt] *adj* çok gizli

top up [tɒp ʌp] *v* doldurmak

torch [tɔːtʃ] *n* el feneri

tornado [tɔː'neɪdəʊ] *n* kasırga

tortoise ['tɔːtəs] *n* kaplumbağa

torture ['tɔːtʃə] *n* işkence ▷ *v* işkence etmek

toss [tɒs] *v* atmak

total ['təʊtᵊl] *adj* tam *(bütün)* ▷ *n* toplam

totally ['təʊtᵊlɪ] *adv* tamamen

touch [tʌtʃ] *v* dokunmak

touchdown ['tʌtʃˌdaʊn] *n* gol *(Amerikan futbolunda)*

touched [tʌtʃt] *adj* duygulanmış

touching ['tʌtʃɪŋ] *adj* dokunaklı *(konuşma)*

touchline ['tʌtʃˌlaɪn] *n* taç çizgisi

touchpad ['tʌtʃˌpæd] *n* akıllı dokunuş

touchy ['tʌtʃɪ] *adj* hassas

tough [tʌf] *adj* sağlam

toupee ['tuːpeɪ] *n* yarım peruk

tour [tʊə] *n* tur *(gezi)* ▷ *v* tura çıkmak; **guided tour** *n* rehberli tur; **package tour** *n* paket tur; **tour guide** *n* tur rehberi; **tour operator** *n* tur operatörü; **Are there any sightseeing tours of the town?** Kent turunuz var mı?; **How long does the tour take?** Tur ne kadar sürüyor?; **I enjoyed the tour** Turdan çok zevk aldım; **Is there a guided tour in English?** İngilizce rehberli turunuz var mı?; **What time does the guided tour begin?** Rehberli tur kaçta başlıyor?; **When is the bus tour of the town?** Tur otobüsü ne zaman kalkıyor?

tourism ['tʊərɪzəm] *n* turizm

tourist ['tʊərɪst] *n* turist; **tourist office** *n* turizm bürosu; **I'm here as a tourist** Buraya turist olarak geldim

tournament ['tʊənəmənt; 'tɔː-; 'tɜː-] *n* turnuva

towards [tə'wɔːdz; tɔːdz] *prep*...e doğru *(yön)*

tow away [təʊ ə'weɪ] *v* arabayı çekmek

towel ['taʊəl] *n* havlu; **bath towel** *n* banyo havlusu; **dish towel** *n* kurulama havlusu; **sanitary towel** *n* ped; **tea towel** *n* mutfak havlusu; **Could you lend me a towel?** Bana bir havlu verebilir misiniz?; **Please bring me more towels** Birkaç tane daha havlu getirir misiniz lütfen?

tower ['taʊə] n kule

town [taʊn] n şehir; **town centre**
n şehir merkezi; **town hall** n
belediye binası; **town planning** n
şehir planlama

toxic ['tɒksɪk] adj zehirli

toy [tɔɪ] n oyuncak

trace [treɪs] n belirti

tracing paper ['treɪsɪŋ 'peɪpə] n
aydınger kağıdı

track [træk] n engebeli yol

track down [træk daʊn] v izini
sürmek

tracksuit ['trækˌsuːt; -ˌsjuːt] n
antreman giysisi

tractor ['træktə] n traktör

trade [treɪd] n ticaret; **trade
union** n sendika; **trade unionist** n
sendikacı

trademark ['treɪdˌmɑːk] n marka
(ticaret)

tradition [trə'dɪʃən] n gelenek

traditional [trə'dɪʃənªl] adj
geleneksel (töre)

traffic ['træfɪk] n trafik; **traffic
jam** n trafik sıkışıklığı; **traffic
lights** npl trafik ışıkları; **traffic
warden** n trafik memuru; **Is the
traffic heavy on the motorway?**
Otoyolda trafik yoğun mu?

tragedy ['trædʒɪdɪ] n trajedi

tragic ['trædʒɪk] adj trajik

trailer ['treɪlə] n römork

train [treɪn] n tren ▷ v eğitmek;
Does the train stop at...?
Bu tren... da duruyor mu?; **How
frequent are the trains to...?**
... treni hangi sıklıkta geliyor?;
I've missed my train Trenimi
kaçırdım; **Is the train**

wheelchair-accessible? Trende
tekerlekli sandalye girişi var mı?;
Is this the train for...? ... treni bu
mu?; **The next available train,
please** Bir sonraki tren lütfen;
**What time does the train arrive
in...?** Tren... a kaçta varıyor?;
What time does the train leave?
Tren kaçta kalkacak?; **What times
are the trains to...?** ... tren
saatleri nedir?; **When is the first
train to...?** ... a ilk tren kaçta?;
When is the last train to...? ... a
son tren kaçta?; **When is the next
train to...?** ... a bir sonraki tren
kaçta?; **When is the train due?**
Tren kaçta geliyor?; **Where can I
get a train to...?** ... trenine
nereden binebilirim?; **Which
platform does the train leave
from?** Tren hangi platformdan
kalkıyor?

trained ['treɪnd] adj eğitilmiş

trainee [treɪ'niː] n kursiyer

trainer ['treɪnə] n eğitmen (spor vb)

trainers ['treɪnəz] npl lastik spor
ayakkabısı

training ['treɪnɪŋ] n eğitim (kurs);
training course n eğitim kursu

tram [træm] n tramvay

tramp [træmp] n (beggar) serseri,
(long walk) taban tepmek

trampoline ['træmpəlɪn; -ˌliːn] n
tramplen

tranquillizer ['træŋkwɪˌlaɪzə] n
sakinleştirici

transaction [træn'zækʃən] n
işlem

transcript ['trænskrɪpt] n
belge (döküm)

transfer n ['trænsfɜː] transfer ▷ v [træns'fɜː] transfer; **How long will it take to transfer?** Transfer ne kadar sürer?; **I would like to transfer some money from my account** Hesabımdan para transferi yapmak istiyorum; **Is there a transfer charge?** Transfer ücreti var mı?

transform [træns'fɔːm] v dönüştürmek

transfusion [træns'fjuːʒən] n kan aktarımı; **blood transfusion** n kan nakli

transistor [træn'zɪstə] n transistör

transit ['trænsɪt; 'trænz-] n transit; **transit lounge** n transit yolcu salonu

transition [træn'zɪʃən] n geçiş

translate [træns'leɪt; trænz-] v tercüme etmek

translation [træns'leɪʃən; trænz-] n tercüme

translator [træns'leɪtə; trænz-] n tercüman

transparent [træns'pærənt; -'peər-] adj saydam

transplant ['træns,plɑːnt] n aktarım (doku/organ)

transport n ['træns,pɔːt] taşıma ▷ v [træns'pɔːt] taşımak; **public transport** n toplu taşıma

transvestite [trænz'vestaɪt] n transvestit

trap [træp] n tuzak

trash [træʃ] n çöp

traumatic ['trɔːmətɪk] adj travmatik

travel ['trævəl] n seyahat ▷ v seyahat etmek; **travel agency** n seyahat acentası; **travel agent's** n seyahat acentası; **travel sickness** n araba tutması; **I don't have travel insurance** Seyahat sigortam yok; **I get travel-sick** Seyahat bulantım var; **I'm travelling alone** Tek başıma seyahat ediyorum

traveller ['trævələ; 'trævlə] n yolcular; **traveller's cheque** n seyahat çeki

travelling ['trævəlɪŋ] n seyahat etme

tray [treɪ] n tepsi

treacle ['triːkəl] n melas

tread [tred] v adımlamak

treasure ['treʒə] n define

treasurer ['treʒərə] n veznedar

treat [triːt] n birine ufak bir armağan alma ▷ v davranmak (muamele)

treatment ['triːtmənt] n muamele

treaty ['triːtɪ] n anlaşma (tarih)

treble ['trebəl] v üç katı

tree [triː] n ağaç

trek [trek] n zahmetli yürüyüş ▷ v zahmetli bir yürüyüşe çıkmak

trekking ['trekɪŋ] n **I'd like to go pony trekking** Ata binmek istiyorum

tremble ['trembəl] v titremek

tremendous [trɪ'mendəs] adj çok büyük

trench [trentʃ] n siper

trend [trend] n moda akımı ▷ v trend olmak

trendy ['trendɪ] adj modaya uygun

trial ['traɪəl] n duruşma; **trial period** n deneme süresi

triangle ['traɪˌæŋgəl] n üçgen

tribe [traɪb] n kabile

tribunal [traɪ'bjuːnəl; trɪ-] n mahkeme

trick [trɪk] n dolap (hile) ▷ v kandırmak

tricky ['trɪkɪ] adj dolambaçlı

tricycle ['traɪsɪkəl] n üç tekerlekli bisiklet

trifle ['traɪfəl] n önemsiz şey

trim [trɪm] v kesip düzeltmek

Trinidad and Tobago ['trɪnɪˌdæd ænd tə'beɪgəʊ] n Trinidad ve Tobago

trip [trɪp] n yolculuk (kısa); **business trip** n iş seyahati; **round trip** n gidiş dönüş yolculuk; **trip (up)** v tökezlemek; **Have a good trip!** İyi yolculuklar!

triple ['trɪpəl] adj üç katı

triplets ['trɪplɪts] npl üçüzler

triumph ['traɪəmf] n zafer ▷ v yenmek

trivial ['trɪvɪəl] adj önemsiz

trolley ['trɒlɪ] n servis masası; **luggage trolley** n bagaj trolleyi; **shopping trolley** n market arabası

trombone [trɒm'bəʊn] n trombon

troops ['truːps] npl birlikler (askeri)

trophy ['trəʊfɪ] n kupa (spor)

tropical ['trɒpɪkəl] adj tropik

trot [trɒt] v tırıs gitmek

trouble ['trʌbəl] n güçlük

troublemaker ['trʌbəlˌmeɪkə] n güçlük çıkaran

trough [trɒf] n yalak

trousers ['traʊzəz] npl pantolon

trout [traʊt] n alabalık

trowel ['traʊəl] n mala

truant ['truːənt] n **play truant** v okuldan kaçmak

truce [truːs] n ateşkes

truck [trʌk] n kamyon; **breakdown truck** n çekici; **truck driver** n kamyon şoförü

true [truː] adj gerçek (söz)

truly ['truːlɪ] adv gerçekten

trumpet ['trʌmpɪt] n borazan

trunk [trʌŋk] n ağaç gövdesi; **swimming trunks** npl yüzücü şortu

trunks [trʌŋks] npl yüzücü şortu

trust [trʌst] n güven ▷ v güvenmek

trusting ['trʌstɪŋ] adj güvenen

truth [truːθ] n gerçek (doğruluk)

truthful ['truːθfʊl] adj dürüst

try [traɪ] n çaba ▷ v çabalamak

try on [traɪ ɒn] v denemek (giysi)

try out [traɪ aʊt] v denemek

T-shirt ['tiːˌʃɜːt] n tişört

tsunami [tsʊ'næmɪ] n tsunami

tube [tjuːb] n tüp; **inner tube** n iç lastik; **test tube** n deney tüpü; **tube station** n metro istasyonu

tuberculosis [tjʊˌbɜːkjʊ'ləʊsɪs] n tüberküloz

Tuesday ['tjuːzdɪ] n Salı; **Shrove Tuesday** n büyük perhizin arife günü; **on Tuesday** Salı günü

tug-of-war ['tʌgɒv'wɔː] n halat çekme oyunu

tuition [tjuː'ɪʃən] n öğretim; **tuition fees** npl öğretim ücreti

tulip ['tjuːlɪp] n lale

tummy ['tʌmɪ] n karın

tumour ['tjuːmə] n ur

tuna ['tjuːnə] n ton balığı

tune [tjuːn] n melodi

Tunisia [tjuːˈnɪzɪə; -ˈnɪsɪə] n Tunus

Tunisian [tjuːˈnɪzɪən; -ˈnɪsɪən] adj Tunus ▷ n Tunuslu

tunnel ['tʌnəl] n tünel

turbulence ['tɜːbjʊləns] n çalkantı

Turk [tɜːk] n Türk

turkey ['tɜːkɪ] n hindi

Turkey ['tɜːkɪ] n Türkiye

Turkish ['tɜːkɪʃ] adj Türk ▷ n Türkçe

turn [tɜːn] n dönme ▷ v dönmek

turn around [tɜːn əˈraʊnd] v arkaya dönmek

turn back [tɜːn bæk] v geri dönmek

turn down [tɜːn daʊn] v geri çevirmek

turning ['tɜːnɪŋ] n kıvrım

turnip ['tɜːnɪp] n şalgam

turn off [tɜːn ɒf] v kapatmak

turn on [tɜːn ɒn] v açmak

turn out [tɜːn aʊt] v ışığı söndürmek

turnover ['tɜːnˌəʊvə] n sermaye devri

turn round [tɜːn raʊnd] v arkaya dönmek

turnstile ['tɜːnˌstaɪl] n turnike

turn up [tɜːn ʌp] v boy göstermek

turquoise ['tɜːkwɔɪz; -kwɑːz] adj türkuvaz renkli

turtle ['tɜːtəl] n su kaplumbağası

tutor ['tjuːtə] n özel öğretmen

tutorial [tjuːˈtɔːrɪəl] n ders (özel)

tuxedo [tʌkˈsiːdəʊ] n smokin

TV [tiː viː] n TV; **plasma TV** n plazma TV; **reality TV** n biri bizi gözetliyor

tweet [twiːt] v tweet atmak

tweezers ['twiːzəz] npl cımbız

twelfth [twɛlfθ] adj onikinci

twelve [twɛlv] number oniki

twentieth ['twɛntɪɪθ] adj yirminci

twenty ['twɛntɪ] number yirmi

twice [twaɪs] adv iki kere

twin [twɪn] n ikiz; **twin beds** npl çift yatak; **twin room** n çift yataklı oda; **twin-bedded room** n çift yataklı oda

twinned ['twɪnd] adj kardeş (şehir)

twist [twɪst] v bükmek

twit [twɪt] n avanak

two [tuː] num iki

type [taɪp] n tip ▷ v yazmak (daktilo/bilgisayar)

typewriter ['taɪpˌraɪtə] n daktilo

typhoid ['taɪfɔɪd] n tifo

typical ['tɪpɪkəl] adj tipik

typist ['taɪpɪst] n daktilograf

tyre ['taɪə] n lastik; **spare tyre** n stepne; **Can you check the tyres, please?** Lastikleri kontrol eder misiniz lütfen?; **The tyre has burst** Lastik patladı

u

UFO ['juːfəʊ] *abbr* UFO
Uganda [juːˈgændə] *n* Uganda
Ugandan [juːˈgændən] *adj*
Uganda ▷ *n* Ugandalı
ugh [ʊx; ʊh; ʌh] *excl* ığğ
ugly ['ʌglɪ] *adj* çirkin
UK [juː keɪ] *n* birleşik krallık
Ukraine [juːˈkreɪn] *n* Ukrayna
Ukrainian [juːˈkreɪnɪən] *adj*
Ukrayna ▷ *n (language)* Ukraynaca
(dil), (person) Ukraynalı *(kişi)*
ulcer ['ʌlsə] *n* yara *(ülser)*
Ulster ['ʌlstə] *n* Kuzey İrlanda
ultimate ['ʌltɪmɪt] *adj* son
ultimately ['ʌltɪmɪtlɪ] *adv* eninde
sonunda
ultimatum [ˌʌltɪˈmeɪtəm] *n*
ultimatom
ultrasound ['ʌltrəˌsaʊnd] *n*
ultrason
umbrella [ʌmˈbrɛlə] *n* şemsiye
umpire ['ʌmpaɪə] *n* hakem

UN [juː ɛn] *abbr* Birleşmiş Milletler
unable [ʌnˈeɪbəl] *adj* **unable to** *adj*
yapamamak
unacceptable [ˌʌnəkˈsɛptəbəl] *adj*
kabul edilemez
unanimous [juːˈnænɪməs] *adj*
oybirliğiyle
unattended [ˌʌnəˈtɛndɪd] *adj*
sahipsiz
unavoidable [ˌʌnəˈvɔɪdəbəl] *adj*
kaçınılmaz
unbearable [ʌnˈbɛərəbəl] *adj*
dayanılmaz
unbeatable [ʌnˈbiːtəbəl] *adj*
yenilmez
unbelievable [ˌʌnbɪˈliːvəbəl] *adj*
inanılmaz
unbreakable [ʌnˈbreɪkəbəl] *adj*
kırılmaz
uncanny [ʌnˈkænɪ] *adj* tekinsiz
uncertain [ʌnˈsɜːtən] *adj* belirsiz
uncertainty [ʌnˈsɜːtəntɪ] *n*
belirsizlik
unchanged [ʌnˈtʃeɪndʒd] *adj*
değişmemiş
uncivilized [ʌnˈsɪvɪˌlaɪzd] *adj*
ilkel
uncle ['ʌŋkəl] *n* amca
unclear [ʌnˈklɪə] *adj* net değil
uncomfortable [ʌnˈkʌmftəbəl]
adj rahatsız
unconditional [ˌʌnkənˈdɪʃənəl]
adj koşulsuz
unconscious [ʌnˈkɒnʃəs] *adj*
bilinçsiz
uncontrollable
[ˌʌnkənˈtrəʊləbəl] *adj* kontrol
edilemez
unconventional [ˌʌnkənˈvɛnʃənəl]
adj göreneklere uymayan

undecided [ˌʌndɪ'saɪdɪd] *adj*
kararsız

undeniable [ˌʌndɪ'naɪəbᵊl] *adj*
inkar edilemez

under ['ʌndə] *prep* altında

underage [ˌʌndər'eɪdʒ] *adj* reşit
olmayan

underestimate [ˌʌndərɛstɪ'meɪt]
v hafife almak

undergo [ˌʌndə'gəʊ] *v* geçmek
(deneyim/ameliyat)

undergraduate [ˌʌndə'grædjʊɪt]
n üniversite mezunu

underground ['ʌndəˌgraʊnd] *adj*
yerin altında ▷ *n* yeraltı harekatı

underline [ˌʌndə'laɪn] *v* altını
çizmek

underneath [ˌʌndə'niːθ] *adv*
altında ▷ *prep* altında

underpaid [ˌʌndə'peɪd] *adj* düşük
ücretli

underpants ['ʌndəˌpænts] *npl*
şort *(erkek iç çamaşırı)*

underpass ['ʌndəˌpɑːs] *n* alt
geçit

underskirt ['ʌndəˌskɜːt] *n* jüpon

understand [ˌʌndə'stænd] *v*
anlamak

understandable
[ˌʌndə'stændəbᵊl] *adj* anlaşılır

understanding [ˌʌndə'stændɪŋ]
adj anlayış

undertaker ['ʌndəˌteɪkə] *n* cenaze
kaldırıcısı

underwater ['ʌndə'wɔːtə] *adv*
sualtı

underwear ['ʌndəˌwɛə] *n* iç
çamaşırı

undisputed [ˌʌndɪ'spjuːtɪd] *adj*
tartışmasız

undo [ʌn'duː] *v* açmak *(paket,
fermuar vb)*

undoubtedly [ʌn'daʊtɪdlɪ] *adv*
kuşku götürmez bir şekilde

undress [ʌn'drɛs] *v* soyunmak

unemployed [ˌʌnɪm'plɔɪd] *adj*
işsiz

unemployment
[ˌʌnɪm'plɔɪmənt] *n* işsizlik

unexpected [ˌʌnɪk'spɛktɪd] *adj*
umulmadık

unexpectedly [ˌʌnɪk'spɛktɪdlɪ]
adv umulmadık bir şekilde

unfair [ʌn'fɛə] *adj* haksız

unfaithful [ʌn'feɪθfʊl] *adj*
sadakatsiz

unfamiliar [ˌʌnfə'mɪljə] *adj* aşina
olmayan

unfashionable [ʌn'fæʃənəbᵊl] *adj*
modaya uymayan

unfavourable [ʌn'feɪvərəbᵊl;
-'feɪvrə-] *adj* elverişsiz

unfit [ʌn'fɪt] *adj* sağlıksız

unfollow ['ʌn'fɒləʊ] *v* takibi
bırakmak

unforgettable [ˌʌnfə'gɛtəbᵊl] *adj*
unutulmaz

unfortunately [ʌn'fɔːtʃənɪtlɪ] *adv*
ne yazık ki

unfriend ['ʌn'frɛnd] *v*
arkadaşlıktan çıkarmak

unfriendly [ʌn'frɛndlɪ] *adj*
düşmanca

ungrateful [ʌn'greɪtfʊl] *adj*
nankör

unhappy [ʌn'hæpɪ] *adj* mutsuz

unhealthy [ʌn'hɛlθɪ] *adj* sağlıksız

unhelpful [ʌn'hɛlpfʊl] *adj*
yardımcı olmayan

uni ['juːnɪ] *n* üniversite

unidentified [ˌʌnaɪˈdɛntɪˌfaɪd] *adj* kimliği belirsiz

uniform [ˈjuːnɪˌfɔːm] *n* üniforma; **school uniform** *n* okul üniforması

unimportant [ˌʌnɪmˈpɔːtˀnt] *adj* önemsiz

uninhabited [ˌʌnɪnˈhæbɪtɪd] *adj* meskun olmayan

unintentional [ˌʌnɪnˈtɛnʃənˀl] *adj* kasıtsız

union [ˈjuːnjən] *n* birlik; **European Union** *n* Avrupa Birliği; **trade union** *n* sendika

unique [juːˈniːk] *adj* eşsiz

unit [ˈjuːnɪt] *n* ünite

unite [juːˈnaɪt] *v* birleştirmek *(kişileri)*

United Kingdom [juːˈnaɪtɪd ˈkɪŋdəm] *n* Birleşik Krallık *(İngiltere)*

United States [juːˈnaɪtɪd steɪts] *n* Birleşik Devletler *(Amerika)*

universe [ˈjuːnɪˌvɜːs] *n* evren

university [ˌjuːnɪˈvɜːsɪtɪ] *n* üniversite

unknown [ʌnˈnəʊn] *adj* bilinmez

unleaded [ʌnˈlɛdɪd] *n* kurşunsuz; **unleaded petrol** *n* kurşunsuz benzin; **...worth of premium unleaded, please** ...lık kurşunsuz benzin lütfen

unless [ʌnˈlɛs] *conj* olmadıkça

unlike [ʌnˈlaɪk] *prep* farklı olarak

unlikely [ʌnˈlaɪklɪ] *adj* olasılık dışı

unlisted [ʌnˈlɪstɪd] *adj* liste harici

unload [ʌnˈləʊd] *v* boşaltmak *(yük)*

unlock [ʌnˈlɒk] *v* kilidi açmak

unlucky [ʌnˈlʌkɪ] *adj* şanssız

unmarried [ʌnˈmærɪd] *adj* evlenmemiş

unnecessary [ʌnˈnɛsɪsərɪ; -ɪsrɪ] *adj* gereksiz

unofficial [ˌʌnəˈfɪʃəl] *adj* resmi olmayan

unpack [ʌnˈpæk] *v* boşaltmak

unpaid [ʌnˈpeɪd] *adj* ücreti ödenmemiş

unpleasant [ʌnˈplɛzˀnt] *adj* hoş olmayan

unplug [ʌnˈplʌɡ] *v* fişten çekmek

unpopular [ʌnˈpɒpjʊlə] *adj* popüler olmayan

unprecedented [ʌnˈprɛsɪˌdɛntɪd] *adj* daha önceden olmamış

unpredictable [ˌʌnprɪˈdɪktəbˀl] *adj* ne yapacağı belli olmayan

unreal [ʌnˈrɪəl] *adj* gerçek dışı

unrealistic [ˌʌnrɪəˈlɪstɪk] *adj* gerçeklerle bağdaşmayan

unreasonable [ʌnˈriːznəbˀl] *adj* mantıksız

unreliable [ˌʌnrɪˈlaɪəbˀl] *adj* güvenilmez

unroll [ʌnˈrəʊl] *v* açmak *(rulo/ sargı)*

unsatisfactory [ˌʌnsætɪsˈfæktərɪ; -trɪ] *adj* tatmin edici olmayan

unscrew [ʌnˈskruː] *v* sökmek *(vida)*

unshaven [ʌnˈʃeɪvˀn] *adj* traşsız

unskilled [ʌnˈskɪld] *adj* niteliksiz

unstable [ʌnˈsteɪbˀl] *adj* dengesiz

unsteady [ʌnˈstɛdɪ] *adj* sallanan

unsuccessful [ˌʌnsəkˈsɛsfʊl] *adj* başarısız

unsuitable [ʌnˈsuːtəbˀl; ʌnˈsjuːt-] *adj* uygun olmayan

unsure [ʌnˈʃʊə] *adj* emin olmayan

untidy [ʌnˈtaɪdɪ] *adj* dağınık

untie [ʌn'taɪ] v çözmek *(bağcık)*

until [ʌn'tɪl] *conj* kadar *(zaman, olay vb)* ▷ *prep* kadar *(yer)*

unusual [ʌn'juːʒʊəl] *adj* alışılmadık

unwell [ʌn'wɛl] *adj* iyi değil

unwind [ʌn'waɪnd] v açmak *(sargı)*

unwise [ʌn'waɪz] *adj* akıllıca olmayan

unwrap [ʌn'ræp] v açmak *(paket)*

unzip [ʌn'zɪp] v fermuarı açmak

up [ʌp] *adv* yukarıya

upbringing ['ʌpˌbrɪŋɪŋ] *n* yetiştirilme

upcycle ['ʌpˌsaɪkəl] v illeri dönüştürmek

update *n* ['ʌpˌdeɪt] güncellemek ▷ v [ʌp'deɪt] güncellemek

uphill ['ʌp'hɪl] *adv* yokuş yukarı

upload ['ʌpˌləʊd] v yüklemek

upper ['ʌpə] *adj* üst

upright ['ʌpˌraɪt] *adv* dik

upset *adj* [ʌp'sɛt] keyfi kaçık ▷ v [ʌp'sɛt] keyfini kaçırmak

upside down ['ʌpˌsaɪd daʊn] *adv* baş aşağı

upstairs ['ʌp'stɛəz] *adv* üst katta

uptight [ʌp'taɪt] *adj* gergin *(sinirleri yay gibi)*

up-to-date [ʌptʊdeɪt] *adj* güncel *(yenilenmiş)*

upwards ['ʌpwədz] *adv* yukarıya doğru

uranium [jʊ'reɪnɪəm] *n* uranyum

urgency ['ɜːdʒənsɪ] *n* ivedilik

urgent ['ɜːdʒənt] *adj* ivedi

urine ['jʊərɪn] *n* idrar

URL [juː ɑː ɛl] *n* URL

Uruguay ['jʊərəˌgwaɪ] *n* Uruguay

Uruguayan [ˌjʊərə'gwaɪən] *adj* Uruguay ▷ *n* Uruguaylı

us [ʌs] *pron* biz; **Please call us if you'll be late** Gecikeceğiniz zaman lütfen bize haber verin

US [juː ɛs] *n* Birleşik Devletler

USA [juː ɛs eɪ] *n* ABD

USB stick [juː ɛs biː stɪk] *n* USB bellek

use *n* [juːs] kullanım ▷ v [juːz] kullanmak; **It is for my own personal use** Bu benim kişisel kullanımım için

used [juːzd] *adj* kullanılmış

useful ['juːsfʊl] *adj* yararlı

useless ['juːslɪs] *adj* yararsız

user ['juːzə] *n* kullanıcı; **internet user** *n* internet kullanıcısı

user-friendly ['juːzəˌfrɛndlɪ] *adj* kullanıcı dostu

use up [juːz ʌp] v harcamak

usual ['juːʒʊəl] *adj* alışılagelmiş

usually ['juːʒʊəlɪ] *adv* genellikle

U-turn ['juːˌtɜːn] *n* U-dönüşü

Uzbekistan [ˌʌzbɛkɪ'stɑːn] *n* Özbekistan

V

vacancy ['veɪkənsɪ] n açık iş
vacant ['veɪkənt] adj boş (daire, ev, sandalye)
vacate [və'keɪt] v tahliye etmek
vaccinate ['væksɪˌneɪt] v aşılamak
vaccination [ˌvæksɪ'neɪʃən] n aşı (tıp); **I need a vaccination** Aşı yaptırmam gerek
vacuum ['vækjʊəm] v vakumlamak; **vacuum cleaner** n elektrik süpürgesi
vague [veɪg] adj belirsiz
vain [veɪn] adj kendini beğenmiş
valid ['vælɪd] adj geçerli
valley ['vælɪ] n vadi
valuable ['væljʊəbəl] adj değerli
valuables ['væljʊəbəlz] npl değerli eşyalar; **I'd like to put my valuables in the safe** Değerli eşyalarımı kasaya koymak istiyorum; **Where can I leave my valuables?** Değerli eşyalarımı nereye bırakabilirim?
value ['vælju:] n değer
vampire ['væmpaɪə] n vampir
van [væn] n üstü kapalı yük aracı; **breakdown van** n kurtarma aracı; **removal van** n taşınma kamyonu
vandal ['vændəl] n vandal
vandalism ['vændəˌlɪzəm] n vandalizm
vandalize ['vændəˌlaɪz] v tahrip etmek
vanilla [və'nɪlə] n vanilya
vanish ['vænɪʃ] v yok olmak
vape [veɪp] v elektronik sigara içmek
variable ['vɛərɪəbəl] adj değişken
varied ['vɛərɪd] adj çeşitli
variety [və'raɪɪtɪ] n çeşit
various ['vɛərɪəs] adj çeşitli
varnish ['vɑːnɪʃ] n cila (vernik) ▷ v cilalamak; **nail varnish** n tırnak cilası
vary ['vɛərɪ] v çeşitlilik göstermek
vase [vɑːz] n vazo
VAT [væt] abbr KDV; **Is VAT included?** KDV dahil mi?
Vatican ['vætɪkən] n Vatikan
vault [vɔːlt] n **pole vault** n sırıkla atlama
veal [viːl] n dana eti
vegan ['viːgən] n vegan; **Do you have any vegan dishes?** Vegan yemeğiniz var mı?
vegetable ['vedʒtəbəl] n sebze; **Are the vegetables fresh or frozen?** Sebzeleriniz taze mi, dondurulmuş mu?; **Are the vegetables included?** Sebze de dahil mi?

vegetarian [ˌvɛdʒɪ'tɛərɪən] *adj* vejetaryen ▷ *n* vejetaryen; **Do you have any vegetarian dishes?** Vejetaryen yemekleriniz var mı?; **I'm vegetarian** Vejetaryenim

vegetation [ˌvɛdʒɪ'teɪʃən] *n* bitki örtüsü

vehicle ['viːɪkᵊl] *n* araç *(otomobil)*

veil [veɪl] *n* peçe

vein [veɪn] *n* damar

Velcro® ['vɛlkrəʊ] *n* cırt bant

velvet ['vɛlvɪt] *n* kadife

vendor ['vɛndɔː] *n* satıcı

Venezuela [ˌvɛnɪ'zweɪlə] *n* Venezuela

Venezuelan [ˌvɛnɪ'zweɪlən] *adj* Venezuela ▷ *n* Venezuelalı

venison ['vɛnɪzᵊn; -sᵊn] *n* geyik eti

venom ['vɛnəm] *n* zehir

ventilation [ˌvɛntɪ'leɪʃən] *n* havalandırma

venue ['vɛnjuː] *n* yer

verb [vɜːb] *n* fiil

verdict ['vɜːdɪkt] *n* jüri kararı

versatile ['vɜːsəˌtaɪl] *adj* çok yönlü

version ['vɜːʃən; -ʒən] *n* versiyon

versus ['vɜːsəs] *prep* karşı

vertical ['vɜːtɪkᵊl] *adj* dikey

vertigo ['vɜːtɪˌɡəʊ] *n* yükseklik korkusu

very ['vɛrɪ] *adv* çok; **It's very kind of you to invite us** Bizi davet ettiğiniz için çok teşekkürler

vest [vɛst] *n* atlet

vet [vɛt] *n* veteriner

veteran ['vɛtərən; 'vɛtrən] *adj* emektar ▷ *n* emektar

veto ['viːtəʊ] *n* veto

via ['vaɪə] *prep* yoluyla

vicar ['vɪkə] *n* papaz yardımcısı

vice [vaɪs] *n* kötülük

vice versa ['vaɪsɪ 'vɜːsə] *adv* ya da aksine

vicinity [vɪ'sɪnɪtɪ] *n* çevre

vicious ['vɪʃəs] *adj* kötü

victim ['vɪktɪm] *n* kurban *(kişi)*

victory ['vɪktərɪ] *n* zafer

video ['vɪdɪˌəʊ] *n* video; **video camera** *n* video kamerası

videophone ['vɪdɪəˌfəʊn] *n* video telefon

Vietnam [ˌvjɛt'næm] *n* Vietnam

Vietnamese [ˌvjɛtnə'miːz] *adj* Vietnam ▷ *n (language)* Vietnamca *(dil)*, *(person)* Vietnamlı *(kişi)*

view [vjuː] *n* görüş

viewer ['vjuːə] *n* izleyici

viewpoint ['vjuːˌpɔɪnt] *n* bakış noktası

vile [vaɪl] *adj* kokuşmuş

villa ['vɪlə] *n* villa; **I'd like to rent a villa** Bir villa kiralamak istiyorum

village ['vɪlɪdʒ] *n* köy

villain ['vɪlən] *n* hain *(kötü)*

vinaigrette [ˌvɪneɪ'ɡrɛt] *n* sirkeli salata sosu

vine [vaɪn] *n* asma *(bitki)*

vinegar ['vɪnɪɡə] *n* sirke

vineyard ['vɪnjəd] *n* bağ *(uzum)*

viola [vɪ'əʊlə] *n* viyola

violence ['vaɪələns] *n* şiddet

violent ['vaɪələnt] *adj* şiddet uygulayan

violin [ˌvaɪə'lɪn] *n* keman

violinist [ˌvaɪə'lɪnɪst] *n* kemancı

viral ['vaɪrəl] *adj* viral; **go viral** *v* viral olmak

virgin ['vɜːdʒɪn] *n* bakire

Virgo ['vɜ:gəʊ] n Başak burcu
virtual ['vɜ:tʃʊəl] adj sanal;
   virtual reality n sanal gerçeklik
virus ['vaɪrəs] n virüs
visa ['vi:zə] n vize; **Here is my visa**
   Vizem burada; **I have an entry
   visa** Giriş vizem var
visibility [ˌvɪzɪ'bɪlɪtɪ] n görüş (göz)
visible ['vɪzɪbªl] adj görünür
visit ['vɪzɪt] n ziyaret ▷ v ziyaret
   etmek; **visiting hours** npl ziyaret
   saatleri
visitor ['vɪzɪtə] n ziyaretçi; **visitor
   centre** n ziyaretçi merkezi
visual ['vɪʒʊəl; -zjʊ-] adj görsel
visualize ['vɪʒʊəˌlaɪz; -zjʊ-] v
   gözünde canlandırmak
vital ['vaɪtªl] adj önemli
vitamin ['vɪtəmɪn; 'vaɪ-] n vitamin
vivid ['vɪvɪd] adj canlı (parlak)
vlog [vlɒg] v video blogu
vlogger ['vlɒgə] n video blog yazarı
vocabulary [və'kæbjʊlərɪ] n
   sözcük dağarcığı
vocational [vəʊ'keɪʃənªl] adj
   mesleki
vodka ['vɒdkə] n votka
voice [vɔɪs] n ses
voicemail ['vɔɪsˌmeɪl] n sesli
   posta
void [vɔɪd] adj geçersiz ▷ n boşluk
   (uzay, geometri)
volcano, volcanoes [vɒl'keɪnəʊ,
   vɒl'keɪnəʊz] n volkan
volleyball ['vɒlɪˌbɔ:l] n voleybol
volt [vəʊlt] n volt
voltage ['vəʊltɪdʒ] n voltaj;
   What's the voltage? Voltaj ne
   kadar?
volume ['vɒlju:m] n hacim

voluntarily ['vɒləntərɪlɪ] adv
   gönüllü olarak
voluntary ['vɒləntərɪ; -trɪ] adj
   gönüllü
volunteer [ˌvɒlən'tɪə] n gönüllü
   olmak ▷ v gönüllü olmak
vomit ['vɒmɪt] v kusmak
vote [vəʊt] n oy ▷ v oy vermek
voucher ['vaʊtʃə] n kupon; **gift
   voucher** n hediye çeki
vowel ['vaʊəl] n ünlü (gramer)
vulgar ['vʌlgə] adj kaba (insan)
vulnerable ['vʌlnərəbªl] adj
   savunmasız
vulture ['vʌltʃə] n akbaba

W

wafer ['weɪfə] *n* gofret
waffle ['wɒfᵊl] *n* waffle ▷ *v* gevelemek
wage [weɪdʒ] *n* ücret
waist [weɪst] *n* bel
waistcoat ['weɪsˌkəʊt] *n* yelek
wait [weɪt] *v* beklemek; **wait for** *v* beklemek; **waiting list** *n* bekleme listesi; **waiting room** *n* bekleme odası
waiter ['weɪtə] *n* garson
waitress ['weɪtrɪs] *n* kadın garson
wait up [weɪt ʌp] *v* yatmayıp beklemek
waive [weɪv] *v* vazgeçmek
wake up [weɪk ʌp] *v* uyanmak
Wales [weɪlz] *n* Galler
walk [wɔːk] *n* yürüyüş ▷ *v* yürümek; **Are there any guided walks?** Rehberli yürüyüş var mı?; **Do you have a guide to local walks?** Yerel yürüyüşler için rehberiniz var

mı?; **How many kilometres is the walk?** Yürüyüş kaç kilometre?
walkie-talkie [ˌwɔːkɪ'tɔːkɪ] *n* telsiz
walking ['wɔːkɪŋ] *n* yürüme; **walking stick** *n* baston
walkway ['wɔːkˌweɪ] *n* yaya yolu
wall [wɔːl] *n* duvar
wallet ['wɒlɪt] *n* cüzdan *(erkek)*; **I've lost my wallet** Cüzdanımı kaybettim; **My wallet has been stolen** Cüzdanım çalındı
wallpaper ['wɔːlˌpeɪpə] *n* duvar kağıdı
walnut ['wɔːlˌnʌt] *n* ceviz
walrus ['wɔːlrəs; 'wɒl-] *n* deniz aygırı
waltz [wɔːls] *n* vals ▷ *v* vals yapmak
wander ['wɒndə] *v* dolaşmak
want [wɒnt] *v* istemek
war [wɔː] *n* savaş; **civil war** *n* iç savaş
ward [wɔːd] *n* (*area*) bölge *(seçim)*, (*hospital room*) koğuş; **Which ward is… in?**… hangi koğuşta?
warden ['wɔːdᵊn] *n* bekçi; **traffic warden** *n* trafik memuru
wardrobe ['wɔːdrəʊb] *n* gardrop
warehouse ['wɛəˌhaʊs] *n* depo
warm [wɔːm] *adj* ılık
warm up [wɔːm ʌp] *v* ısıtmak
warn [wɔːn] *v* uyarmak
warning ['wɔːnɪŋ] *n* uyarı; **hazard warning lights** *npl* tehlike uyarı ışığı
warranty ['wɒrəntɪ] *n* garanti; **The car is still under warranty** Arabanın garantisi var
wart [wɔːt] *n* siğil
wash [wɒʃ] *v* yıkamak; **car wash** *n*

oto yıkama; **I would like to wash the car** Arabayı yıkamak istiyorum

washable ['wɒʃəbᵊl] *adj* **machine washable** *adj* makinede yıkanabilir; **Is it washable?** Bu yıkanabilir mi?

washbasin ['wɒʃˌbeɪsᵊn] *n* lavabo; **The washbasin is dirty** Lavabo kirli

washing ['wɒʃɪŋ] *n* çamaşır; **washing line** *n* çamaşır ipi; **washing machine** *n* çamaşır makinesi; **washing powder** *n* çamaşır tozu

washing-up ['wɒʃɪŋʌp] *n* bulaşık yıkama; **washing-up liquid** *n* bulaşık deterjanı

wash up [wɒʃ ʌp] *v* bulaşık yıkamak

wasp [wɒsp] *n* eşekarısı

waste [weɪst] *n* israf ▷ *v* israf etmek

watch [wɒtʃ] *n* kol saati ▷ *v* gözetlemek; **digital watch** *n* dijital saat

watch out [wɒtʃ aʊt] *v* dikkat etmek

water ['wɔːtə] *n* su ▷ *v* sulamak; **drinking water** *n* içme suyu; **mineral water** *n* maden suyu; **sea water** *n* deniz suyu; **sparkling water** *n* maden suyu; **watering can** *n* bahçe sulama bidonu; **a glass of water** Bir bardak su; **Can you check the water, please?** Suyu kontrol eder misiniz lütfen?; **How deep is the water?** Suyun derinliği ne kadar?; **Is hot water included in the price?** Fiyata sıcak su dahil mi?; **Please bring more water** Biraz daha su getirir misiniz?; **There is no hot water** Sıcak su yok

watercolour ['wɔːtəˌkʌlə] *n* suluboya

watercress ['wɔːtəˌkrɛs] *n* su teresi

waterfall ['wɔːtəˌfɔːl] *n* şelale

watermelon ['wɔːtəˌmɛlən] *n* karpuz

waterproof ['wɔːtəˌpruːf] *adj* su geçirmez

water-skiing ['wɔːtəˌskiːɪŋ] *n* su kayağı; **Is it possible to go water-skiing here?** Burada su kayağı yapmak mümkün mü?

wave [weɪv] *n* dalga ▷ *v* el sallamak

wavelength ['weɪvˌlɛŋθ] *n* dalgaboyu

wavy ['weɪvɪ] *adj* dalgalı

wax [wæks] *n* balmumu

way [weɪ] *n* yol; **right of way** *n* geçiş hakkı; **It wasn't your right of way** Yol hakkı sizin değildi; **She didn't give way** Yol vermedi

way in [weɪ ɪn] *n* giriş *(yer, nokta)*

way out [weɪ aʊt] *n* çıkış

we [wiː] *pron* biz

weak [wiːk] *adj* zayıf *(karakter)*

weakness ['wiːknɪs] *n* zayıflık

wealth [wɛlθ] *n* varlık *(zenginlik)*

wealthy ['wɛlθɪ] *adj* varsıl

weapon ['wɛpən] *n* silah

wear [wɛə] *v* giymek

weasel ['wiːzᵊl] *n* gelincik *(hayvan)*

weather ['wɛðə] *n* hava *(meteoroloji)*; **weather forecast** *n* hava tahmini; **Is the weather going to change?** Hava değişecek mi?; **What awful weather!** Hava çok berbat!; **What will the weather be like tomorrow?** Hava yarın nasıl olacak?

web [wɛb] n ağ; **web address** n internet adresi; **web browser** n internet tarayıcı

webcam ['wɛb,kæm] n internet kamerası

webmaster ['wɛb,mɑːstə] n webmaster

website ['wɛb,saɪt] n internet sitesi

webzine ['wɛb,ziːn] n online magazin

wedding ['wɛdɪŋ] n düğün; **wedding anniversary** n evlilik yıldönümü; **wedding dress** n gelinlik; **wedding ring** n yüzük (nikah); **We are here for a wedding** Buraya bir düğüne geldik

Wednesday ['wɛnzdɪ] n Çarşamba; **Ash Wednesday** n Büyük perhizin ilk Çarşambası; **on Wednesday** Çarşamba günü

weed [wiːd] n yabani ot

weedkiller ['wiːd,kɪlə] n yabani ot öldürücü

week [wiːk] n hafta; **a week ago** bir hafta önce; **How much is it for a week?** Bir haftalığı ne kadar?; **last week** geçen hafta; **next week** gelecek hafta

weekday ['wiːk,deɪ] n hafta içi

weekend [,wiːk'ɛnd] n hafta sonu; **I want to hire a car for the weekend** Hafta sonu için bir araba kiralamak istiyorum

weep [wiːp] v ağlamak

weigh [weɪ] v çekmek (ağırlık)

weight [weɪt] n ağırlık

weightlifter ['weɪt,lɪftə] n halterci

weightlifting ['weɪt,lɪftɪŋ] n ağırlık kaldırma

weird [wɪəd] adj acaip

welcome ['wɛlkəm] n karşılama ▷ v karşılamak; **welcome!** excl hoşgeldiniz!

well [wɛl] adj afiyette ▷ adv iyi ▷ n kuyu; **oil well** n petrol kuyusu; **well done!** excl aferin!; **He's not well** Hiç iyi değil

well-behaved ['wɛl'bɪ'heɪvd] adj iyi yetiştirilmiş

wellies ['wɛlɪz] npl lastik çizme

wellingtons ['wɛlɪŋtənz] npl lastik çizmeler

well-known ['wɛl'nəʊn] adj tanınmış

well-off ['wɛl'ɒf] adj hali vakti yerinde

well-paid ['wɛl'peɪd] adj yüksek maaşlı

Welsh [wɛlʃ] adj Gal ▷ n Galli

west [wɛst] adj batı ▷ adv batıda ▷ n batı; **West Indian** n Batı Hint Adaları; **West Indies** npl Batı Hint Adaları

westbound ['wɛst,baʊnd] adj batıya doğru

western ['wɛstən] adj batı ▷ n kovboy filmi

wet [wɛt] adj ıslak

wetsuit ['wɛt,suːt] n balıkadam kıyafeti

whale [weɪl] n balina

what [wɒt; wət] adj ne, nasıl ▷ pron ne, nasıl; **What do you do?**

Ne işle meşgulsünüz?; **What is it?**
Bu nedir?

wheat [wiːt] *n* buğday; **wheat
intolerance** *n* buğday alerjisi

wheel [wiːl] *n* tekerlek; **spare
wheel** *n* stepne; **steering wheel** *n*
direksiyon

wheelbarrow ['wiːlˌbærəʊ] *n* el
arabası

wheelchair ['wiːlˌtʃeə] *n* tekerlekli
sandalye; **Can you visit… in a
wheelchair?**… a tekerlekli
sandalyeyle gidilebilir mi?; **Do you
have a lift for wheelchairs?**
Tekerlekli sandalyeler için asansör
var mı?; **Do you have
wheelchairs?** Tekerlekli
sandalyeniz var mı?; **I need a
room with wheelchair access**
Tekerlekli sandalye girişi olan bir
oda istiyorum; **I use a wheelchair**
Tekerlekli sandalyedeyim; **Is there
wheelchair-friendly transport
available to…?** Tekerlekli
sandalyeye uygun ulaşım var mı?;
**Is your hotel accessible to
wheelchairs?** Otelinizde
tekerlekli sandalye girişi var mı?;
**Where is the nearest repair
shop for wheelchairs?** Tekerlekli
sandalye tamiri için en yakın
dükkan nerede?; **Where is the
wheelchair-accessible
entrance?** Tekerlekli sandalye
girişi nerede?

when [wɛn] *adv* ne zaman ki ▷ *conj*
ne zaman; **When does it begin?**
Ne zaman başlıyor?; **When does it
finish?** Ne zaman bitiyor?

where [wɛə] *adv* nerede ▷ *conj*

nerede; **Can you show me where
we are on the map?** Nerede
olduğumuzu haritada gösterebilir
misiniz?; **Where are we?**
Neredeyiz?; **Where are you
staying?** Nerede kalıyorsunuz?;
Where can we meet? Nerede
buluşabiliriz?; **Where is…?**…
nerede?; **Where is the gents?**
Erkekler tuvaleti nerede?

whether ['wɛðə] *conj* şayet

which [wɪtʃ] *pron* hangi; **Which is
the key for this door?** Bu kapının
anahtarı hangisi?

while [waɪls] *conj* iken ▷ *n* sırada

whip [wɪp] *n* kırbaç; **whipped
cream** *n* köpük krema

whisk [wɪsk] *n* çırpıcı

whiskers ['wɪskəz] *npl* bıyık

whisky ['wɪskɪ] *n* viski; **malt
whisky** *n* malt viskisi; **a whisky
and soda** bir viski soda; **I'll have a
whisky** Ben viski alayım

whisper ['wɪspə] *v* fısıldamak

whistle ['wɪsᵊl] *n* ıslık ▷ *v* ıslık
çalmak

white [waɪt] *adj* beyaz; **egg white**
n yumurta akı; **a carafe of white
wine** Bir sürahi beyaz şarap

whiteboard ['waɪtˌbɔːd] *n* beyaz
yazı tahtası

whitewash ['waɪtˌwɒʃ] *v*
badanalamak

whiting ['waɪtɪŋ] *n* mezgit

who [huː] *pron* kim; **Who am I
talking to?** Kiminle
görüşüyorum?; **Who is it?** Kim o?;
Who's calling? Kim arıyor?

whole [həʊl] *adj* bütün *(tüm)* ▷ *n*
bütün *(tamamı)*; **for the whole of**

June bütün Haziran boyunca
wholefoods [ˈhəʊlˌfuːdz] *npl* doğal yiyecek
wholemeal [ˈhəʊlˌmiːl] *adj* kepekli undan yapılmış
wholesale [ˈhəʊlˌseɪl] *adj* toptan satış ▷ *n* toptan
whom [huːm] *pron* kime, kimi
whose [huːz] *adj* kime ▷ *pron* kimin
why [waɪ] *adv* niçin
wicked [ˈwɪkɪd] *adj* hain *(cadı vb)*
wide [waɪd] *adj* geniş *(yayvan)* ▷ *adv* ferah *(geniş)*
widespread [ˈwaɪdˌsprɛd] *adj* yaygın
widow [ˈwɪdəʊ] *n* dul *(kocası/karısı ölmüş)*; **I'm widowed** Dulum
widower [ˈwɪdəʊə] *n* dul *(kocası/ karısı ölmüş)*
width [wɪdθ] *n* genişlik
wife, wives [waɪf, waɪvz] *n* karı *(eş)*
Wi-Fi [waɪ faɪ] *n* wifi
wig [wɪg] *n* peruk
wild [waɪld] *adj* yabani
wildlife [ˈwaɪldˌlaɪf] *n* vahşi doğa
will [wɪl] *n (document)* vasiyet, *(motivation)* irade
willing [ˈwɪlɪŋ] *adj* istekli
willingly [ˈwɪlɪŋlɪ] *adv* seve seve
willow [ˈwɪləʊ] *n* söğüt
willpower [ˈwɪlˌpaʊə] *n* irade
wilt [wɪlt] *v* solmak
win [wɪn] *v* kazanmak
wind¹ [wɪnd] *n* rüzgar ▷ *vt (with a blow etc.)* esmek *(rüzgar)*
wind² [waɪnd] *v (coil around)* esmek *(rüzgar)*
windmill [ˈwɪndˌmɪl; ˈwɪnˌmɪl] *n* değirmen

window [ˈwɪndəʊ] *n* pencere; **shop window** *n* vitrin; **window pane** *n* pencere camı; **window seat** *n* cam kenarı koltuğu; **I can't open the window** Pencereyi açamıyorum; **I'd like a window seat** Koltuğum pencere kenarında olsun; **May I close the window?** Pencereyi kapatabilir miyim?; **May I open the window?** Pencereyi açabilir miyim?
windowsill [ˈwɪndəʊˌsɪl] *n* pencere pervazı
windscreen [ˈwɪndˌskriːn] *n* ön cam; **windscreen wiper** *n* cam sileceği
windsurfing [ˈwɪndˌsɜːfɪŋ] *n* rüzgar sörfü
windy [ˈwɪndɪ] *adj* rüzgarlı
wine [waɪn] *n* şarap; **house wine** *n* ev şarabı; **red wine** *n* kırmızı şarap; **table wine** *n* yemeklik şarap; **wine list** *n* şarap listesi; **a bottle of white wine** Bir şişe beyaz şarap; **Can you recommend a good wine?** İyi bir şarap tavsiye edebilir misiniz?; **This wine is not chilled** Bu şarap soğutulmamış
wineglass [ˈwaɪnˌglɑːs] *n* şarap kadehi
wing [wɪŋ] *n* kanat; **wing mirror** *n* yan ayna
wink [wɪŋk] *v* göz kırpmak
winner [ˈwɪnə] *n* kazanma
winning [ˈwɪnɪŋ] *adj* kazanan
winter [ˈwɪntə] *n* kış; **winter sports** *npl* kış sporları
wipe [waɪp] *v* silerek temizlemek; **baby wipe** *n* ıslak bebek mendili

wipe up [waɪp ʌp] v silip temizlemek

wire [waɪə] n tel; **barbed wire** n dikenli tel

wisdom ['wɪzdəm] n zeka; **wisdom tooth** n yirmi yaş dişi

wise [waɪz] adj akıllı

wish [wɪʃ] n dilek ▷ v dilemek

wit [wɪt] n nükte

witch [wɪtʃ] n cadı

with [wɪð; wɪθ] prep ile

withdraw [wɪð'drɔ:] v çekmek

withdrawal [wɪð'drɔ:əl] n çekme

within [wɪ'ðɪn] prep (space) içinde, (term) içine

without [wɪ'ðaʊt] prep onsuz

witness ['wɪtnɪs] n tanık; **Jehovah's Witness** n Yehovanın Şahitleri; **Can you be a witness for me?** Tanıklık eder misiniz?

witty ['wɪtɪ] adj esprili

wolf, wolves [wʊlf, wʊlvz] n kurt

woman, women ['wʊmən, 'wɪmɪn] n kadın

wonder ['wʌndə] v merak etmek

wonderful ['wʌndəfʊl] adj harika

wood [wʊd] n (forest) koruluk, (material) tahta (ağaç)

wooden ['wʊdᵊn] adj ağaç/tahta

woodwind ['wʊd,wɪnd] n ağaç üflemeli (çalgı)

woodwork ['wʊd,wɜ:k] n ağaç işleri

wool [wʊl] n yün; **cotton wool** n pamuk

woollen ['wʊlən] adj yünlü

woollens ['wʊlənz] npl yünlüler

word [wɜːd] n sözcük

work [wɜːk] n iş ▷ v çalışmak; **work experience** n iş deneyimi; **work of art** n sanat eseri; **work permit** n çalışma izni; **work station** n çalışma köşesi; **I'm here for work** Buraya iş için geldim

worker ['wɜːkə] n işçi; **social worker** n sosyal hizmetler görevlisi

workforce ['wɜːk,fɔːs] n işgücü

working-class ['wɜːkɪŋklɑːs] adj işçi sınıfı

workman, workmen ['wɜːkmən, 'wɜːkmɛn] n işçi

work out [wɜːk aʊt] v çözmek

workplace ['wɜːk,pleɪs] n işyeri

workshop ['wɜːk,ʃɒp] n atölye

workspace ['wɜːk,speɪs] n çalışma alanı

workstation ['wɜːk,steɪʃən] n çalışma köşesi

world [wɜːld] n dünya; **Third World** n Üçüncü Dünya; **World Cup** n Dünya Kupası

worm [wɜːm] n solucan

worn [wɔːn] adj eskimiş

worried ['wʌrɪd] adj endişeli

worry ['wʌrɪ] v tasalanmak

worrying ['wʌrɪɪŋ] adj endişe verici

worse [wɜːs] adj daha kötü ▷ adv daha kötüsü

worsen ['wɜːsᵊn] v kötüleşmek

worship ['wɜːʃɪp] v ibadet etmek

worst [wɜːst] adj en kötü

worth [wɜːθ] n değer; **Is it worth repairing?** Tamir ettirmeye değer mi?

worthless ['wɜːθlɪs] adj değersiz

wound [wuːnd] n yara ▷ v yaralamak

wrap [ræp] v sarmak; **wrapping**

paper *n* paket kağıdı
wrap up [ræp ʌp] *v* paketlemek
wreck [rɛk] *n* enkaz ▷ *v* berbat
etmek
wreckage ['rɛkɪdʒ] *n* enkaz
wren [rɛn] *n* çalıkuşu
wrench [rɛntʃ] *n* burma ▷ *v*
burmak
wrestler ['rɛslə] *n* güreşci
wrestling ['rɛslɪŋ] *n* güreş
wrinkle ['rɪŋkəl] *n* kırışık
wrinkled ['rɪŋkəld] *adj* kırışmış
wrist [rɪst] *n* bilek
write [raɪt] *v* yazmak
write down [raɪt daʊn] *v* yazmak
writer ['raɪtə] *n* yazar
writing ['raɪtɪŋ] *n* yazı; **writing
paper** *n* yazı kağıdı
wrong [rɒŋ] *adj* yanlış ▷ *adv* yanlış;
wrong number *n* yanlış numara; **I
think you've given me the
wrong change** Sanırım yanlış
para üstü verdiniz; **The bill is
wrong** Hesapta bir yanlışlık var;
You have the wrong number
Yanlış numara

X

Xmas ['ɛksməs; 'krısməs] *n* Noel
X-ray [ɛksreɪ] *n* röntgen ▷ *v*
röntgenini çekmek
xylophone ['zaɪlə,fəʊn] *n* ksilofon

yacht [jɒt] *n* yat *(tekne)*
yard [jɑːd] *n (enclosure)* avlu, *(measurement)* yarda
yawn [jɔːn] *v* esnemek
year [jɪə] *n* yıl; **academic year** *n* akademik yıl; **financial year** *n* mali yıl; **leap year** *n* artık yıl; **New Year** *n* Yeni Yıl; **Happy New Year!** Mutlu Yıllar!; **last year** geçen yıl; **next year** gelecek yıl; **this year** bu yıl
yearly [ˈjɪəlɪ] *adj* yıllık ▷ *adv* her yıl
yeast [jiːst] *n* maya
yell [jɛl] *v* bağırmak
yellow [ˈjɛləʊ] *adj* sarı; **Yellow Pages®** *npl* Sarı Sayfalar
Yemen [ˈjɛmən] *n* Yemen
yes [jɛs] *excl* evet
yesterday [ˈjɛstədɪ; -ˌdeɪ] *adv* dün
yet [jɛt] *adv (interrogative)* artık, *(with negative)* henüz ▷ *conj (nevertheless)* yine de

yew [juː] *n* porsuk ağacı
yield [jiːld] *v* ürün sağlamak
yoga [ˈjəʊgə] *n* yoga
yoghurt [ˈjəʊgət; ˈjɒg-] *n* yoğurt
yolk [jəʊk] *n* yumurtanın sarısı
you [juː; jʊ] *pron (plural)* siz, *(singular polite)* siz, *(singular)* sen
young [jʌŋ] *adj* genç
younger [jʌŋə] *adj* daha genç
youngest [jʌŋɪst] *adj* en genç
your [jɔː; jʊə; jə] *adj (plural)* sizin, *(singular polite)* sizin, *(singular)* senin
yours [jɔːz; jʊəz] *pron (plural)* sizinki, *(singular polite)* sizinki, *(singular)* sizinki
yourself [jɔːˈsɛlf; jʊə-] *pron* kendin, *(intensifier)* kendin, *(polite)* kendin
yourselves [jɔːˈsɛlvz] *pron (intensifier)* kendiniz, *(polite)* kendiniz, *(reflexive)* kendiniz
youth [juːθ] *n* gençlik; **youth club** *n* gençlik klubü; **youth hostel** *n* gençlerin kaldığı otel

Z

kuraklık); **time zone** *n* zaman dilimi

zoo [zuː] *n* hayvanat bahçesi

zoology [zəʊˈɒlədʒɪ; zuː-] *n* hayvanbilim

zoom [zuːm] *n* **zoom lens** *n* zoom merceği

zucchini [tsuːˈkiːnɪ; zuː-] *n* kabak

Zambia [ˈzæmbɪə] *n* Zambiya

Zambian [ˈzæmbɪən] *adj* Zambiya ▷ *n* Zambiyalı

zebra [ˈziːbrə; ˈzɛbrə] *n* zebra; **zebra crossing** *n* şeritli yaya geçidi

zero, zeroes [ˈzɪərəʊ, ˈzɪərəʊz] *n* sıfır

zest [zɛst] *n (excitement)* haz, *(lemon-peel)* limon kabuğu

Zimbabwe [zɪmˈbɑːbwɪ; -weɪ] *n* Zimbabwe

Zimbabwean [zɪmˈbɑːbwɪən; -weɪən] *adj* Zimbabwe ▷ *n* Zimbabweli

zinc [zɪŋk] *n* çinko

zip [zɪp] *n* fermuar; **zip (up)** *v* kapatmak *(fermuar)*

zit [zɪt] *n* sivilce

zodiac [ˈzəʊdɪˌæk] *n* burçlar kuşağı

zone [zəʊn] *n* bölge *(savaş,*